State and Status
The Rise of the State and Aristocratic Power in Western Europe

State and Status is an examination of the rise of the centralized state and its effect on the power of the aristocracy during the sixteenth, seventeenth, and eighteenth centuries in the British Isles and in France and its eastern periphery.

Arguing that states emerged in Western Europe as powerful political-geographical centres rather than nation-states or national states, Samuel Clark examines and compares the centres and peripheries of these two large regional zones, focusing not only on England and France but also on Wales, Scotland, Ireland, Savoy, and the Southern Low Countries. This wide-ranging and multi-faceted work shows how the state shaped the aristocracy and transformed its political, economic, cultural, and status power.

Theoretically significant and conceptually sophisticated, *State and Status* is the first book to link the anti-functionalist historical sociology of Western Europe with the functionalist or neo-functionalist tradition. It is also the first sociological analysis in many years of the evolution of status in Western Europe.

SAMUEL CLARK is associate professor of sociology, University of Western Ontario.

State and Status

The Rise of the State and Aristocratic Power in Western Europe

S A M U E L   C L A R K

McGill-Queen's University Press
Montreal & Kingston • London • Buffalo

© McGill-Queen's University Press 1995
ISBN 0-7735-1226-8 (cloth)
ISBN 0-7735-1249-7 (paper)

Legal deposit second quarter 1995
Bibliothèque nationale du Québec

Printed in Canada on acid-free paper

This book has been published with the help of a grant
from the Social Science Federation of Canada, using
funds provided by the Social Sciences and Humanities
Research Council of Canada. Publication has also been
supported by the J.B. Smallman Publication Fund,
Faculty of Social Science, University of Western Ontario.

McGill-Queen's University Press is grateful to the Canada
Council for support of its publishing program.

Canadian Cataloguing in Publication Data

Clark, Samuel, 1945–
    State and status : the rise of the state and aristocratic
    power in Western Europe

    Includes bibliographical references and index.
    ISBN 0-7735-1226-8 (bound) –
    ISBN 0-7735-1249-7 (pbk.)

    1. Aristocracy (Political science) – Europe – History –
    18th century. 2. Aristrocracy (Political science) – Europe
    – History – 17th century. 3. Power (Social sciences) –
    Europe – History – 18th century. 4. Power (Social
    sciences) – Europe – History – 17th century. 5. State,
    The. I. Title.

    HT647.C53 1995   305.5'2'09409   C95-900206-5

Typeset in New Baskerville 10/12
by Caractéra production graphique, Quebec City

To Frances Searle and
the memory of Claude Robert Searle

Contents

Tables, Maps, and Figures

MAPS

FIGURES

Acknowledgments

I want to thank the Duke of Argyll for permission to reproduce his coat of arms on the cover of this book. Needless to say, this permission does not imply that his Grace has had any input into the views contained in the book.

It gives me great pleasure to express my gratitude to a number of institutions and their staff for the services they have rendered and the courtesy they have shown me: in Belgium, the Bibliothèque royale Albert 1er and the library of the Université libre de Bruxelles; in France, the Bibliothèque nationale and the Institut de recherches sur les civilisations de l'occident moderne; in Wales, the National Library of Wales and the library of the University College of Wales, Aberystwyth; in Ireland, the library of Queen's University, Belfast; in Scotland, the library of the University of Edinburgh; and in England, the Institute of Historical Research. The Social Sciences and Humanities Research Council of Canada made several research grants, without which this project could not have been completed. The University of Western Ontario has provided excellent facilities and paid my salary for the entire period during which I worked on this project, including a sabbatical leave. I would like to make special mention of the assistance provided by Sylvia Côté and our departmental staff, and also the interlibrary loan staff at the D.B. Weldon Library. I also want to thank Karen Stanbridge and Tena Van Rys for their invaluable assistance, and David Mercer for the maps. At McGill-Queen's University Press I have been pleased to work with Philip J. Cercone, Joan McGilvray, and Donald H. Akenson. And I am most grateful to Rosemary Shipton for her fine editorial contribution.

I have sought in this book to advance the work of others in the sense that I both accept and reject assertions they have made. Evolutionary theorists, geo-economic historians, Marxists, neo-functionalists, and the status school are among the groups of social scientists on whose work I have built in this manner. Two scholars in particular have had a noticeable effect on my thinking, Charles Tilly and Roland Mousnier, though I have substantially modified their arguments in an effort to carry them forward. I am most grateful as well that both men read parts of the manuscript and gave me valuable criticisms. George Comninel and I have vigorously criticized one another's work, but in a spirit of friendship and mutual admiration. And Paul Janssens also deserves special mention. Paul and I independently came to recognize the importance of state regulation of aristocratic status, but we shared many ideas and observations on the European aristocracy in a fruitful scholarly interaction. In addition, his work has provided a singular contribution to the knowledge I have acquired of the Belgian nobility.

In addition to these scholars, I have pestered a large number of able historians who have given unselfishly of their time to lend me a hand in one way or another. Belgian historians were the first to be exploited, including Etienne Hélin, Etienne Scholliers, Karen Nicholas, Johanna Maria Van Winter, Paul De Win, Jean Stengers, Paul Servais, and Jean Jacques Heirwegh. French historians who have assisted me include Jean Nicolas, T.J.A. Le Goff, Guy Chaussinand-Nogaret, Theodore Evergates, J.B. Henneman, Jean-Pierre Brancourt, Michael Sibalis, Gail Bossenga, Orest Ranum, William Reddy, James Wood, Maurice Bordes, Jonathan Dewald, Robert Isherwood, Ellery Schalk, Allan Forrest, and Pierre Boulle. Among English historians Maurice Keen, J.D. Alsop, R.O. Bucholz, David Crouch, M.L. Bush, F.A. Dreyer, Roger Manning, and J.R. Lander have been extremely helpful. Although small in number, Welsh historians have been gracious and accessible. I am exceedingly grateful to R.R. Davies, Philip Jenkins, and David Howell. Scottish historians have been very obliging, T.C. Smout, Frances Shaw, R.L. Emerson, Rosalind Mitchison, K.M. Brown, and David Stevenson. I began my research on the aristocracy of Western Europe having already established a number of friendships among Irish historians. Old friends who have assisted this study include David Miller, Karl Bottigheimer, James S. Donnelly Jr, Gary Owens, and Louis Cullen. I am also indebted to Katherine Simms. Other scholars who have given of their time or assisted me in some other manner include I.K. Steele, R.L. Henshel, Anthony Santosuosso, T.F. Sea, Myron Gutmann, Marie-Thérèse Bouquet-Boyer, Robert Walters, David Nock, L.M. Heller, Donald Von Eschen, Stan Barrett, Geoffrey Symcox, Neil Smelser, M.P. Carroll, and Kevin McQuillan.

Peter Neary has been a source of helpful encouragement and wise advice for some twenty years of my life. My parents and family have been patient and understanding of the long time that it has taken to complete this book. My dear Claudia has once again borne the heaviest burden.

The book is dedicated to my parents-in-law. They were the first to arouse my interest in Belgium and supported this project in many ways.

State and Status

Introduction

This study examines the effect of the rise of the state on the power of the aristocracy in Western Europe. More precisely, it considers the aristocracy in the British Isles, Belgium, Luxembourg, and France (including Savoy); it treats primarily the Early Modern period (1500–1800), focusing especially on the eighteenth century; and it concentrates on the differentiation of power, by which I shall mean the relative separation or fusion of various types of power – economic, cultural, political, and status.[1] A second volume will explore the relationship between different types of elite power in Western Europe during the nineteenth century.

COMPARATIVE HISTORICAL SOCIOLOGY AND THE MAKING OF MODERN EUROPE

In the past two decades we have seen a remarkable increase in comparative historical sociology, and a healthy literature is developing on comparative historical methods. The comparative method that has the most similarity with conventional sociological methodology – what most sociologists learn as undergraduates – is correlation analysis. Here one tries to identify associations by taking variation among regions on one variable and correlating it with variation on one or more other variables. As units of analysis one can use countries, regions, or local jurisdictions. Sociologists are not the only ones who correlate. Historians implicitly do it all the time, usually by explaining events or deducing cause from the differences they find between the country, region, or local jurisdiction they are studying and other places.

Correlation analysis is, however, risky business. We need to worry about the comparability of the data. We may be led to ignore differences within territories. Specialists can misunderstand or oversimplify other countries. And then we have Galton's problem (named after the English psychologist and eugenist, Sir Francis Galton), that our cases may not be independent. Countries and cultures have mutual effects on one another, and similarities may ensue from imitation and diffusion rather than similar independent causes.

These potential difficulties have led some sociologists to a different kind of comparative historical research that focuses on the evolution of large processes or transformations in a number of countries.[2] Countries cease to be units of analysis whose characteristics can be correlated to identify causes or conditions; instead they become part of a greater transformation. For example, a correlation analysis of fertility decline in Europe would try to determine what social conditions characterized societies with sharply falling birth rates as compared with those where the rates fell more slowly. In contrast, demographic change in one country could be studied as part of a larger historical process of demographic transformation. Following this strategy, we do not seek to generalize from "cases," but instead we endeavour to understand whether and in what ways different countries shared a common experience.

This new mode of comparative history has developed not only because correlation analysis has come to be seen as problematic, but also because there has been a renewed interest in the fundamental inquiry that dominated classical sociology. The early sociologists were interested in the character of the society in which they lived and the processes by which that society came into being. The vast social transformation that occurred in Western Europe during the eighteenth and nineteenth centuries was their underlying concern. They studied history in order to understand how things got the way they were. True, Karl Marx may have wanted to develop general laws of economic systems. Nonetheless, he was most of all interested in the evolution of capitalism in Europe. It was a similar interest in European history in Max Weber's work that led Edward Shils to criticize Weber as "historicist."[3] An interest in the making of Modern Europe was less manifest in the work of Herbert Spencer and Emile Durkheim, each of whom thought he was developing a timeless theory of human evolution, but the history and character of the society in which they lived had an enormous effect on the "general" theories of evolution they developed.

For better or for worse sociology has been shaped by the particular intellectual epoch in which it was born, the geographical location of its founding fathers, and the questions that excited these scholars. Insofar as they misunderstood the changes that had taken place in Western Europe over the preceding millennium – and in some ways they understood them badly – their misconceptions have become part of the set of theoretical assumptions on which sociology is based; they continue to be taught every semester to sociology students, graduate and undergraduate, in many parts of the world. I have great doubts about the validity of taking sociological models developed for the understanding of European history and applying them to Asia, Africa, the Middle East, or Latin America. It is even more disconcerting to see this going on if one believes, as I do, that these models are seriously flawed even for the understanding of European history. How they are flawed therefore should command the attention, not just of historical sociologists who are specializing in European history, but of sociologists across the world.

In taking up the questions posed by the classical sociologists, we obviously want to avoid the mistakes they made. Perhaps the most serious is the Whiggism that characterized much of their work. They interpreted history in the light of what they knew happened later. Although Herbert Butterfield's famous article[4] was written more than sixty years ago, both historians and historical sociologists are still giving into this temptation. Indeed, avoiding the Whig fallacy becomes all the more difficult when one seeks to identify major transformations. We also have to be careful not to impose a major transformation or large process on a country or a locality. The involvement of any particular region in a major transformation is what needs to be demonstrated and analysed; we cannot assume it. Even if a region is involved in a large process, its experiences may be very different from others that are also involved. We need to develop a more effective kind of large-process analysis that does not neglect these differences.

From the days of the classical theorists, sociologists have also had a fondness for formulating overloaded concepts that combine a large number of different phenomena; often they assume that by doing so they are providing an explanation for these phenomena. Students of major transformations and large processes in Europe have had a predilection for the invention of holistic typologies and embracing concepts that include a number of different transformations or processes. The classical theorists each had their own holistic typology. Weber gave us "traditional" and "rational legal" authority. Durkheim proposed that the best way to compare societies was by distinguishing between "mechanical" and "organic" solidarity. Marx's concepts of feudalism and capitalism have had by far the most long-term impact. Unfortunately, they have been defined in different ways, even among Marxists, leading to disputes that really hinge on different definitions. They have also acquired systemic assumptions. Many Marxists have come to treat capitalism as a system with its own "logic" or "functional" requirements. This systemic conceptualization led to a particularly sterile debate known as the "modes of production controversy."[5]

Among the historical sociologists studying the making of Modern Europe, treatment of capitalism as a system is most clearly visible in the work of Immanuel Wallerstein. According to Wallerstein, since the sixteenth century the social structure and economic development of European countries has been reciprocally related to their position in a "world system." Also systemic is George Comninel's conception of capitalism in his study of the French Revolution. He denies that agricultural capitalism emerged anywhere in France in the eighteenth century. It was not even present in a nascent, weak, or partial form, because nowhere in France was "agricultural production caught up in the specific logic of capitalist accumulation."[6] Similarly, Ellen Wood talks about the "logic" of capitalism and its inherent "laws of motion."[7]

Contrast this approach with Charles Tilly's to the development of capitalism. Rather than attempting to define capitalism and then establish where and when it developed, Tilly has chosen to focus on a specific process that is usually associated with capitalism – namely, proletarianization. In doing so he is seeking to avoid entanglement in debates that hinge on the meaning of capitalism. He is trying to explore a concrete historical process that can be clearly defined, to explain it and to examine its impact.[8] More than any other sociologist, Tilly has inspired and set the agenda for this kind of study of major transformations and large processes in Western European history.

I think, however, that we have come to the point at which the agenda could use some revision. The historical sociologists studying Western European history have favoured some changes at the expense of others. Interest has focused primarily on economic development – for some, nothing else seems to matter – but other transformations that have not been neglected include the disappearance of the peasantry, the demographic transition, the development of national states, urbanization, and the evolution of collective action.[9] Unfortunately, other processes that are germane to the discipline of sociology have been slighted. These include differentiation and the evolution of status, to which we shall return in a moment, but it is equally regrettable that so many of the historical sociologists who study Western Europe are unwilling to utilize Talcott Parsons's pattern variables, especially universalism versus particularism, and achievement versus ascription. Notwithstanding the respect that the historical sociologists have for Weber, only a few have followed in the footsteps of Reinhard Bendix and engaged in historical research on the major Weberian processes of rationalization and bureaucratization. Nor have many historical sociologists studying Western Europe taken any interest in the differences that the Chicago school identified between "folk" and "urban" societies, including secularization, a decline in social cohesion, the impersonalization and segmentation of social relationships, and increasing individualism.[10] Simply because one cannot agree with many of the underlying assumptions of these schools of thought does not mean that one should avoid the questions they were trying to answer and the concepts they developed.

LARGE PROCESSES

The large processes that will be the primary concern of this study are commercialization, centralization, differentiation, and the evolution of status.

Commercialization

Of these processes the least attention will be devoted to commercialization, but it must be given some consideration because it had significant effects on the other processes in which we are interested. In order to avoid overloading this concept, one should always distinguish between different types of commercialization. Obviously one needs to differentiate between agricultural and non-agricultural commercialization. For our purposes, it is also essential to distinguish between short-distance and long-distance trade. And we want to understand the distinction made by E.W. Fox between "travel" and "transport."[11]

"Travel" versus "Transport"

In Fox's theory, travel refers to the movement of persons or beasts, while transport refers to the movement of goods. Until the nineteenth century, large-scale transport (enough to support an urban concentration) was easier and cheaper over water than land, while large-scale travel (most significantly the movement of troops) was easier and cheaper over land than water. Communication (the sending of messages) was also faster over land than water. Long-distance trade usually took place over water, while short-distance trade took place over land. Social organization, especially coercive and authoritarian social organization, was easier over land, while urbanization usually took place near the sea or on navigable waterways. In theory, one should find powerful military monarchies in hinterland areas, where they govern many small urban centres and rural communities as a result of the relative ease with which such areas can be administered and troops sent overland. Large urban centres, in contrast, are more difficult to administer and control because they are less accessible to troops. Thus large urban centres generally belonged to federations of cities rather than to monarchical states. Short-distance trade characterized the hinterland regions, while long-distance trade took place among water-based urban centres. Social cooperation was achieved primarily through coercion in land-based states, but less so in water-based states, thus enabling other modes of cooperation, such as negotiation and mutual dependency, to be used in the organization of social life.

Of course, the scholars who have developed this model are fully aware that the reality was more complicated. Most centres in Europe were on navigable water; and even the most water-based cities were not inaccessible to troops. So the distinction is one of degree: more or less water-based versus land-based, more or less urbanized, more or less authoritative and coercive, more or less monarchical, relatively long versus relatively short-distance trade.

Fox asserted that, historically, we can divide Western Continental Europe into three major zones: a commercial Atlantic zone consisting of the west coast of France; a "mainland zone" consisting of Paris and the non-coastal region around Paris; and a commercialized and urbanized "Rhineland corridor" running from the Low Countries to northern Italy.[12] The French monarchy was obviously based on the mainland region, though it came to rule over commercialized regions as well. Urban societies struggled to resist the efforts of monarchies to exploit the wealth of more commercialized urban centres. The great conflicts of Early Modern Western Europe, so the argument goes, had more commercialized societies up against more monarchical ones. Differences between England and France can be understood as differences between a more water-based and a more land-based state and society.[13]

Of course, Fox was not the first to recognize the difference between water-based societies and land-based societies, and the dichotomy is well known inside and outside the academic world. Yet, given this familiarity, the systematic thought devoted to it and the volume of research done on it have been remarkably sparse. Despite frequent (often glib) allusions to "maritime societies" and "land societies," European historians have largely ignored Fox. Recently, however, a group of scholars are taking the model more seriously.[14] Projects are under way that seek to put the model to the historical test, to modify it to make it more useful and historically accurate, and to overcome the simplicity which characterized the original formulation by Fox and which still characterizes many of the references to the dichotomy by students of European history.

In addition to the Foxian model itself, one version of the paradigm that I shall both employ and seek to modify has been put forward by Tilly. It is based on the distinction between states built on coercion (for example, Russia and Brandenburg) and those built on capital (for example, Genoa, Dubrovnik, and the Dutch Republic). The former relied for troops on massive peasant populations, which were usually mobilized by subduing or forming alliances with the aristocrats who controlled these peasants. The latter relied for defence on commercial wealth, which was used to pay for ships and troops. Tilly's view is that the region from the Low Countries to northern Italy was politically fragmented because the urban centres in this region had the capital to resist conquest by coercive states. He also conceptualizes a third type of state, capitalized-coercive states, which are a mixture of the first two types. England and France were capitalized-coercive states. They became national states before either of the first two types, but eventually national states predominated. The capitalized-coercive states developed immense national armies, usually conscripted, creating forces that the commercialized city-states could not withstand.[15]

Centralization

Centres and Peripheries

One of the first sociologists to talk about centralization was Norbert Elias in a work published in 1939; it had little impact, however, being translated into English only in 1982.[16] More influential was the work of Edward Shils, who proposed that every society has a centre of order, symbols, and values that people hold as sacred. Shils was using the word centre as a metaphor; the centrality he was thinking of had "nothing to do with geometry and little with geography."[17] Although not a sociologist, Stein Rokkan had a marked influence on sociology and generated interest among sociologists in centres and peripheries.[18] Rokkan's centres were not geometrical (peripheries were not equidistant from the centre in all directions), but they were unmistakably geographical. Indeed, one of Rokkan's contributions was to link social, economic, and political characteristics with geographical location, yielding a "conceptual map of Europe."

Meanwhile, an even more influential centre-periphery model was emerging from Marxist circles. Dependency theory argued that the so-called underdeveloped countries in the world can only be understood if we recognize that they constitute peripheral economies in world capitalism, which is centred in Western Europe and North America.[19] This perspective has been the basis for an abundance of literature and two related perspectives: internal colonialism and world-system theory.[20] Taken together, these Marxian or semi-Marxian approaches have had a profound and far-reaching impact, but they have also been subjected to extensive criticism. From the perspective of this study, two of their weaknesses are especially serious. First, in early dependency theory insufficient regard was given to differences among peripheral countries. Although much has been done to overcome this criticism, there is still a reluctance among many to face up to the fact that some peripheral countries evolve very differently from others. Second, dependency theory and world-system theory both focus almost exclusively on economic centres to the neglect of other kinds of centres. Wallerstein's centre is strictly an economic centre. His model appears simplistic alongside those of Rokkan and Shils, which recognize the possibility of different political, economic, and cultural centres.[21] Shils's centres may be metaphorical, but that does not mean we should ignore them. A geographical centre can indeed be a source of symbolic integration and identification; and symbolic centres can be as powerful as economic centres. What we need to do with Shils's theory is quite literally to bring it down to Earth.

The Rise of the State

We all realize that something very significant happened to the state in Western Europe between the fifteenth and the nineteenth centuries. One common way of describing how the state changed is to talk about the emergence of the "nation-state." The term "nation" does not create great difficulty. It can be defined as a large group of people sharing the same culture and heritage. Rightly or wrongly, and whatever the word used (*Volk*, nation, people), the phenomenon has been perceived for centuries. Gerald of Wales, a Welsh writer of the twelfth century, identified the distinctive characteristics of the Welsh people and referred to Henry II as "king of the English."[22]

The concept of "nation-state," however, is more problematic. Most often it refers to a state that rules a large group of people sharing the same culture and heritage. The trouble is that few such states have developed in Western Europe, or anywhere else for that matter. Most states rule culturally heterogeneous populations. An alternative is to define a nation-state as a state whose people believe they meet the above conditions. Yet this definition would still exclude some European states and would certainly exclude Canada, the United States, and Australia, as well as most of the Third World. A third definition of nation-state, the most satisfactory in my view, is provided by Michael

Mann, who uses the term to describe states that centrally control territories within which economic exchange, culture, law, classes, and the like are increasingly uniform and are bounded by the state's borders.[23]

Finally, a number of students of the subject have turned instead to the concept of "national state." Tilly defines national states as "states governing multiple contiguous regions and their cities by means of centralized, differentiated, and autonomous structures."[24] These national states can be distinguished from empires, federations, and city-states. Tilly insists that, historically, national states have appeared only rarely. The emergence of national states, he thinks, distinguishes the development of the state in Europe from state formation in other parts of the world.

It is certainly true that state formation in Europe was distinctive in certain ways, just as European culture, kinship structure, and economic organization are in certain ways distinctive. Yet is the European state generically distinctive? Although city-states do not have multiple contiguous regions, most federations and empires do. Relatively speaking, city-states and federations do not centralize political power, but empires do. All these state structures may have differentiated and autonomous structures. As Tilly himself has shown, part of the history of state formation in Europe has entailed processes similar to what we would associate with empires or city-states. Most of the region that is now Belgium was thought to be a part of empires until 1814. Although one could call England a "nation," there has been no national state that we are justified in calling England since 1536, when Wales and England were united. England was part of an emerging state eventually called the United Kingdom, which in turn was part of the British Empire.

I am not suggesting that we should avoid ever using the concept of nation-state or national state. These terms can have value for analysing the states that have ultimately emerged. For the Early Modern period, however, rather than trying to find one term that subsumes the important political changes that were taking place, we should draw up a list of the processes that we generally have in mind when we talk about the "rise of the state" and then study as many of them as seems feasible – their development, consequences, and interrelationships. Table 1 provides a non-exhaustive list. While almost all the processes listed in this table will be considered in the chapters that follow, I have chosen to give the most attention to the first process: the centralization of political power over a delimited territory. I have done so for three reasons. First, the territorial centralization of political power was, in my view, the most critical process in the rise of the state and determined many of the other processes. Second, as Mann has noted, only

Table 1
Major Processes in the Rise of the State

Centralization	The centralization of political power over a delimited territory.
Size	Growth in the size of the state (in personnel and budget).
Functions	Growth in state functions and intervention in society.
Differentiation	Increase in differentiation in the institutions, personnel, and functions of the state.
Force	Greater monopolization of force by the state.
Control	Increase in social control by the state.
Mobilization	Increase in the capacity of the state to mobilize resources.
Nationalism	Increasing use of nationalism or national identification to mobilize resources.
Standardization	Greater uniformity within the jurisdiction of states.

the state possesses centralized territorial power.[25] Other institutions have become larger, more differentiated, and able to mobilize more resources, but no institution has centralized power territorially in the way the state has done. Third, a centre-periphery perspective is the most useful for understanding the aristocracies in which I am interested. Centripetal and centrifugal forces have interested French historians more than English historians. True, centralization has recently gone out of favour among historians, even many French historians. One of the aims of this project is to revive interest in centralization as a major process, indeed to persuade English historians to give it more consideration than they have done, while at the same time avoiding the Whiggism that marred earlier work on it. I do not regard centralization as an inevitable or unilinear process. On the contrary, I shall give considerable attention to the accidents of history that led to the development of the two political centres in which I am interested. As is the case with other large processes, it is not the study of centralization that has been wrong, but the Whiggish study of centralization.

Obviously, in this study the "rise of the state" does not refer to the evolution of the idea of the state in an abstract sense.[26] Nor, in my conceptualization, is it a cultural revolution,[27] though it has had enormous impact on culture, as I shall seek to demonstrate.

Differentiation

It is well known that division of labour or function was the paramount concept in the life work of Herbert Spencer and to a lesser extent

Durkheim. Both were of the opinion that as societies advanced they became more differentiated in this sense.[28] It is less often observed that Marx implicitly treated differentiation. Actually, he emphasized both dedifferentiation and differentiation. On the one hand, he believed that capitalism would undermine the division of labour among workers, reducing them all to unskilled machine attendants. On the other hand, he insisted that capitalism would give rise to greater class polarization. And some things he wrote implied an increase in differentiation between economic power and other kinds of power.

This has been one of the most vexed questions in Marxist writings. Most Marxists accept the view that a basic difference between feudalism and capitalism is that surplus is extracted primarily through non-economic coercion in feudal societies, but primarily through economic coercion in capitalist societies. In feudal societies a lord employs a variety of pressures, including force, to oblige the peasant to surrender a surplus.[29] In capitalist societies this is unnecessary. Cultural, political, and military powers are withdrawn from those who control the means of production. There is now a division of labour between those who wield cultural, political, and military power (their job is to protect the capitalist system as a whole) and the capitalists (they are able to use their economic power to make labourers sell their labour power because workers no longer have any alternative). Although capitalists may exercise a certain amount of political power indirectly, capital inevitably gives those who control it more economic power than cultural or political power.

While in principle this transformation is accepted by the majority of Marxists, the matter becomes more complicated because it is closely related to quarrels among Marxists over the relationship between base and superstructure. Can economic and non-economic coercion be distinguished? Is the superstructure (especially the state) autonomous from economic forces? Does economic power prevail over all other types of power in capitalist societies? The debate has a historical dimension. European absolutism may be seen as a fusion of economic and political power, in which case taxation in absolutist states represents a "centralized feudal rent,"[30] or it may be seen as a more differentiated structure that promotes the interests of autonomous economic elites and national economies. The surprising thing is that in all this debate Marxists have mostly ignored the historical process by which economic and non-economic domination became differentiated.[31]

Most consideration of differentiation has been given by structural functionalists. Parsons built his theory of evolution and change on this concept, which was further developed by Neil Smelser and S.N. Eisenstadt.[32] Jürgen Habermas, in his enterprise of merging structural functionalism with historical materialism, has rediscovered processes of differentiation, though he does not equate them with social evolution, or at least not as much as the structural functionalists have been inclined to do.[33]

The concept has also been revived by neo-functionalists, who argue that it is the best analytical tool we have for understanding modern societies.[34] They have been very critical of the way Parsons treated differentiation. Parsons failed to investigate the causes of differentiation, did not recognize the complex historical process by which differentiation took place, assumed that its development was non-problematic because it was functionally superior, neglected power and conflict, ignored the role of concrete groups, and emphasized the integrative effects of differentiation.[35] Today, neo-functionalists call for historical research to show how differentiation developed.[36] Rather than smooth and automatic, the differentiation process may be "uneven"; it may be slowed down by opposition; or it may advance in some sectors more than in others, or in some regions more than in others.[37] As Smelser has shown, differentiation may be impeded by modernizing forces and it may occur for reasons that have nothing to do with functional adaptation.[38]

I am delighted with this call for historical specificity linked to a general theoretical model of differentiation. Indeed, one of the motivations behind the present study is to contribute to the intellectual project that the neo-functionalists have proposed. I caution, however, that in the historical research this project requires, the concept of differentiation has to be used very carefully. It has become overloaded. This can be blamed on Parsons, who took the relatively simple notion used by Spencer and Durkheim and added a large theoretical baggage, which the neo-functionalists have not seen fit to question. Thus differentiation means not only more division of functions and specialization, but also greater specificity of roles, impersonalization, the decline of ascriptive criteria, higher rates of social mobility, bureaucratization, the rise of political parties, the lessening in the importance of social status, secularization, the decay of primordial ties, and more.[39] Conceptualization of this kind impairs historical analysis. The historical exploration of differentiation requires that it be separated from other processes and that we distinguish between different types of differentiation.

In addition, to repeat what I have said about other processes, we need to avoid any assumption that differentiation is natural or inevitable. In spite of their self-proclaimed liberation from the errors of earlier structural functionalists, the neo-functionalists have not given up such assumptions. Parsons would not really have had much trouble with the assertion that differentiation has been "uneven" or that it has involved conflict. He would have had much more trouble with the idea that there has been no underlying societal force leading to greater differentiation.

As said, this book is primarily concerned with the differentiation of power. Among those influenced by structural functionalism, Suzanne Keller has made the best-known contribution to this subject. She argues that elites are more differentiated in modern society than in earlier social formations. Modern "strategic" elites are highly specialized, and their power is limited to their functional sphere.[40] The differentiation of power was also treated by sociologists who used to talk about "status crystallization" and "status inconsistency," the former referring to a situation in which a person enjoys similar rank on various dimensions of stratification, the latter referring to a situation where rank is dissimilar (for example, one's wealth is substantially greater than one's prestige). These sociologists were interested mainly in the consequences of status crystallization and status inconsistency, especially the psychological consequences. They concerned themselves less with the causes of these phenomena and little with their long-term evolution. Yet, in contrast with Keller and structural functionalists, they did assume a certain tendency toward dedifferentiation.[41]

Status

Although I shall give much attention to status crystallization and status inconsistency, I do not adopt these terms because I shall use the term status in a different sense. Henceforth status does not mean rank on a dimension or several dimensions of stratification, but instead denotes positive or negative social evaluation. It is one dimension of stratification, synonymous with prestige or esteem. Status is a type of power, the power to elicit respect. It is derived from the possession or presumed possession of characteristics that people admire or are told they should admire. This possession enables a person to obtain special treatment.

Sociologists pay more heed to class than to status. In the sociological literature on the making of Modern Europe, the evolution of status has been almost completely neglected since Elias's *Court Society*. Sociologists with such contrasting approaches as those of Wallerstein, Barrington Moore, and Perry Anderson treat the European landed elites simply as classes, be they feudal or capitalist. One can even find references to the French nobility as a class.[42]

The exception is a school of thought, which we can call the "status school," whose members hold that one of the most consequential processes that has taken place in the evolution of Modern Europe is the transition from a society that was differentiated primarily by status to one that is differentiated primarily by class. In sociology the idea can be found in the work of T.H. Marshall, Bendix, and more recently B.S. Turner.[43] The argument has some similarity to the notion in legal history of a transition from "status to contract" as the basis of civil law. In the mid-nineteenth century H.S. Maine used these terms to describe the evolution of modern society; more precisely, he suggested that the kinship statuses of primitive society had gradually given way to the free contractual relationships of modern society.[44] On the whole, few sociologists have carefully analysed the status-to-class transition. Yet many have made brief references to it, sometimes describing it as a transition from a society of "estates" to one of classes.[45]

Among historians the most prominent members of the status school have been Roland Mousnier and Jerome Blum.[46] Mousnier's basic thesis was that pre-industrial Europe was not a society of classes, but rather a society of status groups legalized as estates or orders. The reason why class was less important than status, according to Mousnier, was that the production of material goods was valued less than it would be later; and an economic market had not developed sufficiently to provide the conditions necessary for class formation. Blum was convinced that the evolution of European society can best be comprehended as the transition from one holistic type to another, from a traditional order to a "modern class society."[47] All European societies went through the same stages of development.

Many of those who have advanced this line of argument hold that the development of class society in place of status society was related to economic change. Consequently, the decline of status society occurred earlier in certain countries than in others. Common is the view that status society declined earlier in England than in France and that status was not as important in eighteenth-century England as it was in eighteenth-century France.

This study is based on the conviction that research on status needs to be reoriented away from this concern with variation in its importance. The widely accepted assumption that status is more important in some societies than in others has never been tested, much less proven. This study is not designed to provide such a test, though I shall demonstrate that status was no less important in eighteenth-century England than in eighteenth-century France. More significantly, I hope that this undertaking will persuade readers that there is a better strategy for the investigation of status. This strategy involves analysing variation in status according to four variables, which I have listed in table 2.

Table 2
The Four Variables of Status

Differentiation	The extent to which status is differentiated from other kinds of power, especially economic, cultural, political, and military power.
Criteria	What characteristics or possessions are accorded status (for example, wealth, erudition, military valour, athletic ability).
Ascription	Whether status is ascribed hereditarily.
Institutionalization	The extent to which stable norms and values regulate the distribution of status and the rights and duties associated with it.

Throw several five-year-olds together and status quickly comes to have an effect on their interaction, but it is not well institutionalized. In most other contexts the institutionalization varies between this extreme and situations where it is rigidly controlled. When status is well institutionalized it becomes a position in a status hierarchy with certain rights and obligations. Most people hold both institutionalized and non-institutionalized status, and it is possible for them to lose one more than the other – non-institutionalized status more than institutionalized status (a king who comes to be regarded as a fool) or vice versa (a king who is forced to abdicate but is still highly respected).

Status may even be institutionalized in law, in which case it becomes a "legal status." Some writers make a sharp distinction between status in the sense of social evaluation and status in the sense of a legal status. Weber, in contrast, saw the two as linked.[48] Most sociologists have tried to maintain the connection, but without providing a clear understanding of it.[49] In my view it is understandable if one considers a legal status to be the institutionalization in law of the special treatment that status receives. In other words, special treatment can vary in its degree of institutionalization from almost imperceptible courtesy or snubbing to a legal status. Special treatment can be positive or negative. Positive treatment may consist of respect, honour, deference, praise, rights, or legal privileges, while negative treatment may take the form of disrespect, dishonour, humiliation, penalization, or the imposition of penalties or legal disabilities.

Variables 3 and 4 in table 2 determine the extent to which status is freely allocated. Where status is not based on birth and is less institutionalized, individuals will have comparatively more opportunity to raise or lower their own status and comparatively more choice in deciding whom they will evaluate highly and in acting on the basis of their evaluations. When special treatment becomes a legal status, people may be forced to accord privileges or rights even though they personally do not admire the individual or even agree with the basis of the legal status.

Anyone doing research on the institutionalization of status must answer two sorts of questions. First, to what extent is status institutionalized? Second, how is it institutionalized? How do norms and values of status develop? Who articulates them? How are they enforced? Are they codified in law or are they just accepted norms? The answers to these questions should be compared among societies and over time.[50]

A word on the concept of class. This study will focus largely on status to the neglect of class, not because its author in any way rejects class analysis, but because we have not seen enough status analysis of Western European history, at least by sociologists. Whether one believes that there were classes in pre-revolutionary France ultimately depends on how one defines class. It is possible to maintain a definition of class which insists that its members be collectively conscious and active, or that it is structured on the production of material goods. Yet the real issue is whether this helps us in our efforts to understand the Old Regime. Is the concept of class useful or not for understanding this society? The large number of fine studies that employ the concept for Early Modern Europe by Brenner, Tilly, Lachmann, Dewald, Porchnev, Comninel, and many others has, I think, demonstrated that the answer is yes.

THE COMPARATIVE PROJECT

The Comparison of England and France

Contrasts between England and France have formed the basis for many of the conclusions drawn about the making of Modern Europe. Differences between the two have been used to explain economic development, the evolution of agrarian society, state formation, and political revolution.

English Superiority

Traditionally, England has been made to look better. Consciously or unconsciously, many academics as well as non-academics have believed in the superiority of the English over the French, economically, politically, socially, and/or (though less often) culturally. The English were militarily superior, but at the same time less militaristic and more civilized – less torn by class conflict, more willing to compromise, less given to fits of revolutionary passion. They were more religiously tolerant. Their state finance was superior and their taxation more equitable. England was more "advanced" than France in evolutionary terms; capitalism was more developed; there was more structural differentiation; and, to a greater extent, status had given way to classes and contract. One Frenchman, François Crouzet, spent much of his career trying to assess the assumption of English economic superiority and published a collection of his papers on the subject under the title *De la supériorité de l'Angleterre sur la France: l'économique et l'imaginaire XVIIe–XXe siècles.*

Stereotypes of Aristocrats

This bias can be found in literature on the Early Modern European aristocracy. For many years the predominant stereotypes placed the English aristocracy in a favourable light and the French aristocracy in an unfavourable light. The English was more open and competent, less privileged but shrewder, and possessed of an uncanny ability to adapt to social change. English aristocrats spent more time on their landed estates, managed them more efficiently, were more bourgeois, helped promote industrialization, loved liberty, and opposed autocracy.[51] The French nobility, in contrast, was regarded as more privileged, closed, reactionary, and unwilling to accept its social responsibilities and adapt to the changes that were occurring around it. It still clung to a traditional agricultural system and to seigneurial rights. It exploited the peasantry without making any significant economic contribution.[52] Greater nobles "were cooped up in a perpetual house-party at Versailles," while the remainder huddled in the countryside, ignorant, "without any sort of political influence."[53] Most nobles lived a degenerate life of gambling and extravagant expenditure, driving themselves hopelessly into debt; they were bribed with sinecures and pensions to accept their loss of power; and they brought the French Revolution on themselves through their petty selfishness.[54]

Until recently, most sociologists have been inclined to go along with the traditional view, in whole or in part. Vilfredo Pareto accepted it in whole. He had the notion that elite circulation is caused by the psychological and moral degeneration of upper classes. The pre-revolutionary French nobility was one of his favourite examples of a declining, degenerate elite, which was too weak and cowardly to stand up against an emerging bourgeois counter-elite, while at the same time too greedy and self-indulgent to relax its exploitation of the masses. There was little mobility into the nobility under the Old Regime. This meant that it was starved of new blood and that opposition from frustrated members of the bourgeoisie built up against it. In contrast, the English landed elite was more open and more willing to yield "where yielding was called for" in order to maintain its power.[55]

Although Moore rejected the assumption that the French aristocracy was more closed than the English, he believed that it was less commercialized, that it was less actively involved in farming and the sale of agricultural produce on the market, and that it played no significant role in French society or in politics. "By the time of Louis XIV," he wrote, "the nobility seemed reduced to a role of magnificent indolence at Versailles or else of peaceful vegetation in the provinces." French nobles made no contribution towards transforming the French economy; they merely "squeezed" peasants for all they were worth, using traditional modes of surplus extraction.[56] Bendix concluded that the upper French nobility was without power, that the crown sought to degrade them, and that they constituted a heavy burden on the peasantry.[57] Eisenstadt classified both France and England as advanced "bureaucratic empires," but he saw the aristocracy as more reactionary and inflexible in France than in England.[58]

Wallerstein shared the view that the English aristocracy, or a major segment of it, was more capitalist than the French nobility. In England a merger took place between "the nobility and the new merchant-gentry" in the seventeenth century. Most of the aristocracy became transformed into a capitalist class, whereas in France it did not. The English Civil War represented the triumph of the aristocracy, which "was in fact the triumph of the capitalist classes."[59] In England, according to another sociologist, power shifted to a rising landed and urban middle class, whereas French society was still divided into a peasantry and a "feudal" aristocracy.[60] In the words of two other sociologists, the breakdown of the European "caste" society "was most bloody in France where the lid was kept on the longest and the castes most clearly separated. The English nobility seemed almost to aspire to become bourgeois."[61]

One of the earliest works to challenge the stereotype of the French nobility was Robert Forster's study of the nobility in the Toulouse region during the eighteenth century. He argued that most nobles were neither poor *gentilshommes campagnards* nor extravagant and decadent men of leisure, but rather conscientious and resourceful managers of agricultural estates.[62] Shortly thereafter, conventional views on noble privilege in France during the eighteenth century were called into question by Betty Behrens.[63] Other writers began to overcome the simplistic assumptions in the literature about the role of the nobility in business.[64] Doubt was raised about the alleged strengthening of conservatism, escalation of barriers to social mobility, and increase in demands on peasants during the eighteenth century – the so-called aristocratic reaction.[65] The most irreverent revisionist was Guy Chaussinand-Nogaret, who suggested that the French nobility of the eighteenth century sought to abolish privilege, took on bourgeois values, was the true capitalist class, and played an important role in the Enlightenment.[66] Most recently, Jonathan Dewald has argued that the conventional view of the Old Regime as a traditional corporatist society of orders is a vast oversimplification which ignores the modern characteristics of the aristocratic culture of the seventeenth century, in particular its individualism.[67]

A reassessment of the English aristocracy has also emerged. In two volumes of a series on the European nobility and one volume on the English aristocracy, M.L. Bush undertook to demonstrate that there was a general European nobility of which the English peerage and gentry represented simply one variant.[68] Although distinctive in certain ways, the English aristocracy "had much in common with continental nobilities."[69] John Cannon challenged the notion that the eighteenth-century English peerage was open and that it experienced embourgeoisement.[70] Lawrence and Jeanne Stone presented a similar case for the landed gentry in three English counties for the sixteenth to nineteenth centuries.[71]

We should not, however, declare the conventional stereotypes demolished altogether. Some of the revisionist protestations are exaggerated, and many of their assertions are unsubstantiated by evidence. Certainly there were real differences between England and France and between the English and French aristocracies. A comprehensive new understanding of these differences has not yet been constructed to replace the old stereotypes. Most of the revisionists have focused on the aristocracy in either England or France, without systematically comparing them. Until more comparative research is done, it is too early to set the record straight. Yet it is possible at this time to pull together and try to explain the intersocietal differences that can now be perceived. It is also possible to undertake a sociological analysis that makes use of the detailed research thus far done by historians on the subject. We now have available not only the above literature, but also a number of learned monographs on the nobility in what is today France, Belgium, and Luxembourg.[72]

The Comparative Geographical Scope
We are also in a position to extend the geographical scope beyond England and France. There are some particular reasons for bringing in Wales, Scotland, and Ireland along with England. England has too often been treated as a separate unit. An increasing number of scholars have become dissatisfied with this departmentalization of research and writing and have undertaken or are advocating a "Britannic" approach, pointing to the interconnectedness of the history of the

British Isles.[73] It is impossible to understand economic development or the role of the state, even in England itself, if this larger structure is overlooked. Nor is it possible to study the aristocracy in one of these countries taken alone, since aristocratic membership overlapped among them.

Worse still is to compare England alone with France, including Brittany, the Midi, and so forth. If we are going to compare England with France, then we should take only the French core area, which, if we mean the economic core, would be the northeast, or, if the political core, Paris and its region. In neither case would we arrive at conclusions like those that are currently drawn in such comparisons. A better plan, however, is to include not only peripheral parts of France, but also some peripheral regions beyond French borders that were under French influence, and to compare all of these, not just with England but with Wales, Ireland, and Scotland as well. This is not to suggest that these peripheries were all the same. On the contrary, one of the things we discover by broadening our geographical scope is that England and France had very different peripheries. These differences can be best appreciated by comparing the British peripheries with peripheral countries on France's eastern frontiers. Even the latter were not all the same and, in order to capture their differences, I have chosen to focus especially on two that diverged significantly – Savoy and Belgium.

Some problems are created by this approach. First, no claim can be made that the countries provide independent cases. We must constantly keep this in mind as we assess the impact of causal factors that are shared by more than one country. Second, the availability of secondary source material is not equivalent for all of them. Far more material can be found for England and France than for Savoy, Belgium, Wales, Ireland, or Scotland. Moreover, the literature available on the smaller countries does not always cover the same subjects. We know more, for example, about the historical evolution of the aristocracy in Belgium than in Ireland or Scotland. On the other hand, more work has been done on landlord-tenant relations for Ireland and Scotland than for Belgium.

Yet we simply cannot go on comparing England by itself with continental European countries. England, or more precisely southern England, was a core with an extensive and heterogeneous periphery. This periphery must be taken into account in conclusions one draws about English state and society, just as one needs to include all of France in any conclusions one draws about France.

Thus, in this study, a comparison will be made between two large European zones, southern England and its peripheries and the Paris region with its peripheries.

Comparative Methodology

The comparative methodology adopted in this project is one that brings together the examination of multinational transformations with correlation analysis. In a sense, the two methodologies are opposites. The former assumes intersocietal effects, generating large processes involving more than one country; the latter assumes independent cases. So long as we understand this and are careful about our conclusions, the two strategies can be effectively used in the same enterprise. Indeed, by combining correlation analysis with large-process analysis we can do much to overcome the weaknesses of correlation analysis.

We also bring to bear two different modes of causal explanation, the first based on observed association and the second based on observed sequence. The former has led to broad generalizations – in some cases rather bold generalizations, which I hope other scholars will evaluate and amend. Committed specialists may not like these sections because they move away from the rich complexity of individual cases, but they should be happier with those sections in which I give my countries separate and more descriptive (if highly condensed) treatment in an effort to demonstrate the long chains of events that have shaped the evolution of major processes. What has happened in each of the countries I am studying has resulted from centuries of sequential events that have carried both states and aristocrats in similar or different directions.

Organization of the Book

Since I shall be examining four large processes, it may be helpful to the reader if I indicate their relative importance and in what chapters of the book each is treated. The process in which I am most interested is the differentiation of power, above all the differentiation of status power from other types of power. This subject is not discussed in Part One (though the groundwork for it is prepared in these chapters), but it is discussed in every chapter in Part Two ("Aristocratic Power"). The ultimate objectives are to determine if aristocratic power was more differentiated in the British Isles or in our continental zone, to explain the differences we find, and to draw whatever conclusions we can about general processes of differentiation.

Second in importance is the transformation of status. It is linked to the first process insofar as I focus on the differentiation of status power, but I am also interested in what happened to status as a subject in its own right. This issue too is not considered Part One. It is mentioned in every chapter in Part Two, but is the subject primarily of the first two, chapter 4 ("The Decline of Lordship") and chapter 5

("Status Power"). My aim in these two chapters is to identify and explain differences in the structure of aristocratic status that evolved in our two geographical zones.

Third in importance is the development of political centres. This subject comes first in the book, in Part One ("Centres and Peripheries"), where I seek to describe and explain the emergence of two centres of political power in Western Europe, to compare them, and to account for their differences, especially differences in the political relations between centres and peripheries. In doing so I also try to give the reader the political background for the analysis of aristocratic power that follows in Part Two. Thus I emphasize those aspects of the development of the two political centres that I think help us to analyse aristocratic power.

The fourth process is water-based commercialization. As I have already indicated I am less interested in this process in itself than in its effect on the above processes. In other words, it is primarily the variation we can correlate that concerns us here. Differences among our countries in terms of the Foxian model are outlined in Part One, while discussion of the effects of these differences on the aristocracy is to be found in Part Two.

All of the above concerns are branches of a larger interest in social evolution and the making of Modern Europe. I first became interested in the subject of this book because I wanted to evaluate some of the evolutionary assumptions implicitly built into the literature (both sociological and historical) on Western European development, particularly some of the evolutionary assumptions that have been built into comparisons of England and France. In my view evolutionary assumptions need to be introduced explicitly into our analysis and confronted with history. I do this primarily in Part One and in the Conclusion to Part Two.

This work is intended for a number of different audiences: historians who study European history; sociologists who know considerable European history; other sociologists who know very little European history; and students in courses on elites, stratification, aristocracies, the making of Modern Europe, and the rise of the state. Even historians can be divided into specialists in different countries and periods, whose knowledge can be very dissimilar; what is well known to a French Medieval historian will not likely be well known to an Irish Early Modern historian, and so on. Consequently, many subjects I discuss will be new to some readers, but commonplace to others. This is a problem in both Part One and Part Two, but especially in Part One. Thus I strongly recommend that those having considerable familiarity with any of my countries skip sections in Part One. On the other hand, the introductory material in Part One, especially on the smaller countries, should be useful to many readers. One of the objectives of writing this book has been to make sociologists, historians, and students more knowledgeable about smaller European countries.

NOTE ON PLACES

In the Early Modern period Savoy was not a French province, but rather a duchy of the state of Piedmont-Savoy ruled by the House of Savoy. Most of what we now call Belgium was in the seventeenth century known as the Spanish Low Countries; in the eighteenth century they came under Austrian rule and were known as the Austrian Low Countries. Some parts of present-day Belgium were semi-autonomous principalities outside the Spanish/Austrian Low Countries, the largest of which was the Principality of Liège. On the other hand, Luxembourg was then part of the Spanish/Austrian Low Countries. We can refer to what is now Belgium and Luxembourg as the South-Netherlandish provinces, the Southern Netherlands, or the Southern Low Countries, though these names were not used by contemporaries. I usually refer to what is now the Kingdom of the Netherlands as the Northern Low Countries, though in the seventeenth and eighteenth centuries they were called the United Provinces. At the risk of offending the Irish, I often use the term "British" to refer to England, Wales, Scotland, and Ireland, but Britain or Great Britain refers only to England, Wales, and Scotland.

PART ONE

Centres and Peripheries

1 France

We can begin with some easy observations about political centralization in Western Europe. There is no justification for characterizing it as a unilinear process. Not only is the future trend unclear, but if there has been a pattern in the past it has been a cyclical one, in which long periods of slow centralization have been broken by periods of little change or decentralization. The vast political structure centred in Rome, which enjoyed extensive power over much of this part of the world, collapsed in the fourth and fifth centuries, leaving almost no political centres of any significance. The Carolingians exercised a measure of extensive centralized power in the eighth century, but the breakup of this empire led to a decentralization of power once again. During the remainder of the Middle Ages the church and the Holy Roman Empire (a term used from the twelfth century to refer to the Germanic and Italian confederation that succeeded the Carolingian Empire) represented the only centralization of power, but the authority of the church was fragmented with the Protestant Reformation in the sixteenth century. Meanwhile, regional centres were emerging, some of which were able to establish political control over reasonably well-defined territories, which invariably included other centres. Paul Kennedy is being careless when he says that "political fragmentation" in Europe was responsible for the competition that eventually made Europe more powerful than other parts of the world.[1] It was not political fragmentation but the rise of regional centres that generated the competition Kennedy is emphasizing.

In the part of Western Europe that is the focus of this study, two pre-eminent centres came to dominate. What got these centres started and how did the bipolarization come about? What kinds of centres were they? What were the major differences between these centres and their peripheries and why did these differences develop? To what extent and in what ways did they centralize power? What kinds of power did central and peripheral political institutions have? How much autonomy did peripheries enjoy? These are the questions to which Part One is devoted. I also want to evaluate in evolutionary terms the states we will be discussing. What historical evidence do these chapters bring to bear on evolutionary theory?

THE FRANKISH KINGDOM AND THE RISE OF PARIS

The island in the Seine River that is today called the Cité originally became a centre of habitation for the Parisii tribe of Celts, who lived there in the first century BC, because it provided protection. The bridges they built rendered it important for its cross-roads as well. In Roman times the town was politically subordinate to Senones (Sens), but several Roman emperors stayed in Lutetia, as they called it, for varying periods of time. Julian (Roman emperor 361–3) constructed a palace in Lutetia while he was at war with the Franks.

When the Roman Empire disintegrated, the strongest of the Germanic peoples who came to control Gaul were the Visigoths. Their heartland was the Garonne River valley, and their political centres were Bordeaux and Toulouse. A France whose political centre was Bordeaux or Toulouse would have been very different from the France that eventually emerged. However, the hegemony of the Visigoths was destroyed by the Frankish invasion. In 508 the Merovingian ruler, Clovis, made Paris his capital. No concrete evidence remains of his reasons for doing so, but historians have speculated that it was because Paris had demonstrated its defensive advantages during the preceding wars, which it survived better than most other towns, and because Clovis and his wife venerated Saint Geneviève, who was buried there and with whom they wanted to share a mausoleum.[2] They took up residence in Julian's palace, where they established central administration and a small court, which followed Clovis when he travelled.[3]

This (quite limited) centralization was undermined by the fragmentation of the Merovingian kingdom. Although the capitals of Clovis's sons (Reims, Orléans, Paris, and Soissons) were all in the same general region, and though Paris was the seat of government during those periods when the Frankish kingdom was united, the rule exercised by

Merovingian kings became gradually weaker, and political power less centralized, until their dynasty was displaced by the Carolingians, Charles Martel and his descendants, who ruled from the eighth to the tenth centuries.

The Carolingian Empire was not highly centralized. Its strength lay in the delegation of power over vast areas to a ruling elite loyal to the Carolingian dynasty. In varying degrees, some regions had considerable independence. The Carolingians found Brittany especially difficult to subdue. Military victories could not be turned into political control owing to the political fragmentation of the region.[4]

Like the Merovingian, the Carolingian rulers were peripatetic. The king and his court were on the move because the transport of what they consumed was inconvenient. The king also travelled to administer his kingdom and to engage in military campaigns. Yet Charlemagne did spend much of his time at one or another of his royal villas, most of which were located in or near the Ardennes. The abundance of game for hunting and the hot springs made Aix-la-Chapelle his favourite residence. "He enjoyed the exhalations from natural warm springs," recorded Einhard, "and hence it was that he built his palace at Aix-la-Chapelle, and lived there constantly during his latter years until his death."[5] The royal court eventually came to spend most of its time in Aix-la-Chapelle. Charlemagne's heir, Louis the Pious, was less peripatetic than his father, and Aix-la-Chapelle was turned into a real capital.[6]

It was a land-based political centre. The differences that Fox identified between commercial European zones engaged in long-distance trade and agricultural zones engaged in local trade were only just emerging in this part of Europe. Although Aix-la-Chapelle was in what Fox calls the Rhineland corridor, this corridor was not as commercialized and urbanized as it would later become. Fox fully recognizes that the Carolingian Empire was primarily a non-commercial empire.[7] It did not include the maritime Venetians, who successfully resisted conquest.

The subsequent geopolitical history of Europe was greatly shaped by two characteristics of the Frankish kingdom: Carolingian royal authority was patrimonial, and the ninth-century Franks, even their ruling dynasties, practised partible inheritance. Louis the Pious was an only son. His sons, however, all claimed a share of the empire. The Treaty of Verdun of 843 divided it among the three surviving. Charles the Bald received the western portion; Lothaire 1 got the central portion, which ran from the Low Countries south into Italy and came to be known as Lotharingia; and Louis the German inherited the eastern portion, east of the Rhine. Lothaire 1 died in 855. In 870 Charles the Bald and Louis the German each took a share of Lotharingia.

Map 1

The division of Europe in the ninth century had enormous long-term impact. It created a newly defined Frankish kingdom, whose territorial limits remained remarkably durable and have formed the basis of modern France. The areas defined by the treaty were ethnically extremely heterogeneous, a characteristic that has persisted until recent times. Yet this heterogeneity makes the long-term impact of the ninth-century division all the more remarkable and significant.

Another consequence of this division was that the political centre of this Frankish kingdom was no longer Aix-la-Chapelle. In the years following the Treaty of Verdun there was really no political centre. The heartland of the possessions of Charles the Bald was Aquitaine. His mother lived in Tours in the Loire Valley and administered his possessions from there while he campaigned. Carolingian control over these possessions was fragile and frequently disrupted by invaders. Nevertheless, over the following centuries Paris and its environs emerged as the political centre of the Frankish kingdom. Paris was already a comparatively large town by the year 800, with an estimated 25,000 inhabitants. Yet other towns in Europe were just as large or larger (for example, Metz with 25,000 persons, Milan also with 25,000, Seville with 35,000, Cordova with 160,000), while other towns were not much smaller (for example, Tours and Reims each with 20,000 persons). Over the next four hundred years Paris grew dramatically in population, reaching an estimated 110,000 inhabitants by 1200 and 228,000 by 1300, when it had the largest population of any city in Europe. The next most populous city in what is now France was Rouen, with perhaps only 50,000 persons. London may have had only 45,000.[8]

The growth of Paris can be attributed to at least three factors.[9] First, Paris became a centre of learning, drawing students and scholars from across Europe. Second, trade on the Seine River, mostly short-distance trade, was increasing. And, third, the Frankish crown was transferred from the Carolingians to the Capetians. In 888 Eudes, count of Paris, was elected king of the Western Franks by the great lords. He was succeeded by a series of Carolingian rulers, but in 987 his descendant, Hugh Capet, was elected king by the great lords and with the support of Adalberon, archbishop of Reims. This happened after the Carolingian ruler, Louis v, died without heir. Paris was once again the seat of the crown. Despite the trade along the Seine, it was primarily a land-based town. This fact permanently shaped the character of the kingdom.

DECENTRALIZATION AND CENTRALIZATION

The tangible power of the descendants of Hugh Capet reached little beyond their immediate region, essentially bounded by the Seine, the Marne, the Beauvronne, the Oise, and the Nonette, an area that eventually came to be known as the Ile-de-France. Outside the Ile-de-France, royal public authority, with rights of justice and taxation, was in most areas appropriated by dukes, counts, and castellans in the tenth and eleventh centuries.[10] Historians have quite rightly emphasized this decentralization of authority, but several cautionary remarks are in order.

First, in some areas public authority had never really been centralized, so it is misleading to talk about a decentralization of authority. Second, political power became more centralized in the hands of dukes or counts (as in Normandy, Savoy, and Champagne), at least by the twelfth or thirteenth centuries, if not earlier.[11] Indeed, the fragmentation of royal power in the tenth and eleventh centuries had been partially the result of the concentration of intensive power within some (not all) jurisdictions. It will be difficult to understand the development of intensive political power within some states (the two in which we are most interested are England and Savoy) without recognizing this concentration of intensive power in France during this period of decentralized power. Third, these dukes and counts were vassals of the French king, and generally acknowledged his overlordship, notwithstanding the fact that they often did not do his bidding. And, finally, the territorial sovereignty established by the Carolingians made the Ile-de-France the nominal centre of a vast region whose rough boundaries, if far from indisputable, had a historical justification in the Treaty of Verdun. The Capetians were recognized as the kings of the *regnum francorum*, if not its effective rulers. The king did not have intensive power over this kingdom, but did enjoy some measure of extensive power.

Over the course of the late Middle Ages and the Early Modern period, political power became more centralized as a result of three processes. First, the French monarchy enlarged the area over which it effectively ruled. The methods of territorial aggrandizement were not limited to conquest; they also included treaty, marriage, inheritance, purchase, and feudal rights. Artois was obtained as a dowry by Philip Augustus in 1180. The lord of Dauphiné, Humbert III, ceded Dauphiné to France in 1343 on condition that the eldest son of the French king would thenceforth be known as the "Dauphin." Burgundy was seized by Louis XI in 1477 after the death of Charles the Bold. He also inherited Provence in 1481. Brittany was acquired through a combination of force and royal marriages – the marriage of Anne of Brittany to two successive French kings, and that of her daughter Claude to a third French king.

Territorial expansion was not a steady march forward. The twelfth century saw a large portion of the western part of the Frankish kingdom fall into English hands via the Angevin dynasty. During the thirteenth century French kings were able to make considerable headway in ousting the English from the Continent. This progress was threatened during the Hundred Years' War (1337–1453). However, though the English won major victories, when the war came to an end they had been largely driven from continental soil. The danger to the French monarchy on the west was thus diminished, enabling it to commit more resources to expanding to the east. In fact, eastward expansion was limited until the seventeenth century, a century that saw the acquisition of frontier principalities along the northern, eastern,

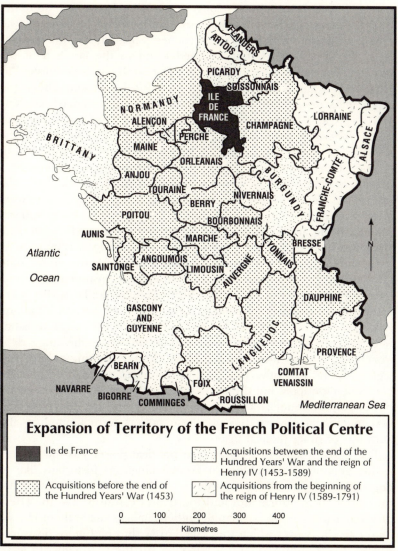

Expansion of Territory of the French Political Centre

■ Ile de France

▣ Acquisitions before the end of the Hundred Years' War (1453)

▤ Acquisitions between the end of the Hundred Years' War and the reign of Henry IV (1453-1589)

▨ Acquisitions from the beginning of the reign of Henry IV (1589-1791)

0   100   200   300   400
Kilometres

Map 2

and southern borders. The seventeenth-century acquisitions came mainly as outcomes of territorial exchanges by treaty at the end of wars.

The second process that centralized political power was the strengthening of royal authority. Again, it was not a steady secular development. During the Hundred Years' War royal authority collapsed almost completely. Yet as a result of the war, many French people came to believe that the crown was the basis of their security. The monarchy emerged from the war much stronger than it had been when hostilities began. During and after the war, royal military and fiscal power was greatly enhanced. Royal authority reached a peak during the reign of Francis I (1515–47), but it declined again in the last half of the sixteenth century during the Wars of Religion. It was re-established by Henry IV (1589–1610), who laid the basis for the pre-eminent period of French state-building in the seventeenth century under Louis XIII (1610–43) and Louis XIV (1648–1715). Major rebellions, known as the Frondes, erupted in the mid-seventeenth century during the minority of Louis XIV, when an Italian, Cardinal Mazarin, was in charge of the state. The failure of these revolts was followed by a greater concentration of political power in royal hands. Provincial institutions became more accommodating to the will of the crown; local government was put under more royal control; tax collection was reformed; the army was enlarged and reorganized; and the bureaucracy was increased in size so that agents of the monarchy were in force throughout the kingdom. Although by twentieth-century standards we might think that law and order were insufficiently established, by seventeenth- and eighteenth-century standards they were respected to a remarkable extent throughout the French kingdom. France was a land of lawyers, judges, and courts, whose legal decisions were generally binding on the population, and where the king's right to rule was for the most part accepted. The French king enjoyed full legislative and executive power. He did not, as we shall see, have a complete monopoly, but the executive function in France was carried out largely by councils and agents of the crown. He also possessed certain judicial powers, though these powers were limited by the authority of other judicial institutions.

The third process that centralized political power was the decline in the geographical mobility of French kings. As historians like to emphasize, Medieval kings moved around a lot. Some changes that took place in the thirteenth and fourteenth centuries had the effect of making them more peripatetic; other changes made them less so. As the territory over which they ruled grew they had more provinces to visit, roads improved, and it was safer for the royal court to leave the Paris region. On the other hand, travelling for food gradually became less imperative as agriculture became more commercialized and the crown had more cash with which to buy it. Moreover, the expansion in the number of provinces ruled by the French king made it impossible for him to rule through personal attendance as kings had once done.

Even in the thirteenth century the peripateticism was generally within close proximity of Paris. True, Louis VIII (1223–6) spent half his time away from Paris, campaigning or exercising the right of *gite*. Yet the Paris region was still favoured. A record of the expenses of his household indicates the presence of Louis at Paris thirty-five times, Melun a dozen times, Compiègne a dozen times, and St Germain twenty times.[12] Except for military campaigns and crusades, Louis IX (1226–70) did not often leave the Paris region. He spent a good deal of time at his hunting lodges and other favourite places, but these spots were usually within a day's journey of Paris.[13] There was little decline in peripateticism between then and the sixteenth century. The court of Francis I was often on the move. "Never during the whole of my embassy," complained a Venetian ambassador, "was the court in the same place for fifteen consecutive days."[14] In the early part of his reign, Francis was careful to visit many of his provinces. As a rule, however, he stayed in one residence during the winter and spring, and travelled only during the other seasons, usually to hunt and to enjoy life away from congested and unhealthy Paris. He spent much time in the countryside of the Loire valley and the Ile-de-France. He did not live permanently in Paris, but he carried out substantial alterations to the Louvre to make it the principal royal residence. No other town had as many royal visits as Paris.[15]

In the seventeenth century, kings became more sedentary. Louis XIII was mostly either in Paris or at his hunting lodge near Versailles. Louis XIV went from one residence to another in the early years of his reign, but he was much less mobile after he took up residence in the new palace at Versailles in 1682. Paris was the royal residence and the centre of the government for almost seven years after the death of Louis XIV. In 1722 Louis XV (1715–74) returned to Versailles. In one respect he was more sedentary than Louis XIII or Louis XIV; he did not try to lead his armies. On the other hand, in order to overcome his boredom, he moved frequently among his principal residences (Compiègne, Rambouillet, Fontainebleau, Marly, Choisy), thus diminishing the importance of Versailles in comparison with its pre-eminence during the reign of Louis XIV.[16] Nonetheless, all the royal residences were reasonably near to Paris, which was their central point.

Royal administration became geographically centred even earlier than royal residence. Ironically, the weakness of the Capetians actually helped to get this process started. What administration the Capetians possessed was concentrated in Paris, providing the basis on which a royal bureaucracy was later built. Institutions that evolved out of the *curia regis*, most notably the Parlement of Paris and the Chamber of Accounts, were also located in Paris. The Parlement of Paris, sedentary in Paris from 1302, became the superior court for a large part of France, and eventually the most powerful political institution in the kingdom, with the exception of the monarchy. Kings often visited Paris solely to attend it. Admittedly, some state institutions had to move about with the king. An English visitor to the court of Henry III (1574–89) remarked that the councils "in the which be handeled matters of greatest importance in the realme" (he was referring to the Great Council, the Privy Council, and the Council of the Cabinet) must "continuallie followe the Court."[17] Again, however, they usually remained in the Paris region.

The Dialectic of the French State

However, when we talk about the centralization of the French state we need to be precise. In some respects, it became highly centralized, the most centralized in Europe. Yet in other notable ways it was not centralized. A remarkable characteristic of the Old Regime was the coexistence of forces of political centralization along with marked political fragmentation, creating a particular dialectic that affected aristocratic power. The fragmentation ensued partly from cultural diversity, some of which will be treated in chapter 8. Here I want to examine certain characteristics of the French state that contributed to the fragmentation.

Piecemeal Expansion

The French state was assembled piecemeal, province by province over centuries. New acquisitions had different customs and institutions; they often had been ruled by different powers; and they were typically annexed under different circumstances and different agreements. Some provinces were gained and lost, and then later regained. Some were brought under the lordship of a member of the royal family, but not fully integrated into the kingdom until later. Anjou and Auvergne were seized by Philip Augustus, but Anjou was not fully integrated until the late fifteenth century and all of Auvergne not until the early seventeenth century. Artois was lost and regained and was only made permanently a part of France by the Treaty of the Pyrenees in 1659. Angoumois was ceded to the English in 1360, reconquered in 1373, but not fully integrated until the seventeenth century. Orléanais was part of the royal demesne of Hugh Capet, but was usually held by a member of the royal family and was not fully integrated until the seventeenth century. Although the seventeenth century saw a remarkable increase in state unification and standardization, the acquisition of additional frontier territories in that century created new sets of relationships between the crown and the provinces.

Limitations on Royal Power

It is now recognized that French kings were not as determined to concentrate power in their hands and to undermine provincial bases of power as historians once thought. Often the extension of royal authority was a result of other things the crown was trying to do, such as establishing military security in a region or collecting more revenue. The French monarchy was "absolutist" in the sense that the power of the state was, relatively speaking, concentrated in the hands of the sovereign rather than shared with other institutions. However, the power of the French crown was not boundless by any means, and we cannot dismiss restrictions on royal power as merely vestiges of the past that were gradually being eroded.

The power of the crown was limited by law. The king was restricted not only by his own edicts and ordinances, and by Roman and customary law, but also by the widespread notion of *lois fondamentales*, which represented something resembling a constitution and prescribed the relative rights and limitations of various state institutions, including the crown.

The people at the time saw nothing inconsistent with swearing obedience to the king, while at the same time resisting the encroachment of royal power. Political centralization and fragmentation were not regarded as contradictory during the Old Regime, whatever we might think. In order to understand how this was possible we must again recognize the heritage of the *regnum francorum*. During the eleventh and twelfth centuries the idea of a unified French kingdom coexisted with the reality of a multitude of almost independent principalities. As French kings sought to turn this idea into a reality, they had to work with rather than against the constituent elements of the kingdom. Even after royal authority had been extended, a measure of the autonomy and distinctiveness of the various provinces persisted and was accepted as natural by the crown. The king ruled by negotiation and compromise with provincial magnates and institutions. No two provinces were ruled in the same way. Both the state bureaucracy and judicial institutions formed a complex and elaborate network of overlapping jurisdictions, generating constant conflicts and confusions of powers.

The Parlement of Paris was the premier *parlement*, but there were also twelve provincial *parlements*. They were intended to provide justice and administration that would take into account regional differences and would be composed of persons whose origins lay in the particular province. The towns in which these *parlements* were located formed provincial political centres of considerable importance.

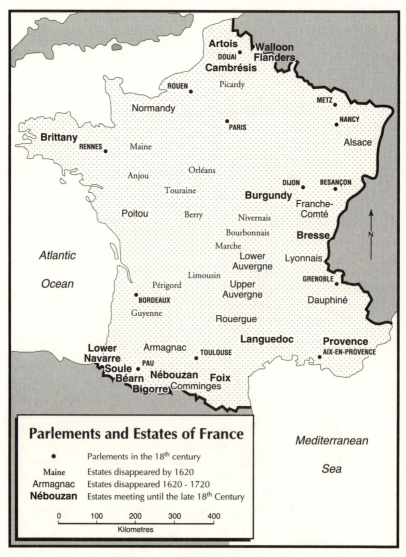

Map 3

The next most powerful provincial institutions were political assemblies known as "estates." They emerged during the thirteenth and fourteenth centuries. The growing financial needs of kings and of their great vassals induced them to call together representatives of those groups whose cooperation was deemed necessary for the raising of revenue. Estates were most influential in the fourteenth and fifteenth centuries. During this period nearly all the provinces had them.

After the Hundred Years' War the monarchy was able to abolish many estates or to refuse to convoke them, but in various parts of the country they remained important in the political processes of the fifteenth and sixteenth centuries.[18] Further decline came during the reigns of Henry IV and Louis XIII. Cardinal Richelieu, Louis XIII's chief minister, succeeded in eliminating many of the provincial estates and ruled instead with *élections,* bodies of royal officers who transmitted royal orders to the parishes and collected taxes directly. All the same, in the eighteenth century certain provinces, most of them known as the *pays d'états,* still had provincial estates, some of which were sufficiently powerful that the king and his men had to pay close attention to them.

Although Medieval kings sometimes called the Estates General, typically they negotiated with local or provincial estates. The limited power of the Estates General in France is not hard to understand given the political fragmentation of the kingdom. Political organization at the provincial level was too strong to enable a central representative body to dominate political life. Most people wanted to be represented, or had the means to be represented, in provincial institutions; they did not usually cooperate with assemblies claiming wider territorial jurisdiction. French kings were inclined to accept these realities and to negotiate with provincial institutions, or indeed with even more local bodies.[19] Eventually, the absence of a central representative assembly came to be to the crown's advantage. In the seventeenth and eighteenth centuries it was the nobility that wanted the Estates General to be called, and the crown that was opposed. Only a strong central assembly could have resisted the growth of royal power, but the Estates General did not meet from 1614 to 1789. Thus, the crown could whittle away at the power of provincial estates, province by province, without facing any united resistance.

All the same, French royal absolutism was limited by the fact that the state was not composed just of the crown and its agents. An unfortunate tendency prevails among some writers to equate the French state with the crown, but the state included a large number of other institutions, and these institutions were not disappearing. *Parlements* were not on the wane. Provincial estates had been reduced in number and power, but during the eighteenth century they were not experiencing any further decline. Some efforts were made to establish new assemblies in the last half of the eighteenth century and the Estates General met in 1789. Of course, Louis XVI did not know that he would be overthrown when he summoned the Estates General. We can only speculate what would have happened in the 1790s to political assemblies if there had been no revolution.

Patrimonialism and Bureaucracy

Finally, fragmentation of power resulted from the patrimonial character of the French state. We have seen that the Carolingian rulers
enjoyed patrimonial rights to their authority. These rights were transferred to the Capetian kings, even if, initially, the patrimonial authority
was limited to the Ile-de-France. As the state expanded, patrimonial
authority was asserted over newly acquired territories, especially those
obtained by inheritance or marriage. Even conquered territories would
become part of the king's patrimony or the patrimony of a member
or branch of the royal family. More remarkable still, the patrimonial
character of the king's staff did not diminish as it increased in size.
The monarchy enlarged the state bureaucracy by making a patrimonial
claim to political power.

If one likes to classify states as belonging to different types, then the
best label to apply to the Early Modern French state is that it was a
patrimonial bureaucratic monarchy. It was ruled by a king with a
relatively large administrative bureaucracy over which the king was
considered to have proprietary rights. Patrimonial bureaucratic monarchies should not be treated as transitional societies between feudalism
and capitalism. They constitute one of the most prevalent social formations in world history and cannot be dismissed as merely transitional.

As the French state evolved, its patrimonial bureaucracy became
both alienated and overgrown. Until the mid-fifteenth century, buying
and selling offices was informal. Official royal venality appeared
during the fifteenth and sixteenth centuries. During the reign of
Francis I it became a regular source of revenue, and French sovereigns
persisted in resorting to it in the following centuries. The decisive step
forward in the routinization of venal offices came in 1604 when the
paulette or *droit annuel* was introduced, which permitted offices to be
inherited if the holders paid an annual fee. This gave office-holders
greater patrimonial rights over offices, while it gave the crown a
regular source of income.

In order to continue to raise revenue, the crown sometimes confiscated offices several times, requiring owners to buy them back. The
monarchy was also able to erect new offices on top of old ones. This
practice provided new sources of revenue and diluted the status and
authority of the offices already created. It was the power of the crown
to make new offices in this way that gave rise to the overgrown
patrimonial bureaucracy that was characteristic of Early Modern
France. At the same time, the sale of offices alienated royal authority.
A gradually increasing portion of the ownership of the state was lost
to the monarch and invested in office-holders over whom he did not
have complete control. The venality of offices also undermined the

effectiveness of the state apparatus. Viewing their posts as their private property, officials considered themselves free to do as they pleased and to pursue their own interests as much as those of the crown. Those who did not own offices often complained about their sale. Many who did own an office also complained. Pierre de l'Estoile (a bureaucrat in a judicial record office who kept a diary during the last quarter of the sixteenth century) wrote that the sale of offices was "contrary to all law and reason," as a result of which "it is not possible to imagine a more tortuous and deformed crab than the order and state of France."[20]

Richelieu, though recognizing the validity of many criticisms of the venality of offices, nonetheless insisted that it was better than the abuses that would be committed "if the distribution of offices depended simply on the will of the kings," in which case offices "would depend as a consequence on the favour or artifice of those who enjoyed more influence over them."[21] We should not assume that patrimonial bureaucracies whose offices were owned by their incumbents were altogether archaic. In a ground-breaking article published over two decades ago, J.A. Armstrong argued that it was not true that the most modern bureaucracy in the seventeenth and eighteenth centuries was the one that conformed best to the Weberian model. In France, a strong commitment to bureaucratic rationality and innovation developed in spite of the patrimonial character of the state. Inheritance of office could, in fact, help to build a dedicated state-service elite.[22] It has often been asserted that the venality of office increased loyalty by giving purchasers a vested interest in the state and its survival. Although I shall later express some reservations about this argument, there is no doubt that the venality of office was a central element in a complex of inducements built into the French state which helped to secure the cooperation of elites.

Moreover, the French king was not limited to creating venal offices. The extraordinary power acquired by the crown enabled it to institute offices that were not venal and thus less independent of royal authority. The traditional way of doing so was to appoint a *commissaire*, a person who was given a special commission by the king for a defined period. A major political phenomenon of the seventeenth century was an increase in this method of augmenting royal authority. The most important *commissaires* were the *intendants de justice, de police et de finances*, usually known simply as intendants. They oversaw the administration of the provinces, in some cases very closely. They were men of the political centre. The fathers of more than half the intendants of the period 1652–1715 were from Paris, and almost another quarter from districts close to Paris (such as Ile-de-France, Soissons, Normandy,

Flanders, and Artois); over two-thirds of the intendants themselves were from Paris, and another one-sixth from districts close to Paris. It is true that earlier ancestors were usually from the provinces. Indeed, 78 per cent of a sample of eighteenth-century intendants were from families established in Paris for less than a hundred years. Yet only 16 per cent of the sample were the first in their families to establish themselves in Paris.[23]

During the seventeenth and eighteenth centuries the French royal bureaucracy was becoming increasingly staffed by professional civil servants, like those in the *bureaux de commis* under the royal councils, the secretaries of state, and the controller general of finances. By the late eighteenth century the secretaries of state were being made into real ministries.[24] Departments were strictly organized, the size of their staffs enumerated, appointments and salaries regulated, and expenses monitored. On the basis of this information, reasonably accurate budgets were calculated.[25] Technical bureaucrats were in a strong position in France as a result of the bias of the French bureaucracy in favour of technical specialists and the better training of such specialists. A landmark in European administrative history was the founding of the Ecole des Ponts et Chaussées in 1747, which both trained technological experts and integrated them into the state administration.[26]

These professional bureaucrats were not in a separate world from that of venal *officiers*. They interacted with one another both professionally and socially. Indeed, most professional state servants, including the intendants, were venal office-holders and came from the same social background. It is, what one historian has called, the "paradox of venality" that French state patrimonialism, while in certain respects impeding reforms that would have made the state apparatus more efficient, made possible the social mobility that brought new and more able men into the governing elite.[27]

Thus patrimonialism and bureaucratic differentiation were not incompatible. Nor were patrimonialism and absolutism. Patrimonialism had for long both increased and decreased the power of the French crown. It was by claiming the state as their private property that French kings expanded their power, but largely for fiscal reasons this patrimony was constantly being transferred to office-holders. Limitations on royal power were not just what was left over from earlier state forms as the new state emerged. They were also an outcome of the development of the patrimonial bureaucratic state.[28]

The French state in the eighteenth century was not a federal state. Nor was it any longer a "divaricated" or "heteronomous" state, to borrow some terms from Samuel Finer.[29] I have referred to it as fragmented, but one could argue that "amalgamated," "assembled," or "aggregated" would be more accurate. John Brewer has suggested that the French crown "superimposed" a centralized apparatus over a regionally diverse and particularistic society.[30] I find this metaphor misleading because the state created by the crown had itself strong tendencies towards fragmentation. Although political power became massively more centralized during the late Middle Ages and the Early Modern period, it is not clear that this was the direction in which political power was moving in the eighteenth century. One can point to the growth of the state bureaucracy in Paris during the eighteenth century, but one can also point to a process of decentralization and a decline in royal power after 1750. This decline is usually attributed to the personal weaknesses of Louis xv and Louis xvi in comparison with Louis xiv, or to the degeneration of the Old Regime, but I would argue that a certain measure of fragmentation was normal, as were periods of time when the power of the central government appeared to diminish.

LAND-BASED STATE

Water-based commercialization had evolved further in France, taken as a whole, than in Prussia, Austria, or Russia. France became part of two major long-distance trading regions. The first of these will be discussed at greater length in chapter 2. It developed in the tenth to twelfth centuries and included northern Italy, southeastern France, the Low Countries, and trading centres that linked these areas, most notably Champagne. The other region was the Atlantic seaboard. It evolved later, from the twelfth and thirteenth centuries, when Bayonne, Bordeaux, La Rochelle, and Nantes emerged as trading centres. Initially, commercial exchanges rarely went further than Spain or England, but gradually the Atlantic became an alternative route for trade between the Mediterranean and the Low Countries. To this of course was eventually added the Atlantic colonial commerce, which totally transformed the west coast of France. In the twelfth century the Bretons were not sea people, but the passage of ships around their coast drew them into maritime activity in the thirteenth century. The Bretons, in particular those of Saint-Malo, became seafarers more than merchants. Brittany was the leading maritime province in France in the eighteenth century.[31]

In France, long-distance internal trade was impeded by tolls and duties, but was facilitated by the road system (perhaps the finest in Europe in the last century of the Old Regime) and promoted by the demand created by population density, especially in the Paris region. One of the historical processes that some versions of the Fox model underestimate is the way in which political centres attract population and thereby become centres of trade. For the same reason, industry, especially the manufacture of luxury goods, was drawn to Paris and its surrounding region. Manufacturing could also be found in the northeast, in or near Arras, Lille, Rouen, Amiens, Reims, and Sedan. Yet the striking feature of French industry was its dispersion throughout many parts of the country in small towns and rural cottages.[32] Most noteworthy is the fact that most Atlantic ports were not backed up by substantial concentrations of industry in their immediate hinterland, an exception being shipbuilding located near some ports.

There was nothing seriously wrong with the performance of the French non-agricultural economy in the eighteenth century. In 1720 France participated in 8 per cent of world trade, Britain, 15 per cent; both participated in 12 per cent in 1780. It has been estimated that from 1700 to 1789 France's agriculture grew by 25 per cent, its industry by 80 per cent, and its trade by 196 per cent.[33] Yet France, again taken as a whole, had not become as commercialized as the Low Countries or England had by this period. Although French trade grew spectacularly in the eighteenth century, it was still less than British trade per capita. At the beginning of the eighteenth century, industry and trade represented 45 per cent of the total economic output in England, but only 25 per cent in France.[34] Equally significant, Paris did not dominate France economically in the way that it dominated it politically. Not only trade and industry, but also agricultural commercialization in the Paris Basin and finance in the city were a consequence of its large population and political importance, not the cause. And, depending as it did on the population of Paris, the trade that was centred in the Paris region was mainly short-distance trade rather than long-distance trade.

Many characteristics of French state and society stemmed, at least in part, from its relative land basis. This fact becomes evident in any discussion of the French military or state finance.

Military Power

It can no longer be argued that the rise of the state was the simple result of changes in the means of waging war, but such changes, during the late Middle Ages and the Early Modern period, did expand the territory that a land-based political centre could control. The most critical changes were the utilization of firearms and fire-powered canons, the increasing use of specialized forces (cavalry, infantry, and artillery), the growth in the size of infantries, the centralization of command and strengthening of discipline, and the maintenance of larger standing armies during peacetime in order to have trained forces prepared to act quickly. These changes required more mobilizing capacity – to pay for larger infantries, for firearms and new canons, and for fortresses built in such a way that they could withstand the new canons. Admittedly, remote areas remained difficult for land-based political centres to control, or were often not worth the cost of controlling. Yet political power increasingly came to be exercised by those centres that had the greatest mobilizing capacity. No area, however remote, could escape this power if the centre was willing to commit the resources it could mobilize. Cities and smaller castles were equally vulnerable to the military power of centres. Only other powerful political centres could resist determined conquest by such a centre.

Theoretically, a land-based state depended on its control over more territory in order to raise its mobilizing capacity. Whereas water-based centres could raise their mobilizing capacity by expanding commerce, a land-based centre, to the extent that it was a land-based centre, relied on augmenting the resources it could extract from land and a large rural population. The French crown succeeded in enlarging the land resources it could extract more than any other political centre in Western Europe (though, as I have stressed, it did so by other means in addition to war and, in the process, acquired control over water-based economic centres). This also meant, of course, that France had a long frontier that had to be defended.

Militarism was given high priority by the French state and carried inordinate prestige in society. Particularly during the reign of Louis XIV, war enjoyed exalted status. Military expenditures represented a major portion of the state budget, even in peacetime. For example, in 1726 some 54 per cent of the budget (minus servicing the debt) went to the military, roughly 47 per cent to the army, and about 7 per cent to the marine. The percentages were 58 (42 and 16) in 1751, 48 (35 and 13) in 1775, and 43 (29 and 14) in 1788.[35] During certain periods, considerable effort was made to improve the navy. French ships were often larger, faster, and better designed than British ships.[36] Yet, as the above figures indicate, most of the money for the military went to the army, not the navy. Often the navy was seriously impaired by a shortage of financial resources.[37]

It was on the land that the French were superior. France had been the first state to establish a standing army. The *compagnies d'ordonnance* were formed in 1445 by Charles VII. By roughly half a century later the king employed some regiments enough that we can refer to them as a standing army. Eventually, cores of regiments were maintained after troops were disbanded, and these cores were steadily increased in size.[38] In the early seventeenth century the French army was still a

Table 3
Number of Effectives in Army per 10,000 Inhabitants

Year	France	Austrian Low Countries	Piedmont-Savoy	British Isles
1693	200*			50*
1700				23
1705			216	
1706			177*	
1710	143*			87*
1733			260*	
1738	61		184*	
1745			233*	
1747			349*	126*
1760	117*		223	
1763	137*	43*		193*
1765			217	
1773		51		
1780			228	
1783				41
1786		73		
1787			225	
1789	65			

Asterisk indicates that the country was then at war. These figures cannot be taken as exact. The inclusion or exclusion of foreign regiments, ordnance regiments, mobilized militia, etc., can cause estimates of effectives to vary. In addition, most population figures are only rough estimates. See note 39 for sources.

multiform collection of almost autonomous regiments. Louis XIV and his ministers, however, transformed it into a well-organized fighting force under royal control, which grew in size (though not steadily) during and after his reign. In the period 1635 to 1659, the size of the army had been in the neighbourhood of 150,000 men. It fell to 72,000 in 1666, rising to perhaps 134,000 during the following year of war over the Spanish Low Countries. The Dutch War led to an increase to almost 280,000 men. In the following period of peace the number was reduced drastically, but was still an impressive 138,000 men, which swelled to 158,000 until the War of the League of Augsburg, when it enlarged again, reaching 400,000 in 1693.[40] During the eighteenth century French armies were not as superior in size to those of other European countries as they had been in the last half of the seventeenth century, but, as shown in table 3, they were still relatively large per capita. Recruitment tended to come disproportionately from the north and east. Provinces close to land frontiers were generally overrepresented, while coastal provinces were underrepresented, with the exception of Normandy and the northeastern coastal regions. The lowest rate of recruitment into the army was from Brittany.[41]

Taxation and Finance

There was a common pattern to the development of taxation in Western Europe. In the Middle Ages, princes were expected to pay for normal operations with income from fines, feudal dues, customs, crown lands, and various fees. They were to ask for more revenue, "extraordinary" as opposed to "ordinary" revenue, only during periods of crisis when the demands of war required additional funds. The objective of most sovereigns was to increase extraordinary revenues so they were not tied to war or defence – in other words, to make them ordinary revenues. Various tax structures evolved out of this constant process of negotiation, and recent scholarship has made us familiar with this phenomenon.[42] While it was found in the majority of European countries, the way in which negotiations were carried out and the institutions that developed along with the negotiations varied significantly. First, the more land-based a state was, the more it negotiated with landed aristocrats; the more water-based it was, the more it negotiated with urban merchants. Second, the political organization of the state made a significant difference. In France, the crown had no strong central political assembly to which it could turn; rather, the sovereign negotiated with a great number of corporate bodies, town governments, local or provincial assemblies (often ad hoc), and different groups in society, including Jews.[43]

In the course of the Hundred Years' War, lasting changes occurred in French taxation. The prolonged emergency enabled the crown to raise revenue without the consent of the Estates General. In the reign of Charles VII, the crown assumed the right to collect *tailles* without calling the Estates General; it also established a permanent *taille*, which became the cornerstone of French taxation.[44] At the close of the Hundred Years' War the French monarch had the most revenue of any Western European ruler and was less dependent on the royal demesne than perhaps any other.[45] In the sixteenth century, during reign of Francis I, tax collection was brought under more central control, primarily by the establishment of one receiver for all revenues. Under Henry IV, revenue was augmented by boosting indirect taxes and by reorganizing tax farms.[46] French kings gradually placed themselves in a strong position to increase state revenue to meet the rising costs of the Early Modern state. The data we have indicate that royal taxation increased more than threefold between the beginning of the seventeenth century and the final years of the Old Regime, even when the effect of inflation and population growth is controlled.[47]

Thus French state finance could not have been as ineffective as most people believe, and some recent writers have come to its defence.[48]

Yet, insofar as the earlier criticism was justified, what were the reasons? What was wrong with French state finances?

First, the methods of collecting taxes and borrowing money have been subjected to a continuous stream of criticism. One view is that French financial officers were corrupt and incompetent. This assumption was especially popular in the seventeenth and eighteenth centuries. A second opinion holds that the people involved were trapped in an archaic system that was not of their own making; not the people but the structure was at fault.[49] As J.B. Collins has asserted, royal taxation developed only by the crown's accepting a large measure of regional variation and particularistic rights.[50] Worse still, tax collection and state financing were in the hands of officers who enjoyed considerable autonomy from the crown, who were, in fact, private businessmen with patrimonial claims to state financing.[51] A substantial portion of the total was siphoned off before it reached the crown, though most of this was perfectly legal, the money going to provincial state expenditure, the costs of collection, and interest charges. The government sold hereditary and life annuities, which Colbert tried unsuccessfully to abolish. There was no state bank. The Scots banker, John Law, established a national bank in 1718, the Banque royale, but it was merged with a colonial monopoly, the Compagnie des Indes, which soon collapsed. The crown was left, for the remainder of the Old Regime, to rely on annuities and financiers.[52]

In addition, though there has been some exaggeration, the significant number of tax exemptions in France reduced the income of the state. The problem was all the more serious because the greatest number of exemptions were from the payment of the *taille*, the major land tax on which the state depended. As a consequence, the tax burden in France rested heavily on a small tax base consisting of surplus-producing peasants and local trade. This configuration placed low limits on the amount of revenue that could be extracted, overburdened those on whom the state depended, and made the system seem unfair in the eyes of those who were paying.

Finally, French state finance was affected by the nature of the French economy, which did not produce as much commercial surplus per capita that could be taxed by the state as did the British or Dutch economy. The French crown was consequently often in debt to governments or bankers in other countries. Henry IV, for example, was in debt to the British crown and the Estates of Holland, as well as to Swiss and Italian bankers and German princes and towns.[53]

It is not a simple matter to estimate how much royal income came from different sources. According to a list of receipts for 1549, the *tailles* yielded 53.8 per cent of the royal revenue, while excise taxes (the *gabelles* and *aides*) together yielded 18.7 per cent. Only 3.6 per cent was registered as coming from the royal demesne, and no income was shown as coming from what we would call customs. Yet this record was no doubt incomplete.[54] Export-import duties were first levied by the state in 1369 with the *imposition foraine*.[55] They were consolidated along with other transit duties in 1581 as part of the *cinq grosses fermes*.[56] According to figures put together by J.R. Mallet, a clerk in the late seventeenth and early eighteenth centuries, some 4 per cent of royal revenue came from the *cinq grosses fermes* during the years 1600 to 1654.[57] Again, however, the figures are unsatisfactory, in this case for a number of reasons: the *cinq grosses fermes* collected transit duties on goods moving within France as well as those moving into and out of the kingdom; the *cinq grosses fermes* did not collect all import-export duties; and the base we are using does not include all state revenue. Further estimates are available for the eighteenth century from Mathias and O'Brien. Their research suggested that late in the century, 3 to 4 per cent of royal tax revenue came from customs.[58] Indirect tax revenue represented about half of royal tax revenue in the eighteenth century.[59] It should be noted that indirect taxation includes the *gabelle* and also taxes on agricultural produce, most notably wine. Not surprisingly, there has been considerable debate over whether the agricultural sector or the urban sector was overtaxed.[60]

The fundamental problem for the French state was that the major tax on which it relied, the *taille*, became less and less adequate to meet its needs, but the slow growth of the agricultural economy, the unpopularity of the tax, and its perceived unfairness made it difficult to increase. For a land-based state this was an unfavourable situation, when combined, as it was, with massive expenditures, primarily owing to military activity. Some historians are convinced that if France had not been almost constantly at war its finances might have been put on a sound basis. They point out that those reforms that were instituted generally came during periods of peace, and that many reforms worked well until undermined by war expenditures.[61]

THE FRENCH STATE IN EVOLUTIONARY TERMS

For an evolutionist, our discussion so far suggests a mixed assessment of the French state: centralized, but in significant respects decentralized; patrimonial and in some ways undifferentiated, but in other ways differentiated, organized, and professionalized; financially incumbered, but still able to mobilize immense resources. France had the largest land-based armed forces in Western Europe. It also had, as a result of the reforms of Michel Le Tellier and his son, the Marquess of Louvois, the most bureaucratically organized army, despite the persistence into the eighteenth century of venality.

Consequently, from the second half of the seventeenth century, France was a greatly feared military power. The leading rivals of the French were the Habsburgs and the British. Against the Habsburgs, they expanded their territory in the seventeenth century and held their own in the eighteenth. Against the British, they experienced heavy overseas losses in the eighteenth century, but were generally able to frustrate British continental threats. Although the Seven Years' War was a disaster, the last great struggle between the two powers before the French Revolution occurred during the American War of Independence, when France played a major role in the defeat of the British.

2 Lotharingia

By the Treaty of Verdun, Lothaire 1 obtained the middle portion of
the Carolingian Empire. We can say that his kingdom covered approximately what is now the Kingdom of the Netherlands, the Kingdom of
Belgium, Germany west of the Rhine, eastern France (Lorraine,
Alsace, Franche-Comté, Savoy, Dauphiné, and Provence), western Switzerland, and much of northern Italy. Flanders did not go to Lothaire 1,
but I shall include it in what I call Lotharingia. Although my concern
is primarily with the seventeenth and eighteenth centuries, for historical reasons I think the term "Lotharingia" is the most appropriate
one we can use to refer to this region.

Broadly speaking, Lotharingia corresponds with what Fox calls the
Rhineland corridor, the relatively urbanized and commercialized territory that stretched from the coast of Flanders to Venice. It linked
the Mediterranean economic world with that of the North Sea. The
centres of long-distance trade and finance in Lotharingia changed
over the centuries. In the Early Modern period, Marseilles became the
largest French trading centre on the Mediterranean at the expense of
other ports in that area. The Champagne fair towns had been
extremely active in the twelfth and thirteenth centuries, but were
replaced first by the Genevan fairs and later by the fairs of Brabant
(Antwerp and Bergen op Zoom), Frankfort, Besançon, and Lyons.[1]
Comparatively speaking, Genoa and Venice were not as pre-eminent
as they had once been. Nor was Bruges. Indeed, though still crucial
for European trade, by the seventeenth and eighteenth centuries
Lotharingia had, in relative terms, lost some of its trading importance

to other routes, most notably the Atlantic and Baltic sea routes. Yet these two sea routes converged in the Low Countries. Antwerp and Amsterdam, each in turn, were leading European economic centres.

At the same time, many parts of Lotharingia were not very urbanized or commercialized. Urbanization was obviously inconsiderable in higher regions, such as the Ardennes and the Alpine parts of Savoy, Dauphiné, and Provence, but it was modest as well in most of Lorraine, Upper Alsace, and Franche-Comté. Only the southern and northern extremities of Lotharingia were sea-based. Plenty of Lotharingian people lived in relatively land-based societies, though long-distance trade may have passed through their territories.

FROM POLITICAL CENTRE TO POLITICAL PERIPHERY

Before Lothaire I died in 855, Lotharingia was divided into three kingdoms, one for each of his sons. These kingdoms were coveted by the Frankish realm to the west and the Germanic realm to the east. Charles the Bald eventually seized most of Lotharingia, but the collapse of the Frankish kingdom left this region politically fragmented. To restate a point made in chapter 1, this fragmentation does not deny the emergence of smaller jurisdictions where intensive power became concentrated, such as Flanders and other principalities in the Low Countries. Yet only the Northern Netherlands eventually emerged as a major European power in the seventeenth and eighteenth centuries. For extended periods small states remained independent or semi-independent, avoiding amalgamation with larger states. Even today the area contains several comparatively small European states.

Urbanization and commercialization certainly constitute one of the reasons for this fragmentation, as Tilly argues. The best examples for him are the Northern Netherlands, Venice, and other city-states in northern Italy. Indeed, as I have already observed, Venice had been able to resist Carolingian conquest. Strasbourg also illustrates the point. In 1262 it liberated itself from its bishop and became a "free town." When Alsace was annexed by the French in the seventeenth century, Strasbourg was the last to be taken over. Its failure to remain independent was the result, at least in part, of its economic decline, which made it unable to maintain its neutrality and protect itself against the armies of the great powers during the wars of the seventeenth century.

Clearly, however, since comparatively greater urbanization and commercialism did not characterize all of Lotharingia, it cannot be fully understood as a band of capital-intensive states.[2] It also needs to be understood as a periphery among centres. For centuries it was one of the most contested regions in Europe. To the east was the Holy Roman Empire, in which some Lotharingian states were included. Those writers who assume that centralization is progress have not had much respect for the Empire, but a number of historians have challenged the conventional contempt. It has been argued that the Habsburg emperors provided leadership in foreign policy, defence, and law, within the framework of an effective federation that met the needs of the people of the region and the period.[3] Moreover, within the Empire two centralized states emerged, Prussia and Austria, the latter also headed by the Habsburgs.

France too had an interest in Lotharingia; French rulers repeatedly sought to dominate the region and to annex parts of it. The British, after the loss of Calais in 1559, gradually realized that it was impractical for them to try to hold any territory in this or any other part of continental Europe, but they had no small interest in denying control to others, usually the French. Spanish interest in Lotharingia came when Spain was linked up with the Low Countries, Franche-Comté, and the Duchy of Milan. The papacy also had a vested interest in this region, at least in northern Italy.

The slowness with which Lotharingia was incorporated into the larger states surrounding it was primarily due to the fact that the great powers sought to keep one another from holding these small states on a permanent basis. The small states were often able to play European powers off against one another. When faced with a threat from one big neighbour, they could seek aid from another. During the Thirty Years' War Lorraine looked to the Empire for help against threats of French annexation, while the Alsatians solicited protection from the French against the Empire. At the end of the war France acquired rights over Alsace in the Treaty of Westphalia, though only Upper Alsace was clearly ruled by the French. For a number of reasons, one of which was the efforts of Alsatians to preserve their rights by appealing to the Empire, it was not until 1681 that Alsace was fully annexed by France.

The Burgundian dukes had tried to unify a substantial segment of Lotharingia. Begun by Philip the Bold in the late fourteenth century, the Burgundian state reached its peak under Philip the Good in the mid-fifteenth century. In addition to the Duchy of Burgundy and other parts of what is now France, this state comprised most of the Northern and Southern Netherlands, with the notable exception of Liège.

As a rule, in continental Europe, political centres were only secondarily economic centres. This was true of Paris, Berlin, and Vienna. If the Burgundian state had survived it would have meant a very different

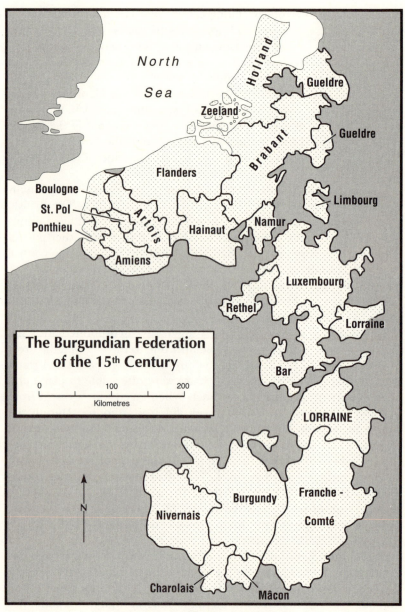

North
Sea

Holland

Gueldre

Zeeland

Gueldre

Brabant

Flanders

Limbourg

Boulogne
St. Pol
Ponthieu

Artois

Namur

Hainaut

Amiens

Luxembourg

Rethel

Lorraine

The Burgundian Federation
of the 15th Century

0   100   200
Kilometres

Bar

LORRAINE

N

Burgundy

Franche -

Nivernais

Comté

Charolais

Mâcon

Map 4

structure of states in Europe, not only because a powerful state would have emerged in Lotharingia, but also because the region that would have become the political centre of this state was primarily an economic centre – Flanders and Brabant. True, the United Provinces eventually became a powerful political and economic centre, but did not include as much of Lotharingia as a Burgundian state would have done.

To take the position that the particular pattern of political centralization that eventually emerged in Western Europe was inevitable requires that we ignore many events in history, but none more than the sudden death without a male heir of Charles the Bold, killed in battle with the Swiss at Nancy in 1477 – an accident of history that led to the collapse of the Burgundian state. The only thing that was perhaps predictable was the acquisition after his death of different segments of the state by the powers that lay to the east and to the west, the greater part going to the Habsburgs through the marriage of Maximilian I of Austria to Mary of Burgundy, daughter of Charles the Bold. As a result, the emerging Burgundian kingdom between France and Britain, on the one side, and the Empire, on the other, was cut short.

The marriage in 1496 of Philip the Handsome (son of Maximilian I and Mary of Burgundy) to Joannna the Mad added Spain and its dominions to the Habsburg lands because she eventually inherited Castile and Aragon. Their heir was Charles V, who became ruler of Germany, Austria, Italy, Spain, and all of the Habsburg lands in Lotharingia. Insofar as this empire had a political centre it was again Flanders and Brabant. It is interesting that northern Lotharingia was the political centre of the two largest European empires since the Roman Empire – that of Charlemagne, which was centred in Aix-la-Chapelle, and that of Charles V. However, in both cases we are talking about very weak political centres. Although Charles V was born and brought up in the Netherlands, his empire was not unified and there was no central administration. Charles himself was the only unifying force, and he was usually on the move. When he abdicated in 1555, he explained his weariness at a ceremony in Brussels: "I have made frequent voyages: nine into Germany, six into Spain, seven into Italy, ten into the Low Countries, four into France, two into England, and ten into Africa, in peace and war, forty altogether."[4]

Charles's abdication made Lotharingia into a political periphery by dividing his possessions between his son, Philip II, and his brother, Ferdinand, the former receiving Spain, the Duchy of Milan, Franche-Comté, and the Netherlands, while the latter became the Holy Roman

Emperor and got the eastern portions centred in Vienna, which he had in fact already been looking after. Philip had been brought up in Spain; his largest possession was Spain; and after visiting the Netherlands he returned to Spain in 1559 to live and rule. As a consequence, the seat of the sovereign to whom the people of the Low Countries, Franche-Comté, and the Duchy of Milan owed allegiance became the distant capital of Madrid. During the same period Alsace was becoming politically peripheralized as well. Strasbourg was a leading centre of Protestantism in the sixteenth century, yet its political power was at the same time declining. The centre of gravity of the Empire moved eastward and Alsace became a periphery.[5]

In the 1560s the Netherlanders revolted against Spanish rule. For almost a hundred years the struggle of Spain to preserve its power in the Low Countries was a critical factor in Lotharingian history, not only in the Low Countries, but also in those other parts of Lotharingia used by the Spanish to supply their northern army – the so-called Spanish Road. At various times Spain sought to acquire control over more of Lotharingia. In 1617 an agreement was signed between Spain and the Archduke Ferdinand of Styria, in which the Spanish promised to support Ferdinand's candidacy for the emperorship in return for his consent to Spain having Alsace; but the agreement never went into effect.[6] Most of the time Spain opted for a strategy of wooing the Lotharingian small states and persuading the great powers to accept their neutrality. For their part, the rulers of the small states became very skilled at using the Spanish interest in the Road to enhance their own dignity and sovereignty, demanding, for example, that permission to enter their lands be requested on every occasion.[7] The Spanish strategy for a long time met Spanish needs. It eventually fell victim, however, to the decline of Spanish power in Europe and the rise of French hegemony. During the seventeenth century France increasingly came to dominate much of Lotharingia and was able to use this domination to cut off the Spanish Road.[8]

It is not feasible in this study to give equal attention to all of Lotharingia. Some parts of it were taken over by France before the French Revolution, such as Franche-Comté, Alsace, and Lorraine. I shall give them the same share of attention I give other parts of France. Beyond French borders, Savoy and the Southern Low Countries have been selected as case studies for two reasons. First, as I indicated in the introduction, they provide interesting contrasts with one another. Secondly, they were more peripheral than other parts of Lotharingia (the Northern Low Countries, Switzerland, and northern Italy) and were under greater French influence.

THE DUCHY OF SAVOY

In the Middle Ages, Savoy was a semi-autonomous county of the Holy Roman Empire, from 1416, a duchy. The counts of Savoy, like many other continental counts and dukes, were able to concentrate considerable intensive power in their hands during the twelfth and thirteenth centuries. And they were able to expand this intensive power by acquiring new territories (outside the original county) during the thirteenth to fifteenth centuries. They did so through military pressure, conquests, strategic marriages, purchases, and the rights of the Holy Roman Emperor, who granted the counts of Savoy feudal superiority over certain lands owing him allegiance.

The dukes became very adept at playing the great powers off against one another. Admittedly, some dukes were better at it than others. Charles III (1504–53) fared badly against Charles V and Francis I, oscillating between the two, in the end losing much of his territory to Swiss and French occupation. He died in 1553 and was later succeeded by his son, Emanuel Filibert (1558–89), who was at the time in the service of the Habsburgs. For a number of reasons, one of which was his success in this service, the Habsburgs assisted him in regaining the majority of his territories, which were accorded to him by the Treaty of Cateau Cambrésis in 1559.[9] Emanuel Filibert was generally skilful at handling the great powers, most notably Spain. The Spanish needed his cooperation to keep open the Spanish Road. A minister in the Spanish government told Philip II that the territorial integrity of Savoy "matters more to Your Majesty for the passage to the Netherlands, than it does to the Duke."[10]

Emanuel Filibert was succeeded by Charles Emanuel I (1580–1630), who was less effective in dealing with other states. He sought to recover lost lands and to extend his territory, but the result was a loss of territory and a weakening of the state, with the consequence that his successors were forced to accept French domination, which persisted until the reign of Victor Amadeus II (1675–1730). For his first fifteen years as duke he too was forced to accept French bullying, but in 1690 Victor Amadeus broke with France and formed an alliance with the Empire. Although he experienced numerous reverses and frustrations, Victor Amadeus was on the whole successful at playing more powerful countries off against one another. He switched allegiance several times between France and the Empire for his own purposes and was even able to get the British and Dutch to contribute to the survival and expansion of his state, primarily by financing his armies.[11] After the War of the Spanish Succession (1702–13) he acquired Sardinia, thus

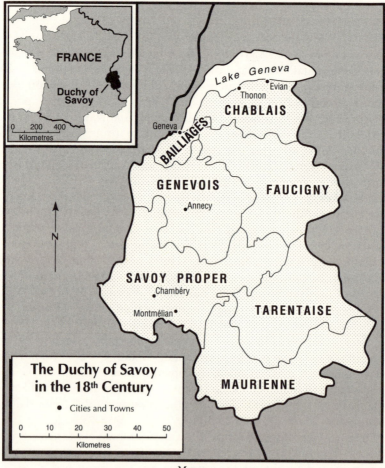

Map 5

becoming king of Sardinia. The rulers and statesmen of the great
powers regarded him as shameless and unprincipled. "I could hardly
conceive he was so impudent a knave," wrote an exasperated George
Stepney, British envoy in Vienna, accusing the duke of a volte-face in
1703. "After such infamous usage as this, mankind ought to detest
him and all that belongs to him."[12]

In the Middle Ages the centralization of power in Chambéry had
been limited by the peripateticism of the counts and their councils,
the fondness of the counts for other residences (particularly Ripaille
on Lake Geneva), and the fact that the estates did not meet in one
place. Nevertheless, the administrative and judicial heart of the state
was located in Chambéry. While the sovereign's council still travelled

with him, the centre of justice was the Resident Council of Justice at Chambéry, which had been set up by Count Aymon in 1329.

Emanuel Filibert, however, moved the capital to Turin, with the result that the state became more Italian than French and the Duchy of Savoy became peripheral. He abolished the estates and advanced the concentration of political power in the hands of the (now removed) central government, though a chamber of accounts and a superior court or Senate, as it was called, both in Savoy, limited this centralization. The Senate enjoyed judicial, legislative, administrative, and ecclesiastical powers, with magistrates that were more professional than French *parlementaires*.[13]

The other major architect of absolutism in Piedmont-Savoy was Victor Amadeus II. As we shall see, the nobility of Savoy was never the same after he was finished with it. During his reign the superiority of "despotism" was openly asserted. Local government was restructured and the authority of the Senate was diminished. The Chamber of Accounts was abolished altogether. The crown launched an attack on venal offices and tried to replace them with trained, professional civil servants. Towns and regions lost much of their autonomy. The fiscal system was reformed. Most of all, the introduction of intendants radically altered the political structure of the whole state. Intendants dispatched from Turin were modelled after French intendants, but were under tighter control by the central administration. They enjoyed administrative, fiscal, military, and, to a lesser extent, judicial powers.[14]

It is essential not to exaggerate the control that Turin exercised over Savoy. The distance between the two, the mountains that had to be crossed to travel from one to the other, the prestige of its traditional institutions, and the historical relationship between the House of Savoy and the province meant that it was in fact one of the more autonomous of the mainland provinces of the House of Savoy.[15] All the same, the power of the central government over the Duchy of Savoy after the changes introduced by Victor Amadeus II certainly exceeded the control of any other centre over a peripheral region that is treated in this volume.

The Medieval County of Savoy had obviously been a land-based rather than a sea-based political centre. The territory was mountainous, economically poor, relatively unurbanized, certainly not a centre of capital, and with little industry. Comparatively speaking, agriculture was not very productive, though it varied greatly within the duchy. Important crossroads were located in Savoy for long-distance trade. There was, however, considerable competition among Alpine regions for this trade, and it brought only meagre benefits to these regions, mainly from tolls and from providing travellers with food and lodging.

With the exception of the grain and certain primary products that were exported, in particular to Geneva and Lyons,[16] the Savoyard economy was largely separate from this long-distance trade. Even short-distance trade was modest in comparison with other regions. Indeed, commercialization was so limited in the economy that the people frequently did not have the cash to pay taxes. In 1611, for example, members of the community of Saint Paul (near Yenne) were forced to sell communal land in order pay a war contribution because they could find no "means to pay by levy, loan or otherwise as a result of the lack of money in this region."[17] With relatively little trade and industry, the business community was small and had slight impact, while the legal community was large and defined the values and way of life of urban society.[18]

Piedmont was the most populated, urbanized, and economically productive among the lands governed by the House of Savoy. (In the fifteenth century the dukes of Savoy had acquired Geneva, but lost it in the early sixteenth century.) Piedmont's greatest non-agricultural economic asset was its textile industry, especially its silk production. Yet Turin was actually a finance centre more than a manufacturing or trading centre. In comparative terms, Turin was a small metropolis, whose demographic growth, like that of Paris, was primarily a consequence of its political importance. In comparative terms, Piedmont was not a highly commercialized or urbanized region, and not involved in much long-distance trade.

It is true that the sources of revenue on which the dukes of Savoy depended were somewhat different from those of the typical land-based state as a result of the long-distance trade that passed through their lands, on which they were able to levy tolls. However, they also depended heavily on land taxes and those consumption taxes that extracted revenue from the less commercialized as well as the more commercialized sectors of the economy. The tax voted by the Estates of the Duchy of Savoy at their last meeting in 1560 became a permanent tax, initially a *gabelle*, in a few years converted into the *taille*, but then made half a land tax and half a tax on salt and other food products.[19] In addition, the dukes frequently forced the population or specific groups to pay special levies for war. And, while the venality of offices did not reach French-like proportions, the dukes were forced to resort to it in order to meet their expenses. They imposed taxes on the inheritance of offices and required forced loans from office-holders.[20]

Although the counts used a variety of methods to expand their territory, the most decisive in the Middle Ages had been their unusual military power, which was the result of the martial competence of a number of the Medieval counts and the warlike character of the population from which they could mobilize an army. The reconstruction of the state by Emanuel Filibert and Victor Amadeus II increased this military power further. Emanuel Filibert established a potent military organization drawing on Swiss mercenaries and other professionals for the core of his force, supplemented by contingents selected from a large conscripted militia that he organized among the peasantry.[21] Some indication of the priority given to the military is provided by the fact that members of this militia enjoyed legal privileges.[22] Almost continuous war and foreign subsidies enabled Victor Amadeus II to militarize his country all the more. Even during peace time, military expenditures represented more than half of all state expenditures. Admittedly, this was not really any more than the French state was spending, but during major wars foreign subsidies enabled the dukes of Savoy to supply an army far larger than they could have managed from their own resources. As shown in table 3 in the preceding chapter the House of Savoy had a larger army per capita than any other country in this study.[23]

Historians should pay more attention to Piedmont-Savoy because it provides an extreme example of a land-based state. This is the principal reason I have chosen to give it special treatment. Whereas France became at least partially a water-based state, Piedmont-Savoy remained almost entirely a land-based state. We see here in magnified form the vicious circle between war and political centralization that was characteristic of land-based states. War created a need for armed force and a more centralized administration, which in turn enabled the dukes to impose their will on peripheral regions. The militarism of the central state both necessitated and assisted the development of new means of taxation. The coercive force available to them was vital domestically and internationally. After the War of the League of Augsburg, Victor Amadeus gave a demonstration of how he meant to rule by using his troops against the rebellious district of Mondovì: it fell under military occupation in 1698; rebel forces were defeated in 1699; its leaders fled or were executed; and assemblies and the possession of arms were banned.[24] It was a style of rule that was applied, in varying degrees, to all parts of Piedmont-Savoy. At the same time, the success of the dukes in war and in international diplomacy raised their prestige. Whatever they may have thought of Victor Amadeus's scruples, most observers acknowledged his courage.[25] And his way of dealing with the great powers made him a hero to many of his people. The grandeur of the dukes helped them to overcome opposition to reforms.[26] There was considerable loyalty to the House of Savoy. The ideal towards which the dukes were striving was reflected in a few words off-handedly written in a medical survey of life in Chambéry in the late eighteenth century. "The Savoyards are good soldiers, much attached to their Prince and their *Patrie*."[27]

THE PRINCIPALITY OF LIEGE

Liège was very different. It had long been a centre of economic activity. The oldest coal mining and metallurgical industry in Europe were in this region. In the eighteenth century, wool spinning and weaving were intense and the principality had developed a flourishing urban armament industry and an active nail industry in the countryside, both of which served mainly foreign markets. The principality had long had an active business bourgeoisie. Its merchants were known in the markets of Brussels, Antwerp, Cologne, and Koblenz. Some wealthy industrialists could be found in the eighteenth century.[28] Although Liège itself had no direct access to the sea, its prosperity depended heavily on its proximity to water-based economies. Much of what was produced in Liège was exported to the densely populated parts of the Low Countries closer to the sea. The large Liégeois nail industry relied heavily on exports to the United Provinces, where the shipbuilding industry created an exceptional demand for nails.[29]

The Principality of Liège was not a territorially unified region as is the Belgian province of Liège today. It consisted of islands of territory surrounded by Austrian provinces, the main island large and elongated, other islands small, some minuscule. Liège evolved in the tenth and eleventh centuries as a semi-autonomous principality governed by a prince-bishop. There was constant and often successful pressure to control it by other sovereigns, either directly or by installing a relative or dependent as prince-bishop. The autonomy of Liège waxed and waned through the Middle Ages and the Early Modern period. Although it avoided absorption by the Burgundians, it was not able to prevent considerable Burgundian interference in its affairs. The principality became the pawn in struggles between the Burgundians and the French. It was forced to accept submissive treaties with the dukes of Burgundy and to accede to their candidates for prince-bishop. As a result of its resistance to this interference, the city of Liège was eventually sacked and pillaged by Charles the Bold in 1468. It was reconstructed, and the Perron (symbol of its communal rights and freedoms) was returned by Mary of Burgundy after the death of her father in 1477. The principality's neutrality was eventually recognized by its more powerful neighbours in 1492, but during the sixteenth century it came under the increasing domination of the Holy Roman

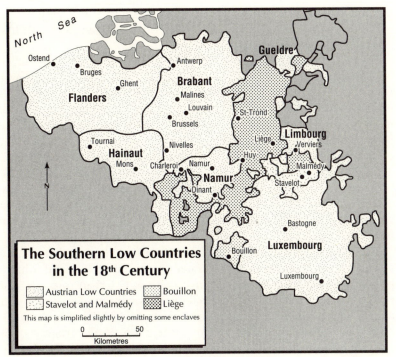

Map 6

Empire, whose protection it received in return for supporting Imperial interests. The prince-bishop managed to keep the principality out of the revolt of the Low Countries in the sixteenth century and was thus able to escape incorporation by either side. It was sometimes impossible, however, for Liège to avoid being drawn into larger power struggles that surrounded it. As a member of the Empire it was led to declare war on France during the War of the League of Augsburg, as a consequence of which it was bombarded and severely damaged by the French in 1691. Yet at other times the French were regarded as protectors against the Empire and against the Spanish/Austrian Low Countries. During the eighteenth century the French went to great lengths to win the allegiance of the Liégeois.[30] All the great powers interfered in the affairs of the principality. Not only the Austrians, but also the Prussians, the Dutch, and the French could be found supporting one or another candidate in elections.[31] The Liège Revolution of 1789 was supported by the Prussians.

Nonetheless, the significant fact is that there was no long-term increase or decrease in the autonomy of the principality until the late eighteenth century. Whatever designs the great statemakers of Europe had on this fragmented patch of the Continent, Liège enjoyed as much autonomy in the Early Modern period as it had in the Middle Ages. What explains this independence?

Here surely is a case where the autonomy of a small state can be explained by its economic strength. Did Liège use its economic resources to pay for the military forces necessary to preserve its independence? No. The principality was and remained incapable of defending itself militarily. It will be seen that the economy of the principality was not totally irrelevant to its survival. Yet it is absolutely clear that Liège's independence was not owed to the armed force it could mobilize by means of its economic resources, but rather to the protection of more powerful neighbours. Although it could become a battleground for these neighbours, and often paid a heavy cost because it could not defend itself, it survived as an autonomous state until the 1790s.

The military weakness of Liège corresponded with that of the prince-bishop. Economic development went hand in hand with a public determination to defend civil liberties.[32] Urban interests had played a critical role in the Medieval institutionalization of such rights and in the establishment of comparatively powerful political assemblies – most notably, the Estates of Liège. As a result, urban groups constituted a strong voice in this assembly during the Early Modern period. Also powerful in the Estates of Liège was the church, or, more precisely, the Chapter of Saint Lambert, whose canons constituted the clerical estate and had the right to elect the prince-bishop. The power of the prince-bishop was also constrained by the Tribunal of XXII, which was established at the end of a bitter political conflict in the fourteenth century. It was to be composed of four canons, four nobles, and fourteen delegates from the towns, whose function it was to hear complaints from the public against episcopal functionaries.[33] It was a valued institution in the eighteenth century for the protection of civil rights.[34]

In the fourteenth and fifteenth centuries a major portion of the state revenues in the principality came from land taxation, but by the eighteenth century mainly indirect taxes were levied.[35] Two conditions explain why the state could rely on indirect taxes. The first is the intense economic activity that was carried out in the principality, insuring relatively good returns from duties levied on trade and consumption within the principality, but also on exports and imports. These export-import duties were further enhanced, however, by political fragmentation. The Liégeois were able to levy duties on goods that passed through their scattered lands, some of which were going only from one part of the Spanish/Austrian Low Countries to another.

THE SPANISH/AUSTRIAN LOW COUNTRIES

The Spanish/Austrian Low Countries consisted of six major provinces: the Counties of Flanders, Hainaut, and Namur, and the Duchies of Brabant, Limbourg, and Luxembourg. Ruling over each was, in a strict legal sense, a separate sovereign, a count or a duke, but from the Burgundian period the separate roles were in fact all performed by the same sovereign. Whereas the Principality of Liège was semi-autonomous, the Habsburgs exercised direct sovereignty over the Spanish/Austrian Low Countries. And whereas Liège formed part of the Holy Roman Empire, in the Early Modern period the Spanish/Austrian Low Countries did not.

The Netherlands, both Northern and Southern, have formed one of the most economically active regions of Europe. From the eleventh to the sixteenth centuries the way was led by Flanders and Brabant. In the seventeenth and eighteenth centuries it was the Northern Low Countries that excelled. In the nineteenth century it was southern Belgium.

In the sixteenth century, Antwerp became the northern terminus of the Lotharingian long-distance trade route and stood as the leading centre of finance and trade in northwestern Europe.[36] The war with Spain and the closure of the Scheldt by the Dutch in 1585 led to the decline of Antwerp and the rise of Amsterdam. Despite this shift, the ports and towns of the Spanish/Austrian Low Countries remained active in long-distance trade during the seventeenth and eighteenth centuries, particularly Ostend, which took part in the Atlantic-London-Netherlandish-Baltic trading network, though less so than ports in the Northern Low Countries. Flanders was one of the most water-based regions of Europe. So was Brabant, though less so than if the Dutch had not blocked the Scheldt. Wallonia was much more land-based, especially Luxembourg. Nevertheless, the Spanish/Austrian Low Countries were, taken as a whole, more water-based than France, and plainly far more water-based than Savoy.

Urban development in the Netherlands had been precocious. The importance of towns dates from the twelfth century in Brabant and earlier still in Flanders. Compared with most of Europe, Flanders, Brabant, and even Hainaut formed a comparatively urbanized part of Europe in the eighteenth century. Although Hainaut could boast few populous towns, one quarter of the population was urbanized in 1784.[37]

Political Development

Politically it has been a different story. After the breakup of the Carolingian Empire, the Low Countries fragmented into a dozen or

more principalities or provinces, whose dukes and counts owed nominal allegiance either to the king of France or the German emperor.
Even during the reunification of the greater part of the Low Countries
in the fourteenth and fifteenth centuries under the House of Burgundy, the provinces were ruled individually. Nonetheless, the assimilation under the Burgundians of the sovereignty of each province in
a single person did much to centralize political power. Although most
provincial institutions were not abolished, common structures were set
up to administer the territory as a whole; each province had its own
governor and council, while a Great Council was established for the
larger realm.[38] The balance of power between the estates and the
sovereign shifted in some measure towards the latter and taxation
increased, especially under Charles the Bold (1467–77).

Under Charles v, those who advised the governor-general in the
Low Countries were organized, on the basis of administrative specialization that had developed gradually, into three collateral councils: the
Council of State, the Privy Council, and the Council of Finance. A
major attempt to centralize power was undertaken by his son, Philip ii,
but it met with fierce opposition. From the first days of his reign,
Philip ii was unpopular with the Netherlanders. Whereas his father
had been a Fleming, he was very much a Spaniard and preferred to
rule the Low Countries through Spanish administrators. The Netherlanders did not like being ruled by foreigners. Even Maximilian i's
popularity had been negatively affected by the fact that he was German. Philip the Handsome (1494–1506) had been more popular
because he was born in the Low Countries. Philip ii was considered
a foreigner, all the more when he sought to strengthen the power of
the sovereign at the expense of local elites and tried to impose religious conformity. Dissatisfaction began with Philip's efforts to reduce
the power of privileged groups in the Low Countries – the nobility,
the clergy, and the towns.[39] It grew rapidly as a result of his determined
policy of suppressing Protestantism. And it was ignited by the appointment of the Duke of Alba as governor-general, sent to quell the unrest
that had broken out. Although the "terror" of Alba was exaggerated
by contemporary writers, his administration did see the establishment
of a special tribunal to try opponents, a large number of death
sentences, including the execution of two leading nobles, and tax
increases without the approval of the estates.[40]

A number of reasons can be given for the success of the Dutch
revolt. One of these is consistent with the geo-economic model of Fox
and his followers. The geography of the Low Countries was an obstacle
to Spanish military action. The great number of water courses made
the transportation of an army difficult, especially since the Dutch were

willing to flood their own land in order to impede the movement of the Spanish army. Moreover, the sea route from Spain to the Low Countries was obstructed by the Sea Beggars (a fleet in the service of the Prince of Orange and manned by exiled Netherlanders) as well as by a deterioration in English-Spanish relations and a French Protestant navy.[41] The Spanish were then forced to depend on the overland route, the problematic Spanish Road. In the mid-seventeenth century an Englishman wrote that the success of the Dutch had been due to "their strength in shipping, the open Sea, their many fortified Towns" and the "lowness and plentiful Irriguation" of the land, which made it "unpassable for an army when the winter but approaches."[42]

Tilly's model is also supported by the Dutch case. Philip II faced severe financial problems in fighting the war. It might have been better for the Spanish if the Netherlanders had all revolted together; a rebellion of this kind might have been put down once and for all. The revolt, however, developed slowly, was repeatedly rekindled, and dragged on and on. Thus the Spanish were forced to maintain a large army in the Low Countries for decades. It was beyond their capacity to support financially, with the result that the wages of the army were almost always in arrears.[43] In 1575 Philip was forced into bankruptcy – a restructuring of his debts that solved his immediate problems, but made the long-term financing of the war still more difficult. In fact, it became hard even to arrange the transfer of money to the Low Countries. To make matters worse, his enemies were comparatively "capital-intensive," to use Tilly's term, enjoying reasonable financial resources to pay for the fight. Indeed, they were able to impair one source of borrowing for Philip – the financial institutions in the Low Countries. In some ways it was the perfect example of a commercialized and urbanized small state resisting control by a monarchical state.

Yet we should not depend too much on this line of argument. In the sixteenth century it was the Southern Low Countries that had the greater economic centres (Bruges, Ghent, Brussels, and Antwerp), but the Southern Low Countries returned to Spanish rule. Furthermore, despite Philip's financial problems, Spain still commanded resources that surpassed those of the Low Countries.[44]

In addition to the geo-economic reasons for Dutch success, there was a critical geo-political reason: the intentional and unintentional assistance given to the Dutch by other powers, assistance that the Dutch pursued with intense diplomatic efforts, though not always with success. The Turks may have been the most help to the Netherlanders, by periodically diverting Spanish attention and resources in the direction of the Mediterranean.[45] Spain gave higher priority to the Turkish threat than to the Dutch revolt. France was torn by civil war during a good part of the last half of the sixteenth century, and so could play only a limited role, but the French did make financial contributions to the rebels, and the Duke of Anjou (brother of Henry III, king of France) temporarily assumed the role of sovereign of the Netherlandish provinces in the early 1580s.[46] The English government and population provided greater assistance, particularly financial aid; they interfered with Spanish borrowing in England, donated money to the Dutch cause, assisted Protestant refugees, confiscated Spanish property, and attacked and destroyed Spanish ships. The English were the first to assist the Netherlanders openly and to sign a treaty of alliance with the rebels.[47] The English were, however, playing a delicate game. Much as they loved to make trouble for the Spanish, they preferred to have the Spanish rule the Low Countries than the French. The English government therefore provided enough support to keep the revolt going, but not enough that Spanish power in the Low Countries would collapse altogether.

Still, even with all this assistance, the outcome of the revolt was not inevitable. The fact that the Spanish held the Southern Low Countries is clear evidence that in spite of everything that was against them they might have won the war, in which case the story to be told in this book would have been very different.

In the event, the revolt made the Northern Low Countries a political as well as an economic centre, where political interests were often subordinated to economic ones. It had the opposite effect in the Southern Low Countries, which had to face the rigours of Philip's absolutism. Philip persisted in relying on force to rule the southern provinces and to try to repossess the northern ones. Yet this determination ultimately waned. With a view towards gaining the allegiance of South-Netherlanders he decided that their lands should pass (rather than to his son) to his daughter, Isabella, who would marry the governor-general of the Spanish Low Countries, Albert, archduke of Austria. Together they were to rule the Spanish Low Countries as monarchs so that these provinces would enjoy more autonomy than they had been permitted during Philip's reign. It is true that foreign policy, defence, military justice, and finance were still controlled by the Spanish king, with the help of separate administrative structures staffed by Spaniards. Yet the transfer of authority to the archdukes was still a major concession to the South-Netherlandish autonomy, and their rule was in most respects decentralized.[48]

As a result of the decline of Spanish world power in the seventeenth century, these centrifugal forces were not undermined by the death of Archduke Albert in 1621 and the return of the Spanish Low Countries to direct rule from Spain. Spain no longer had the strength to enforce its will in the Low Countries. The Spanish were still unable to supply their army there by sea. From 1622 the Spanish Road was also closed.[49] With the contraction in their military power and international stature in the seventeenth century, they could only maintain sovereignty over the Spanish Low Countries by abandoning any further drive towards centralization and absolutism. The Spaniards concerned themselves largely with foreign affairs and military matters, leaving internal administration up to the governor general and the Netherlanders.[50] Thus, while the seventeenth was a century of state centralization in France, the evolution towards greater political centralization and absolutism that had begun in the Southern Low Countries under the Burgundians, and was carried further by the Spaniards in the sixteenth century, abated in the seventeenth century.

Estates

Political assemblies in the Low Countries go back at least to the twelfth century. As in France, however, it was primarily during the thirteenth and fourteenth centuries that such institutions established themselves in the different provinces of the Low Countries.[51] Based on his research on Flanders, Jan Dhondt insisted that these institutions did not originate in the need of the sovereign for money, nor as a consequence of the structuring of society in carefully defined orders, but rather they had their origin in struggles for power among various socio-economic groups in society; only later did the fiscal requirements of the sovereign play a determining role. To begin with it was the wealth and power of vassals that demanded representation. By the thirteenth century a new power had arisen, that of the towns, which eventually surpassed the power of the vassals and even rivalled the authority of the sovereign. As in Liège, in Brabant and Flanders these urban groups were crucial in the development of political assemblies.[52] More recently Willem Blockmans has reaffirmed this line of argument and has tried to extend it to other parts of Europe. He has been able to show that the distribution of power in political assemblies could vary considerably from one region to another. In some the clergy were the most powerful, in others the nobility, in still others the third estate. Moreover, it was not always these three groups that were represented.[53]

While this thesis may underestimate the importance of the fiscal requirements of the sovereign, its emphasis on struggles for power and the variability of estate representation is generally accepted. Flanders and Brabant offer good illustrations of this variability because towns were so powerful in these provinces in the thirteenth and fourteenth centuries.

The authority of political assemblies in the Low Countries diminished under the Burgundians until the death of Charles the Bold. Mary of Burgundy was then forced to accept a reassertion of their powers. This revival was followed by a gradual weakening of the estates under Philip the Handsome, Charles v, and Philip ii. Of special significance was the victory of Charles v over the town of Ghent; in response to their refusal to grant him a subsidy he wanted, he took control over the town's representation in the Estates of Flanders. During the seventeenth and eighteenth centuries a further decline in the power of the estates occurred. There was an expansion of royal authority over the composition and deliberations of the estates. The central government often bullied estates into decisions they would not otherwise have made. Many town representatives came to be appointed by the central government, and the approval of taxes became routine.[54]

On the other hand, at least they had estates. In contrast with France and Savoy, provincial estates could be found in almost all the provinces of the Spanish/Austrian Low Countries in the seventeenth and eighteenth centuries and their traditional authority was far from eliminated. The fundamental source of that authority was control over revenue. In the Spanish/Austrian Low Countries, direct taxes and some indirect taxes were levied by the estates, while only indirect taxes were levied by the sovereign. In general the estates gave the central government what it wanted, but in doing so they could exercise considerable influence or constrain the actions taken by the central government, which frequently made concessions to the estates or anticipated their wishes so that things would run smoothly. This was especially the case with respect to "extraordinary revenues" (usually for war), as opposed to "ordinary." The former could vary and concessions could be extracted by the estates for a large extraordinary subsidy. The cooperation of the estates was almost essential for borrowing money; their revenues were normally the security for loans. The estates were also entrusted with many functions by the central government and often took initiatives themselves to make improvements in their provinces. Relative to other people living in the Austrian Low Countries, those who belonged to the estates enjoyed considerable political power.

There were no Estates General. In an effort to give the Low Countries greater political unity, Philip the Good had organized the Estates General in 1463. However, they exercised little authority after 1585 and never convened after 1632. As in France, they were caught between two opposing forces: provincial particularism and evolving absolutism. The regional particularism that made the provincial estates strong also made it difficult for them to cooperate with one another. They would not give up any of their powers to the Estates General, much less allow themselves to be replaced by a more centralized assembly. If the Estates General failed to advance political unity, the sovereign could see no point to them and so had little reason to convene them.[55]

Austrian State Building

As a result of the War of the Spanish Succession, the Habsburg Low Countries were transferred to the Austrians. What sort of state was this and how did the Southern Low Countries fit into it? For one thing, it was an eastern absolutist land-based state ruling over a western society characterized, as we have seen, by a relatively developed economy and strong urban centres. For another, despite its land basis, in comparison with other eastern absolutisms and also with Spanish absolutism, Austrian absolutism was less militaristic. In addition, like their Spanish counterparts, the Austrian Habsburgs administered an assortment of territories whose heterogeneity was even greater than the heterogeneity of the territories ruled by the French monarchy. And, finally, Maria Theresa (1740–80), and even more her son Joseph II (1765–90), pursued an active policy of what they considered to be political modernization, the objective of which was to undermine the power of privileged groups and to centralize state administration and improve its efficiency. The underlying motivation was a determination to strengthen the Austrian state, in particular the hereditary lands, in order to withstand the Turks and to meet the challenge of other European powers, most of all Prussia.

In the Low Countries the Austrians improved the professionalism of the state bureaucracy. More account was taken of administrative competence in the appointment of officials. More authority was invested in the governor general's minister, the "plenipotentiary minister." There was a centralization of authority at the expense of the provincial governors and, to a lesser extent, the governor general, all of whom increasingly became figure-heads.[56] The direct authority of the chancellor over South-Netherlandish affairs was strengthened by the abolition in 1757 of the Supreme Council of the Netherlands, which had been the principal advisory body on governing the Austrian Low Countries and had been regarded as too pro-Netherlandish. The functions of the Privy Council were augmented. Eventually Joseph decreed sweeping reforms designed to transform the political, religious, and educational structure of the society and to undermine the position of the nobility, the guilds, and the urban patriciate of the towns.[57]

How effective were the Habsburgs as statemakers in the Southern Low Countries? The most serious problem was their inability to defend these lands and their interests against other powers. The Spanish Habsburgs had to give into the closure of the Scheldt by the Dutch and accept the loss of considerable territory to France during the seventeenth century. There were no comparable losses in the eighteenth century, but the Southern Low Countries provided a major battleground for the War of the Spanish Succession. The region was occupied by various foreign armies, so that there was really no clear sovereignty over these provinces until the Austrian Habsburgs firmly secured control in 1716. One of the agreements that ensued from this war was the Barrier Treaty between Austria and the United Provinces, by which 35,000 troops were to be stationed in the Austrian Low Countries, three-fifths of whom were to be provided by the Austrians and the remainder by the Dutch. The Dutch troops were to be maintained at the expense of the Austrian Low Countries, which in addition were required to furnish a heavy subsidy to the Estates General of the United Provinces and to pay off earlier debts owing to the United Provinces. As a consequence, the Austrian Low Countries, under the terms of the treaty, owed the Estates General of the United Provinces 2,100,000 florins annually.[58] To this burden and humiliation were added the invasions and occupations of the subsequent period, the most prolonged of which came during the War of the Austrian Succession (1740–48). Austrian rule was re-established in 1748 when Maria Theresa's right to the sovereignty of the provinces was recognized, though she lost other parts of her dominions. This was followed by a long period of peace in the Low Countries. On balance, the Austrians did better during the eighteenth century than the Spaniards had done during the seventeenth century. Nevertheless, in the end their rule proved to be as precarious. It was brought to a conclusion with a revolution and two French conquests.

Although the Low Countries were comparatively sea-based, they were highly vulnerable to land-based conquest and were ruled by land-based centres. The people were used to large armies. During the late sixteenth and early seventeenth centuries the Spanish army in the Low Countries, the Army of Flanders, averaged about 65,000 men, more than half of whom were from outside the Low Countries (Spain, Italy, Burgundy, Germany, and the British Isles). By 1664, however, this army was reduced to 11,000 men.[59] During the eighteenth century most of the troops required by the Barrier Treaty were foreigners, but the Austrians gradually built a number of "national regiments," recruited primarily from the Austrian Low Countries. It was a difficult task. The South-Netherlanders were not especially militaristic and would not

Table 4
Province of Origin of Effectives in National Regiments of the Austrian Low Countries, 1786–87

Province	Number of effectives	Number of effectives per 10,000 inhabitants
Brabant and Malines	3,689	56
Flanders	3,148	39
Luxembourg	2,037	91
Hainaut	1,430	50
Namur	752	80
Limbourg	605	61
Tournai and Tournaisis	338	42
Gueldre	39	15
TOTAL	12,038	53

The total number of effectives per 10,000 inhabitants differs from the figure for 1786 in table 3 because table 3 includes effectives recruited from outside the Austrian Low Countries. See note 60 for source.

accept conscription or volunteer in great numbers. As shown in table 3 in the preceding chapter, even during the second half of the century, when the number increased significantly, the total size of the national regiments relative to population was small in comparison with the armies of most other continental countries, though the peak of 17,000 men in 1780 did represent a respectable ratio. As shown in table 4, Flanders and Brabant provided the largest absolute number of effectives, but relative to population the more land-based Luxembourg, Namur, and Limbourg provided the largest number. The availability of alternative employment is not likely the explanation for these differences. Flanders was heavily overpopulated at this time. As historians have found in other countries, there appears to be a relationship between army recruitment and distance from the sea, a relationship that is consistent with the Foxian model.

The proportion of state revenue coming from indirect taxes (excise, tolls, and customs) rose in the eighteenth century, exceeding one-half in 1782, while land taxes provided only about a third, though it should be understood that, as in France, some of the indirect taxation was levied on agricultural products, such as wine, beer, spirits, wheat, and meat.[61] Needless to say, indirect taxes yielded proportionately more in more urbanized parts of the country.[62] One historian estimated that, during the second half of the eighteenth century, customs duties raised 20 to 25 per cent of state revenues, but in 1780 we know that they accounted for only 16 per cent.[63] In any case, customs certainly brought in more than the 3 to 4 per cent they did in France. Table 5

Table 5
Customs Revenues of the Austrian Low Countries in 1780

	Customs revenue (florins)	Revenue per capita (florins)
Brabant and Malines	968,000	1.5
Flanders	1,370,500	1.7
Luxembourg	326,500	1.5
Hainaut	112,000	0.4
Namur	74,000	0.8
Limbourg	90,750	0.9
Tournai and Tournaisis	91,000	1.1
Gueldre	21,250	0.8
TOTAL	3,054,000	1.3

See note 64 for source.

indicates that in 1780 the two sea-based provinces yielded more customs revenue per capita than most of the land-based provinces, but
the contribution was remarkably high in Luxembourg, no doubt because goods going elsewhere had to be transported across the borders,
as was the case in Savoy and Liège.

Tax revenue did not match expenditures, and large-scale borrowing
was necessary. This was the usual way of raising extraordinary revenue,
and full advantage was taken of the capital available in the Northern
and Southern Low Countries.[65] Yet the government went from one
financial crisis to another, particularly in the first half of the eighteenth century; at times it was not able to pay full wages to troops and
civil servants, meet its obligations under the Barrier Treaty, or pay all
the interest due to creditors.[66] Taxes were low and the population was
firmly resistant to any increases; taxes were often not fully paid.[67] In
addition, the economy of the Southern Low Countries had experienced difficulties in the period since the separation of the north,
though it was still more commercialized and industrialized than most
other parts of Europe.

The financial situation improved after 1750. Two principal reasons
have been given. First, economic expansion augmented returns from
customs; second, Maria Theresa terminated payments to the United
Provinces after the War of the Austrian Succession.[68] Her government
also introduced new tariffs, renegociated revenue agreements with
some provincial estates, improved the financial administration, and
established a state lottery. Under these new circumstances, state
finances in the Austrian Low Countries were certainly healthier than

French finances during the second half of the eighteenth century, though borrowing continued to be necessary.

In certain respects the Austrian state bureaucracy was more effective and efficient than the French. It was not as infested by venality. True, offices had been sold since the fourteenth century, under the form of *engagère d'office*. The practice persisted during the Austrian regime at all levels of administration, despite efforts to curtail it.[69] A fee or tax, known as a *médianate*, was also charged on the assumption of an office. Yet, in the Low Countries, venality of office was never as pervasive, neither in its scale nor in its consequences, as it was in France; and it declined in the late eighteenth century.[70] This decline gave the Habsburgs greater control over their bureaucracy than could be claimed by the Bourbons.

POLITICAL CENTRALIZATION

An Anachronistic Empire?

If we compare the development of the state in the countries discussed in this and the preceding chapter, the similarities are as striking as the differences. Although France, Piedmont-Savoy, and the Habsburg dominions were very different as states, the same movement towards the centralization of power was characteristic of all three. The exception was Liège. It was not ruled directly by the Habsburgs, but was merely part of the Holy Roman Empire. To this extent its relationship to the Habsburgs resembled that of Hanover, Saxony, Brandenburg, and Bavaria. In contrast, the Austrian Low Countries belonged to the Austrian dominions, which also included Bohemia, Moravia, Hungary, Austria, and Tyrol. Maria Theresa and Joseph II were not seeking to build a unified and centralized state out of the Holy Roman Empire; but they were endeavouring to do so out of these states over which they exercised direct rule. The fact that this state did not endure does not mean that we can relegate it to the status of an anachronistic empire. In the territories that they ruled directly, Maria Theresa and Joseph were consciously trying to do what the French, the Prussians, and the House of Savoy were doing to centralize power.

It is true that, as a result of dynastic marriages and inheritances, but also as a result of trading territories with other European states, the Habsburg lands were geographically dispersed. This dispersion must not, however, be overstated; most of their possessions formed a solid bloc in Eastern Europe. Moreover, we should not necessarily see dispersion as anachronistic and characteristically imperial. Dynastic marriages and trading territories were elements of European kingship that gave rise elsewhere to what we call nation-states or national states. There is nothing distinctively imperial about dynastic marriages and trading territories, nor the non-contiguity that could result from them.

Yet it was very difficult to construct a unified, centralized state with non-contiguous territories. The Habsburgs were aware of this as they watched their rivals build states. Charles v allowed his lands to be divided because he perceived the impossibility of effectively ruling them all. Philip ii saw only too clearly that the geographical distance between Spain and the Low Countries made them difficult to hold. Joseph ii sought unsuccessfully to exchange the Austrian Low Countries for Bavaria.[71] In 1781 he visited the South-Netherlandish provinces, but he was the first Habsburg sovereign to do so since Philip ii.

That even centralizing states can have problems if some of their territory is non-contiguous is demonstrated by the experience of the House of Savoy when it acquired Sicily and then Sardinia. The Treaty of Utrecht (1713) gave Sicily to Victor Amadeus ii. He was unable, however, to centralize power as he had done in Piedmont-Savoy and lost Sicily in a few years for a number of reasons, but certainly including the logistical difficulty created by the considerable distance from the state's centre in Piedmont to the island possession and the presence of hostile powers between the two. In compensation he acquired Sardinia. Yet he was unable to force upon this island the kind of centralization that he was putting into place in Piedmont-Savoy, again for a number of reasons, but clearly in part because of the geographical separation of Sardinia from the principal possessions of the House of Savoy.

Nonetheless, the Austrian Habsburgs and the House of Savoy enjoyed remarkable success during the seventeenth and eighteenth centuries in building centralized states. The stimulus that interstate competition could give to state reorganization and reform is no where better demonstrated than in the Habsburg dominions under Maria Theresa and Joseph ii, who took up the challenge of increasing French and Prussian power to strengthen the state which they headed. In a different way, Piedmont-Savoy was also a remarkable accomplishment in state building. It too is forgotten, again because it did not survive into the twentieth century.

Capital-Intensive Path versus Coercion-Intensive Path?

Tilly wrote *Coercion, Capital, and European States* out of dissatisfaction with unilinear models (including his own) of the making of European states; they assumed that states evolved through a steady process of political centralization. Such models could not, he felt, account for the great variety of types of states that can be found in different centuries; in particular, they could not account for the fragmented states that were found in Lotharingia during the Middle Ages and the Early Modern period. He came to the conclusion that these states were able to evade forces of political centralization because they were capital-intensive.

Although it cannot be denied that a variety of types of states have existed in different periods of European history and that the emergence of the modern state has not been a unilinear process, it is not clear to me that states in Lotharingia escaped the forces of centralization affecting other European countries or that capital-intensive is the best way of characterizing the development of states in this region. First, I have suggested that a large centralized state may well have emerged in Lotharingia but for the death of Charles the Bold without a male heir. Second, I have argued that the principal reason for the political fragmentation of Lotharingia was not the concentration of capital in this region, but rather that the region was a buffer zone between large central powers. Thus the development of regional political centres explains not only the emergence of states in France and the British Isles, but also the political fragmentation of Lotharingia. Tilly's explanation for political fragmentation in Lotharingia results from a tendency to see the Northern Low Countries as the model Lotharingian state, which is, in my view, a mistake. Only some of the Lotharingian states owed their autonomy to commercialization and capital, while all of them (even to some extent the Northern Low Countries) owed their autonomy to the struggle among great centralizing powers. There was no one path to the modern state, but there was one force – regional political centralization – that played a greater role than any other.

3 The British Isles

The centre-periphery structure of the British Isles was based on certain well-known social and economic differences between the southeast and the rest of the islands. It was under the Romans that these differences first began to emerge. In the southeast the Romans established a commercialized urban society, literate and bureaucratic, linked with the Continent. Ireland was never invaded. What is now Scotland was invaded, but Rome had to withdraw its forces to serve elsewhere.

Some writers have stressed that peripheral regions in the British Isles have higher altitudes.[1] They have pointed out that highland regions were more pastoral, less wealthy, unable to support a dense population, inaccessible, and difficult to conquer. It is true that much of the territory the Romans failed to subdue has higher altitudes than the southeast, yet the peripheral regions in the British Isles are obviously not all characterized by high altitudes. Ireland for the most part is not. Distance from the southeast has been a greater factor. Roman settlers were not anxious to locate in far-off regions; and, militarily, these regions were costly to hold, requiring that armies be transported and supplied around the coast of Britain or across the Irish Sea. Controlling regions so far removed from the centres of Roman power did not seem worth the resources it required.

THE RISE OF CENTRES IN THE MIDDLE AGES

Before the Normans

The withdrawal of the Romans from the British Isles led to a remarkable process of deurbanization and political decentralization. The

Anglo-Saxons were not inclined to form towns. Their people interacted and traded at non-urban central places.[2] They were also less
concentrated in the southeast than the Romans, though they did not
altogether undermine the regional differences created by Roman
colonization.

The Scandinavians, whose major invasions began in the late eighth
century, initially set up coastal ports and were slower to push inland.
In what is now England they placed themselves largely along the
eastern coast. Scandinavians also settled in Ireland and in northern
Scotland and the western islands, where the Romans and the Anglo-
Saxons did not go. In some ways the Scandinavians reinforced the
divergence between the southeast and other parts of the islands, while
in other respects they altered the earlier pattern by effecting change
in parts of the British Isles well beyond the southeast.

By the ninth and tenth centuries the post-Roman decentralization
was being reversed. The Anglo-Saxon kings established their position
first in Wessex and then all across southern England and north into
Mercia. Royal authority was exercised by means of sealed writs. The
Anglo-Saxon kings possessed a comparatively differentiated administration and considerable powers of taxation. It is true that local autonomy persisted in many areas, particularly Danish areas, but the
concentration of power intensified further under the Danish king
Cnut (1017–35).[3]

Less well recognized is the fact that monarchies were expanding
their power in other parts of the British Isles as well. Kenneth
MacAlpin, king of the Scots, acquired the Pictish throne during the
ninth century. He and his descendants extended their territory and
struggled to conquer the Lothians. It was Malcolm II (1005–34) who
succeeded in doing so. Malcolm was continuously on the move, but
his power base was the heartland of the Scoto-Pictish kingdom, the
region between the River Forth/Firth of Clyde line and the mountain
range that runs from Ben Nevis to the North Sea near Stonehaven.[4]

Although what little unity this kingdom had was shattered by dynastic struggles, reunification was achieved by Malcolm III (1058–93).
He had lived in England during the reign of his predecessor, Macbeth.
He also married Margaret, sister of Edgar the Aetheling, the refugee
English heir after the Norman Conquest of England. These influences
had lasting impact on the history of the British Isles. They led to
stronger ties between the Scottish crown and the English. They also
brought about a growth in English-speaking Lothian influence over
the Scottish crown and a decrease in the influence of the old Gaelic-
speaking heartland.

In post-Scandinavian Ireland the title of king was reserved for the
ruler of a *tír*, roughly the size of a modern county. Consolidation

Map 7

increased further in the eleventh and twelfth centuries, and the size of the territories over which kings ruled expanded. The officialdom serving these kings became larger and more differentiated; kings were more directly involved in legislation and punishment; they centralized ecclesiastical organization and developed a theocratic ideology of kingship; and they copied the ritual of other European monarchies.[5]

Admittedly, these Irish kingdoms were not as powerful or as differentiated as the monarchy in England. Even the Scottish kingdom did not have the administrative apparatus of the English crown. Also, Scottish kings sometimes acknowledged the superiority of English kings.[6] One could argue, however, that all parts of the British Isles were moving in a similar direction towards regional kingdoms. If observers had been asked in the mid-eleventh century to predict the future political structure of the British Isles, they might have predicted what actually happened, but could just as easily have predicted the consolidation of one or two kingdoms in Ireland and another two or three in Britain, perhaps with, perhaps without, an independent kingdom of Northumbria or York.

The Normans and Angevins

Such a prediction would have been foolish at the end of the century. By then the Normans had introduced a new force in the British Isles. Even then what happened was far from inevitable, but the Normans did eventually unify the islands and further the centralization of power in the southeast to a greater extent than ever before. The kind of rule they imposed varied from one part of the British Isles to another. These differences can be related to more general differences in state formation across Western Europe.

There were two ways in which Medieval rulers expanded their political power. The first was "intensive-expansion": dukes or counts began with a comparatively tightly organized duchy or county and then extended their rule over new territories through conquest or other means, seeking to maintain the intensity of their authority, though not always successfully. The other way was "extensive-expansion": rulers have an extensive claim over a large territory, which they gradually make good by destroying or undercutting those who have rivalled their authority. While no states were formed exclusively along one route as opposed to the other, French state formation came closer to the second than did Savoyard state formation. Norman state formation followed the intensive route, but only in Normandy and England, not in the rest of the British Isles.

The intensive power established by William in Normandy was extended into England.[7] William forged a powerful monarchy in England by two means: by coercion, sometimes savage coercion, and by exercising rights that he claimed he inherited from the Anglo-Saxon monarchy. This did not happen overnight. In 1066–67 William acquired control over little more than the southeast. There was resistance to further expansion, but in the years 1068–75 William severely crushed rebellions in the southwest, the Midlands, and the north, where he confiscated lands and reinforced royal authority.[8] In strategic

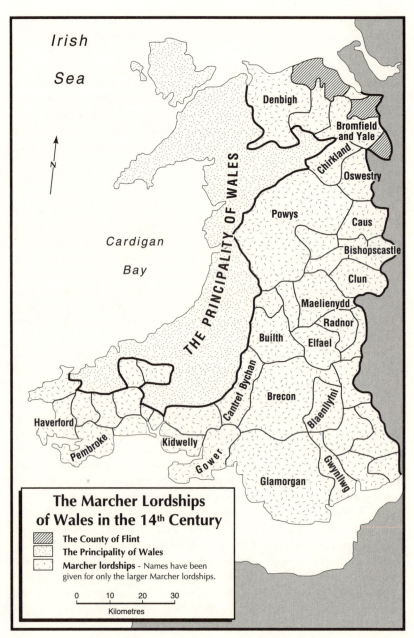

Irish Sea

Cardigan Bay

THE PRINCIPALITY OF WALES

Denbigh

Bromfield and Yale

Chirkland

Oswestry

Powys

Caus

Bishopscastle

Clun

Maelienydd

Radnor

Builth

Elfael

Cantref Bychan

Brecon

Blaenllyfni

Gwynllwg

Haverford

Pembroke

Kidwelly

Gower

Glamorgan

The Marcher Lordships of Wales in the 14th Century

The County of Flint

The Principality of Wales

Marcher lordships - Names have been given for only the larger Marcher lordships.

0   10   20   30

Kilometres

Map 8

areas he granted compact blocs of land to his closest allies. From Kent to Chester large blocs were entrusted to his half-brothers and several other loyal followers.[9]

William relied on much the same methods in Wales, but he did not conquer Wales as he did England. Two reasons have been offered by historians. First, the Norman methods of warfare, with the emphasis on castles and well-coordinated cavalry, did not have the same advantages in Wales that they did in England. Guerilla warfare with lightly armed foot-soldiers was more effective in Wales. Second, an occupation of Wales by a Norman king, even if possible, was not worth the costs it would have entailed; he simply could not have committed the necessary military and financial resources. Instead, military commands were created. In return for restraining Welsh raids, Norman lords were given extraordinary powers and were encouraged to raid or invade Wales as they pleased.[10]

In contrast with their conquest of England, the Normans formed separate Norman regions in Wales. Norman lords brought settlers with them, both French and English, and others followed. They settled mostly in what was called the "March" – a wide swath of land shaped like a reversed L. In other parts of Wales, power was fragmented among a great number of native Welsh lords, though occasionally one lordship would become, at least for a period, hegemonic. The Norman kings did not have intensive authority over either region. True, the power of the crown should not be underestimated. Norman kings did achieve a measure of domination over Wales without conquest; even the great Marcher lords were left in no doubt about the sovereignty of the crown.[11] The dissimilarity with England is, nonetheless, unmistakable.

What happened in Ireland under the Normans has some resemblance with Wales. In the year 1169 a number of Norman lords went to Ireland to help the King of Leinster. They did so without the authorization of Henry II, but two years later he followed in an effort to establish royal authority over both Gaelic and Norman lords. He built royal castles in what is now Limerick, Waterford, Cork, and Dublin. The political fragmentation of Ireland, like Carolingian Brittany, made partial takeover of the island relatively easy, but complete conquest difficult. As in Wales, separate regions developed in Ireland. In parts of the island the native rulers were left undisturbed in return for giving fealty to the English king. In other areas, landownership was transferred from Gaels to Anglo-Norman lords and heavy settlement occurred. By the end of the thirteenth century territory representing over two-thirds of Ireland had been taken over by the Anglo-Normans.[12]

Crown rule over Anglo-Norman Ireland was in one respect very different from crown rule over Anglo-Norman Wales. Henry II made Ireland a separate lordship under his son John. His eventual plan was that it would be a separate kingdom.[13] John was provided with a royal army, a royal court, and royal officers, including a chancellor, seneschal, steward, and chamberlain.[14] Ireland had its own royal councils and officials located in its own capital. In Wales no political centre of this kind was formed.

Beyond Dublin, on the other hand, English rule in Ireland was not unlike its rule in Wales. True, Norman lords in Ireland did not have the regal rights enjoyed by the lords of the Welsh March. Yet it was nearly impossible to impose intensive authority over much of Ireland. As a result, Norman lords in Ireland enjoyed considerable autonomy. Crown control over Gaelic Ireland was even less intensive, much like its control over native Wales in the same period. English kings depended on the defences afforded by Norman lords and on the personal submission of Gaelic lords.

The arrival of the Normans in Scotland was different from their arrival in England, Wales, or Ireland. Although not without opposition, they came by royal invitation. Admittedly, one could argue that the Normans also came to Ireland by invitation. In fact, because the Normans were asked by the King of Leinster to help him against his enemies, some historians insist that there was no Norman invasion or conquest of Ireland. Yet the Norman arrival in Ireland was certainly much less peaceful than it was in Scotland. The Scottish king, David I (1124–53), had lived in England in his youth, was the brother-in-law of Henry I, and married the widow of the Earl of Northampton. He brought Normans to Scotland, gave them positions, and granted them lands. He reorganized the Scottish government, modelling his reforms on other European monarchies, especially the Norman monarchy of England. However, Normanization was limited to only a part of the country and barely affected the Highlands and Western Islands, where the authority of the crown was, as in native Ireland and Wales, at best extensive.

Political and Economic Centres

Although power was far less centralized than it would be later, we can nevertheless identify the three most powerful centres in the British Isles during the tenth to twelfth centuries: the southeast of England; the Anglo-Norman Pale in Ireland; and eastern Scotland and the area around the Firth of Forth.

It is not difficult to understand why London became a powerful centre, given its strategic and economic advantages. The Thames River provided access to the interior, and London was safer than coastal places from raids, yet it could be reached by boats coming from both Scandinavia and the Continent. London started as a Roman supply depot. It became the wealthiest community in the Roman province, an economic and a political centre, and a crossing-point of the road system. Eventually it replaced Colchester as the capital of Roman Britain.

The town went into decline after the Roman withdrawal, but, along with other towns, it recovered in the ninth and tenth centuries. The Scandinavians contributed significantly to trade and urban formation in the British Isles through the sea ports they founded.[15] At the same time, England was gradually becoming a part (though still very much an outer part) of the European commercial region identified by Fox. This commerce contributed to the growth of a number of towns besides London, some of which, most notably York, were not located in the southeast. It should also be recognized that this commerce connected with an agricultural hinterland, and so the southeastern economy was both land-based and sea-based. Furthermore, urban growth in this period had political as well as economic causes. The Saxon kings played an important role. They developed a number of Roman towns, including not just London, but also Canterbury, Southampton, Exeter, Colchester, and others.[16] They also founded several new towns, such as Hastings, Dartmouth, Tamworth, Wilton, and Taunton.[17] Alfred the Great (871–99) reconquered London from the Scandinavians and rebuilt it. London was a significant conquest because it was on the nebulous frontier between Danish and Saxon territory. This added to the natural conditions that made it important strategically. London was the key town to be held by any group in its attacks on or resistance to others.[18]

The town lost some of its pre-eminence when it was absorbed into the Saxon kingdom. Nonetheless, the southeastern part of the country remained the centre. The itineraries of the Wessex kings did not generally include territory north of the Thames; the same was true of the itineraries of Cnut and Edward the Confessor.[19] These kings were always on the move. Insofar as they had a seat it was Winchester, but London was the largest town, with an estimated 15,000 persons in the year 1000.[20] In 1053 Edward rebuilt the monastery and palace in Westminster. When he invaded England, William I almost immediately set himself up in Westminster Palace and began to construct the fortress that subsequently became the Tower of London.[21] Yet he did not spend much time in England. In his absence his agents were located in London, Westminster, Winchester, and Kent. When he was in England his court did not stay long in one place. He supposedly held great councils three times a year: Christmas at Gloucester, Easter at Winchester, and Whitsuntide at Westminster, but this schedule may have been more an ideal than a reality.[22] William Rufus (1087–1100) remained in England more than did William I, except in the later years of his reign when he was in Normandy ruling while his brother was on crusade.[23] By the last half of the eleventh century London had a population of perhaps 25,000; the next largest were Winchester and York, with probably in the neighbourhood of 6000 to 8000 persons.[24]

Edinburgh became a centre because it combined both military and economic advantages. Like London, it had early origins. It was a centre for the Gododdin, a British tribe that lived in southeastern Scotland. They chose it for the security that could be obtained by building a fort on one of its two hills. Edinburgh remained a minor centre, however, until the reign of Malcolm III. His residence and royal court were at Dunfermline, but Malcolm built a hunting lodge at Edinburgh and spent considerable time there. In 1076 he also built a chapel for his wife Margaret at the highest point on the Castle Rock. In 1128 David I (who was their son) constructed Holyrood Abbey in memory of his mother. In economic terms, Edinburgh was not a leading centre, but David did make it one of a number of burghs built with crown sponsorship, later to be called "royal burghs." They were usually selected for their defensive advantages. Most royal burghs were in eastern regions; thirty of the forty burghs in 1210 were in the eastern half of Scotland.[25]

Although established and protected by the political power of the crown, these royal burghs were intended to be economic centres. They enjoyed special privileges, including economic monopolies. Most Scottish long-distance trade was with England, the Low Countries, and northern Europe, including the Baltic. It was conducted largely from the east coast and the Firth of Forth. Scotland engaged in more long-distance trade than one might expect, judging by its economy. In this it was much like Brittany, whose thriving ports were not backed up by a prosperous hinterland. Later, James VI allegedly referred to the economic activity on the Forth estuary as gold fringe on a beggar's mantle.[26] Trade was concentrated in the same region as royal political power. It was not Edinburgh's economic potential that first attracted rulers to it. Be that as it may, Edinburgh was located in the region that became the economic centre of Scotland.[27]

Dublin had later origins than London or Edinburgh because it was founded by the Scandinavians. One of the Scandinavian camps in

Ireland had been placed at the mouth of the Liffey and subsequently grew into the town of Dublin, which became the capital of a small Scandinavian kingdom and an important centre in the Scandinavian world.[28] It was taken by the Normans and their Irish allies in 1170, from which time it was the centre of the Anglo-Norman state and society in Ireland. The core of the Anglo-Norman colony in Ireland was what would eventually come to be known as the Pale, roughly the present-day counties of Dublin, Louth, Meath, and parts of Kildare, though the area considered to make up the Pale varied from one time period to another. Like London, Medieval Dublin was an economic as well as a political centre. Dublin merchants traded with Chester and Bristol especially. No small quantity of herring, grain, wool, and hides was exported, and cloth and salt were imported, mainly through Dublin, Drogheda, Waterford, Cork, and Galway. For a country whose economic production compared unfavourably with that of many others, the Irish were engaged in a remarkable amount of long-distance trade.[29] In this respect Ireland was like Brittany and Scotland.

Of course, if we compare the three centres in the British Isles, we must recognize that the concentration of power was greater in south-eastern England than in the other two centres.[30] Still, the three centres had some very noticeable similarities. All the central regions were good agricultural lowlands, at least relative to other parts of their respective countries. All three towns that eventually became capitals (London, Dublin, and Edinburgh) were on inland waterways, though the traffic on these waterways differed greatly. All three regions were on the east coast, partly because most conquests had proceeded from east to west, and partly because the east coast enjoyed more proximity to trading centres in Scandinavia and on the Continent than did other parts of their respective countries, or, in the case of Dublin, proximity to ports in Wales and England. London, Edinburgh, and Dublin were both economic and political centres in a way that Paris was not. This is not to say that the British Isles were at this time more commercial-ized than the Continent, only that the political centres in the British Isles were located in areas relatively favourable for long-distance trade. Although Paris was situated in a good agricultural lowland region, and on a river that reached the sea, its location was not especially advan-tageous for international commerce. Other continental places were much better situated for long-distance trade.

The English Crown and Its Territory

The Normans built on the strength of the Anglo-Saxon monarchy to establish the most powerful crown in Western Europe. The shire and hundred courts gave them the basis on which to fashion a structure of local justice. In addition, people could take their grievances to the *curia regis*, which led to the development of central royal courts and to a royal body of law known as Common Law. Henry I (1100–35) dispatched judges to every shire to hear civil and criminal cases. Henry II (1154–89) institutionalized the circuit of courts that was under the jurisdiction of royal judges.

This intensive power in England coincided not only with the extensive power the crown came to enjoy over the rest of the British Isles, but also with considerable power over continental territory. The Norman kings ruled over Normandy as well as England, but the continental reach of the English crown grew even greater under Henry II. The seat of his government was Westminster, the home of the Exchequer and royal court,[31] but he was actually an Angevin, son of Geoffrey Plantagenet, count of Anjou. His continental inheritance included Brittany and Anjou. His marriage to Eleanor of Aquitaine and his succession to the throne of England made him perhaps the greatest ruler in Europe. With the conquest of Ireland, the Angevin Empire stretched from Ireland to the Pyrenees. Henry was born at Le Mans; he spent most of his life on the Continent, died at Chinon, and was buried at Fontevraud.[32] His successor, Richard the Lionheart (1189–99), was born and raised in England. Yet in the ten years he reigned, he spent only six months in England; most of the time he was in Anjou or Aquitaine.[33] The Angevin Empire was both sea-based and land-based. One of the advantages that Richard and his father had over their enemies was more money with which to pay soldiers, buy allies, and build fortifications.[34] They could also use English trade for diplomatic purposes. Richard was able, for instance, to use the threat of cutting off trade with Flanders to force the Count of Flanders to ally with him against Philip Augustus.[35]

These advantages notwithstanding, the Angevin Empire was short lived. Richard faced the expansionism of Philip Augustus and numerous uprisings (often supported by Philip) in his lands, but he was able to hold on to most of the empire he had inherited from his father.[36] It was during the reign of his brother John (1199–1216) that the big losses came; he failed to hold on to Poitou, Normandy, Maine, Touraine, Brittany, and Anjou. Some territories were later recovered, but almost all continental possessions were lost at the end of the Hundred Years' War, though England was not forced to give up its last foothold on the Continent, Calais, until Mary's reign. Why did the English crown lose its continental possessions to the French?

First, even Henry II, who put it all together, conceived of his domains as a loose imperial federation rather than a unified state. He wanted them to be apportioned among his heirs, so they would all enjoy sovereignty over at least some territory. Some lands were granted as dowries for Henry's daughters.

Second, while the English crown could mobilize resources for seizing continental districts, it had trouble mobilizing resources to retain them. The English were able to hire mercenaries, control the Channel, move quickly around the French coast, and win battles, but they needed to put into action their land-based military and financial resources to keep large territories. It was difficult to persuade elites in England that holding large continental territories was worth the cost. The ordinary revenues of English kings were insufficient for continental wars. They time and again sought to find ways of persuading their barons to join them in continental campaigns and/or supply them with arms, men, and money for these purposes. It was no accident that major English losses occurred during the reign of John, who was frequently in conflict with his barons.

To these problems may eventually have been added a decline in royal power. In a recent work, J.R. Lander has pointed to the limitations of the English monarchy during the late Middle Ages.[37] He has emphasized a decrease in the arbitrary power of the crown, a weakening of royal control over taxation, the absence of a standing army, the small size of the state bureaucracy, the failure of royal justice to enforce the law, the increasing role of Parliament, the takeover of local government by the county gentry, and growing corruption. Whether the English crown was actually less powerful in the fifteenth century than it had been in the twelfth century is perhaps debatable. What is clear, however, is that, whereas in the twelfth century the English crown was manifestly more powerful than the French, this was not the case after the Hundred Years' War.

The forfeiture of continental territory by the English crown and a decline in its power in England coincided with a loss of territory in Ireland. Although it is impossible to draw a distinct boundary between Anglo-Norman and Gaelic Ireland, historians estimate that Anglo-Norman control fell from about two-thirds of the country at the end of the twelfth century to less than half in the mid-fifteenth century.[38] Strategically, Ireland was less vital to England than its continental neighbours. An invasion of England across the English Channel was easier than across the Irish Sea. Until the end of the Hundred Years' War the English crown preferred to invest its resources in continental military activity than in crushing the Irish.[39]

To a degree the same was true with respect to Scotland. Controlling Scotland, like controlling Ireland, required a long-term investment of resources that the English simply could not manage. Scotland, like

Ireland, was treated during the Hundred Years' War as less significant strategically than continental territories.[40] Nevertheless, in noteworthy respects the relationship between Scotland and England differed from the relationship between Ireland and England. Most obviously, Scotland and England were not separated by a body of water. An invasion of England through Scotland was a perpetual threat, and Scottish raiding into northern England a perpetual torment. And the alliance that developed between Scotland and France (from the thirteenth century, if not earlier) made it difficult to ignore the Scots. At the same time the Scots were more politically unified than the Irish. The importance of this unity was never more clearly demonstrated than in the early fourteenth century, when Robert I brought the Scots together to overturn the conquest of Scotland by Edward I; he defeated the English led by Edward II at the Battle of Bannockburn in 1314.

In one respect the loss of continental possessions re-enforced London as a political centre, since English monarchs were on the Continent less often and could concentrate their attention on their English kingdom. Nonetheless, it was over a declining empire that the English political centre ruled.

The exception was Wales. In the years 1240 to 1256 English royal power increased dramatically in native Wales. It subsequently slipped, but was re-established under Edward I.[41] Edward compelled into submission Llywelyn ap Gruffudd, the leading Welsh lord. When Llywelyn rebelled, Edward defeated him in battle and forced the native Welsh to accept direct English rule. Edward's conquest of Wales was not, like his conquest of Scotland, reversed under his less able successor. Eventually, native Wales became a principality of the heir apparent to the English throne. It was put under tighter royal control than many parts of England. Ironically, the March of Wales, which was less Welsh and was geographically closer to southeastern England, was more independent of the English crown than the Principality of Wales, though I hasten to add that most of the great Marcher lords lived in England and had large English landed estates.

THE SUBORDINATION OF THE PERIPHERY

The Tudor Revolution

The idea of a "Tudor Revolution" is most associated with G.R. Elton.[42] He asserted that under the Tudors, and in particular during the period in which Thomas Cromwell was the king's closest adviser (1532–40), English state administration became more differentiated and functions formerly fused in the royal household came to be performed by departments of state, at least to a greater degree. This thesis has been challenged by critics, who insist that power remained heavily concentrated in the royal household and that the changes that occurred during Cromwell's period were not the result of a conscious plan of reform, as Elton believed, but were in fact responses to power struggles, struggles that were very much centred in the royal household.[43]

With respect to England itself, I shall not try to resolve this argument. My concern is with the transformation in the relationship between the political centre and the peripheries, which has been given little attention in the debate. The relationship that came to exist in the Early Modern period between England and the British peripheries was not predetermined. If other things had happened in the Tudor period, the centre-periphery structure of the seventeenth and eighteenth centuries might have been very different.

During the Tudor period royal control over northern England was extended. A Council in the North, set up by Richard III in the late fifteenth century, became the major instrument for the governing of the north. In 1537 Cromwell reorganized the council and entrusted it with more responsibility. There is good reason to believe that Cromwell also wanted to restructure Irish government. He tightened the control of London over the Irish administration and reduced the autonomy of Irish leaders.[44]

Central power over Wales also increased. In 1471 Edward IV had established a Council in the Marches to oversee the property of the Prince of Wales in the principality and the Marches. Henry VII reactivated this council as a first step towards better government of Wales. He named special commissions to try to improve law and order. More dramatic changes came when Cromwell took over in the 1530s and the hard-nosed Rowland Lee, bishop of Lichfield, was appointed president of the Council in the Marches in 1534. Lee ruthlessly enforced law and order. Further legislation against lawlessness was enacted, and commissions of the peace were issued.[45] From 1536 to 1543 the Acts of Union between England and Wales were passed. They shired Wales, awarded the Welsh representation in the English House of Commons, extended English law to Wales, and put an end to the independence of the Welsh March. Administrative and judicial institutions were integrated. The Welsh court system did, however, keep some differences from the English. The Council in the Marches was not abolished, but invested with more administrative authority in order to advance royal control over Wales. It sat in Ludlow and in 1543 received statutory powers in Wales and in a number of English counties.[46]

Similarities in the way in which Cromwell approached the different peripheries may suggest that he had a master plan for the British Isles, but he may also have been responding to similar problems in these peripheries.[47] In any case, historians have certainly come to reject any notion that the whole political transformation that took place in northern England, Wales, and Ireland between the beginning and the end of the Tudor period was the result of a long-term project. Different political leaders in sixteenth-century England had different projects for the peripheries, and all were forced to cope with events and circumstances beyond their control and with limitations to their power.

Certainly, the remarkable transformation in Ireland between the beginning and the end of the Tudor period was even less the product of a consistent program. Whatever Cromwell had in mind, Ireland was handled very differently. It was not integrated politically as was Wales, but raised, in 1541, from a lordship to a kingdom, a separate kingdom, keeping its separate Parliament and administration, though its monarch was also the monarch of England and Wales. Royal authority was not respected in Ireland as much as it now was in Wales. English rulers would have been quite happy if Ireland did not exist. At this time it was not worth the resources that were required to subdue it. Yet it could not be ignored because France and Spain threatened to use it as a base for attacking England, because losing it would have been a blow to English prestige, and because rebellions could not simply be ignored.

Not surprisingly, therefore, the policy towards Ireland of the English state shifted from one strategy to another, usually in an effort to deal with recurring crises. If there was a pattern it was one of oscillation between two strategies: a moderate strategy, which sought to increase royal authority by introducing reforms, conciliating powerful members of the society, and Anglicizing Gaelic leaders; and a coercive strategy, which tried to increase royal power by appointing strong-willed governors and crushing opposition by force.[48] The first strategy kept failing as a result of factional struggles in English and Irish politics and the inability of Irish leaders to convince the English that they were trustworthy. The second strategy, on the other hand, required the replacement of the existing elite and the stationing in Ireland of an army, which was very expensive. Since a large body of water, of course, separates Ireland from England and Wales, if the English were to adopt a military-coercive strategy they had to have at least some armed force there on a long-term or permanent basis. They could not move troops in and out very easily as the great powers could do in Lotharingia. The second strategy also encouraged the confiscation of land since land was the basis of the power of the existing elite, and the normal (and least expensive) reward for the new politicians and officials. Thus the second strategy led to confiscation and settlement.

At first English leaders tried to make garrisons in Ireland self-financing by providing troops with land, but even this program proved too expensive for the English crown. Elizabeth time and again approved and then resisted plans to establish garrisons.[49] Yet the repeated efforts to subdue Ireland and to introduce New English administrators and settlers alienated both the Gaelic and most of the Old English population. Considerable hostility developed between the Old English and the New English. The crown was gradually forced to commit the necessary resources to intervene in these struggles and to crush rebellions that broke out in the last half of the sixteenth century. Eventually, at the turn of the century, a rebellion in the north and a Spanish invasion in the south pushed the English into a complete conquest of Ireland.[50]

Ireland under the Stewarts and the Hanovarians

In this way an intense struggle emerged between two groups, in which membership was defined by religion. Under the early Stewarts, Protestants gained advantage relative to Catholics, but the Old English Catholics were still a powerful force. A rebellion of Gaelic Irish Catholics began in Ulster in 1641 and was subsequently joined by many Old English. A parliament of Catholics known as the Confederation of Kilkenny met in 1642 and efforts were made to strike a deal with Charles I, who was then struggling with rebellion in England; they would support the king in return for concessions to Catholics.[51] Yet there were too many factions with diverse interests and goals. In 1649 Oliver Cromwell conquered Ireland, and the rights of all Catholics, Old English and Gaelic, were nullified. The Restoration in 1660 improved the situation for Catholics. The accession in 1685 of James II (a Catholic) brought further benefits. However, the Glorious Revolution (1688–89), which overthrew James, effected a destruction of Catholic power in Ireland, from which Catholics would not recover until the nineteenth century. In March 1689 James arrived in Ireland and sought to use the country as a base for regaining his kingdoms. He came with a number of French officers and twenty-two ships.[52] On 1 July 1690 he was defeated at the Boyne River by William of Orange. James fled again to France. His supporters were eventually defeated in 1691. Although they were able to obtain guarantees of the protection of Catholic rights in the Treaty of Limerick, the terms of this treaty were subsequently violated by the Protestant-dominated Irish Parliament. A series of crippling laws were passed, known as the Penal Laws, which denied Catholics political, social, and economic rights.

Catholics also lost almost all their land. Confiscations had actually begun under Mary Tudor in 1556. Then land was confiscated from the Gaelic Irish and passed into the hands of Protestants and Old English Catholics. From the reign of Elizabeth, however, the objective of the Confiscations became displacing Catholic owners, Old English as well as Gaelic. Major confiscations occurred in the early seventeenth century, in the mid-seventeenth century (after the Cromwellian conquest), and in the late seventeenth century (after the Williamite victory). The proportion of land owned by Protestants also increased as a result of the conversion of Catholic landowners to Protestantism or the inheritance of land by Protestant rather than Catholic descendants, a fact emphasized by F.G. James, who argues that historians have underestimated the continuity of the Irish elite in the seventeenth and eighteenth centuries.[53]

In any case, the change in the religious affiliation of the landed elite was dramatic. It has been estimated that as late as 1640, nearly 60 per cent of the land in Ireland was still owned by Catholics. After the Confiscations of the mid and late seventeenth century, the proportion was cut to 14 per cent.[54] It certainly fell still further in the eighteenth century; according to Arthur Young, an Englishman who wrote books on his travels in several countries in the late eighteenth century, it was only 5 per cent by 1776.[55] This was the golden age of the Protestant Ascendancy in Ireland.

British rule in Ireland reached a crisis in the 1790s. Organized opposition to the existing political and social order escalated.[56] In 1798 a rebellion broke out led by the United Irishmen, who wanted to create an independent Irish state. Then, on 22 August 1798, a French army landed in County Mayo, on the west coast of Ireland, under General Humbert. It united with Irish rebels and peasants, and successfully penetrated into the country until it was defeated by an English army in County Longford on 8 September. Never before had a continental army posed as great a threat.

Two years later, 2 August 1800, the centuries-old Irish Parliament met for the last time. The Act of Union, which went into effect in 1801, united the British and Irish Parliaments, as they remained for over a hundred years.

Scotland under the Stewarts and the Hanovarians

Scotland and England were generally on unfriendly terms during the fourteenth, fifteenth, and sixteenth centuries, their relations disturbed by frequent border clashes, occasional pitched battles, assistance provided by the English to Scottish rebels, and Scottish interference in

English affairs, most notably during the Wars of the Roses. Consequently, one of the surprises of British history is the fact that the Scottish and English crowns united in 1603. It was the result of a series of not easily predictable historical events and developments: previous dynastic marriages; the celibacy of Elizabeth 1; discontent in Scotland with French overbearance; the Protestant Reformation; and the overthrow of Mary Queen of Scots and her imprisonment and execution by the English, as a result of which her son James VI was raised as a Protestant in Scotland – all of which brought James to the throne of England.

The union of the English and Scottish crowns had a decisive effect on the centralization of political power in the British Isles. What had been a political centre in its own right became peripheral. James VI moved to London and only once returned to Scotland. As king of both Scotland and England, his resources were greatly enlarged and he was more independent of unruly factions in Scotland.[57] The Highlands and Western Islands felt the royal presence more in the seventeenth century than previously, though they remained beyond the full control of the crown. The efforts of his son, Charles 1, to tighten relationships with Scotland, introduce religious reforms, and undermine the power of the greater aristocracy led to rebellion in Scotland, but (as in Ireland) the fall of Charles brought even more central control. In 1651 Cromwell invaded Scotland and incorporated it into England on disadvantageous terms for the Scots. "I do truly think," declared Cromwell, "they are a very ruined nation."[58]

The Restoration re-established Scotland as a separate political entity. In 1707, however, England and Scotland amalgamated into one kingdom and their two parliaments were united. The Scots, or at least some of them, sought entrance into the British market and wanted to eliminate the economic disadvantages inflicted by English mercantilism on Scotland. For their part, the English wanted to bring Scotland under better political control. England was also trying to make itself less vulnerable to a French invasion through Scotland. And union was one solution to the succession crisis created by the refusal of the Scottish Parliament to accept the Hanovarian Succession without "limitations."

Scotland entered into political union in 1707 by a treaty whose tone implied that a partnership was being formed between two equal kingdoms. The content of this treaty and the political realities in which it was drafted leave little doubt about the inequality of the alliance. Scotland was much smaller in population and poorer. The Scottish Privy Council, which had been the king's ministerial body in Scotland, was abolished by the British Parliament shortly after the union of 1707, thus removing a separate and Scottish institutional structure for governing Scotland. The Scots were, however, able to use the treaty to preserve their church and legal system.[59]

Thus the seventeenth and early eighteenth centuries saw the transfer of central political power from Edinburgh to London. The eighteenth century saw the subordination of all of Scotland, including the Highlands and Western Islands, to this central power. All the same, Scotland was a long way from the centre, and the role of the state was limited at this time. Some measures were taken to advance royal authority in the Highlands and Western Islands during the first half of the eighteenth century. In 1715 an abortive rebellion broke out of Scottish "Jacobites" – supporters of the Stewarts who sought to restore them to the throne. It pushed the government into a disarming act in 1716 and another in 1725. A network of roads was built and a "Black Watch" formed in 1739 to police the Highlands and Western Islands. Yet the power of the central state was still remarkably limited, and the authority of the crown in the Highlands and Western Islands could be ignored to an extent that was unimaginable almost anywhere in France. The full submission of the Highlands and Western Islands did not take place until after the defeat of another Jacobite rising that began in 1745. It was led by the young Charles Edward Stewart, better known to history as Bonnie Prince Charlie. His failure was followed by harsh repression and a renewal of the Disarming Act. For these and other reasons, the king's law came to the Highlands and Western Islands as they never had before.[60]

THE CENTRALIZATION OF POWER

Comparisons of England and France have customarily been confused and contradictory as a result of a failure to recognize that the state that was emerging in the British Isles in the Early Modern period was, like the French state, in some ways comparatively centralized, while in other ways it was not. The two major forces of political centralization in the British Isles were the Westminster Parliament and the crown, but parliaments also provided the basis for peripheral autonomy in Scotland until 1707 and in Ireland until 1801.

Parliament

England
Needless to say, it was in England itself that the Westminster Parliament centralized political power earliest and most effectively. It was a central rather than a provincial institution. Within England there were no provincial estates as there were in most continental countries.

Westminster Palace became the normal site. Under the reigns of Edward I and Edward II, Parliament met in Berwick, Carlisle, York, Lincoln, and Stamford as a result of military engagements in the north. Between 1338 and 1377, in contrast, every meeting was at Westminster.[61] Of fifty parliaments meeting between 1377 and 1422, forty-two were held there.[62]

If we ask ourselves why England had a powerful central parliament, the answer, paradoxically, lies in the comparatively powerful centralized monarchy that emerged in England during the late Anglo-Saxon period and under the Normans. The English monarchy created the centralized parliament in the thirteenth and fourteenth centuries in order to raise money and mobilize support, usually for military ventures. Eventually this centralism limited the power of the crown because it enabled elites to unite in opposition to it. English kings were faced with an institution that brought together persons from across the country, rather than provincial assemblies that could have been undermined one at a time in the way that French monarchs reduced the number of provincial estates.

The Commons was first an extension of the royal council. During the thirteenth century the "knights of the shire" and burgesses of the towns were sometimes invited when the council met to obtain their support for this or that undertaking. In the 1330s they began to meet separately. This eventually proved to be a source of power for the Commons by enabling them to act independently of the Lords. Urban elites were not as critical in the early evolution of the English Parliament as they were in the emergence of estates in Flanders and Brabant. Nonetheless, urban compliance with taxation was essential if the crown wanted to tap the commercial wealth of the country, and one of the reasons for the rising power of the Commons in the late Middle Ages was its claim to speak for the commercial sector.

These three factors – centralism, the autonomy of the Commons, and the role of the commercial sector – were partly responsible for the successful defence and enlargement of the powers of Parliament in the revolutions of the seventeenth century. They were not the cause of these revolutions. Altogether too much has been written on the causes of the English Civil War. Since almost all revolutions in world history have multiple causes, it is not surprising that wide differences of opinion exist on the causes of the English Civil War. The list includes religious conflicts, the growth of capitalism, the rise of the gentry, the opposition between "court" and "country," the weakness of the English state, state fiscal crisis, demographic crisis, and the rise of commercial classes.[63] Less attention has been devoted to explaining why the English revolutions of the seventeenth century succeeded.

One writer who has tried is Michael Kimmel. He has compared the outcome of the English Civil War with that of the Frondes. In seeking to explain why the former succeeded and the latter failed, he emphasizes the strength of the French crown as compared with the English crown, the unity of resistance to the crown in England, the greater ideological cohesiveness of the English rebels, and the interests of French office-holders in the existing state.[64]

Kimmel's explanation rings true, though greater emphasis might be placed on the fact that the English rebels had the institutional unity and leadership provided by a centralized and autonomous political assembly. Neither the *parlements* nor any other institutions in seventeenth-century France provided a similar basis for challenging the crown. In addition, it is necessary to take into account the backing provided to the rebels in England by urban commercial interests. Support for the revolt against Charles I came particularly from commercialized and urbanized England, more specifically from water-based districts. Recent research shows that anti-royalist members were elected to the Long Parliament disproportionately from coastal and riverine constituencies.[65] True, far from all commercial men opposed the crown. As we might expect, those enjoying monopolies granted by the monarchy, which included many of the great overseas merchants, were mostly on the side of the king. Conversely, some peers and many members of the gentry opposed the king. Nor should we conclude that a conflict between more commercialized and less commercialized England was a major cause of the Civil War. Nonetheless, the geographical correlation cannot be ignored. It indicates the role played by commercial and urban England in the struggle against royal power.

The consequences of the revolts of the seventeenth century were various, but the conventional emphasis on the strengthening of the powers of Parliament is certainly justified. The increase in royal power under the Tudors and early Stewarts was arrested, indeed reversed. At the end of the seventeenth century, Parliament was in a stronger position than at the beginning. By overthrowing two kings in one century, Parliament left a message for later sovereigns. More concretely, the Long Parliament abolished the Star Chamber, the councils of Wales and the North, and the ecclesiastical Court of High Commission. The Bill of Rights of 1689 declared the illegality of many of the actions taken by James II and reaffirmed the principles of parliamentary government. Twelve years later the Act of Settlement established the Hanoverian succession and, in the process, reaffirmed the limitations on the monarchy. Parliamentary approval was necessary for the king or queen to leave the country, and Parliament had control over judges. George I was king thanks to an act of Parliament; he depended on parliamentary approval for his revenue; and he had to appoint ministers who had the confidence of the House of Commons. In the eighteenth century, Parliament, meeting more often than in previous centuries, had almost full control over revenues.[66]

Wales

The Westminster Parliament centralized political power for the Welsh as well – later than for the English, but earlier than for the Scottish or the Irish. No separate Welsh Parliament had to be abolished to integrate the Welsh into the English political structure. True, this integration was hampered by the unwillingness of the English to give the Welsh a share of seats in the House of Commons proportionate to their population. In 1750, with twenty-seven representatives, they had fewer than seven members per 100,000 persons in the Welsh population, while the English had more than eight for every 100,000 in their population. Still, Parliament provided a focus for Welsh grievances that would not otherwise have been available. And Parliament certainly exercised as much power over Wales as it did over England.

Scotland

The Scottish Parliament began as a royal council of magnates and prelates summoned to advise the king. Eventually, as was the case in England, urban elites also participated. Burghs were first summoned in order to obtain their consent to specific financial contributions.[67] As Parliament evolved, only those towns in Scotland that were summoned were liable to pay the taxes voted by Parliament. Consequently, the crown was particularly anxious to get burgh representatives to attend Parliament; and in Scotland the organization of urban representation in Parliament came earlier than the organization of shire representation. It was only the royal burghs that obtained the right to be summoned to Parliament.[68]

Political power was less centralized in Scotland than in England, with the result that Parliament was weaker. Not surprisingly, the Scottish Parliament acquired a normal central meeting place later than the English Parliament. It convened in numerous locations, especially often at Holyrood or Edinburgh, but frequently at St Andrews, Stirling Castle, or Scone, and now and then at Roxburgh Castle, Aberdeen, or Perth. Edinburgh did not became the regular site until the reign of James III (1460–88).[69]

The power of the Scottish Parliament should not, however, be underestimated. Historians once believed that the Scottish crown controlled Parliament through the Lords of Articles, but more recent research has modified this view. In the fifteenth and sixteenth centuries the Lords of Articles were not altogether compliant in their relations with the monarchy, and they in turn did not altogether dominate Parliament.[70] Moreover, the Scottish Parliament became more powerful during the seventeenth century.[71]

With the Act of Union of 1707, the centripetal power of the British Parliament could now draw Scots to the centre as it did the English and the Welsh. Like the Welsh, however, the Scots did not acquire a share of seats in the House of Commons proportionate to their population. With only forty-five members in 1750, Scotland had fewer than four representatives in the House of Commons for every 100,000 persons in the population – a number significantly worse than that for Wales and less than half that for England. Of course, population was not the standard that people of the eighteenth century used for determining political rights and responsibilities; their standards, especially wealth, were ones that greatly favoured those living in the centre over those in the periphery. Nonetheless, as we shall see, the Union of 1707 enabled some Scots to play a greater role in the political centre.

Ireland
The Irish Parliament was closely modelled on the English Parliament, as indeed were a large number of institutions and offices in Anglo-Norman Ireland. It too evolved out of councils of great lords called together to advise the king, to which were eventually added representatives of other groups in the population. Representatives of counties and towns were initially summoned in the late thirteenth century and then more often in the fourteenth century.

Yet Parliament and its role differed in certain respects between England and Ireland. First, whereas the Scottish and English Parliaments were central assemblies in the sense that they developed around the person of the king, the Irish Parliament was more like provincial estates in France. In Ireland the king's leading tenants did not meet directly with the king himself, who was in England, but instead with the chief governor or "justiciar." Second, Parliament was more often circumvented in raising revenue from the population in Ireland than in England.[72] Third, the centralization of political power in England made the Irish Parliament weak, just as it made the English Parliament powerful. And, finally, the Irish Parliament represented only a part of the country, the most Anglicized part.

In the sixteenth and seventeenth centuries it came to represent the whole of the country, but it also met less often; Elizabeth had only three parliaments and James I only one.[73] Furthermore, its powers had become more carefully defined and in a way that made it a subordinate parliament for three centuries. Poynings's Law, which had been enacted by the Irish Parliament in 1494, stipulated that statutes had to be approved by the crown and Privy Council in England before they were submitted to the Irish Parliament, which could approve or reject them, but not amend them.[74] Considerable English legislation applied to Ireland because it was enacted by the king. Laws disadvantageous to Ireland, such as the Navigation Acts, which restricted Irish trade, could be passed by the English Parliament and imposed on Ireland, while the Irish Parliament was restricted by Poynings's Law. The "Sixth of George 1" or Declaratory Act of 1720 further strengthened the superordinate position of the English Parliament by stipulating that it could enact legislation binding on Ireland.[75]

On the other hand, the fact remains that in the eighteenth century, Ireland, unlike Scotland, had a separate parliament. And whereas the French provincial political assemblies lost power in the Early Modern period, the Irish Parliament gained somewhat greater power. English domination could be counteracted in a number of ways. The Irish had often sought to engage England in legal struggles using different interpretations of their constitutional relationship. Already in the seventeenth century the Irish Parliament had acquired the authority to introduce legislation by passing the "Heads of Bills" – bills beginning with "we pray that it may be enacted" rather than "be it enacted," thus enabling the Irish Parliament to initiate legislation despite Poynings's Law.[76] In the aftermath of the Williamite victory over James, the Irish Parliament was able to reassert its power because William depended on the Protestant political elite to resist the supposed Jacobite threat in Ireland.[77] From the late 1690s it met more regularly and used its control over taxes to bargain with the English. In the eighteenth century a magnificent meeting place was constructed in College Green. Eventually the Irish Parliament won an amendment to Poynings's Law that gave it more legislative authority, and the "Sixth of George 1" was repealed.[78]

Thus the abolition of the Irish Parliament in 1801 reversed a process that was moving in the direction of greater parliamentary autonomy for the Irish. As a result of the Union of 1801 the Irish acquired representation at Westminster, though, like the Welsh and the Scots, they were not accorded a share of the seats proportional to their population. With 100 seats, the Irish had just over two representatives in the British House of Commons per 100,000 persons in their population. At this time the Scottish had just under three, the Welsh more than four, and the English more than five.

Royal Power

Although the Medieval Scottish crown had been strong enough to preserve Scottish independence, it was not a powerful monarchy in comparative terms. Fifteenth-century Scottish kings failed to tax regularly; they were not wealthy; and Scottish institutions of central government were not well developed.[79] They were also peripatetic. James III (1460–88) tried to rule Scotland almost entirely from Edinburgh, but James II (1437–60), James IV (1488–1513), and James V (1513–42) often travelled about the kingdom granting charters and meting out justice.[80]

In this respect James V was like his French contemporary, Francis I, and unlike his English contemporary, Henry VIII. Henry did not go on the numerous progresses that kept Francis's court touring about.[81] Elizabeth went on numerous progresses until the 1580s. James VI of Scotland travelled considerably before he assumed the crown of England, and even for a period thereafter. He became more sedentary, however, after his trip to Scotland in 1617.[82] By the eighteenth century, British monarchs travelled little in the British Isles. They often moved from one residence to another. These were largely, however, in the London area: St James's, Windsor, Kensington, Hampton Court, and Richmond. George I visited Hanover and made progresses to the country residences of some peers, but his movements were usually seasonal migrations from St James's to Kensington Palace to Hampton Court.[83] George II went to Hanover every second year and in 1743 even took to the field in the War of the Austrian Succession. Nevertheless, like his father, he spent most of his time moving around the London residences, his favourite being Windsor, followed by Kensington.[84] No British monarch went to Scotland between the 1630s and the 1820s.[85] Neither did one go to Ireland, except for James II and William III, who met there to fight.

By the Early Modern period the British crown was less powerful than the French vis-à-vis other state institutions. If there was a Tudor Revolution, it did not lead to a centralized absolutist state like those emerging on the Continent. Yet it is essential not to exaggerate this weakness. In the eighteenth century, Parliament had more control over finances than it did at the beginning of the seventeenth century, but this was not altogether to be regretted from the sovereign's point of view. The severe financial problems that plagued the crown in the early seventeenth century had been overcome. By the early eighteenth century the monarch and his or her ministers could rely on regular revenue from taxation approved by Parliament. These changes did not assure the king or queen of all the money he or she needed (particularly, as we shall discover, for the royal household or for building palaces). They did, however, give the crown more financial security.

The powers enjoyed by the British king or queen were different from those enjoyed by the Austrian, French, or Savoyard monarchies. The most critical was his or her power to influence Parliament through his or her prestige, patronage, and selection of ministers. He or she also had control over appointments to the House of Lords and considerable influence over elections to the House of Commons. Without the support of George I or George II, Robert Walpole would not have survived. This support was as critical as his parliamentary majority; in fact, it was a prerequisite of his parliamentary majority.[86] Although the crown did not use its right to veto legislation after Anne, the threat of it could still be used to influence Parliament.

WATER-BASED STATE

Like France, the British Isles in the seventeenth and eighteenth centuries were both land-based and water-based. However, along a continuum between these two theoretical poles, the British Isles were closer to the water-base pole than were Savoy and France. Within the British Isles the English economy, or at least that of southern England, was more commercialized and more involved in long-distance trade than was the Welsh, Irish, or Scottish. Let us consider a few of the consequences, or presumed consequences, of these differences.

Military Power

Theoretically, water-based states are less militaristic primarily for two reasons. First, they have less need for territorial expansion and a growing population because they can extract resources from an expanding commercialized economy. Second, they have less need for a defensive army, because they can rely on a navy, which requires less manpower. To what extent do these theoretical generalizations fit the British Isles?

It is certainly clear that, from the end of the Hundred Years' War, English leaders became less and less interested in continental territory. The cost of seeking to maintain or acquire such territory did not seem warranted. England's takeover of the British Isles was also in many ways hesitant. This hesitancy may be explained partly by a lack of interest in territorial expansion.

Yet other factors were more decisive in accounting for England's slowness in taking over its periphery. Furthermore, the takeover did eventually occur and was no less coercive for being slow in coming;

the conflicts in Ireland in the 1640s and in Scotland in the 1740s led to brutality on both sides. Although England did not have much ambition for continental territory in the seventeenth and eighteenth centuries, it certainly involved itself in continental struggles. And it did manifestly engage in overseas expansion.

There is considerable truth in the oft-made claim that England did not require a large army to defend itself, but could rely on building a powerful navy. The government of Henry VIII is usually credited with initiating the process by which Britain became a major naval power. Although generally unsuccessful at naval warfare, this government did advance the shipbuilding program and improve naval administration. It was believed that protection of southern England from invasion could be impeded more effectively by means of naval control of the Channel than by maintaining a large army on the southern coast. An invasion through Ireland or Scotland was also a threat. Indeed, this threat was a major factor in the subordination of the peripheries to English control. Yet the English were slow to accept the costs of meeting this threat. In comparison with Lotharingia, the British periphery was not as strategically important. England had neither the need nor the capacity to protect Ireland and Scotland with large armies in the way that continental powers protected their borders. British land power was particularly weak under Elizabeth and the early Stewarts, and remained weak during the seventeenth century when British involvement in continental wars was limited.

The Civil War, however, demonstrated the ability of the British to mobilize substantial land forces. It may also have increased the militarism of British society even though the New Model Army as such was disbanded after the war.[87] The Civil War creates some difficulty for the Foxian model. In this theory, conflicting groups in a water-based society are more likely to negotiate their differences than in a land-based society because they do not have enough coercive power to impose their will on one another. Yet the English Civil War and the Glorious Revolution contributed to the strengthening of the powers of Parliament. Insofar as these revolts involved the mobilization of large armies, they provide evidence contrary to the theory, evidence that the institutional structure that most promoted negotiation in the British Isles existed as a result of the capacity of certain people in the society to put together fighting forces.

In any case, in the late seventeenth century the British state was led to expand its land warfare as it was drawn into continental struggles to a greater extent than it had since the mid-fifteenth century. This happened mainly for three reasons: a continental leader became king of the British Isles; British leaders became more fearful of the expansionism of Louis XIV; and Jacobites were actively trying to solicit continental support for their movement to overthrow the monarchy. As a consequence, British military activity became more land-based. The size of the standing army increased. New peaks were reached with almost every war, and the number of effectives usually did not fall after a war to the former peacetime level. During the Seven Years' War the total reached some 203,000 men (including German mercenaries).[88]

Figure 1 and table 6 show that in the eighteenth century Britain actually spent proportionately more on the military than did France, at least if the years for which we have French data were not unusual. In the seventeenth century British armies were much smaller than French armies per capita, but table 3 in chapter 1 indicates that this was less true in the eighteenth century.[89] Indeed, during the Seven Years' War the British army was larger per capita than the French.

This is not to say that British military activity does not conform at all to the theoretical water-based state. Although in both Britain and France more was spent on the army than the navy, a higher proportion went to the navy in Britain. While English ships were not as a rule superior to French ships, their gunnery and seamanship were generally better.[90] The French likely had larger armies per capita than the British in most years during the eighteenth century. There were certainly fewer troops per capita stationed in the British Isles during peacetime. Many British people still believed in the "blue-water" strategy: British wealth would be used to pay mercenaries and subsidize foreign armies and British naval superiority would be used to resist continental powers and to damage their commerce.[91] People associated armies with continental absolutism, a sentiment intensified by their experiences, as they remembered them, with the armies of Oliver Cromwell and James II. The notion that Britain did not have a standing army in the eighteenth century was a myth, made necessary by the immense opposition to having one. Charles II referred to the field regiments he preserved as "guards" to overcome hostility in Parliament.[92] An especially vigorous campaign against a standing army came during and after the War of the League of Augsburg, which forced William to disband most of his army in the closing years of the seventeenth century, leaving only 7000 men in England.[93] Parliament continued to put limits on the number of effectives. It would only accept a standing army if its existence and strength depended on parliamentary approval, which was given every year in the renewal of the Mutiny Act.[94]

The size of the British army was also limited by demographic factors. The English population was much smaller than the French. One might expect that the British state could draw on the population available

Figure 1
Military Expenditure of Britain, 1701–93

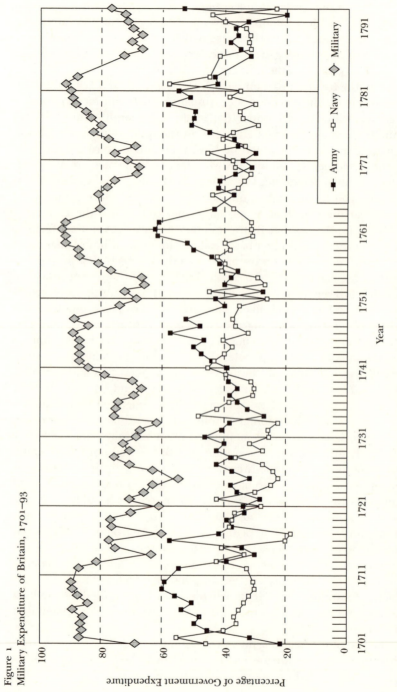

Government expenditure excludes debt charges. Ordnance has been included in army expenditure. See note 95 for source.

Table 6
Military Expenditure as a Percentage of Government Expenditure of Britain and France
for Selected Years

	Britain			France		
Years	Total military	Army	Navy	Total military	Army	Navy
1726	62	38	24	54	47	7
1751	69	43	26	58	42	16
1775	83	45	38	48	35	13
1788	71	38	33	43	29	14

Government expenditure excludes debt charges. Ordnance has been included in army
expenditure. See note 96 for sources.

in less water-based Ireland and Scotland (many Scots and Irish served
in continental armies), but such was only partially the case. In the last
half of the seventeenth century (except during the reign of James II)
and the early eighteenth century the Scots and the Irish, including
Protestant Irish, were regarded as untrustworthy.[97] Some Scots in the
armed services remained loyal to the Stewarts, and many more were
suspected of such loyalty.[98] These suspicions were kept alive by the
Jacobite rebellions of 1715 and 1745. Jacobite connections could
impair the career of a Scottish soldier; the Fourth Earl of Balcarres
was handicapped by his father's and brother's role in the Jacobite
rebellion of 1715.[99] Many Scots did, however, serve in the armed
forces during the eighteenth century, and the number that became
officers shows that negative prejudices towards Scots did not have
much effect on promotions. In the first half of the eighteenth century
generally about one-quarter of the regimental officers in the British
army were Scots, while the Scottish population constituted only about
one-eighth of the population of the British Isles. Almost one-fifth of
the colonelcies were held by Scots from 1714 to the end of the Seven
Years' War.[100]

Prejudices against the Protestant Irish also declined and they too
became well represented in the officer corps. By the middle of the
eighteenth century one-quarter of the officers in the British army were
Irish.[101] On the other hand, the largest population in the peripheries,
the Catholic Irish, were excluded altogether. Political leaders were afraid
to arm Catholics, especially for home defence. Recruitment of Catholics
did gradually develop in the second half of the eighteenth century, but
the full potential of the Catholic population of Ireland was not exploited
until the French Revolutionary and Napoleonic Wars, when perhaps
one-third of the British army was composed of Irishmen.[102]

Finally, the British army was weakened by a crippling organizational structure that appalled George I, who came to Britain with continental notions about how a military force should be organized. There was not one unified administration. The secretary at war, the Treasury Board, the master-general of the ordnance and the Board of Ordnance, the paymaster-general, and the Commissioners for the Sick and Wounded were all involved.[103] And the purchase of officer ranks in the army persisted longer in the British Isles than it did on the Continent. Not only did it fail to insure that those appointed to lead troops were the best qualified, but the system was also plagued by corrupt practices, such as bribes for the acquisition of a commission and appointment to office solely for the purpose of selling the office at a profit.[104] William III, George I, and George II made efforts to abolish the system, but merely managed to bring it under some regulation. Even this regulation was only partially successful, as were the regulations introduced by Lord Barrington, secretary of war from 1755 to 1761 and 1765 to 1778.[105]

Without denying the overall success of the blue-water strategy, its difficulties must be clearly recognized. The days of mercenary warfare had been declining. Subsidies to the armies of other countries were still worthwhile, but they depended on forming alliances with those countries. Impressive as the navy was, naval "dominance" was a difficult thing to achieve. The navy did little to help Britain accomplish its continental objectives.[106] Raids on the French coast were not terribly successful operations. Britain could indeed attack the commercial ships of other countries, but it too was vulnerable to such attacks, dependent as it was on trade. Worst of all, a country with a strong navy and a weak army can easily get itself overextended, acquiring sovereignty over more territory than it can hold with its land forces. The small number of troops in Britain often left the state with insufficient resources to contain public unrest.[107] In 1768 the quartermaster-general was afraid that if troops were sent to Newcastle to suppress riots, other parts of Britain would be left defenceless; in 1774 the secretary of war was worried that possible rioting in Manchester would not be controlled because four battalions had been sent to America.[108]

The most serious trouble came in Ireland and Scotland. This happened in spite of the fact that a larger standing army was kept in Ireland during the eighteenth century than ever before. By then the threat of a continental invasion of Ireland was taken more seriously. The landing of James II with a continental army in 1689 had made Ireland a vital place in European power struggles and dramatically increased the strategic importance of Ireland in the minds of both Irishmen and Englishmen.[109] In addition, the Catholic population of the country was regarded as ripe for rebellion. And Ireland provided a way of dodging English opposition to a standing army; the Irish Parliament, fearful of rebellion or invasion, was not opposed to a standing army for the same reasons as the British Parliament.[110] The British Parliament would accept for Ireland what they would not accept for England. The Irish army became a reserve force that the government could call upon when needed. It was spread about the country in dispersed barracks and was frequently called upon to enforce law and order.[111] The number of troops in Ireland was set at 12,000 men in 1692 and remained at this level until 1769. The Irish component (or "establishment") of the British army was then increased to 15,000, but only 12,000 were kept in Ireland.[112]

It was inadequate for the task. While this was a large army by British standards, it represented only about forty per 10,000 persons in the Irish population. Inevitably, some regions in Ireland evaded the king's rule, the most notorious of which were the southwest, south Ulster, and Iar Connacht (the region west of the town of Galway). By the second half of the eighteenth century, some success had been made in establishing law and order in these areas (less so in Iar Connacht).[113] Nonetheless, security in Ireland was still uncertain as a result of the weakness of British land forces. Indeed, for a number of reasons the last half of the eighteenth century saw an increase in collective violence.[114] During the American war the size of the army in Ireland was reduced to dangerous levels. To defend themselves from invasion, leaders in local communities formed militia in 1778. This "Volunteer" movement came to number at least 25,000 men, perhaps 40,000.[115] In the event, it did not have to defend Ireland from invasion, but instead was used by the Irish Parliament to back their demands with the threat of military force. The Volunteers were instrumental in the political gains that the Irish Parliament won in the late eighteenth century. They illustrated very clearly the vulnerability of British rule.

By the eighteenth century a relatively large number of garrisons were also maintained in Scotland to resist possible invasion and prevent rebellion, though they were not as dispersed as the army in Ireland. As mentioned above, however, the government was not able to enforce the king's rule in most of the Highlands and Western Islands until the last half of the eighteenth century. Bonnie Prince Charlie was able to form a Jacobite army because so many clans in the Highlands and Western Islands had lived outside the law and because the army in Scotland was at the time reduced to 3000 men as a result of continental commitments.[116] When the Rebellion of 1745 broke out, troops were hastily returned from Flanders, but not before the Jacobite army was able to invade south as far as Derby. The Jacobites retreated and were eventually defeated at Culloden 16 April 1746. Still, it had been a frightening experience for the Hanovarian regime. The king simply did not have enough troops to go around.

Taxation and Finance

The evolution of royal taxation in England was precocious. Anglo-Saxon kings collected a national tax, the geld, employing a staff of royal officers. With the aid of Domesday Book, the Normans developed the system further, coming to rely on central institutions to legitimate taxation. If a Medieval king wanted to lead an expedition against the Scots or raise additional revenues, he obtained agreement from his council, later his parliament, rather than through negotiations with local bodies. English kings did not as routinely as French kings turn to corporate bodies, specific social groups, town governments, or local, provincial, or ad hoc assemblies. Instead, they generally negotiated with one council or later one bicameral parliament. The exceptions were in Ireland and the Principality of Wales. There historians have found something similar to the negotiations we encountered in France. In Ireland some revenue was raised through local levies. Consent for taxation was obtained by making bargains with individual lords and local communities, though the existence of a parliament in Ireland led to tax procedures closer to the English practice. A regular pattern of parliamentary subsidies was established after 1380, but the continuation of local taxation limited the sum that could be raised by general taxation.[117]

The British were especially resistant to taxation and insisted even longer than people in other countries that the king live of his own. In England, additional exactions were accepted only for war and defence. New taxes that did not accord with traditional conceptions of just taxation generally failed.[118] During the sixteenth century the distinction between ordinary and extraordinary revenues broke down, but a pretence could be made that the traditional rules were being followed.[119] Like the French monarchy, the British crown had to indulge in a variety of manipulations to obtain the revenue it needed: forced loans, debasement of coinage, sale of land, and sales of honours or offices. The last mentioned, however, did not compare in magnitude with the sale of offices in France.

Initially, crown lands were the major source of royal revenue in England, apparently responsible for around 60 per cent of revenue in the reign of Henry II. Yet, by the reign of Edward I, hereditary crown revenues (which includes justice) represented only 32 per cent of royal revenues, while customs represented 25 per cent and lay taxation and subsidies 24 per cent. Under Edward III and Richard II, customs became the largest single source, followed by hereditary crown revenues and lay taxation and subsidies.[120] The same was later true under Elizabeth.[121] Customs revenue depended to a considerable extent, however, on English agriculture, especially on the export tax on wool. It is true that with the development of the English cloth industry from the mid-fourteenth century, wool exports declined. This was disastrous for royal revenue since wool exports were taxed much more heavily than cloth exports. Nevertheless, taxation reflected the combined water and land basis of the English state and society. In many places long-distance trade fostered agricultural commercialization both by promoting urban population growth and by encouraging and facilitating the export of agricultural products. The Foxian model should not lead us to think that agriculture is an important resource only in land-based societies. True, land-based states depend more heavily on agriculture, but if an economy is exceedingly land-based, agriculture may not be commercialized enough to provide sufficient resources. Again doubt is raised about the simple dichotomy of land and political centralization versus water and political fragmentation. A combination of land and sea provided greater resources for political centralization than a relatively non-commercialized agricultural society. This was all the more true in the case of England as a result of special circumstances that increased returns from crown lands, which also constituted a larger source for the English crown than for the French, as a result of the lands in England seized by the crown during the Norman Conquest, the acquisition of land of extinct or attainted aristocratic families (though land acquired by attainder was often restored to the family),[122] and the confiscation of church property (though most of this land was alienated by 1640).

The massive growth in demands on the treasury as a result of the wars of the late seventeenth and eighteenth centuries led to heavier taxation. Property taxes were raised, but they did not meet the new requirements, and attempts to correct regional inequities in the land tax were unsuccessful.[123] In desperation the government turned to higher excise taxation, a course strongly opposed by the country gentry in the House of Commons. This opposition may seem curious, since increases in land taxes would certainly have hit them harder than increases in excise taxes. Yet what concerned them most was parliamentary control over taxation. Their antagonism towards excise taxation was based on the view that, once these taxes were established, they would be difficult for the Commons to control, in contrast with the land tax, which they could and did preserve as an "extraordinary" tax to be voted every year. The government was able to raise excise taxation only by adding to it one product at a time.[124] The percentage of annual government revenue coming from excise rose from a mean of 35 per cent in the first quarter of the eighteenth century to a mean of 47 per cent in the second and third quarters and 45 per cent in the fourth quarter. The percentage derived from customs did not increase during the eighteenth century; the mean was 23 per cent in the first quarter, 27 per cent in the second, 24 per cent in the third, and 22 percent in the fourth.[125] The percentage raised by customs was somewhat higher than the comparable figure of 16 per cent or more for the Austrian Low Countries, and much higher than the 3 or 4 per cent in France, if those figures are correct.[126] Altogether, indirect taxes (customs and excise) were providing about two-thirds to three-quarters of government revenues in mid-eighteenth-century Britain, as compared with perhaps half in the Austrian Low Countries and in France. Thus, though historically the Southern Low Countries were more water-based than Britain, in the eighteenth century British taxation conformed more to the theoretical water-based state than did taxation in the Austrian Low Countries.

In the eighteenth century, state finances in Britain were healthier than they were in France in spite of a huge increase in government expenditure during the century. The right of Parliament to raise taxes was not disputed; a growing commercial economy provided a lucrative source of revenue; the capacity of the state to raise money also made it easier to borrow; and short-term debts were transformed into long-term funded debts.[127] Parliament stood as a watchdog over both the collection of revenue and its expenditure. The administration of tax collection was now more centrally and bureaucratically organized.[128] Britain became one of the most successful countries in Europe at extracting the maximum revenue from its economy.

Yet this success should not be exaggerated. The data suggest that the British and the French states were about equally effective at mobilizing resources through taxation. It is now well known that in the eighteenth century the British state raised far more revenue per capita than the French state, but this difference has been overestimated by leaving out Ireland and by basing comparisons on taxes collected by the central government, excluding local taxes. In addition, it is necessary to take into account the relative capacity of populations to pay. If we do so, we find that the comparative extractive power of each state varied over the course of the eighteenth century. In 1725 a London worker had to labour eight days to pay his quota of state taxation, compared with ten for a Parisian worker; in 1790 a London worker had to labour eighteen days to pay his quota, while a Parisian worker had to labour only fourteen.[129] Similarly, if the health

Figure 2
Cost of Servicing State Debt in Britain, 1701–93

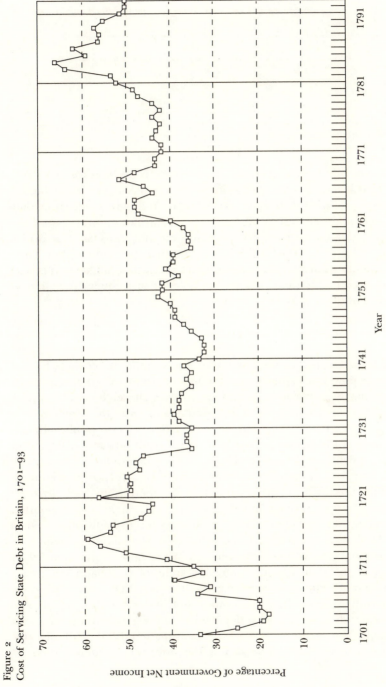

Percentage of Government Net Income

Year

Table 7
Debt Charges as a Percentage of Government Net Income of Britain and France
for Selected Years

Years	Britain	France
1726	48	34
1751	42	28
1775	42	41
1788	56	55

See note 131 for sources.

of a state is judged by its debt charge, there is no basis for classifying the British state as greatly superior to the French. Figure 2 and table 7 demonstrate that, in Britain, debt charges as a percentage of income were generally at least as high as in France, if not higher, again if the years for which we have French data were not unusual. The British state had a better system for borrowing than the French, but it was not without its problems, one of which was its vulnerability to financial crises, which repeatedly erupted as a result of frequent deflation in public confidence in the system.[132]

WEAK OR STRONG?

The British state was once regarded as "weak." The crown's lack of coercive power was well recognized. Indeed, some writers accepted the myth that Britain had no standing army in the eighteenth century. The bureaucracy was small in comparison with the French state bureaucracy. It has been estimated that only 16,000 public officials (90 per cent of whom were in finance) served the state in Britain in 1797, in contrast with 300,000 in France just before the Revolution.[133] Of course, this French figure includes many venal offices that contributed little to the "strength" of the state, but there is no doubt that the effective bureaucracy was much larger in France. Writers often pointed out, moreover, that the British bureaucracy was as badly organized as the French, if not worse. Little uniformity was found between one department and another, or even within the same department.[134] In much of the state apparatus the hierarchy of command was loose. Considerable emphasis was given to the fact that county officials, especially justices of the peace, were not under central control. The political system was for long depicted as one big gravy train, in which principle and democratic representation mattered little and jobs and state contracts mattered most. Public money was frequently invested for private profit. Those who officially held a position did not necessarily perform its functions, and many positions were simply sinecures. While there was less venality of office in the British Isles than in France, state positions could take on a patrimonial character. Most posts in the civil service did not go to the best-qualified candidate, but to the one with connections. Partiality in favour of relatives and friends was normal. Appointments to the revenue administration were used to create vacancies in the House of Commons, to win over political factions, and to provide for friends in financial distress; peers and politicians sought posts for their dependants; positions were applied for as marriage provisions; and those with any administrative ability were often in the minority.[135] Even the British excise administration, which was probably the most efficient, was still in some ways patrimonial.[136] Historians have found bribery, payoffs, and other kinds of corruption throughout the state bureaucracy. The smuggling in which Robert Walpole was engaged was notorious, as well as the fortune he made as paymaster-general.[137]

Some historians have argued that this was quite acceptable by the norms of the day, yet the inefficiency and corruption did garner plentiful public criticism. Certainly, politicians who were not on the gravy train sought to take advantage of public disgust, until, of course, they got on. In any case, many writers have exalted the British state as better precisely because of its deficiencies. Regrettable as the corruption might have been, the impotence of the state meant that it was not as repressive as absolutist states on the Continent. The smallness of the bureaucracy and the military weakness of the state were actually praised as essential to the development of liberal institutions in the British Isles.

This applause must be understood in the context of the liberal intellectual tradition in the British Isles that called for a minimalist state. This tradition had a profound influence on early sociology, an influence that was particularly marked in the work of Herbert Spencer, who distinguished between "military" societies, in which the power of the state is oppressive, and "industrial" societies, where the power of the state is restricted. Spencer believed that the latter were more advanced in evolutionary terms.[138] Parsons did not glorify weak states, but considered societies to be more advanced where the functions performed by the state were more restricted and civil society was more autonomous. Early Modern absolutist states were in this sense behind the British state in social evolution.[139] Similarly, Wood, a Marxist, alleges that the subordination of the state to civil society in Early Modern England was just what we should expect from the first capitalist society.[140]

Yet there were some bothersome problems with this line of thinking. A few people wondered if Spencer's negative attitude towards military states was not inconsistent with his more general view that the societies that are most evolved are those that survive the struggle of the fittest. L.T. Hobhouse recognized this inconsistency and worried about how the best society in terms of human values would be able to win out over the fittest society according to the principles of natural selection.[141]

None of this caused any difficulty for the alternative, more continental, intellectual tradition, which always regarded powerful states as more advanced. The great thinker of this tradition was G.W.F. Hegel, who equated social evolution with the development of a powerful state. Marx was aware of the role of concentrated political power in the making of capitalism and the structuring of capitalist societies. Weber recognized, with much apprehension, the concentration of power in the state bureaucracies of modern societies. Dietrich Rueschemeyer has argued that the coercive power of the state was necessary for the emergence of the division of labour.[142] The recent literature on interstate struggles and military-fiscal resources directly challenges Spencer's dichotomy, arguing that the most advanced societies have the greatest military resources, which enable them to prevail in international struggles for power.[143]

We should not be surprised, therefore, to discover a revisionist view that England really had a powerful or "strong" state in the seventeenth and eighteenth centuries. Wallerstein, as could be expected, took the position that the "strongest" states were those that were dominant in the "world system"; in the seventeenth century, the United Provinces were the strongest, followed by England and then France.[144] R.J. Holton has argued that the English state was more "effective" than the French state.[145] John Brewer has used the same word to describe the English state, attributing its "effectiveness" to the very absence of coercive features that might be associated with "strong" states.[146] He minimizes the effects of the purchase system, patronage, and corruption and puts the emphasis on the development of professional civil servants from the late seventeenth century.[147]

Michael Mann has made a useful distinction between "despotic" power and "infrastructural" power; and Karen Stanbridge has developed this conceptualization further in a comparison of the French and British states and their relationships with their North American colonies during the seventeenth and eighteenth centuries. Despotic power refers to "the range of actions which the elite is empowered to undertake without routine, institutionalized negotiation with civil society groups," while infrastructural power is "the capacity of the state to actually penetrate civil society, and to implement logistically political decisions throughout the realm."[148] I think one could also say that infrastructural power refers to the capacity of the state to mobilize resources to achieve its objectives. Again there is an evolutionary assumption in this theoretical distinction. Mann surmises that state infrastructural power has gradually increased over the ages.[149]

If we rank our states according to the despotic power of the sovereign, beginning with the most despotic, we should place them in this order: Savoy, France, the Spanish/Austrian Low Countries, and the British Isles. It is more difficult, however, to rank them in infrastructural power. In some respects the British state had more infrastructural power than the French state: it plainly had greater sea power; it ruled over more colonies; there was less venality of office; and the authority of the king or queen in Parliament was accepted in all of England and Wales, if not in all of Ireland and Scotland. Although the difference was not as great as most writers have assumed, the British state also had greater capacity to mobilize fiscal resources. In other respects, however, the British state had less infrastructural power than the French. Even including all the British Isles, it ruled over a smaller population; its control over this population was less intensive; the authority of the state was less respected in the peripheries; even in England less direct authority was exercised by the centre in the localities; the state bureaucracy was smaller; and so was the army. If we are talking about the magnitude of infrastructural power in absolute terms, it is clear that, within Europe, the French political centre was more powerful. Indeed, in this part of the world no other state exercised as much power over as many people as the French state.

Conclusion

Chapters 1 to 3 enable us to draw, in addition to the above conclusions, some comparative conclusions about relationships between centres and peripheries in Western Europe, conclusions that will be useful in subsequent discussions, especially when we treat the political power of the aristocracy. How do we explain the fact that some peripheries enjoyed greater political autonomy than others?

The first factor affecting peripheral autonomy was the military capacity of the political centre to enforce its will on the periphery. By this capacity I mean not just whether it could send an army to the periphery, but whether it could afford to keep one there, or send one repeatedly. As a result of certain geographical impediments and the military weakness of the crown within the British Isles, this capacity developed only slowly in the British Isles. In the Principality of Wales it became established in the thirteenth and fourteenth centuries. It was not established in all of Scotland until the mid-eighteenth century. It was largely established in Ireland in the seventeenth century, but British rule in Ireland had some militarily weaknesses even in the late eighteenth century.

Although in the last half of the sixteenth century and in the early seventeenth, Spain relied heavily on force to govern the Low Countries, its capacity to do so declined steadily during the latter century. The Austrians improved matters in some measure. They did not face rebellion in the Low Countries until the Liège and Brabant Revolutions of 1789, which they were able to suppress militarily. Yet the rebels, or the most radical faction among them, were carried to victory by the French, and the Austrians could do little about it.

The capacity to use force to govern was much greater in France and Savoy. Savoy was the quintessential land-based state that needed to build up a large military force to defend itself among the European states and thus had the military power to rule with comparatively less regard for the sensitivities of peripheral elites. During the Religious Wars, the capacity of the French centre to control its territory was weak. Nonetheless, France subsequently evolved into one of the most successful states in Europe at imposing the rule of the crown throughout its territory. Eventually, of course, the crown was overthrown, but the French Revolution began at the political centre and was primarily a revolt of the centre. It did not result from weak control of the centre over the peripheries.

The second factor affecting peripheral autonomy was the importance of the periphery in international power struggles. In general, political centres sought most to undermine the political autonomy of regions over which there was international competition.

Autonomy persisted longer in the peripheries of the British Isles not only because they were difficult to control militarily, but also because they were strategically less crucial. Indeed, the two factors reinforced each other; the English did not think they needed to build large armies to defend their peripheries, which then made these peripheries all the more difficult to control or defend when the time came. Peripheral autonomy was permitted the longest in the part of the British Isles furthest from the Continent – the Highlands and Western Islands of Scotland. After the Union of the Crowns of 1603, the English would certainly have preferred a loyal and law-abiding population living in the region, but an uncontrolled peripheral population could be tolerated in Scotland to an extent that would have been intolerable in France, even in Brittany, and certainly in Lotharingia.

One critical part of the history of English-Irish relations was the increasing but reluctant and inconstant recognition by the English of Ireland's strategic importance. Only from the late sixteenth century was the perceived importance of Ireland sufficient to lead to complete military domination of the island. The role of the Irish in the English Civil War raised English anxieties about Ireland, but the attitude of the English towards Ireland was still revealed in the Cromwellian plan to transplant Catholics (mainly landowners) to Connacht, a most extraordinary policy. One can hardly imagine Louis xiv adopting a similar policy in Lotharingia or even in Brittany. The last thing a continental power wanted was a disloyal population near its frontiers.

As we have seen, however, the arrival of James ii in Ireland with French assistance revived English concern about the strategic importance of Ireland. Paradoxically, it was recognition of this importance that led William both to grant Catholics favourable terms in the Treaty of Limerick and to turn around and accept the annulment of these concessions by the Irish Parliament. There was little that the English government could do to prevent this outcome, because the ascendancy of Protestants in Ireland was now seen as crucial to keeping the continental powers out of their back door.

Even in the eighteenth century, however, though English will was generally imposed on the Irish, Ireland was permitted to have a separate Parliament. This was primarily because that Parliament was in the hands of Protestants, whom the English felt they could trust. So long as the Irish elite seemed to accept its dependence on the English and so long as Ireland remained constitutionally subordinate to England, union had no appeal to the English.

It became clear, however, in the late eighteenth century that Ireland had the potential for considerable autonomy; and, indeed, a measure of autonomy was realized. To this was added increasing violence in Ireland, a rebellion by the United Irishmen, and a French invasion. It would be a vast oversimplification to say that the continental threat was the principal cause of the Union of 1801; the abolition of the separate Irish Parliament was the result of a number of forces. Yet one of them certainly was English opinion that an Ireland politically united with Britain would not be as vulnerable to the continental threat as a semi-independent Ireland had been. The unrest and the invasion also had an effect on the Protestant elite in Ireland. Although a substantial number of Protestants opposed union, many others were becoming convinced that union would help them resist Catholics.

Whereas the English for long tried to ignore Ireland, no European powers ignored Lotharingia. Control over parts of Lotharingia, or preventing others from gaining control, was fundamental to the policies of all the great powers. Those political centres with claims to Lotharingian territory generally sought to limit autonomy and to abolish provincial institutions, but they were not always able to do so. This was most evident in the Spanish/Austrian Low Countries. Philip II tried to reduce local autonomy in the Low Counties. For reasons given above, his efforts were unsuccessful. The Northern Low Countries became completely autonomous; and in the Southern Low Countries provincial institutions persisted. In contrast, the dukes of Savoy were able to destroy the provincial autonomy of the Lotharingian regions under their control.

Another general pattern is apparent. Blockmans has proposed that representative institutions varied in Medieval and Early Modern Europe, particularly between those found in comparatively agricultural societies and those found in more urbanized societies. He believes that representative institutions were generally more vigorous in the latter.[1] Among the countries I am studying there was a tendency for political assemblies to be more powerful and to survive longer in centres that were as much economic as political. Thus political assemblies that met in the South-Netherlandish provinces, in London, in Edinburgh, and in Dublin were comparatively strong. Within the Southern Low Countries, estates were most powerful in the relatively urbanized and commercialized provinces: Flanders, Brabant, and Liège. Estates were abolished everywhere in Piedmont-Savoy. In France the pattern was more complex. No estates met in Paris from 1614 to 1789. Estates did survive in the eighteenth century in Languedoc, Artois, and Brittany, which were comparatively commercialized. Yet other comparatively commercialized regions, such as Normandy and the Bordeaux area, did not have estates in the eighteenth century.

Thus there appears to be a correlation, but an imperfect one, between commercialism and the power of political assemblies. Insofar as there was a tendency for economic centres to be more likely to have political assemblies, why was this the case?

As I have already suggested with respect to Liège, it was not that elites in the more urbanized parts of the Southern Low Countries had the financial resources to employ armies that defended them against the great political centres. Perhaps more to the point was fear of harming the goose that lays the golden egg. Reluctance to exacerbate financial problems by alienating economic elites may have been one factor among others that helped preserve provincial institutions in more commercialized areas.

Blockmans implies a closely related reason. Political assemblies were especially vigorous in economic centres because urban elites added their support to efforts being made by other groups to impose their advice on the sovereign. Indeed, the sovereign frequently turned to urban elites to obtain their backing for his demands for revenue from urban populations. The Medieval commercialization of the Netherlandish economy generated an unusually aggressive urban elite, which had a dramatic effect on the development of estates. Blockmans's thinking is very much influenced by Flanders, as is mine. It was the extreme case. Here urban elites actually spearheaded the development of political assemblies and dominated them.

Yet any effort to explain the survival of estates in the seventeenth and eighteenth centuries by means of the urban factor runs into certain difficulties. Intense commercialism in Britanny was limited to coastal ports. Otherwise the province was not comparatively commercialized. Moreover, though further research is required, it would not seem that urban elites played a critical role in the development or preservation of the Breton estates. The Third Estate was not a strong independent force in the Estates of Brittany during the seventeenth and eighteenth centuries. Efforts of the crown to reform or weaken the estates were thwarted primarily by the nobility, not the urban representatives, many of whom were under the control of either the crown or members of the nobility. The theory encounters some difficulty even in the Southern Low Countries. By the seventeenth and eighteenth centuries, Flanders was not the economic centre that it once was, and its estates were no longer as powerful as they once were. Urban representation in the estates of the Southern Low Countries was in some cases controlled by the sovereign. It could also be weaker than that of the other estates. And the most active business elite in the Southern Low Countries was not usually invited to share much of the power of the estates.[2] As I have argued, some credit can be given to urban elites for the power of the British parliaments in the seventeenth century, but the British Isles on the whole were less urbanized than the Low Countries and the role of landed elites was critical in the development of parliamentary power. The urban factor provides only a partial explanation.

I would suggest that, in addition, the contingencies of power struggles between crown and political assemblies determined the outcome in each case. That is why we do not find a perfect correlation between commercialism and the strength of political assemblies. Different forces in different cases enabled some estates to preserve a measure of power. In the Southern Low Countries it was clearly the loss of the Dutch War and the decline in Spanish power during the seventeenth century that enabled estates to survive. In England the Civil War and the Glorious Revolution upheld parliamentary authority. And in Ireland the dependence of the government of William III on the loyalty of the Protestant Ascendancy gave new life to a parliament whose power had been declining.

A critical contingent factor was the set of circumstances under which a peripheral territory was annexed. Languedoc was incorporated into France with promises of a *parlement* and the right of the estates to be consulted before taxes were levied.[3] Royal acquiescence to the powers of the Estates of Brittany was a condition for the union of Brittany and France. Similarly, respect for the constitution of Béarn was a condition for its union; in particular the French crown accepted control of the estates over taxation.[4] We can observe something of a parallel between the latter two cases. The union of France and Brittany occurred after Anne of Brittany became queen of France; the union of France and Béarn occurred after Henry of Navarre became king of France. In contrast, when the dukes of Savoy went to Turin, Savoy lost its estates. The difference was that Brittany and Béarn were separate countries being united with a larger centre, while Chambéry was simply losing its status as a political centre, much as if the king of France moved to Bordeaux. Savoyard elites could not bargain for concessions or guarantees as conditions for union. In a situation similar to that of Béarn, the Scottish Parliament survived the Union of the Crowns in 1603.

PART TWO

Aristocratic Power

4 The Decline of Lordship

In a general sense, lordship refers to a relationship of authority in which a higher-status person, the lord, was owed deference, loyalty, and services. Beyond this simple definition, disagreement flourishes among historians about its meaning. For some, the right to exercise justice is the defining feature of lordship. For others, economic benefits constitute a critical characteristic. For still others, rights to land are essential to the concept. Some historians have insisted that the term "lordship" refers to a situation where there was a clearly defined territory, a "seigneurie" or "manor," which was the area of jurisdiction of the lord and the basis for rendering services. Yet it was possible to find lordship without justice, land, seigneuries, or manors. Retaining or bonding usually did not involve any of these characteristics. Instead, a man attached himself to a lord in return for protection, maintenance, and/or payments.[1]

In table 8 I have characterized lordship in terms of the four variables of status outlined in the introduction. Lordship may be considered a historically specific variant of the patron-client tie, and feudalism a historically specific variant of lordship.[2] From the decline of the Roman Empire until at least the end of the Middle Ages, ties of lordship, kinship, community, and religion were the primary basis of social organization in Western Europe. While the four often reinforced one another, the significance of lordship was precisely that it could introduce a new bond among people that did not depend on kin or communal ties or religious authority. Although many anthropologists have studied patron-client ties, few anthropologists or sociologists have

Table 8
The Status Characteristics of Lordship

Differentiation	Normally status coincided considerably with political power. It also coincided with economic power if lords controlled land, but it was the fusion of status with political power that was a fundamental characteristic of lordship.
Criteria	It was primarily leadership that was being accorded high status. This legitimated the authority possessed by the lord.
Ascription	Lordship was largely an ascribed status, though perhaps not as much as is generally assumed. It was possible to acquire lordship in other ways besides inheritance; it was certainly possible to lose it; and lords varied in their ability to command loyalty or obedience.
Institutionalization	The status of lord was relatively well institutionalized. In most cases, it was legally recognized as inherent in a position with rights and obligations.

studied lordship. Most sociologists have allowed themselves to be guided by the Marxian conception of feudalism, which focuses primarily on its economic characteristics. Weber and those influenced by Weber have taken more interest in lordship, but Weber seriously mistook the essence of lordship. Lordship was often legitimated by tradition, but not necessarily. The essence of lordship was contract, which was usually explicit and might be restated or renewed several times during the life of the lord or the follower. Contract is not, as some sociologists think, a unique feature of modern society.

FRANCE, SAVOY, AND THE SOUTHERN LOW COUNTRIES

Early French lordship was deconcentrated and became more so in the tenth and eleventh centuries when the royal public authority was dispersed among dukes, counts, and castellans. In the following centuries, powers of lordship were gradually recovered by the crown, but the dispersion of the tenth and eleventh centuries continued to have consequences and to make French society different from English society.

In the late Middle Ages the feudal relation at the higher levels of society gradually gave way to the *alliance*.[3] It was not totally new; the distinction between *alliance* and feudalism was not a sharp one; and the one did not simply displace the other. The *alliance* was similar to what English historians have called "bastard feudalism." It was a retaining contract, typically between lords. Whereas feudal relationships were usually based on land and involved payments by the inferior to the superior, land was less often involved in retaining, and the payments were the reverse: a less powerful lord owed loyalty to a more powerful lord in return for privileges, maintenance, and various kinds of compensation. Knights, lawyers, and administrative officials could also be linked to a lord through an *alliance*. Fewer references to *alliances* survive in the documents from the fifteenth century, but there is ample evidence of reciprocal service between persons of relatively high social standing. First comes what historians call clientage, subsequently state patronage. By state patronage I mean patronage in which the benefits supplied by the patron consist of state income, offices, and/or services. The growth in the power of the state explains this transition. The state gradually succeeded in eliminating warfare among lords, thus making *alliances* less important for lords from a military point of view; at the same time, the state became the major source of political power, making smaller lords and petty nobles dependent on patrons with influence in political centres to represent their interests.

Relations of lordship between lord and peasant also changed. During the twelfth and thirteenth centuries many communities, both urban and rural, purchased franchises that reduced or fixed their obligations to their lord and thus freed them from the arbitrary exactions that implied servitude.[4] Also by the thirteenth century the crown had encroached on private rights of jurisdiction. Many of the services owed to lords were commuted into money payments.[5] In the late Middle Ages the seigneurial right to tax was substantially limited by the crown. By the end of the sixteenth century, seigneuries were bought and sold. As a rule, seigneurial obligations owed by peasants were now inherent in the land they occupied, not in their person. In the seventeenth and eighteenth centuries there were further royal encroachments on seigneurial authority, especially justice. The seigneurie might be little more than an administrative unit, subject to the jurisdiction of higher state administrative authority. By the eighteenth century many of the obligations owed to seigneurs had been given up. This was especially true in the Southern Low Countries, where seigneurial monopolies and payments due to the lord such as relief and *formariage* had been reduced or had fallen into disuse.[6] In addition, seigneurial dues that had been set at a fixed monetary value decreased in real terms through inflation.[7]

As a consequence, by the eighteenth century seigneurial dues formed a minor component of the agricultural economy in many areas. In the Flemish district of Aalst, by the second half of the eighteenth century, seigneurial dues represented 1.13 per cent of the gross agricultural product as compared with proprietary rent, which represented 25.4 per cent, tithes 9.1 per cent, and taxes 13.4 per cent.[8] Seigneurial dues were only slightly higher in the Duchy of Savoy, at least in those parts for which we have data; in the early eighteenth century seigneurial dues represented 4.4 per cent of the gross agricultural product in Faucigny and 6.3 per cent in the province of Savoy.[9]

The same picture emerges if we examine seigneurial rights or dues as a proportion of landed revenue.[10] This proportion was 17.3 per cent in Faucigny and 14.2 per cent in the province of Savoy.[11] Seigneurial dues in the seigneurie of Pont-St-Pierre in Normandy yielded 92 per cent of total revenues in 1398–9 (29 per cent if we exclude *rentes*), but only 23 per cent in 1740, 30 per cent in 1765, and 11 per cent in 1780 (20, 23, and 8 per cent respectively if we exclude *rentes*).[12] For other parts of France for which data are available, such as the district around Toulouse and Bordeaux, the proportion was generally 8 per cent or less.[13] T.J.A. Le Goff gives the example of one noble family with eighteen seigneuries scattered throughout Lower Brittany whose income from fixed seigneurial dues came to 13 per cent of its total revenues.[14]

Yet lordship did not disappear. With modifications, seigneurial rights were preserved in customary law when it was edited in the sixteenth century.[15] Obligations to a lord that endured included relief and *saisine, banalités, droits de mutation*, the *terrage*, the seigneurial *taille*, and the *cens* or *servis*.[16] In Savoy the lord had the right to a share of the produce of a herd grazing on high pastures; in certain Savoyard regions the seigneurs had the right to send their herd on the high mountain pastures three days before the villagers.[17] The lord often enjoyed exclusive rights to fishing and hunting. Most lords had local political and judicial powers, to which I shall return in a later chapter. Although serfdom as such had been abolished, those peasants subject to *mainmorte* were regarded as serfs and their lands could be appropriated by the seigneur should they die without children. More than half the peasantry in Savoy were *mainmortables*.[18] While in most districts seigneurial dues had ceased to be a considerable source of revenue, in some they still were. In Upper Auvergne in the mid-eighteenth century the proportion varied from one *élection* to another, ranging from 22.5 per cent to 41.7 per cent. In the Duchy of Meilleraye, 40 per cent of the revenues may have come from seigneurial dues in the 1770s. In Pont-St-Pierre *banalités* yielded as much as a percentage of total revenue in some years of the eighteenth century as they had in the fifteenth century.[19]

The continued importance of seigneurial obligations is attested by the litigation, claims of hardship, and denunciations to which they gave rise.[20] Arthur Young found peasants in Berry who "complained so heavily of these burdens, that the mode of levying and enforcing them must constitute much of the evil; they are everywhere much more burdensome than apparent, from the amount which I attribute to that circumstance. Legal adjudications, they assert, are very severe against the tenant, in favour of the seigneur."[21]

The "aristocratic reaction" of the eighteenth century has been exaggerated. Yet the widespread belief in a "feudal reaction" (that is, the alleged increase in demands on peasants) may have had some truth to it. It is conceivable that there was a double reaction – possibly greater exertion on both sides to better their positions.[22] Or it may be that one is simply witnessing the normal validation of rights undertaken by every generation of seigneurs.[23] At any rate, the evidence that has been collected to support the notion of a feudal reaction reveals, at the very least, the survival of lordship in France, Savoy, and to a lesser extent the Southern Low Countries during the last century of the Old Regime.

Above all, the prestige of being a seigneur persisted and the status was sought after by nobles and commoners alike. Acquisition of a seigneurie raised the standing of the purchaser and brought with it specific honourary rights, such as a privileged position in the church, rights to display one's coat of arms in certain places, and oaths of fidelity.[24] Although the monetary value of the *cens* was usually not much, it continued to have considerable symbolic value.

THE BRITISH ISLES

England

The lordship established in England by the Normans was relatively centralized, militaristic, and closely connected with land. It acquired these characteristics as a result of three forces. First was the influence of lordship in Normandy, where authority was less dispersed than it was in France as a whole and where William had been able to overcome opposition to his rule and to establish that lands were held in return for military service.[25] Second was the influence of Anglo-Saxon lordship, which was based on military service and land grants.[26] Third was the conquest itself, which enabled William to impose the kind of lordship he wanted, and in particular to set stringent conditions for grants of land. Land was awarded for relatively precise terms of military service. The sovereign's rights were firmly institutionalized.[27] William's power in Normandy had been closely tied to bonds of kinship, and those who helped him lead the conquest of England were mostly his kinsmen.[28] The legal formalism of the feudalism that they established in England, however, led to the evolution of a kind of lordship that was comparatively independent of kinship.

The English king's vassals owed heavier obligations to the king than did the French king's vassals. They also had less autonomy from the king. We do not find many great territorial magnates, at least not to the extent that one finds them in France. The exceptions that prove the rule were the border regions and areas outside England, which were more difficult to control – northern England, the Welsh March, and most of Ireland. In England, public authority was vested in the hands of the crown, with the result that lordship was private and domestic instead of public.[29] Under William and his successors, royal justice developed in a way that it did not on the Continent, offering an alternative to the lord's justice.[30]

English feudalism was transformed in significant ways during the twelfth and thirteenth centuries. Most land held in fief came to be inherited. This process both changed the character of the lord-vassal relationship and denied lords land to enfeoff more vassals. In the thirteenth century vassals began to evade feudal incidents, particularly those owed to the crown. Military services were increasingly converted into monetary compensation.[31] Fewer communities were enfranchised in England than in continental countries during the twelfth and thirteenth centuries, but community charters were not unknown.[32] English serfdom declined in the late fourteenth and fifteenth centuries.

The retaining of followers persisted into the late Middle Ages and indeed may have expanded as feudalism declined. Certainly most historians regard bastard feudalism as a late Medieval phenomenon, an assumption that is rejected by J.M.W. Bean. He argues that its prototype is located in the lord's household.[33] In any case, bastard feudalism did not last. In the fifteenth century considerable opposition arose to retaining, especially to the interference by lords in judicial processes on behalf of their followers; this opposition came primarily from the House of Commons and the crown.[34] Retaining decreased in the sixteenth century, giving way, as did *alliances* in France, to clientage and state patronage, though the aristocratic violence associated with retaining was slower to subside.

Feudal obligations were also reduced during the sixteenth century. Henry VIII sought to increase revenues from feudal incidents by enacting the Statute of Uses in 1536. The Statute of Wills of 1540, however, turned things around and seriously damaged royal feudal revenues.[35] Feudal tenures were to all intents and purposes eliminated in the political upheavals of the seventeenth century. Wardship was abolished in 1646 and all feudal tenures were turned into free and common socage, leaving them without incidents. The legal fiction of feudalism was not abolished until the twentieth century with the Law of Property Act of 1922, which went into effect in 1926. The institution was, however, long since moribund.

The crucial question is how much life lordship still had in the seventeenth and eighteenth centuries. If we try to answer this question, we soon find ourselves in the midst of a debate in English history over tenurial arrangements, agrarian class structure, and the rise of capitalism.

One side is best known in the work of R.H. Tawney, who argued that as early as the sixteenth century traditional rural society in England was being destroyed by the forced removal of many peasants from the land. This transformation was not necessary for economic progress, but was carried out so the fruits of the expanding agricultural economy would go to great landlords.[36] More recently the forced removal of peasants has been emphasized in a series of articles by Robert Brenner.[37] Although comparisons between Western Europe and Eastern Europe formed part of Brenner's argument, it is the contrast he drew between England and France that is relevant here. Brenner sought to explain the development of agrarian capitalism in England as a product of agrarian class structure and class struggle. In England class struggle led to a victory of lords over peasants; in France the peasants, with the help of the state, successfully resisted the expropriation of the land by lords. Rights acquired by the French peasantry in the late Medieval period (such as the use of commons, fixed rents, and secure hereditability) were strengthened. French absolutism entrenched peasant society, and this in turn prevented the development of agrarian capitalism. In contrast, English landlords used fines and enclosures to eliminate customary tenants and to convert copyholds to leaseholds. The failure of peasant revolts to prevent lords from seizing their land doomed English peasant society to extinction and made possible the rise of agrarian capitalism.

On the opposite side were those who had challenged Tawney's argument – Eric Kerridge, Joan Thirsk, and others.[38] They rejected the claim that the English peasantry was in a weak position. They maintained that English copyholders often banded together to defend themselves in royal courts or in manorial courts; there they were protected by manorial custom, which survived into the seventeenth century and in some areas even into the eighteenth. These writers have emphasized the persistence of copyhold, manorial courts, and manorial dues. In some places the number of copyholds actually increased in the seventeenth century.[39] Agricultural communities were still dependent on a lord to protect their common interests and to enforce manorial custom. Enclosing and sometimes even engrossing were "amicable" in many parts of the country, and opposition declined during the seventeenth century as their benefits came to be generally recognized, except in a few regions such as the East Midlands.[40] Leases were not forced on tenants, but were often preferred by them.

Even fellow Marxists have criticized Brenner for underestimating the role that peasant resistance played in the transformation of English agrarian structure. This resistance was a major factor in the decline of serfdom that came after the peasant uprising of 1381.[41] More recently, Comninel has argued that it was the absence in English Medieval lordship of the *seigneurie banale* that explains the development of agrarian capitalism in England. The term refers to the appropriation of public authority by lords that took place in France during the tenth and eleventh centuries,[42] but not in England, where lords did not acquire jurisdiction over freemen. As a result, when serfdom disappeared in France the public authority that had been appropriated by lords did not go with it, while in England the decline of serfdom diminished seigneurial authority. However, the separation of public authority and the development of Common Law, which this separation made possible, led in England to the protection of freehold peasant tenure by the Common Law and the royal courts. By an ironic twist, this protection provided the basis for the property rights that lords came to enjoy over the land, property rights that enabled them to reorganize their landed estates in a way that French lords could not. Comninel criticizes Kerridge and his allies for failing to explain how the property relations emerged in England that made agrarian capitalism possible.[43]

This debate has clarified several things that bear on our inquiry. As Thirsk and others have insisted, customary tenure, manorial courts, and some manorial dues persisted in England. As many as one-third of all landholders may still have held by customary tenure in the late seventeenth century, though less than one-third of the land was probably under custom.[44] Copyhold tenure for three lives was by far the most widespread form of landholding in the southwest of England during the sixteenth and seventeenth centuries.[45] Royal courts frequently judged claims based on manorial customs and sometimes protected manorial custom.[46]

Certain seigneurial obligations persisted. Heriot, in particular, survived in many places; in some areas so did thirlage, reliefs, and labour dues. Quit-rents were also collected by many lords.[47] Hence, the difference between England and France has been exaggerated with regard to manorial rights and obligations. Indeed, there may have been a "feudal reaction" in England as well as in France. Many English landowners, like French seigneurs, tried to increase revenues within the manorial apparatus in the sixteenth, seventeenth, and eighteenth centuries, efforts that certain historians refer to as "fiscal seigneurialism."[48] Neglected seigneurial rights were frequently revived. Both landlords and tenants could be found researching manorial documents, in some cases stealing and altering them, in order to advance their claims.[49] Lords also asserted seigneurial rights to natural resources and fishing. Maintaining rights to natural resources became more rather than less important as the English economy developed.

Nevertheless, a major transformation did take place in English agrarian structure in the Early Modern period. As Comninel says, in France seigneurs enjoyed the private appropriation of public authority. This was not the case in England, with the result that when serfdom declined, tenants achieved greater freedom from the obligations of lordship.[50] In addition, there is no denying the proletarianization, enclosures, engrossment, and shift from customary to contractual tenures in England. The number of copyholders declined, while the number of leaseholders, tenants-at-will, and yearly tenants increased.[51] It is also hard to deny the decline in manorial rights and obligations between landlords and tenants. Many manorial courts were still operating, but a large number had also disappeared. Increasingly, they were unable to cope with disputes or were passed over in favour of royal courts.[52] Both tenants and lords could undermine lordship in their struggle to protect their interests. Where manorial courts still operated, tenants could use them to resist the seigneurial demands of a lord. Where they no longer met, their demise could be used by tenants to call into question the seigneurial rights of the lord. For example, the customary tenants of Aylsworth in west Sussex disputed their landowner's claim to seigneurial rights on the manors of Racton and Woodmancot on the grounds that the court baron had not met for at least fifty years.[53]

Wales

At the local level, the Welsh *maenor* and *maenol* had some similarities with the Anglo-Norman manor; in both England and Wales dues and services were rendered to a lord. As a consequence, the transition from Welsh lordship to Anglo-Norman manorialism was not difficult.[54] Yet early Welsh lordship and Anglo-Norman feudalism differed in a number of critical ways. Early Welsh lordship was tribute more than territorial lordship. In England all land was considered ultimately to be the property of the king, but in Wales land was owned by kinship groups. The bond of man to man was more important than ties based on land, though the two were generally complementary. Welsh lordship was more egalitarian and decentralized than English feudalism. Indeed, there were usually several kings in Wales, and no clear distinction was made between kingship and lordship.[55]

The English crown established a precarious overlordship in native Wales. Native lords were generally not displaced, but agreements were made with them. Henry II invaded Wales, not to incorporate it into the English state, but to demand submission from Welsh kings. Native Welsh lordship was abolished, however, by Edward I after his conquest of Wales in the late thirteenth century. It is true that manors persisted; and dues and services continued to be collected from the peasantry. The Welsh also had their own version of bastard feudalism. A Welsh leader commonly had a retinue, known as a *plaid*.[56] The Welsh custom of *arddel* also persisted, by which lords brought criminals into their service and protected them. So lordship was still alive. Yet much less of the authority and rights of lordship were invested in Welsh lords and much more in the crown than was the case before the conquest.

The fascinating thing is that it was in the most Normanized part of Wales that robust lordship persisted the longest. The lordship established by the Normans in the Welsh March during the eleventh century remained autonomous longer than did native Welsh lordship. The relationship of the Marcher lords to the crown was altogether different from the relationship between native Welsh lords and the crown. The Marcher lords were conquerors, while the native Welsh lords were conquered. Like English lordship, Marcher lordship was feudal. Unlike English lords, however, these lords enjoyed regal rights. Marcher lords had the right to engage in war and make peace. The king's writ did not run in the Marcher lordships. No royal officers, courts, or judges were to be found in the March. Although the king granted these lordships and could destroy a Marcher lord, he otherwise relied on the obligations the Marcher lords might feel towards him as their lord and king, or on other personal links he might have with them.[57]

Marcher lords typically supervised their lordships closely and made all significant decisions. They claimed almost unlimited power over those who lived in their lordships.[58] The earls of Arundel asserted the right to change laws, "to declare, to add or to reduce the ... laws, customs and services of their lordship whenever and howsoever it pleases them."[59] The judicial authority of Marcher lords was broadly defined and intensive.[60] The basis for this authority lay in their military power and in the defensive responsibilities entrusted to them by the English crown. Military vigilance was necessary and military tenurial duties continued to be required until at least the late thirteenth century.[61]

In the late Medieval period agrarian social relationships in Wales underwent great change. The Welsh customs of partible landholding were eroded in the fourteenth and fifteenth centuries. Services were commuted into money rents, and serfdom largely disappeared as a distinct status.[62] A series of charters granted by Henry VII between 1505 and 1508 abolished various ancient dues and payments in certain regions of the Principality of Wales.[63] Under the Tudors there began the conversion of customary tenures to tenancies-at-will, yearly tenancies, and leaseholds.[64] Like English landowners, Welsh landowners were able to carry out such conversions because the majority of Welsh peasants had lost their traditional rights to the land, though the traditional rights in native Wales were different from those in England.

The Marcher lordships were greatly undermined by the state restructuration that united England and Wales in 1536–43. Seigneurial judicial authority was taken away from Marcher lords. The following century saw the termination of feudal tenures in Wales as in England. Manor courts in Wales were not dissolved, but were restricted, most of their jurisdiction going to the quarter or petty sessions. The courts leet ordered the maintenance of roads and bridges, took care of stray dogs, reprimanded merchants for selling bad meat or illegal ale and for overcharging, and prevented the illegal construction of cottages on common land.[65] By the eighteenth century many manor courts were in a sorry state. Their operation was characterized by neglect and laxity.[66] In some parts of Wales manorial dues continued to be exacted. Here, too, there was fiscal seigneurialism. Cases can be found where manorial dues were employed to increase landed income.[67] Landowners used their rights of lordship to lay claim to natural resources.[68] It was even possible to find *cymorthas* (contributions to lords in material difficulty); they were banned by the Acts of Union, but were demanded by the lords of the Manor of Brecon even in the 1740s.[69] As in England, leaseholds replaced the seigneurial bond. What remained of manorial obligations typically came to be thrown in with a long list of covenants.

Ireland

Most of the regions discussed thus far – on both sides of the English Channel – saw an extension of royal power and a decrease in autonomous lordship from the thirteenth to the sixteenth centuries. Two exceptions were Gaelic Ireland and the Scottish Highlands and Western Islands. In Gaelic Ireland autonomous lordship did not decline, but strengthened.

It was said in chapter 3 that in post-Scandinavian Ireland high kings were establishing their authority over other kings and lords. High kingship was, however, undermined by the Norman invasion.[70] As in Wales, the English established royal lordship. When Henry II arrived in Ireland in 1171, some Irish lords submitted to him.[71] Irish lords became tenants and vassals of the crown, though on rather vague terms, and feudalism was introduced into the Norman region. Otherwise the spread of feudalism was limited. In marked contrast to Wales, where the native region was brought under royal control in the late thirteenth century, English royal control over native Ireland remained weak until the seventeenth century. English power undermined Irish native kingship, but did not undermine native lordship. The result was a fragmentation of Gaelic Ireland into a great number of lordships. By the late Middle Ages much of Ireland had become a land of warlords, what the English called "chief captaynes."[72] Gaelic lordship remained stronger, covered more of the territory, and lasted longer than did native Welsh lordship.

In pre-Scandinavian Ireland, clientship had been the fundamental basis of aristocratic domination. The lord received food and personal services from his clients, while the clients enjoyed the protection of the lord.[73] Like native Welsh lordship, Gaelic lordship in Ireland was a tribute lordship based more on military force than on the ownership of land.[74] Lordships became more militaristic over the course of the Middle Ages. Submissions were not made freely, but were extorted by coercion.[75] Lords engaged retainers and mercenaries; these relations, like those of English bastard feudalism, entailed payments from the lord to followers rather than tributes to the lord.[76] Property was vital, but it was not granted in the same way as it was granted by English feudal lords. As in early Wales, it was owned by kinship groups. Usually there were two landowning classes: the leading families from whom the chief lord was chosen; and subordinate septs who rendered economic and military service to the leading families.[77]

Although Anglo-Norman estates in Ireland were organized on the principles of English manorialism, Anglo-Norman and Gaelic lordship became in certain respects similar, especially in areas where there was the most contact between the two. In the sixteenth century Anglo-Norman lords were said to "folowyth the same Iryshe ordre and kepeith the same rule" as "the kinges Iryshe enmyes."[78] Most Anglo-Norman lords had Gaelic followers.[79]

During the sixteenth century the Tudors sought to undermine Irish lordship by establishing the direct lordship of the crown over subordinate lords, thus separating them from their overlords. Yet in the same period they also recognized the lordship of magnates who could be helpful to the crown.[80] In the 1540s the English undertook a policy of "surrender and regrant," whereby an Irish chief surrendered his land to the English crown, submitted to the English sovereign as lord, and foreswore jurisdictional independence; the land would then be returned to him and, if a prominent and powerful lord, he might receive a title.[81] Rather than abolishing lordship the English central government was at this time trying to control it and limit its autonomy, by giving it official recognition. The program enjoyed some success, though many Gaelic lords remained outside its reach. The crown tried to avoid upsetting the balance of power among Gaelic lords, but these agreements did extend royal power and did undermine the authority of some Gaelic lords over smaller lords by establishing a direct relationship between these smaller lords and the crown.[82] Similarly, the "composition" of Connacht and Munster during the last half of the sixteenth century (in which "presidencies" were established as an alternative to the authority of lords) and the abolition of "coign and livery" weakened Gaelic lordship, but did not destroy it.[83]

Far more serious was the abolition of Irish law and land tenure as well as the enactment of legislation aimed directly at undercutting Gaelic lordship. The greatest change occurred during the reign of James I when Irish law (known as Brehon law) was abolished and English Common Law was extended to Ireland. As a result, even Gaelic landowners, especially smaller owners, could be found seeking secure titles under English law.[84] Assize judges were dispatched to all parts of the country and armed retinues were made illegal.[85] A proclamation of 1605 prohibited any dependency on lords in Ulster. All inhabitants of Ulster were declared "the free natural and immediate subjects of his majesty" who should not be referred to as "the natives or natural followers of any lord or chieftain whatsoever."[86] The combined result of these forces was to undermine the great Gaelic lordships.[87] Gaelic lordship was, of course, also undermined by the decline of the Gaelic aristocracy. The Proclamation of 1605 was followed two years later by the "Flight of the Earls"; two Ulster lords, the Earl of Tyrone and the Earl of Tyrconnell, moved to the Continent. These were powerful Gaelic lords. Their departure weakened Gaelic lordship in Ulster, all the more when their lands were confiscated and reorganized.

What would have occurred without the large-scale confiscations that took place in Ireland is difficult to say. At any rate, the new owners acquired land on extremely advantageous terms and with few restrictions.[88] In their relationship with the peasantry, the new owners almost enjoyed a *tabula rasa* and were consequently able to organize their properties with comparative freedom. In most cases, they established landed estates on the current English model.

Even in Ireland, however, lordship persisted into the late seventeenth and even eighteenth centuries. The earls of Ormond enjoyed palatinate jurisdiction until 1715.[89] New tenants on the Ulster plantations had to attend the manorial court, paying a nominal fee ("leet money" or "head silver") to the seneschal of the manor.[90] Tenants might be "bound" to a manor to do suit or suit and service at the manor court; they could also be obliged to use the manorial mill.[91] Manorial obligations were exacted less often outside the long-settled counties, such as Kilkenny, Meath, and Wexford,[92] though eighteenth-century estate records for the O'Callaghan lands in southwestern Tipperary indicate that manorial dues (such as labour days on the landlord's demesne, provision of horses and carts, and Michaelmas goose) were still being demanded.[93] In the late eighteenth century there was a revival of manor courts, and legislation in 1785 strengthened their authority.[94]

Scotland

Like Wales and Ireland, Medieval Scotland became divided into a largely feudalized region, the Lowlands, and a less feudalized region, the Gaelic-speaking Highlands and Western Islands. Along with other Norman institutions, feudalism was introduced into Scotland by David I in the twelfth century. Although it penetrated much less into the Highlands and Western Islands than into the Lowlands,[95] feudalism had a more protracted influence on Scottish society, even in the Highlands and Western Islands, than it did elsewhere in the British Isles. Land law in Scotland became feudalized in the sense that it recognized the coexisting rights of a superior and a vassal rather than direct ownership by an individual or a kinship group. This feudal land law institutionalized a lordship that could be in opposition to Highland Gaelic lordship, which was based on kinship ties. A Gaelic lord was generally known as a "chief." Many feudal superiors were not chiefs, while some chiefs were not feudal superiors. Indeed, some chiefs were almost landless or had only small estates. Many enjoyed powers of chieftainship that went far beyond the power they could enjoy as feudal superiors. The distinctive characteristic of Scottish chieftainship is that chiefs could mobilize men of their surname living as tenants on other men's lands.

When the two kinds of lordship did coincide, the power of the lord could be enormous. Sir Henry Lee (an English knight and landowner in the service of Elizabeth I) once remarked: "In what place in the world will kin, friends and servants adventure more for their lords?"[96] In late Medieval Scotland we find large provincial lordships, in both the Highlands and the Lowlands, which were ruled almost as separate states. Scotland also experienced an especially vigorous phase of bastard feudalism, known in Scotland as bonding. From the mid-fifteenth century until the early seventeenth century, contracts in the vernacular, known as bonds of manrent, were drawn up between lords and followers.[97] What is striking in Scotland is the presence of robust lordship in which there was little direct connection between land and service. Both clanship and bonds of manrent have this characteristic, in contrast with the feudalism with which they coexisted.[98]

As in Ireland and Wales, the story of Scottish lordship is one of its gradual destruction, but this process ebbed and flowed, with the result that it was long and drawn out. It began with a deterioration in the autonomy of some of the provincial lordships in the fifteenth century and eventually the forfeiture in 1493 of the most powerful provincial lordship, the Macdonald Lordship of the Isles. Yet the fall of the Macdonalds benefited the Campbells in the west, the Gordons in the east, and the Mackenzies in the north.[99] Bonds of manrent also emerged after the destruction of the Lordship of the Isles. However, the growth in the role of the church in Reformation Scotland undermined bonding in the sixteenth and seventeenth centuries. The church altered attitudes towards violence and took over the functions of private justice performed by kinship and lordship.[100] After the Union of the Crowns in 1603, the style of royal rule changed and the autonomous powers of lords were less tolerated until they were abolished almost entirely after the defeat of the Jacobites in 1746. Gradually, as elsewhere, lordship had been replaced by state patronage.

Meanwhile, relations between lords and peasants had also been changing. Like their English counterparts, Scottish lords were comparatively free to reorganize their estates. Again one can debate the security of tenure enjoyed by customary tenants, in this case the "kindly" tenants, whose situation was not unlike that of English copyholders.[101] These kindly tenants enjoyed moderate rents, security of tenure, and the right to pass their holdings on to heirs.[102] This protection was, however, eroded in the seventeenth and eighteenth centuries.[103] The commercialization of landlord-tenant relations over the course of the seventeenth and eighteenth centuries also turned tenant-followers into mere tenants. Some Scottish landlords tried to reorganize their estates to increase revenues.[104] At the same time, many chiefs in the Highlands came to face serious financial problems that had a negative effect on their prestige, their power, and their ability to assist followers, as well as forcing them to boost the economic demands they made on their tenants. Scottish lords found themselves in a vicious circle in which commercialization weakened lordship, which in turn made landlord-tenant relations more commercialized. In one of a number of references he made to the inverse relationship between lordship and rents, Samuel Johnson observed in 1773 that "the Chiefs, divested of their prerogatives, necessarily turned their thoughts to the improvement of their revenues, and expect more rent, as they have less homage."[105]

However, the significance of Scottish lordship lies not so much in its decline. It lies in its persistence. Lordship endured longer here than anywhere else in the British Isles. The tenures that were the most unmistakably seigneurial were wardholding and *feu ferme*. It was the responsibility of wardholders to perform various duties, one of which was military service, and to pay wardship and other casualties. In the seventeenth century wardholding was in decline and casualties were usually paid in a fixed sum of money. By the eighteenth century it was common only in the Highlands and Western Islands.[106] *Feu ferme*, however, was not in decline. Tenants holding by *feu ferme* were obliged to pay a perpetual fixed *feu* duty. In the fifteenth and sixteenth centuries large-scale feuing of church lands took place; and over time *feu ferme* was replacing wardholding.[107] Like peasant proprietors on the Continent, wardholders and feuars were *de facto* owners of their holdings, but obliged to pay seigneurial dues to a superior. Manorial "customs" were also persistent in Scotland. Milling rights could be as entrenched as any continental *banalité*. Tenants could even be obliged to repair, thatch, and maintain the lord's mill.[108] Consent of the superior was necessary for marriage and for the alienation of land, though such rights were coming to be regarded as archaic in the eighteenth century.[109]

Until 1747 Highland and Lowland lords enjoyed rights of justice known as "heritable jurisdictions," which preserved independent courts and entrusted sheriffships and other offices to local lords as a hereditary right. In the first half of the eighteenth century there were still more than two hundred heritable jurisdictions.[110] Although higher courts had significantly undermined their powers in the seventeenth and eighteenth centuries, they continued to be in charge of much of the local justice.[111] Finally, another indication of the persistence of lordship was the ability of clan chiefs in the Highlands or Western Islands to call out military forces even in the late eighteenth century. Impressed as he was with the decline of lordship, Johnson also gave some remarkable examples of its survival. Sir Allan Maclean was

the Chieftain of the great clan of Maclean, which is said to claim the second place among the Highland families, yielding only to Macdonald. Though by the misconduct of his ancestors, most of the extensive territory, which would have descended to him, has been alienated, he still retains much of the dignity and authority of his birth. When soldiers were lately wanting for the American war, application was made to Sir Allan, and he nominated a hundred men for the service, who obeyed his summons, and bore arms under his command.[112]

CAUSES AND CONSEQUENCES OF THE DECLINE OF LORDSHIP

Causes

Differences in the persistence of lordship between the British Isles and the continental countries were not as pronounced as most of the comparative literature has indicated. Still, there was a difference. Lordship survived longer on the Continent than in the British Isles. Why?

The most obvious factor is the state. Bush has suggested that, in general, states supported lords in the struggles they might have with peasants, but were often led to undermine lordship in an effort to renovate society and/or to increase state revenues.[113] This generalization would lead us to expect comparatively land-based states to move harder against lordship because they depended more heavily on taxing peasants.

On the Continent this certainly seems to have been the case. The most land-based state was Savoy, and there lordship came under the most determined attack. Victor Amadeus II initiated it by revoking many fiefs and ordering a survey of seigneurial rights. His heir, Charles Emanual III (1730–73), initially abandoned the project, but decrees dated in 1762 required the abolition of *mainmorte* and other seigneurial obligations on royal land and adjusted taxes to encourage the freedom of other serfs. An edict issued in 1771 abolished *mainmorte* on all estates, making peasants direct subjects of the duke. His heir, Victor Amadeus III (1773–96), suspended the execution of this legislation, but allowed it to resume in 1778. It was carried on during the following years, to be completed by the French revolutionary regime in 1792.[114]

France was less land-based than Savoy, and seigneurialism was not subject to the same ruthless measures it faced in Savoy, at least not until the French Revolution. Yet the crown did take measures to undermine seigneurialism. Kings and many of the dukes and counts encouraged the franchises in the twelfth and thirteenth centuries, perhaps in some cases even imposing them on reluctant lords.[115] In the Early Modern period royal agents interfered with the functioning of the seigneurial regime. Dewald found that in the Norman village of Pont-St-Pierre the state helped to make seigneurial authority expensive and vexatious.[116] Hilton Root's research directly supports Bush's thesis. He has shown that in northeastern Burgundy the growth of royal power weakened lordship. It was in the interest of the crown to protect the financial position of peasant communities to enable them to pay royal taxes. Intendants regarded seigneurs as a threat to the financial solvency of peasant communities. They consequently tried to weaken seigneurial rights, to help peasants resist demands made by their lord, and to protect communal lands.[117]

Finally, the Spanish/Austrian Low Countries were less land-based than France and here the central state did the least to undermine lordship. Indeed, the crown often supported seigneurs in their struggles with peasants. As late as 1759, for instance, legislation was enacted to make it more difficult for peasants to evade seigneurial dues levied on the sale of a property by pretending that the property was being rented.[118] The Habsburgs certainly encroached on seigneurial justice, but primarily in an effort to improve the administration of justice and to increase the uniformity of law, not in an effort to undermine lordship.[119]

Another variable could also, however, be accounting for this correlation. As Bush fully recognizes, the likelihood that the state would move against lordship was also determined by the power of the state to do so. The dukes of Savoy may have had greater reason to go after seigneurial rights because they depended so heavily on the peasantry for revenue, but they also had more power to do so. By contrast, in the Spanish/Austrian Low Countries, the central state tolerated lordship at least partly because it could not afford to alienate provincial elites and there were no intendants to undermine the local power of the aristocracy as there were in Savoy and France. The Habsburgs did not seriously attempt to dismantle seigneurialism until 1787, when Joseph II tried to abolish seigneurial justice as part of his reform package; however, when it provoked revolution, it had to be withdrawn.

During the eleventh to fourteenth centuries the French crown had little choice but to tolerate autonomous lordship. Whatever its contribution to the enfranchisement movement in the twelfth and thirteenth centuries, it certainly did not succeed in confiscating seigneurial authority over the peasantry. The fiscal burdens of the state were largely added to those of lordship.[120] The expansion of the French state in the fifteenth and early sixteenth centuries did not change this situation. On the contrary, in order to win the loyalty of elites who were brought into the French state through annexations, the crown usually recognized existing seigneurial rights. Leaving lordship alone was one of the ways in which the French crown persuaded lords to accept the growth in royal authority and, in particular, to accept the taxation of their peasants. Once this orientation towards lordship became established, it was difficult to dislodge, even as circumstances changed. Royal toleration for lordship declined only gradually. In the seventeenth and eighteenth centuries, Canada was colonized by establishing seigneuries. If the French crown did take action that threatened seigneurial rights, the *parlements* often used their very considerable powers to defend them. Although *parlementaires* were nobles of the robe, most owned seigneuries; and the French *parlements* were in principle opposed to the undermining of traditional privilege by royal power.

The preceding discussion compares continental countries with one another. If the comparison is broadened to include the British Isles, at least one of the conclusions we have drawn is called into question. The British Isles were less land-based than the continental countries, at least France and Savoy, but lordship declined earlier. The effect of state power could also be questioned, at least if one believes that the British state was less powerful than the French state. This would, however, be a mistake. It is clear that the power of the English crown in the twelfth and thirteenth centuries was a critical factor in the decline of lordship in the British Isles. For reasons already given, the English crown was able to establish a relatively centralized feudal structure in the post-conquest period. The close relationship that was thus created between the monarchy and the magnates had an enduring effect. The crown would not tolerate much seigneurial autonomy in England. The English crown also had no hesitation in undermining the judicial powers of local lords through royal justice. It was not just that the king was running courts that were not under the control of local lords; it was also that in doing so he was promoting Common Law, a distinguishable body of law to which all freemen were subject. Appealing to royal courts became one of the ways in which English villeins gained freedom, though it was a slow process that was often unsuccessful.

If we now ask ourselves why lordship declined in the British peripheral regions, the simple answer is that, as the power of the English monarchy extended over the peripheries, it established with lords in these regions the same kind of relationship it had with lords in England. Yet this did not happen smoothly and steadily; it was not always apparent that this was the goal of the English rulers; and the peripheries varied in the time it took for this change to occur.

The earliest region outside England was native Wales, undoubtedly because the conquest of Wales by Edward I was so thorough. Ironically, the Marcher lordships could not be abolished because they were held by Anglo-Normans, not native Welshmen, with the result that autonomous lordships persisted there until the jurisdiction of the English state was enlarged to include the March in the sixteenth century. Pre-conquest Wales illustrates the alternative ways in which the limitations of royal power helped to preserve lordship: in native Wales, hostile lords over whom the king had limited influence exercised power; in the March, the king permitted autonomous lordship to be enjoyed by those he believed would deal with the hostile lords and keep order in the king's name.

The situation in Ireland remained for long similar to that of pre-conquest Wales. Total conquest of the island was nearly impossible and the crown was forced to allow considerable autonomy to Anglo-Norman lords who could handle Gaelic lords. Only when royal power reached throughout Ireland in the seventeenth century could the English crown begin to treat Irish lords in a way that was more to its liking. Even in the late sixteenth century the government depended on Irish lords, including Gaelic lords, to control other lords.[121] It was the peace of the early seventeenth century that strengthened the power of the crown sufficiently that it was no longer dependent on Irish lords to enforce the royal will and was able to reorganize local government in a way that undermined lordship. There was at the same time some willingness in Gaelic Ireland to accept English land tenure, but the main reason for this willingness was a fear felt by Gaelic landholders that they would lose their land if it were not recognized according to English law, which was all too clearly replacing Irish law as the English state expanded its power.

Finally, Scotland demonstrates better than any other part of the British Isles the critical role of state power. Given the way in which the Scottish crown ruled, it is not surprising to find that lordship remained robust in Scotland in the period before the Union of the Crowns. After the Union of the Crowns the monarchy did become more powerful, but it was still less powerful in Scotland than anywhere else in the British Isles, with the result that lordship persisted longer here than elsewhere. When lordship was destroyed, it was destroyed by the state. Both heritable jurisdictions and wardships were done away with in the "reforms" imposed by the government after the Rebellion of 1745. It is true that wardships were already in decline, but the demise of heritable jurisdictions was certainly the work of the state.

The major cause of the decline of serfdom in the Middle Ages was the struggle fought over centuries by peasants to rid themselves of the stigma of servitude by rising in revolt, evading servile obligations, fleeing to towns or newly settled land, challenging their lord in court, or buying their freedom or substituting payments for servile obligations. Although these forces help us to understand why serfdom declined in France and the Low Countries before it did in England, they do not explain why, in the end, lordship declined earlier in the British Isles than in these continental countries. It certainly cannot be argued that lordship declined earlier in the British Isles because the British peasantry was more powerful.

What explains more are differences in the interests of various parties, and, in particular, differences in the interests of lords. In addition to the way in which the state undermined lordship, we need to recognize how the state shaped the structure of lordship, which in turn affected its durability. In France, Savoy, and the Southern Low Countries the structure of lordship was declivitous during the eleventh, twelfth, and thirteenth centuries; in other words, seigneurial rights and obligations were greater at lower levels of the hierarchy. This meant that everyone in the chain, except the lowest serf, had more to lose and less to gain from the abolition of lordship, since everyone, again excluding the lowest serf, was owed more than he or she owed. All efforts made by those above the lowest serf to maximize their interests served to reinforce lordship. When vassals revolted against their obligations to the king or prince, they did not seek to cripple the whole system; on the contrary, they sought to exercise all the more lordship over their subordinates.

As a result of the power of the crown, lordship was less declivitous in England. Most notably, the rights of the king over his vassals were more burdensome than the rights of the French king over his vassals. Consequently, the English vassals had more interest in the decline of feudal dues than did vassals of the French crown. The exception that proves the rule was the lordship of the Welsh March. The dues owed to the king by Marcher lords were comparatively limited, and thus Marcher lords had no interest in undermining lordship. In England, by contrast, vassals were willing to relinquish their rights of lordship over peasants, or at least they were willing to do so if they could evade their own obligations and if they could extract a return from the peasants by other means.[122] Pressure was often put on the English king by his vassals to give up the financial benefits of feudal incidents. It is this kind of pressure that explains the *volte face* of Henry VIII when he enacted the Statute of Wills of 1540; the Statute of Uses had benefited the king much more than his vassals, with the result that they fiercely opposed this effort to strengthen the feudal revenues of lords.[123]

Another closely related variable was the manner in which aristocrats enjoyed power in the local community. In France aristocrats depended on seigneurialism to maintain political power. I shall discuss the political power of the aristocracy in more detail in a later chapter, but at this stage it can simply be recorded that, in contrast with the English crown, the French crown did not use members of the local landowning elite as agents for local administration. Insofar as landowners sought to exert power in their community, they relied primarily on the maintenance of their seigneurial authority, which survived the decline of serfdom. English lords maintained their political power in the local community in a different way, not as lords but as justices of the peace, sheriffs, and lords lieutenant. Thus English landowners did not have as much reason to protect lordship in order to hold on to their political power in the local community.

Similarly, much of the literature leads to the conclusion that their economic power did not depend on lordship. In the Early Modern period lords in the British Isles were able to exploit their land more successfully by converting from manorial to leasehold tenures. Customary tenures provided some security to peasants in the British Isles, but the persistent efforts of landlords to undermine customary tenure was in the end largely successful. By doing so lords in the British Isles were able to obtain higher returns from their land. They might at the same time lose many of the manorial rights they enjoyed, but could allow this to happen because, on balance, leaseholds were more profitable.

Seigneurs in France, Savoy, and the Southern Low Countries did not as often undertake such a tradeoff because they were not as often in a position to force peasants to accept leaseholds. Thus, rather than relinquish seigneurial rights and convert to leaseholds, lords in France and the Southern Low Countries made a greater effort to maintain seigneurial rights. The evolution of peasant proprietorship in France, Savoy, and the Southern Low Countries helped to preserve lordship because lords depended on seigneurial dues as a source of revenue. Seigneurial dues provided a means to extract revenue from peasant proprietors.

As an explanation for the decline of lordship, this kind of argument tends to equate customary tenure with lordship, and leaseholds with the demise of lordship. It is certainly true that seigneurial dues became institutionalized as part of the customary normative structure and, to some extent, shared its fate. Yet the essence of lordship is contract. Thus there is nothing inherently antithetical between lordship and leaseholds.

Particularly instructive is the case of Scotland. If land tenure and rents were more seigneurial in eighteenth-century Scotland than elsewhere in the British Isles, they were not more customary. Not only did kindly tenure decline in the seventeenth and eighteenth centuries, but even in the sixteenth century rights of kindness were generally enjoyed only with a landowner's cooperation.[124] When church lands were feued out, a good number of kindly tenants had the means to purchase their holdings, but many others lost their customary rights as new owners took over the properties; for this and other reasons, "kindness" was less often recognized in the seventeenth and eighteenth centuries.[125] The terms on which land was held were primarily contractual, often in the form of leases or "tacks." These leases were usually short, generally one to six years, and the rights to the land enjoyed by tenants were weak. Many tenants had no leases at all.[126] The point I am making is that seigneurial dues persisted despite this shift from customary to contractual tenure. Indeed in Scotland and elsewhere in the British Isles manorial obligations were often written into leases.[127] Contractual tenure did not necessarily undermine lordship. What it did, for reasons given above, is make lordship unnecessary. One kind of contract could be replaced by another.

Finally, the most hotly debated cause of the decline of lordship is commercialization.[128] While many argue that its effects have been exaggerated, few would insist that it played no role at all. First, it increased the interest of lords in procuring money; this made them more agreeable to the sale of charters and the commutation of dues. Second, it increased the wealth or financial liquidity of peasants, thus enabling them to purchase charters or commute servile obligations. Indeed, the high price of most charters in the twelfth and thirteenth centuries made commercialization, if not a sufficient condition, certainly a necessary condition for enfranchisement. Commutation in itself undermined lordship, but in addition the conversion of seigneurial dues into money payments could, if payments were fixed, cause them to decline over time as a result of inflation. Third, commercialization increased the size and attraction of towns and in other ways promoted peasant geographical mobility. Fourth, in making some (though not most) peasants wealthier, commercialization not only enabled them to buy their way out of obligations, but also raised their aspirations and expectations. Undoubtedly one of the major causes of the decline of serfdom was the inconsistency between the wealth of some peasants and their legal status. Those who organized communities to buy their freedom or challenge their lord were usually wealthier peasants. Fifth, with commercialization, the character of lordship changed. It came to be based less on political power and status, and instead was based, at least more so, on economic relations. Commercialization monetized the landlord-tenant relationship. The seigneur was more likely to regard tenants as a source of revenue. This both damaged the relationship and induced the lord to give up seigneurial rights, such as justice, if they were no longer worthwhile in economic terms. Commercialization undercut lordship by turning land into a commodity that was bought and sold. And finally, though commercialization could increase the value of seigneurial monopolies, it could also undermine them by providing economic alternatives.

The enfranchisement of communities in the twelfth and thirteenth centuries appeared earliest in more commercialized regions of Europe – northern Italy and other parts of Lotharingia, the Paris Basin, and French wine districts.[129] Similarly, in the Early Modern period, though the correlation was far from perfect, seigneurialism in France was weaker in more commercialized agricultural regions, most notably in the Paris Basin. Most historians attribute the fact that seigneurial burdens were lighter in the Southern Low Countries than in most of France to the greater commercialization of the economy. Certainly one finds numerous cases in these provinces of the commutation or purchase of seigneurial dues.[130] The pattern actually varied within the Southern Low Countries. In some areas, particularly in the Duchy of Luxembourg, commercialization was more limited and thus had little effect on seigneurialism. It was primarily in Brabant, Flanders, and Liège that commercialization subverted lordship.

Savoy provides us with the opposite case. Here the poverty and absence of commercialization frustrated the efforts of the dukes of Savoy to abolish lordship. An edict of 1561 permitted peasants to free themselves from *mainmorte* on the payment of a proportional sum, but few were able to take advantage of it.[131] Even when the dukes succeeded in abolishing lordship in the eighteenth century, the poverty of the peasant communities and the lack of liquidity in many regions created difficulty.[132] "The well-to-do of the parishes are not generally over-burdened with funds to lend to peasants," wrote the intendant of Genevois in 1773 about communities under his jurisdiction. "There is no great number of persons who are in a state to offer advances, since there is in this region an appalling shortage of cash, all the more because, for the past few years, it had to leave the region in order to provide for the subsistence that was lacking."[133]

Yet once more we have to be careful. Commercialization does not always weaken lordship. The geographical correlation in the twelfth and thirteenth centuries between the enfranchisements and commercialization is not perfect and is subject to differing interpretations.[134] In the Early Modern period commercialization in Eastern Europe did not undermine serfdom. Even in Western Europe landowners could modernize within the old framework. In some relatively commercialized regions in France, such as Berry, seigneurialism had a strong hold in the eighteenth century. Conversely, lordship can be found decaying in regions that were not exceptionally commercialized. The case of

Wales is instructive. Wales was not as commercialized as many parts of France and the Southern Low Countries, where lordship persisted longer. Given the limitations of comparative analysis, one will never know for certain why this was the case, but it was possibly the expectations established by the centre that were critical. Commercialization in Wales itself may not have been responsible for undermining lordship; indeed, commercialization led a large number of Welsh lords to use their seigneurial rights to increase their profits.[135] What was perhaps more important was the commercialization in the region of the political centre, which was southern England. The major provinces in the Southern Low Countries (Flanders, Brabant, and Liège) were highly commercialized, but their centres (Spain and Austria) were less so. Neither Wales nor the Southern Low Countries can be treated as an independent case. They were both influenced by their centres. On the Continent the predominant values and norms in the society respected the traditional rights of lords. In spite of commercialization, agrarian society in the Southern Low Countries continued to be organized on a seigneurial basis. Things changed in our continental countries only when the centres took the lead in abolishing lordship – the reforms of Joseph II in the Austrian Low Countries, the reforms of the House of Savoy in Piedmont-Savoy, and the abolition of lordship by the French revolutionary government in 1792.

In contrast, the centre that influenced Wales had seen lordship decline relatively early as a result of three of our variables (the role of the state, tenurial arrangements, and commercialization). Thus landowners and even many tenants in Wales came to believe that English tenure was superior and so gradually conformed to it. In Ireland the landowners who reorganized agrarian society on the English model actually migrated to Ireland with English ideas, which they were comparatively free to introduce after the revolutionary upheavals of the seventeenth century.

Consequences

The transformation and gradual disappearance of lordship has had a dramatic impact on human social relationships. Some of the above causes of its decline were also consequences. The rise of the state contributed to the decay of lordship, but the decay of lordship also facilitated the rise of the state. Commercialization undermined lordship, but the decline of lordship created the greater freedom that was necessary for commercialization. The decline of lordship has also made possible higher rates of social, occupational, and geographical mobility. It has significantly affected modes of domination; lordship has been replaced by alternative modes, primarily capitalist and bureaucratic. And the disappearance of lordship has reduced the personalism and particularism of social relationships. Here I am referring not to a decrease in affect; relations of lordship were not usually based on emotional ties. Yet they were personal and particularistic in the sense that the relations linked individuals, could vary depending on the individuals involved, and were in some sense regarded as singular, even if general norms often governed the expectations of the relationship. The death or defeat of one's lord, or some disagreement with him, could alter one's life completely. Finally, since lordship fused power, its decline made possible a greater differentiation of power. In addition, lordship itself became more differentiated; that is to say, it did not fuse status and political and economic power as much as it had in the Middle Ages, instead becoming primarily a form of economic power. Thus, if all one knew was what happened to lordship, one would expect that aristocratic power became more differentiated in the Early Modern period. One would also expect that the differentiation of aristocratic power was most advanced in those countries where lordship had declined or was transformed the most, that is, in the British Isles. The following chapters will demonstrate that, as a result of other changes taking place, such expectations correspond only partly to what actually occurred.

5 Status Power

France, Savoy, and the Southern Low Countries

HISTORICAL EVOLUTION OF THE MEDIEVAL NOBILITY

The status of "noble" is even more difficult to define than that of "lord." Indeed, it can really be understood only by examining the individuals and groups to whom it was applied. It is not very useful to seek to establish the origins of the nobility in a particular period. What we instead have to do is to determine what the values and norms were that were associated with the status and what the rules were for determining who was and who was not a noble in any given period.

The best-known statement on the Medieval unfolding of the continental nobility was published by Marc Bloch in 1940.[1] Influenced considerably by Paul Guilhiermoz, Bloch proposed that before the middle of the twelfth century the nobility existed only as a vaguely defined status group; the criteria for membership were then not always clear; and the acquisition of the status was not nearly as difficult as it would become later. The transformation of this "de facto class," as he called it, into a "legal class" occurred between about 1130 and 1250 and was primarily a result of two developments: knighthood was increasingly the primary criterion for membership in the nobility; and knighthood became a hereditary right. In this way a new nobility was created in the twelfth and thirteenth centuries.

This thesis has been challenged by a large number of scholars. It is not without significance that many of these challenges have been based on regional studies. The strongest criticism of the Bloch thesis came from historians studying the Southern Low Countries.[2] Two points of disagreement stand out.

First, the Belgian historians argued that there was a nobility before the twelfth century. It was more clearly defined than Bloch allowed; it was based on birth; and the same families predominated over time. The Belgian historians emphasized the continuity between the Carolingian nobility and the nobility of the twelfth century, rather than a new nobility emerging in the twelfth and thirteenth centuries. Second, these historians have insisted that nobility was not identical to knighthood. Admittedly, there was a rise in the status of knight as the title was adopted by nobles. Eventually, young men in noble families were expected to become knights. Yet the fusion of knighthood and nobility took place at different times in different regions. In some regions it did not occur at all. The notion that knights were nobles did not develop in Brabant until the Burgundian period.[3] The evolution of noble status in France may have conformed more closely to Bloch's model than it did in the Southern Low Countries, but the Belgian thesis has been accepted, in whole or in part, by many French historians as well.[4]

A modified version of the Bloch thesis was proposed by Georges Duby. While he acknowledged considerable continuity between the Carolingian nobility and that of the twelfth century, he insisted on an early fusion of nobility and knighthood, at least for a region near the Cluny Abby in the Mâconnais. He believed that the eleventh and early twelfth centuries saw a significant transformation. In this period the nobility came to be united by chivalry, and nobles adopted the title of knight; families began to trace their kinship ties more genealogically than horizontally; male descent was strengthened; and the *ban* was appropriated by castellans. Together these forces led to the development of a "genuine" nobility – relatively closed, privileged, homogeneous, and based on ancestry in the male line.[5] Critics have responded that the early fusion of nobility and knighthood was not typical, that gradual evolution and continuity characterized the Medieval nobility, and that a nobility with privileges predated the appropriation of the *ban*.

Despite the weight of evidence that supports the Belgian position, the Bloch-Duby thesis provides some valuable insights. Its emphasis on change as opposed to continuity is helpful. In particular, the idea that the concept of nobility could be imprecise, and more so in some periods than in others, is well founded. This is the point that is crucial for my argument. It is likely that there was no nobility in the sense of a legally defined, hereditary group before 1000.[6] Even later, the way in which the word *nobilis* was used differed from one region to another, and even from one document to another. The term does not appear very often. Other words were frequently employed to refer to members of the elite, such as *domini, potentes, magnates, optimates,* and *principes.*[7] Robert Fossier found that neither *nobilis* nor these alternatives were used often.[8] Usage was imprecise and an exact juridical definition difficult to achieve.[9] Jane Martindale believed that there was a nobility in the early Middle Ages, but not in the sense in which the word was used in the Early Modern period. The Modern concept of nobility has been imposed on the Middle Ages. Then it was a vague quality.[10] Even when it became a juridical status, it was impossible to enforce as a result of the fragmentation of political power. In the fourteenth and fifteenth centuries noble status still depended primarily on public acceptance and life style.[11] While noble status was often associated with the power of the sovereign, the state did not play an active role even in the late Middle Ages in restricting noble status to those who were legally entitled to it. Nor was the state able to do much to control the assumption of noble privilege.

Although a person was usually accepted as a noble if his or her ancestors were noble (more so after the eleventh century, according to Duby), noble status was not based exclusively on birth. In an influential article presented in 1961 and published in 1962, Edouard Perroy described how the nobility was penetrated by new members in Forez during the late Middle Ages. New nobles emerged almost imperceptibly from the peasant population by accumulating wealth and military obligations that rendered them indistinguishable from the lesser nobility. Eventually they would come to be regarded as nobles.[12] The fact that membership in the nobility was determined by customary law made ennoblement by prescription easier.[13] It needs to be stressed that in order for ennoblement by prescription to occur it was necessary for the would-be noble to adopt a noble life style, to be accepted by the nobility, and to acquire a fief and/or engage in military service – processes that Paul Janssens has called "social assimilation."[14] This was the most frequently travelled route into the nobility during the late Middle Ages.[15]

THE STATE INSTITUTIONALIZATION OF ARISTOCRATIC STATUS

Everyday people at all levels of society made decisions about who was and who was not a noble. Least institutionalized were the decisions made in casual interaction, or avoidance of interaction, that occurred in the street or at the market. Rather more subject to norms were the decisions made about who was to be invited to a social event or a private or public gathering. Still more institutionalized was the order of precedence on such occasions. We could also trace the evolution of decisions on noble status made at tournaments and by chapters, religious and military orders, and colleges that were reserved for the nobility. Finally, the state often made decisions about who was and who was not a noble.

During the late Middle Ages and the Early Modern period state institutionalization of aristocratic status came to assume greater weight. Sociologists and historians have paid considerable attention to the relationship between the aristocracy and the state, but have generally ignored one of the most significant aspects of that relationship: the role of the state in the institutionalization of aristocratic status. By the eighteenth century a whole new connection had developed between the state and the nobility. This was true in a great number of respects. I shall focus principally on privilege, ways of becoming noble, and proof of noble status.

Privilege

One can draw a distinction between seigneurial privilege and noble privilege. Not all nobles possessed seigneuries, and not all seigneurs were nobles. Moreover, it is not possible to explain both in the same way. The persistence of seigneurialism has been treated in chapter 4. Now it is necessary to offer some explanation of noble privilege, at least to make an effort to understand why it endured in the Early Modern period.

Even before the late Middle Ages, nobles on the Continent enjoyed a number of privileges by customary law. These could include exemption from taxes and seigneurial dues, the right to be tried by equals, the right to refuse a challenge by a non-noble, precedence in public functions, and the right to fight on horseback. A major development during the late Middle Ages was the addition of new privileges granted or legitimated by the state. These included special political representation, judicial privileges, and further tax exemptions.

These privileges were largely a consequence of the need of the crown to maintain the cooperation of powerful interests in society. The significance of the fact that the French crown raised revenue by negotiating with numerous groups in the society now becomes apparent. In doing so it often accepted their privileges or claims to privilege. It might even accord them new privileges. All this was done usually in return for the payment of a tax or subsidy (often for a specific purpose, such as a military campaign) or for an understanding not to interfere with the levying of a tax. French kings would have preferred to negotiate with the Estates General, but never found this satisfactory. Even when the consent of the Estates General or a general council was obtained, it was often not enough; powerful groups in the country had to be persuaded to cooperate.[16]

This explanation for tax exemptions is supported by the fact that nobles were not the only ones who came to have privileges. The urban bourgeoisie often did as well, particularly in Flanders and Brabant, but even in much less urbanized regions, such as Savoy.[17] Yet in relatively land-based states it was the nobility whose cooperation was vital. A Medieval sovereign in a relatively land-based state had to rely heavily for revenue on taxing the peasantry and could not tax them unless nobles agreed to allow the money to be collected from those whom they regarded as their subjects.[18]

In the fourteenth century French kings were gradually acquiring the power to tax without consent. They continued, however, to need the political support of different groups, especially the nobility. Continental monarchs had difficulty coping with private violence. Keeping it under control meant keeping nobles conciliated, including petty nobles.

Continental rulers did not have equal difficulty managing nobles. Not surprisingly the nobility enjoyed fewer tax privileges where they had historically enjoyed less political power, such as in Flanders.[19] Nobles usually acquired privileges when the crown was in a difficult situation, particularly when it was in need of money or assistance for war. This was notably the case during the reign of the French king, Philip the Fair (1285–1314). The exemptions of the nobility did not rise in a straight line over the course of the late Middle Ages; they oscillated according to the political circumstances in which the parties found themselves. Significant tax concessions to the nobility came during the chaos of the reign of Charles VI (1380–1422) and during the reign of Charles VII (1422–61), whose situation made it impossible for him to alienate the lesser nobility by taxing them.[20] Eventually, continental monarchs reached a situation in which they did not have to play to groups in the population for their support, but by then noble privilege had become so entrenched that it was difficult to abolish. The result was that major noble privileges, most significantly exemption from the *taille*, were legitimated by the crown.

There was another reason for the persistence of aristocratic privilege on the Continent. In the chapters that follow we shall repeatedly return to the subject of the value placed on military activity by the aristocracy and the military role played by aristocrats in our different countries. Here the main conclusions can be summarized, leaving the details of the argument for later. First, the militarism and military role of the Western European aristocracy declined in the Early Modern period, but by no means disappeared. Second, the military role of the French and Savoyard nobility was most likely greater than that of the British aristocracy, but the difference was smaller than historians have generally assumed. Although more research needs to be done on the subject, the data we have suggest that British aristocrats were over-represented in the army. Finally, though again we should not overstate the difference, the military ethos of the continental nobility was greater than that of the British aristocracy. The continental nobility manifestly prided itself on its military role, which was used to justify privilege. Tax exemption, in particular, was justified on the grounds that it compensated noble families for their assistance to the prince in war.

Nevertheless, during the seventeenth and eighteenth centuries continental monarchs became interested in reducing the cost of aristocratic privilege to the state. They also wanted to rationalize it, to standardize it across regions, to make tax exemption seem less arbitrary, and to eliminate fraud. Many of the king's servants thought that the unfairness of taxation largely accounted for opposition to it. They sought to limit noble exemption from the *taille*. They also invented new taxes that the nobility had to pay, such as the *capitation*, the *dixième*, and the *vingtième*. These taxes did not in fact capture much noble wealth. All the same, historians no longer assume that the French nobility was undertaxed relative to other European elites.[21] And the willingness of the French crown to interfere with noble privilege was clear enough.

The erosion of noble privilege was relatively advanced in the Southern Low Countries. By the seventeenth century there were only a few tax exemptions for nobles in Flanders and Brabant.[22] Only in Hainaut, Luxembourg, and Limbourg were nobles exempt from excise duties.[23] In Hainaut only seigneurs of high justice and nobles belonging to very old families enjoyed real tax exemption.[24] In Namur nobles were exempt from taxes on their home and business, and were also exempt from military and excise taxation; but in 1769 these exemptions were pruned.[25] One of the last to go was the privileged position of the nobility of Luxembourg, which was abolished in 1771.[26]

During the sixteenth century Emanuel Filibert tried to standardize taxation in Piedmont-Savoy, but not with much success. The duke who followed him, Charles Emanuel 1, legislated an edict in 1584 for the reform of the *taille*. Exemptions were limited to *biens anciens* of the church and (in the words of the edict) "the property of gentlemen who were vassals and descended from an *ancienne race* and others of *qualité noble,*" recognized as such before the introduction of the tax. Those who were ennobled later had to wait fifty years for exemption.[27] Charles Emanuel also sought to establish a new cadastre in 1601. As a result of intense opposition, these reforms largely failed.[28] Further reform did not come until the reign of Victor Amadeus II. He required new nobles and the bourgeoisie to pay the *quartiers ordinaires* of the land tax for the first fifty years after their ennoblement, but not the *quartiers extraordinaires.*[29] In 1731 his successor, Charles Emanuel III, proclaimed that exemptions would be allowed only for feudal properties of members of the nobility and *ancien patrimonie* of the church. Only a small number of owners were able to show the required documentation and, consequently, merely 12 per cent of the land in the possession of nobles was deemed to be feudal.[30]

It must be understood, however, that continental monarchs were not trying to eliminate noble privilege altogether. To repeat, the primary objective was to reduce the cost to the state of noble privilege and to make it seem less arbitrary. Many privileges were supported by the crown, especially symbolic privileges, which did not cost it anything. The French crown made its greatest effort ever to increase the heraldic privileges of nobles in legislation enacted in 1760, late in the Old Regime.[31] While the Habsburgs were unhappy with tax privilege, they were not in general opposed to political privilege.[32] Moreover, the assault on tax privilege in the Low Countries was led by the third estate, not by the crown.[33] Even in Savoy noble privilege was not abolished; rather, it was limited and standardized.

The conflict between the nobility and the state over privilege during the eighteenth century did not represent a new development foreshadowing the abolition of privilege. Privilege had been a source of contention in the Middle Ages as it was in the eighteenth century. What was different now was that the state, and particularly the crown, had become more interventionist.

Ennoblement

Gradually the state was also coming to play a larger role in the admission of new members into the nobility. There were two processes: first, a decline in community appointment of nobles, which was replaced by royal appointment; and, second, an increasing monopolization by a ruler, at the expense of other rulers, of the right to create nobles within a given territory. The progression was not linear, but halting and haphazard, buffeted by struggles among princes. Nonetheless, the authority to issue letters of nobility became, like minting gold coins, a measure of sovereignty.[34] Ennoblement of commoners in the Low Countries increased during the Burgundian era. The Burgundian dukes created nobles without consulting the French monarchy in order to advance their claim that the House of Burgundy was a sovereign dynasty. Ennoblements were also linked to the political centralization undertaken by the Burgundians. To gain the allegiance of the diverse population of the territories they had brought together, to reward those who had assisted them, to limit the number of persons enjoying tax exemption, and to strengthen their sovereignty, the Burgundian dukes were anxious not only to establish their prerogative to bestow noble status, but also to prevent other rulers from doing so for persons residing in their lands. In 1448 Duke Philip the Good went so far as to demand redress from the French king, Charles VII, because the latter had "illegally" granted ennoblement to some of his (the duke's) subjects.[35]

When France, after the death of Charles the Bold, recovered the Duchy of Burgundy and the County of Artois, Louis XI declared that ennoblements were among the treasonous acts of the late duke.[36] Subsequently, he permitted these ennoblements to stand for the citizens of Arras, though he did not accept the duke's right to have granted them. By the Treaty of Arras of 1482, Louis XI recognized ennoblements granted by Maximilian and Mary to certain inhabitants of Artois on condition that these persons took out letters of confirmation, which the French king was willing to issue at no cost.[37] Louis XII went further, confirming by legislation the royal monopoly on ennoblement.[38]

In Savoy, edicts issued by Emanuel Filibert and legal suits against usurpation increased the control of the dukes over ennoblement in the sixteenth century. Ennoblements came to be granted routinely by letters patent in return for financial payments or in reward for services to the duke. Between 1561 and 1600 a remarkable 110 ennoblements were granted, between 1601 and 1640, no fewer than 126.[39]

In the Spanish/Austrian Low Countries letters of ennoblement were limited to a few regions during most of the sixteenth century.[40] Philip II established a state monopoly on access to the nobility in the last decade of the century. Subsequent Habsburg rulers routinely elevated persons to the nobility and improved the administrative procedures for ennoblements, which were increasingly placed under greater central control by the sovereign and the Supreme Council of the Netherlands in Madrid, and then later in Vienna.[41] The royal monopoly over ennoblement was consolidated in the years 1641 to 1658.[42] Specialized institutions emerged for the regulation of aristocratic status. The Heraldic Chamber advised the Privy Council on questions of noble status, regulated coat of arms, and performed numerous functions with respect to ennoblements: receipt of applications, validation of facts contained in applications, transmission of applications to Madrid or Vienna, and registration of ennoblements.[43] The Austrian Habsburgs, as Holy Roman emperors, also enjoyed the authority to ennoble and grant titles in the Principality of Liège. Indeed, this particular authority was one of a limited number of prerogatives that the emperor could exercise over the principality without consulting the prince-bishop.

We have some data on ennoblements in France from the fourteenth century, at least those registered with the Parisian Chamber of Accounts. It would seem that no ennoblements were registered from 1345 to 1349. In the last half of the fourteenth century an average of 15.4 ennoblements were registered per year. The rate subsequently fell. The figure for the fifteenth century was 6.9 per year, for the sixteenth century, 7.6, for the first half of the seventeenth century, 9.5, and for the eighteenth century, 11.3.[44] Thus, after an early burst of enthusiasm, there was a fall in the number and then a pattern of gradually rising ennoblements. The rate of increase may, however, have been little different from the rate of expansion of the total French population. This does not negate the significance of the growth, but it does mean that eighteenth-century French kings were no more generous than earlier ones relative to the number of aspirants.

Many people today assume that letters of nobility could be easily purchased in France during the Old Regime. This was true in only certain years. Although Louis XIV had once expressed disapproval of the sale of honours, lamenting the "infinite number of usurpers, without any title, or with title acquired for money without any service,"[45] in the years 1694 to 1715 he himself blatantly sold letters of nobility at the relatively low price of 6000 livres. Additional costs made the real price higher, perhaps reaching 10,000 livres. It was still a bargain, and a large number of commoners took advantage of it. Some 700 letters were issued and sold in the period.[46] Financial problems resulting from the War of the League of Augsburg initially provoked this sale of honours. It is interesting to see the king trying to justify the sales in terms of the right of a sovereign to create nobles in reward for service to the country. In the preamble to the Edict of March 1696 we find Louis proclaiming:

Unless noble origins and antiquity of family, which confer so much distinction among men, are merely the gift of blind fate, the title which is the source of nobility is a gift from the Prince, who knows how to reward appropriately the important services which subjects render to their homeland. These services, so deserving of the gratitude of sovereigns, are not always rendered arms in hand. Zeal is shown in more ways than one; and there are occasions when, by devoting one's possessions to the upkeep of the troops defending the state, one becomes worthy, to some degree, of the same reward as is given to those who shed their blood to defend it.[47]

The year 1715 marked the end of the major phase of venal elevations to the nobility in France. For the rest of the eighteenth century, royal letters of ennoblement were accorded primarily on the basis of merit. Although fees were charged, ennoblement was not a fiscal device in the way it had been during the period 1694 to 1715.

A study of ennoblements in Provence during the eighteenth century has found frequent reference in the letters to services to the state. Qualities such as virtue, zeal, and loyalty were also mentioned, but no references appeared to "race" and only a few references to "distinction." Some 27 per cent of the ennoblements went to persons active in municipal politics; this participation was usually noted as one of the reasons for ennoblement. In general, the letters reflected the values of the monarchy rather than those of the local nobility.[48] Chaussinand-Nogaret has suggested that in the country as a whole there was a radical change after 1760, with a greater emphasis on merit and bourgeois values of achievement.[49]

The state came to play a rather different role with respect to ennoblement by office. This path to nobility evolved with the need of the crown to reward and inspire loyalty among those holding state appointments, and, equally important, to strengthen the authority of servants of the state by raising their status relative to that of the people over whom the sovereign ruled. Yet by the seventeenth and eighteenth centuries most ennobling offices in France were venal. Thus ennoblement by office, even more than letters of ennoblement, contributed to the coffers of the state.

Before the sixteenth century, ennoblement by office in France was arbitrary and precarious.[50] Special privileges were enjoyed by the Medieval *commensaux*, who were officers of the court, the Maison du roi, and the Maison royale. The *noblesse de cloche* or *noblesse municipale* can be traced to the fourteenth century. The municipal offices of a number of towns were made ennobling in reward for their loyalty during the Hundred Years' War. The practice continued in later years. Offices were made ennobling in Cognac and Issoudun, for example, as a reward for the loyalty of these towns during the Frondes. Magistrates of certain courts, most notably the *parlements*, were accorded noble status. This kind of ennoblement was not, however, officially recognized until the sixteenth century and was based on customary law until the seventeenth, when it was rendered more institutionalized by a flood of jurisprudence and a number of royal edicts. When venal offices became hereditary in the early seventeenth century, the ennoblement of lineages through office was fully institutionalized. Few military offices were ennobling until 1750, when a royal edict made the higher ranks of the army ennobling.[51] Thus in the eighteenth century the crown institutionalized what had been the classic route to the nobility during the Middle Ages.

It is extremely difficult to estimate the number of ennoblements by office in a given period, for several reasons: in most cases ennoblement by office was not immediate, usually coming into effect only after a certain period of time or in a second generation; one person might hold more than one office; and ennobling offices were often filled by persons who were already noble. Jean Meyer estimated that ennobling offices created some 2000 new nobles in the eighteenth century, but Chaussinand-Nogaret subsequently argued for a figure of 5500.[52] Even if Chaussinand-Nogaret was overestimating, ennoblements by office clearly outnumbered those by letter. This was not the case everywhere. In Lorraine, for example, there were more ennoblements by letter than by office.[53] According to James Wood's data, admittedly for an earlier period, the same was true in Bayeux, an *élection* in Lower Normandy.[54] As a rule, however, purchasing an ennobling office was the usual way in which commoners became nobles in France during the seventeenth and eighteenth centuries. It was in this manner that nobility was most often purchased, not through the purchase of letters of ennoblement. Ennoblement by office obviously involved the state in a direct way, but it did not increase the control of the crown over ennoblement.

There were no ennobling offices in the Principality of Liège. In the Spanish/Austrian Low Countries ennoblement by office developed later than it did in France, only in the seventeenth century. Hereditary nobility was accorded to members of the collateral councils and the Great Council of Malines, as well as presidents of the provincial councils of justice; personal nobility was awarded to members of the provincial councils of justice, to councillors or secretaries of the monarch, to lieutenants of the fiefs of sovereign seigneuries, and to members of the Imperial Academy of Sciences and Literature.[55] Moreover, though the proportion was declining, the Habsburgs issued a larger number of letters of ennoblement to state functionaries than to persons of any other occupational category.[56] Yet the number of ennobling offices was smaller in the Spanish/Austrian Low Countries than in France. Given that there was also less venality of office in the Spanish/Austrian

Low Countries, we can conclude that buying an office was not the typical way for commoners to acquire noble status in the Spanish/ Austrian Low Countries as it was in France. This meant that the crown had greater control over who became a noble.

It is possible, of course, that ennoblements in the Spanish/Austrian Low Countries were still purchased, if letters were sold by the sovereign. This is a subject on which more research is needed. Janssens made a distinction between "venal" ennoblements and "fiscal" ennoblements. Ennoblements are venal if the price and volume that are sold are influenced by the demand; they are fiscal if the price and volume are influenced by variations in the state's need for revenue. His conclusion was that neither condition was obtained in the Spanish/ Austrian Low Countries. Large numbers of requests for ennoblement were rejected. The demand constantly exceeded the offerings, without resulting in an adjustment of the price. Although fees were occasionally raised to meet fiscal crises (in the years 1629–32, for example), on the whole they were relatively stable in the seventeenth and eighteenth centuries. They were certainly substantial and represented a source of revenue for the state, but they were lower than what could have been imposed.[57] And some candidates were exempted in part or in whole from the payment of fees. During Austrian rule, 113 recipients of titles were excused from paying fees, along with at least thirty recipients of noble status and twenty-four persons knighted.[58] We certainly find nothing in the Southern Low Countries comparable to the sales that occurred in France.

Another way in which the state controlled aristocratic status was through confirmations and rehabilitations of nobility. Even families confident of their noble status could seek letters to confirm it. Those whose claim was more dubious had all the more reason to obtain letters. Families who lost their noble status through *dérogeance* could have it restored by the crown.[59] A comprehensive edict of 1616 for the Spanish Low Countries provided that families who had "soiled their nobility by some mechanical activity" or "by some base occupation" could obtain letters of rehabilitation from the sovereign.[60] As a rule, fees were charged for these confirmations and rehabilitations.

In France, monarchs might revoke ennoblements if they became worried about the excessive creation of nobles, more often because revocations were typically accompanied by provisions that noble status could be maintained on the payment of a fee, or because new letters of ennoblement were later issued in return for payment. Ennoblements of the preceding twenty, thirty, or even more years were revoked by the French crown in 1598, 1634, 1640, 1664, and 1667; in most cases, noble status was restored for a fee. An edict of 1692 and a declaration of 1696 levied a premium on those whose noble status had been reinstated after the revocation of 1664, while those who had been raised to the nobility since 1664 had to make an additional payment to preserve their status. The ennoblements created in the years after 1689 were all revoked in 1715, but then all those who had been ennobled by letters from 1643 to 1715 received confirmations in return for contributions to the royal treasury.[61]

Titles

Continental monarchs gradually acquired control over aristocratic titles. The most control was achieved over the highest titles, in France the "dukes and peers," which actually refers to four different statuses: peers, count-peers, duke-peers, and dukes. During the tenth and eleventh centuries, dukes and peers were relatively autonomous vassals of the French king. Between the late thirteenth century and the late sixteenth century they became dependent on the monarchy. New dukes and peers owed their elevation to the king, who could increase the number holding these ranks as he wished.[62]

The same was true of other aristocratic titles. "Counts" and "viscounts" were originally administrative positions, but eventually turned into honorific titles. The meaning of the word "baron" in the Middle Ages had little connection with its use in the Early Modern period. "Marquess" was also metamorphosed. It was first used to refer to royal officers in charge of marches, but eventually became a noble rank. The crown could raise individuals to all these titles. In contrast with the British Isles, however, where the crown had a monopoly, a person could also acquire a title in France by purchasing a *marquisate*, a *comté*, a *vicomté*, or a *baronnie*. The crown had a monopoly only over the making of dukes and peers.

The crown also took control of the making of knights. Louis IX claimed that only he had the authority to create knighthood.[63] The idea that knights could dub other knights, especially on the field of battle, declined only slowly. Yet eventually knighthood became hereditary and the crown acquired a monopoly over the creation of new knights. In the Spanish/Austrian Low Countries the title was usurped by some officeholders, but the crown never officially accepted this state of affairs.[64] In a general edict on noble status enacted in 1754, Maria Theresa affirmed that "no one could call himself or title himself a Knight unless he was created and made a knight by Ourself or by the Princes our Predecessors."[65] Since only knights could create other knights, diplomas of knighthood granted by Albert and Isabella had been issued in the name of Albert alone. By the eighteenth century, however, the sovereign's right to confer knighthood had become sufficiently established that Maria Theresa could ignore this requirement. She created knights in her own name.[66]

Etiquette and Ceremony

In addition to regulating aristocratic status by creating nobles and by revocations, confirmations, and rehabilitations of nobility, institutions of the state endeavoured to monitor aristocratic clothing, decorations, funerals, points of honour, heraldry, appellations, and the proper form of letters for different ranks.

Behaviour in royal courts came under increasing regulation during the sixteenth and seventeenth centuries. This subject will reappear in later chapters, but it can be said here that the crown encouraged and even required the development of elaborate norms of behaviour that prescribed the proper comportment of people according to their rank; at the top level of the hierarchy almost every individual had his or her own rank and rights of etiquette.[67] These rules of rank were observed in everyday behaviour, but were even more carefully observed during any kind of ceremonial, where great attention was accorded to rights of precedence. The crown frequently had to adjudicate quarrels among nobles over precedence.

Honour and Duelling

Nobles had always been greatly concerned about their honour – the public recognition of the qualities that gave them high status, or at least they thought gave them high status. Princes might be asked to verify the honour of a noble or to intervene when a noble believed that his name had been dishonoured. In addition, the crown not infrequently dishonoured a noble who had opposed the sovereign or engaged in some other activity considered unworthy of a person of high birth. The Tribunal of the Marshals of France had jurisdiction over disputes and insults among aristocrats. Until the mid-sixteenth century it could authorize duels.[68] Duelling increased during the sixteenth and seventeenth centuries. In one respect state supervision of duels declined; duels were less often authorized by the king or his agents.[69] Yet, on the whole, state regulation expanded as a result of the increasing efforts of the crown and the *parlements* to reduce the number of duels. Henry IV and Louis XIII issued edicts against them, but with little effect. Louis XIV's attack was more consequential. He tried to prevent duels by establishing more regular procedures for the resolution of disputes and for control over insults. He instituted

penalties for insults or assaults.[70] His edicts also changed the relationship between the crown and duels. Whereas formerly the king, as the
leading noble of the realm, was supposed to be concerned about
disputes of honour among his *gentilshommes*, Louis xiv saw himself as
the absolute ruler decreeing what was best for the nobility.[71] Louis xv
promulgated a final edict against duels at the time of his coronation,
and a point-of-honour court heard 624 cases from 1725 to 1790.[72]

Heraldry

During the Middle Ages heraldic devices were subject to little regulation, at least by public authorities.[73] Officers to enforce regulation
were only gradually developing. Initially heralds went from castle to
castle, had little prestige, and performed minor functions, such as
transmitting messages and announcing the names of contestants at
tournaments. By the end of the thirteenth century their situation
became more secure. They were appointed by lords and regularly paid.
By the late fourteenth century their status had risen markedly. In this
period most heralds were still commissioned by lords and formed part
of their service. Naturally, kings also had heralds. Little by little heraldry came under more royal supervision. The crown was consciously
trying to develop institutions for overseeing it. In the early fifteenth
century Charles vi organized the royal officers of arms in the College
of Heralds. French kings of arms were elected by the heralds and the
pursuivants, whose choice was approved by the sovereign.[74]

From 1615 royal heralds in France were chosen by the king and
linked to the Grande Ecurie. In the same year the office of *juge d'armes*
was established.[75] The occupant of this post oversaw armorial bearings,
but also ratified letters of ennoblement and confirmations of nobility;
he too was designated by the crown. The right to display arms was not
limited to any segment of the population, but the right of a family to
its particular coat of arms was in theory protected by these heraldic
officers and by the courts whom they advised. Also protected was the
exclusive right of the eldest male to the full coat of arms and the
exclusive right of nobles to use crests. Numerous royal edicts were
issued by the French crown in the sixteenth, seventeenth, and eighteenth centuries forbidding commoners to use crests.[76] In 1696 a
French royal edict sought further to regulate the display of coats of
arms, to establish new institutions for this purpose, and to draw up a
general armorial. It was primarily a fiscal measure; all armorial bearings had to be registered, for which there was a fee. The ordinance
of 1760 tried to have all coats of arms registered and to limit their
use to nobles and certain categories of commoners. Although again

fees were charged, this measure, unlike that of 1696, was not designed principally to raise revenue for the French state. Its purpose was to increase state regulation of heraldry and to restrict the use of armorial bearings. It was never put into effect because it was rejected by the Parlement of Paris as contrary to customary law.[77]

Unlike their English counterparts, French heraldic officers did not have the right to grant coats of arms. This right was reserved for the king. While the French crown made less use of it than did monarchs in other countries, from the sixteenth century concessions were more frequent and usually accompanied by ennoblement.[78] Also from the sixteenth century, jurists held that all changes in armorial bearings had to be submitted for the sovereign's approval. This view was not based on any law, but it became increasingly common for anyone who took up a coat of arms or changed her or his arms to have it registered.[79] In addition, the French king possessed the power to degrade armorial bearings as punishment for desertion or lese majesty.

State control over heraldry also increased in the Spanish/Austrian Low Countries. The Edict of 1616 forbad the assumption of the arms, crest, or crown of another family. Relying heavily on customary law, it tried to formalize rules for distinguishing the coat of arms of the head of the family from those of cadets. It also stipulated conditions for the assumption of the armorial bearings of noble or extinct families and sought to regulate the use of crowns according to aristocratic status.[80] Eventually the Edict of 1754 provided a fine of 300 florins for anyone who displayed a crown that was reserved for titled persons, even in the case of a son who adopted the crown of his father with the latter's consent. A decree of 1662 required that coats of arms printed on cards had to be submitted to heraldic officers for approval.[81]

Regulation of heraldry was undertaken not only by supervision of its utilization and by enactments against "abuses," but also by providing for exceptions to the rules. In the Spanish/Austrian Low Countries a change in the ancient coat of arms of a seigneurie could not be made, except by authorization of the sovereign. The coat of arms of a noble family could be appropriated by the purchaser of its seigneurie if he or she obtained letters patent from the sovereign. The coat of arms of a family that had died out could be assumed with royal consent. A son could adopt the blazon of his mother, with the permission of the sovereign.[82] Almost anything was possible at the pleasure of the sovereign.

Usurpation

As the state sought to increase its control over aristocratic status, it tried to undermine community allocation of status and to limit alternative ways in which status was institutionalized. As early as the thirteenth and fourteenth centuries the French crown made attempts to restrict ennoblement by fief. Through a gradual process that culminated in the Ordinance of Blois of 1579, ennoblement by fief was brought under control in France, not by preventing commoners from procuring noble lands, but by restricting their right to claim nobility as a consequence.[83] A commoner would be permitted to own a noble fief on payment of a fee (*franc-fief*) to the crown. This did not, however, make one a noble. "Commoners or non-nobles, buying noble fiefs," it was clearly stated in the Ordinance of Blois, "are not thereby ennobled, whatever the revenue of the fiefs they have acquired."[84] Similarly, by the eighteenth century possession of a noble fief in the Principality of Liège did not "create the presumption of nobility"; it was even asserted that this had been the case from the fourteenth century.[85] In the Spanish/Austrian Low Countries the name of a noble associated with a fief or seigneurie could not be assumed by anyone acquiring the fief or seigneurie.[86] Although a commoner aspiring to noble status might still buy a noble fief for this purpose, one usually sought letters of ennoblement as well, or purchased an ennobling office. A noble fief was extremely helpful for the ennobling process, but its value had declined relative to these other acquisitions.

Parallel efforts were made to curb usurpations. A series of French edicts in the last half of the sixteenth century, most notably the Ordinance of Amboise of 1555 and the Ordinance of Orléans of 1560, provided for fines for the usurpation of noble status.[87] The Habsburgs legislated against the usurpation of noble status, noble titles, noble privileges, and marks of nobility, as did the prince-bishops of Liège.[88] Heraldic officers had the job of exposing and documenting usurpation.[89] Usurpers were frequently brought to court. In France, Savoy, and the Southern Low Countries, royal officials might initiate prosecution or villagers could take action against persons who were not paying the *taille* if their noble status was in doubt. In the Habsburg Edict of 1595 all law officers were granted the authority to prosecute, but during the seventeenth century these powers were restricted to heraldic officers and the provincial councils. Until 1744 heraldic officers travelled from one town to another seeking out nobles whose claims to status were doubtful, usually bringing their cases before the Heraldic Chamber to decide if they should be sent to court. It was up to those who asserted noble status to prove their case; the heraldic officers did not have to prove the contrary. Defendants who lost had to pay a fine and the cost of the prosecution.[90]

Usurpers could also be hunted down by establishing royal commissions to inspect noble credentials. In France these inquiries came to be known as *recherches* or *reformations*, the earliest of which were in the fifteenth century. They were ordered on numerous occasions in the sixteenth century, were most frequent in the seventeenth century, and then almost disappeared after the reign of Louis xiv. The commissions were often demanding, requiring nobles to present unquestionable "proofs" of their status. Titled nobles were frequently not bothered and, occasionally, old established families were accepted as noble without proof, or with weak documentation.[91] Still, some commissions forced many noble families in the region to establish the validity of their claim to noble status. The rejection rate could be high. In 1696, in the *généralité* of Paris, 40 per cent of the nobles were rejected. In the 1660s the rejection rate was 34 per cent in the *généralité* of Tours and 29 per cent in Brittany. Even lower rates, such as 15 per cent in Normandy, 10 per cent in Bayeux, and 13 per cent in Beauce, would be enough to cause significant social repercussions. It is true that some of those rejected had their status subsequently restored, but this did not undermine the claim the state was making to determine noble status.[92]

Most writers have stressed the fiscal aim of the French *recherches*. The objective was to put false nobles back on the *taille* roll. It is true that the burden of the *taille* was apportioned by parish; what a noble or false noble did not pay, fellow parishioners had to make up. Yet the ability of the parish to meet its obligations was threatened if there were many nobles or false nobles in the parish. Also beneficial to royal revenues were the fines that were levied on usurpers and the fees that could be charged for restoring the noble status of families whose credentials were rejected in a *recherche*.[93] Rejecting a person's claim to noble status might also force him to purchase an ennobling office, again bringing financial returns to the state. Another objective was to make the *taille* seem less illegitimate to the population by correcting some of its abuses and by improving its fairness, or at least its appearance of fairness. Let us notice, for example, that the *recherche* of 1634 in Normandy was part of a larger undertaking by Richelieu to rationalize taxation, a rationalization that also involved a reduction in the *taille*.[94] Still another motivation was a determination to combat usurpation for social and political reasons, in line with the more general royal endeavour to regulate aristocratic status. The *recherches* were not just concerned with the payment of the *taille*. Some were aimed at the usurpation of titles and the evasion of the *franc-fief*, which had primarily symbolic significance.

Although in much of this matter remarkable similarity existed between the Southern Low Countries and France, the role of the state in the institutionalization of aristocratic status was in important respects different in the two countries. First, there were more ennobling offices in France than in the Southern Low Countries. Second, French kings issued a large number of edicts that affected the nobility, but never an all-embracing measure to pull this legislation together and render it consistent. By contrast, in addition to a good number of separate edicts and rulings, several comprehensive statutes were enacted for the Spanish/Austrian Low Countries by the Habsburgs in an effort to regulate aristocratic status as effectively as possible. The first part of the Ordinance of 1595 covered the use of titles, marks of honour or nobility, coats of arms, and other symbols of status; the second part regulated titles and designations. The next major measure was the Edict of 1616, which elaborated on the Ordinance of 1595. Finally, the Edict of 1754 consolidated and amended the preceding legislation and also added new injunctions. Especially in the earlier legislation, an effort was made to codify and, where necessary, modify customary law. In some cases, exceptions were permitted for certain regions in conformity with local custom.[95] Yet the overall effect of the legislation was to increase state intervention in aristocratic law and to standardize it throughout the Spanish/Austrian Low Countries.

The same cannot be said, however, for the Principality of Liège. The people of this territory were not subject to the above legislation, but rather to the customary law of the principality, the legislation of the prince-bishops and the estates, and the customs of the Holy Roman Empire. There were some enactments on aristocratic status by the prince-bishops, such as those alluded to earlier that were designed to combat usurpations. The institutionalization of aristocratic status by the state was not, however, as advanced in Liège as it was in the Spanish/Austrian provinces.

Finally, it is worth observing that no *recherches* were conducted in the Southern Low Countries, at least not like those in France. The sovereign could call on all nobles to furnish "proofs" of their status. This was done by the prince-bishop of Liège, Maximilian-Henry of Bavaria, in 1662, when those who claimed noble status were given three months "to produce in our Privy Council their Diplomas, titles, or authentic proofs of their Nobility and titles."[96] The decree was renewed in 1687, 1692, and 1699. The Emperor Charles VI reaffirmed it in 1712 and commanded all nobles in Liège to provide their proofs within the next two months on pain of loss of noble status.[97] Yet this was a far cry from the large-scale *recherches* in France. And there was little of this in the Spanish/Austrian Low Countries. As a rule, the assault on usurpations of aristocratic status in the Southern Low Countries was carried out by prosecuting violators.

Differences between the legislation enacted in France and in the Spanish/Austrian Low Countries did not stem from general differences in the extent to which law was codified. In fact, the homologation of customs evolved more slowly in the Southern Low Countries than in France. Instead, differences between the Bourbon and Habsburg methods of regulating aristocratic status reflect a greater Bourbon concern with the fiscal consequences of aristocratic status and a greater Habsburg concern with protecting aristocratic status and controlling abuses. It was a difference of degree, but still a difference. The French crown was more willing to use its authority over aristocratic status to raise revenue. And when it sought to control usurpation, it did so in a manner that was profitable or thought to be profitable to the crown.

THE STRUGGLE OVER ARISTOCRATIC STATUS

The processes I have been describing inevitably led the state to become more involved in power struggles over aristocratic status, struggles in which the state typically sought to undermine the ability of people to increase their status on their own or to control the criteria by which status was accorded. First, the state struggled with commoners seeking to acquire noble status without going through "proper" channels – without buying an ennobling office or obtaining a royal letter of ennoblement. It was simply impossible to eliminate usurpation altogether. The purchase of a fief, often with the fabrication of a false genealogy, was still one way of becoming a noble in the eighteenth century. Usurpers, particularly wealthy ones, could stymie prosecution in many ways.[98]

Second, the state struggled with nobles. The attitude of many nobles towards the crown was ambivalent. They expected the state to put down usurpations. They were also very proud of the special relationship they enjoyed with the monarch. Yet they did not like to see agents of the crown deciding who was and who was not a noble. They were especially outraged when old noble families were declared usurpers because they did not have satisfactory documentation. Many members of the old nobility even denied the very right of the state to create nobles. The snubbing of *anoblis* and the *noblesse de robe* by the *noblesse d'épée*, which I shall discuss below, implied a rejection of the state's right to ennoble. Or at least it implied that, if the state could create a noble, it could not create a true noble, a *gentilhomme*, only the noble community could do that. The *noblesse d'épée* was willing to accept certain new nobles, most obviously those who were ennobled for military service. Ennoblement for other services to the state was accepted by some members of the *noblesse d'épée*, but many bitterly opposed ennoblement by office or by the purchase of letters.

The authority of the state over noble status was to a degree constrained by customary law. A major route to the nobility, through marriage, was regulated by custom, and the state had no way of controlling it. The rehabilitation of *noblesse dormante* in Brittany was authorized by the Breton Custom and hence did not require royal letters of rehabilitation.[99] Most of the privileges enjoyed by the nobility were theirs by virtue of customary law, making it difficult, though far from impossible, for the state to regulate them.

Different state institutions often opposed one another. The decentralized political structure of the Spanish/Austrian Low Countries beget coordination difficulties between central and provincial heraldic officers.[100] Confusion and conflict resulted from the multiplication of authority. Actions taken by the provincial councils and the heraldic officers were at best disconnected and at worst in manifest conflict.[101] Heraldic officers might also clash with municipal authorities, as they did with those of Antwerp for a long period in the eighteenth century. Heraldic officers even quarrelled with one another over differences in orientation, vested interest, and jurisdiction.[102]

In France the most intense struggles within the state pitted the crown against judicial institutions. The *parlements* often went out of their way to defy the king. I have already noted that the heraldic Ordinance of 1760 never became law because it was rejected by the Parlement of Paris. The French *parlements* often tried to block ennoblements or the granting of new titles, or to restrict the rights of *anoblis*, in particular among the municipal nobility.[103] On a number of occasions the Parlement of Paris refused to register peers named by the crown.

Rulers often struggled with one another over aristocratic status. This was particularly true, of course, in the Empire and other regions governed by the Habsburgs. In the Low Countries it was repeatedly necessary to forbid the use of titles granted by foreign princes and to affirm in letters patent the exclusive right of the Habsburgs to create nobles.[104] However, given the international character of the nobility, it was a difficult practice to control.

Control over the regulation of aristocratic status was greatly affected by war and changes in sovereignty. The Dutch war increased usurpations in the Low Countries.[105] The regulation of aristocratic status was frequently undermined during the wars of the seventeenth and eighteenth centuries. In the eighteenth century the Habsburgs believed that usurpations and illicit ennoblements multiplied as a result of the weakening of the sovereign's authority during the War of the Spanish Succession, during the War of the Austrian Succession, and even (though to a lesser extent) during the troubled period between these two wars. The irregularities of the period led Charles VI to decree in 1724 a stricter control of ennoblements and subsequently to develop plans for new legislation, which Maria Theresa eventually carried out.[106] In 1718 Charles annulled diplomas of nobility granted by the King of Spain during the War of the Spanish Succession. A treaty in 1725 validated these ennoblements, provided that Austrian approval was obtained within a year.[107]

The War of the Austrian Succession raised even more questions of sovereignty. Between the death of Charles Albert in January 1745 and the crowning of Francis Stephen of Lorraine as Holy Roman emperor in October, the Empire was ruled by Charles Albert's son, Maximilian-Joseph, elector of Bavaria. Shortly before the end of his term he granted complete powers of ennoblement to Count Jean-Jacques of Zeyl, to his eldest son, and to the eldest sons of his male descendants. The hereditary knights created by the count's son, François-Antoine of Zeyl, chamberlain of the Elector of Bavaria, were invalidated in the Austrian Low Countries in 1761 by the Privy Council. In the Principality of Liège, however, the count was able to have his powers recognized and to create nobles of the Holy Roman Empire, which were registered in Frankfort. The result was that a number of families in Liège owed their nobility to the auxiliary or to his delegate and the validity of their status was still being debated in the nineteenth century.[108]

Aristocratic status in Savoy was theoretically controlled by the House of Savoy in Turin, but these rulers had to cope with problems similar to those posed by the Low Countries for the Habsburgs. Frequent military occupations, periods of uncertain sovereignty, and the service of Savoyards in Imperial armies meant there were nobles who owed their status to other rulers. It was often necessary for Turin to assert its right to deny recognition to such nobles.[109]

The French state did not face such problems because it suffered fewer disruptions of sovereignty. Yet periods of civil unrest during the sixteenth and seventeenth centuries did create difficulties. Usurpations certainly increased during the Wars of Religion. The Court of Aids of Paris thought the same thing happened during the Frondes. It was said that in both periods many of those who took up arms assumed noble status.[110] In Béarn, property ennobled its possessor. This continued to be the case even after union with France as a result of the special political status of Béarn.[111]

Obviously neither the Habsburgs nor the Bourbons had complete control over their state apparatus. The authority of both was undercut not only by estates and *parlements*, but also by the independence, ineffectiveness, corruption, and in some cases anti-royalism of persons in the state bureaucracy. The French monarchy, for example, could find courts of aids recognizing persons as noble whose status was highly doubtful. One of Colbert's aims for the *recherche* of 1668 was to rescind ennoblements by courts of aids.[112]

At the time, it was thought that the regulation of aristocratic status was less well organized in France than in other European countries. Things were less chaotic in the Spanish/Austrian Low Countries than in its large neighbour to the south, despite periods of uncertain sovereignty. Yet there were problems enough in the Low Countries, where the kings of arms often took it upon themselves to certify the noble status of old nobility in return for a fee.[113] Intentionally or unintentionally, state officials could legitimate a false pretension by acknowledging it in a public act, a problem that the archdukes tried to combat by prohibiting any public officer from knowingly attributing nobility to persons who were not really noble, on penalty of a fine of 100 florins for each contravention.[114] Heraldic officers could not be controlled because they could play one state authority off against another.[115] Provincial bodies could easily exceed their authority. The Council of Brabant, for example, had the right to rehabilitate patricians who had belonged to one of the privileged lineages of Louvain or Brussels. In 1658, however, the crown had to overrule the council when it restored a patrician, not only to his lineage, but also to noble status. Philip IV made it clear that in the Spanish Low Countries only the sovereign had the right to rehabilitate nobles.[116]

Prosecutions in the Spanish/Austrian Low Countries came in spurts, interrupted by long periods of inactivity.[117] Many usurpers were able to avoid prosecution. A lawyer with a provincial council might frustrate a prosecution because the usurper was a colleague.[118] Heraldic officers also did not always perform their job properly. Usurper and heraldic officer often came to a deal.[119] One trick was for a usurper to bribe a heraldic officier, who would commence legal proceedings against the usurper (to prevent other heraldic officers from doing so), but then let the case drag on.[120] The most serious problem of all was the sale of ennoblements by heraldic officials. In spite of numerous efforts to suppress it, such practices continued.[121] The most fantastic example is that of Jean and Pierre-Albert de Launay. Jean de Launay became a pursuivant of arms in the Spanish Low Countries. With an imaginary genealogy and letters patent that he wrote himself, he claimed to be a baron of the Holy Roman Empire. He repeatedly granted authentic-looking certificates of nobility in return for payments. Eventually he was taken to court. He fled to Holland and later settled in the part of

Flanders acquired by France during the seventeenth century, where he appropriated the role of herald of arms, there resuming his frauds, for which he was ultimately condemned to death. Meanwhile his brother, Pierre-Albert, also became a herald of arms and sold false coats of arms and certificates of nobility.[122]

State control over aristocratic status could, in the eyes of the nobility, distort its distribution as a consequence of the state's tendency to use it as a means to raise revenue. As we have seen, this was a far greater problem in France than in the Southern Low Countries. The sale of letters of nobility by Louis XIV supplemented royal revenues, but at the expense of discrediting his regulation of aristocratic status. Heraldry was also abused by the French crown for financial reasons. As a consequence of the Edict of 1696, some people who did not have coats of arms, or at least did not display them, were forced to register them with the intendant.[123]

This kind of manipulation of aristocratic status to raise revenue diminished in France during the eighteenth century. The Heraldic Ordinance of 1760 was not enacted for fiscal purposes. Noble status was not sold in the blatant manner that was characteristic of the turn of the century. Yet the most serious problem still remained. The French monarchy, by using the sale of ennobling offices to raise revenue, thereby denied itself control over the bulk of ennoblements. Ennoblement by office did not decline in the eighteenth century; in fact, it increased.[124] This was a self-inflicted limitation on royal control over aristocratic status that was found in France to a far greater extent than in any of the other countries we are looking at in this book. It has to be acknowledged that it was not beyond the power of the French king to deny the privilege of ennoblement to this or that office or set of offices. It was difficult, however, for him to prevent a given individual from buying an ennobling office that was for sale. Moreover, since the majority of ennoblements in France were by office, the most distinguished and wealthiest persons in the society did not need to beseech the crown for letters of ennoblement. This had the effect of lowering the value of royal ennoblements. Whereas in the Southern Low Countries persons of exceptional wealth and stature turned to the sovereign for letters of ennoblement, in France such persons bought an ennobling office or were already ennobled by office. Those who sought letters of ennoblement from the king were generally of relatively modest social standing.[125]

A similar problem existed in Savoy, despite the unusual power of the dukes. Ennoblement by office developed largely outside the control of the House of Savoy. In 1582 the members of the Chamber of Accounts took the liberty of attributing noble status to themselves, the magistrates of the Senate, and certain other office-holders. This right was never officially recognized by the sovereign, but was also never contested. Consequently, it became a regular avenue of ennoblement in the seventeenth century. After the Chamber of Accounts was done away with in 1720, the Senate attested by decree to the noble status of its own members and their descendants.[126]

Even in the Spanish/Austrian Low Countries ennoblement by office engendered problems. The Edict of 1595 made no mention of it. The Edict of 1616 alluded to it. Yet it did not specify what offices were ennobling. The result was considerable confusion, and the king of arms repeatedly requested rulings by the sovereign or the Privy Council on the validity of ennoblements by office. A ruling of 1643 from the Privy Council verified that the office of president of a provincial council ennobled the person who held it and also his descendants. On numerous occasions it was necessary for the monarch or the Privy Council to put down the pretensions to noble status of office-holders or members of certain occupational groups, most notably lawyers and military men. The kings of arms took some lawyers to court for calling themselves nobles.[127]

Obstacles to crown control over aristocratic status are well illustrated by the problems encountered in the French *recherches*. The *recherches* contributed to perceived abuse as much as to its elimination. Because their resources for presenting their case before a commission were weak, many families locally recognized as "true" nobles lost noble status, while usurpers with such resources were confirmed or, more commonly, were able to have their status restored.[128] The whole process was biased in favour of the most influential and the wealthiest. Even the testimony of witnesses was under this spell; it was hard for commissioners to obtain witnesses to testify against the pretensions of a powerful family in the community.[129] For all these reasons, the *recherches* were often immensely unpopular with the French nobility.

As fiscal measures, the *recherches* had mixed success. Considerable revenue was certainly derived from fines and from the fees levied for the restoration of noble status. The *recherches* also contributed to the rationalization of tax collection, added names to the *taille* roll, and perhaps improved the legitimacy of the tax by reducing the number of fraudulent exemptions. Yet it is amply clear that many fraudulent exemptions escaped detection, and not a small number of exemptions survived even for persons specifically rejected by a commission.[130] Few of the *recherches* were ever completed; and in any given area it was rarely all those claiming noble status who were affected by the commission.[131] Furthermore, the evidence we have suggests that it was the small fry, not big taxpayers, who were the most often investigated and thus were most likely to be placed back on the *taille* rolls.[132] Finally, not all the income from fines went to the state. It was common to farm out the collection of fines; and the view was widespread that more money went into the hands of the *traitant* than into the coffers of the king.[133]

Very few *recherches* were undertaken during the eighteenth century. There is disagreement among French historians over why they declined in number. Some believe the *recherches* were abandoned because they were failures. Others argue it was because the *recherches* were generally successful, or because the seriousness of the problems they were meant to solve gradually diminished. By the end of the reign of Louis XIV the collection of taxes had been regularized and the most scandalous inequities eliminated. The *recherches* were designed to confront the problems created by the great number of usurpations during the sixteenth century, problems that no longer existed by the eighteenth century. Furthermore, the French crown sought to tax the nobility in other ways and therefore gave less attention to exemptions from the *taille*.

To sum up, on the whole the state regulation of aristocratic status was more effective in the Spanish/Austrian Low Countries than it was in France. This was especially true in the last half of the eighteenth century. In chapter 2 we saw that Austrian rule over their provinces in the Low Countries became more firmly established in the second half of the century. This change was reflected in the regulation of aristocratic status, which underwent a number of reforms and was certainly more effective than it had been earlier. Although many fundamental problems persisted and efforts at reform were still often frustrated, by the standards of the time the state regulation of aristocratic status was impressive in the Austrian Low Countries.[134]

CONSEQUENCES OF THE STATE INSTITUTIONALIZATION OF ARISTOCRATIC STATUS

However successful or unsuccessful, state regulation of aristocratic status was clearly not without consequences. Some indication of these consequences has been provided in the course of the preceding discussion and more will come out during later chapters. Here I can remark on several obvious effects.

State Accreditation and the Decline of Spontaneous Ennoblements

First, it is clear that the development of ennobling offices, the use of letters of ennoblement, the suppression of ennoblement by fief, the prosecution of usurpers, and the *recherches* all led to a situation in which noble status came to be regarded as requiring state accreditation, even if state accreditation was subject to venality and corruption. Indeed, the corruption of state officials contributed to the reinforcement of state authority over noble status by encouraging usurpers to turn to the state for help. Whereas in the Middle Ages usurpation was under the control of the nobility itself, whose members had the power to decide whether to accept a usurper as a noble, in the seventeenth and eighteenth centuries the state and its officials assumed greater control over usurpation.

Nobles themselves came to feel the need for state recognition. This was especially true of those whose noble status was in doubt. In the Spanish/Austrian Low Countries the services of the Heraldic Chamber were utilized most by immigrants and by those on the border between noble and bourgeois status.[135] Yet even those with a long lineage of noble status could seek the endorsement of the state. And among all parties it became accepted that it was extremely advantageous, if not absolutely necessary, to have "proofs." This requirement was stressed by L.N.H. Chérin in the introduction to his collection of French royal legislation on the nobility.[136] The *recherches* in France made a significant contribution to this process and helped to transform the character of the French nobility. Although few *recherches* were carried out in the eighteenth century, the effect of the earlier *recherches* persisted. They helped to establish the principle that noble status required documentation. Indeed, the *recherches* themselves became historical documents of varying credibility attesting to the noble status of families.[137] Other ways of proving noble status remained helpful, but increasingly proof of noble status came to depend on the state.

A second consequence of the expansion in the role of the state in the institutionalization of aristocratic status was a decline in the frequency of what Mousnier called "spontaneous" ennoblement, that is, ennoblement by prescription. This change has been documented by Jean-Marie Constant for the Beauce. His data show a decline in the sixteenth and seventeenth centuries in ennoblement for military service and by fief, while ennoblement by office rose.[138] This is not to deny that ennoblement by prescription continued in France; but it was becoming probably less common and certainly less often successful. When many old nobility were concerned enough to provide "proofs" of their noble status, it was harder to achieve ennoblement by prescription.

Third, the growing role of the state led to a shift in the conception of noble status. What took place was not altogether new. Rulers and state officials had always tried to shape the aristocracy to suit their needs. The expansion in state regulation of aristocratic status, however, strengthened conceptions of noble status consistent with state interests. Service to the state became the principal justification. The ennoblement of magistrates was not the result of a public consensus that this was the most important function performed in the society; the public was never asked its opinion on the subject. The exalted status of the high-court justices and other high state officials was instead the result of the power of institutions of the state to accord honour to those who served it.

Closely related to this conception of a nobility of service was the idea that what distinguished nobles from the rest of society was "merit." By the eighteenth century the elevation of persons to the nobility by letters patent was almost always justified by reference to merit (though not only merit). At the same time many members of the *noblesse d'épée* were giving more emphasis to merit as the basis of their noble status, and particularly to the notion that noble lineages gave their children examples to follow and that the noble life style afforded them the kind of upbringing that made them superior to commoners. In the seventeenth and eighteenth centuries there was a growing emphasis on the education and moral preparation of the nobility.[139]

Yet the transformation that occurred in the conception of the nobility during the Early Modern period went deeper still. Ever since sovereigns began to ennoble, a tension existed between two opposing conceptions of the source of nobility: that the sovereign could make someone a noble, or that all the sovereign could do was to acknowledge the nobility already existing in a person. Gradually from the thirteenth to the eighteenth centuries the first notion came to prevail over the second. The idea that the crown did not have the capacity to create a noble never disappeared. Nonetheless, those who held such a view were on the defensive in the face of ennoblements by letter and large numbers of ennoblements by office.

Paradoxically, conceptions of noble status became at the same time more genealogical. While the state was pushing a nobility of merit, it was also undermining traditional ennoblement by prescription. As Ellery Schalk has shown, there emerged in France a greater emphasis on birth as a criterion of noble status. Before the seventeenth century, though most nobles owed their noble status to birth, an ideological conviction prevailed that nobility was acquired by virtue. Then noble status in France was, theoretically at least, based on vocation, specifically the military vocation.[140] In the late sixteenth century there developed an increasing reliance on blood, lineage, and race, a concept originally used to refer to qualities sought in the breeding of animals.[141]

The Habsburg Edict of 1595 described the nobility as "those who descend from old noble race of blood and house."[142] Birth received greater emphasis in the literature from the early seventeenth century. Although Schalk does not consider the role of merit in the eighteenth-century view of the nobility, he documents the development of pedigree as the primary criterion of noble status. Valour no longer made one a noble. The *recherche* mentality was now ascendant. Proof of ancestry became a requirement. The obvious inconsistency between these notions and the evolving emphasis on ennoblement for merit created acute contradictions in eighteenth-century France.

Internal Heterogeneity

The view is widespread in sociology that status groups are relatively homogeneous, enjoy collective consciousness, and are capable or can easily be made capable of collective action. Whereas classes may or may not have these collective characteristics, status groups always do. These assumptions are derived from Weber's writings on status. Weber believed that members of status groups conformed to a particular life style and interacted more often with one another than with members who did not belong to their group.[143] Summarizing the Weberian perspective on this subject, Frank Parkin writes:

The problem with classes is that they are too heterogeneous and internally divided to act as a concerted force for any length of time. There is in fact something rather improbable about the notion of a social class being cast in the role of a social actor. Status groups, on the other hand, are generally moral communities. They are more likely to have a powerful sense of their own common identity and of the social boundary separating them off from others, especially if there is a racial, religious or ethnic component present. As a consequence they can be more readily mobilized for collective ends.[144]

These assumptions can be made true by definition; that is, we can define status groups as moral communities and contrast them with heterogeneous classes. However, if we have here something that is more than a definition, then that something must be the following proposition: people who enjoy high or low status as a result of possessing the same characteristic(s) are more likely to form homogeneous communities with a capacity for collective action than are people who have the same relation to economic resources or the means of production; in Weberian terms, common "status situation" is more likely to give rise to homogeneous and collectively organized communities than is common "class situation."

When put in these non-tautological terms, the proposition is clearly unproven. We can observe numerous esteemed characteristics in many societies (intelligence, beauty, skill, weight, height, honesty, wit, composure, generosity, loyalty, chastity – the list could go on and on) that do not give rise to homogeneous communities with the capacity for collective action. Those who argue that status groups are homogeneous and cohesive usually have ethnic or communal groups in mind; while common status characteristics may contribute to the solidarity of such groups, they have other sources of attachment that draw members together (such as language, religion, presumed common ancestry, and cooperative social relationships). There has been little systematic sociological research on other kinds of statuses to determine if they generate homogeneous and cohesive communities more often than common economic interests or relations to the means of production.

Most sociologists would consider the European aristocracy to be a quintessential example of a homogeneous status group with the capacity for collective action. Yet Bush has demonstrated that in its heyday the European nobility was extremely heterogeneous.[145] Moreover, the state institutionalization of aristocratic status increased this heterogeneity. It did so by making or maintaining as nobles in a legal sense persons who did not conform to the general social characteristics of the nobility. The extent to which this was the case cannot be fully appreciated until we have investigated aristocratic wealth, political power, and culture, but it is possible to say a few words here about several of the major divisions within the nobility.

Pedigree

The state made it possible for commoners to become nobles, legally at least, without going through the traditional process of social assimilation. It has to be allowed that almost all new nobles came from the upper strata of society. However, from those strata a diverse group could be drawn. Legally, people had only to meet the conditions set by the state – purchasing an ennobling office or receiving a letter of ennoblement – to gain admission. Socially, they would not be accepted as full nobles, but once admitted they contributed to the diversity of the nobility. Simultaneously, the state increased the importance of birth as the basis for aristocratic status. The nobility had always been differentiated according to pedigree (old nobility enjoying higher status than new nobility), but these differences became more acute in the Early Modern period as a result of state institutionalization of aristocratic status.

To be sure, new nobility and old nobility in some measure assimilated. New nobles usually tried to conform to noble characteristics. A businessman who was ennobled or who bought an ennobling office might give up business; certainly some of his sons would.[146] The new nobility imitated the old nobility and purchased seigneuries. They sent their children to the same academies as old nobles. And they intermarried with the old nobility. At the same time, old nobles were taking on the characteristics of the new nobility, becoming more educated and urban.

The division in the continental nobility between old and new nobles was, nevertheless, a persisting one. Mobility into the nobility insured that new nobles entered as quickly as those who preceded them were assimilated. All nobles tried to distinguish themselves from new entrants. Those who enjoyed a long line of noble ancestors did all they could to make their pedigree known. Real differences in values and life style existed between old and new nobility.[147] Old nobility were, of course, the most likely to espouse the race concept of nobility. Noble ancestry could be calculated by "quarters," but more often it was based simply on the number of generations or "degrees" of nobility. One could find the number of degrees or quarters proclaimed in various places, on sepulchres, for example; or a certain number of degrees or quarters might be required to be admitted to an order, society, noble chapter, and the like. Most nobles thought that a person had to have four generations of nobility to be a true noble, a *gentilhomme*. The state regulation of aristocratic status could institutionalize these differences by conceding to old nobles rights or privileges denied to new nobles. An example we have come across already is the reform of taxation carried out by the dukes of Savoy.

Robe and Sword

The state institutionalization of aristocratic status also led to the related cleavage between the *noblesse de robe* and the *noblesse d'épée*. In France and Savoy it was ennoblement by office that produced the *noblesse de robe*. In the Southern Low Countries it was ennoblement by office plus the ennoblement by letters of persons employed by the state that created this new status category in the nobility.[148]

Narrowly defined, the *noblesse de robe* included only the magistrates of the sovereign courts; broadly defined, it included all office-holding nobles. Narrowly defined, the *noblesse d'épée* included only nobles who took up arms; broadly defined, it included all nobles who were not members of the robe. Whether or not a noble pursued a military life, he and his family could consider themselves to be members of the nobility of the sword on the grounds that their ancestors had served in arms. Observers found more group consciousness and explicit identification with the nobility of the sword in France and Savoy as a result of the relative militarism of these two countries, at least in comparison with the Southern Low Countries.

It has to be conceded that, like old and new nobility, sword and robe were to a degree assimilating, even in France and Savoy. Much of the wealth of the robe was in land.[149] Marriages between robe and sword were not uncommon. Some *parlementaire* families could boast a long noble lineage. A robe family could easily send one or two sons into the army. Conversely, many office-holders were from families of the *noblesse d'épée*.[150] As a result, it was not unusual for the same family to have some members in military service, while others were in law. Many social institutions served to integrate the two groups; it has been argued that the Parisian salons of the seventeenth century performed this function.[151]

An overlap between the two groups – such that it is impossible to treat them as exclusive of one another – does not, however, invalidate the differences. Rather than distinct social groups, robe and sword were differences along a continuum. Differences there certainly were. Nobles who undertook a military career lived quite a different life from those who did not, and the professionalization of the army increased these dissimilarities during the seventeenth and eighteenth centuries. A military career was a much riskier one, not only because of the danger of physical injury or death, but also because advancement depended on unusual skills and good fortune.[152] On the other hand, the *noblesse d'épée*, especially the court nobility, was generally indulged by the crown more than the *noblesse de robe*.[153] Military training and/or an education designed for entrance into the royal court was more common among the *noblesse d'épée* than among the *noblesse de robe* and reinforced the distinction between the two groups.[154]

The social differentiation between sword and robe could have a considerable effect on behaviour. Most sword families identified with the *noblesse d'épée*. Writers from sword families could be found criticizing or belittling the robe, and vice versus. The sword believed they were superior to the robe and often snubbed them. There were numerous disputes over precedence at public ceremonies. Robe and sword were often ideologically opposed and usually had dissimilar values. We can compare the libraries they left when they died. In the inventories of the libraries of the magistrates of the Senate and the Chamber of Accounts of Savoy, law, history, literature, and religious works were the most often found.[155] Unfortunately, no study of the libraries of sword nobility in Savoy has been done, but these inventories can be compared with the library of the Marquess of Pont-St-Pierre at his death in 1700: little literature, nothing by classical authors, no legal treatises, nor works of philosophy. His son, when he died in 1754, left a library that differed somewhat from that of his father; philosophical works found a place, including works of Rousseau and a French version of Pope's *Essay on Man*. Yet, like his father, he was most interested in history, geography, and the Christian religion; there was only a smattering of ancient literature, little classical French literature, and no books dealing with the law.[156]

From Lord to Noble

As a result of the decline of lordship and the institutionalization of aristocratic status, the relative significance of two distinguishable statuses in continental society shifted. Whereas in the Middle Ages noble status was only one of a number of aristocratic statuses and was secondary to lordship, by the eighteenth century the status of noble had become unquestionably the foremost aristocratic status on the Continent.

These two aristocratic statuses had noteworthy differences in terms of the four variables of status listed in the introduction to this book. First, nobility separated status from other kinds of power to a greater extent than did lordship. It cannot be denied that nobles usually had other kinds of advantages and privileges. In the Middle Ages these included landed wealth, fiefs, lordship, and freedom.[157] Nonetheless, nobility was a more differentiated status than was lordship. It was primarily prestige.

Second, nobility was more hereditarily ascriptive and more closely tied to kinship than was lordship. While lordships were usually inherited, they could also be acquired in other ways, and few lords went through life without changes in the persons who owed them loyalty. The importance of kinship to the bond of lord and follower could vary. In some cases, kinship was used to legitimate the authority of the lord and to reinforce the loyalty a man owed to his lord. In other cases, kinship had little to do with such loyalty. Indeed, as I mentioned in chapter 4, when so many social bonds in Medieval Europe were intertwined with kinship, lordship stood out as a leading non-kinship bond in the society. Thus the decline of lordship was the decline of a status that was not as firmly based in kinship as most social ties in the society.

If Duby was right, the type of nobility that was to be characteristic of Europe emerged between the tenth and the mid-eleventh centuries when certain members of society started to claim status on the basis of male lineage rather than lordship or other affiliations they could establish with powerful persons.[158] Certainly, the essence of noble status as it emerged in Medieval Europe was the claim to a prestigious lineage. Thus the institutionalization of noble status that occurred in France, Savoy, and the Southern Low Countries in the late Middle Ages and the Early Modern period meant the strengthening of a kinship-based status. Indeed, the emphasis on birth was increasing in the Early Modern period. If in the long run the importance of kinship for elite status has declined in continental Western Europe, it has not been a consistent trend.

OBJECTIVES OF STATE REGULATION OF ARISTOCRATIC STATUS

Why did the state become more involved in the institutionalization of aristocratic status? The most obvious reason is that it had financial payoffs, or at least so it was thought. If one were to study only France one might conclude that this was the overwhelming reason, but the institutionalization of aristocratic status in the Southern Low Countries helps us to recognize that the state was interested in aristocratic status for other reasons as well. Even in France aristocratic status served as a reward for loyal citizens or servants of the state. Hence it was desirable that the right to provide such rewards be monopolized by the state. In addition, control over aristocratic status became identified with sovereignty. Certainly by the end of the Middle Ages heads of state were set against ennoblement of their subjects by foreign rulers. The "proper" institutionalization of aristocratic status also became identified with stability and effective rule. The objective of Philip II in the legislation of 1595 was "to put everything in good order and provide regulation" for those over whom he ruled.[159] In more general terms, state authority over aristocratic status inevitably developed along with the growth of centralized states because status, as Weber insisted, is a kind of power. Status power was confiscated just as other kinds of power were confiscated. State control over the power to elicit respect expanded at the expense of individual and communal control. Awarding status distinctions was "one of the most visible demonstrations of our power," thought Louis XIV.[160] In the extreme, one could imagine a sovereign telling his or her people: "You shall respect whom I tell you to respect." Things had not gone anything like this far in eighteenth-century France, Savoy, or the Southern Low Countries. Yet, relative to the Middle Ages, the state had come to assume such authority to a greater degree.

This development contributed to the overthrow of the Old Regime. By the late eighteenth century more and more French people were tired of being told whom they should respect. And, as a consequence of the increasing role of the state in the institutionalization of aristocratic status, the state became the target of this discontent in a way that would not have occurred in the Middle Ages. Then the king would not have been blamed for aristocratic privilege. Even in the eighteenth century people recognized that royal authority over aristocratic status was subject to severe limitations. Nevertheless, just as the state had become the source of aristocratic accreditation, it had also come to be seen as the means by which aristocratic rights to respect and privilege could be abolished.

The British Isles

It is well known that the status structure found in the British Isles during the Early Modern period was unlike the status structure just described. Little effort has been made, however, even by historians, to explain the differences. Those explanations that have been offered or implied point to the earlier rise of capitalism and class society in England. This line of argument gives insufficient attention to status in its own right, treating it as an epiphenomenon of the economy and the class structure. It also fails to appreciate that the differences in status structures were not the result of one or two causal forces, but the product of a great number of mostly unpredictable historical events and developments over centuries of history.

THE INSTITUTIONALIZATION OF ARISTOCRATIC STATUS

Lords in Parliament

Although lordship declined in the British Isles during the late Medieval and Early Modern periods, another very different "lord" emerged, a lord that gave the British aristocracy a unique element with no equivalent anywhere else in Europe.

England and Ireland
Historians once assumed that those who were summoned to the king's council in the twelfth and thirteenth centuries were the tenants-in-chief of the king. We now know that persons who were not tenants-in-chief were often present and that not all tenants-in-chief were

called. Whom the king summoned depended on the business of the moment. The council called together by the Irish justiciar usually consisted of those magnates whose consent was valued or who were near at hand.[161] In the course of the fourteenth century, the English and Irish lists of those summoned became more fixed, and an invitation to appear became a privilege claimed by some magnates. In both England and Ireland, to be summoned now signified high status. Little by little the right to attend became more hereditary. In 1313 some 61 per cent of those summoned to the English Parliament were later succeeded by an heir. By 1401 no less than 85 per cent of those summoned were succeeded by either a male heir or a man married to or descended from an heiress. At the same time, the numbers summoned fell from ninety-nine to forty-six.[162] In other words, the eldest sons of a declining number of aristocratic families were being personally called. New members (that is, those personally summoned who had not inherited the right) were at first simply added to the summons list, but eventually they were granted the right to attend by the crown, much as nobles were ennobled on the Continent.[163]

The Commons represented localities or communities associated with localities, in contrast with most continental political assemblies, which represented status groups. Yet, because they met separately, the Commons as a whole became a separate status group from the lords. In Ireland the representatives of counties and towns eventually came to form an integral part of Parliament, but they were excluded from the council. They were forced to stand behind a bar, while the justiciar, his ministers, and the lords sat.[164]

Aristocrats who were not personally summoned could come to the English or Irish Parliament in this manner and sit with the burgesses. This was an unusual feature of English and Irish political assemblies. It was possible for continental nobles to become representatives of the third estate, but as a rule they did not. The parliamentary cleavage in both England and Ireland was between the "lords," who were summoned to the upper chamber by name with individual writs, and those in the lower chamber, who were picked by their communities as representatives in response to a summons sent to the shire or town. Gradually the notion developed that the lords temporal summoned to the upper chamber were nobles, while those summoned to the lower chamber were not.[165] The idea was resisted. As late as 1483 it is possible to find a document referring to "many and divers lords spiritual and temporal and other nobles and notable persons of the Commons."[166] The word "Commons" did not mean "commoner." It referred instead to the communities represented in the lower chamber. Yet those who were personally summoned to the upper house enjoyed a distinct, more elevated aristocratic status; they were variously referred to as the "nobility," the "peerage," or the "aristocracy."[167] Initially only the peerage was referred to as an estate, but by the fifteenth century, following the French, many people referred to the lords temporal, the lords spiritual, and the Commons as the "three estates."[168]

The process I have just outlined was one in which the state institutionalized status differences. These differences proved to be extremely important in the British structure of aristocratic status. The explanation is to be found in the Medieval evolution of Parliament. This is not to deny that political leaders adapted to existing status distinctions. Obviously when a twelfth-century king called on members of the society to support and advise him he took existing status differences into consideration, summoning greater barons and tenants-in-chief more often than men of lesser status. Yet at this time there was no institutionalized convention. The institutionalized convention evolved later and it was this convention that created the very clear aristocratic status distinctions in England that were quite different from those on the Continent.

The English and Irish peerages were much smaller than the continental nobility. In the late eighteenth century an estimated 300 to 600 nobles per 100,000 persons could be found in the Austrian Low Countries and about 1000 to 1500 in France.[169] Irish peers represented perhaps only 5 to 6 per 100,000 persons in Ireland in the eighteenth century. English and Welsh peers represented about 2 to 3 per 100,000 persons in England and Wales in the late eighteenth century; even if one includes members of their extended families, they made up an estimated 30 to 40 per 100,000 persons in the population. Although most English and Irish peers were large landowners, collectively they owned only a small proportion of the land. It has been estimated that peers owned 8 to 10 per cent of the land in England in the late seventeenth century.[170]

The English crown and its representative in Ireland controlled summonses to the two parliaments and thus enjoyed a monopoly over ennoblement in this sense. People were made peers for different reasons: to strengthen the government in the houses of lords, to offset the power of an overmighty magnate, to honour war heroes or give public recognition to a military career, to reward those who served the monarch or the government, or to elevate the status of the relative of a peer. During the reigns of James I and Charles I, English and Irish peerages were sold, the returns going mostly to friends or servants of the king.[171] Even later, appointments were made to the Irish peerage of persons who had no connection with Ireland. English political interests and social climbing among English elites determined many elevations to the Irish peerage. As a result, some half of the Irish peerage rarely or never attended sessions of the House of Lords, at least in the early eighteenth century.[172]

Scotland

The Scottish Parliament emerged more independently. Its character was a product of intersocietal forces and indigenous conditions, making it in some ways similar to the English Parliament and in other ways different. There is no doubt that the English Parliament was a model for the Scottish. The English helped to organize parliaments during Edward I's rule over Scotland, and the English Parliament served as an example.[173] English influence was also evident in the Act of 1428, which stipulated that members of the greater nobility receive individual summons to attend Parliament. Yet the evidence is lacking to demonstrate that the king (James I) was seeking to imitate the English Parliament or structure of aristocratic status. The making of the Scottish peerage was the result primarily of the development in the years 1350 to 1450 of a distinguishable group of greater barons or lords of Parliament, whose claim to noble status was honorific and personal more than it was territorial.[174]

These lords were different from English and Irish lords in a number of respects. First, though a clear distinction was made between lords and others who came to parliament, there was no "house of lords" in Scotland; the Scottish Parliament was unicameral. Second, in Scotland a baronage persisted below the peerage. The Medieval Scottish baronage had been a large group, not just the tenants-in-chief of the crown, but all those enjoying baronial jurisdiction.[175] Most of these barons were excluded from the peerage as it developed, partly as a result of their own neglect in coming to Parliament. Many barons, even tenants-in-chief of the crown, had resisted attendance because they sought to impede the centralization of power in the hands of the monarchy and because they did not want to assent to taxation sought by the monarch. Royal efforts to persuade barons to show up at Parliament or to send spokesmen did not enjoy much success until the sixteenth century. By the late sixteenth century the barons were more eager to participate.[176] By then, however, the right to attend Parliament had been redefined and only a small number of greater barons came by right as peers. The lesser barons, along with freeholders and burgesses of the royal burghs, sent representatives.[177] Whereas in England the title of baron eventually became the preserve of peers, this did not happen in Scotland, where there were barons who were not peers.

These barons did not, however, enjoy as high a status as the lords whose rank became institutionalized by Parliament, a fact that illustrates again how, in the British Isles, state structures shaped the structure of aristocratic status. Certain differences notwithstanding, on the whole, the structure of the Scottish peerage came to conform to that of the English. This process was completed with the Union of Parliaments in 1707, though even after the union the Scottish peerage persisted as a distinct status group because Scottish peers were not all given seats in the British House of Lords. Rather, they could elect only sixteen of their number to sit among the British Lords.

Why did this kind of peerage develop in the British Isles and not on the Continent? In England the reason was clearly two-fold: first, the concentration of power in the crown, and, second, primogeniture and contingency factors that limited the size of the House of Lords. The power of the crown meant that it could assemble the great lords of the realm and hope for their support, in contrast with the French crown, which could not count on the cooperation of the great dukes and counts. The power of the English crown also gave the great lords of the realm reason to want to be summoned to the king's council, in order to share in his power. The structure of aristocratic status might still have been similar to that found on the Continent if Medieval English kings had not restricted the number of those personally summoned to their parliaments and if the inheritance of this right had descended to all the children. By the seventeenth and eighteenth centuries this aristocratic status would have been held by a large number of persons. This would, of course, have made the houses of lords unwieldy, but this does not explain why it did not happen. Some estates on the Continent, those of Brittany for example, were large and unwieldy.

The Irish House of Lords was under the same crown as the English House of Lords and represented only the Anglo-Norman population of Ireland. It is thus not surprising that it evolved similarly to that of England. The similarity between the English and Scottish lords is more difficult to explain. The Scottish crown did not enjoy as much power as the English, resulting in certain differences between the two parliaments, most notably the reluctance of some Scottish lords to attend Parliament. Yet the Scottish crown was powerful enough to attract the majority of the great lords. It also made a certain effort to follow the English example. And primogeniture served, as in England, to limit the number of lords of Parliament.

Privilege

Perhaps the greatest dissimilarity in the institutionalization of aristocratic status between the Continent and the British Isles was the larger set of privileges enjoyed by continental aristocrats. Admittedly the differences have been exaggerated. British aristocrats did enjoy some privileges, most obviously the right of peers to sit in one of the parliaments. Peers also possessed certain minor economic advantages in the law of debt.[178] Sons of peers had special privileges at universities.[179] And, as we shall see, certain political offices were customarily reserved for peers. Many references have been made in the historical literature to the right of peers to be tried by other peers, but this was not necessarily an advantage, in some situations actually increasing the likelihood of conviction.

The gentry had some customary privileges. It was well accepted that to hold certain offices it was necessary to own considerable landed property. Attention should also be drawn to the sumptuary legislation regulating personal consumption (especially attire) according to status, though in England sumptuary legislation was repealed in 1604 and almost no further legislation was enacted thereafter.[180] In addition, persons of high status might be entitled to special rights with respect to handgun laws, not to mention the privileges that the gentry enjoyed by virtue of game laws.

Nevertheless, it is indisputable that fewer aristocratic privileges, certainly privileges attached to a status, were accepted by the state in the British Isles than in France, Savoy, or the Southern Low Countries. Why? This is a difficult question that deserves more research than it has received. Critical factors include English Common Law, and the emerging concepts of nobility and commoner; as the gentry came to be regarded as non-noble, it was more difficult for them to lay claim to special privilege. We also need to recall the way that English kings obtained support and raised revenue. If the king needed assistance or money for a venture, he persuaded his council or Parliament to go along with it rather than negotiating with local bodies or political assemblies. He did not therefore need to grant tax exemptions to special-interest groups in order to obtain support or money. Members of the king's council could, of course, receive benefits in return for their cooperation; and merchants might be given special treatment in return for granting loans to the crown. Yet these were in the nature of individual favours, not privileges accorded to groups in the population. Otherwise, the magnates in Parliament cooperated with the king in return for recognition of the powers of Parliament, confirmation of the judicial rights of freemen, acknowledgement of certain limitations on royal power, or general concessions. Magna Carta is only the best-known example of concessions of this kind extracted from an English king.

In Ireland and the Principality of Wales, the situation was slightly different. It was mentioned in chapter 3 that historians have found that English kings raised money in these two countries by negotiating with individual lords and local communities. Whether, under different circumstances, the practice in Wales and Ireland would have led to aristocratic privilege, as happened on the Continent, is impossible to say. I suspect that the pressure to conform to the English pattern would have been too powerful. It is hard to imagine Irish or Welsh lords being granted tax exemptions that their English counterparts did not enjoy. In any case, taxation by consent of parliament did eventually develop in Ireland and Wales.

Why did English kings less often than French kings turn to specific groups in the population for support or revenue? It was primarily the result of the power of the central government, including not only the power of the crown, but also that of Parliament. Thus even when an English king was personally weak and desperate for money, the raising of revenue was more centralized in England than it was in France. French kings, with or without the acquiescence of the Estates General, had to bargain with local bodies to raise revenue. Even when the French crown became able to tax without consent, it had to allow privileges in order to keep various interest groups from opposing it. The strength of the central government in Medieval England made this unnecessary for English kings. The fact that the French method of taxation was followed to some degree in Wales and Ireland, where the authority of the central government was weaker, supports this explanation.

In addition, of course, the English king received larger sums than did the French king from sources that did not require as much cooperation from powerful groups in the society, namely crown lands, customs, and later excise. These alternative sources of revenue had a further consequence: the English crown did not have to tax land as heavily as did continental monarchies. The reliance of the latter on this source in the late Middle Ages meant that land taxes were higher on the Continent than in the British Isles. Consequently, English landowners paid less in taxation than continental nobles would have paid if they had been subject to their share of land taxes. Instead of granting the aristocracy tax exemptions, the English crown tried, for a long time, to live of its own. It also allowed landowners to be under-assessed.[181] Indeed, if one compares taxation in England and on the Continent during the fifteenth and sixteenth centuries, it is tempting to conclude that these monarchies evolved two different ways of persuading their respective aristocracies to accept the growing fiscal demands of the state: tax exemptions in the continental case, under-assessment in the English case. In fact, this way of putting it exaggerates the control that the crown had over the process, which really consisted of a constant struggle to meet yearly expenses in ways that were politically acceptable to those with power in the society.

Native Nobilities and the Rise of the Gentry

During the Middle Ages, nobilities existed in the British Isles similar to those that could be found at the same time on the Continent. The Latin term *nobilis* was often applied to the members of these groups. Native nobilities were eventually deinstitutionalized in the British Isles, but it was a long process varying from one part of the islands to another.

England

Contemporaries often referred to the Anglo-Saxon thanes as nobility, and historians have followed suit.[182] This nobility was replaced by a smaller Norman nobility, whose members owed their aristocratic status primarily to the land they held of the king, not their noble lineage, despite the importance of kinship ties among the Norman elite. Moreover, royal law soon became applicable to all freemen, not just aristocrats.

Still, the word *nobilis* was used to refer to most barons and large landowners. It was not until the peerage began to emerge as a distinct status group that the wide use of the term "noble" began to decline. K.B. McFarlane suggested that before 1300 the English gentry was unmistakably a nobility. He believed that from 1300 to 1450 it is unclear whether the gentry were part of the nobility. After 1450 it was difficult to see them as part of the nobility.[183] I think the transformation took longer. In the sixteenth and seventeenth centuries members of the gentry were still sometimes referred to as "lesser nobles" and equated with the untitled nobility on the Continent. It was in the sixteenth century that Sir Thomas Smith (a scholar and statesman, secretary of state of Elizabeth) referred to the peerage as the *Nobilitas major* and the gentry as the *Nobilites minor*; it was in the seventeenth century that Edward Chamberlayne (an author and royal tutor) referred to members of the gentry in like fashion as *nobiles minores*.[184] And some historians have adopted similar terminology.[185] Nevertheless, what had once been familiar use of the term "noble" had become exceptional by the late seventeenth century. Then one finds more references to "the nobility and the gentry," clearly implying that the latter was not part of the nobility.[186]

The process by which the English gentry lost noble status might remind some readers of the old "rise of the gentry" debate of the 1940s and 1950s. For those unfamiliar with this quarrel, R.H. Tawney and, later, Lawrence Stone argued that during the last half of the sixteenth century and the first half of the seventeenth the English gentry acquired greater power and wealth vis-à-vis the "aristocracy" (in this case meaning principally the old peerage), while H.R. Trevor-Roper, focusing on the lesser gentry, asserted that the gentry experienced a decline in this period.[187] By stressing the gentry's loss of noble status I may give the impression that I am taking the side of Trevor-Roper and those who have subsequently supported his position. I am not suggesting, however, that the gentry underwent a decline in status. I am saying there was a change in the way status was institutionalized. Relative to the larger population, the ordinary member of the English gentry remained as high in status as the ordinary member of the French nobility.

Moreover, there was no decline in their landed wealth, at least not in general. On the contrary, the average size of landed estates increased from the fourteenth to the eighteenth century. It is true, however, that there has been insufficient recognition of the concomitant process of losing noble status. The rise of the gentry involved two closely related processes, one in which birth or pedigree became less important and another in which land became more important as criteria of aristocratic status. Some words of caution are necessary here. Birth remained the source of most titles. Even for the remainder of the aristocracy we are talking about a relative shift. People continued to take ancestry seriously.

The social basis for the rise of the gentry in England lay in historical developments and proprietary patterns that contributed to an increasing concentration of landownership. Customs of landholding and inheritance that emerged in England during the Middle Ages facilitated the creation and maintenance of large landed estates. In addition, many freeholding peasants or small landowners were forced to yield their properties to greater landowners, often as a consequence of heavy indebtedness. Finally, the dissolution of the monasteries and the sale of monastic land by the crown contributed significantly to the rise of the gentry.

Wales

The free *uchelwyr* were regarded as noble in the Middle Ages. They had special legal rights and obligations. They were fighting men and considered themselves to be of royal stock.[188] In the late Middle Ages the distinctiveness of their status diminished.[189] This resulted from a drastic weakening in their military strength and authority. It was also promoted by a breakdown in the distinction between free and unfree, with the result that freedom ceased to be an aristocratic status.[190] And it ensued from the imposition of an English-type status structure on Wales. The higher elite consisted of those holding English peerages, while they were served by a gentry composed at least partially of descendants of the Welsh nobility.

The rise of the gentry in Wales is especially revealing. During the Middle Ages freeholders were more numerous than they were in England. Land ownership lay in the hands of kin groups, and inheritance was largely partible. Hence, properties were small. The greater concentration of landownership that eventually occurred in the seventeenth and eighteenth centuries resulted from the earlier deterioration of Welsh land customs and the penetration of primogeniture and other English customs.[191] As in England, land also became more concentrated through confiscation of wastes and commons, marriage alliances, land purchases, and seizure of land that had been used as security for loans. Land was purchased from small proprietors, but was in addition made available by the sale of church and crown property; more land also came on the market during the Civil War.[192]

The decline of an aristocracy based primarily on birth did not come easily in Wales. Many small landed estates could still be found in the seventeenth and eighteenth centuries. The rise of the gentry was up against strong forces in Wales. Gradually, however, the English emphasis on land was accepted; land became the principal criterion of aristocratic status.[193] The *uchelwyr* evolved into a gentry, but a gentry that preserved certain characteristics stemming from its historical origin. The Welsh gentry put greater emphasis on birth than did the English gentry. Pride in lineage among families of Welsh gentry, some with very modest landholdings, amused the English.[194]

Scotland

The metamorphosis was even slower in Scotland. The Scots had a tradition that all freeholders were considered noble. Although the arrival of the Normans and the introduction of feudalism by David I put a new layer of feudal aristocracy over this native nobility, the native nobility survived. Even in the fourteenth and fifteenth centuries freeholders were regarded as nobles by most members of the population.[195] This native nobility failed to obtain state recognition. The evolution of the Scottish peerage, the decline of privilege, and the conscious attempt to imitate the English made such legitimation unlikely. Admittedly, noble status continued to be recognized, if not for all freeholders, at least for large landowners. The differentiation of the landed aristocracy into peers and gentry was less clear-cut than in England.[196] And in many areas the concentration of landownership was limited in the seventeenth century; in the Western Isles, for instance, little land changed hands in spite of the indebtedness of many landowners.[197]

Nevertheless, in other regions of Scotland the ownership of land was becoming more concentrated. The legal basis for this trend was provided by Scottish feudal land law, which institutionalized primogeniture.[198] A special case was the Northern Isles, where a rise of the gentry coincided with the displacement of "udal" (allodial) tenure by feudal terms of landholding.[199] In many parts of the country, more property had come into the hands of private landowners before the Reformation as they acquired the superiority of church lands. The feuing of kirklands also made land available to landowners who were trying to build larger landed estates, though initially the feuing of kirklands also transferred considerable property to small landholders.[200]

Land was gradually becoming more determinant of gentry status. In the seventeenth century a gentry on the English model was emerging. The closer ties with England in the sixteenth century and the Union of the Crowns in 1603 effected marked changes in Scottish life and manners. According to Jenny Wormald, it was then that "gentleman" took on the English meaning.[201] Highland chiefs were regarded as noble by their followers, even if the state did not acknowledge their nobility. Yet such notions coexisted with the view that the term "noble" should be reserved for someone with a title.

Ireland

Across the Irish Sea, the fate of the native nobility was, in comparison, cataclysmic. Before the arrival of the Normans, a distinction had been made in Ireland between nobles and commoners on the basis of a number of criteria, including birth, wealth, and clientage. A noble was a person with a large number of clients; the more clients one had, the more noble one could claim to be.[202] It was a relatively fluid status structure; there was considerable upward and downward mobility; and struggles were waged among and within families for domination. This status structure endured after the arrival of the Normans, and the native nobility was recognized in most of Ireland until the end of sixteenth century.

When English rule over Ireland expanded in the sixteenth century, the English sought to Anglicize the native Irish nobility. A small number of Gaelic lords became peers through the program of surrender and regrant. In the first half of the seventeenth century there seems to have emerged a greater desire among the Gaelic nobility to integrate into the Anglo-Irish gentry, as evidenced by an interest on their part in Anglo-Irish heraldry.[203] This development was cut short by the Confiscations. True, some Gaelic families kept their land by converting to

Protestantism or by passing land to Protestant descendants. Many of the dispossessed owners, however, became middlemen on landed estates purchased by Protestants. Some were driven west or forced to flee to the Continent. A small number were able to remain Catholic and yet survive among the landowners of the eighteenth century.

In Ireland the rise of the gentry was dramatic. It occurred in little more than a century. Pedigree quickly became less important because so much of the elite established in the seventeenth century was new, without a long ancestry in which they could take great pride. It must be acknowledged that James has shown that roughly a quarter of the eighteenth-century Irish peers who were active in the House of Lords were descended from Gaelic or Old English landowning families. Still, the majority of peers were New English.[204] Some of these peers had family histories that were modest before their ancestors came to Ireland. This was even more true of the gentry, many of whom had non-aristocratic backgrounds. Similarly, the decline of small proprietorship in Ireland happened much more suddenly than in Wales or Scotland. During the seventeenth century, property rapidly became concentrated in fewer hands as a consequence of the Confiscations and the adoption of English laws of property.[205]

In sum, at different times in different parts of the British Isles the native nobilities were replaced by a peerage/gentry structure of aristocratic status, a structure that had first emerged in England. By the eighteenth century the English status structure predominated everywhere. This happened for a number of reasons. Similar social and economic developments in England and certain parts of the periphery contributed to the outcome. To a degree, the English structure of aristocratic status was consciously imitated. Yet the most critical factor was that the English state took over the British Isles, and it did not recognize native nobilities. Although particular members of a native nobility could be elevated to the peerage, these native nobilities as such did not obtain the state accreditation that we now understand was so important to the status of the nobility on the Continent. Those who did have state recognition were the peers and certain ranks in the gentry (knights and baronets). For these title-holders, recognition by the state was vital. The status of the untitled gentry and those enjoying merely the title of esquire was, however, much less regulated than was the case for nobles in our continental countries.

Heraldry

It would be inaccurate, however, to say that there was no state regulation whatsoever of gentry status in the British Isles. In certain respects the state regulated the legal status of the gentry by regulating the use of coats of arms. Legal control over coats of arms was stricter in England and Scotland than in our continental countries. Only members of the nobility or gentry were supposed to have them. In England the College of Arms was empowered to enforce this restriction. In Scotland it was the king of arms, known as the lord lyon, who had this power. He had a court of chivalry and the authority to pass judicial judgements.[206] Not only did the lord lyon verify who had the right to bear coats of arms, he also recognized clan chiefs. The chief alone had the right to undifferenced arms. By the seventeenth century the lord lyon was insisting that the assumption of a chieftainship without his permission was unlawful.[207] The notion that members of the gentry were nobles was most strongly held among those who were concerned with coats of arms, and the largest number of references to the gentry as a nobility is found in their literature. The kings of arms presumed it was their prerogative and duty to validate noble status.

As in Medieval France, in Medieval England the majority of heralds were in the service of powerful lords and carried out a variety of functions. Yet in both countries the regulation of heraldry expanded with the evolution of the state. The late thirteenth century provides us with the earliest indication of the employment of heralds by an English king. We have evidence of the presence of a king of heralds (later known as king of arms) in 1276. Heralds came to be referred to by names of office; the earliest of these names in England would seem to have been that of "Carlisle," which was conferred in 1327. The English Court of Chivalry began to acquire jurisdiction over heraldry by the late fourteenth century, a prerogative institutionalized during the following century. In 1417 a royal proclamation forbid the self-assumption of arms. During the fifteenth century it became routine for kings of arms to grant them in the name of the crown. By the sixteenth and seventeenth centuries heralds had established the custom of calling on members of the gentry to validate their coats of arms. Those who could not prove a just claim to a coat of arms were obliged to sign a form forsaking pretensions to gentility. Penalties were levied for the improper use of arms.[208]

While there was a resemblance between these "visitations" and the French *recherches*, there were significant differences. In England it was the right to a coat of arms that was being recognized, not noble status. The English visitations did not have the fiscal functions of the French *recherches*. And the regulation of heraldry in England and Scotland was even less effective than the regulation of noble status on the Continent. The English heralds failed, for example, to keep painters from usurping their functions and providing people with coats of arms.[209] Furthermore, the heralds were primarily interested in making sure that people did not adopt someone else's coat of arms, rather than restricting coats of arms to a small elite. What the lord lyon was most fussy about was that only one person in each generation use undifferenced coats of arms.[210] So long as other branches differenced their coats, he was not greatly concerned. Finally, though the heralds were supposed to certify the gentry status of those who adopted coats of arms, wealth (especially landed wealth) was the criterion used to determine who had the right to assume arms, at least in England.[211]

It is true that the belief persisted, especially in Scotland, that those who had coats of arms were "gentlemen," even "nobles"; the claim is still made today. Nevertheless, the use of arms has always been widespread in England and Scotland among persons of a range of social circumstances.[212] The Scottish love for coats of arms undermined them as a symbol of aristocratic status.

Heraldry was much less indigenous to Ireland than to England and Scotland.[213] Until almost the eighteenth century, heraldry in Ireland was largely limited to the Anglo-Irish community – in fact, the urban Anglo-Irish community. The heraldic college in Ireland was known as the Ulster Office; the chief heraldic officer was the Ulster king of arms, or just Ulster. The office was really a branch of the English College of Arms.[214] It was established for political reasons as part of the English effort to extend its authority in Ireland during the sixteenth century, but its power outside the Pale was thin indeed. Although by the eighteenth century the Ulster Office had acquired control over coats of arms in most of the country, its regulation was still ineffectual.

The irony was that in the eighteenth century the Ulster Office was kept busy validating the genealogies of Irish emigrants who had fled to the Continent. These emigrants were trying to establish their right to membership in the continental nobility and sought to prove generations of noble status in Ireland. Thus a British institution was drawn into providing the kind of state accreditation of noble status that had developed on the Continent, but which did not develop in the British Isles. Continental rulers and governments were not convinced of the reliability of British status regulation and, in particular, of the Ulster Office. Several governments passed legislation to prevent abuses arising from the practices of British heraldic offices.[215] An Austrian count of Irish extraction complained about this kind of legislation and other restrictions imposed by Maria Theresa:

This new law of hers is very severe and hard against all Britanik subjects because she requires any genealogy out of Ireland should be attested by the Lord Lieutenant, or Lords Justices of the Kingdom, that it is really and truly the work of the King and Herald of Arms; this even is not sufficient but it must be attested by her own ambassador at the Court of England that it is the true subscription of the Lord Lieutenant and Lords Justices. She goes further and requires that the English Ambassador at her Court at Vienna should supper attest any genealogy that is provided with these requisites has PLENAM FIDEM and no contradiction or objection is to be admitted against it.[216]

CHARACTERISTICS OF THE BRITISH STRUCTURE OF ARISTOCRATIC STATUS

The structure of aristocratic status that emerged in the British Isles differed from the structure of aristocratic status found on the Continent in a large number of ways, some of which are already apparent, others of which will become apparent in subsequent chapters. Three characteristics can be mentioned here.

First, the British aristocracy was not divided into a *noblesse d'épée* and a *noblesse de robe*. To be sure, state service could become an avenue of upward mobility and admission into the landed elite. The British office-holding elite was very different, however, from the continental *noblesse de robe*. Most obviously it was much smaller. In the British Isles the crown did not indulge in a massive creation of offices for the sake of selling them as did the crown in France. And the working bureaucracy was smaller in the British Isles than it was in France. Moreover, state offices in the British Isles were not ennobling as they were in our continental countries. Purchase of land, admission to the social world of the gentry, acquisition of a title, procurement of a peerage – these were separate processes.

More plausible is to argue that there was an equivalent in the British Isles of the continental *noblesse d'épée*. The differences in the military role of the French and British aristocracies were not as great as many writers have assumed. On the other hand, the military ethos of the French or Savoyard aristocracy was greater than that of the British aristocracy. Even more to the point, military service was not for the British peerage or gentry the basis of their aristocratic status. Peers were defined by their right to sit in a parliament and members of the gentry primarily by their pedigree, ownership of land, and life style – neither of which depended on military service. Admittedly, military activity had ceased to be a defining characteristic of the continental nobility, but many continental noble families clung to it as the basis of their identity in a manner that was simply not found in the British Isles. For these reasons, a social cleavage between robe and sword did not exist in the British Isles as it did in France, Savoy, and the Southern Low Countries.

Another difference between the British and the continental aristocracy was that the former was less differentiated than the continental nobility. Not all aristocratic statuses were equally differentiated from other kinds of power; nobility was more differentiated than peerage, peerage more than gentry, gentry more than lord. Unlike the status of continental noble, the status of peer was not purely one of prestige, if for no other reason than that it was impossible to be a peer without the political power that was enjoyed by the right to sit in a parliament. Although unusual, it was possible to be a peer without land, but land was a prerequisite for membership in the gentry, making gentry status less differentiated. In other words, in the British Isles the relatively undifferentiated status of lord was replaced by more differentiated statuses, but these statuses were less differentiated than that of continental noble. The status of gentry was also, as we have seen, less institutionalized by the state than that of noble, further increasing, I shall argue, the probability that it would be fused with other kinds of power.

A third difference was that the British aristocracy was more homogeneous. The British peerage was comparatively homogeneous because it was small and the criteria used by the crown in creating peers was very restricted. The British gentry was more heterogeneous than the British peerage, but less heterogeneous than the continental nobility because admission into and membership in the British gentry required certain socially recognized characteristics, the most critical of which was the ownership of considerable land. If one did not have these characteristics one could not enter the gentry; if one lost them, one fell out of the gentry.

Along with these differences between British and continental status structures there were also, of course, a good number of similarities that are apparent or will become apparent. On both sides of the English Channel lordship was largely replaced by other aristocratic statuses. On both sides aristocratic status became more institutionalized at a national level. On both sides some members of the aristocracy enjoyed political privilege. On both sides the crown had the right to grant individuals certain aristocratic statuses. On both sides there were important status distinctions within the aristocracy. And on both sides great importance was attached to status.

Evidence abounds of concern for status and status symbols in British society. Precedence was of the gravest concern. Every county had its pecking order, which was carefully observed by anyone who was brave enough to draw up a list of the gentry. Petty confrontations could occur over precedence at ceremonies, such as funerals. Great quarrels erupted over the precedence of English, Irish, and Scottish peers.

Members of the British peerage and gentry engaged in as much status consumption as members of the continental nobility, perhaps more. Lavish entertaining, the construction of marvellous country houses, extravagant landscaping, the keeping of an excessive number of servants and other dependants, and elaborate funerals were primarily a matter of status. Heraldry was also, of course, a status symbol, and one that was a greater passion in England and Scotland than in most continental countries. Despite the stress on land as a criterion of aristocratic status, British families could still take considerable interest in their genealogy and they encouraged or commissioned family histories.[217]

British aristocrats also competed for titles. Men were constantly petitioning and politicking for new titles. Many title-holders were anxious to raise their title. Old nobility invariably wanted a higher title to keep up with or ahead of newly appointed families.[218] In no way can it be argued that interest in these titles was dying with the "modernization" of British society or the rise of capitalism. All the titles had taken on new significance in the Early Modern period, and one, that of baronet, was a new honour created by James I in 1611.

And, of course, land itself was a symbol of status in the British Isles. The profitability of land will be discussed in the next chapter. Here I can just point out that, even when provided with better alternatives for investment, British people bought land for reasons of social standing and to gain admission into county society.

REASONS FOR DIFFERENCES IN THE ROLE OF THE STATE

Why did the state play a greater role in the institutionalization of aristocratic status in our continental countries than in the British Isles? Can we explain these differences as a consequence of royal "absolutism" on the Continent versus "liberalism" in the British Isles? Does the lesser state institutionalization of aristocratic status in the British Isles reflect the evolutionary advancement of England, at least in liberal terms, over continental countries? Bush has suggested that in absolutist states ennoblement was more often by grants of patent or office, whereas in "constitutional polities" ennoblement could occur by "assumption."[219] This thesis is further developed by Janssens. Differences in the status structures between England and the Continent are to be explained, he argues, by the greater liberalism of English society and the "less monarchical" character of its state. Absolutist states wanted to control status, as they wanted to control everything else, to an extent that the English state did not. Ennoblement of state servants by office or by letters patent distinguished an absolutist state, while social assimilation of new nobility and ennoblement of persons from the private sector was characteristic of a liberal state. According to Janssens, the Spanish/Austrian Low Countries were in a transitional period of emergent liberalism during the eighteenth century.[220]

There is considerable merit in this thesis. Insofar as the British state was less powerful than the French in the seventeenth and eighteenth centuries, it is not surprising that it was less able to control aristocratic status. A good example is sumptuary legislation in England, which reached its peak when the Tudors increased the power of the state, but then disappeared, likely because it was unenforceable.[221] In the seventeenth and eighteenth centuries the sovereigns of our continental countries could be more arbitrary in the decrees and regulations they issued on aristocratic status. More precisely, the regulation of aristocratic status in the British Isles was to a degree constrained by the power of the English landed elite vis-à-vis the crown. The manipulation of status to raise revenue for the crown was brought to a halt by the English Civil War, and it would have been difficult for any subsequent monarch to have resorted to it again. Nor could a British monarch have arbitrarily revoked noble status; revocation required conviction for treason or some other serious offence.

Savoy was at the opposite extreme. The dukes of Savoy could treat the aristocracy in a manner that British rulers would never have dared. They did not fear alienating nobles;[222] on the contrary, they delighted in their total power over the nobility, who, in the words of Victor Amadeus II, relied "on us to use them as we see fit."[223]

Between these two extremes, the Southern Low Countries were probably closer to the British and France was closer to Savoy. The French *recherches* suggest that the French crown had more power to force unpopular regulation on the nobility than did the Austrian. Similarly, one of the reasons ennoblement was more venal in France than in the Southern Low Countries may have been that the crown was powerful enough to impose venality in spite of noble opposition.

This is, however, about as far as this line of thinking can be carried. In certain respects the regulation of aristocratic status was greater in the Spanish/Austrian Low Countries than in France or Savoy, even though Habsburg rule was less absolutist. The French king and the duke of Savoy may have been able to force nobles to accept regulation they did not like, but these rules did not regulate aristocratic status any more than did the Habsburgs. On the contrary, the enactments of the French and Savoyard crowns look disorganized and spasmodic along side the Habsburg legislation of 1595, 1616, and 1754.

The proposition that differences in the way in which aristocratic status was institutionalized between the British Isles and the Continent can be explained by absolutism versus liberalism also runs into difficulty when one tries to argue that the development of the British peerage as a distinct status group or the loss of noble status by most of the British aristocracy resulted from British liberalism. These both occurred before the emergence of British liberalism and resulted from the power of the English crown in the Middle Ages, a power that led to the formation of the peerage and enabled the crown to ignore many claims to privilege. This royal power was limited to England, the Pale of Ireland, and, from the late thirteenth century, the Principality of Wales. It took longer for English royal power to expand over the British Isles than for French royal power to expand over what is now France. Eventually it did so, however, and, consequently, native nobilities were undermined throughout the Isles. The English crown recognized peers, but did not recognize the ordinary gentleman as a noble with privileges. What was left was a gentry that was "free" of state control. This "freedom" was not the product of British liberalism; rather, it resulted from the capacity of the crown to refuse to recognize native nobilities, and the spread to other parts of the British Isles of the structure of aristocratic status that originally appeared in England.

This structure was also the consequence of certain characteristics of English state fiscality, characteristics that in turn stemmed from the relationship between the state and the economy. The Bourbons and to a lesser extent the Habsburgs were interested in controlling aristocratic status, not only because they wanted to have power over it, but also because tax exemptions for the nobility made it necessary to restrict noble status. Similarly, the practice of selling nobility and ennobling offices to raise revenue made French kings more concerned about restricting ennoblement by prescription than would otherwise have been the case.

The argument that the lesser state institutionalization of aristocratic status in the British Isles reflects the evolutionary advancement of England over continental countries is hard to sustain when we think about long-term changes. The very idea comes from a peculiarly English Whiggish perspective. On the Continent, unregulated aristocratic status was Medieval and state institutionalization of aristocratic status was modern. Even in the British Isles state control over titles increased in the late Middle Ages and in the Early Modern period. The British peerage developed in the late Middle Ages; it is as much an Early Modern and Modern phenomenon as a Medieval one.

6 Economic Power

Land

Power over the Peasantry

Some continental peasants were owners holding their land as *allodia*. Many were tenants enjoying customary tenure that gave them *de facto* ownership. If we define proprietorship as the right to sell, an estimated 40 to 50 per cent of the land in France was owned by the peasantry in the eighteenth century.[1] This percentage varied enormously from one district to another in France, as it did also in Lotharingia. In the Genevois province of Savoy the peasantry may have owned as much as 60 per cent of the land.[2] In the Southern Low Countries peasants owned a smaller proportion of the land, often as little as 10 per cent, but then in some places 50 per cent.[3]

Nevertheless, historians are agreed that on average much more of the land was owned by its occupiers in our continental countries than in the British Isles, where proprietary rent and contractual tenures (tenancies-at-will, yearly tenancies, and leaseholds) were proportionately greater.[4] The rate of return from land could be affected by these dissimilarities. Rents for contractual tenancies were usually higher than those for copyholds, and thus the conversion to contractual tenancies in some British districts enlarged landed income.[5] Peasants enjoying *de facto* or *de jure* ownership could not be threatened with eviction or increases in rents, though it was possible to exercise some muscle by means of seigneurial rights, even reviving or threatening to revive old seigneurial claims that had fallen into disuse. To the extent that continental agriculturalists had such security, the power of aristocrats over them was constrained. At the other extreme were yearly tenancies and tenancies-at-will. Leaseholders were comparatively independent of the landowner's economic power if they had long leases, but when leases came up for renewal their situation was more precarious. Written leases that have survived reveal the great number of demands an owner could make on a tenant wanting to renew his or her lease.

Several cautionary remarks are, however, in order. First, contractual tenants were not totally powerless against landlords. Tenants enjoyed a certain measure of protection from English royal courts. Moreover, rough treatment by a landlord was almost everywhere restrained by communal pressure. And a "good" tenant could threaten his or her landlord with leaving as much as the landlord could threaten him or her with eviction. Many yearly tenants or tenants-at-will in the British Isles enjoyed *de facto* security of tenure. It is only in comparative terms that we can say that British landowners were in a stronger position than continental ones.

Second, the contractual versus customary difference between the British Isles and the Continent should not be over-emphasized. Contractual tenures were more prevalent on the Continent than has often been realized. In addition, though changes taking place were complex, in some continental districts there was an increase in leasing during the seventeenth and eighteenth centuries and a decline in customary tenures, either because direct farming by owners was decreasing or because owners were trying to replace customary tenures with term leases.[6] In many parts of France, especially in the west and the south, aristocrats depended heavily for income on contractual sharecropping, known as *métayage*. The terms of letting for *métayers* were usually short and precarious. We also saw in chapter 4 that proprietary rent must have represented a not insignificant portion of landed income for most aristocrats, as indicated by the small percentage of income coming from seigneurial dues in many areas.

At the same time we observed in chapter 4 that copyhold tenure persisted in many parts of the British Isles during the seventeenth and eighteenth centuries. Copyholders enjoyed considerable security and paid low fixed rents – rents of assize, quit rents, reserved rents.[7] In areas of the North, tenants enjoyed "tenant right," which gave them security of tenure as compensation for border service until the 1620s and 1630s.[8] In Ulster there emerged in the late eighteenth and early nineteenth centuries, if not a new customary tenure, at least a new custom affecting landlord-tenant relations, known as the Ulster Custom. It gave tenants the right to sell the "interest" in their holding to a new tenant.[9]

Furthermore, dissimilarities between Ireland and Britain point to other variables besides the customary/contractual variable that must be taken into account in trying to explain the greater economic power of landowners in Britain. In important respects the landlord-tenant relationship in eighteenth-century Ireland was like the British and unlike the continental. Proprietary rent and contractual tenancy had become the predominant forms in Ireland as in England. Peasant proprietorship as found on the Continent was rare. Yet at the same time marked contrasts existed between Irish and English landlord-tenant relations. Three closely related differences were especially critical. The first was the practice of granting long leases. In England during the seventeenth and eighteenth centuries, landlords generally (though not in all areas) tried to reduce the number of years for which leases were granted, to rely less on fines, and to allow rents to be determined by market forces. This did not occur in Ireland. Second, the subletting of land was more common in Ireland. Owners of Irish estates often preferred to turn management over to an agent or a middleman. There was then nothing to stop the middleman from further subletting the holdings. The third difference between Irish and English landlord-tenant relations was the greater fragmentation of holdings in Ireland, as a result of which the owner of Irish land, insofar as he or she dealt with them at all, was dealing with a different kind of tenantry than the owner of English land. A shortage of Protestant tenants also undermined the economic bargaining power of Irish landowners, particularly in the North.[10] It was this weakness that led to the development of the Ulster Custom, which further undercut the landlord's power. For all of these reasons the economic power of landowners over their tenantry was less than one would expect if only the customary/contractual difference were considered.

Nonetheless, putting it all together, the economic power of British aristocrats over the peasantry was on average greater than that of continental aristocrats. Scottish landowners were especially powerful. Legally they could raise rents and accept the highest bidder – what the people called "rouping." Tenants were well aware that if evicted by their landlord, they were not likely to find land elsewhere. It was difficult to obtain land from an owner who belonged to a different clan. And the Scots were distrustful of strangers; tenants from other regions were often not accepted without a testimonial from their former landlord or minister.[11]

Even in the Highlands and Western Islands the peasantry suffered from insecurity. Control was exercised either by landowners themselves or by their "tacksmen" – middlemen who were usually close relatives of the landowner. As a result of this kinship tie, subletting did not undermine the owner's power over the peasantry as much as it did in Ireland. Although the tacksmen themselves held by lease, leases were otherwise unusual in the Highlands and Western Islands. Virtually all the occupiers were tenants-at-will or yearly tenants to the tacksmen, who thereby enjoyed, in strict legal terms, the power to retain or dismiss tenants at their pleasure. Typically the tacksman was an integral part of the society in which he lived and therefore subject to social pressures to conform to norms of the fair treatment of tenants and followers. Yet considerable power lay in their hands, and arbitrary use of this power was far from unknown.[12]

Scottish peasants got the worst of both regimes. Obligations of lordship persisted longer than elsewhere in the British Isles, while at the same time customary protection of tenants declined, except for those who held by *feu ferme*. Peasants relied heavily on maintaining a cooperative relationship with their landlord, often based on real or fictitious kinship ties. Tenants frequently invoked a presumed kinship tie in an effort to persuade their landlord to treat them leniently. Until the late eighteenth century, appeals of this kind were in many cases successful, but the vulnerable position of Scottish tenants was revealed by the clearances that took place in the late eighteenth and nineteenth centuries.

Role in Agriculture

It is widely believed that British landowners were more active in agriculture than continental nobles. Yet it is also well known that demesne farming declined in the British Isles during the late Middle Ages and the Early Modern period. It is now also generally recognized that notions of British "capitalist landowners" are misleading. The British agricultural revolution was carried out primarily by tenant farmers, not landowners. At the same time, Robert Forster's contention that many provincial nobles in France tried to manage their estates efficiently has come to be widely accepted.[13]

The fact of the matter is that many continental nobles farmed their own lands. Most *gentilshommes campagnards* could ill afford not to do so.[14] Rules of *dérogeance* did not prohibit nobles from farming their own lands of no more than four *charrues*. In Savoy they could farm their own lands and even, if necessary, those of another.[15] Nobles might also be found supervising the agricultural practices of peasants.

Sharecropping, in particular, required the landowner to become more involved in the productive process than was the case for landlords who leased to tenant farmers.[16] Arthur Young found French landlords supplying a share of livestock, seed, implements, and harnesses to *métayers*.[17]

Where dues or rents were paid in kind or partly in kind, seigneurs or landowners might have to market the agricultural produce. This was also the case in the British Isles, especially in Scotland, but on the whole landowners were less involved in marketing produce in the British Isles than they were in our continental countries. English landowners were not as active in the wool trade as were French nobles in the wine trade.[18] Sharecropping also involved the landowner in agricultural marketing more than did other forms of land tenure. In the course of the eighteenth century there was a change in marketing practices. French noble landlords gave up the traditional method of marketing through small brokers; instead, they held the produce until the most favourable moment to sell.[19] In Vannes they sold their grain for cash to merchants or agents, and they were known to drive a hard bargain.[20]

Yet the conventional belief that French nobles were less active in agriculture was based on a real difference, a difference that significantly affected their comparative economic power. The evidence available suggests that the British Isles had more "improving landlords" – landlords who, in farming demesne land, were willing to make investments in the enterprise and to experiment with new methods of agriculture. A larger number of British landowners also took an interest in the agricultural activities of their tenants, encouraging them to make improvements and to adopt new techniques and perhaps helping them finance these innovations, though not typically carrying them out themselves.[21] The demesne farm in the British Isles was often managed by the landlord out of an interest in agriculture, while in France when an aristocrat engaged in farming himself it was typically out of necessity and usually on a small scale. Most French nobles freed themselves from such cares if they could, whereas in the British Isles even peers could be found directing, in person or by post, the management of their estates, often making decisions about matters of detail.[22] Even Forster, in his defence of French provincial nobles, admits that it was rare for them to alter crop courses, plant forage crops, or improve livestock in the way that the English did.[23]

Moreover, it was noted in chapter 4 that landowners also played a role in reorganizing British agriculture by facilitating the transfer of land to large tenant farmers. Although it was the large farmer, not the landowner, who was the capitalist, the role of landowners was still instrumental. Admittedly, many French seigneurs and landowners also tried to reorganize agriculture, and in particular to acquire more control over communal lands, but they were neither as active nor as successful as British landowners in this regard.

Several explanations can be offered for these differences. The paramount factor was the economic power of British aristocrats over the peasantry. British tenants posed less resistance to the interest a landowner might take in farming. French peasants were bound together by greater communal solidarity and customary norms, such as *vaine pâture* and *parcours*, which made it difficult for a seigneur or owner to introduce significant changes. In addition, the fact that continental nobles had proprietorial control over a smaller percentage of the land than British aristocrats meant they had less power to reorganize or improve farms. Their seigneurial rights did give them certain powers over peasant proprietors, but these were circumscribed and certainly did not draw seigneurs into much agricultural improvement. The effect of tenurial regimes is revealed both by comparing the British Isles with the Continent and by making comparisons within the British Isles. Landowners whose land was held in non-customary tenure could regulate the husbandry of their tenants in a way that landowners whose land was let in customary tenure could not.[24] As leases developed in England, they often stipulated care of the owner's property and sometimes rules of husbandry.[25] Scottish landlords had more freedom to improve their estates, particularly to improve their tenantry, than any other group of landlords we are studying. The economic power of Scottish Lowland landowners over tenants permitted them to assist large farmers in transforming Scottish agriculture in the eighteenth century. A good proportion of the land was engrossed and enclosed, thus forcing out many small tenants.[26]

Differences in power over the peasantry do not, however, account for the failure of continental landowners to innovate on farms they let contractually. There must, then, be additional factors that need to be considered in order to explain the smaller role of the continental nobility in agriculture.

Certainly one other factor was the way in which aristocratic status was institutionalized in the British Isles, where a landed estate was more essential to aristocratic status than in France, Savoy, or the Southern Low Countries. Thus it was all the more critical that the land be made profitable so that the owner was not forced to sell it. A continental noble whose agricultural properties were losing money could sell them and invest the proceeds in other ways, and yet remain a noble. True, ownership of a fief reinforced noble status even in the eighteenth century, but by this time acquisition of a fief did not confer noble status on a person, and loss of a fief did not deprive one of it. In contrast, members of the British gentry who lost all their land would lose gentry status.

The fact that continental nobles were less often resident on their estates would obviously also decrease the likelihood they would devote much time to agriculture. The aristocracy in our continental countries was more urbanized than the aristocracy in the British Isles. A larger proportion owned little or no land, and even among those who did own land a larger proportion lived in towns. This resulted from a considerable movement of nobles to continental cities and towns in the Early Modern period. At the same time the ennoblement of office-holders further increased the proportion of the continental nobility that was urban. Many urban nobles kept a house in the country, but it was often not their principal residence, and some had no country residence at all. By comparison, British landowners less often lived in urban centres, or if they did, they visited their country estates more frequently than continental nobles. This enabled them to play a greater role in the rural economy.

Historians who have made this kind of argument can find support in a comparison of the role of landlords in England and in Ireland. The failure of Irish landowners to improve agriculture has been iden-tified as a major cause of the backwardness of the Irish economy.[27] Irish landowners have gone down in history as one of Europe's worst landowning classes, while English landowners are considered one of Europe's best, certainly its most economically progressive, enlight-ened, and conscientious. Yet the curious thing is that probably about a fifth of the land in Ireland was owned by proprietors living in Britain. Many of the rest were descendants of people who had come to Ireland from England in the previous one or two centuries. Many landowners resident in Ireland were related by blood or marriage to British families. Almost all Irish landowners shared the values, aspirations, and interests of the British gentry. They were exposed to the same literature and had much the same education. The same technology was available to them. Why were they such bad landlords?

Part of the answer is that they were not so bad. One can find many Irish landlords who invested in their properties, enclosed land, fos-tered agricultural innovation and improvements, assisted peasants in the acquisition of further knowledge of agricultural techniques, and constructed estate villages, market houses, and roads.[28] Another part of the answer lies in the difficult relationship that prevailed between landlord and tenant as a result of their differences in religion and ethnicity. In addition, partible inheritance among the peasantry contributed to the fragmentation of holdings. And much of the subletting was carried out by farmers and middlemen, not landowners.

Insofar as Irish landowners themselves were not as improving as English landowners, the primary reason was clearly the higher rate of absenteeism. The presence of resident landowners obviously encouraged involvement. In rural areas, resident landowners usually had little else to keep them busy, except for hunting and building. Whatever an agent might do, the absentee owner himself or herself was not as much involved in this management as a resident owner would be. Thus absenteeism almost certainly gave Irish landowners less economic power over agriculture. Whether it was also responsible for the poor management of estates in Ireland is another question. One cannot say that the property of a resident landowner was necessarily better managed than that of an absentee. It depended on the agent. A poor agent could be extremely destructive of the interests of either the owner, the tenants, or both. In 1782 Lady Louisa Conolly complained about the agent on an estate that her husband had inherited in County Londonderry:

It is the estate that came to him by the death of the late Lord Conyngham, and which has been so neglected that an agent of his had done exactly what he pleased there, and set leases that Mr Conolly is obliged to break ... I am not sorry that we are to stay a fortnight, as in that time we may hear how the poor peasants have been used, which I believe has been very indifferently, according to the custom of many places in Ireland where there is no head landlord resident in the neighbourhood.[29]

One Irish gentleman complained about the neglect of estates by Irish landowners and their mistaken faith in agents, many of whom were chosen with little care. "We see but few agents that take any pains to make their employers acquainted with the situation or condition of their estates," he lamented.[30] It is, of course, difficult to say if Irish agents were generally worse than English agents. We do know that the former were more often the younger sons of minor gentry. This was not, however, the critical difference. What mattered was the ability of the owner to monitor the behaviour of his or her agent. If a landowner were resident or could visit the property regularly, he or she would not run the same risk of damage to property or income from a bad agent.

Exploitation of Natural Resources
Seigneurs and landowners could earn considerable income from timber. This was especially the case in England, Scotland, the Ardennes,

large parts of Savoy, and the hilly regions of France. A striking case
was the seigneurie of Durbuy in the Ardennes. The revenue from the
woods rose from less than half the seigneurial dues in the late 1730s
to more than twice in the 1770s. The difference subsequently
declined. Nonetheless, the woods continued to yield more income
than seigneurial dues.[31] The same was true of the seigneurie of Pont-
St-Pierre in Normandy.[32]

In the British Isles, common minerals were the property of the
landed proprietor. Some owners worked their mines directly, while
others leased them out for long terms. It is well known that landed
wealth in Durham, Staffordshire, and Cornwall, for example, was
heavily based on mining, but examples of landowners exploiting
resources under their property can also be found in Cumberland,
Shropshire, Nottinghamshire, and South Wales, especially Glamorgan.[33] The most successful coal entrepreneurs in Scotland during the
seventeenth century were landowners who mined their land directly.
In the eighteenth century the newer coalfields found in the Clyde
Basin were exploited in the majority by independent lessees. All the
same, landowners were still active.[34]

In the Principality of Liège, minerals under the ground belonged
to the proprietor as they did in the British Isles, while in Hainaut they
belonged to the seigneur, though the sovereign enjoyed rights to
precious minerals (gold, silver, iron, and lead).[35] In France, mining
was originally a seigneurial privilege, but since the fifteenth century
the monarchy had imposed a 10 per cent tax; and in 1744 it claimed
ownership of the subsoil. In fact, however, it was the seigneur who
continued to control the exploitation of the resources under the land
and the decree of 1744 helped the larger seigneurs to force out the
small operators.[36]

Thus natural resources constituted a potential source of income for
aristocrats in several of our countries, or, more precisely, in specific
regions of several of our countries. It was least important in Ireland
because natural resources were less plentiful there. Yet, even in Ireland, landowners were prominent in the exploitation of natural
resources.[37]

Returns from Land

How good was land, then, as a source of investment and income? In
one sense, no doubt, it provided a secure investment. Land could
generate profit by rising in value and it was not subject to as much
risk as most other financial ventures. Such profits, however, could only
be realized if a family sold land and reduced its total ownership. This
was something they did, as a rule, only when deep in debt.

Meanwhile, the income yielded by land was often irregular. It was not rare for a landowner to be driven into bankruptcy when he or she could not meet financial obligations because, often as a result of hard times, tenants were in arrears. Moreover, the income from land was usually less than what it would be from many of its alternatives. In France it was known for people to realize 1 to 2 per cent on land, while they could get 5 per cent from merchants; they could even be found borrowing money to buy land at these rates.[38] In mid-eighteenth-century England the average return on land through rent was about 3 or 4 per cent per annum, after costs were deducted.[39] The experience of a Dublin businessman, Sir Nicholas Lawless, later Lord Cloncurry, indicates the cost that could be borne by those who invested in land. The estate of Abington, County Limerick, which he purchased in 1775, "cost £26,000, which producing but £650 yearly is at the rate of forty years purchase, or only 2½% for the money – hitherto a dear bargain." In 1778 he had several loans paying 5 per cent as well as government debentures realizing 4 per cent. Although by the 1790s Sir Nicholas was realizing as much from his landed estates as he was from alternative investments, this was only possible because rents rose unusually rapidly.[40]

I think we should conclude that landed income kept up with inflation better in the British Isles than in our continental countries, but it would be foolish to insist that landed incomes on the Continent were completely inflexible. Some seigneurial dues were paid in kind, in which case they could rise with inflation. The same was true of *métayage*. Even the Norman *rente foncière* could be adjusted to meet price inflation.[41] Nonetheless, to the extent that there was a difference between aristocrats in the British Isles and those in our continental countries, it was that the former had more flexible income, primarily because seigneurial dues and customary rents were more often fixed than proprietary and contractual rents. British aristocrats also relied for their incomes on fines and natural resources, both of which were relatively flexible. And the inclusion in many rental agreements of demands for payments in kind and labour dues, the value of which fluctuated with prices, further increased the flexibility of income from contractual tenancies. The larger number of enclosures in the British Isles also made a difference, enabling rental revenues to advance with the general elevation of prices.[42]

It must be understood that all this flexibility required effort on the part of landowners. A landowner who did not take advantage of the natural resources on or under the property, or one who let land on long leases, would not have benefited from rising prices. However, Scottish and English landowners did not generally get themselves caught with long leases, at least not as often as Irish landowners.

Unfortunately, it is not possible to make reliable comparisons of rents between the British Isles and the Continent, but we can compare yields, which would have had a considerable effect on rents. B.H. Slicher van Bath once estimated that yield ratios in England and the Low Countries exceeded 4:1 during the Middle Ages, reached 6:1 in the early 1600s, and were close to 10:1 in the late 1700s, while in France they did not exceed 4:1 even in the eighteenth century.[43] His figures have, however, been revised and there is now considerable debate on this subject, some historians arguing that the differences were greater, others that the differences were less.[44] Michel Morineau contends that the differences in yields between England and France are greatly reduced if the comparison is confined to the large north-western region from Flanders to Brittany.[45] In any case, there is still a difference, one that would lead us to conclude that income from agriculture was higher in England and the Low Countries than in France.

Returns from land also varied with commercialization, which increased the surplus that could be appropriated by the landlord and also intensified competition for land, thereby driving rents upward. Thus landed incomes were generally higher in southern England, the Low Countries, and the Paris Basin, in contrast with areas of less commercialization, most notably western parts of Ireland and Wales, northern England, the Scottish Highlands and Western Islands, many areas in the French Midi and in Savoy, and even a few parts of the Low Countries, Luxembourg, for example.

Office-holding

Estimating returns from land does not capture all the benefits to be enjoyed by being an aristocrat, and especially not those benefits ensuing from the rise of the state. Sovereigns had always used a variety of rewards – pensions, lands, profits of state, employment, and outright gifts – to secure the support of aristocrats, both the great and the small. One of the benefits of aristocratic status was a certain entitlement to the munificence of the crown, reinforced by the personal contact with the monarch that might go with such status. With the rise of the state in the late Middle Ages and the Early Modern period, some of these rewards became more important than others. Those increasing most in importance were state offices.

In all our countries aristocrats sought offices. In the British Isles they were valuable as a result of the relatively strict adherence to primogeniture. Aristocratic families often took care of non-inheriting sons by finding them a good government job. In Scotland the pressure for offices was intense because the effects of primogeniture were made more severe by the greater financial problems of the Scottish aristocracy. The extraordinary use made of patronage for the governing of Scotland (to be discussed in the next chapter) has often been attributed in part to the desperate need of the Scottish elite for state positions. The value of office-holding for the Irish aristocracy can be illustrated by the fact that in 1783 some 37 per cent of the 150 Irish peers held or had held office in the royal household, in the central government, in the foreign service, or in the armed services, or had been or were colonial governors.[46] True, many offices were costly. The duties and life style of a statesman could easily exceed the remuneration provided. Often the reason that aristocrats were appointed to offices was that only they could afford to run the losses that some of these positions entailed. Arthur Chichester had to be given substantial grants of land in Ireland before he was appointed lord deputy in 1605 so he would be able to meet the expenses of high office, but the lands proved insufficient for this purpose and he was in financial difficulty throughout his career.[47] Most offices were, however, profitable and represented a useful source of income for aristocratic families who could acquire them.[48]

We shall see later in this chapter that the inheritance practices that prevailed on the Continent did not penalize younger sons to the extent that British practices did. On the other hand, the landed estates that were being divided up in Savoy, France, and the Southern Low Countries were usually not large enough to sustain the life style considered appropriate to noble status. In 1743 Karel F. van de Werve of Antwerp was described as belonging to "an ancient very noble and distinguished family, of conduct worthy of his birth, but deprived of proportionate means." His candidature for burgomaster in 1772 was promoted on the grounds that he was "in need of help" because he was "burdened with a large family, with little means, and too much integrity to increase it through indirect means."[49] Fortunately for such people, the Austrian government was sympathetic towards hard-pressed nobles and gave them preference in appointments to state offices.

In France, state offices were investments that one purchased in expectation of a return. Revenues of state office were lower in Savoy than in France. Most striking, given their status, was the inadequate remuneration of magistrates of the Senate and the Chamber of Accounts, as a result of which most of those who held the post had to have considerable alternative resources.[50] Yet state office formed a crucial part of the income of many Savoyard noble families.[51]

The problem, of course, was the capital needed to purchase an office. Wealthy noble families could obtain them, but they were hardly a means by which to find employment for a younger son in a noble family that was experiencing financial hardship. Indeed, an impoverished noble family would have found it a struggle to pay the *paulette*. Offices were less expensive in the Southern Low Countries. The *médianate* was typically less than the cost of offices in France, and the nobility was given a 50 per cent discount. Yet many nobles still could not afford them, especially in poorer regions such as Luxembourg.[52] As in the British Isles, some positions, such as membership on a provincial council in the Austrian Low Countries, did not generate much income, certainly relative to the life style that people thought a councillor should enjoy.[53] A poor noble could entertain greater hopes of pursuing a military career than a bureaucratic one, but even a military career was costly.

In this regard the major difference between the British Isles and France was that, by the eighteenth century, the monarchy in the former had less wealth to bestow than did the monarchy in the latter. This difference had not existed in the sixteenth century, but by the end of the seventeenth century the British crown had enough difficulty meeting its household expenditures, let alone lavishly subsidizing the aristocracy. Court offices were limited in number and not especially rewarding; and sometimes the pay for such offices was in arrears.[54] In addition, the British bureaucracy was smaller than the French, providing fewer offices to dispense. On the other hand, the power of the French crown to bestow offices was constrained by the venality and inheritance of offices in France.

Non-agricultural Rental Revenue

Non-agricultural rental revenue included income from urban land and buildings, government securities, annuities, and other investments that provided a steady return. They were a vital source of income for the aristocracy in all our countries. In the British Isles the bulk of urban property was owned by large landowners. In many cases the landlord played an active role in urban development; the role of the Fifth Earl (First Marquess) of Donegall in the building of Belfast is a case in point.[55] In most instances, urban rents constituted only a small proportion of the income of these owners, but in some instances the urban rents were significant.

Nobles in our continental countries were even more dependent on this source of income because a greater proportion of them owned little or no agricultural land. They supported themselves, sometimes in high style, sometimes in a rather modest style, by investing. The most popular were loans to the government. As Daniel Dessert has shown, investors in France included all nobles with money, robe and sword, and especially the very wealthy high nobility. Nobles lent directly to the king or purchased state annuities or the right to collect many royal fees or taxes. Noble fortunes constituted a major source of borrowing for all the tax farmers and other financiers. Women, in particular widows, were prominent. The whole system of state financing in France could not have functioned without these aristocratic investors.[56]

Non-agricultural Business

Aristocratic status was enjoyed by people who engaged in non-agricultural economic activity and by people who did not. Insofar as aristocratic status was a factor, it simply raised or lowered the probability that an individual would be found undertaking non-agricultural business. Some characteristics associated with the aristocracy increased the probability; other characteristics reduced it.

One factor that made it less likely to find aristocrats in business was the historical position of the aristocracy in the economic structure; they were primarily seigneurs or landowners and traditionally depended on land for their income. This was more the case in the British Isles than on the Continent, but the majority of aristocrats were oriented towards the land on both sides of the English Channel.

A second factor was the strong tendency for many successful members of the aristocracy to enter politics or state service rather than to engage in business. Consequently, many successful aristocrats were simply too busy to engage directly in business activity, especially in the British Isles.

The third factor, and the one that I want to discuss at the greatest length, consisted of a certain set of values and norms that discouraged economic activity. There was a snobbish view towards work. Aristocrats customarily made a virtue of avoiding it. Leisure was a symbol of aristocratic status. They also made distinctions among different kinds of work. Obviously military, intellectual, and religious effort had higher status than manual labour, but they also had higher status than business. Such attitudes were found among aristocrats in all five countries, but were strongest in Savoy and most of France and weaker in most of the British Isles and in parts of the Southern Low Countries.

There are several reasons why opposition to non-agricultural business was weaker in most of the British Isles and in parts of the Southern Low Countries. One is maritime trade, which seems to have encouraged a more flexible frame of mind. Within France, attitudes towards business were most favourable and rules of *dérogeance* were least enforced in coastal centres. The right of the nobility of Marseilles to engage in maritime trade was granted by the crown in the sixteenth century.[57] In Brittany the traditional custom allowed nobles to relinquish their noble status temporarily if they engaged in overseas trade; their *noblesse dormante* would be restored if they gave up trade.

The Irish aristocracy was divided in its attitude towards business between an older elite with a favourable disposition and a newer elite with less interest in business. In the past the aristocracy had been more active in business (especially in foreign and colonial ventures) than they were in the eighteenth century. The new aristocracy was drawn disproportionately from landed, military, and administrative groups in the English population. They came to Ireland to establish landed estates and to live like the gentry. They regarded business as more derogatory than the older aristocracy. During the eighteenth century the values of these new aristocrats were hegemonic in Irish society. Even Catholics came to accept them, though Catholics were relatively active in trade in the eighteenth century, because they had better continental connections than Protestants, because they were excluded from other pursuits, but also because they still retained some of the older values that were less hostile to non-agricultural economic activity.[58]

What impact did the rise of the state have on such attitudes? The principal effect on the Continent was the development of royal legislation on *dérogeance*, both for and against nobles engaging in business. Many statesmen and officials wanted to stimulate the participation of nobles in business and they were often able to persuade the king to support them. As a result, legislation was enacted to encourage aristocrats to enter business. Even in Savoy, a land-based state, Emanuel Filibert tried to interest the nobility in commerce and issued edicts proclaiming that wholesale commerce did not entail *dérogeance*.[59] In France a few enactments sought to undermine rules of *dérogeance* in the fifteenth and sixteenth centuries, but the bulk of the legislation appeared in the seventeenth and eighteenth centuries. The French crown frequently issued special decrees to assure nobles that engaging in commerce would not threaten their noble status. And some merchants were ennobled.[60] In the Spanish/Austrian Low Countries nobles were encouraged to enter wholesale trade in edicts of 1694, 1698, 1722, and 1736, in the last of which *commerce en gros* was referred to as an "honourable occupation."[61] Explicit permission was often given to individual nobles in the Southern Low Countries to undertake wholesale trade without incurring *dérogeance*. Noble status was restored for some families whose members had engaged in commerce. And a considerable number of men of commerce were ennobled in the eighteenth century, more than in any other occupational group except for functionaries.[62]

No effort was made to disguise the objective. In both France and the Southern Low Countries, contemporaries believed that the failure of nobles to engage in business weakened the economy. Whether the aristocracy should engage in business was an issue in France to a greater extent than anywhere else. There was more literary opposition to it, but also more literary encouragement of it.[63] Such encouragement could also be found in the Southern Low Countries. In 1765 Nicolas Bacon, a deputy councillor of commercial affairs, expressed the hope that nobles in the Austrian Low Countries would follow the example of the English and Dutch nobility and engage in trade.[64]

The state was not, however, of one mind on the question of *dérogeance*. While some state activity sought to undermine norms of *dérogeance*, other state activity reinforced it. It is not often realized that the very notion of *dérogeance* evolved with the state institutionalization of aristocratic status. It originated in the fourteenth century and further developed thereafter.[65] In 1435 French nobles lost exemption from the *taxe de huitième* if they sold their wine directly "because it is not the place of a noble to be a tavern keeper."[66] In 1560, in the first year of the reign of Charles IX, it was "forbidden of all *gentilshommes* to engage in trade" on pain of losing their privileges and paying the *taille*. Charles also rejected a request of the nobility of Touraine to engage in trade without loss of noble status and privileges.[67] Although legislation encouraging nobles to enter business became predominant during the seventeenth and eighteenth centuries, the earlier enforcement of *dérogeance* had successfully institutionalized the traditional aversion to business activity.

In addition, even during the seventeenth and eighteenth centuries the position of the French crown was contradictory. One of the reasons it did not give up rules of *dérogeance* altogether was that it did not want businessmen to enjoy noble tax exemptions. Royal officials frequently tried to force nobles to pay more tax on the grounds that they were engaged in business activities or were farming more than the four *charrues* for which they enjoyed exemption. In 1756 legislation was drawn up, though not enacted, strengthening the law of *dérogeance*.[68] It should be conceded that, in the eighteenth century, nobles who possessed unambiguous proof of noble status could engage in business activity with less fear than their ancestors. Yet in other ways the new requirements of verification discouraged business activity. Nobles otherwise willing to engage in business might hesitate for fear of losing noble status or its privileges. This kind of fear reached a peak during the periods of the French *recherches* because economic activity was frequently used by commissioners to justify denying noble status and forcing a person to pay the *taille*. The French king might make high-sounding pronouncements that encouraged nobles to engage in business, but at the same time he was sending commissioners into the provinces looking for any reason they could find to deprive families of noble status and force them to pay the *taille*. Inevitably many nobles remained cautious.

Attitudes in the more commercialized parts of the Southern Low Countries may have been more favourable to nobles engaging in business than in most of France, but the Spanish/Austrian Low Countries were ruled by conservative land-based centres, where enthusiasm was comparatively restrained. The legislation of 1616, regulating aristocratic status in the Spanish Low Countries, institutionalized *dérogeance*, though it did not specify the occupations that "soiled" noble status. As I said in chapter 5, it enabled nobles who had engaged in a derogatory activity to obtain letters of rehabilitation from the sovereign. It was, however, only with this royal rehabilitation and if the person gave up the derogatory activity that he or she could enjoy noble status. In 1650 Philip IV ordered the governor general to enforce this requirement because the Council of Brabant had been supporting those who were ignoring it.[69] In the same period the Madrid government was fighting with the Privy Council over the rights of English merchants living in the Low Countries who wanted to engage in trade while at the same time claim noble status.[70] In 1651 Philip reaffirmed the interdiction against foreign nobles enjoying "the privileges, honours, and immunities possessed by nobles in the Low Countries, unless they first give up and abandon their said profession and obtain my letters of rehabilitation."[71] Wholesale trade was encouraged by royal enactments. Nevertheless, it was stipulated in the legislation of 1694 that one needed "particular permission from his Majesty" to engage in it.[72] Shortly thereafter the famous printer of religious works, Balthasar Moretus, whose father had been ennobled in 1692, had to request special permission to continue his printing business after he was ennobled.[73]

The legislation that gradually loosened restrictions in the Spanish/Austrian Low Countries on noble business activity came primarily as a result of demands from the Low Countries made by the provincial councils, the Privy Council, and the Council of State, whose members generally wanted restrictions on noble business activity to be abolished. The central government usually did not want to go much further than encourage nobles to engage in wholesale commerce. It did not like the idea of businessmen enjoying privilege.

We can now turn to factors that increased the number of aristocrats engaging in non-agricultural business activity. Landownership induced many aristocrats to engage in economic activities that were related to the exploitation of resources found on or under their land. Ironically, it was often aristocrats who lived in economically less developed regions (in Scotland, Savoy, and Luxembourg, for example), where such resources were sometimes more plentiful, who were drawn in this way into non-agricultural activity.[74] Yet in all our countries we find them overrepresented in mining, lumbering, and metallurgy.[75] Metallurgy was in some ways a traditional form of economic participation and grew naturally from the exploitation of land, while in other ways, especially with regard to the size of some enterprises, it was a modern type of economic activity.[76]

Aristocrats were more likely than non-aristocrats to enjoy royal privileges or receive state contracts. This was particularly true in France. Although his efforts were not very successful, Colbert created royal companies in order (among other things) to provide opportunities for the nobility to participate in business.[77] French aristocrats were also not above creating their own monopolies that were as restrictive as those of the traditional guilds. Until the reforms of A.-R.-J. Turgot (finance minister to Louis XVI), a landowners' syndicate in Provence had a monopoly over the sale of wine in Marseilles.[78]

A major factor that brought aristocrats into non-agricultural business was their wealth. Those aristocrats who were poor or unable to obtain credit did not engage in much non-agricultural economic activity,[79] but those with considerable wealth or with the credit necessary to obtain loans were very likely to undertake at least some business venture. Even in Scotland many landowners had access to capital and were comparatively willing to make long-term investments that did not bring immediate returns.[80] Furthermore, aristocrats were often able to get themselves into state positions where they could use tax money to make investments out of which they could profit.

As a consequence, aristocrats were overrepresented in economic activities requiring large amounts of capital. Because it was regarded as less derogatory, aristocrats were especially willing to invest in wholesale and overseas trade. They were also overrepresented in moneylending, finance, and banking. Even Irish landowners were relatively active in banking,[81] but the continental aristocracy was generally more often engaged in finance than the British. In most of Europe, lending money to the crown was regarded as serving the crown and thus in keeping with noble values.[82] On the Continent, nobles were also more likely to engage in state finance than in trade or industry as a result of the geographical pattern of political and economic power: towns that were primarily political rather than economic were frequently centres of finance. In Toulouse and even Luxembourg, for example, financial administration was a means to greater affluence.[83]

Among the various financial roles in which they took part, members of the older nobility in France were more commonly found among investors than among financiers. Financiers usually came from recently ennobled robe families.[84] Yves Durand has provided a statistical analysis of 220 of the 223 persons who became *fermiers généraux* (including *adjoints*) from 1726 to 1791. Of the 220, some 65 per cent were nobles when they joined. How long they or their families had been nobles is known for about 90 per cent of them, among whom 28 per cent were first generation (most of whom were ennobled by office before joining the *fermiers généraux*), 60 per cent were second or third, and 12 per cent were fourth or more. Of the remainder who became *fermiers généraux*, 34 per cent were sons of persons who had purchased an ennobling office, while another 34 per cent purchased an ennobling office themselves after joining the *ferme*, thus becoming nobles during or after their term.[85]

Norms of *dérogeance* led aristocrats to prefer anonymity when they engaged in business activity. This could mean investment in joint-stock companies or even the use of *prête-noms*.[86] In many cases participation was relatively passive and only small amounts were invested, especially in the same enterprise. Nevertheless, one historian has estimated that almost a thousand landowners took part in various company ventures launched in England between 1575 and 1630, representing almost 16 per cent of the total number of investors.[87] Ironically, for a number of reasons, there was a tendency for the aristocracy to be active in the most modern forms of industry, those requiring the most capital investment, those outside the control of guilds, those with the most capitalist organization, and those that were most innovative. Even in the textile industry, in which the nobility were not especially prominent, when they did play a part it was usually in relatively innovative enterprises and outside the control of guilds.[88]

Aristocrats were also active, especially in England and Scotland, in the regulation of industry, in leadership roles, or in some other way encouraging economic development, even when they did not participate themselves.[89] They were frequently appointed to boards set up to encourage one industry or another. In Scotland and Ireland landowners played an instrumental role in the linen industry. The Scottish Board of Trustees for Manufactures was dominated by landowners.[90] Most of the linen market halls in the Lagan Valley were constructed by landowners.[91] They were often active in building roads, canals, ports, or other components of the infrastructure.[92]

On the whole, the English aristocracy was the most involved in non-agricultural economic activity, primarily because anti-business values were weaker in England, because the aristocracy was in a good position to exploit natural resources on the land, because its rules of inheritance encouraged family members to find careers off the land, and because, as we shall conclude below, it was also the wealthiest. Surprisingly, the Scottish landowners may have been the second most involved. Although this aristocracy was not especially wealthy, it was in a good position to exploit natural resources, its rules of inheritance encouraged younger sons to enter business, and aristocratic ideological opposition to business was very weak in Scotland. The Irish and continental aristocracies were all less involved, but the differences were not as great as the traditional stereotypes of the aristocracy once led us to believe. Prejudices against business and the absence of natural resources explain why the Irish were less active. A number of factors encouraged nobles on the Continent to engage in non-agricultural economic activity: they were more urban than British landowners; they were involved in state finance; and they could obtain state privileges in certain types of economic ventures. Yet ideological opposition to non-agricultural economic activity was greater on the Continent.

WEALTH, INCOME, AND ECONOMIC POWER

Differences between Continental and British Aristocracy

The wealth of continental nobles varied greatly. In the Beauvais region studied by Pierre Goubert, half the noble revenues in the 1690s belonged to thirteen great families, none of whom lived in the region.[93] In the *élection* of Bayeux the poorest half of the nobility enjoyed less than 10 per cent of the income, while the wealthiest tenth enjoyed over half the income; this was the situation in both the sixteenth and the seventeenth centuries.[94] In Savoy during the eighteenth century roughly 20 per cent of the nobility enjoyed 60 to 70 per cent of the revenues of the group. Some 28 per cent of the nobility employed 70 per cent of the servants.[95] It was often the case that a limited number of nobles owned great properties, while most nobles owned small estates. In Genevois, for example, only 15.3 per cent of the nobles owned more than 100 hectares (247 acres), but those who did monopolized 67.8 per cent of the noble-owned land.[96]

There really was a poor nobility. In Saint-Brieuc in Brittany, one-third of the nobility was reduced to begging. In Plouha over half the nobility was exempt from the *capitation* because they were too poor.[97] In the Beauvais region studied by Goubert, some third of the nobility would have to be categorized as *pauvres honteux*.[98] One source suggested that two-thirds of the nobility of Savoy could not afford a noble life style.[99] "At Boussy," it was recorded, "Jacques de Motz cultivated his own land and lived in a house without locks: no furniture, no linen, no clothes; his wife 'never had more than one dress' and she went barefoot." Things got so bad that "the couple fought with fire logs and frying pans in scenes that were notorious in the parish."[100] Poverty among the nobility was more serious in Savoy and especially in Brittany than it was elsewhere, but it was also widespread in the Midi. Indeed, everywhere in France, even in Paris, poor nobles were to be seen living in a state of perpetual embarrassment because their standard of living did not accord with their aristocratic status.

We do not find poor gentry in England as we find poor nobility in France. In certain respects, this made for greater equality in the English aristocracy than in the French nobility. Yet inequality characterized the British aristocracy as well because some British aristocrats were fabulously rich. In the late seventeenth century the annual income of the Earl of Devonshire was over £17,000, while the Duke of Newcastle took in about £25,000. Incomes of other great peers in the early eighteenth century were over £20,000.[101] This was at a time when a good lawyer earned £100. The weight of the evidence indicates that land distribution within the English aristocracy became even more unequal during the eighteenth century. F.M.L. Thompson has estimated that the proportion of the land owned by the "great landlords" was 15 to 20 per cent in the seventeenth century, but rose to 20 to 25 per cent by 1790.[102] Although the reasons given by J.H. Habakkuk for the increased concentration of landownership in the first half of the eighteenth century have been challenged, the trend in favour of large landowners has been confirmed by most subsequent studies.[103]

Estimates of the income of the aristocracy as a whole are available for England and France. They show that only 14 per cent of the French nobility earned more than 10,000 livres (£400), compared with the 23 per cent of the English gentry that earned more than £625; less than 1 per cent of the French nobility earned more than 50,000 livres (£2000), whereas 8 per cent of the English gentry earned more than £2000.[104] While these estimates could no doubt be improved, they do support the general presumption that the English aristocracy was wealthier than the French. This is not to deny that many of the "parish gentry" in England had limited resources, especially in more northern counties. A good number were not lords of manors or even free-holders. Many were copyholders, often tenants on large crown manors. Their level of material affluence would be little different from that of yeomen. There were also younger sons whose livelihood was uncertain. The number of poor aristocrats was, however, much larger in France. Although France was a wealthy country and some French nobles were very rich, the average wealth of French nobles was generally lower.

As well as poor nobles, a good number of continental nobles owned little or no land because they had alternative investments. Many of the *noblesse de robe* resided in urban centres and lived primarily off non-agricultural and non-seigneurial investments. The average size of noble estates in France in the eighteenth century has been estimated at 370 acres.[105] It is thought that the nobility in France owned 20 to 25 per cent of the land; even the nobility and the bourgeoisie together owned only 40 to 45 per cent.[106] Estimates for the Southern Low Countries reveal that the nobility owned 10 to 25 per cent of the land. For Savoy the figure is 17 per cent.[107]

Thompson has estimated that in the eighteenth century 60 to 85 per cent of the land in England was owned by the peerage and gentry.[108] Some of the sources he was forced to use are of doubtful reliability. Nonetheless, his analysis suggests that the distribution of land was relatively stable over time. Thus we can make use of a survey whose reliability is not in doubt, which was carried out in the 1870s, if we keep in mind that some change may have taken place in the preceding hundred years. This return showed that 55 per cent of the land was in the hands of owners of 1000 acres or more.[109] A similar survey carried out in Ireland in the 1870s showed an even greater concentration; 78 per cent of the land was owned by landowners with estates of 1000 acres or more.[110]

The one kind of economic power that many French aristocrats did enjoy more than their British counterparts was financial power. Many aristocrats were investors, usually purchasers of government securities. Some were also financiers. French financiers were extremely wealthy, but a greater source of economic power than their personal fortunes was the money they controlled. The state depended on both financiers and aristocratic investors to supply it with the credit it needed to operate. It should be allowed that political leaders had considerable power over financiers. Royal ministers, in particular the comptroller general, could make or break the career of a financier. Yet the two were really mutually dependent and often bound together socially and politically.[111] The crown could not afford to alienate major financiers, while financiers were at the mercy of the crown to honour its obligations. It is also true that the economic power of financiers was fragmented. The crown itself, however, regularly sought to consolidate financiers into larger farms, the largest of which was the General Farm established by Colbert.[112]

We cannot generalize, however, from these noble investors or financiers to the nobility as a whole. Because they were generally not as wealthy as British aristocrats, most continental nobles did not have much capital of their own to invest. Continental aristocrats were certainly as active in wholesale trade as British aristocrats, perhaps in industry as well. They were not, however, as enterprising in exploiting the natural resources of the land as the English, Welsh, or Scottish aristocracy. Nor were they as enterprising in increasing the agricultural productiveness of their landed estates, though many engaged themselves in farming. And they did not have the same power over the rural economy that most British landowners had, with the result that they did not reorganize agriculture in the way that British landowners did. Altogether, it is clear that British aristocrats enjoyed more economic power than nobles in France, Savoy, or the Southern Low Countries. Why?

Reasons for Differences

Although many aristocrats were ruined by getting into non-agricultural ventures, on the whole non-agricultural business increased aristocratic economic power. It has been remarked several times that the return on non-agricultural investments was generally better than on land. The income from non-agricultural business was also more elastic than income from land and could provide seigneurs or landowners with a new infusion of badly needed cash, especially in regions where peasants were poor and often paid their rent in kind and/or irregularly. Since the English aristocracy was overall the most involved, they benefited the most from non-agricultural economic activity. Along with other impediments mentioned above, continental nobles were restricted by rules of *dérogeance*, which limited their participation in non-agricultural business and led them to play roles in which they exercised only limited economic power, such as rentiers or silent partners.

British aristocrats enjoyed more economic power (both personal wealth and power over the rural economy) because more of them had converted to contractual tenures and because their landed incomes were more flexible. While agricultural commercialization helps to explain many regional differences in landed income it does not explain differences between the British Isles and our continental countries, since both had their share of commercialized and non-commercialized regions. Similarly, higher yields increased the economic power of some English landowners, but the same cannot be said for many landowners in other parts of the British Isles whose land was inferior in quality to that of many continental landowners. On the other hand, a larger proportion of the land was owned by the aristocracy in Ireland, Scotland, and northern England than in most districts on the Continent.

Why did the British aristocracy own more land? Most writers have quite rightly stressed the smaller proportion of the land owned by the church and the peasantry. But there are additional reasons. We have repeatedly noticed the consequences of the more careful adherence to primogeniture in the British Isles. Along with the use of strict settlement, it helped to preserve estates over generations and even enabled them to expand. Differences in rules of inheritance created variation within the British Isles. It has been suggested that Welsh landowners were not as wealthy as English owing not only to poor soil conditions in much of Wales and its less commercialized economy, but also to partible inheritance customs that had formerly prevailed and had not disappeared altogether in the seventeenth and eighteenth centuries.[113]

The norms of inheritance followed by the nobility in our continental countries, known as *partage noble*, varied from one region to another according to customary law. A few examples are provided in table 9. Although less partible than the norms followed by continental non-nobles, *partage noble* was generally more partible than the norms followed by the British gentry. It is true that many inheritances were less partible than custom prescribed, but this did not negate the difference between the Continent and the British Isles. The long-term effect was to reduce the wealth of the continental aristocracy relative to the British.

This effect was compounded by differences in the way in which aristocratic status was institutionalized. Members of the British aristocracy had more land than their continental counterparts because landed wealth was a requisite for membership in the status group. It should be granted that it was difficult to become a noble in France, Savoy, or the Southern Low Countries without wealth, which was needed to buy an office, meet the wealth requirements that could be put on obtaining a title, live a noble life style, and/or buy a fief. Yet it was possible to remain a noble without land or with very little. Technically, one could be a British peer without land, but anyone belonging to the British gentry was, by social definition, the owner of a landed estate. There was a minimum level of landed wealth, albeit not unambiguously defined, but at least enough that most members of the gentry could conform to a certain life style.

Table 9
Noble Inheritance Prescribed by Several Customs of France

Custom of Toulouse	Two-thirds of the patrimony was entailed for the eldest son, while the other half was shared by all the children (including the eldest son); if five or more children had a claim on the estate, half of it was entailed.
Custom of Brittany	Two-thirds went to the eldest son and one-third to the other sons; the eldest son also enjoyed other rights, such as the right of *préciput*, which was usually worth 5 per cent.
Custom of Paris	The eldest received two-thirds of the noble lands when two children had a claim on the inheritance, or one-half when more than two children had a claim; non-noble land was divided equally among all children; and the right of *préciput* gave the eldest son the choice of the château or the principal manor.
Custom of Troyes	The *préciput* was limited to the principal manor and the *vol du chapon*.
Custom of Bordeaux	Noble property was accorded to the eldest son, leaving other children their *légitime*, paid to sons half in land half in money and paid to daughters entirely in money.
Custom of Anjou	The eldest son, in addition to his *préciput*, received two-thirds of the rest of the property and even the remaining third, his brothers and sisters enjoying only usufruct.
Custom of Normandy	For both noble and non-noble families this custom demanded that the patrimony be equally divided among all sons, leaving very little if anything for daughters unless there were no sons.

See note 114 for sources.

The position of daughters and younger sons differed greatly between the British Isles and the Continent. Comparatively strict adherence to primogeniture disinherited daughters and younger sons in British aristocratic families. Younger sons who did not inherit land were forced to withdraw from the gentry and to find work in the government, the armed forces, business, the professions, or the church. Only if they were able to make enough money doing so or if they married into wealth could they regain full membership in the gentry by purchasing a landed estate. Although this was possible, it was difficult. In Cumbria only one younger son in the gentry was able to succeed in gaining readmission between 1680 and 1750.[115] In contrast, all the children of a continental nobleman inherited noble status, even if they inherited little or no land. In addition, the British practices permitted younger sons to engage in economic activities that contributed to the wealth of the lineage rather than becoming a drain on it. Differing attitudes towards economic activity and rules of *dérogeance* were even more significant in their effect on younger sons than on other members of aristocratic families. Younger sons in continental noble families inherited noble status and with it the reluctance to partake in derogatory occupations.

Priorities of State and Society

The economic differences between the British Isles and the Continent also resulted from differences in the priorities of state and society.[116] The efforts made by the French crown to persuade nobles to take up business were always secondary to its efforts to persuade them to serve the state, as office-holders and soldiers. The foremost objective of the political centre was to increase its administrative and military power in Europe. The French crown was more interested in the political loyalty of the nobility and in using its status to support state goals than in mobilizing nobles to improve the economy. A state official in Bayonne compared France with Holland and emphasized that in France "genius prefers glory and the profession of arms ... which had prevented serious attention being paid to commerce, which had never been regarded as a serious business."[117]

It is true that the economy was given high priority by the *agronomes* and by the physiocratic movement led by François Quesnay (physician of Louis xv) and Victor Riquetti, marquess of Mirabeau. A large number of publications were produced and agricultural experiments were carried out by enlightened seigneurs, churchmen, and members of the landed bourgeoisie. Physiocrats were obsessed with the economic role of agriculture and mining, which they considered more important than trade or industry to the economy. Land formed the basis of wealth. The health of the economy therefore depended on how successfully the resources of the land were exploited. The physiocrats tried to persuade French landowners to take greater interest in agriculture and to improve the farming on their estates. By the middle of the eighteenth century, agricultural progress had become a noticeable concern of the French elite.[118]

Obviously, however, this did little to encourage nobles to enter into non-agricultural enterprises (with the exception of natural-resource exploitation). Furthermore, the *agronomes* and physiocrats were driven primarily by English example and influence, an influence that emerged in the eighteenth century and was not really a powerful force until the nineteenth century. Perhaps most well known was Jethro Tull, whose writings were translated into French by Duhamel du Monceau. Yet his methods were subjected to criticism as well as praise. Improvers remained small in number and their influence limited.[119]

Scottish improvers also made England a model to follow, but their situation was altogether different. Scottish improving writers who felt a sense of inferiority vis-à-vis England could seek a solution in the Union.[120] The coincidence of their economic and political centres pushed them in this direction, thus avoiding the conflicts faced by French improvers. The latter had to try to persuade their countrymen to emulate England economically even if Paris was their political centre. The French physiocrats had difficulty reconciling their economic philosophy with the nature and ideology of the state in France. In spite of their support for free trade, they typically came to the conclusion that they could live with French absolutism.[121] Most physiocrats worked in the government. They did not challenge the traditional order and did not wish to imitate the English state in the way they wished to imitate the English economy. They wanted to combine a market society with an authoritarian government.[122]

The French state recognized the importance of a strong economy for its own objectives. Yet one of the consequences of the pre-eminence of the political centre was more state intervention in the economy than was the case in the British Isles. The result is well known: government regulation, state enterprises, royal monopolies, economic privileges, and so on. Under Henry IV, state assistance was provided to silk, tapestry, rug, glass, and soap industries, and state regulation was instituted to improve the quality of products.[123] Richelieu himself assumed the title of *grand maître du commerce et de la navigation* and used various measures to encourage trade and industry.[124] Above all, Colbert brought state intervention and regulation of the economy to a peak. Although there was less regulation in the eighteenth century, even at the end of the Old Regime most industries, and especially the metallurgical industry, were subject to intense state regulation.[125] Much of it was evaded, of course, but this does not call into question the character of the relationship between state and economy in Early Modern France. Legislation encouraging nobles to enter business needs to be seen in the context of this state regulation of the economy.

Geographically, commercial interests were on the periphery, not at the centre. The French royal bureaucracy was controlled by men from the northern inland regions rather than the commercial men of the sea ports.[126] The former saw the economy as a fiscal resource of the state and a machine to be managed by governmental regulation. They were most interested in protecting the peasantry as a tax source, and, in order to do so, were quite willing to prevent seigneurs from reorganizing the agrarian structure in more profitable ways.

In Savoy, administrative effectiveness and military power were emphasized even more than in France; and commerce was even lower in priority. Although the dukes of Savoy encouraged nobles to enter business, their enthusiasm was always restrained by their much greater concern to get nobles (as well as other members of the population) to serve the prince in arms.[127] A military ethos predominated at the court of the dukes of Savoy.[128] Nobles in Savoy did seek to exploit the natural resources on their lands and did engage in related economic activities, such as metallurgy. Otherwise, however, they pursued a way of life that can only be described as traditionally aristocratic.[129] Commerce enjoyed higher status in Flanders, Brabant, and Liège than it did in most of France and Savoy, but the political centres that ruled over these provinces were less commercially oriented.

The Differentiation of Status and Economic Power

There was a circular relationship between status power and economic power. To a certain extent, status could be used to increase economic power, especially if status brought one into contact with the crown, which was a source of economic benefits for the aristocracy in all the countries we are examining. To an even greater extent, indeed a much greater extent, the reverse was also true: economic power could be used to raise status, through the purchase of titles, land, fiefs, ennobling offices, aristocrat life style, education, and so on.

For a number of reasons this link between economic power and status power was closer in the British Isles than on the Continent. Sure enough, in our continental countries one can find considerable fusion of status and economic power. On average, titled nobles enjoyed higher status and more wealth than high-court magistrates, who enjoyed higher status and more wealth than most nobles, who enjoyed higher status and more wealth than bourgeois members of society. To a significant degree, however, status and economic power were differentiated. Many nobles were not as wealthy as members of the bourgeoisie and some were as poor as peasants. Most high-court magistrates were less affluent than many merchants who had lower status, while they were wealthier than some of the old nobility who enjoyed higher status.[130] In addition, other than their wealth, continental nobles did not have much direct economic power. Financiers were the exception. While they certainly enjoyed high status, coming, as they did, from rising robe families, they did not enjoy the highest status in the kingdom, which was reserved for the great nobility. Although lending money to the crown was not viewed as derogatory, this does not mean that it had high status. Financiers were regarded negatively in French society, at best as people who performed a sordid task, at worst as swindlers. They were frequently made the scapegoats for French financial crises. Most aristocratic investors, in contrast, avoided the stigma attached to finance by remaining anonymous.[131]

Those aristocratic investors whose wealth was sufficient that the crown and the financiers depended heavily on them were, in Dessert's view, the most powerful people in the country. Since many were members of the high nobility, high status and economic power were fused in them to a greater extent than elsewhere in Old Regime France. Dessert estimates that there were several hundred such investors.[132]

Otherwise, status and economic power were less correlated than in the British Isles. British peers had higher status and were on average wealthier than baronets and knights, who had higher status and were on average wealthier than the untitled gentry, who had higher status and were on average wealthier than the rest of the population. Although the difference should not be exaggerated (and there is no need for my argument to exaggerate it), the poor gentry in the British Isles were, in relative terms, fewer and not as hard up as the poor nobility on the Continent. The British aristocracy did not possess as much economic power in finance as the French nobility, or at least a segment of the French nobility, but, with the partial exception of Irish landowners, they enjoyed greatly more power over the agricultural economy and played a role in agricultural change that would have been impossible for the continental nobility.

Was the Aristocracy a Class?

This chapter reveals the economic heterogeneity of the Western European aristocracy. Wealth, income, and economic power varied greatly within the aristocracy, even within the old nobility. So did the sources of wealth, income, and economic power. In some respects this variation was greater in the British Isles, where aristocrats engaged in more non-agricultural economic activity and where some aristocrats were extremely wealthy; in other respects it was greater on the Continent, where more of the aristocracy owned little or no land and relied primarily on non-landed investment or state income and where many nobles were incredibly poor.

The continental nobility was in no sense a class, unless we are prepared to exclude economic characteristics from our definition of class. Continental nobles formed a status group. Members of this group belonged to several different classes, most commonly the landed class, but other classes as well. It is perhaps possible to refer to the British aristocracy as a class, since almost all British aristocrats depended on land for most of their income and land helped to define group membership in a way that it did not for the continental nobility. Yet the British aristocracy was also a status group and members of this group engaged in a variety of economic activities.

7 Political Power

France, Savoy, and the Southern Low Countries

THE DIFFERENTIATION OF POWER IN THE MIDDLE AGES

Fusion of power was the rule in the Middle Ages. True, power was more differentiated in those regions where dukes or counts centralized political power. In Savoy, for example, judicial power was comparatively differentiated from administrative/political power. The castellans and bailiffs exercised mainly the latter and enjoyed limited judicial power; serious cases were handled by judges with legal training.[1] Even in these more centralized regions, however, power was to a considerable degree undifferentiated. The status of lord blended a number of different kinds of power. It included both status power and political power; and it combined more than one type of political power. The seigneur or the seigneur's agents performed what we would distinguish today as political, administrative, and judicial functions. Judicial authority was inseparable from other powers in the minds of the people and reinforced other powers. Judicial authority also protected other seigneurial rights. Seigneurial courts were used to oblige defaulting tenants to pay their dues. Seigneurs with high justice enjoyed prerogatives that other seigneurs did not enjoy. Seigneurs also had military power. Many lords were military men and, in addition, were owed military service. The bond of lordship was the principal means of mobilizing an army.

Although the status of noble was more differentiated than that of lord, in the Middle Ages it also brought together several kinds of power. Not all nobles were lords, but almost all lords were nobles. (The major exception was the ecclesiastical seigneurie.) To this extent the status of noble was fused with the status of lord and other powers of lordship. Yet even nobles who were not seigneurs enjoyed more than just status power. The most significant was military power. While peasants could be mobilized for short periods, it was usually young men from noble families who made fighting a vocation. This was increasingly the case during the twelfth to fourteenth centuries as the status of knight rose. Every powerful lord would have in service young men from noble families, some local, some from far away. No great lord could survive without the adherence of a large number of nobles, whose allegiance was sought in order to increase military power and to keep them from serving enemies. Great lords were not always successful in doing so, and even when they were they had to acknowledge the bargaining power of armed nobles and treat them favourably to maintain their loyalty.

TAMING THE FRENCH MAGNATES

Monarchies generally used four strategies to deal with regional magnates: (1) co-opt: persuade magnates to give up their regional power in return for a share in the central power; (2) delegate: allow magnates to rule a region in return for their acknowledgement of the crown as overlord; (3) destroy: curtail or destroy the regional power of magnates; and (4) undercut: leave magnates with some power and perhaps nominally in charge, but transfer most of their political power to lower-status officials under tighter crown control.

Before the sixteenth century the French crown employed the first three strategies, but delegation predominated. The king permitted the independent dukes and counts to govern on his behalf. Even when the crown began to exercise more authority, considerable power was still delegated. Regiments of the French army long remained under the control of princes of the blood or the greater nobility; and large forces could be mobilized only with the assistance of these magnates even in the seventeenth century.[2] The governors of the provinces were normally members of the greater nobility. The monarch enjoyed the right of appointment, but great families often came to expect a governorship almost as a customary right. It was the responsibility of the governor to assure public order, administer army regiments, and prepare the province against possible invasion. The result was enormous military power in the hands of great families, especially during the

Wars of Religion. Governors published ordinances, collected taxes, interfered in the administration of justice, and intervened in local government.[3] They and other great noble families established large clienteles through which they exercised political power.[4]

Over time many nobles were co-opted. The nobility and the crown became reciprocally interdependent during the fourteenth and fifteenth centuries. By 1484 many nobles sought to serve the king.[5] Typically higher clergymen, often members of noble families, served as the king's administrative servants. The royal councils in the fifteenth and sixteenth centuries brought together members of the greater nobility. Francis I placed considerable confidence in the greater nobility to administer the affairs of state; both the Council of Affairs and the Privy Council were dominated by high nobility.[6]

However, the delegation of power to French magnates had been less than voluntary on the crown's part. French kings had not exercised much control over the great dukes and counts, and had often been unhappy with the arrangements they had with them. Consequently, they generally tried, when they could, to undermine great magnates more than to co-opt them. By the late Middle Ages they had succeeded in doing so in some regions, while not in others, but by the end of the sixteenth century all the great lay territorial peerages were gone. In most cases they were assumed by the crown. (The exception was Flanders, which was held by the Emperor; it ceased to be a French peerage when Francis I relinquished sovereignty over the County of Flanders.[7]) By the seventeenth century the majority of dukes and peers were nobles raised to higher status by the crown; they were not in a strong position to threaten its authority.[8]

During the seventeenth century the army was centralized and control over regiments was taken out of the hands of the princes of the blood and the greater nobility. Richelieu dismantled the fortified castles of difficult nobles, restricted the travel of some of the most illustrious families, and limited their personal contact with the king.[9] Richelieu, Mazarin, and Colbert used two methods to undermine the political power of the governors and other members of the greater nobility.[10] First, they replaced governors not deemed sufficiently loyal to the crown and transferred many powers of the governors to royal agents who could be controlled more easily from the political centre. This was facilitated by the fact that the governorships were ultimately revocable by the crown and there were very few of them; the crown could undo one at a time. Second, they established simultaneously their own clienteles, what historians have called administrative clienteles, in place of the great noble clienteles. The decline of the great noble clienteles in the seventeenth century and their replacement by administrative clienteles was one of the most significant developments in the history of Modern France.[11] Note that both these methods – the insertion of new agents of the crown and the building of new clientele networks – involved undercutting the political authority of the greater nobility. Richard Lachmann has proposed a metaphor that is the opposite of Brewer's notion that the French crown superimposed a centralized apparatus over French society. Lachmann thinks the French crown established "vertical absolutism"; before the greater nobles were subdued the French crown was already bypassing them and forming direct ties underneath them with local officials and corporate bodies.[12] The revolts of the princes and the greater nobility in the seventeenth century, that of Chalais (1626), Montmorency (1632), and Cinq Mars (1642), and then the Fronde of the princes, further persuaded the crown that most of them were untrustworthy and that their power had to be undercut.

NOBLES AT THE FRENCH POLITICAL CENTRE

The Older Nobility

Of course, the crown did not find all the greater nobility untrustworthy, and some leading nobles exercised considerable power in the new scheme of things. Yet their access to power now became increasingly dependent on their access to the king. The royal court was the arena in which political factions struggled with one another. In order to govern, the king had to control these factions, and he sought to do so in the court by skilfully playing one off against another. As nobles became more urbanized and as the greater nobility lost its territorial power, it attended court more often than in earlier periods. The court was practically a bourse of patronage where influence with the king was exchanged for payments or loyalty to a patron. Some aristocratic families generally supported the king and formed his faction. Considerable political power was combined in the hands of members of these families.[13] Courtiers and officers in the royal household had direct personal contact with the most powerful individual in the kingdom. Louis xiv frequently consulted with members of the high nobility who attended court.[14]

The power of the court may have reached even higher levels during the reigns of Louis xv and Louis xvi. They were not able to manipulate court factions as skilfully as could Louis xiv. Court nobles, like the Duke of Richelieu (grand nephew of Louis xiii's chief minister), developed skills at charming the court or maneuvring factions. We should not assume that these factions were all petty self-serving cliques playing games. One of the most powerful factions in the eighteenth century was the *parti dévot*, which opposed the Jansenists during the reign of Louis XV. It included the Queen, the Dauphin, and the king's daughters, as well as the Duke of La Vauguyon (governor of the royal children), the Count of Argenson (minister of war), Lamoignon de Blancmesnil (the chancellor), and the Bishop of Mirepoix.[15]

The court enjoyed not only political power, but status power as well. This was so for two reasons. First, membership in the household or attendance at court was prestigious in itself. Second, the majority of those attending court were nobles, often from the most illustrious families in the kingdom. It is probably valid to say that no institution in Early Modern France, saving the monarchy itself, fused political power and status power more than the royal court. There was a widespread public perception of the court as extremely powerful. Many people believed, as did E.J. Sieyès (an abbé, then politician and writer during the French Revolution), that "it is the court that has reigned and not the monarch."[16]

This perception was, however, an exaggeration. The political power of the court rested on the royal person. This is demonstrated by the political power that could be enjoyed by royal mistresses, most notoriously Madame de Maintenon and Madame de Pompadour. Some courtiers did hold political posts outside court. Yet one part of the traditional wisdom that has not been disproven is that the most powerful offices outside court did not go to the princes of the blood, the dukes and peers, or other members of the greater nobility, in particular during the reign of Louis XIV. This exclusion began under Louis XIV's predecessors, but he went further than they had. His High Council was a small informal group composed of ministers of state; none belonged to the older nobility. Although his Privy Council included some nobility of the sword, it was dominated by recruits from the nobility of the robe (broadly defined).[17] As a rule, the most serious business of government was kept secret from the court. Great nobles sometimes had to seek the help of a royal minister or a personal secretary to get something from the king.[18]

Some great nobles, such as the Duke of La Rochefoucauld (son of the well-known writer), were given prestigious court positions with little political power.[19] There was a clear differentiation between ministerial families and high aristocratic families. The sombre clothes of the ministers contrasted with the colourful clothes worn by courtiers.[20] The former enjoyed more political power than the latter, but less prestige. As a result, members of ministerial families eagerly sought marriages into the high nobility, which Louis XIV was willing to permit and which did something to reduce the difference between the two.[21]

The greater nobility regained some lost ground after the death of Louis XIV. The regent, Philip of Orléans, made an effort to bring the older nobility into the councils of state. He put together the "Polysynodie" – six councils, half of whose members were nobles. Unfortunately for the nobility, the Polysynodie did not turn out to be very effective.[22] It was brought to an end in 1718, resulting in a decline in the presence of the older nobility at the centre of political power. Nevertheless, during the eighteenth century members of the older nobility played a more prominent part in the royal administration than they had under Louis XIV. Their role was particularly marked in the ministries of foreign affairs and war. Examples of nobles of long ancestry who occupied these ministries in the eighteenth century include the Duke of Choiseul, the Duke of Aiguillon, and the Marquess of Argenson, all ministers of foreign affairs under Louis XV, the Marquess of Castries, minister of war under Louis XV, and the Count of Saint-Germain, the Marquess of Ségur, and the Duke of Broglie, all ministers of war under Louis XVI. Usually one or two titled nobles sat on the High Council, but in some years there were none. François Bluche has investigated the social origins of royal ministers (*chanceliers, gardes des sceaux, contrôleurs généraux,* and *secrétaires d'état*) who served between 1718 and 1789. Only about 15 per cent were of what he calls *origine chevaleresque* or *ancienne extraction*.[23] This is certainly an over-representation. They were, however, greatly outnumbered.

By and large French kings wanted to prevent princes of the blood and other members of the greater nobility from acquiring a share in state authority by membership on an inner council. This concern was likely present in the minds of kings in earlier periods. Yet in earlier periods, especially during the Hundred Years' War and the Wars of Religion, the crown frequently had no choice but to ask members of the greater nobility to attend inner councils; their territorial power made it necessary. This territorial power, however, was all but demolished by the end of the seventeenth century. Kings had more liberty to choose advisers who had two essential qualities they most wanted: loyalty and competence.

Members of the greater nobility sometimes filled less powerful state offices, but not often. It was embarrassing for a nobleman from one of the great French families to occupy a minor position, certainly if orders had to be taken from a commoner or a noble of lower status. Only in the diplomatic corps do we find a significant number of persons from the greater nobility. This was the case because great nobles saw service of this kind as sufficiently prestigious that it did not threaten their status, because such nobles were regarded by the crown as sophisticated enough to be diplomats, because the representatives of the king to other royal courts needed to have high status, and because diplomacy was closely related to military service.

Although some members of great families became brokers in the new administrative clienteles, these brokers were more often lesser nobles.[24] They were more willing to subordinate themselves to a minister in Paris, to become his *créature*. Like the greater nobility, they had a long tradition of (mainly military) service to the crown, of which they were extremely proud. Some noble families recognized that the crown had developed new needs, which it was appropriate for nobles to meet. Indeed, the tradition of royal military service convinced many nobles that they had a special right to royal posts. They not infrequently complained if they were not favoured. While the members of the greater nobility would not deign to occupy minor government posts, many lesser nobles were only too glad to do so. The venality of offices, however, impeded state service by members of the lesser nobility for reasons given in the preceding chapter, mostly financial. Financial problems also restricted the educational opportunities of a large number of nobles. The nobility had become much more educated in the Early Modern period, but far from all nobles were educated, even in the eighteenth century.[25]

We have some data on the number of nobles holding state office. In his study of French intendants serving from 1652 to 1715, J.M.W. Dawson found that less than 6 per cent of the families of these intendants could trace nobility back six or more generations, and only about 30 per cent could trace it four or more generations.[26] Over time the new nobility was aging. Thus it is not surprising to find that the number with four or more generations increased to 40 per cent in the eighteenth century.[27] The old nobility was also poorly represented on sovereign courts. According to Bluche, only 5.7 per cent of those who entered the Parlement of Paris in the eighteenth century were from families that were ennobled before 1500, and about a quarter of these were ennobled by office.[28] Dewald gives us the percentage of the *parlementaires* of Rouen whose fathers were non-office-holding nobles. The figure fluctuates between 13 per cent and 22 per cent in different periods from 1539 to 1638.[29] William Doyle found that only four of 127 *parlementaire* families in eighteenth-century Bordeaux could trace their nobility to a period before the sixteenth century.[30] J.B. Wood's findings are rather different. He has given us data for Bayeux that include positions of varying importance. He found that in the period 1463 to 1666 the old nobility outnumbered the new nobility in the most powerful state and judicial offices; the new nobility outnumbered the old nobility in middle-level posts; and the old nobility outnumbered the new nobility among lawyers, notaries, and sergeants. For Wood, however, a century is enough to make one an "old" noble.[31]

The military revolution had a profound effect on the nobility. The most valuable fighters in the Middle Ages were knights who had been able to undertake long years of training and who could purchase a first-class horse and the necessary armour and equipment. As large infantries and artillery increased in relative importance, the advantages enjoyed by the nobility declined. The new firearms required a different kind of expertise, which young nobles often did not acquire. The new fire-powered canons did not make fortresses less suitable for defence, but did undermine the defensive capability of the small fortresses that minor lords had been able to build in the Middle Ages to protect themselves and their small armies.[32] The increase in the size of armies and the centralization of command undermined the autonomous military power that French nobles had enjoyed even in the sixteenth century. To pursue a military career was now to become a member of a professional army under the increasingly tight command of the crown, the ministry of defence, and military officers.

All the same, the French nobility continued to play a significant role in the military. Young men from old sword families were not usually interested in a bureaucratic career. They had inherited values from a long ancestry of military service. *Gloire* for them was to be found on the field of battle, not behind a desk. This does not mean that most noblemen had a military career. While members of older noble families might all claim martial ancestors, the majority of men in the seventeenth or eighteenth century could not justify their noble status and privileges because they served in arms. Yet a major contribution to the defence of the realm was still made by French nobles. French kings believed that the nobility, despite its limited numbers, was indispensable in the armed forces. To be sure, some nobles could not afford to join the army because they could not purchase the equipment, and many nobles were barred from the officer corps for lack of financial resources.[33] Nonetheless, rare was the family of long noble ancestry that did not have at least one son pursuing a military career. The older nobility was the symbol of the military ideals that still enjoyed great esteem in French society. Many people believed that the nobility was necessary to promote the courage and discipline in the army that would make it victorious. It was rather a myth, but one that the crown consciously promoted. The sovereign encouraged nobles to join the army and assume positions of leadership. This encouragement did not decline during the Early Modern period. On the contrary, in the eighteenth century the crown became increasingly concerned that members of old noble families were having difficulty rising in the military hierarchy. Eventually an edict of 1781 (the Ségur edict) required evidence of four quarters of nobility on the father's side for promotion to the level of sublieutenant.[34]

Jean-Marie Constant's research on the careers of nobles in the Beauce shows an overwhelming tendency for those from families ennobled before 1500 to enter the military or the Maison du roi. Between 1500 and 1700 no fewer than 222 out of 224 nobles who entered state service and came from families ennobled before 1500 entered the military or the Maison du roi; in the last time period he considered, 1660–1700, all seventy-nine of the pre-1500 nobles serving the state did so in the military or in the Maison du roi.[35] Those who entered the military or the Maison du roi outnumbered those undertaking an ecclesiastical career. Altogether the military and the Maison du roi drew 57.8 per cent of those who pursued a military, administrative, or ecclesiastical career in the generation 1500–60, 70.3 per cent in the generation 1560–1600, 73.9 per cent in the generation 1600–60, and 76.7 per cent in the generation 1660–1700. Somewhat surprisingly, Constant discovered that it was the eldest son who was the most likely to enter the military or the Maison du roi. Not surprisingly, he discovered that the older nobility were well represented among military officers.[36]

Wood has found that in Bayeux during the period 1463 to 1666 a majority of noblemen did not engage in military service, about a third took part in one or two campaigns, and about 15 to 20 per cent had military careers. He indicated that the old nobility of the sword, indeed a small number of families, monopolized the military officer corps.[37] André Corvisier estimated that 20 to 25 per cent of French noblemen engaged in some military activity during their lifetime.[38] Louis XIV took the administration of defence out of the hands of the older nobility, but the older nobility still dominated the officer corps. David Bien has estimated that in the late eighteenth century a remarkable 95 per cent of officers of regiments of the line were from noble families.[39] Examples of older nobility in command of military forces in the eighteenth century are provided by the Marquess of Bouillé, the Marquess of Castries, and several members of the Noailles family, the Ségur family, the Broglie family, and the Croy family, especially the Prince of Croy-Solre.

How much political power did this military presence give the nobility? In the twentieth century we are accustomed to seeing civil authorities overthrown by the military, and in many countries today the civil government has to appease military leaders out of fear of a military *coup d'état*. Given the presence of the nobility in the military and the autonomy of powerful military nobles, and given the dependence of the sovereign on these nobles to raise and command regiments even in the seventeenth century, one might have expected to see numerous military *coups* in the Early Modern period, as well as evidence that some rulers lived in fear of their armies. Such evidence is not altogether lacking, and the second Fronde was certainly a revolt of powerful military nobles. Yet the second Fronde was much more than a military *coup*. What is in general striking is the lack of pressure of the military on Early Modern rulers.

An explanation for this phenomenon would be a major study in itself, but some reasons might be suggested. Critical was the fusion of civilian and military commands. In Early Modern Europe the sovereign was the highest military commander and therefore had ultimate authority over the military, even though elements in the military could sometimes operate relatively autonomously. Today we differentiate military and political power, a separation that works fine so long as the military accept that their position is subordinate, but one that creates a struggle between military and civilian leaders wherever the military are not willing to do so. Moreover, in the twentieth century, command over the military has become more unified. A small number of generals enjoy authority over the entire state army, in some cases the entire state military, with perhaps the exception of a presidential guard. Thus military leaders are able to unite the army to carry out a *coup d'état*. The irony is that the very fragmentation of Early Modern armies may have helped preserve sovereigns from such *coups*. No military noble had control over the entire army such that he could turn it against the crown. The Noble Fronde demonstrates clearly the power enjoyed by great military nobles, but also their weakness. The rebellious nobles were unable to unite the nobility and the military against the king.[40]

To sum up, some members of the old nobility enjoyed political power in the central state, especially in the royal court, but on the whole the political power of this group declined drastically during the seventeenth century and recovered only a little, if at all, during the eighteenth century. The principal role in the state played by these nobles was in the army, a role that brought political power only to those who moved on to a successful career in the world of politics that surrounded the king.

The New Nobility of the Robe

The new nobility, composed of those ennobled by letters or by office in the sixteenth, seventeenth, and eighteenth centuries, was more involved in state institutions than the older nobility and consequently enjoyed more political power. This power often ran in families. If we look for the family background of the incumbents of any particular office in the seventeenth or eighteenth century we usually find that their fathers or uncles, and often grandfathers, held state office. This meant that most nobles holding state office in eighteenth-century France had either purchased an ennobling office or had inherited nobility from someone who had purchased an ennobling office. I think that this nobility should be referred to as "new," but not because they were all *nouveaux riches*, if by this we mean that they had achieved spectacular social mobility in one generation. The families of about a fifth of the nobles who sat on the Parlement of Paris from 1715 to 1771 acquired their nobility in the sixteenth century, and over half joined the nobility in the period 1600 to 1715.[41] Almost a fifth of the families who had members in the Parlement of Bordeaux under Louis XVI could trace their nobility to the sixteenth century, while over a third were ennobled in the seventeenth century.[42]

Despite the willingness of some young men in robe families to undertake a military career, there was no takeover of the military by a new nobility as there was of the officialdom. Military offices were not ennobling until the mid-eighteenth century. The Edict of 1750 made certain grades in the military ennobling and provided for exemption from the *taille* for others.[43] It came too late, however, to have much effect. If it had been enacted in the sixteenth century, the character of the French nobility in the eighteenth century might have been very different. A "new nobility of the sword" might have emerged along with the new nobility of the robe.

The brokers in the new administrative clienteles of the seventeenth century were, if not lesser nobles, often members of the nobility of the robe.[44] The new nobility of the robe also provided recruits for the *commissaires*. Only a small percentage of intendants did not inherit noble status – those from just 6 per cent of the families studied by Dawson, just 2 per cent of the families studied by Vivian Gruder.[45] Most intendants came from families in the new nobility of the robe broadly defined. Some 21 per cent of the fathers for whom Dawson was able to obtain data were financial officers, 12 per cent local administrators, 43 per cent *parlementaires*, 20 per cent members of the Great Council, 32 per cent *maîtres des requêtes*, and 22 per cent intendants.[46] No less than 97 per cent of the intendants in Gruder's sample came from families ennobled by specific acts rather than immemorially; 83 per cent came from families ennobled by office.[47] Intendants had subdelegates of different kinds. Their social origins varied greatly depending on their duties, but they were often lawyers, local officials, or lower-court judges or councillors.[48]

Royal ministers who were not from old noble families were generally from the new nobility of the robe, again broadly defined. Of the ministers studied by Bluche, only three were of non-noble origin. Over half owed their noble status to an ennobling office. Here especially it is important to emphasize that these ministers were not predominantly *nouveaux riches*. Although only about 15 per cent of those who held the ministerial offices studied by Bluche were nobles of *origine cheval-eresque* or *ancienne extraction*, an additional 35 per cent could trace their nobility for more than two hundred years.[49]

How much political power did those who held the above positions have? The greatest influence over the king was enjoyed by his ministers, most of whom were also at the head of a network of clientele. Yet they had the least independence of the crown. Although the royal hands were not altogether free, kings normally decided whom they appointed as ministers and they were able to remove those they no longer favoured. The eighteenth century was littered with disgraced ministers, the victims of royal whim and/or political intrigue.

Officially the intendants enjoyed remarkable power. Their judicial authority consisted of the right to oversee the administration of justice, investigate alleged irregularities, hear complaints, and insure that laws were obeyed. Their police role required them to enforce royal decrees and maintain law and order. In the *pays d'états* the intendant represented the crown vis-à-vis the estates. The intendants gradually acquired *tutelle* or trusteeship over local government. And, most important and contentious of all, they oversaw the collection of royal taxes.[50]

Yet in the historical literature one can find two contrasting stereotypes of the royal intendant. The first picture is that of a powerful official, unsympathetic to local vested interests, backed up by the authority of the crown, and able to impose the will of the central state on the locality. The second picture is that of a beleaguered royal official, desperately trying to follow directives from Paris in a hostile environment with only a small staff and thus forced to make compromises with local interests.[51] The reason we have such contrasting stereotypes is that the experiences and characteristics of intendancies varied greatly from one province to another and even from one time period to another within the same province. Often a weak intendant was replaced by a strong intendant or vice versa; or an intendant on bad terms with local elites was supplanted by one who was more accommodating. William Beik has demonstrated that in Languedoc, during the reign of Louis xiv, intendants needed the support of elements in the provincial elites to function; with such support they could work successfully with local interests.[52]

On the other hand, we certainly have evidence, some of it striking, of opposition to local power on the part of intendants. They sometimes went out of their way to portray themselves as champions of the weak and the poor. It was not unusual for intendants to denounce local elites and to attack privilege.[53] Intendants were frequently engaged in struggles with provincial estates. The last intendant of Burgundy, Antoine-Jean Amelot, criticized the nobility in the Estates of Burgundy for unfairly distributing the tax burden and for using subterfuge to reduce the weight of the *vingtième* on the nobility.[54] In 1788 the intendant of Besançon tried to persuade the government to renounce the recently restored Estates of Franche-Comté because they were a tool in the hands of the nobility.[55]

The *parlements* were also a source of power for the newer nobility. The Parlement of Paris had jurisdiction over a large area centred in Paris, representing between one-quarter and one-third of the kingdom. The jurisdiction of a provincial *parlement* did not necessarily conform to the province in which it was situated; the jurisdiction of the Parlement of Toulouse, for example, included not only all of Languedoc, but also considerable parts of Guyenne, Gascony, Quercy, and Foix.[56] Most of the provincial *parlements* were in provinces that had been integrated into France at the end of or after the Hundred Years' War. They were in regions that were relatively far from Paris and/or bordering on other European states; this was not the case for the Parlement of Rouen, not really the case for the Parlement of Rennes, but it was the case for the Parlements of Aix, Bordeaux, Toulouse, Besançon, Grenoble, Pau, Metz, Douai, Nancy, and Dijon. If the Parlement of Toulouse was not unusual, during the reign of Louis xiv the powers of *parlements* became strengthened while at the same time better serving the interests of the crown.[57]

The registration, proclamation, and interpretation of laws was the duty of the *parlementaires*. It was necessary to have royal edicts registered with the appropriate *parlement* for them to have the force of law. *Parlements* sometimes refused to register a law, or at least resisted registration or amended the legislation. This is what forced the crown to cooperate with them and make concessions. In addition, *parlements* often objected to government measures by means of a remonstrance (supposedly confidential but frequently leaked to arouse public opinion).[58]

It should be acknowledged that there were definite limitations to the authority of the *parlements*. They had no power to enforce their decisions. Over time, but especially under Louis xiv, their authority tended to become more differentiated, largely judicial as opposed to political and administrative. And the king had the authority to overrule a *parlement* by appearing himself at a session. Known as a *lit de justice*, this personal appearance was an effective check on the power of the *parlements*.

Yet it was not possible for the king to attend more than a small proportion of sessions of the thirteen *parlements* in the kingdom. Ultimately the king's will might prevail, but the *parlements* could make governing the country very difficult for him. In contrast with ministers and intendants, *parlementaires* were not chosen by the king and could not be removed without great difficulty. The king could really bring a recalcitrant *parlement* under control only by banishing it from its province. Thirty members of the Parlement of Besançon were exiled in 1759. In 1771 René-Nicolas Maupeou, Louis XV's chancellor, abolished a number of *parlements*, including the Parlement of Paris, and exiled the magistrates, putting in their place new courts. In 1774, however, Louis XVI, responding to popular pressure, sacked Maupeou and restored the *parlements*. In August 1787 the Parlement of Paris was removed to Troyes, but it was allowed to return in November. In May 1788 all the *parlements* were dismissed and supplanted by new courts. They were reinstated in September.

I mentioned in chapter 1 that some historians believe that the crown used venal offices – in addition to their obvious and primary fiscal function – to bond elites to the state by providing them with an interest in its stability. This is an oversimplification. Attached to the state they may have become, but not necessarily attached to the crown. The French state in the eighteenth century was a diverse, segmented structure, within which a large number of forces pulled, sometimes together, sometimes in opposition. While many venal office-holders were loyal servants of the king, many were not. And it is significant that during the eighteenth century the most powerful opposition to royal authority anywhere in the kingdom came from venal office-holders.

PROVINCIAL BASES OF POWER

France

Estates potentially gave the nobility their greatest provincial power base. The distribution and magnitude of this power varied with three conditions. First, it varied with the composition of the noble estate. The composition of several noble estates is given in table 10. Some were very exclusive, with the result that they contributed to power inequality within the nobility. This inequality did not strengthen newer nobility over old, or robe over sword. On the contrary, older nobles were generally favoured and sometimes *anoblis* were excluded, or at

Table 10
Composition of Several Noble Estates

Burgundy	Those with four generations of nobility and possessing fiefs.
Artois	Those with one hundred years of paternal nobility and ownership of a local seigneurie.
Béarn	Twelve great barons and the possessors of five hundred seigneuries or lay abbeys.
Nébouzan	Eight barons, twelve seigneurs, and the *capitaines* of four castles. Commoners holding noble lands and seigneurial lands could sit with the nobility.
Lower Navarre	Those who possessed noble land or houses in the province plus those selected by the king.
Bigorre	A small number of seigneurs with the right of entry by letters patent, plus all those who possessed any one of twelve baronies or seventy seigneuries.
Languedoc	Twenty-three barons, who happened to enjoy this privilege as a historical right.
Brittany	All old nobility were entitled to attend meetings of the estates, but the number attending varied from several hundred to nine hundred.
Walloon Flanders	The nobility as a group was not represented in the estates, but there were four noble *grands baillis* selected by four *seigneurs hauts justiciers* (the king, the prince of Soubise, the count of Egmont, and the duke of Orléans).

See note 59 for sources.

least efforts were made to exclude them.[60] Yet members of the old nobility could be excluded as well. Restrictions on membership in noble estates often seriously divided the old nobility.

Second, the power that estates gave nobles varied with the power of the noble estate vis-à-vis other estates. The noble estate could be weaker than the third estate or the clerical estate. This was the case in some of the provinces of the Pyrenees and also in Languedoc, where the estates were dominated by the clergy.[61] Yet in most other provinces, Franche-Comté and Brittany, for example, the noble estate was powerful relative to other estates.

Third, the power that estates gave nobles varied with the power of the estates as a whole. The rise of the state had increased administration and public works in the provinces, and some estates were extremely active in this sphere.[62] The majority of estates also had some leverage over taxation. They could obtain concessions in return for approving taxes expeditiously. Even Louis xiv sometimes had to write to officials, nobles, and clergymen seeking their assistance on a question coming before the estates of a particular province.[63] Agents sent to Paris by the Estates of Brittany were received by the crown as it might receive the envoys of a foreign power.[64]

Vis-à-vis the crown, the authority of the estates in the seventeenth and eighteenth centuries is the subject of some disagreement. The conventional wisdom has been that the crown gradually undermined the estates, that estates fought hard against this process, and that they enjoyed success in a few provinces, but not as a general rule. The assumption has been that the power of the crown and the power of the local elites were zero-sum; that is, as royal power expanded, that of local elites declined.

Recently, it has been argued that centre-periphery relations were not so conflictual. We now have a better understanding of the way in which privilege was used to attach provincial elites to the central state.[65] Sharon Kettering has proposed that the French political centre used patron-client ties to integrate the periphery with the centre. Brokers mediated between the two and helped ministers in Paris to control provincial elites, and especially to control the estates.[66] The crown was not, in general, hostile towards local elites and determined to undermine their power. Daniel Hickey has demonstrated that the extension of royal power in Dauphiné did not come about as a result of a determined effort on the part of the crown to destroy the political power of local elites, but mostly as a consequence of persistent efforts of the king's men to collect revenue.[67] Beik shows that in Languedoc Louis XIV strengthened his authority by supporting local elites and provincial institutions, both the estates and the Parlement of Toulouse, whose power was not undermined to the extent that one might assume. Under Louis XIV the estates and the Parlement spent less time wrangling and more time governing the province. They were able to prevent increases in taxes and to restrict the flow of tax money out of the province. Indeed, many members of the local elite profited from royal taxes as much as did the crown. The jurisdiction of the Parlement was strengthened and the court became less resistant to royal authority. The elites of Languedoc were not ideologically opposed to royal power. Rather, they appreciated the necessity of sturdy royal authority in their province.[68]

These arguments are sound, especially the assertion that the political power of crown and local elites was not necessarily zero-sum. The conventional wisdom is not, however, altogether wrong. The fact of the matter is that the powers of estates did decline as royal power increased. By the eighteenth century provincial estates persisted in only about one-third of the kingdom.[69] In addition, the power of those still in operation had been reduced, primarily by making them agents of the crown. The estates in the north of France, in particular, had become little more than royal tax collectors; the Estates of Walloon Flanders were allied with the crown in opposition to the bulk of the provincial nobility, which was politically weak.[70] Beik does not deny that from 1632 to 1685 the rights of the Estates of Languedoc were curtailed. At the same time the crown acquired considerable influence over the membership of the estates. For these and other reasons, both the clergy and the nobility in the Estates of Languedoc were generally subservient to royal demands.[71]

Moreover, there is no denying the very real and repeated confrontations between the crown and many *parlements* or estates. Even the *parlement* of Toulouse sought to protect provincial rights, albeit in the king's name.[72] Estates might or might not have the kind of working relationship with the crown that Beik found in Languedoc under Louis xiv. The most anti-centrist were the Estates of Brittany. In 1717 the estates were dissolved because they declined to grant the king the *don gratuit*. A rebellion by some nobles in 1718 was severely crushed and four leaders were executed.[73] Further struggles between the crown and the Estates of Brittany occurred a number of times during the remainder of the eighteenth century. In many of these struggles the Estates of Brittany joined forces with the Parlement of Rennes against the crown.[74]

Estates, like provincial *parlements*, were most often found in provinces that were far from Paris and/or bordered on the jurisdictions of other European states. Only Brittany offers something of an exception to this generalization. Yet the primary difference between the geographical distribution of *parlements* and that of estates is that there was no central assembly of estates. The Parlement of Paris was a source of centralized power that benefited primarily the new nobility of the robe.

Parlements and estates in provinces that bordered on another European state posed special security problems for the crown. One of the reasons Richelieu wanted to subdue the *pays d'états* was that many of them were near frontiers. The bulk of the territories annexed during the seventeenth and eighteenth centuries became what were called the *pays des contributions, pays d'impositions*, or *pays conquis*; the main ones were Flanders, Hainaut, Roussillon, Franche-Comté, Alsace, and Lorraine. They were ruled more directly than other parts of France – without estates, *élections*, or any corps of financial officers. The political power of the French crown seems to have been laid on new provinces with an especially heavy hand. Maritime Flanders and Hainaut came into a very different political system when they were transferred from the Habsburg countries. Both were deprived of their estates.[75]

Yet for the same reasons that these frontier territories were strategically important, they could not be treated in a draconian manner. The loyalty of their populations was both important and problematic. Agreements at the time of union were often used later by provincial elites to support their opposition to the crown, as, for example, when the Estates of Brittany declared in 1718 that the Contract of Union of 1532 was being violated.[76] Provincial elites in annexed territories often used treaties signed by France with other states as though they were written constitutions, and years later could be found claiming that these treaties were being violated by the French crown, though such claims were frequently unsuccessful.[77]

In some cases annexation was preceded by a wooing period, during which the population of the prospective province, and especially its elites, were treated with care. While their permission was not necessary for annexation, annexation would be more difficult if local elites were opposed to it. Before the annexation of Alsace, the French crown had established itself as the protector of Alsatian liberties against the Empire. Close ties developed between French elites and Alsatian elites, especially urban elites. During the Thirty Years' War Protestant seigneurs in Alsace looked for protection from France. Alsatian princes and towns accepted French occupation on the understanding that their privileges would be respected and that they would rejoin the Empire at the end of the war. Similar assurances with respect to traditional privileges were contained in the Treaties of Westphalia. In poorly defined terms, they made the French king protector of Alsace. From 1648 to 1679 Alsace was under French control, but not integrated into the rest of France. French sovereignty at this time was fragile, and discontent in the population had to be avoided. No radical change was made in the administration of the province, and Imperial institutions were not eradicated.

After the Treaty of Nijmwegen Alsace was further integrated into France. The loyalty of the Alsatian nobility to the Empire was overcome. They were persuaded to swear allegiance to the French king. The autonomy of the counts of Hanau-Lichtenberg was recognized. Although an intendancy was established in Alsace during the Thirty Years' War, it was slow to become effective. The intendancy did not replace existing political institutions, but took them over and reorganized them. The controller general of finances who wrote in 1701 "that it was unnecessary to touch Alsatian customs"[78] was exaggerating, but the French certainly made an effort to respect Alsatian institutions. France acquired Alsace by claiming to defend its liberties. It was then rather awkward to turn around and trample on these liberties.[79]

Thus, while the *pays d'impositions* were certainly treated differently from other French provinces, their annexation did not change the fundamental character of the French Early Modern state. This character, as I stated in chapter 1, was shaped on the one hand by the centralizing pressure of the state, but on the other by cultural and regional diversity, by the piecemeal manner in which the French state grew, by the provincialism of many state institutions, and by limitations on royal power. As a result of these countervailing forces, members of the French elite varied between those whose interests lay in this centralization and those whose interests lay in opposing it. Although recent qualifications have been helpful, it is still clear that a centre-periphery struggle shaped much of the political life of Early Modern France. Measures adopted by the crown allegedly in the interests of the kingdom were often perceived by people in the provinces as contrary to their rights and interests.[80] Edicts and communications between the central government and provincial elites were full of hyperbole and bold denunciations, each side seeking to gain advantage over the other.[81] The centralist ideology of state officers in Paris was in many ways contrary to much of public opinion.[82]

The Spanish/Austrian Low Countries

The circumstances in which nobles found themselves in the Spanish/ Austrian Low Countries were in some ways similar to those of nobles living in French *pays d'états* – just more so. From the Habsburg bifurcation of the sixteenth century, when sovereignty over the Low Countries passed to Spain, South-Netherlandish nobles played little role in the government of the Habsburg lands. Nobles were overrepresented among leaders of the revolt against Spanish rule. After the revolt, the political power of the nobility declined in both the Northern and the Southern Low Countries, but for different reasons. In the north it declined primarily as a result of the increase in power of urban elites. In the south it declined as a result of the repressiveness and absolutism of Spanish rule.[83] In the immediate aftermath of the revolt, some nobles were executed and others fled abroad or lost their property.[84] Another revolt of the nobility in 1632 failed for lack of support. This attempt was not severely repressed, but the greater nobility withdrew from the affairs of state and experienced a further loss in power.[85] Eventually the greater nobility of the Spanish/Austrian Low Countries recovered, but the centralization of political power during the Austrian period meant they never regained their former position of power.

No South-Netherlandish nobles were at the top of the state hierarchy during Austrian rule. The governor general was a prince of the blood, from 1744 to 1780 Charles of Lorraine, Maria Theresa's brother-in-law. In her government the highest civil servant who helped her rule over the Austrian dominions was Prince Kaunitz; he came from an Austrian noble family. For governing the Netherlands, Maria Theresa relied heavily on the advice of Count Tarouca, a noble, but not a South-Netherlander, though he had lived in the Austrian Low Countries.[86] The administration of the Austrian Low Countries was under the authority of the Supreme Council of the Netherlands, which sat in Vienna and was presided over by Count Tarouca. When this council was abolished in 1757, greater authority was invested in the Imperial Chancery, which favoured more centralized control. The governing of the Austrian Low Countries was primarily in the hands of the plenipotentiary minister in Brussels, who was usually a noble, but not a South-Netherlander. From 1748 to 1753 the plenipotentiary minister was Antoine Othon, marquess of Botta-Adorno, who was an Imperial military and state officer, born in Pavia. He was replaced by Count Charles de Cobenzl, a professional diplomat from a great family of Austrian state servants. When he died in office in 1770 the new plenipotentiary minister was Georges Adam, prince of Starhemberg, who belonged to a great Austrian noble family and had previously been ambassador to France.[87]

Nobles had once been well represented on the Council of State. Noble representation on this council declined after 1632; by the time it was regained in the eighteenth century, most of the powers of the Council of State had been transferred to one of the other collateral councils and membership on this council had become almost honorific.[88] State offices in Brussels were filled mainly by South-Netherlanders, some of whom were from noble families, but the majority of whom were not. The chief president of the Privy Council was, from 1758 to 1783, Patrice François de Neny, whose father, Patrice MacNeny, had immigrated from Ireland and had pursued a successful career in the Austrian administration and was appointed secretary of state and war in 1724.[89]

Thus, as in France, the power of the older nobility was undercut by the centralized monarchy in the seventeenth and eighteenth centuries. Yet the Habsburgs did not establish vertical absolutism to the extent that it was established in France. At the provincial level the older nobility exercised considerable power. Again we see the consequences of the fact that the control of the Spanish over their territories in the Low Countries decreased during the seventeenth century with the decline in Spanish military power. As the Spanish allowed power to decentralize in the seventeenth century, they came to rule on the basis of the support of those members of the nobility and the urban elites whose power was entrenched at the provincial and local levels, while the greater nobility, who were less provincial, were more excluded.[90] Provincial governors were chosen from the greater nobility, but, as in France, they had lost much of their authority.[91] On the other hand, there was an unmistakable bias to the advantage of the nobility when an appointment was made to a provincial council. Not only was the *médianate* reduced by half for members of the nobility, but some of the provincial councils had a number of seats reserved for the nobility.[92] These magistrates were referred to as *conseillers nobles* or *de courte robe*. During the eighteenth century the number of *conseillers nobles* was in decline. Yet a growing proportion of nobles were ordinary magistrates, not *conseillers nobles*.[93]

South-Netherlandish nobles had a better chance of obtaining a state position than French nobles because in the Southern Low Countries there was less venality of office. In addition, though some evidence of royal favouritism towards the appointment of nobles to political posts can be found in France, such favouritism seems to have been more pronounced in the Southern Low Countries. It was motivated by a desire to raise the status of government office, while at the same time using the revenue of office to restore or preserve the economic position of nobles. True, to a large extent, it was the newer nobility of the robe that was selected, while the older nobility was passed over or awarded diplomatic or honorary posts. The number of older nobles in state positions was also restricted by the lack of qualified individuals. Nonetheless, if there was a difference between the Austrian Low Countries and France in the representation of the old nobility in state office, it was certainly that they were better represented in the former than in the latter.

An even greater source of power for the nobility of the Spanish/ Austrian Low Countries was provided by the provincial estates. Although the authority of the estates declined in some ways during the seventeenth and eighteenth centuries, these institutions were still meeting regularly in all the major provinces of the Spanish/Austrian Low Countries (with one exception) and they played an important role in the political process until the French Revolution. This contrasts sharply with the situation in France and it is interesting to note that the one exception in the South-Netherlandish provinces was West Flanders, where representative institutions disappeared at the time this territory was acquired by Louis XIV and where they were not reestablished when it was returned to the Habsburgs by the Treaty of Utrecht.[94]

The progress that was made by the Habsburgs during the last half of the eighteenth century in raising royal revenue was partly offset by

the increasing financial needs of the monarchy. Ironically, modernization of the state under the Austrians contributed to the power of the
provincial estates vis-à-vis the sovereign. The Habsburgs did not have
the same success as the French monarchy in circumventing the control
of estates over taxation. They also came to depend on the provincial
estates to provide security for loans. It is true that they had the greatest
success at undermining the control of the estates over taxation in
Flanders, the most populated and wealthy province. It is also true that
the approval of ordinary taxes had become routine in some provinces.
However, agreement to extraordinary taxes was not routine. Estates
could extend their powers beyond their fiscal competence by attaching
conditions to the approval of extraordinary taxes.[95] Other powers
enjoyed by provincial estates included the right to recognize a new
sovereign (each province recognizing its duke or count), the right of
approval of changes in the provincial constitution, the right of remonstrance to the sovereign, and control over the administration of provincial revenues.[96]

The power of the noble estate relative to other estates varied greatly.
There was no noble estate as such in Flanders. The nobility merely
had the right to attend the meeting of the estates. Yet the nobility of
Flanders had for long sought to infiltrate the urban elite and some of
the power of the Estates of Flanders accrued to nobles as individuals;
many of the representatives of the clergy and of the towns in Flanders
were nobles.[97] In the Estates of Brabant the clergy and the nobility sat
together, votes were taken separately, and then the Third Estate had
to ratify their decision; thus all three estates had a veto power. This
was also true for important decisions made by the Estates of Hainaut
and Namur.[98]

The exclusiveness of the noble estate varied. Even great nobles
could be excluded if they did not have sufficient fiefs or seigneuries
in the province. In Luxembourg, Namur, and other provinces a certain
number of generations or quarters of nobility were required, with the
result that only a minority of the nobility belonged to the noble estate.
In the Duchy of Limbourg and the Lands of Outremeuse it was
necessary to possess a seigneurie with high justice and to have eight
quarters of nobility. From 1587, only titled nobility were admitted to
the Estates of Brabant. Even this rule was too open for this noble
estate, which subsequently imposed still tighter restrictions. These
were not the only provinces where the representativeness of the noble
estate declined during the seventeenth or eighteenth century.[99]

The South-Netherlandish nobility was active in military service, but
less so than the French nobility. The Habsburgs and their military
commanders wanted the officer corps to be composed largely of

nobles, and, consequently, they established military schools to train the lesser nobility for military careers and favoured the nobility in promotions. The number of South-Netherlandish nobles who were interested in a military career was insufficient, however, to avoid promoting commoners, whose elevation was also assisted by the venality of military offices. Thus the proportion of officers who were noble was lower than in the French or Prussian army, though this was partly offset by ennobling some of them and allowing others to usurp noble status. We cannot attribute this bourgeois presence entirely to the fact that the Austrian Low Countries were relatively water-based, since the Habsburg army was, as a whole, less aristocratic than the French or Prussian army. Yet it is significant that the recruitment of noble officers in the Austrian Low Countries was proportionately the highest from two relatively land-based provinces, Hainaut and Luxembourg.[100]

Liège

Throughout the history of Liège there were recurrent political encounters between the prince-bishop and factions within the principality, in particular the nobility, over the authority to be exercised by the prince-bishop and the rights to be enjoyed by the nobility and other groups in the society. The prince-bishop operated under constitutional constraints and his powers were restricted, as seen in chapter 2, by the estates and the Tribunal of XXII. The control that the estates came to have over taxation constituted, as in the Spanish/Austrian Low Countries, a severe limitation on the authority of the sovereign. In contrast with those of the Spanish/Austrian provinces, the Estates of Liège enjoyed legislative power, which they shared with the prince-bishop. A piece of legislation became law only if more than half the members of each estate gave approval. The consent of the estates was also necessary for the prince-bishop to declare war or form alliances. His powers were particularly restricted by the Chapter of Saint Lambert, which had to be consulted on almost all important decisions.

A prince-bishop could endeavour to overcome these constraints on his power in several ways. He could seek to control the membership of the institutions with which he had to contend. The prince-bishop and the canons enjoyed reciprocal powers of appointment: the canons selected the prince-bishop, but the prince-bishop chose half the canons. (The other half were appointed by the pope.) While canons could act independently of the prince-bishop, over time it was possible for him to alter the composition of the chapter to his liking. The prince-bishop had a say as well in the selection of representatives of the Third Estate. Since 1684 the choice of delegates for the Third Estate had been taken out of the control of the democratic communal councils and brought into the hands of the prince-bishop and an urban aristocracy.[101]

The authority of the prince-bishop could also be strengthened by the backing of foreign powers. Constitutionally, the maintenance of the privileges and rights of the prince-bishop was guaranteed by the emperor and by the council of a group of Imperial states known as the Circle of Westphalia, which included Liège. Yet prince-bishops were willing to turn to almost any foreign ruler for assistance. A repeated scenario was the following: the prince-bishop sought to reinforce his position, thereby increasing opposition to his rule, forcing in extreme cases his flight, which might, if he could manage it, be followed by foreign interference to reinstal him and re-establish his authority. More commonly, a prince-bishop simply used an alliance with another sovereign to impose his will, with the threat of outside intervention hanging over the opposition.

All the same, Liège was no absolutist state. If the prince-bishop could turn to other states for aid, so could his opposition. The best example is provided by the Grignoux, who sought French backing in their contest with the prince in the 1630s and 1640s; so vital was this support that the Grignoux were crushed when it was withdrawn in 1648.[102] It was also a common practice in Liège for the nobility or other political factions to seek the backing of popular forces, even the city mob, in their struggles with one another. Moreover, there is no denying that the people of Liège enjoyed unusual constitutional rights. The prince-bishop of Liège was constitutionally weaker than the dukes and counts of the Spanish/Austrian provinces vis-à-vis other political institutions, and his position was less secure.[103]

As in other parts of the Southern Low Countries, we have here a relatively urbanized society with political institutions that the nobility was able to use to preserve some of its power, in this case considerable power. The majority of those who sat as representatives of the Third Estate and the chapter belonged to families of the nobility of the robe, while the Noble Estate was composed largely of members of the older nobility.[104] However, the prince-bishop exercised more control over the Third Estate and the Clerical Estate than over the Noble Estate. Thus it was the old nobility that had greater autonomous power. Noble representation in the Estates of Liège was exclusive, perhaps even more exclusive than it was in the Spanish/Austrian Low Countries.[105] In addition, though the newer nobility were well represented in state offices, certain state offices were reserved for the older nobility.[106]

Savoy

If the provinces of the Southern Low Countries in certain respects resembled the French *pays d'états*, the Duchy of Savoy in certain respects came to resemble the French *pays d'impositions*. The relative powers of the sovereign and the provincial institutions contrasted sharply between the Low Countries and Piedmont-Savoy, though both were members of the small-state belt between France and the Empire. The difference is to be explained, as suggested in chapter 2, at least partly by the military tradition of the House of Savoy and its coercive power, in contrast with the declining military power of Spain in the seventeenth century. It also resulted from the comparative weakness of urban centres in Savoy.

As a result of the intensive power enjoyed by the House of Savoy in the county during the twelfth and thirteenth centuries and the close relationship of the counts with the nobility of this region, many nobles were co-opted by the counts. The castellans were normally nobles. The nobility was represented in the estates, which possessed considerable power in the fifteenth century. *Charges auliques* were the preserve of older families. The council that travelled with the count and advised him was composed of members of the high nobility, along with church-men and legal men.[107]

In the sixteenth century, Emanuel Filibert reduced the political power of the nobility of the Duchy of Savoy significantly by making Turin the capital, by naming Piedmontese to major posts, by assuming more direct control over castellans and selecting non-nobles for the office, by permitting the estates to fall into desuetude, and by setting up new local government offices (the *prefetti* and the *juge-mage*).[108] A number of circumstances coincided to bring this about. Emanuel Filibert reportedly believed that he was entitled to reorganize the state because he had regained possession of his territories by force. He also felt no obligation to his subjects because they had cooperated with the French during the occupation. And the nobility had been reduced in numbers as a result of war and disease.[109] It is noteworthy, however, that the sovereign courts (the Senate and the Chamber of Accounts) survived, whereas the estates did not. This reflected the balance of power in the duchy. The former were more useful to the duke than the estates and they represented the legal bourgeoisie, which was a comparatively powerful force in Savoyard society.

We saw in chapter 2 that in Piedmont-Savoy, as in France, political centralization was achieved mainly through the crown and the state bureaucracy, and primarily during the reign of Victor Amadeus II. The effect was to undermine noble power significantly. The duke greatly increased the number of state positions going to trained professionals. He also imposed more Piedmontese on the administration of Savoy.[110] The nobility themselves were partially responsible for the fact that few could be found among state administrators; they regarded many government posts as beneath their station. Yet Victor Amadeus did not encourage them to pursue careers in his bureaucracy. He was not keen on appointing members of old Savoyard families because they were generally opposed to his program of centralization and were too much under the influence of the local population.[111] He liked to make all appointments himself and to advance career bureaucrats. Out of sixteen intendants of Savoy in the eighteenth century whose birth could be determined by Jean Nicolas, only two were older nobility, while two were the sons of *anoblis*; all the remainder were commoners, mostly with legal training.[112] All governors of the duchy were high nobles, but in most years a noble from Piedmont.[113]

Admittedly, the nobility of Savoy was not excluded altogether. Members of noble families were often able to move up the diplomatic hierarchy and into the court. As in France, the royal court provided for contact between the sovereign and the most illustrious families of the older nobility.[114] And the nobility served the state in arms. The size of the army in Piedmont-Savoy provided the nobility with good career openings in the military. In addition, many Savoyard nobles served in other armies, especially the French.[115] Nicolas found that at the beginning of the eighteenth century half of the noblemen of Savoy had at some time engaged in military service.[116] And when nobles from Savoy did receive powerful positions in the state bureaucracy, it was usually through a military career. The numbers were small, however, and left most members of the older nobility excluded.

Under Victor Amadeus II the political power of the newer nobility of Savoy also declined. Both the Senate and the Chamber of Accounts tried to resist the political centralization undertaken by Victor Amadeus and sought to defend provincial rights and noble privilege.[117] In response, he abolished the Chamber of Accounts and reduced the authority of the Senate, especially its political and administrative authority. Some of its powers were transferred to the intendants, while the Senate became a more specialized institution, entrusted with specific judicial authority. Selection for the Senate was determined mainly by judicial experience, and the presidency was typically accorded to a Piedmontese.[118]

In comparative context, therefore, Savoy provides an example of a peripheral region where a provincial base for political power was nearly absent for the older nobility, and strictly limited, though not absent altogether, for the newer nobility. It was almost a complete opposite to the Southern Low Countries, especially the Principality of Liège. The political power of the nobility was undercut even more than in France, creating a variant of vertical absolutism. To the extent that it was not vertical absolutism it was because the nobility did not even enjoy the nominal power that was preserved for the high nobility in France.

The relationship between the nobility of Savoy and state officials, particularly intendants, could be a difficult one. The intendants were lower in status, without the financial resources to live ostentatiously, but with more political power. They frequently resented the airs of the nobility of Savoy and thought them pompous. Most were opposed to the tax privileges of the nobility and to the seigneurial system. One of the reasons that seigneurialism was eventually abolished in Savoy is that it was repeatedly criticized by Piedmontese officials who had more influence in Turin than did the Savoyard nobility.[119]

Interestingly, the strongest force helping to overcome the political weakness of this nobility was provided by France. The relationship with France of the nobility of Savoy was similar to that of the nobility of Alsace and Liège. As said, many members of the Alsatian elite were favourably disposed towards France because they saw it as their protection against the Empire. A good number were willing to accept annexation to France for this reason. Similarly, different political groups in Liège could turn to France for support against the Empire or against other factions in the principality. Elites in Savoy were even more positive about France than those in Liège or Alsace, not surprisingly in view of Turin's program to reduce the power of the Savoyard nobility. When the centre of the House of Savoy moved eastward and the Duchy of Savoy became a peripheral region, the duchy came under increasing French influence. After 1630, when Charles Emanuel died, French domination over the state of Piedmont-Savoy as a whole expanded and the Duchy of Savoy was turned into a French satellite.[120] Victor Amadeus was largely successful in removing French control over most of his dominions, but he never eliminated French influence in the Duchy of Savoy, which was occupied by the French during the War of the League of Augsburg and the War of the Spanish Succession.

During the seventeenth and eighteenth centuries French annexation of the Duchy of Savoy was regarded by many people as likely, even inevitable. The French sought to control it for strategic reasons, while the dukes were not wholly committed to holding on to it. Victor Amadeus II was willing to exchange it for Milan. Hence Savoyard elites were placed in an awkward position, especially during French occupations, not knowing on which horse they should lay their bets. The

French tried to take advantage of their dilemma to draw them away from the House of Savoy. During French occupations the authority of provincial institutions and the Savoyard nobility was increased and local customs were generally respected. When Victor Amadeus resumed control over Savoy after the French occupation of the 1690s, he dismissed senators and other office-holders appointed by the French.[121] Although this may have driven the pro-French faction into submission, it did nothing to reduce pro-French sentiments in the Savoyard nobility. Thus, they welcomed the next French occupation. It is somewhat amusing, of course, to see the elites of Savoy engaging Victor Amadeus in his own game; just as he played Britain, France, Spain, and the Empire off against one another, they were playing him off against France. The ironic long-term result was to make the elites of Savoy willing to accept annexation by a state every bit as centralizing as the government in Turin.

LOCAL POWER

The seventeenth and eighteenth centuries saw a general decline in the local political power of the nobility in France and Lotharingia. The timing of this decline and the pace at which it occurred varied from one region to another, and some of this variation can help us understand the reasons for the process.

The power of the nobility in the local community varied with its presence in that community. Several further variables determined the strength of such presence. These include the proportion of the land in the district owned by the nobility and the rate of absentee ownership. It is clear that in France the increasing urbanism of the nobility had a negative impact on its local political power. The withdrawal of nobility from the local community played a part in the decline in its influence in the Norman community studied by Dewald.[122] The small number of resident nobles rendered the nobility a weak force in many parts of the French Alps, such as Briançonnais in Dauphiné.[123] A similar situation came to exist in Savoy. Although not the major reason, the geographical distribution of the Savoyard nobility helped to undermine its local political power. The nobility of Savoy had a high rate of urban residence. Some 85 per cent of the nobility was found in the lower valleys and populated areas, more than a quarter in the town of Chambéry.[124] Especially in the higher altitudes, the absence of the nobility reduced its power.

The local power of the nobility varied with the solidarity and autonomy of the peasantry, which were generally greater in France than in the British Isles. French peasants met regularly in village assemblies,

which followed rules laid down in custom. Led by the wealthier peasantry, these assemblies sometimes challenged the power of the local
nobility. They often engaged in lawsuits against local seigneurs. Within
France, peasant solidarity and autonomy were relatively greater in
remote areas, especially those of high altitude, perhaps because peasants were more often left alone, perhaps because more of the land
was held communally.[125] Most noted for their collective spirit were the
Waldensians or Vaudois of the southwestern Alps (who, having been
treated as heretical in the Middle Ages, had become Protestants in the
sixteenth century). Their religious solidarity was as much a consequence of their communal solidarity as their communal solidarity was
a consequence of their religious solidarity.[126] Peasant solidarity may
explain or partially explain why, in France, lords and peasants were at
one another's throats most of all where comparatively more of the
land was held communally, which was especially true in the northeast,
while there was less conflict where less of the land was communal,
such as the west.[127] Yet peasant solidarity was also greater where village
government was more organized, and this was more often the case in
southern France than in the Paris Basin.[128]

The local political power of the nobility was dramatically affected
by the strength of seigneurialism. The authority to appoint local
administrators was enjoyed by countless numbers of seigneurs. Many
seigneurs had the power to convoke village assemblies and may have
had the right to be present at any meeting of the assembly.[129] In the
eighteenth century one still finds seigneurial courts of high justice as
well as a multitude of courts of low justice.[130] Altogether there may
have been twenty or thirty thousand seigneurial courts in France.[131]
Seigneurs appointed judges to seigneurial courts. As a result of the
costliness of rights to higher justice, many seigneurs relinquished
them. In contrast, lower justice, where disputes among peasants were
adjudicated, was more often retained. This was bad enough for peasants, forcing them to stay on the good side of the local seigneur, but
what was worse was that seigneurial courts also adjudicated disputes
between seigneurs and peasants. Thus in those parts of France where
seigneurialism remained hardy, seigneurial rights gave nobles a direct
source of political power. The comparative weakness of seigneurialism
in the Southern Low Countries reduced the local power of the nobility,
though in other ways the South-Netherlandish nobility was comparatively powerful. Seigneurialism was the last source of political power
in the local community enjoyed by the nobility in Savoy after the
centralizing reforms of Victor Amadeus II.

On the whole, however, the political power of seigneurs had
declined more than other types of power. Although the *seigneurie*

banale helped lordship survive longer on the Continent than in the British Isles, it was certainly less inclusive than it had once been. The considerable domination that lords had enjoyed over the daily life of serfs had long since disappeared. Although the position of seigneur still carried considerable prestige, peasants did not as often as before turn to their seigneur to assist them in dealing with powers beyond their local community. The military obligations of peasants to their seigneur had been either eliminated or transformed into the means for recruitment into armed forces under the control of the crown. The crown no longer required the cooperation of the seigneur to levy taxes on peasants. The commutation of dues had decreased the political and increased the economic character of seigneurial authority. Seigneurial consent had become easier for peasants to obtain on the payment of a fee. Seigneurs were more willing than in former centuries to alienate tenants (and thus undermine their loyalty) in order to exact dues or exploit communal lands. Even where seigneurial powers of justice survived, the number of cases coming before seigneurial courts was declining by the eighteenth century.[132] Those lords who had yielded all or some of their seigneurial jurisdiction because of its cost were giving up political power in order to preserve or increase economic power.

In general terms it can be said that the undermining of lordship by the state affected the nobility in two ways. First, seigneurs found their political and judicial powers appropriated by various office-holders, ranging from *parlementaires* to intendants and their subdelegates. Second, if a seigneur was engaged in a struggle with his tenants, he could find them supported by state agents. This happened to seigneurs in northeastern Burgundy.[133] In Savoy seigneurs frequently complained that Piedmontese officials tried to undermine seigneurial power.[134] In the Southern Low Countries the state did less to undermine seigneurialism than in France or Savoy, but even here seigneurs could find their peasants supported in one way or another by the state.[135]

The problem for the nobility was that seigneurialism had been its major source of local political power. What this meant was that, in order to preserve local power, nobles were forced to defend seigneurialism, an increasingly unpopular institution and one that some continental governments were unwilling to protect. Seigneurialism declined later on the Continent than in the British Isles, but to the extent that it did decline it undermined the political power of the aristocracy more.

In both France and Savoy intendants played a major role in weakening the local political power of the nobility. The power of seigneurs over village assemblies had been essentially supervisory; in the seventeenth and eighteenth centuries intendants took over much of that supervision.[136] Often a local noble could establish a relationship with the intendant, but he might have no more influence with the intendant than many of his tenants.[137] The power of the local nobility was limited against an uncooperative intendant. Even historians who are unimpressed with the powers of intendants concede that they were generally unpopular with local elites.[138] One of the major purposes of the intendancies was, in fact, to eliminate "abuses" and violence being committed by local nobles and notables.[139] They could be asked to adjudicate disputes among nobles. They were also required to inform against duelists.[140]

NOBLE COLLECTIVE ACTION

When we look at the historical literature on collective action by the European nobility we find two intellectual traditions, both with considerable evidence to support them. The first, which most historians would identify with Mousnier, though he is far from its only exponent, is the corporatist tradition. It holds that within each country the continental nobility formed a politically unified group. It was not "fragmented" or "internally subdivided."[141] Insofar as Early Modern Europe was not corporatist it was because a new society was beginning within the old, a new society that would eventually replace the society of orders. The best-known political manifestation of the society of orders was, of course, the estates, but even outside the formal structure of estates one can find nobles coming together and engaging in collective action. Some recent research provides examples of this kind of noble collective action.[142]

Very different is another line of argument, in the tradition of Alexis de Tocqueville and Pareto, which emphasizes the political disunity of the continental nobility. Some recent research also supports their view. Dewald's evidence of individualism in French aristocratic culture throws doubt on the ideological basis of the corporatist society.[143] The role of some members of the nobility in liberal movements and in the Enlightenment (which I shall discuss in the next chapter) is further evidence of this individualism. It is also evidence of deep ideological divisions within the French nobility since many other nobles were extremely conservative. Some historians argue that the direction taken by the French Revolution was significantly affected by the fact that the nobility could not get its act together, indeed, that many nobles tried to use the political instability of 1788 and 1789 to assail one another.

In an analysis of the *cahiers de doléances*, John Markoff and Gilbert Shapiro discovered less agreement among the nobility than among the Third Estate.[144]

Much of the opposition within the nobility was between robe and sword. The two often came into political conflict. In the Provincial Council of Luxembourg the *courte robe* (nobles of the sword) squared off against the *longue robe* (nobles of the robe).[145] In the Principality of Liège the Noble Estate, composed of nobility of the sword, was politically opposed to the Clerical Estate, the Chapter of Saint Lambert, which was controlled by the nobility of the robe.[146] The Parlement of Bordeaux and the local nobility of the sword fought against one another for control during the political crisis of 1789.[147]

Opposition was not, however, always between robe and sword. The great differences in wealth that were emphasized in the preceding chapter were as much a source of hostility within the nobility as pedigree or robe and sword. Indeed, many historians have argued that the higher aristocracy of the sword was allied with the *parlementaires* and that the real conflict in the nobility was between the plutocratic elite and the nobility of modest means. Politically the former was comparatively powerful and closely linked with the central state, while the latter was politically weak and disorganized. The wealthy nobility of the sword did, it is true, sometimes endeavour to assist the poor nobility of the sword, but this assistance was often provided in an effort to soothe poor nobles, who generally felt abandoned and excluded by the *grands*. The exclusiveness of many noble estates was also a source of stress within the old nobility. In many provinces the bulk of the nobility resented the power of the noble estate and in some provinces those excluded even engaged in political struggles to undermine the power of the noble estate.

Nor was the *noblesse de robe* fully united, though this depends a bit on what we mean by the *noblesse de robe*, whether the term refers strictly to members of the sovereign courts or more generally to those ennobled by office. Obviously the former (such as *parlementaires*) often came into conflict with the latter (such as intendants). Yet even the *parlementaires* were far from united. French *parlements* frequently came into conflict with one another.

More fundamentally, many historians now reject the assumption that the political institutions of the Old Regime were, or ever had been, primarily emanations of the corporatist structure of the society. While it is agreed that estates facilitated noble collective action, it is no longer agreed that they emerged historically on the basis of a division of society into status groups.[148]

It would be unwise to declare either of these traditions the right one. Groups of nobles certainly did engage in collective action and use their shared status as a basis of solidarity, but they did not consistently do so; they often opposed or undercut one another; and many other political battles took place in which members of the nobility were involved. Status was only one of a number of forces that determined the shape of alliances and conflicts in the Old Regime.

THE DIFFERENTIATION OF POWER

With the rise of the state, political power became less differentiated from status power in some ways and more differentiated in others. Insofar as estates, seigneurs, and the royal court continued to enjoy political power, the fusion of status and political power endured. The great *parlementaire* families enjoyed significant prestige and political power. Elites of the day were adept at getting status power and political power to reinforce each other. Monarchies used their increasing political power to enhance their status, and their status to enhance their political power. Strict attention to aristocratic status hierarchy was employed to undermine the political power of the higher nobility and the princes of the blood, especially in the court of Louis xiv.[149] Status denigration was often used to undermine political power. The king's men frequently tried to weaken the political power of those with whom they were struggling or negotiating by reducing their status through insults and rudeness.[150] Aristocracies tried to do the same. They would invoke their status and rules of precedence in political struggles. This was true at all levels, but an especially good example can be found in the struggle during the sixteenth century over precedence at coronation ceremonies between the peers and the princes of the blood.[151] Similarly, nobles sought to use their aristocratic status to increase their political power by citing their status as a reason for appointing them to state positions. Having sufficient status to approach the king or other politically powerful persons was invaluable in seeking an office or other resources. Contacts in the royal court were especially important for a military career or for procuring military resources.[152]

Nonetheless, political power and status power were becoming more differentiated. The older nobility lost more political power than prestige and thus discontinuity increased between the two kinds if power. Some nobles occupied prestigious positions deprived of their former political authority. A large number of the older nobility had little or no political power, especially at the political centre and in provinces without estates. Even in provinces with estates, nobles might not enjoy significant political power because the noble estate was weak or its membership restricted and because royal power was encroaching on the local political power of the aristocracy, in particular on the political power of seigneurs, which had declined more than their economic or status power. The higher *parlementaires* enjoyed greater political power than status power in comparison with the dukes and peers or other members of the higher nobility. Many state officials, particularly royal ministers, intendants, and subdelegates in the intendancies, enjoyed greater political power than prestige because they were either commoners or members of the newer nobility of the robe. In the provinces the intendant enjoyed more real political power than the governor, but he had to exercise that power carefully because the governor invariably enjoyed higher aristocratic status.[153] Other provincial nobles posed less of this kind of problem, but intendants and their subdelegates were constantly forced to impose royal authority over persons who enjoyed more prestige in provincial society.

The British Isles

THE DIFFERENTIATION OF POLITICAL POWER IN THE MIDDLE AGES

It is evident from our earlier discussion of lordship that the lordships of the Welsh March, northern England, Scotland, and Ireland fused status power and political power, as well as different types of political power. Even in England, lordship fused power. Before they came to England, Norman lords had been accustomed to exercising judicial authority over their vassals and did not give it up easily. Although restricted by customary law, lords in England possessed considerable judicial power and could severely punish their villeins.[154] They also enjoyed military power, which was based on the armed service owed to them by their tenants. Indeed, the number of tenants owing military service to a lord was the primary measure of his power.[155]

However, as was the case in Savoy and other jurisdictions where dukes or counts were able to centralize it, power was in fact comparatively differentiated in post-conquest England, primarily because kings assumed some powers of lordship but not others. They confiscated judicial authority more than most other kinds of power. Yet even judicial authority was not entirely confiscated, not all of it equally. Forceful as he was, Henry II was careful not to interfere in affairs that were generally recognized as the prerogative of the lord.[156] English kings particularly avoided intruding in the tenurial relations between peasants and lords. And the king's justice came to be reserved for the free, while villeins were left to manorial justice. In the late twelfth and the early thirteenth centuries the Angevin monarchy was able to establish its right to treat even unfree villeins as subjects and to tax them and recruit them for military service.[157] Yet officially these same villeins had no rights in the royal courts. An English lord's jurisdiction was not as embracing as that of a French lord, but within his jurisdiction he was permitted by the crown to do with his tenants whatever was allowable under manorial custom.

TAMING THE MAGNATES

Like continental monarchs, English kings delegated power to regional magnates, and co-opted, destroyed, and undercut them.

Southern England

The Norman kings by and large destroyed the power of the Anglo-Saxon magnates. In the following centuries the crown employed a mixture of strategies in dealing with Norman magnates – delegation and co-optation, gradually shifting to co-optation in the sixteenth and seventeenth centuries. Destruction was usually experienced only by certain families or even just certain individuals, typically those who had revolted against royal power. Even the attainders of the Wars of the Roses were used merely to control particular aristocrats, not to cut down their families, and certainly not to cripple magnates in general. Most attainders were reversed.[158]

For their part, the magnates in southern England sought to force the crown to share its authority with them. They did so for the same reason that England developed a strong central parliament – because the English monarchy was powerful. This power did not make magnates powerless. On the contrary, they often exercised considerable influence over the sovereign. When they dominated the country, they did so through rather than in opposition to royal power. The remarkable number of English monarchs who were deposed obviously reflects not the weakness of the English monarchy, but the consistent efforts of English magnates to have a king with whom they could work or to replace him by someone with whom they could work. A less drastic course of action was to push their way into royal councils that advised the king. Admittedly, English kings did have difficulty persuading some magnates whom they summoned to attend their council meetings, later their parliaments, but the problem was not as serious in England as it was in many other European countries. Indeed, English magnates tried to go a step further and to join or replace the inner counsellors of the king by establishing a commission elected by the "prelates, earls and barons" and responsible to them to supervise the king as closely as possible.[159] Alternatively, magnates frequently opposed rule by the king and his closest advisers, pushing instead for rule by the larger king's council.[160]

Most writers have emphasized the reduction in the power of the magnates effected by Tudor monarchs. In Lachmann's terminology, the Tudors established "horizontal absolutism"; that is, they secured control over the magnates and undermined their influence over the local community, which fell into the hands of the gentry.[161] The Tudors curtailed the violence for which magnates were responsible, interfered with castle building, and reduced the number of retainers. The influence of great families over the gentry diminished. Sheriffs, justices of the peace, and commissioners were now oriented towards the monarch in London, on whom they depended for appointment.[162] The militia was reorganized in 1573, making the crown less dependent on the personal followings of magnates. The number of peers who served on the King's Council, which became the smaller Privy Council, decreased sharply.[163] The power that the crown achieved over the peerage is evidenced by its ability to secure convictions when peers were tried by their fellow peers. Only one peer was cleared by his colleagues under Henry VIII.[164]

Yet this kind of argument can easily become oversimplified. We do not want to think of the crown as inexorably overwhelming the magnates. There is not much evidence of magnate resistance to what the Tudor monarchs were trying to do. The majority of the magnates favoured a reduction in aristocratic violence. Each may have wanted to hold onto his own retainers, but most were not opposed to the decline in retaining in general. They stopped building castles at least partly of their own accord because they no longer felt a need for them.[165] Although the gentry had become more independent of the peerage, most peers enjoyed a following among the gentry. If there was anything new it was that members of the gentry increasingly looked for support to the magnates who enjoyed some influence in the political centre. It was this influence that came to determine the power of a magnate.[166]

The crown was not so much seeking to undercut or destroy the power of the magnates as to use their prestige and authority to achieve royal objectives. No less than 67 per cent of the 301 working peers during the Tudor period held a commission of the peace, many several commissions. A good 25 per cent were appointed county lord lieutenant, in some cases to more than one county. Some 27 per cent undertook diplomatic missions. A remarkable 31 per cent held a post at the royal court. And 43 per cent of the peers served on the King's/ Privy Council, over half of whom inherited their peerage. The reduction in the size of the Council had a dramatic effect on the political power of peers, especially those who inherited their peerage, but they were not excluded altogether. Nineteen peers who inherited their peerage served on the Privy Council in the last half of the sixteenth century – not a paltry figure given the small number of such peers and the reduced size of the Council.[167] The reduction in the size of the council decreased the number of peers who could be on it, but increased the power of those who were. And some of the non-peers on the Privy Council were related to peers. For example, Sir Henry Sidney, a privy councillor from 1575 to 1586, was the husband of Mary Dudley, who was closely related to three peers who also sat on the Privy Council – her father, the Duke of Northumberland, and two brothers, the Earl of Leicester and the Earl of Warwick. Sir Thomas Heneage, a privy councillor from 1587 to 1595, was the husband of Mary Browne, who was the daughter of Viscount Montague and widow of the Earl of Southampton.

The Welsh March and the North

Until the sixteenth century the crown delegated authority to the magnates of the Welsh March and the North. These elites enjoyed more autonomous power in their regions than was true of magnates in southern England. In the fifteenth and sixteenth centuries the crown governed the North by means of "wardens," who were usually selected from great northern families.

The delegation of power to the Welsh Marcher lords had been voluntary on the part of the crown and it was generally satisfied with the arrangement for a long time. Individual Marcher lords had sometimes been displaced, but remarkably little effort was made to increase royal authority at the expense of Marcher lords as a group. The same was the case in northern England. Although the relationship here was less cooperative, the conflict between northern magnates and the crown has been exaggerated. Even the Pilgrimage of Grace (1536–37), which has been interpreted as a rebellion of northern magnates against the centralization of power, was (as well as many other things) more in the nature of a revolt of one political faction in London against its loss of power, and was not in fact supported by the five northern earls (Shrewsbury, Derby, Cumberland, Westmorland, and Northumberland).[168] The Northern Rising (1569–70) involved some of the northern earls, but it too was connected with struggles for power in London;

the rebellious lords were members of a pro-Catholic faction that wanted a reconciliation with Spain, the restoration of Mary Queen of Scots, and a recognition of her claim to the English throne.[169]

As a result of its relative satisfaction with delegation in the Welsh March and the North, the crown did not endeavour to destroy the power of magnates, certainly not completely, as it brought these regions under direct rule. It is true that during the Tudor period the government came to depend less on the magnates for defence of the North, relying more on paid troops.[170] More gentry and professional men were to be found on the Council in the North and comparatively fewer members of the great families. The council was incorporated as an administrative arm of the central state and was eventually restricted in power. After the mid-sixteenth century many of the wardenships went to southern peers.

Yet these changes were partly forced on the crown because it had difficulty finding suitable people.[171] During the period following the Pilgrimage of Grace there was a vacuum of power in the North, forcing the government to seek alternatives to magnate rule. For a time Henry VIII assumed the position of warden of the North himself and selected deputies from the gentry.[172] The Northern Rising also removed or disqualified members of great aristocratic families from political office. Nevertheless, in the last half of the sixteenth century, before and after the Northern Rising, several members of leading aristocratic families in the North held wardenships. William, third Lord Dacre; George, third earl of Cumberland; and Lords Henry and Thomas Scrope served as wardens of the West March. Thomas, seventh earl of Northumberland, served as warden of the East and Middle Marches. Lord Henry Hunsdon was warden of the East March. Ralph, third Lord Eure, served as warden of the Middle March. Henry, second earl of Rutland, served as warden of the East and Middle Marches and president of the Council in the North.

This council should not be seen as a means for destroying or under-cutting the position of the great families of the North. In addition to the above peers, all of whom sat on the council, other northern peers on the Council in the North during the last half of the sixteenth century included Sir Henry Percy, later eighth earl of Northumberland; Henry, second earl of Cumberland; William, second Lord Eure; Henry and Charles, fifth and sixth earls of Westmorland; John, sixth Lord Lumley; Edward, third earl of Rutland; and Cuthbert, seventh Lord Ogle.[173] What was the case was that northern peers did not enjoy as much power in the political centre as did peers in southern England. They were decidedly absent from the Privy Council in the last half of the sixteenth century.

In short, the English crown did not endeavour to destroy or under-cut the power of the Welsh or northern magnates, but at the same time it did not co-opt them at the centre to the extent that magnates from southern England were co-opted. For their part, the magnates did not vigorously challenge the way in which they were being treated. Most magnates in the Welsh March put up little resistance to their loss of autonomous power in the sixteenth century. The crown had no difficulty appropriating what remained of their regal powers by the Acts of Union of 1536 to 1543. One is inclined to argue that the magnates of the North put up greater resistance, though much depends on how one interprets the Pilgrimage of Grace and the Northern Rising. In any case, the majority of northern magnates acquiesced to the centralization of power under the Tudors.

Scotland

The strategy of delegating power and co-opting some magnates, while destroying or partially destroying the power of others, was pursued most manifestly by Scottish kings. Magnates in Scotland, like those in the Welsh March and the North, had more territorial autonomy than did magnates in southern England.[174] Fewer royal resources account for this in large part, but recent scholarship has stressed the cooper-ative relationship that existed between the crown and the magnates. Scottish kings ruled by establishing personal bonds with the great lords, who cooperated with the crown in preserving order. Thus the Scottish crown allowed magnates to command large areas in the name of the king.[175] At the same time, Scottish magnates saw less reason than did English magnates to try to influence the king. In the late Middle Ages they were more immune from the consequences of central politics.[176] It was for this reason that the crown in Scotland had difficulty persuading some lords to attend Parliament.

The kind of cooperation sought by the crown was threatened by the emergence of the Macdonald Lordship of the Isles in the fourteenth century. The forfeiture of the Lordship of the Isles might seem to represent a shift in strategy from delegation to destruction, but the crown continued to delegate authority or accept the autonomous power of great families. It was noted in chapter 4 that the fall of the Macdonalds increased the power of the Campbells, Gordons, and Mackenzies. Scottish kings did seek to centralize power in their hands. Yet struggles between the crown and the magnates usually involved only a small number of families. Not even the destruction of the Douglases by James II in the mid-fifteenth century was part of a general effort to crush the power of magnates.[177]

Although historians now accord Scottish magnates of the fifteenth and sixteenth centuries more credit than was formerly given them for maintaining law and order, the delegation of power did nonetheless permit considerable lawlessness and violence. More than once Scottish sovereigns were held captive by great magnates; most magnates felt free to use force to protect their interests; and feuds were chronic even in the early seventeenth century. James VI thought it was imperative to "roote out these barbarouse feadis."[178] He attacked the powers of independent chieftains. Legislation in 1597 obliged all landowners in the Highlands and Western Islands to produce valid title deeds or to risk forfeiture of their lands.[179] When he became king of England he possessed vastly greater resources than any previous Scottish monarch. Some chiefs were forced in 1609 to sign bonds, known as the Statutes of Iona, by which they agreed to give up many of their powers and to appear before the Privy Council each year to account for their conduct. In the same year, justices of the peace were established on the English model to try to check the power of Scottish magnates.[180]

And yet most of these undertakings fell far short of James's hopes. The powers of the crown were difficult to extend into the Highlands and Western Islands. Direct rule was frustrated by the distances and terrain that had to be traversed to reach most parts of the west and north of Scotland, by the absence of roads, and by the bellicosity and solidarity of the clans. Many chiefs simply ignored the Statutes of Iona. The justices of the peace were not as effective in Scotland as they were in England.[181]

The crown continued to rely heavily on delegation. It entrusted whole regions to the Campbell earls of Argyll, the Gordon earls of Huntly and Sutherland, and the Mackenzie earls of Seaforth.[182] One of the most significant developments in the Highlands and Western Islands in the fifteenth to seventeenth centuries was the rise of the House of Argyll, the senior branch of the clan Campbell.[183] They acquired their dominant position in two ways: by establishing an extensive power network in the Highlands and Western Islands, securing the loyalty of cadet branches over a large geographical area;[184] and by obtaining the support of the central government, in return for keeping the peace in the Highlands and Western Islands. This hegemony required the destruction of the power of the major rivals of the Campbells, primarily the clan Donald, for which the Campbells were rewarded with the greater part of the MacDonald mainland possessions.[185] The power of the violent clan McGregor was also destroyed, though members of the clan survived in hiding or by temporarily altering their surname.[186] This destruction of other clans continued in the eighteenth century. The failure of the Jacobite rebellions was critical. They were supported by a good number of Highland clans out of opposition to the Campbells. The Jacobite defeat in 1746 led to executions, property confiscations, the eradication of heritable jurisdictions, and a prohibition of the kilt. The autonomous political power of many Highland families was destroyed.

Like lordship, delegation persisted longer in the Scottish Highlands and Western Islands than anywhere else in the British Isles. Yet the role of the House of Argyll was undergoing considerable change. Campbell politicians became not just the crown's agents in the Highlands and Western Islands, but also the representatives of Scottish interests in the political centre.[187] No aristocratic family in the British Isles made the transition from delegation to co-optation more successfully than the House of Argyll. They did so, however, at the expense of other aristocratic families in the Scottish Highlands and Western Islands.

Ireland

As the effective rule of the English over Ireland contracted in the late Middle Ages, the crown was forced to delegate more power to magnates in Gaelic regions and in areas of Anglo-Norman settlement outside the Pale. It was an unsatisfactory arrangement from the royal point of view, particularly in Gaelic regions, where powerful lords paid little attention to the king's nominal authority. Some control over Gaelic lords was exercised by Anglo-Norman magnates, on whom the crown had to depend to protect the English from the Gaelic Irish. In addition, certain Anglo-Norman lords were delegated extraordinary formal political authority. Such authority came to be exercised in the late fifteenth and early sixteenth centuries by the Fitzgeralds, earls of Kildare. The most successful was Gerald Fitzgerald, eighth earl of Kildare, who was governor of Ireland for the better part of the period from 1478 to 1513.

It is not surprising, however, that a king like Henry VIII and a chief minister like Cromwell would find the autonomous authority of the Kildares intolerable, especially in view of their Yorkist sympathies. The Kildares were led into rebellion in the 1530s. The ninth earl died in the Tower of London and his son was executed in 1537. The fall of Cromwell in 1540 was followed by a less coercive strategy under the governorship of Anthony St Leger. It was he who undertook the program of surrender and re-grant. And in varying degrees some delegation of authority to Anglo-Norman magnates was tried on several later occasions. Yet for the most part this method of ruling Ireland was gradually replaced after the fall of the Kildares by government through a deputy of English birth supported by a standing garrison and controlled more tightly from London.[188] No Anglo-Norman lord in the subsequent period enjoyed the authority that had been exercised by the Kildares. The increasing militarism of English rule was accompanied by an effort to shift power to the New English. Over time, and often as a result of rebellion, the power of most traditional Anglo-Norman dynasties was destroyed.[189]

The delegation of authority to Gaelic chiefs had always been out of necessity, especially in comparison with royal delegation in England and the March of Wales. Gaelic lords repeatedly rose in revolt and routinely inflicted violence on their enemies in both the Gaelic and the Anglo-Norman population. The last uprising led by a Gaelic magnate was that of Hugh O'Neill, earl of Tyrone, in 1595–1603. He overcame an English army in August 1598 at the Battle of the Yellow Ford, but was defeated himself in December 1601 at the Battle of Kinsale, despite Spanish assistance. It was the failure of this rebellion that undermined the position of Gaelic magnates in Ulster and led Tyrone and Tyrconnell to their "flight." A certain number of Gaelic and Old English aristocrats remained powerful. Some took part in the rebellion of 1641, though it is indicative of what was happening to Gaelic aristocrats that the military commander was Owen Roe O'Neill, nephew of Hugh O'Neill, who had served in the Spanish army since 1610. Eventually, political power was transferred to New English aristocrats. Their relationship with the crown was very different. Even the greatest of them did not exercise the autonomous power that had once been enjoyed by Gaelic and Anglo-Norman magnates in Ireland.

Native Wales

Native Wales was unique. Here magnate power was destroyed earlier than anywhere else in the British Isles. In the late thirteenth century, Edward I quite simply dispossessed and disinherited the leading Welsh families and undertook a massive program of building castles, which were used as centres of government administration and as a means of military domination. Edward's settlement degraded the great Welsh dynasties to powerlessness. He declared that all the lands of native Wales had escheated to the crown. Many Welsh dynasties lost their lands.[190]

Although lands were granted to Anglo-Normans and a new aristocracy emerged, delegation of large powers to autonomous magnates never reappeared in the Principality of Wales. Power at the English centre could be achieved by those Welsh families who could marry into the English or Marcher peerage. Yet Wales continued to be underrepresented in the peerage because Welsh landowners considered sufficiently wealthy and influential to merit a peerage were few in numbers.[191]

In part what happened in Wales was an accident of history. If Llywelyn ap Gruffudd had not been killed in 1282, or if Edward II had won the Battle of Bannockburn in 1314, Wales and Scotland could have followed a more similar path. Nonetheless, the early destruction of magnate power in native Wales is understandable. The English crown found the delegation of authority unsatisfactory in the Principality of Wales during the twelfth and thirteenth centuries in comparison with the delegation of authority in the Welsh March. Native Wales was strategically almost as crucial as the Welsh March, certainly more strategically crucial than Ireland or Scotland, but easier and less costly to conquer and rule directly than Ireland or Scotland, and, unlike the Welsh March, it was inhabited by an "alien race," which the English crown was less likely to trust with delegation.

Conditions for Delegation and Co-optation

There was nothing inevitable about the growth of royal power over all of the British Isles, much less how and when various peripheral magnates were brought under control. The crown adopted or was forced to adopt different strategies for different peripheral elites. By making a few comparisons we are now able to draw some general conclusions about the conditions underlying these strategies. Which strategy was employed was determined by the cost of military conquest and direct rule of the region, the strategic importance of the region, the similarity of the culture in the region to that of the centre, and the character of delegation.

As a rule, delegation was employed for regions of relatively less strategic importance and where the cost of conquest or direct rule was high, though differences in cultural homogeneity produced exceptions to this rule. If sovereigns were relatively confident of the loyalty of magnates in a region (usually as a result of personal ties or some cultural homogeneity), they might permit delegation even if they had the capacity to impose royal authority directly. This was clearly the case in the Welsh March, but the policy of Scottish monarchs with respect to some regional magnates in the Lowlands had a similar character.

What conditions led to co-optation as opposed to destruction? Again cultural homogeneity was a factor. Southern English magnates were co-opted the most, while indigenous Welsh and Irish magnates were destroyed the most. Thus destruction or partial destruction was usually employed where there were greater cultural differences, though if, as in the Scottish Highlands and Western Islands, an area was costly to subdue and of relatively less strategic importance, destruction could be late in coming.

Co-optation was unlikely to be promoted by the crown where delegation had been forced upon it and/or where magnates had previously been relatively uncooperative with the crown. This was clearly the case in Ireland and in pre-conquest native Wales, and was also the case in the Scottish Highlands and Western Islands after the Union of the Crowns in 1603. This variable also provides us with part of the explanation for the differences that emerged between England and France. The crown was less willing to co-opt magnates in France during the seventeenth and eighteenth centuries because delegation and co-optation had been previously forced upon it to a greater extent than was the case in England and because, on the whole, the French crown found its magnates to be less cooperative.

Finally, as we shall see more clearly in the following pages, English and Scottish kings did not undercut the power of great magnates as much as French kings did – they did not build clientele networks directly with the local population and/or invest lower-status royal agents with royal power while leaving great magnates as the nominal head of a region. One could argue that justices of the peace were instituted for this purpose, but they did not become royal agents for undercutting magnate power; indeed the crown had to use great magnates to try to control over-independent justices. English and Scottish monarchs avoided undercutting, not only because they had generally enjoyed a reasonably cooperative relationship with more magnates, but also because they lacked the financial resources to establish a network of professional civil servants in the counties and the peripheries.

THE DIFFERENTIATION OF POLITICAL POWER IN THE EARLY MODERN PERIOD

Royal Court

By the eighteenth century the British royal household and court were weaker than the French, but they gave high aristocrats a fair measure of power, especially in earlier periods, principally as a result of the influence that could be exerted on the king or queen through personal contact.[192] There was great variation from one reign to another in the influence of courtiers and household officers, depending on the personality, habits, and policies of different monarchs.[193] Courtiers and household officers were often favoured in appointments, titles, and grants of land; and a court office was frequently the first step in the career of a young aristocrat.[194] Court factions played a critical role in British politics as they did in French. Attendance at court was essential for political influence. The failure of a prominent politician to attend court implied that he was going into opposition.[195] Ministers had to go to court to demonstrate that they had the confidence of the king or queen and to persuade him or her to support actions that the government was taking.[196] It was difficult for a ministry to survive if it did not have people in the court supporting it, a fact well illustrated by the problems faced by ministries during the period in which George I was influenced by his German courtiers.[197]

Like the French court, the British court was perceived as powerful. Government ministries worried about the influence of court favourites with the monarch. At the very least, the household had considerable control over access to the monarch and over the information that reached him or her.[198] The political power of the British court, again like that of the French court, contributed to the fusion of power because attending court or occupying a household post was prestigious in itself and because most of those attending court or belonging to the royal household were from the peerage or the gentry, except those holding menial positions. Indeed, the highest court offices were reserved for peers. Often the same persons held positions in the royal household and simultaneously occupied powerful political posts outside the royal court. All peers who held a court position obviously combined this with a seat in the House of Lords, but other examples can be found.[199]

For a number of reasons, however, the British royal court eventually came to fuse power less than the French royal court. The primary reason was that there were other sources of centralized power for high-status aristocrats in the British Isles besides the crown. This was less true in France, where only the Parlement of Paris provided an alternative source of centralized power for high nobles. Its functions were very different from those of the British Parliament, which was much more powerful than the Parlement of Paris and a greater source of political power for the aristocracy. As a consequence, though the royal court remained an important source of power, politics in the royal court in England was gradually replaced over the course of the seventeenth and the early eighteenth centuries by "parliamentary/aristocratic politics."[200]

It will be shown in the next chapter that the British royal court waned as an aristocratic cultural centre in the late seventeenth and the early eighteenth centuries. This inevitably weakened its political power. As a result, though ministers had to attend regularly, the court did not attract the country's leaders. Those who came most often to court were members of old families that had had a connection with the court for generations, along with individuals of lesser weight who came to court usually to meet people.[201] The court "serves me for a coffee-house, once a week," wrote Jonathan Swift contemptuously.[202]

Intentionally or not, Parliament restricted the power of the royal court by limiting its financial resources. During the sixteenth century the crown was able to use its own sources of money to finance a lavish court. This remained the case up to and including most of the reign of Charles II.[203] Financial problems, however, forced him to reduce the attractiveness of his court in the later years of his reign. Most subsequent monarchs did not have enough money to run the court properly, and certainly they had nothing like the financial resources that Louis xiv was able to mobilize to fund his court and palaces.[204] The crown was dependent on a subsidy approved by Parliament, first granted under William iii and known as the "civil list." Queen Anne was supposed to receive 40 per cent of the civil list revenue for the royal household, but in fact she never received the amount to which she was entitled.[205] As a result, employees and bills sometimes went unpaid; the staff was trimmed; and many normal court activities had to be limited.[206] The size of the royal household declined from about 1450 under Charles i to around 950 under George i.[207] When White-hall Palace was destroyed by a fire in 1698 it was not rebuilt, and Parliament never came forth with the money necessary to give the British monarch a suitable principal residence.[208] The parliamentary subsidy was increased for the Hanoverians, but they continued to have difficulty covering the costs of their court with the money provided by Parliament, though much of the problem lay in other expenses met out of the civil list.[209]

The weakness of the British royal court (at least as compared with the French) would seem to support the arguments of those historians who have emphasized the importance of party divisions rather than the cleavage between "court" and "country" in English politics.[210] The terms "court" and "country" certainly do not identify two real political factions. Nevertheless, these terms were used by contemporaries. The court supposedly consisted of those who benefited from the wealth and power of London – the crown, courtiers, office-holders, politicians, and statesmen in London, who were all allegedly in league with the City merchants and financiers. They were opposed by the country, those who did not enjoy any of the spoils of power and hence were opposed to paying for them. That made them more hostile towards courtiers and the extravagance of the court, more reluctant to bear the burdens of war, more disgruntled about taxation, and more contemptuous of financiers and merchants.

The misleading use of the term "court party" in the British Isles testifies not to the power of the royal court, but to its weakness. It was precisely because the centre of British politics was more than the court proper that the term "court" came to have a wider meaning in the British Isles. The power that was concentrated in the royal court in France was shared in England by a larger group that did not enjoy power primarily because they were courtiers. In Britain, from the late seventeenth century, membership in the royal court almost never sufficed to make a person politically powerful, with the exception of a few royal favourites. One had to be in the governing ministry, have a seat in the House of Lords or the House of Commons, or hold an important state office. Even in the sixteenth century, though the royal court was the centre of political struggles, it was usually necessary to be more than just a courtier.[211] This necessity increased over the course of the seventeenth century. Whereas in France the ultimate centre of political power was the king and those who surrounded him, in the British Isles the ultimate centre of political power by the eighteenth century was Parliament.

State Offices

Many persons from peerage or gentry families held high state offices. Most lords privy seal, first lords of the Treasury, and secretaries of state were peers or sons of peers; every lord chamberlain, lord president of the Council, and lord lieutenant of Ireland belonged to the peerage, while almost every lord chancellor was a peer.[212] Robert Walpole was not a peer until 1742, when he became the first earl of Orford. He was, however, from the gentry and was the only first lord of the Treasury in the eighteenth century who was not connected with the peerage. Of the twenty-two persons who held this position, sixteen were hereditary peers, four were sons of peers, and one was the grandson of a peer.[213] Every cabinet formed during the eighteenth century had at least one duke.[214] When the Duke of Newcastle became first minister in 1754 he had an inner cabinet containing only one non-peer and an outer cabinet containing two non-peers. A decade later George Grenville was the sole commoner in his (Grenville's) cabinet.[215] Yet he was no ordinary commoner. He was the nephew of Lord Cobham and he married Elizabeth Wyndham, daughter of Sir William Wyndham and sister of the Earl of Egremont. Of the sixty-five persons belonging to cabinets from 1782 to 1820, forty-three were peers and most of the rest were related to peers.[216] Although available statistics are difficult to compare, there can be no doubt that in the eighteenth century the English peerage, proportional to its numbers, was better represented on the high councils of state than the greater nobility in France.

Two closely related reasons are unmistakable. The first has already been indicated: the comparatively cooperative relationship with English magnates that the crown had long enjoyed, which made it more willing to trust them. The second reason is that by the seventeenth century British sovereigns needed to have members of the peerage or greater gentry on royal councils to take advantage of their influence over Parliament. It was obviously necessary to enlist the assistance of peers in order to influence the House of Lords. To control the House of Commons, it was necessary to appease those with influence over the elections that sent MPs to London. Peers were essential for influencing the Commons because many of the members of the Commons were related to peers and/or were their clients. The French king had none of these concerns in selecting close advisers.

The Military

Unfortunately, little research has been done on the role of the aristocracy in the military in the British Isles. The most common assumption among historians has been that English aristocrats were less interested in military life than continental aristocrats. A few historians have, however, raised some doubts.[217] The data I have come across indicate that the peerage and gentry were vastly overrepresented in the military, but, unlike the French nobility, did not enjoy a monopoly of officer positions. In the Indian army only 7.5 per cent of the officers were from the peerage or gentry in the period 1758 to 1774, and 16.5 per cent in the period 1775 to 1804.[218] In contrast, an army list for the British Home army in 1780 shows 40 per cent to be from the peerage or gentry.[219] In 1769 some 70 per cent of the field marshals were peers, 27 per cent of the full generals, 16 per cent of the lieutenant generals, and 10 per cent of the major-generals.[220] Many colonels of regiments were peers.[221] Among thirty-three officers of the Seven Years' War studied by J.W. Hayes, no less than 51 per cent were sons of members of the gentry, and 27 per cent were sons of peers.[222] Many British aristocrats or their sons also served in foreign armies; most prominent were the Scots.

Ideally, we would like to know what proportion of the sons in a sample of peerage or gentry families went into the military, but I have not been able to find such a study. Table 11 provides the results of a

Table 11
Careers of a Sample of Men Listed in *Dictionary of National Biography*:
Percentage Serving at Some Time in Navy or Army

Military service	England and Wales			Ireland			Scotland		
	A Father had no title	B Father had a title	C Impossible to determine	A Father had no title	B Father had a title	C Impossible to determine	A Father had no title	B Father had a title	C Impossible to determine
No military service	91.6	69.5	90.7	84.4	56.3	82.5	92.3	60.0	95.5
Service in navy	3.8	6.9	4.9	1.6	6.3	5.0	1.4	1.7	0.0
Service in army	4.6	23.6	4.4	14.1	37.5	12.5	6.3	38.3	4.6
TOTAL	897	174	453	64	32	40	143	60	66

To be included, a man must have been born in the British Isles and have died in the seventeenth or eighteenth century. The titles were duke, marquess, earl, viscount, baron, baronet, or knight. See appendix for a discussion of methodological problems. See note 223 for source.

sample that I took from the *Dictionary of National Biography*. Unfortunately it was generally impossible to judge from entries in the *Dictionary* whether or not a man's father was a landowner; all that could be ascertained was whether or not the father had a title, and even this could not be determined with certainty in a large number of cases. The analysis is also plagued with certain methodological problems that I discuss in the appendix. As a result, the data need to be interpreted with the utmost caution. In particular, it is not possible to compare these percentages with estimates that have been given for the proportion of the French and Savoyard nobilities who had served in the military at some time.[224]

Yet some tendencies in the table are so pronounced that several conclusions can be drawn with reasonable confidence. In all three countries, sons of title-holders joined the army proportionately much more often than sons of non-title-holders. These data thus support the revisionists, suggesting that the British (including the English) aristocracy was significantly more militaristic, at least in the army, than historians have generally assumed. It is also contrary to what the Foxian model would lead us to expect. Yet we should not reject the Foxian model too quickly. As the model would predict, the British navy was less aristocratic than the British army, and the percentage of sons of title-holders in the army was significantly greater in Scotland and Ireland than in England and Wales.

Moreover, since we have no comparable data for our continental countries, table 11 does not disprove the conventional view that the percentage of the English peerage or gentry entering the military was less than the percentage of the French nobility doing so. It is likely that the rate of participation was lower for the English aristocracy in the seventeenth century when British armies were smaller. For the eighteenth century we just do not know. Further research is necessary with comparable data.[225]

Finally, there remains considerable evidence that the English aristocracy was less militaristic in ethos than the French or Savoyard aristocracy until the late eighteenth century.[226] Opposition to the cost of wars was greater among the country gentry and in the House of Commons than among many other social groups. So was opposition to a standing army.[227] It is difficult to imagine the country nobility in France leading opposition to a standing army. Given the insularity of the British Isles, the English gentry were not persuaded of the need for this kind of force, certainly not a large one, and were suspicious of those who argued in favour of one. This view was not inconsistent with sending their sons, especially non-inheriting sons, into the armed services. Nor obviously was it inconsistent with the participation of many gentry in county militia, which they much preferred because it was managed by the landed elite.[228]

The British House of Lords

The House of Lords had enormous legislative and judicial authority. Although the will of the House of Commons prevailed on financial matters, the upper chamber still had a veto over legislation coming to it from the Commons. In addition, with the removal in 1641 of most of the judicial functions of the Privy Council, the House of Lords became the only court of final appeal.[229]

It must be allowed that the power of the House of Lords declined in the Early Modern period as a result of encroachments from both the crown, on the one side, and the House of Commons, on the other. The objective of the government of the day was to command a majority in the House of Lords. In the eighteenth century it was generally able to do so. If it came to it, the crown could bring the Lords into line by threatening to add new lords to the House. An attempt to remove this royal prerogative failed in 1719.[230]

Recent scholarship has argued, however, that the House of Lords was not the pliant tool of the crown.[231] The lords did not always do what they were told by the ministry. Moreover, when peers supported the governing ministry they often did so because they belonged to the government or governing party and/or because they were bribed with offices, pensions, or concessions to their interests. It is debatable whether these bribes constitute evidence of an absence of principles. They certainly do not constitute evidence of political weakness. Lords were using their political power to serve their private interests.

The British House of Commons

The British House of Commons constituted a major source of power for both the peerage and the gentry. Despite the role played by urban elites in the historical evolution and consolidation of the English Parliament, the power that Parliament enjoyed fell primarily into the hands of the aristocracy. Many members of the House of Commons had always come from landowning families. In fact, knights of the shire had been summoned to the English Parliament before representatives of the towns; most of these knights were gentleman landowners. In addition, it had become not unusual for gentleman landowners to represent boroughs. In the Yorkist Parliaments for which we have data, gentleman landowners outnumbered townsmen two to one, whereas townsmen should have outnumbered the gentry three to one.[232] In elections to the Commons from 1660 to 1689, 77.3 per cent of those obtaining seats were country gentlemen; 52.7 per cent were country gentlemen with no other occupation. The number who were country gentlemen with no other occupation outnumbered those who were businessmen with no other occupation twenty-fold.[233] A shire or borough constituency might be controlled by members of the same family for decades. The Owens of Orielton, for example, dominated the representation from Pembrokeshire, particularly in the years 1660 to 1700, when only twice was the county not represented by an Owen.[234]

Although a British peer himself could not sit in the British House of Commons, his sons (even the heir apparent) could, as well as other dependants. What is more, some members of the Commons belonged to the Irish peerage. John Cannon calculates that among the 558 MPs in the Commons in 1708, seventy were Irish peers or sons of British peers. The number dropped to fifty-four in 1710 and forty-eight in 1713. It subsequently rose, reaching 113 in 1754 and 120 in 1796. In addition, many MPs were baronets or related to baronets. In 1784, for example, 107 MPs were Irish peers or sons of British peers, another 68 were related by blood or marriage to British peers, and another 129 were baronets or related by blood or marriage to baronets.[235]

Immense political power was possessed by those British peers who had clients and relatives in the House of Commons. Scholars such as Richard Lachmann, who stress the autonomy of the local gentry, underestimate the ties that linked the great lords to the lesser lords, and the interlocking lines of patronage and clientage that linked the monarchy with the local society through the great lords. M.L. Bush has quite correctly suggested that some historians have overestimated the gentry's dependence on the great lords during the late Middle Ages and underestimated their dependence during the Modern period.[236] Not a small number of members of the Commons who challenged the crown during the first six months of the Long Parliament were clients of peers.[237] British monarchs did not undercut the power of the high aristocracy to the extent that French kings did.

A seat in the House of Commons was a coveted prize. It was valuable as a source of political power, but it was even more valuable as a symbol of both political power and status power. The reason that most of those elected to the House of Commons were landowners was not the property qualification, which could be evaded.[238] More instrumental was their prestige. And it was to demonstrate that they had such prestige that landed families sought to acquire and maintain the representation of a county or borough in the Commons.

Electoral Power

The relationship between different types of power in the British Isles cannot be fully appreciated without examining as well the way in which landowners used their economic power – their control over land – to exert political power. The contractual tenancy, which had by the eighteenth century become the predominant form of land tenure in the British Isles, put the tenant in a vulnerable position vis-à-vis the landowner. In Scotland the threat of eviction was used by landowners to mobilize military forces, but by the seventeenth and eighteenth centuries the major political function of the threat of eviction in most parts of the British Isles was influence over elections. This source of political power was obviously not available to continental aristocrats for two reasons: peasants did not vote in elections to political assemblies that were as powerful as the British House of Commons; and more of the land on the Continent was owned by the occupiers, who could not be ejected for insubordinate political behaviour.

It has even been suggested that the precocious development of comparatively democratic institutions in the British Isles was the result of the decline of customary modes of tenant security; that is, landowners saw that they could control votes in a way that urban elites could not, and this influenced the extension of the franchise. Except in Scotland, the legal requirement for voting in a county constituency was the ownership of freehold property worth forty shillings per year, but this qualification was interpreted in such a way that a good number of tenants enjoyed the franchise in parliamentary elections. Through various devices, landowners could increase the number of voters on their landed estates by granting leases of certain kinds or by creating fictitious voters.[239] As a result, a landowner's power varied directly with the number of voters on his or her estate.[240]

This view has come under criticism, particularly in the debate over agrarian class structure discussed in chapter 4. Not surprisingly, those who reject the thesis that tenants in the British Isles were subject to arbitrary ejectment are led to reject the notion that they were required to vote for the landlord's candidate. These writers contend that tenants had more security than the above argument assumes and so could not be easily bullied. It has also been maintained that only those landowners who had a patron-client tie with their tenants could influence their voting, and that even these patrons could not take the support of their tenants for granted.[241] Coercion could be counterproductive. The right to vote was a source of status in the British Isles; this status would be diminished if a voter was seen to be the pawn of a landowner. As a result, many landowners failed in their efforts to influence the votes of tenants and could suffer humiliating defeats.[242] The domination of a particular landed family over the representation of a county could be challenged by another landed family or by factions composed of non-landed or marginal members of the landed elite.[243] The costly and active campaigning that candidates frequently entered into is strong evidence to the effect that voters had a choice.[244]

While the revisionists provide evidence of non-deferential voting, they do not deny that there is also evidence available of deferential voting. A tenant often had more than one vote, and the usual practice was to allocate one to the candidate supported by the landlord and the other to the candidate of choice.[245] There are some examples of undisguised intimidation. In 1740 Lord Mansel was assured that "all persons that hold any lands under your lordship is safe and will obey your directions for they dare not do otherwise."[246]

The electoral power of landowners was manifestly the result of their status power and their economic power. Deference is one possible way in which to label this fusion. It is certainly the best term to describe what happened in many cases. Yet the revisionists are quite right that we are not talking about grovelling deference and that voters were not easily malleable. A landowner needed to win the respect and esteem of his or her tenants in order to influence their votes. In the British Isles status power was closely tied to the ownership of land, but it did not come automatically with ownership. The best strategy was enunciated by Thomas Gisborne in his treatise on the duties of persons of various statuses. His advice to a landowner was explicit. "Let him unite the votes of his tenants to his own by argument and honest persuasion (if his conduct towards them has been as it ought, even those means will scarcely ever be necessary): but let him not force their compliance by menaces of expulsion from their farms or forfeiture of his favour."[247]

The situation in towns was different. Yet there, too, landowners had significant electoral power. Although some historians have certainly oversimplified borough representation, the historical record provides us with so many cases in which a single family was consistently elected from a particular borough that it is impossible to accept that the majority of these members of parliament were freely elected. Many towns were "rotten boroughs" (few people lived in them) or "pocket boroughs" (they were effectively controlled by the local landlord). The easiest to control were "manor boroughs," where the land was all owned by the same landowner.[248] In the majority of Irish boroughs, the franchise was held either by members of the corporation or by freemen of the borough and members of the corporation. Admission to the freedom of a borough had generally come to depend on the patron. Borough elections were largely under the control of patrons.[249]

In Scotland the power of landowners over voting was even greater than in England, Wales, or Ireland. There the requirement for voting was forty shillings of superiority or lordship under a Medieval taxation schedule (the "Auld Extent"), or £400 (Scots) of superiority according to contemporary valuation. This created a much smaller number of voters. Although the number rose during the eighteenth century, even in 1788 there were on average only about eighty per county,[250] many of whom would be landlords. There were various ways of increasing the number of voters by bogus transfers of superiority. In this manner a landlord could expand the number of voters among his or her tenants.

Finally, even if elections in the British Isles were characterized by some freedom, the choice of candidates was not. The overwhelming majority of candidates came from landed families, and selecting them was usually in the hands of a small elite group.[251] When they were able to come to an agreement, they could avoid a contest altogether. Until well into the nineteenth century the majority of elections were uncontested. And, when contested, county elections had become so expensive that none but very large landowners could finance them. Anyone else had to have the support of large landed interests.[252] Generally speaking, the greater the wealth and status of a landed family, the greater its electoral power. The most powerful were peers. Cannon has estimated that peers controlled or partially controlled the selection of 105, or one-fifth of the MPs in the House of Commons in 1715; by 1784 it had reached 197.[253]

Lords to Magistrates

England and Wales
If Parliament fused power, it is still possible that power differentiated at the local level. Given the decrease in local seigneurial powers of justice as a result of the encroachment of royal justice, we might expect that in the counties power would be more differentiated in England than on the Continent.

Certainly royal courts developed at the expense of local seigneurial institutions. The Common Law courts and royal judges created a new structure of justice. The major Common Law courts were the Court of Common Pleas, set up in the twelfth century to handle civil cases; the Court of King's Bench, established in the thirteenth century under Edward I and originally concerned exclusively with criminal acts; and the Court of Exchequer, which initially dealt with fiscal disputes but enjoyed an expanding jurisdiction during the fourteenth and fifteenth centuries.[254] In addition, supplementing the Common Law courts, the chancellor's Court of Chancery enjoyed equity jurisdiction. While the rationality of this system and the specialization of the various courts must not be exaggerated, it is clear that even in the thirteenth and fourteenth centuries the English developed a relatively differentiated structure of courts. Moreover, the jurisdiction of Common Law courts was extended to customary tenures in the late fifteenth and sixteenth centuries.

Landowners had also, by the seventeenth century, lost most of their control over manorial courts. It was noted in chapter 4 that these courts were either in decline or had come to be controlled mainly by tenants. Although lordship was still a force, especially as a status, much of the real operational power had been usurped by the tenants, who undertook the day-to-day running of manorial courts. Land stewards, such as Daniel Eaton, who worked for the Third Earl of Cardigan, usually attended manorial courts to defend the interests of their employers.[255] Courts can be found deciding in favour of a landowner over a tenant or of a tenant over a landowner.[256]

And yet, it is one of the curious developments in Early Modern English history that, in spite of the evolution of Common Law and the relatively differentiated and autonomous structure of royal courts, political and judicial power became less differentiated at the local level during this period. While landowners were losing authority as lords, they were acquiring authority through local government office. The most powerful position in county government in England came to be that of lord lieutenant. Lords lieutenant were in charge of the county militia, and they recommended appointments of justices of the peace. By the eighteenth century their military duties had diminished, but they could still be required to command local forces during an emergency. The lord lieutenant was usually a peer. Out of 294 lords lieutenant listed for England and Wales in the eighteenth century, no fewer than 255 were peers or sons of peers.[257]

The office of sheriff originated in the eleventh century as the royal representative in the counties. Annual appointment prevented the government from professionalizing the office as part of a permanent state bureaucracy.[258] However, it declined in prestige during the late Middle Ages and the Early Modern period. By the eighteenth century in most of England and Wales it was falling more often to lesser gentry or newcomers because its duties were regarded as onerous. In Shropshire the office was held by a variety of men during the eighteenth century, including an ironmaster, the son of a draper, and a rich Liverpool merchant.[259] Greater landowners used their influence to avoid the job, not get it. Nonetheless, it remained an office typically filled by a landowner. In Flintshire, sheriffs were always esquires or titled aristocrats.[260] In seventeenth-century Caernarvonshire bitter battles were fought over the office.[261]

Above all, the fusion of local power in Early Modern England and Wales was found in the office of county magistrate or justice of the peace. These commissions were established in the fourteenth century in order to cope with the breakdown of the General Eyre, which was overburdened and unable to prevent widespread lawlessness.[262] In certain respects the judicial system developed by English kings in the twelfth and thirteenth centuries was not working. Seigneurial justice had lost jurisdiction to royal justice more than in other countries. Yet the English state was incapable of mobilizing the resources that would have been necessary to enable royal justice to enforce the law in all the king's lands.

From 1350, the new justices were at work in England, though it was not until 1361 that royal statutes made their function official.[263] When commissions of the peace were introduced into Wales, some politicians did not believe that the Welsh gentry could be trusted with them. In a famous letter written to Thomas Cromwell in 1536, Rowland Lee expressed his view that it was "not expedient to have justices of the peace and gaol delivery in Wales, for there are very few Welsh in Wales above Brecknock who have 10 li. land, and their discretion is less than their land."[264] They were instituted nevertheless and evolved in a manner similar to their counterparts in England.

In the fifteenth and sixteenth centuries the crown struggled to control the justices, usually by appointing outsiders to county benches, typically peers, churchmen, and royal officials loyal to the crown.[265] Such efforts were not particularly successful. Little by little the central government acquiesced to the autonomy of the magistrates. During the first half of the seventeenth century, to a lesser extent even during the second half, some effort was still made to control them. In the eighteenth century, however, they were almost on their own. The central government did not supervise them or even make sure they did anything at all.[266] One difference between English and Welsh commissions is that the Welsh JPs were under more central control by the Council in the Marches, but it was abolished in 1688. In both England and Wales, the lord lieutenant had the authority to supervise the benches. Yet few exercised day-to-day control. Even the appointment of JPs, which was the prerogative of the lord chancellor and the lord lieutenant, could be greatly influenced by the opinion of the local gentry.

Can one argue that justices of the peace constituted a specialized branch of the differentiated legal system that had emerged in England

and Wales? What we know about their origin encourages such an interpretation. The position stemmed from the royal office of keeper of the peace; it had been his function to report any crime and to deliver the accused to a royal judge. During the fourteenth and fifteenth centuries the judicial authority of JPs increased over trespass but decreased over felonies, as many cases went to the Court of King's Bench.[267]

Nonetheless, these centuries also saw justices acquire broader powers that we would call both administrative and judicial. In the late fifteenth century the county benches had wide-ranging jurisdiction, including the regulation of wages, weights and measures, money lending, legal tender, ale houses, and gaming.[268] These responsibilities were added to their authority to suppress numerous offences (such as drunkenness, riot, theft, poaching, and extortion). They enjoyed powers of summary conviction and the right to exercise social control by taking recognizances for the keeping of the peace.[269]

During the sixteenth to eighteenth centuries, the functions of JPs became even less differentiated. After the Glorious Revolution they were entrusted with the right to license Dissenting teachers and churches.[270] In Wales, magistrates became much more active after the dismantling of the Council in the Marches. In both England and Wales they gradually acquired more and more duties that we would regard as administrative, not judicial.[271] Even with respect to justice, the role of the JP was a highly undifferentiated one. A JP was expected not only to make legal decisions, but if necessary to climb on his horse and ride out to enforce them. Their powers were not precisely defined and frequently overlapped with those of other county officials. Magistrates often occupied other offices of local government or sat on other commissions.[272] A list of sheriffs who served in Glamorgan during the sixteenth century shows much the same names as a list of JPs for 1573.[273] No training was required for appointment to the bench; JPs were sometimes named at an extraordinarily young age; and in certain counties particular families dominated the bench.[274] By the eighteenth century JPs were expected to be educated and many had some legal training at the Inns of Court, but these were not professional legal men by any means. Although there was some bureaucratization of the quarter sessions in the eighteenth century, this hardly differentiated the role of the JP. Clerks to the petty sessional division were mostly attorneys. Yet, as a rule, they were not consulted for expert advice by JPs. Instead, they were treated as servants.[275]

The power of the English JPs can, of course, be exaggerated. They were constrained by the authority of other state institutions, especially higher courts. They also constrained one another. Indeed, power struggles among members of the gentry who sat on the bench were almost a constant bane that the population had to endure. Over the course of the eighteenth century, however, the justices became more united and typically reinforced one another's authority. Although a number of officials were elected by the parish – the constables, the churchwardens, the overseers of the poor, and others – all were under the authority of the justice of the peace.

Commissions of the peace fused different kinds of political and judicial power together with status power. Some caution is necessary when we discuss the social characteristics of JPs. They were more diverse than many writers have assumed. Nevertheless, the landed gentry was unmistakably predominant. J.R. Lander has calculated that 128 justices serving in England during the years 1461 to 1509 were clerics, 121 were peers, 80 were legal officials, and 1339 were members of the gentry. An additional 583 could not be identified.[276] The 1573 list of JPs in Glamorgan was composed almost exclusively of members of well-established Glamorgan families.[277] Although lesser gentlemen and newcomers to the gentry could be appointed to the bench, JPs came to form tighter status groups in the eighteenth century, restricting membership to those whom they regarded as acceptable.[278]

There was a property qualification, based on rental value, but it was not a difficult one to surmount. In 1439 it was set at £20. Acts of 1732 and 1745 raised the requirement to £100, but this does not account for the gentry predominance before these enactments; the new requirements did not have a dramatic effect on the composition of the benches. Rather, it was the prestige of landowners in the counties that secured their numerical predominance on the benches, as it did in the House of Commons. In sociological terms, status power was being used to maintain and acquire political (including judicial) power. The relationship, however, was two-way. Membership on the county bench, again like the House of Commons, was used to increase a man's status. Most gentleman landowners wanted the prestige of a commission, whether they had the interest and time for it or not. "Gentlemen are apt to be very pressing to get into the Commission of the Peace," complained Lord Chancellor Hardwicke, "and when they are appointed, to be very backward in Acting."[279] Like balls, hunts, and military drills, the petty and quarter sessions became occasions for symbolic display of their status.[280] The fusion of political power and status power could not be more evident.

All three of the offices – lord lieutenant, sheriff, and justice of the peace – were created by the crown and theoretically appointed by the crown. Why did they come under the control of the aristocracy?

In a few words, it resulted from the fact that the English crown, be it repeated, was in certain respects more powerful, while in other respects less powerful than the French crown. The very centralization of power that we find in England made it possible for the monarchy to tolerate considerable autonomy in local government. The crown might bemoan the corruption and incompetence of the county benches, but at least the gentry in local office did not challenge the unity of the state or the king's right (within constitutional limits) to rule. The French monarchy did not enjoy that same confidence and tended to believe that the localities could be best governed by introducing its own centrally controlled agents to oversee local officials, report to the central government, and enforce central directives. This policy can be detected as early as the reign of St Louis in the thirteenth century, but it reached its fulfilment under Louis XIV.

The British House of Commons also played a critical role in helping the aristocracy gain and retain control over local government. On numerous occasions in the fourteenth century the Commons requested that keepers of the peace be converted into justices of the peace and that local gentry be issued these commissions.[281] And the Commons was instrumental in the augmentation of the powers of justices of the peace in later periods. In the 1740s, for example, Parliament overruled the courts and legislated that magistrates could decide cases that affected their own interests.[282] Finally, Parliament would not have given monarchs the money they would have needed to replace justices of the peace with professionals.

Scotland

The failure of the Scottish crown to monopolize force prevented it from governing the localities. During the first half of the seventeenth century the old Marquess of Huntly still presided over feuds among his dependants in the northeast.[283] Feuds and lawlessness persisted in the Highlands and Western Islands until the defeat of the Rebellion of 1745 and the destruction of the military power of the clans.[284] The authority that had been vested in heritable jurisdictions went primarily to the sheriffs depute when the former were abolished in 1747.[285] Although often members of gentry families, the sheriffs depute were professionals and were paid a salary by the government. Hence justice in Scotland at the local level was now the most professionalized (an evolutionist would have to admit the "most advanced") in the British Isles. The reason was that the government saw the defeat of the Jacobites and the abolition of heritable jurisdictions as an opportunity to professionalize the administration of local justice in Scotland.

There were two other local government offices in Scotland where power was less differentiated. While it cannot be denied that Scottish justices of the peace did not possess the authority of English justices, historians have in the past been too willing to dismiss them.[286] What powers they did have were fused with one another and with other sources of power enjoyed by the landed elite.[287] And most JPs were members of the gentry.

More powerful were the commissioners of supply, again mostly landowners. This institution was established in 1667 to collect the cess, but this relatively specialized function was used as a base for expanded power. Meetings of the commissioners of supply became fora for county opinion.[288] Lowland lairds also met frequently in "county meetings," where they sought, not without success, to exert their influence on political issues of the day.

Other local functions were managed by the aristocracy much as they were in England. Landowners controlled the allocation of poor relief in the parish. They appointed the baillie, who sat in judgement at the court of barony, not only over disputes among tenants, but even over disputes between tenants and their landlord.[289] Many of the same people served as justices of the peace and as commissioners of supply.

Economic power and status power were the foundation of political power in the British Isles. Those who came to share in the authority of Parliament or the commissions of the peace were men of land, wealth, and prestige. The relationships among these different kinds of power were, moreover, circular. Political power boosted economic power and status power, as well as vice versa. Aristocratic political power and status power were plainly less differentiated in the British Isles than in our continental countries. One exception was the royal court. Here status and political power were highly fused, and more so in Versailles than in London. Otherwise, political power and status were less differentiated in the British Isles, especially in Parliament, but also in local government, which gave even lesser gentry a means of combining status and political power. No doubt, political power and status power were differentiated among some of the lesser British gentry or sons of gentry who enjoyed no real political power but laid claim to gentry status. Yet, in contrast with the lesser nobility in our continental countries, these people did not enjoy legal backing for such status claims. Their status was lower just as their political power was weaker. In this way the two coincided more than was the case among the lesser continental nobility, where people with almost no political power still enjoyed the legal status of noble.

PROVINCIAL BASES OF POLITICAL POWER

Neither Wales nor northern England had separate political assemblies or other provincial institutions, except for the Council in the Marches and the Council in the North. Scotland and Ireland had separate provincial institutions, including political assemblies until 1707 for Scotland and 1801 for Ireland.

Scotland

With this separate political assembly the Scottish aristocracy preserved a strong power base in Scotland when the crowns of Scotland and England were united in 1603. As was the case in the Westminster Parliament, the aristocracy dominated the Scottish Parliament, even though urban areas had contributed to its development and preservation. It is true that before the Union of the Parliaments in 1707, Scottish peers and gentleman landowners had not taken over urban representation to the extent that English aristocrats had been able to do.[290] A sixteenth-century act prohibited anyone from representing any district except "the place of that estate in which he commonly professes himself to live."[291] It was not permitted for the eldest son of a peer to represent a burgh or a county.

Nonetheless, collectively the landed elite greatly outnumbered the urban representatives in the period 1603 to 1707. In 1612 and 1617 the number of burgesses attending Parliament was fifty-one and sixty-three, respectively, but the second figure was unusually high. Often fewer than fifty burgesses showed up. The number of barons was similar, though under William and Mary and then again under Anne their number reached over eighty. In 1617 forty-four peers came to Parliament; they equalled or exceeded this number seven times from 1617 to 1661. Thereafter the number was larger, falling below fifty only eleven times and reaching an average of sixty-seven in the Parliament of Queen Anne.[292] Some historians argue that the single chamber made Scottish peers weaker than their English counterparts because they did not have the autonomy of the English House of Lords, while others believe that the unicameral assembly made the Scottish peerage more powerful because the peers could overawe other representatives in a way that English peers could not overawe the House of Commons.

Ireland

The Irish Parliament provided a similar power base for the Irish aristocracy. The Irish House of Commons, like the Westminster Commons, was dominated by landowners of one kind or another. Even members with professional, administrative, or commercial occupations – and there were a few – invariably had a strong landed connection. The business community often complained that the members of Parliament were not sufficiently knowledgable in commerce.[293]

Irish peers were extremely powerful. As in Britain they were not able to sit in the Commons, but their brothers and sons could. Most Irish constituencies were controlled by a great magnate. It should be conceded that men were appointed to the Irish peerage clearly for the purpose of making it more English in its orientation. It should also be conceded that some members of the Irish peerage were Englishmen who took little or no part in Irish affairs. Yet, in spite of all this, the Irish Parliament could represent the interests of the Irish against the English, and in particular against the Westminster Parliament. The "active" Irish peers had Irish roots, and they tended to distrust the British government.[294]

The provincial base for aristocratic power in Ireland was strengthened in the late eighteenth century, albeit for only a brief period. Beginning in the 1750s a "Patriot" movement emerged with the aim of advancing Irish independence and eliminating obstacles to Irish economic development, especially those obstacles that could be blamed on the English. It was this movement that was responsible for the strengthening of the powers of the Irish Parliament in the late eighteenth century. The Patriots were also able to eliminate some of the restrictions that had been imposed on Irish trade and some of the disabilities that had been inflicted on Catholics and other religious Nonconformists. It is impossible not to notice a certain similarity between the rebelliousness of the Irish Parliament and that of the Estates of Brittany. Very different as the two political assemblies were in many respects, both were used by peripheral aristocrats to resist the power of the political centre.

POLITICAL INTEGRATION

It was proposed in chapter 3 that the major forces of centralization in the British Isles were the crown and the Westminster Parliament. How effectively did these forces integrate the peripheral aristocracies?

Crown

It is no coincidence that the two aristocracies whose political integration with the English centre was least difficult provided royal dynasties to the English throne. Although what the Tudors did for the Welsh was circumscribed, many Welsh believed they enjoyed protection and perhaps even special favour because the monarchy had Welsh descent. Political integration of the peripheral aristocracy was also assisted by the Stewart ascension to the British throne in 1603. The downside of the Union of the Crowns for Scottish aristocrats was the move of the king and the transfer of the royal court to London. This was a serious loss, given that one of the major sources of power of the Scottish aristocracy had been the personal relationship that most of its leading members had with the monarch. Distance to London and competition with English aristocrats for the king's time severely weakened the relationship. Initially, the king's bedchamber contained a large Scottish contingent, whose presence caused resentment among English courtiers. Gradually, however, the number of Scottish courtiers and servants declined, and with it the access of Scots to James's ear. By the reign of Queen Anne few Scots were to be found in the royal court, though her physician, John Arbuthnot, was a Scot and some other Scots were in powerful positions, such as John Erskine, earl of Mar.[295]

The importance of the Stewarts for the integration of Scotland and England is demonstrated by the consequences of the fall of the Stewarts. For a number of reasons this did not alienate most Scottish aristocrats or destroy the political unification of England and Scotland, but loyalty to the House of Stewart did coalesce with a number of other forces and occurrences to turn some members of the Scottish aristocracy against England and the Hanoverian monarchy. After he was dismissed by George I, the Earl of Mar led the Jacobite Rebellion of 1715. Even Scots who supported the Hanoverian regime did not feel the attachment that Jacobites felt towards the Stewarts. There was more to Scottish and Welsh integration than loyalty to the crown.

Parliament

In contrast with Ireland, the absence of a separate parliament in Wales and in Scotland after 1707 created the possibility that the Westminster Parliament could integrate the aristocracies of these countries. To what extent did it do so?

The Welsh aristocracy was the first of the peripheries to gain access to the Westminster Parliament. Wales did not have a Medieval parliament, so these aristocrats did not have as much as Scottish or Irish aristocracies to lose through union. Although the lesser gentry did not often join Parliament themselves, their assistance was necessary for the control of parliamentary representation by the greater landowning families.[296]

The presence of Welsh members in the House of Commons was, however, weak. Not only did they have fewer members per capita than the English, but their attendance at the House of Commons was poor. While they regularly sat on committees dealing with Welsh affairs,[297] they typically did not form a cohesive group to represent Welsh interests, but instead were hangers-on to the government or to English political factions. The only noteworthy effort to act as a group during the last half of the seventeenth century or in the eighteenth was their opposition to the award that William III wanted to make of the crown lordships of Denighland and Bromfield-and-Yale to a Dutchman.[298] For most of the eighteenth century the Welsh returned representatives that supported the government.

Welsh seats, even more than English ones, were pursued primarily for their prestige and emoluments. This was the principal manner in which Parliament helped to integrate the Welsh elite into the British political structure. This should not be taken to mean, however, that the Welsh were less principled than the English. Many Welshmen forwent the rewards of political office as a result of Tory and/or Jacobite allegiance. Yet insofar as the Welsh aristocracy was drawn to the political centre and did benefit from political union, it came via the individual rather than the collective rewards of parliamentary activity.

The effect of the Union of the Scottish and Westminster Parliaments in 1707 was also complex. Scottish peers had been in favour of the Union because they had aspired to closer ties with the English peerage and to a share in the latter's power, but the price they paid was the loss of their own parliament, for which little compensation was granted by membership in the British House of Lords – just the sixteen representative peers. A person who held or inherited a Scottish peerage was not permitted to sit in the British House of Lords except as one of the Scottish representatives, not even if he was granted a British title.

Historians have generally held that the Scottish representative peers were even more subservient to the governing ministry than English peers. Again some research has challenged these assumptions.[299] Nevertheless, it is difficult to argue that the Scottish peerage as a body gained political power with the Union of 1707. Formerly they provided almost a third (or fourth if the bishops are counted) of the members in a distinct national Parliament; now they were represented by a mere sixteen noblemen in an assembly containing more than two hundred members. If they were to have any significant political power in the Union they would have to acquire it individually as members of the British political elite through penetration into the British aristocracy. Although the Scottish peerage as a whole was less powerful in the eighteenth century than it had been in the seventeenth century, those peers who could establish contacts or positions of power in London did not lose under the new regime. John Stuart, third earl of Bute, was the most dramatic case in point, though not the most typical. Thanks to his close relationship to George III, which he acquired as his tutor, Bute entered the cabinet when George took the throne and was prime minister from 1762 until 1763. The persisting opportunities for power available to members of the Scottish nobility are reflected in the fact that the major Scottish political factions of the eighteenth century were based on several powerful aristocratic households, those of Queensberry, Hamilton, Atholl, and Argyll.[300]

In 1782 the House of Lords agreed that Scottish nobles with British titles could sit in the House of Lords, a decision made all the more significant as a result of the increase in the number of British peerages awarded to Scots in the closing years of the century.[301] And Scottish representative peers became less willing to bow to the pressures of the ministry and more assertive of their own principles and persuasions. Formerly, election as a representative peer had been regarded by Scottish lords primarily as an honour, a way of raising their status, and only secondarily as a vehicle for promoting the interests of their country.[302] Gradually, however, the representative peers exhibited a greater aggressiveness, an aggressiveness, one historian has argued, that reflected a determination to assume an equal place in the British ruling elite.[303] Curiously enough, Scottish peers were able to provide better representation of Scottish interests the less Scottish they became.

In the seventeenth century the Scottish Lowland gentry had been in a weak position relative to the peerage. They sat as second-class members of the same chamber as the lords. As a result of the Union of the Parliaments in 1707, the Scottish gentry gained access to the very powerful British House of Commons. By one measure this gave them a source of power they had never enjoyed before, especially since Scottish MPs were relatively active. They were more involved with party divisions than Welsh MPs.[304]

We saw in chapter 3, however, that the Scots were represented in the British House of Commons even less than the Welsh. Not surprisingly, little legislation relating to Scotland was enacted during the eighteenth century.[305] We should perhaps not make too much of this since the wheels of Parliament rolled slowly in the eighteenth century and few Scots were anxious to have their lives regulated by the British Parliament. Nonetheless, if an important decision had to be made it was usually made in London. Where English interests came into conflict with Scottish interests, it was rare for the latter to prevail. There was also considerable public opposition to the Scottish factor in British politics. It was not until the late eighteenth century that Scots were admitted in proportionate numbers into the British political official-dom, and even then they were not welcomed in the London adminis-tration to the same extent that they were accepted in the Scottish administration, the military, and the colonial service.[306]

The Union of the Parliaments carried further a long-term process by which political power was relocated to London, with the result that the Scots with the greatest political power were now those who secured influential positions in London or their agents in Scotland.[307] Many members of the great Scottish families, often the most talented mem-bers, left Scotland in search of careers in London or abroad in the British Empire.

Politicians and Patronage in Scotland

Thus the role of the crown and the British Parliament in the integra-tion of the peripheral aristocracies cannot be appreciated without taking into account the way in which patronage was used by both to persuade peripheral elites to be cooperative. Ecclesiastical, military, and civil appointments were overseen by the central government. It was not easy to disregard altogether the abilities of candidates, but those who determined appointments could still favour friends or clients. The parliamentary institutions and the relationship between the crown and magnates that distinguished the British Isles gave rise to a patronage system somewhat different from that found in France. Great aristocrats were more involved in dispensing patronage in the British Isles than they were in France. And patronage became linked to political parties and parliaments in the British Isles. Among the rewards of a seat in a parliament, uppermost in a gentleman's mind was patronage. The party that formed the ministry had access to patronage from which their opponents were largely excluded.

The role of patronage was critical in both Wales and Ireland, but for reasons of space I shall focus on Scottish patronage, which has been the subject of the most historical research and, consequently, is the most illuminating.

It was primarily through patronage that members of the Scottish aristocracy acquired power individually during the eighteenth century and were able to pursue governmental careers first in Scotland, and gradually later in London and the British Empire. In the eighteenth century Scottish patronage was usually in the hands of a leading Scottish politician, sometimes known as the Scottish minister or "manager," who normally held a ministerial post in the cabinet and lived in London. The person who occupied this role did so by virtue of his ability to deliver political support for the government; in return, he was granted considerable influence over Scottish political patronage, which in turn reinforced his political clientage and the support he could deliver to the government. During several periods in the eighteenth century there was no manager, or merely someone who conformed only partially to the role as historians have come to define it. Two Scottish politicians, however, were real managers for extended periods. The first was Archibald Campbell, first earl of Islay and third duke of Argyll. After he succeeded his brother as duke in 1743, he stood as the most powerful clan chieftain in the Highlands and Western Islands. In Scotland, the more limited destruction of magnate power and the prolongation of delegation meant that state patronage fell into the hands of a great territorial magnate. The second archetypical manager was Henry Dundas, from 1802 first viscount Melville, who was the closest colleague of Pitt the Younger, at various times treasurer of the navy, home secretary, secretary of war, president of the India Board, and first lord of the admiralty. Significantly, he did not belong to a great aristocratic family. The evolution from Islay to Dundas personifies the transition from magnate patronage to politician patronage that occurred in eighteenth-century Scotland.

These managers (and others who do not fit our notion of the role so well) performed a double function: they helped the government maintain political control of Scotland, especially control over Scottish representation in Parliament. At the same time they represented Scottish interests at Westminster, albeit not the interests of all Scots. The Scottish manager gave the Scottish landed aristocracy and the better-off townspeople a way of communicating their needs and demands to London when otherwise they would have been almost totally ignored. Although always fearful of losing control, most British ministries found it expedient to give the manager much authority and were willing to accede to many of his demands so long as he could deliver Scottish political support and prevent Scottish representation from upsetting delicate balances of power.

In the last half of the eighteenth century the relationship between the Scottish and English politicians changed. The function of Scottish minister shifted from defending Scottish interests and distributing patronage, as it was in the days of Islay, to winning for the Scots a solid place in the British ruling class and the rewards of British imperialism.[308] Dundas was more a British politician than a Scottish politician in a way that Islay was not.

ARISTOCRATIC EXPERIENCES

Political Centralization

Political centralization, like the other large processes considered in this book, created both similarities and differences among our aristocracies, some of which can be summed up at this point.

First, though there were differences in the roles aristocrats played in the military, we observe a marked similarity as well. If the data we have are not deceiving us, all the aristocracies were overrepresented in the armies that monarchies were building in the Early Modern period. This does not deny that England's military activity was significantly affected by the country's connection with the sea, but it does again mean that we have to be careful in the implications we draw from the Foxian model.

Second, for almost all peripheral aristocrats, their experience was one of being drawn to and profoundly affected by a centre rather than an emerging national state. Both on the Continent and in the British Isles, political centres determined how aristocratic status was institutionalized in the peripheries. In addition, the rise of the state obviously increased political power at the centre and strengthened central state institutions at the expense of provincial state institutions. And we shall see in the following chapter how aristocracies also experienced a centralization of cultural power.

Third, given the great variety of institutions, the similarity in the role of patronage in integrating peripheries with the centre is all the more remarkable. Patronage, and other types of spoils under the control of the central government, were the leading integrating forces in the relationships between peripheral aristocracies and the central state; they were also the principal means by which political centres sought to control local elites and overcome provincial institutions that were resisting centralization.

Yet the experiences of peripheral aristocracies also varied in many ways. At one extreme were those aristocracies that enjoyed considerable autonomy for a long time, but eventually underwent a drastic loss in power. We saw that until the seventeenth century the English were unable and to a degree unwilling to establish full control over Gaelic lords and even Anglo-Norman lords in Ireland. During the seventeenth century this Catholic aristocracy was largely displaced. There were parallels between this and the experiences of some clans in the Scottish Highlands and Western Islands, but the Highland and Western Island clans were not reduced after Culloden to the extent that the Catholic aristocracy in Ireland was reduced after the victory of William of Orange over James II. The treatment of the Vaudois in Piedmont and Dauphiné was similar. Few other examples, however, can be found of this kind of experience in Lotharingia.

More common in Lotharingia were aristocracies that were not destroyed, but whose power was whittled away because their territory had too much strategic importance for them to be left alone. In much of Lotharingia, aristocracies were in the situation of the nobility of Savoy: on the one hand being wooed by great powers, while simultaneously experiencing a significant loss of power.

At the same time other peripheral aristocracies continued to enjoy a certain measure of autonomous power, despite the rise of political centres, because provincial political institutions gave them some leverage with the centre. The Protestant aristocracy in eighteenth-century Ireland, the nobility of the Southern Low Countries, and the nobility in the French provinces that had either estates or *parlements* benefited from this kind of power base. Some aristocrats were thereby able to resist central control, or to use their provincial power base to bargain for a better share in the resources being mobilized by the central authority.

Finally, there were those aristocrats who benefited from the centralization of power either because they held powerful state offices that were in or were linked to the centre or because they participated in central representative institutions. We recognised that the Scottish and Welsh aristocracies had both of these advantages in the eighteenth century, but that their power was circumscribed; their representatives in Parliament were vastly outnumbered and the enjoyment of state offices was limited to certain aristocratic factions. Nevertheless, as individuals, Scottish and Welsh aristocrats who went to the political centre used this method of maintaining or acquiring political power the most effectively, at least among our peripheral aristocracies. Irish, South-Netherlandish, and Savoyard aristocrats used this method the least effectively. In both England and France, aristocrats who were admitted to the royal court benefited from the centralization of power. So did many members of the French nobility of the robe. And so did those who were in other ways connected with powerful networks of clientele. Yet English peers and those members of the English gentry who influenced the choice of representatives for the House of Commons shared centralized power the most.

In the continental countries the new nobility of the robe, or a segment thereof, benefited most from centralization, while the old aristocracy, with the exception of those in the royal court, held on to power insofar as powerful provincial institutions allowed it to resist centralization. This difference between old aristocracy and new aristocracy was not found in the British Isles, where more of the aristocracy could benefit from centralization. Yet in the British Isles as well, some aristocrats did seek to use provincial institutions to resist a loss of power to the centre.

In the final analysis the continental aristocracy was less powerful than the aristocracy of the British Isles. We should not ignore the forces that did support the former's power. First, there was some favouritism towards giving state offices to the aristocracy in the Southern Low Countries, France, and Savoy, though less so in the last two mentioned and least in Savoy. Second, there was a stronger tradition of royal service in the continental aristocracy than in the British aristocracy. Third, by the late seventeenth century and certainly the early eighteenth century, the French royal court was comparatively more politically powerful than the British royal court. Finally, powers of lordship persisted on the Continent in the seventeenth and eighteenth centuries to a greater extent than they did in the British Isles.

On the whole, however, the aristocracy of the British Isles was more politically powerful. The foremost reasons were the co-optation of British aristocrats by the crown, the weakness of central control over royal agents in the counties, and the power that the British aristocracy acquired through parliamentary institutions. Both the British and the continental aristocracies were powerful in local government, but the British more so than the continental, primarily as a result of commissions of the peace. The political power of the aristocracy vis-à-vis the farming population was in the aggregate also greater in the British Isles. And, on the whole, British landowners had better means than continental aristocrats to use their economic power to increase their political power because they had more land, because some of their tenants could vote in elections, and because farmers were comparatively less secure, though this generalization is, of course, subject to numerous qualifications. British aristocrats more often resided in the countryside than continental aristocrats. This added to their capacity to influence their tenants and also meant they were more often involved in the political activities of the local community.

At an abstract level, two variables appear to be the most critical. The power of an aristocracy varied negatively with peripheralization and positively with water-based commercialization. Savoy and non-coastal peripheral parts of France had the politically weakest aristocracies. England had the most powerful. The aristocracies of the Southern Low Countries, Brittany, and Ireland were in between. That landed aristocracies enjoyed more political power where commercial forces were stronger is certainly one of the paradoxes of Western European history. It was not the case in Europe as a whole and is the opposite of what the Foxian model would predict. Part of the explanation is that, if the power of aristocrats was relatively fused, it enabled them to transform agriculture (and thus promote commercialization) and at the same time to seize and preserve power from the crown. To be more specific, it could be argued that English landowners had the power both to commercialize agriculture and to limit the political power of the crown, thus creating a coincidence between commercialization and aristocratic political power. Yet this can provide only part of the answer we are looking for because, first, it works only for England, and, second, in England the coincidence of aristocratic political power and commercialization began before English landowners transformed English agriculture. Thus we need to seek additional explanations. I have stressed the unpredictable results of struggles between centres and peripheries, including the explicit or implicit bargains that might have been made with local elites when a region was united politically with the centre. I have also suggested that the correlation between commercial forces and the political power of the aristocracy is not altogether inconsistent with the Foxian model if we recognize the role of urban elites in helping to place limits on the power of rising monarchies.

Insofar as the elites of Ireland, Brittany, and the Southern Low Countries were politically weak, it was most of all because they had been peripheralized by political centres that were comparatively distant. On the other hand, the elites of these three regions had political assemblies, with at least some power. The reasons for this may have some similarities in the case of Brittany and Ireland: both were by comparison remote regions, with mixed economies (high and low commercialization juxtaposed) and vigorous aristocracies that were able to bargain with centre to preserve or strengthen their political assemblies (at the time of union in the case of Brittany, in various periods when the British crown was dependent on the Protestant-dominated Parliament in the case of Ireland). This kind of struggle was also found in the Southern Low Countries, but in other ways the situation was different; this region was highly urbanized and commercialized with not so much a vigorous aristocracy as a vigorous bourgeoisie. In Savoy the estates did not survive, while the sovereign courts did. Despite some support from the French, the Savoyard nobility never bargained very effectively with the dukes of Savoy and was not supported by a vigorous commercial bourgeoisie. Thus the same forces did not exist that in the Southern Low Countries had led to relatively powerful estates. A number of conditons account for the remarkable differences between the Southern Low Countries and Savoy, but as part of any explanation we need to include the fact that the former (or at least Flanders, Brabant, and Liège) was more commercialized than the latter.

Water-based versus Land-based States

We are now in a position to evaluate how useful the Foxian model has been. It does not help much if we try to turn it into a pair of ideal types. I say this not because we have failed to find the perfect water-based or land-based state – we never find perfect examples of theoretical models – but because we have discovered that most countries are water-based or land-based in some respects more than in others. The exception was perhaps Savoy, which was land based in almost all respects. The military carried high prestige; there was virtually no navy; large numbers of nobles pursued a military career; legal men were more powerful than the business bourgeoisie; the aristocracy enjoyed state-recognized privileges; monarchical power was the most absolutist and coercive; and the decline of lordship was owed more to the role of the state than to commercialization. Yet even here we find a discrepancy: Savoy had the military characteristics of a land-based state more than the state revenue characteristics.

Certainly for our other countries it is more effective to use the model as a set of variables that often go together, but not necessarily. The Southern Low Countries, or at least the provinces of Flanders, Brabant, and Liège, conformed in most ways to what we would expect from water-based states. They were not highly militaristic; the army was not as aristocratic as it was in Savoy; the urban bourgeoisie was politically relatively powerful and, partly as a consequence, the estates were relatively strong; monarchical power was less absolutist and coercive; and the decline of lordship was owed more to commercialization than to the role of the state. On the other hand, we encounter nothing like the navy that was built in the Northern Low Countries; indirect taxation was proportionately not as great as it was in the British Isles; there was a self-conscious *noblesse d'épée* (though less so than in France and Savoy); the nobility enjoyed state-recognized privileges; the Spanish/Austrian Low Countries were ruled by absolutist monarchies; and the urban bourgeoisie had been greatly weakened under these monarchies. Moreover, some of the differences from a land-based society cannot be attributed entirely to water baseness. The power of estates was the consequence of a number of historical forces, and the fact that the army was less aristocratic was a characteristic of Austrian armies in general.

In most respects the British Isles, and especially England, had become more water-based than France. The monarchy had less coercive power;

the state spent far more on its navy; it raised more revenues than our other countries through indirect taxes (especially customs); the aristocracy enjoyed less privilege; and the decline of lordship was owed at least partly to commercialization. Yet the differences were not the same on all these variables. The British Isles were very water-based with regard to taxation, naval expenditures, and aristocratic privilege, but differed from France only a little in certain other respects: by the eighteenth century Britain spent proportionately as much on defence and mobilized large armies for war; and the state played as great a role in the decline of lordship as it did in France. Furthermore, like the Southern Low Countries, some of the differences from a land-based society cannot be attributed entirely to water baseness. The power of Parliament had a number of causes and was in turn responsible for some of the water-base charateristics of the British Isles. In addition, while we cannot say that the British aristocracy was just as militaristic, it does seem that they were highly overrepresented in the army as compared with the general population in the British Isles.

One particular argument that has been made by those who have taken up the Foxian model requires further comment: the proposition that elites exercise power through negotiation in water-based states and through coercion in land-based states. We have found that negotiations between princes and aristocrats were important in both water-based states and land-based states; the thing that differed was the character and structure of these negotiations. Furthermore, though the coerciveness of states may have correlated positively with land baseness, we have found that coercion played an important role in the development and preservation of the powers of representative institutions in the British Isles. It was the coercive power of the English crown in the Middle Ages that led English magnates to want to be consulted by the king, in contrast with the coercive weakness of the French crown, which limited the interest that French regional elites could be expected to take in such consultations. Then, later, it was the capacity of English aristocrats to take up arms and overthrow two of their kings that was critical in the strengthening of the powers of the British Parliament in the seventeenth century.

As Charles Tilly has argued, all states depended on coercion. What varied was the manner in which they raised revenue to pay for it. Without denying the importance of borrowing, I have emphasized more than Tilly does differences in taxation: comparatively commercialized states drew revenues from indirect taxes (especially customs) more than comparatively land-based states did. This difference had all sorts of consequences, the most significant of which for this study was the effect it had on the institutionalization of aristocratic status.

What also varied was the capacity of central states to exercise coercion. This is how the Foxian coercion proposition can be usefully reformulated. The power of political assemblies persisted where the central state lacked the coercive capacity to destroy or weaken them. This was true of both the British and the Spanish crowns during the sixteenth and seventeenth centuries, in marked contrast with French and Savoyard rulers.

8 Cultural Power

MEDIEVAL CULTURES

As a result of invasions, a variety of peoples (Visigoths, Burgundians, Basques, Franks, Bretons, and Scandinavians) inhabited what is now France in the tenth century, though not all of them could be clearly distinguished. A large number of languages and a vast number of dialects were spoken. The majority were romance languages or dialects, but some, most notably the Breton, Netherlandish, and Basque languages, were not. The largest romance groups were the *langues d'oïl*, spoken in the north, and the *langues d'oc*, spoken in the south. The Low Countries were divided into a Germanic northern region and a romance southern region. The boundary or interface between them was approximately the same as the linguistic boundary in Belgium today: a line running just north of Tournai, just south of Brussels, and just north of the city of Liège.

The British Isles were also culturally and linguistically heterogeneous. Before the twelfth century a number of invasions and foreign settlements changed the ethnic composition of English society. Generally natives and invaders assimilated, though some of the native population was forced to move. Many Celts were pushed north and westward by the Anglo-Saxons, where their language endured in some areas. When the Danish arrived they assimilated with the Anglo-Saxons. Danish speakers persisted in particular areas, however. In addition, the arrival of the Normans introduced yet another cultural group. The new Norman aristocracy and monarchy were French speaking. By the time of Henry II, considerable blending had taken place between the English and the Normans. Nevertheless, England was by no means a land of one language.[1]

Cultural heterogeneity was even greater in Wales and Ireland. In the southern districts of Wales along the coast and in the valleys of the southeast, the native population was replaced or reduced to a minority. The Norman and English settlers were determined that the king should treat them differently from the native Welsh and that their culture should be dominant. Yet separation from the native Welsh meant that Norman and English hegemony did not undermine Welsh culture. In Welsh areas the Welsh tongue was not significantly altered, and Welsh customs survived largely intact.[2]

The English lordship of Ireland also followed a pattern of settlement and separation. In the areas of Anglo-Norman settlement, feudal landholding and English Common Law were introduced, while in Gaelic areas the laws, customs, and language of Gaelic society persisted. Gaelic society differed from continental society more than did Anglo-Saxon society. The Gaelic Irish also regarded their culture as much superior to Norman or English culture. This alone would have made the Norman penetration of Ireland different from its conquest of England. In addition, the Anglo-Norman social structure that had developed in England since the Conquest was by its nature relatively inflexible and not easy to blend with Gaelic society.[3] For these and other reasons, natives and newcomers assimilated little. It is true that some Gaelicization of the Anglo-Norman population occurred in the fourteenth and fifteenth centuries. Yet, like Wales, the striking characteristic of Ireland in the twelfth and thirteenth centuries was the juxtaposition of two very divergent cultures.

Two very divergent cultures evolved in Scotland as well, but in a different way. Because the Normans were brought to Scotland by the Scottish crown, there was very early assimilation of the Normans with some of the native population and we do not find an Anglo-Norman enclave. Although Normans assumed a dominant position in the society, no displacement of the existing elite occurred and native culture was not subordinated as much as it was in Wales and Ireland. As in Wales, the Normans brought English people with them. This was not, however, the first incursion of English-speakers into Scotland. The Angles had penetrated the southeast and, by the tenth century, the Anglo-Saxon tongue was spoken by the majority of the population in the Lothians.[4] The result was a plentiful mixture of languages in Scotland, with a Frenchified English emerging as the dominant language in the Lowlands, while Gaelic remained the most spoken language in the Highlands and Western Islands.[5]

The Normans did not pierce the north and west of Scotland. Not only was feudalism imposed less effectively on the Highlands and Western Islands, but the reorganization of the church under David I did not include the Highlands and Western Islands.[6] Indeed, one of the principal consequences of the arrival of the Normans in Scotland was the intensification of differences between the Highlands and the Lowlands. These differences continued to increase during the following centuries and, by the fourteenth century, they had become pronounced.[7]

Of course, the cultural characteristics of the aristocracy were not the same as those of the general population. On the Continent and in the British Isles the aristocracy was both parochial and cosmopolitan during the Middle Ages relative to what it became later. In many respects it was socially and culturally localized; to the extent that it was not localized it reached beyond recognized political boundaries and formed a European elite. Although many nobles were little less parochial than most peasants, others shared in a larger European culture. The Latin language was pan-European in a way that not even English is today. The simultaneous introduction of French into England also increased the linguistic unity of the European aristocracy. The peak was reached under Henry II, who ruled over a large French-speaking aristocracy on both sides of the English Channel.

Almost all aristocrats of Western Europe also saw themselves as belonging to Latin Christendom. The church was the most united institutional structure in Europe and the most centralized power in the sense that geographically its power reached the farthest. This power varied greatly from one pope to another. Christendom was much more united under Innocent III than under Boniface VIII. The church had political and economic power, but much less than its cultural power. Christianity provided or attempted to provide a normative regulation of behaviour on a massive scale and was the symbol of religious faith.[8] It was also the basis for centres of learning throughout Europe – monasteries, cathedral schools, and universities.

The aristocracy enjoyed considerable cultural power. Most high ecclesiastics came from noble families. Yet the fusion of cultural power with status was less than the fusion of economic or political power with status. The ideological function of the clergy was generally kept separate. The role of the theologian was certainly not fused with that of lord or noble. And many theologians were from non-noble families. The explanation is obviously that the values and ideals of noble families, and especially the emphasis on fighting, gave them no advantage over urban elites in making young men into churchmen or scholars.

The ideology that was most closely tied to aristocratic status was, of course, chivalry. Here cultural power was indeed fused with status. We shall return to this subject later in the chapter.

THE CENTRALIZATION OF CULTURE

In the late Middle Ages and the Early Modern period the local and supra-local cultures discussed above succumbed in considerable measure to the cultures of the emerging political centres. Yet there was nothing smooth or inevitable about this process; nor is it an easy one to describe. Culture is not unidimensional. One group may be extremely influential in religious matters, another in literature, still another in art.

The French Centre

Language

Pre-revolutionary French society was multilingual. As the letters to Abbé Grégoire indicate, a substantial number of people in France could not speak French at the end of the eighteenth century; Grégoire estimated that six million people knew no French and that another six million were incapable of holding a conversation in French.[9] Even in regions of *langue d'oïl* a great number of dialects were spoken that varied among villages. In many southern regions, French was rarely used as a spoken language.

One of the reasons for the persistence of many languages and dialects was the ambivalent attitude of the state, at least until the Revolution of 1789. In contrast with the nineteenth and twentieth centuries, in this period language was not regarded as a basis for state-building and was not a political issue. From the fifteenth century the crown was determined to expel Latin as the language of state and culture, but it was largely indifferent to the persistence of the popular languages.[10]

All the same, the growth of the state had a huge impact on the languages of France. Because language was important for justice and administration, the growth of the state had the effect of making the king's language the dominant language. During the late Middle Ages the French spoken by the king gradually began to impose itself as an official, though not often spoken, language in the regions over which the crown came to rule. In the south it had very limited impact until the mid-fifteenth century, but in the late fifteenth century and from the early sixteenth century it became the language of the elite.[11] The major forces operating against the provincial languages were the church, trade, the development of printing, the royal administration, the French Academy, and the cultural power of the French centre. The role of the crown in the sixteenth century is the subject of some disagreement. According to most writers, the Ordinance of Villers-Cotterêts of 1539 ordered the use of the king's French in the administration of justice and forbad the use of any of the popular dialects. In a thesis published in 1933, however, Henry Peyre insisted that "French" (*langage maternel françois*) in this context included the popular languages.[12] In any case, by ordinance or otherwise, the king's French was becoming the language of administration and justice; and demands imposed by the state constituted the most potent force in promoting language assimilation.

The new territories acquired during the seventeenth century created new linguistic problems for the crown. Efforts were made to impose French as the judicial and administrative language, but no effort was made to impose it as the spoken language. Even in justice and administration, though officially French was obligatory, circumspection was used in the application of decrees. French was not required for state affairs in Alsace until 1685, and the edict of that year was not enforced.[13]

In sum, the French state did not vigorously try to drive out the provincial languages, but did, through its growth, make its cultural power felt by promoting the ascendancy of the king's French. Of course, the king's French was an evolving language significantly influenced by other languages and dialects as people moved back and forth between Paris and other parts of the country. The linguistic exchange was not, however, equal. The language that was developing as the language of state was no melange of all the languages and dialects spoken in the country; it was primarily the language of the centre.

The first members of the population to learn the king's language belonged to the higher nobility, the upper bourgeoisie, and the nobility of the robe. In Languedoc during the fourteenth century, nobles spoke French with the king and his agents, but stuck to the provincial language when conversing with their own people.[14] French was accepted by the nobles of Dauphiné subsequent to its union with France in the fourteenth century. In the Bordeaux region the higher nobility used French to communicate with other parts of the country. Increasingly after 1500, French was adopted in order to communicate with the central government and other regions.[15]

True, language was still an important source of diversity among the nobility even in the eighteenth century. In the far coastal regions, in parts of the Midi, and in new territories, such as Alsace, nobles could be found who could not speak French, or spoke it poorly.[16] Most provincial nobles, especially those who lived in the countryside, spoke French with a noticeable accent and with certain differences in usage.[17] Nonetheless, by the end of the seventeenth century it is likely that a majority of the French nobility were either unilingual in French or at least bilingual. By this time Versailles set the standard for oral French, while Paris set the standard for written French.[18]

French was also becoming the most prestigious language in areas beyond French borders, taking over from Italian. Whereas in the sixteenth century the language of the French court was rather Italianized,[19] during the seventeenth and eighteenth centuries French became the genteel language of Europe, spoken in many of the courts. By the reign of Catherine the Great it had become the language even of the Russian court.[20] Needless to say, its hegemony was especially pronounced in Lotharingia. During the French occupation of the sixteenth century, French was imposed as the official language in Savoy.[21] When Turin was made the capital, Italian became the official state language. In Savoy most people spoke local dialects, but the elites spoke French as well. Even communications with Turin were in French.[22] Although German dialects were still spoken by elites in Alsace after annexation, these elites had for some time taken a keen interest in French language and culture, and speaking French was a symbol of high status; Strasbourg became a centre for French studies in the early seventeenth century.[23]

In the Southern Low Countries, French became the language of the most powerful people in the society during the Burgundian period, but there was no attempt on the part of the Burgundians to suppress Netherlandish or to make French the official language.[24] Even in the eighteenth century, French was not the language of the general population. The percentage of the Flemish population who spoke French was still very small. Edicts were printed in either French or Flemish depending on the place. The majority of edicts targeted for Flemish provinces were drafted in Flemish. And, whatever the original text, the public notices were in the language used where they were published.[25] Flemish was spoken in provincial administration, including the estates. Local French dialects were also still spoken, even by the nobility. A book on noble heraldry was published in the provincial language in Liège in the late eighteenth century.[26] And yet French was clearly the hegemonic language of the Southern Low Countries. It was the principal language of the central administration during both the Spanish and Austrian periods of rule. French was spoken by nobles and other high-status persons even in Flemish regions.[27] In the eighteenth century, upward social mobility necessitated learning French and learning it well. And it was French from

Paris, not the indigenous French, that was coming to be spoken by the elites.

Religion

The Reformation constituted a massive breakdown in cultural power. Latin Christendom was never as united as it had pretended to be, but in the sixteenth century that unity was broken as never before. Reform obtained a considerable number of adherents in France. French Protestants, or "Huguenots" as they were called, were most numerous in the provincial towns and in the "Huguenot crescent" – the (not unbroken) band that stretched from Dauphiné across southern France and up the western coast.[28] Protestantism also found fertile ground in parts of Lotharingia – in the Low Countries, Alsace, Geneva, and parts of Piedmont. Thus the geographical distribution of Protestants actually resembled a *U* more than a crescent, a *U* that surrounded Paris at some distance. One can say that Catholicism was the religion of the centre in the sense that there was a tendency for Protestantism to be stronger away from the French political centre, and Catholicism was the religion of the crown, something Henry IV (who converted from Protestantism to Catholicism after he ascended to the throne) was careful not to alter. Although opposition to Protestants was spread throughout the country and was perhaps even more intense in areas where Protestants were comparatively numerous, the seventeenth-century assault on the rights of Huguenots came from the centre and was imposed on the peripheries. Elizabeth Labrousse has suggested that those Catholics who tried to protect their Protestant neighbours were usually motivated by the solidarity of locals against distant powers.[29]

The rights of French Protestants were theoretically safeguarded by the Edict of Nantes of 1598. This edict, along with the armed power of the Protestant population, protected them from the cultural power of the political centre, but over the course of the seventeenth century this protection was eroded and the full power of the crown to dictate religious practice came down on the Huguenots. The disarmament began with the military attack on Protestants in Béarn by Louis XIII, which led to a revolt of Protestants in southern France. This conflict was concluded with the Treaty of Montpellier of 1622, by which many of the Huguenot strongholds were to be neutralized. Yet Protestant strongholds still represented a security threat, a threat that became dramatically clear in 1627 when the English sought to use La Rochelle as the base for an Anglo-French war. Despite three fleets sent from Britain, La Rochelle capitulated to the French crown in 1628. By 1629 most other Huguenot strongholds had fallen. Freedom of worship for Huguenots was guaranteed by the Peace of Alais, but the disarmament of Protestants was carried greatly further by the destruction of their fortresses and the disbandment of their troops. In the following decades Protestants enjoyed relative toleration in France. From the late 1650s, however, their rights were gradually whittled away, partly by strict interpretations of the Edict of Nantes, increasingly by systematic violations of the edict. From the early 1660s commissions went into the provinces to report Huguenot offences. The culmination of this gradual process of escalating persecution was the Edict of Fontainebleau in 1685, which eliminated what was left to protect Protestants in the Edict of Nantes.[30]

The number of Protestants in France began to decline sharply even before the Edict of Fontainebleau. As a result of the Wars of Religion, by the time of the Edict of Nantes they may have constituted as little as 6 per cent of the population. During the seventeenth century the foremost reason for decline was perhaps extinction. Numbers were also lost as a consequence of the defeat of the Protestant rebellion in 1627. The increasing persecution of Huguenots preceding the Edict of Fontainebleau led to conversions and emigration. And, finally, the edict itself resulted in a great number of conversions and large-scale emigration.[31]

Many nobles had entered the Reform movement and battled for the Protestant cause in the Wars of Religion. They had played a crucial role in protecting and leading Protestants.[32] It has been suggested that a third to a half of the nobility were Protestant in the late sixteenth century, but Constant indicates that in the Beauce region approximately one-quarter of the rural nobility were *réformés*.[33] Constant's data also suggest that many nobles remained faithful to the minority religion; more than half the Protestant nobles in Beauce were Protestant until the revocation of the Edict of Nantes.[34] In contrast, it has been estimated that in the *élection* of Bayeux, 40 per cent of the nobility were Protestant in the 1560s, but merely 13 per cent in 1597 and 10 per cent in 1666.[35] And most historians agree that by 1685 few of the high nobility were Protestants. Most Protestant nobles were simple *hobereaux*.[36] Conversions resulted from the attraction of the royal court or royal service and the social costs of remaining Protestant.[37] For example, the commander of the Protestant fortress of Lectoure became a Catholic and turned the fort over to the king in return for a royal pension.[38] Special efforts were made by the crown to convert Huguenots of higher socioeconomic position, such as removing their children and turning them over to Catholic educators.[39] The crown was often acting under pressure from the church and it was not the only force operating to weed out Protestantism among French nobles, but it was primarily responsible. Royal legislation and the necessity of conversion to enjoy the benefits of the state were the major factors.

The Edict of Fontainebleau created the legal fiction that there were no Protestants in France, only "NC" – "New Catholics" or "New Converts." Under this pretence, the crown often protected them in the eighteenth century. Although Huguenot literature published outside France continued to enter the kingdom and to arouse the hatred of Catholic zealots, Protestants were increasingly tolerated, at least during the last half of the century. Eventually the Edict of Versailles of 1787 established religious freedom in France (if not totally), but by then only small communities of Protestants were left.

Repressive as the crown's religious policy was, it was largely one of assimilation. Although some members of French society may have wanted to drive the Huguenots out of France, the crown wanted to convert them. Protestants were offered one inducement after another to become Catholics. After the revocation of the Edict of Nantes, the crown struggled desperately to keep Huguenots from fleeing abroad. Those who converted were generally not harassed further, certainly not by the crown.

Protestantism was not the only nonconforming religion in France during the seventeenth century. A new religious movement within Catholicism began in the first half of the seventeenth century when Cornelius Jansen, the archbishop of Ypres, wrote *The Augustinus*, a controversial anti-Jesuit work on the theory of grace found in the writings of St Augustine. After his death in 1638 his treatise was promoted in France by his friend, the Abbé de Saint Cyran. During the eighteenth century the most serious religious struggle in France pitted Jansenist Catholics against the church leaders. Jansenism in France became associated with Gallicanism and with the political opposition of the *parlements* to the crown. Jansenists were critical of the court and especially of its moral degeneration, or perceived moral degeneration.[40] Wealthier members of the bourgeoisie were over-represented in the movement, which was strongest in urban concentrations.[41] The movement split the nobility. Members of the *noblesse de robe*, led by the *parlementaires* of Paris, were overrepresented among those who took the Jansenist side, while members of the *noblesse d'épée* were overrepresented among those who were anti-Jansenist.[42] However, many sword nobility opposed one another in the Jansenist struggle, as did many members of the robe. Although the crown's objective was to settle the controversy and bring the fighting to an end, its interventions generally had the opposite effect. A bull condemning the Jansenist-leaning work of Pasquier Quesnel was issued by the pope at the request of Louis XIV in 1713. Louis wanted to strengthen the organization and discipline of the church in France. The bull was called *Unigenitus*, which turned out to be rather ironic since, instead of bringing together all French Catholics, it united those Catholics opposed to the crown and the church hierarchy. The conflict reached a peak in the 1750s when the Archbishop of Paris attempted to annihilate Jansenism by denying the sacraments to persons who could not produce a ticket that verified their confession to a priest who had acquiesced to *Unigenitus*.

What needs to be stressed for my argument is that Jansenism had proportionately the largest number of supporters in Paris. Thus in the eighteenth century, in contrast with the sixteenth and early seventeenth centuries, opposition to the French king's religious preferences came especially from the centre, not the peripheries.

The English Centre

Language

At the end of the eleventh century the bulk of the population of England spoke various dialects of Old English, while the elite generally carried on in French. French remained the language of the royal court and the aristocracy as late as the fourteenth century, but by the twelfth to thirteenth centuries most nobles were bilingual.[43] Even during the seventeenth and eighteenth centuries French and Latin continued to be used in certain courts, especially in transcription, and educated members of the peerage and gentry still learned French, but French had declined as a spoken language in this elite. London English came to prevail over other English dialects, and in the seventeenth and eighteenth centuries was used by educated persons in all regions of England. As in France, the emerging dominant language was substantially influenced by other languages and dialects. Migration to London injected much from the provincial dialects into London speech. Again, however, the exchange was not an equal one. Agreement on what constituted the best pronunciation may have begun to emerge as early as the fourteenth century, and definite evidence for it can be found in the sixteenth century. By the end of the seventeenth century a more or less standardized written English had developed.[44] Regional accents persisted longer, even among the peerage, but the language of the centre had established an indisputable hegemony in England.

Religion

The official Reformation in England was carried out by Henry VIII for reasons that were more political and financial than religious. The established church was not destroyed; it was simply renamed and placed under the authority of the English crown. The Church of England was the religion of the state even more than Catholicism was the state religion in France. It is true that in the seventeenth century Catholicism was stronger in the British political centre (especially in the royal court) than was Protestantism in the French political centre. On the whole, however, people who remained Catholic were comparatively more numerous away from the southeast of England – in northern England and Scotland, but especially in Ireland. Thus both Protestantism in France and Catholicism in the British Isles were religions of the peripheries more than they were religions of the centre.

The social characteristics of English Catholics were very different from those of French Protestants. English Catholics had disproportionate support from the landed aristocracy. About 20 per cent of the peerage was Catholic in 1641.[45] Although the number dropped precipitously thereafter, Catholics still made up 12 per cent of the peerage at the beginning of the eighteenth century.[46] Many members of the gentry were also Catholic. The strength of the Catholic community came to rest on the patronage of a Catholic landowner who employed a priest.[47] A conflict emerged between the goal of Catholic landowners to organize relatively autonomous local communities of Catholics and the goal of the secular clergy, which was to weaken lay domination and to establish a church hierarchy with jurisdiction over English Catholics. The gentry were largely successful and Catholic communities generally coagulated in groups around a Catholic landowner.[48] Some members of the Anglican gentry were friends of Catholics, even related by blood or marriage to them, so that it could be difficult to obtain their cooperation in combatting Catholicism. This was true at least in counties with large numbers of Catholic gentry, such as Lancashire, where some justices of the peace were unwilling to enforce the recusancy laws under Elizabeth and the early Stewarts.[49] Catholics were also protected by the crown. James I, Charles I, Charles II, and James II all had Catholic mothers and wives, with the exception of the first wife of James II, who converted to Catholicism and, in any case, died before he became king. They frequently moderated anti-Catholic legislation – suspended its enforcement or granted exemptions. Moreover, magistrates were less than zealous in their enforcement of the law because they never knew whether the next monarch would be Catholic or Protestant.

Be that as it may, the severity of legislation enacted, in the words of an edict of 1609, for "the better discovering and repressing of popish recusants," testifies to the power of anti-Catholic forces in the country. Catholics were first excluded from office by an act of 1558, which required that office-holders take an oath of the queen's supremacy.[50] Another act of the same year required uniformity of common prayer and church service.[51] In 1563 all officers were obliged to take an oath repudiating the authority of the pope.[52] An act of 1570 made it treasonable to be reconciled to Rome or to reconcile another person to Rome.[53] In 1585 priests were excluded from England and it was made a felony to provide shelter for a priest.[54] A 1605 act prohibited Catholics from holding office.[55] The act of 1609 excluded from office those not taking an oath to the monarch.[56] In 1672 an act barred those not willing to swear an oath to the monarch and the Church of England from civil and military office.[57] And, finally, another of 1677 prohibited Catholics from membership in either of the two houses of Parliament. These last two measures make it difficult to claim that persecution of Catholics was diminishing in this period.

We have seen that the number of Protestants in France declined sharply during the seventeenth century. This did not happen to Catholics in England. John Bossy concludes from the available evidence that there were in the neighbourhood of 30,000 to 40,000 Catholics in England and Wales in 1603 (67 to 90 per 10,000 persons in the population), rising to roughly 60,000 in 1641 (110 per 10,000), and reaching 80,000 in 1770 (117 per 10,000).[58] Given the severity of the anti-Catholic legislation and the viciousness of Puritan hostility towards Catholics, it is difficult to explain this difference by arguing that the English were more tolerant. More critical was the role of the crown and the protection, resources, and status provided by the landed aristocracy in England. Protestants in France and Catholics in England who refused to convert put at risk their chances of getting state patronage and largesse. Catholics in England were, however, in a better position for two reasons: first, the crown was less hostile towards them and, second, in England it was easier for landowners to remain on their property, typically in northern England, devoting themselves to estate management and practising their religion with Catholic dependants. In contrast, few nobles could resist the attraction of the royal court and state office in France.

In addition to Catholic Nonconformists, there were in England Protestant Nonconformists, known also as Dissenters. Not surprisingly, English Protestant Nonconformity was in many respects like French Protestantism. This is the intuitively obvious comparison. Less obvious are a few differences and similarities with French Jansenism. Dissenters and Huguenots were anti-sacramentalist and wanted to maintain their own worship, neither of which was the case with French Jansenists. Like French Protestants, English Protestant Nonconformists challenged the official state religion more than did the Jansenists. On the other hand, English Dissenters and French Jansenists (as well as French Huguenots) shared an Augustinian theology of grace. Like Jansenists, English Nonconforming Protestants were opposed to the alleged moral corruption of the court and many tried to shun a lavish lifestyle, though this was more true of the Jansenists than the Dissenters. And French Jansenism and English Protestant Nonconformity split the aristocracy in a way that French Protestantism did not, at least by the late seventeenth century.

In the seventeenth and eighteenth centuries religious opposition in both the British Isles and France came from segments within the religion of the majority – Protestantism in the British Isles, Catholicism in France. These movements were both overrepresented in urban areas and in the centre, but, of the two, British Nonconformity was the less centralized. It was concentrated in London to a lesser extent than Jansenism was concentrated in Paris. It will become more evident as this chapter progresses that the French centre had more cultural power than the British centre.

The British Peripheries

Consciously and unconsciously the English pursued two different strategies with respect to peripheral elites: assimilation and exclusion. Which strategy was pursued varied from one period of time to another and from one part of the British Isles to another.

The Meeting of Peoples

The separation of ethnic groups in Wales and Ireland (in contrast to their intermingling in the Scottish Lowlands) resulted in more ethnic discrimination in Wales and Ireland than in Scotland. When Edward I conquered Wales he reduced the status and authority of the native Welsh elite and put Englishmen in charge of the administration.[59] After a rebellion at the beginning of the fifteenth century, harsh penal laws were enacted. Among their provisions, some specifically denied rights to English persons married to Welsh spouses or to persons who had one parent who was Welsh. Thus the laws sought both to penalize the Welsh and to prevent assimilation. Status discrimination was used to prevent cultural assimilation.

Similarly, in Ireland the Gaelic Irish were not accorded the same rights as the English. Laws discriminated against the Gaelic Irish and explicitly forbad the assimilation of the two peoples. This legislation was repeatedly renewed and finally culminated in the Statutes of Kilkenny of 1366. Here is just a sample of their provisions. They prohibited marriage, fosterage, or concubinage between English and

Irish; Irish minstrels and other entertainers were banned from English districts; Irishmen could not be accepted into English religious houses; and the use of the Irish language, mode of riding, and dress was forbidden.[60]

In both countries, however, this penal legislation actually appeared in the context of increasing assimilation. Indeed, in Ireland the legislation was a reaction to such assimilation. Until the sixteenth century it was the Gaelic culture that prevailed; in the sixteenth century the pressure was reversed. Yet it is in regard to this assimilation that critical differences emerged in the British periphery. Although the Welsh today are in some respects more distinct than the Irish or the Scots, they in fact assimilated to English culture earlier than did the Irish or the Scots. Until the eighteenth century there remained two different worlds in Ireland, however much some people may have straddled them. Even in counties where the two cultures came together producing a "hybrid," one could distinguish in the seventeenth century between Gaelic settlements and Anglo-Norman settlements.[61]

By the late Middle Ages the assimilation of the Scottish population and the Anglo-Norman population was comparatively advanced in the Lowlands. English was the language of most of the Lowlands, the language of state and even of the royal court.[62] This English was, however, a distinctly different dialect from the English spoken in England. The Scottish English was known as *Inglis* or later Scots. Cultural autonomy also persisted, of course, in the Highlands and Western Islands. Although subject to the same crown as the Lowlands, the Highlands and Western Islands did not form part of the same society. It is more helpful to see the Western Islands and many areas in the Highlands as part of a Gaelic society found in Ireland and in Scotland.

Lower levels of inter-ethnic contact resulting from distance and the absence of roads obviously help to explain the slower assimilation that took place in Scotland and Ireland than in Wales. In both Ireland and Scotland it was the western and northern regions that were the least assimilated. Of course, in all three countries there were cultural border districts where inter-ethnic contact occurred. In contrast with Ireland and Scotland, no part of native Wales was very far from those borders. Native Wales was small and half surrounded by the Welsh March. Topography also made a difference. The mountains and islands of northwest Scotland made them especially inaccessible and, consequently, these regions were slowly assimilated, even in comparison with much of Ireland. The level of contact that occurred between native Wales and the Welsh March in the fifteenth century did not occur between Highland and Lowland Scotland even in the seventeenth century. Similarly, distance and obstacles to transportation help to explain the cultural distinctiveness of Lowland Scotland from England and to a lesser extent of Anglo-Norman Ireland from England. These two regions developed a distinctiveness vis-à-vis England that was greater than the distinctiveness of the Welsh March.

The cultural autonomy of the periphery was also affected by the reach of the state. In the thirteenth century Edward I conquered native Wales and brought it under the direct administrative control of the English crown. Although the Welsh were discriminated against in the administration of the principality, this administration did at least bring the two groups into greater contact and Welshmen served in it, albeit with less authority than the English. Consequently, when the Penal Laws were passed it was really difficult to enforce them, and they certainly were not fully enforced.[63] The status of the Welsh further improved under the Tudors. When Henry VII ascended to the throne, Welsh gentry, especially those connected with the Tudors, were given important offices in the Welsh administration. Under Henry VII Welsh landowners were admitted to the higher circles of English society and they could be found in London in greater numbers than ever before. The Penal Laws were not repealed, but exemptions were greatly extended.[64] A policy of exclusion was replaced by one of assimilation. It culminated under Henry VIII in the Acts of Union of 1536 to 1543. Theoretically, this legislation made the English and the Welsh equal before the law.

Finally, the English had greater need for cultural imperialism in Wales than in Ireland or Scotland. Again we witness the consequences of the greater strategic importance of some regions as opposed to others. Wales was more strategically important than Gaelic Ireland or the Scottish Highlands and Western Islands. It just did not matter that much if the people living on Lewis or in Donegal were "barbaric."

Religion

In the sixteenth century Calvinism became the dominant religion in Scotland. In 1560 most of these Calvinists became Presbyterians. In 1690 some broke with the Presbyterian Church to become Episcopalians. In addition, a minority of Catholics persisted into the seventeenth and eighteenth centuries. In Ireland, though the Church of Ireland (the Anglican Church) made a significant number of conversions and the Protestant population was reinforced by Anglican and Presbyterian immigration, the bulk of the population remained Catholic. In contrast, in Wales the majority (though not all) of the population accepted the religion of the centre, though for a long time rather passively. Nonconformity gained considerable support in Wales, while the Counter-Reformation experienced only limited success. Catholicism expanded in Wales under Elizabeth; it was especially strong in the border counties, most of all Monmouthshire. Yet by the end of Elizabeth's reign there were reportedly only 808 recusants in Wales.[65] Documents indicate there were only 1085 Catholics in Wales in 1676.[66]

Little comparative analysis has been undertaken by historians to explain these differences, perhaps because the effect of many variables is almost impossible to evaluate. To what extent, for example, can we explain Calvinism in Scotland by reference to the charisma of a few religious leaders, most obviously John Knox? Can it be argued that there was something in the personality of the Scots or in their culture that predisposed them towards Calvinism? Similarly, is there something in the Irish culture or personality that inclined them towards Catholicism? Did geographical differences play a role – that Ireland and England were separated by sea or that Ireland was closer than Scotland to two Catholic powers, France and Spain, while Scotland, or at least eastern Scotland, was closer to the Northern Low Countries and to Germany?

Clearly one variable was language and cultural differentiation. Most of the clergymen sent by the Church of England to Ireland were unfamiliar with Gaelic society and culture and did not speak the Irish language. Few of the Gaelic population became clergymen in the established church, and those who did had to serve under Englishmen.[67] In contrast, most Catholic clergy were Irish speaking. One could similarly make a case that Calvinism had difficulty penetrating into the Scottish Highlands and Western Islands because Lowlanders spoke Scots, while the Highlanders spoke Gaelic. In Wales, by contrast, the Anglican cause was promoted under Elizabeth by the translation of religious texts into Welsh and by the fact that the new church became and for long remained Welsh-speaking.

The problem with this explanation is that in Ireland we need to explain not only why the Gaelic Irish remained Catholic, but also why those of Anglo-Norman descent did as well. Many of these people were culturally and linguistically similar to the English.

The principal reason that the Old English in Ireland rejected the religion of the centre was that they were less loyal to the crown than were the Welsh. Relative satisfaction with Tudor rule in the early sixteenth century led the Welsh to conform to the crown religion, in a way that the Old English in Ireland were not willing to do. Relations between the Old English and the crown were seriously strained during most of the sixteenth century. The former came to see Anglicanism as something that was being forced on them, while Catholicism was part of a patrimony that needed to be defended. Matters were made worse by the failure of the crown to use monastic land to win the support of the Old English as effectively as it was used in England and Wales. The active support of the state was essential to the success of the Reformation, but the Dublin government remained cautious, hesitating to enforce laws against recusancy, fearful of testing the loyalty of disaffected subjects. Some Irish also remained loyal to Catholicism because they thought it increased their chances of securing continental assistance against the English.

Another problem for the Church of Ireland in the sixteenth century was clerical personnel. The conversion of the existing clergy to the new church faced enormous obstacles, and those who were won over were not very useful. Their incomes were low and they were poorly educated. Many of those who accepted the state's religion wanted English livings. The Church of Ireland could engage new clergy from England. There was, however, a distinct lack of enthusiasm among English clerics about going to Ireland. Inevitably the rate of turnover was unusually high and the preachers not the best of the bunch. And some clerics had livings in both Ireland and England. For all these reasons, the campaign for converting the Irish to the religion of the centre was fatally weak.

The Counter-Reformation in Ireland, though plagued with certain problems of its own, had some advantages. Close ties between Ireland and France provided the clerical personnel to promote Catholicism in Ireland. The Jesuits who came to Ireland were from Anglo-Irish commercial and landed families. The calibre of the clergy produced by the continental colleges in the early seventeenth century was of high standards. The Old English in Ireland saw themselves as participating in a European reform movement.[68]

In the Scottish Reformation, personal ties and opposition to the crown were crucial. Scotland was the only part of the British Isles to have a Protestant Reformation in which the religion of the crown was overthrown. In order to understand how this happened it is essential to recognize the extent to which the Continent was the cultural centre for Scotland. The long historical ties that existed between Scotland and the Continent became in the sixteenth century the bridge by which continental Lutheranism and Calvinism spread from Germany, Switzerland, and the Low Countries to Scotland. Patrick Hamilton (burned in 1528) was a student in Marburg, Paris, and Louvain, as a result of which he came under the influence of Luther. George Wishart (burned in 1546) acquired his Reform convictions in Switzerland. John Knox, the man who is given (perhaps undeservedly) the most credit for the Protestant Reformation in Scotland, put in several years in Geneva studying under John Calvin in the 1550s, though he actually converted to Reform earlier when he was still in Scotland.

The religion these men brought with them became entangled in political struggles in Scotland. Scottish elites were bitterly divided into two factions, one pro-French and the other pro-English. Not surprisingly, Reform became the religion of the anti-French faction; Knox denounced Catholicism and ties with France in the same voice. During the regency of Mary of Guise (the French wife of James v and mother of Mary Queen of Scots), French ties became even stronger and, by 1558, Scotland was becoming a French dependency. In 1560, with military assistance from England, French domination was overthrown and the Scottish Parliament repudiated the authority of the pope. Yet the Scots would not accept the religion of the English centre, for some of the same reasons that the Irish would not do so. They were not about to allow either Paris or London tell them how to worship.

Protestant Settlement and the Penal Laws in Ireland

Heavy Protestant settlement occurred in Ulster. Much of it was organized plantation, but not all. Unsponsored Scottish migration to Counties Antrim and Down transformed the population of these counties. Historians believe that outside Ulster the heaviest concentrations of settlement were in Counties Wicklow, King's, Carlow, and Wexford, though the evidence is incomplete.[69] The sixteenth and early seventeenth-century Confiscations entailed the settlement of English colonists on the confiscated land; in some cases such settlement was a condition of the grant. The Cromwellian Confiscations of the mid-seventeenth century and the Williamite Confiscations near the end of the century put no such obligations on new owners,[70] but settlement still occurred.

It cannot be argued that there was a uniform and consistent English policy towards the Irish population. Objectives and assumptions varied. Some of these objectives and assumptions we can call assimilationist; others, exclusionist. The Confiscations were certainly exclusionist. Catholics were to be forced out of the landowning class; many New English wanted them forced out of the country. The defeat of James II was followed by the flight of some 12,000 Irish troops to join the French army. Edmund Burke compared the subsequent Penal Laws with the Edict of Fontainebleau and the treatment of Huguenots in France.

Is it not most evident that this act of injustice, [the Edict of Fontainebleau] which let loose on that monarch [Louis XIV] such a torrent of invective and reproach, and which drew so dark a cloud over all the splendour of a most illustrious reign, falls far short of the case in Ireland? The privileges which the Protestants of that kingdom enjoyed antecedent to this revocation were far greater than the Roman Catholics of Ireland ever aspired to under a contrary establishment. The number of their sufferers, if considered absolutely is not half of ours; if considered relatively to the body of each community, it is not perhaps a twentieth part. And the penalties and incapacities which grew from that revocation are not so grievous in their nature, nor so certain in their execution, nor so ruinous by a great deal to the civil prosperity of the State, as those which we have established for a perpetual law in our unhappy country.[71]

It should be conceded that Burke had political motives for the case he was making. It should also be conceded that the Penal Laws did not ban Catholic worship as the Edict of Fontainebleau banned Protestant worship. And the Penal Laws were not enforced to the letter. This was also the case, however, with anti-Protestant legislation in France. The major difference was that the Edict of Fontainebleau had one objective, assimilation, whereas the Penal Laws in Ireland had two contradictory objectives, one of which was assimilation (to use status discrimination to impose the religion of the centre), the other of which was exclusion (to use status discrimination to force Catholics out of the elite). The provisions against the aristocracy were the most thoroughly enforced. No Roman Catholic could obtain land from a Protestant through inheritance or marriage. Catholics could not be granted leases of more than thirty-one years. And land could not be let to Catholics at a rent that was less than two-thirds the property's annual value. Catholics were also excluded from political activity. They were not permitted to vote or take a seat in Parliament. Catholic peers who were not willing to renounce their belief in transubstantiation and papal supremacy were excluded from the Irish House of Lords.[72] In 1716 this house voted that any attainted or outlawed peer or his heirs who used his title had committed a breach of privilege against the peerage.[73] Secular clergy were not banned, but measures were adopted to undermine their cultural power.[74]

The churchmen who had come to Ireland in the sixteenth century were assimilationist in the sense that they sought to convert the Irish, even the Gaelic Irish, to the Church of Ireland. Efforts at assimilation were never given up altogether, even in the eighteenth century. The Church of Ireland consistently demanded the enforcement of obligatory church attendance. Beginning in 1733, Charter schools were founded to convert Catholics, growing in number until the 1770s.[75] The Penal Laws imposed partible inheritance on Catholics, but stipulated that the eldest son inherited the entire estate if he became a

Protestant.[76] The result was a goodly number of conversions, intermarriages between Catholic and Protestant families, or transfers of land to descendants who had converted to Protestantism.[77]

Louis Cullen has asserted that the rate of conversion increased during periods in which there was greater fear among Protestants of a Jacobite or Catholic invasion or insurrection,[78] suggesting that if the Church of Ireland had made greater efforts, more conversions might have been possible. Nonetheless, over time the struggle against Catholicism became more discouraging. Even in the sixteenth century Anglican clergy were tempted to settle down in congregations with a reasonable number of adherents of the established church and to leave the job of saving the souls of the Irish to others. As settlers arrived in Ireland during the seventeenth century this temptation became all the greater. It was plainly easier to make Ireland Anglican by encouraging such immigration, and serving these immigrants, than by trying to convert the Irish. The decline in immigration in the late seventeenth century, however, undermined this strategy. What evolved in Ireland was not a Protestant nation, but a society characterized by ethnic privilege and stratification, in which members of the Church of Ireland (and to a much lesser extent Presbyterians) were overrepresented in higher status groups, while Catholics were vastly underrepresented. The aristocracy was composed overwhelmingly of members of the Church of Ireland. Although the effort to make the religion of the British centre the persuasion of the majority of the population had failed, the religion of the centre was the established religion and the one to which the wealthiest and most powerful people in the society belonged.

Anglicization and Its Residues

Over the course of the sixteenth, seventeenth, and eighteenth centuries the Welsh, Scottish, and Irish gentry were Anglicized – but not completely.

The greater selling and buying of land and concentration of landownership in the late seventeenth and early eighteenth centuries increased the number of owners with properties in different parts of the British Isles.[79] This was particularly true in Wales, where English acquired land through purchases, inheritances, and intermarriage. In Glamorgan family extinctions led to a significant change in the composition of the landed elite; the new families that emerged in the eighteenth century were more English, more involved in government service, and more closely linked to commerce.[80]

English culture invaded Wales, especially into the southwest.[81] From the time of the Union of Wales and England, an increasing proportion of the Welsh gentry spoke and wrote English.[82] English acquired a prestige and became a symbol of status differentiation; to speak Welsh was regarded as a sign of lower status.[83] Aristocrats typically conversed and exchanged letters with one another in English. Increasingly their education was in English. There was no education in Wales beyond the grammar school level. Welsh students were sent in especially large numbers to Oxford and the Inns of Court. Jesus College, Oxford, was almost a "Welsh college."[84] Some gentry also increasingly educated their children by private tutoring and travel abroad, neither of which improved their command of the Welsh language.[85]

We should not, however, exaggerate the Anglicization. While some members of the gentry resisted speaking Welsh or could do so only with great difficulty, others were fluently bilingual, and still others spoke Welsh regularly. In many areas, such as Caernarvonshire, a magistrate could not function without speaking Welsh.[86] The lesser gentry were more likely to speak Welsh fluently than were the higher gentry. The minor gentry of the Teifi Valley (which forms the boundary between Cardiganshire and Carmarthenshire) spoke Welsh regularly in the eighteenth century.[87] The higher gentry spent more time in England than did the lesser gentry.[88] It was only the wealthier landowners who could afford to send their children to an English public school rather than a Welsh grammar school, to have them tutored, or to send them abroad to travel. Even in Glamorgan only 10 per cent of gentry boys went to a major English school; most of the remainder were educated at local grammar schools.[89] Yet Glamorgan landed families, especially those from the lowland southern portion of the county, were more closely tied to the English gentry than to the rest of the Welsh gentry. Philip Jenkins found no case of a marriage between a member of the gentry in Glamorgan and anyone from the six northern counties of Wales, while one in ten of the marriages in the Glamorgan gentry took place with persons from southwest England.[90] At the same time that many Welsh landowning families were adopting the "sophisticated" manners of English society, many others still seemed to conform to the model of the rustic Welsh squire. Despite the invasion of English culture, the stereotype of the backward Welsh squire persisted into the eighteenth century and even into the nineteenth.

We see in this period little that could be described as a melting pot. If one likes analogies, a better one would be a magnet that draws some filings to a centre while leaving others. This analogy is also more appropriate than the melting pot for Scotland. Although it remained politically distinct in the seventeenth century, gradually its elite became more Anglicized. Consumption patterns came to conform more closely to those of England. Law and order in the Lowlands, together with English influences, transformed the character of country houses; the new houses were influenced by styles in England, France, and Italy.[91] The Union of the British and Scottish Parliaments in 1707 had a dramatic effect. Although some Scottish institutions persisted, institutional separation was reduced. The importance of Edinburgh declined and a much greater number of Scottish peers and gentlemen found reason to go to London. The distance between Scotland and London made the trip a difficult one, but it also persuaded Scots to stay in London for longer periods when they got there. Another change took place after 1760 when the Scottish economy became stronger. Rentals increased; more expensive tastes developed; and the cost of living rose. Gentlemen improved their residences and estates.[92] From the seventeenth century there was increasing intermarriage between the Scottish and English aristocracy. Gradually the Scots tongue gave way to London English as the language of the peerage and gentry. It is probable that Anglicization occurred in the private correspondence of Lowland landowning families in the seventeenth century.[93] They began to write in English. They also began increasingly to speak English.

The Highlands and Western Islands were also changing in the seventeenth and eighteenth centuries. Along with the commercialization of the landlord-tenant relationship and the deterioration of lordship, a parallel transformation occurred in the life style of lairds in the Highlands and Western Islands. Evidence has survived of payments of hundreds of pounds by landowners in the Western Isles during the seventeenth century on fashionable clothing and accoutrements, luxury foods, and household goods.[94] At the beginning of the seventeenth century many abandoned the saffron shirt, which was the traditional dress of the lairds, and began to imitate the clothing of the gentry of the south of Scotland.[95] The traditional method of raising the children of chiefs and chieftains by fosterage in the family of another member of the clan was replaced by education at home and in Lowland and English institutions.[96] By the mid-eighteenth century many Highland chiefs were university educated and had travelled on the Continent. Some spoke several languages. Visitors to the Highlands and Western Islands found a strange mixture of European aristocratic culture with a primitiveness that would have shocked even a poor French noble.

Even for the Lowland gentry, Anglicization was not all inclusive. The Scottish accent and distinctively Scottish words and sayings were difficult to eliminate. These Scotticisms persisted and they were a source of embarrassment to Scots in London.[97] As a percentage of the landed elite, the number of Scots in London was very small; the absenteeism of Scottish landowners was nothing like that of Irish landowners. Thus most Scots had great difficulty learning English well and getting the right accent. The greater proximity of Wales to England undoubtedly gave the Welsh gentry more practice speaking English with the English, practice that was seriously lacking for many of the Scottish gentry.[98]

The landed gentry of Ireland was also Anglicized, albeit through a different process. The majority migrated to Ireland from England. Many aspects of English life style were brought in or adopted during the seventeenth and eighteenth centuries. Numerous Irish landowners were absentee and spent considerable time in England. Goods were imported and English habits, such as tobacco smoking, became more common.[99] Landowning families began to move out of tower houses and thatched dwellings into more modern country houses. Eventually during the eighteenth century there was a standardization of houses; the box-like Georgian house eventually reached even lesser gentry.[100]

What is perhaps remarkable is that a linguistic difference nevertheless developed. A number of English dialects were brought to Ireland with the immigration of the seventeenth century. These dialects merged as the Anglo-Irish dialect, which developed differently from the standard English dialect that was coming to dominate in higher status groups in England. Standard English did not replace the Anglo-Irish dialect until the nineteenth century. The Irish language and the English spoken by the Old English in Ireland were persisting influences, but lack of contact with England was also a major factor. The distance and water that separated Ireland from England impeded intercourse sufficiently to permit linguistic differentiation. This differentiation was only overcome when methods of transportation improved and when – but not until the nineteenth century – it became more common for children of Irish gentry to go to school across the Irish Sea. Thus, the Irish gentry of the eighteenth century was like the Scottish Lowland gentry – English speaking, but with noticeable differences in accent and usages.[101]

Linguistically the pattern was not altogether dissimilar in France and the British Isles. In both cases the language of the centre became the predominant language of the aristocracy, while the non-aristocratic population remained more linguistically heterogeneous. Within the aristocracy, linguistic diversity in the British Isles was represented in Scotticisms in the English spoken by Lowland Scots, Gaelic spoken in the Highlands and Western Islands, the distinctiveness of the Anglo-Irish dialect, Gaelic spoken in Ireland by the very few remaining Gaelic landowners, Welsh spoken by some Welsh gentry, and regional accents of English spoken in different parts of Wales and England. Within the French nobility, linguistic diversity was represented in regional accents of French spoken in different parts of France, and the preference of many nobles in the Basque country, the Midi, Brittany, Flemish districts, Alsace, and some other places to speak the provincial language more often than French because they were more comfortable in it. One could argue that, with respect to some recently acquired territories, most notably Alsace, the French government was more tolerant towards linguistic diversity, but there does not seem to have been a great difference in the degree of linguistic diversity in France versus the British Isles. The major difference was abroad. French far more than English was spoken by European aristocrats.

With respect to religion there were also some similarities. Most striking is the parallel between Ireland and many parts of France. In both cases the centre did not have sufficient power to impose its chosen religion during the sixteenth century. It was able to do so during the seventeenth century, but only by using draconian measures that entailed the displacement or forced conversion of many aristocrats of the religious minority. Scotland bears some similarity to Alsace. In both cases religious differences developed before union and the acceptance of these differences by the centre was a condition for the acceptance of union by the periphery. Finally, Protestant Nonconformity in the British Isles bears a few similarities with Jansenism in France.

There were, however, more differences in the religious structures than similarities. During the sixteenth century the English crown was able to impose its chosen religion more successfully than the French crown. Protestants in France were remarkably successful at establishing strongholds as a result of the weakness of the French crown.[102] In comparing Scotland and Alsace we must recognize that the relationship between Anglicanism and Presbyterianism was exceedingly different from the relationship between Catholicism and Lutheranism. Jansenism was quite a different kind of nonconformity than Protestant Nonconformity in England. And there was no equivalent in France of the large Catholic population in Ireland. The percentage of the aristocracy in the British Isles that was Catholic was greater than the percentage of the nobility in France that was Protestant. This stemmed from the fact that Catholicism in both the British Isles and in France was proportionately stronger in the aristocracy than among urban elites. Yet the majority of British aristocrats were Protestant, just as the majority of French were Catholic. In both countries, religion was a source of cohesion, which created a bond among aristocrats in different regions.[103] Yet after 1685 religion was more cohesive in France than in the British Isles.

We have already seen that for many aristocrats their experience was one of being drawn to and changed by a centre rather than a developing national state. This was true culturally as well as politically. The culture that aristocrats were led to emulate and in varying degrees to assimilate was not one in which several aristocracies blended together to form a national culture. The culture that prevailed was that of the centre, altered to an extent by peripheral cultures, but unquestionably the culture of the centre to which the peripheries conformed. Aristocrats of the peripheries were not very successful at injecting their culture into that of the centre. When Scottish culture seemed to be succeeding, even a little, English reaction could be nasty, as it was in the 1760s when John Wilkes aroused anti-Scottish passions through his newspaper, mockingly entitled the *North Briton*. Linda Colley's contention that Wilkite Scottophobia was a reaction to a perceived Scottish political and cultural invasion has considerable validity, but does not really strengthen her more general argument that "Britons" were integrating at this time.[104] Despite the increase in the number of Scots securing state positions, Scottish political participation in the centre was still limited in this period and Scottish cultural penetration of England was largely a Wilkite myth, while the Scotsbashing was all too real.

Nonetheless, though Scots were becoming like the English far more than the English were becoming like the Scots, assimilation was indeed occurring among the elites. In principle this process is denied by theories of internal colonialism. Michael Hechter rejected diffusion models that emphasize the assimilation of peripheral cultures with that of the centre. Instead he argued that the cultural distinctiveness of the British periphery resulted from cultural exclusion by the centre, which sought to maintain peripheral groups as separate so that they could be exploited, thus creating a "cultural division of labour." Eventually the peripheries accepted their cultural distinctiveness and tried to use it to organize collective action against the centre.[105] This is all very true, but his own discussion of the British Isles in the Early Modern period demonstrates that the assertion by the centre of its cultural superiority also had the effect of assimilating many people in the periphery.[106] There is an internal contradiction in the dynamics of status and cultural superiority. All high-status groups with cultural power tend to undermine their own position. They help to establish and maintain their higher status by denigrating other cultures and convincing people that their own is superior, all of which leads other groups to imitate this culture. In turn, this imitation serves to undermine the monopoly of the higher status group, unless boundaries can be set up to prevent assimilation.

THE CENTRALIZATION OF ARISTOCRATIC CULTURE

If we turn our attention specifically to what we can call "aristocratic culture," we find a similar process of centralization.

Courts and Chivalry in the Middle Ages

In varying degrees, aristocrats in Western Europe aspired to a common courtly culture during the Middle Ages. This culture was developed at courts and cathedral schools by courtiers and clerics, who sought to educate the aristocracy and instil new values in them.[107] They taught a culture that celebrated the classics. They extolled service to the prince. Fidelity, altruism, and charity were goals to which aristocrats should strive. Young nobles were instructed in proper comportment – the right way to stand, walk, talk, smile, dress, and eat. They must respect the feelings and interests of others.[108] Idealized love and the proper treatment of women also became part of this courtly culture, though some scholars have insisted that there was a considerable satirical element in troubadour songs about courtly love.[109]

A closely related ideology that greatly affected the aristocracy was chivalry. It evolved in the eleventh and twelfth centuries with the following processes: (1) the rise in the status of knights, (2) the celebration of the knight in romance literature in order to motivate young nobles to become knights, (3) the effort of churchmen to contain the violence of warriors, ideally to persuade them to serve God, and (4) the growing importance and skill in battle of horsemen, a development that was made possible by the arrival in Europe several centuries earlier of the stirrup.[110] Those who led this movement usually sought to combine courtly culture, religious devotion, and military ideals. Thus knights were expected to be both learned men and skilled warriors. In the twelfth century an abbot wrote to the Count of Flanders declaring that "neither is manly chivalry of prejudice to learning, nor is a fitting knowledge of letters of prejudice to knightly exercises." Rather, "the union of the two is so useful and so becoming in a prince, that the prince who is not made truly noble by knowledge of letters betrays his status by stooping to the condition of a rustic or even a beast."[111] Knights were also expected to serve God. Their heroes should be ancient saintly warriors, such as Eustache and Sebastian.[112] And they must be courageous and willing to fight alone against overwhelming odds. Meeting these standards was necessary in order to preserve their "honour."

It may come as a surprise to most sociologists that the values and norms of this culture were in certain respects universalistic. This is not to say that knights always behaved in a universalistic manner. Nor is it to say that Medieval culture was in general universalistic. Rather, it is to assert that insofar as the chivalric movement had an impact, it was to make attitudes and behaviour more universalistic than they would otherwise have been. Knights were supposed to follow general normative standards, not just serve the interests of the particular group to which they belonged. It is true that they were expected to fight for their lord and to shield their kin and communities against foreigners. Yet this had always been expected of fighting men. What was new with the chivalric movement was the notion that there were higher moral principles to which knights were bound and which should moderate the aggressiveness with which they defended their lord, kin, or community. Knights were told to refrain from excessive brutality and to protect the weak. Ramon Lull in the *Book of the Ordre of Chyvalry* demanded that knights safeguard women, widows, and orphans.[113] Knights should also think of themselves as belonging to a brotherhood of arms, all members of which were committed to a fair fight and to respect for their opponents. Whatever they actually did, the chivalric movement was universalistic.

From our perspective the crusades of the eleventh, twelfth, and early thirteenth centuries seem particularistic. Europeans invaded the Middle East to assail those of an opposing religion. In their terms, however, the crusading movement contained strong elements of universalism. Knights from across Europe, many of whom had fought against one another, joined forces to serve a cause that transcended the communal or cultural group to which they belonged. The brotherhood of arms made the crusades possible and at the same time was reinforced by the crusades. Within Europe the crusades represented a universalizing force. In 1188, for example, Philip II was forced to seek a peace agreement with the Angevins partly because some of his most powerful nobles were reluctant to fight against other nobles who had, like themselves, participated in a crusade.[114]

It should not astonish us therefore that knights were not often killed in battle. If captured, they were rarely slain; indeed, they might be treated as guests. I grant that they were often kept alive for ransom, and that lower-status fighters did not receive the same privileges. Theoretically, however, they could acquire such privileges if they proved themselves worthy. Many stories were told of young men from humble backgrounds who were able to prove themselves worthy of such treatment.

Not enough emphasis has been given to the fact that chivalry was also an individualistic ideology. Yet this is only to be expected given the emergence of the movement at a time when centralized authority was weak. Knights glorified self-reliance and the solitary soldier. All nobles – not just knights – believed they had a right to autonomous action, and in particular to defend their honour. Kristen Neuschel has analysed this kind of individualism among nobles in sixteenth-century France. She uses it to explain the fact that nobles formed and broke off alliances remarkably freely. A key element in her thesis is that clientage did not control the behaviour of nobles during the sixteenth century as much as historians have generally believed.[115]

This disagreement points to a fundamental contradiction in noble culture. What Neuschel is talking about is the sixteenth-century version of a set of countervailing forces that could be found throughout the Middle Ages. Noble individualism repeatedly ran up against lordship and against the view that knights should serve their lord and be loyal. These countervailing forces created serious tensions, which were the subject of many stories. As a result of the independent-mindedness of knights, they could not always be counted on.

The cultural powerholders – those who generated, transmitted, inculcated, and/or served as models of chivalry – were diverse, more diverse than those who promoted courtly culture. Clerics were obviously the most commonly responsible for literature that tried to persuade knights to become learned, serve their prince and God, and protect women and children. Tutors employed by nobles could do much to fashion chivalric ideals in their young pupils. Chivalry was also spread by troubadours and nomadic minstrels, and nobles themselves propagated chivalry. Writers of chivalric works were nobles of varying status – Ramon Lull (whose father was a companion of King James of Aragon, from whom he received landed estates), Geoffrey de Charny (author of the *Book of Chivalry*, a knight and lord), and Ghillebert de Lannoy (author of *Enseignements paternels* and a counsellor of Philip the Good).[116] Even simple knights shaped the chivalric ideology and culture by providing models and by instructing young aspirants.

Courtly and chivalric cultures were closely associated and mutually influenced one another.[117] Indeed, many of the characteristics that distinguished chivalry from plain military culture stemmed from the courtly movement. Still, there was a difference in emphasis and they should not be conflated into one ideology. Courtly culture was more learned and anti-rural than chivalry. It was less individualistic. It was more concerned with etiquette and comportment. Some people believed that knights lost their virility when they became learned, that knights socialized in courtly culture were self-indulgent, and that the king's men were slick and deceitful in contrast to the honest and simple knight.[118] Moreover, certain courts were more chivalric, others more learned, and still others more concerned with idealizing love. The court of Amadeus VI, the great count of Savoy of the fourteenth century, was mainly a chivalric court; it left the world only a few accomplishments of learning.[119] One of the most learned courts was that of Emperor Frederick II (1211–50) in Sicily; even when on military campaign he carried with him works of Aristotle and Avicenna on pack-mules.[120] The best-known court idealizing love was that of Eleanor of Aquitaine and her daughter Marie of Champagne at Poitiers.[121]

The number of courts that produced courtly or chivalric literature and were known for their achievement of the ideals of one of these two movements was large. Almost every lord holding a castle tried to establish a court of some kind, with at least a few clerics and as many knights as could be attracted and afforded. These "schools" of knighthood provided training for young knights.[122] They were highly participatory. And the larger ones were supralocal. Knights from considerable distances would attend courts, often to participate in tournaments. Both the knights and the courts were peripatetic. Monasteries were also centres of chivalric culture, at least of the Christian mission of knighthood.[123]

During the late Middle Ages monasteries ceased to be the centres of aristocratic culture that they had once been and the number of courts declined. A smaller number of highly exalted courts came to dominate the scene, culminating in the greatest courtly chivalric centre of all, the court of Burgundy in the Southern Low Countries. In its day it outshone all other courts. It was renowned for its learning and literature; it attracted artists and musicians from afar; it imparted chivalric ideals and moulded knights; it staged spectacular tournaments and ceremonies; and it cultivated aristocratic entertainment and pleasures. It effected nothing less than a chivalric renaissance.[124]

From Knight to Courtier

State Control over Aristocratic Militarism and Violence

One reason for the decline of chivalry was the increasing control exercised by princes over knights.[125] This development contributed not only to the state institutionalization of status, but also to the gradual state monopolization of violence. Princes instituted orders of knighthood, in part to persuade nobles to live up to courtly and chivalric ideals, but also to strengthen the less individualistic elements in those ideals and to get knights to serve some larger purpose. Princes tried to use orders to create bonds between themselves and their nobility. It was for this reason that Edward III founded the Order of the Garter in 1348.[126] In the same century Amadeus VI formed the Order of the Black Swan and (more successfully) the Order of the Collar to secure more firmly the loyalty of his men and to counter the growing tendency for military campaigns to be carried out by mercenaries or other warriors without chivalric ideals.[127] Persuading knights to serve the religious mission was the purpose of a number of religious-military orders, the best-known of which are the Order of the Poor Soldiers of Christ of the Temple, or Knights Templar, and the Knights of the Order of the Hospital of Saint John of Jerusalem, subsequently known as the Order of Malta.

The religious-military orders became cut off from knighthood in general, but the non-religious orders had a tremendous impact on noble culture. They promoted chivalry and helped to preserve it longer than it might otherwise have lasted, but at the same time, by undermining its individualism, they made a contribution to its ultimate demise. The Order of the Golden Fleece, founded by Philip the Good in 1430, did much to perpetuate, indeed revive, chivalry. It demanded that all members of the order be learned and honourable, and that they serve God and defend the weak. Its rules required members to be courageous in battle (and specifically prohibited them from withdrawing after the opposing forces had displayed their banners). Magnificent ceremonies were held at the periodic general assemblies of the order.[128]

None of the individualism of chivalry was, however, to be tolerated. Indeed, the dukes of Burgundy employed the Order of the Golden Fleece to help them keep nobles in line. Members had to swear to obey the statutes of the order; when the order met they were to judge the behaviour of their fellow knights and vouch for one another's conduct.[129] The statutes of the Order of the Golden Fleece placed much emphasis on loyalty to the duke, and only to the duke. Knights were obliged to serve the duke in battle; they could not engage in military activity or take long trips without his permission; they had to obey the duke and his deputy in any circumstance that involved the order; and membership in the order signified that one was the duke's man.[130] The order was used as an instrument of state formation. A major purpose was clearly to promote state centralization by creating solidarity among its members and bringing together nobles from the diverse regions over which the Burgundian dukes were trying to rule.[131]

State control over aristocratic militarism and violence was frustrated by the popularity of various substitutes for war, including criminal activities, such as brigandage, abductions of women, and poaching. In England, both poaching and hunting often simulated elements of war.[132] Fox hunting may have been popular because it developed skills that could be useful in a military career.[133] Aristocratic criminal activity was common among continental nobles. Examples of such behaviour abound and popular puns – *gens-tue-hommes* and *gens-pille-hommes* – reflected public recognition of the noble proclivity for violence.[134] The reluctance of some aristocrats to give up private fighting was shown by a growth in the popularity of duels, particularly in France, during the sixteenth and seventeenth centuries. Duels sprang from the determination of many aristocrats to preserve normative codes of chivalric individualism that limited state control.[135] This is not to suggest that duels were the straightforward consequence of crown-noble opposition. Many nobles wanted the king to re-establish judicial duels, supervised by the crown or its agents.[136] They resented not the power of the crown, but what they saw as the unwillingness of the crown to provide ways for nobles to defend their individual honour.

Gradually, over the course of the late Middle Ages and the Early Modern period, individual encounters became less common and fighting meant more often working within a disciplined regiment – leaving warriors with fewer opportunities to demonstrate their skill and courage. Monarchs wanted standing armies with professional full-time soldiers and conscripts who did not have the right to join a military campaign or withdraw from it as they pleased. Only in rebellions or civil wars, such as the Wars of Religion in France, did this kind of autonomy persist. Yet these are exceptions that prove the rule. So is duelling. It rose in popularity precisely because some aristocrats were seeking alternative ways to defend their honour in single combat as single engagements in battle and tournaments declined.

Fighting and duelling among aristocrats was strongly opposed by monarchs, even in Scotland,[137] and by most of the aristocracy as well. In France and Savoy duelling was a marginal movement, one not endorsed by the majority of nobles and certainly not by those nobles in positions of power. Although it persisted even into the eighteenth and nineteenth centuries, under Louis XIV most people were losing interest in duelling.[138] Militarism was encouraged by the crown, but strictly in the service of the crown. Noble opposition to duelling also resulted from the growth of the *noblesse de robe*, whose culture was less bellicose. Finally, as a consequence of the changing social definition of noble status, even in France and Savoy military activity did not define aristocratic status as it had in the Middle Ages, though it continued to do so more in France and Savoy than it did in the British Isles.

Early Modern Courtly Culture

The culture of the Early Modern court drew more heavily on Medieval courtly than on Medieval chivalric culture. This is not to deny that many chivalric elements endured in the court culture of the sixteenth, seventeenth, and eighteenth centuries. Yet the emphasis was now on the courtly tradition more than the chivalric tradition. The Renaissance had a profound impact on court culture, strengthening learning and art as opposed to arms. With the Renaissance the centres of art shifted from the churches and the towns to the princely courts (with a few exceptions, such as the Northern Low Countries).[139] Courtiers were expected to be learned, as we can see from the most influential book that preached court behaviour, *Il cortegiano* by Baldassar Castiglione, first issued in 1528. According to one of Castiglione's authorities on courtly behaviour, the ideal courtier should be "more than passably learned in letters, at least in those studies which we call the humanities. Let him be conversant not only with the Latin language, but with Greek as well, because of the abundance and variety of things that are so divinely written therein."[140] The same authority also indicated that he would not be satisfied with a courtier "unless he be also a musician, and unless, besides understanding and being able to read music, he can play various instruments."[141]

Dress and appearance received greater attention. Extravagance in dress – already pronounced in the Middle Ages – reached new heights that sumptuary legislation did not deter (partly because sumptuary legislation was never very effective and partly because aristocrats were usually exempted).[142] Somewhat contradictorily, manners came to be taken more seriously and a stronger belief in the necessity of self-control emerged. Elaborate rules of etiquette and formal ceremony were developed. Nobles were greatly concerned with the presentation of the body and with bodily purification.[143] Ideally, one should be sensitive to the interests and feelings of others, and should restrain one's own behaviour.[144] The skills that a courtier had to acquire were very different from those of the Medieval knight. In addition to learning, music, and dancing, the Early Modern courtier had to be adept at dealing with other people; he or she was diplomatic, pleasing, ingratiating, and tactful rather than straightforward, forthright, and simple.[145] All other qualities will "not suffice to win him universal favor with lords and cavaliers and ladies unless he have a gentle and pleasing manner in his daily conversation."[146] The culture was one that required disguised manipulation and dissimulated negotiation.[147] The most important rule of all was "to practice in all things a certain *sprezzatura*, so as to conceal all art and make whatever is done or said appear without effort and almost without any thought about it."[148]

The individualism of Medieval noble culture did not die altogether. Far too often we try to understand cultures as internally consistent wholes, when in fact most cultures are full of contradictions. A recognition of these contradictions in seventeenth-century noble culture in France is the very considerable contribution of Dewald's study.[149] He has called historians' attention to the great concern of nobles with understanding themselves as individuals and with individual advancement and performance both inside and outside the court. However, this individualism coexisted with the increasing emphasis on "race" as the basis of noble status and with the growing pressure to conform to a stylized court culture. As it was during the Middle Ages, aristocratic individualism was also in contradiction with corporatist ideology, now reinforced by the state to a greater extent than ever before. Tournaments gradually declined as court entertainment. In Turin, even during the seventeenth century, the shows performed in the central piazza in front of the ducal palaces were still what Geoffrey Symcox calls "feudal-chivalric"; they typically extolled the martial prowess and courage of illustrious nobles. During the eighteenth century the nobility was no longer represented as individuals but as corporate groups; they paraded along with other corporate groups in hierarchical order.[150]

In some respects these observations support the corporatist view briefly summarized in the preceding chapter. Yet in other respects they do not. The corporatist view neglects the individualism that we can find in Medieval noble culture. Many historians assume that whatever individualism there was in Early Modern culture was something new and represented the beginning of the evolution of the society of the future. They would consider the mixture of individualism and corporatism in Early Modern Europe as merely a transitional phenomenon. Those inclined towards the corporatist view would have little patience with the suggestion that Early Modern society was in certain ways more a society of orders than was Medieval society.

Socialization

The methods of aristocratic socialization changed. A major transformation occurred during the fifteenth to seventeenth centuries in the level of formal education acquired by young aristocrats in the British Isles, the Southern Low Countries, and France.[151] In the seventeenth century, French academies designed for aristocratic education became popular among the *noblesse d'épée*. Parents tried to send their children to those academies whose riding master was well connected in court society. The most prestigious of these institutions were linked to the court and to Parisian high society. In addition, there were schools for pages, and other educational institutions even more closely connected with the court. Sons of the great sword families might become "children of honour," who were raised in the royal court; children of lesser nobles might be cadets in regiments of the royal household. During the eighteenth century the academies were gradually replaced by these court institutions (and by Jesuit boarding schools). Most of these institutions manifestly socialized young nobles in court culture. Physical grace, restraint, dancing, fencing, self-beautification, etiquette, riding – all these accomplishments were taught at the academies, which also helped young nobles make useful contacts for their careers.[152]

Resistance

Early Modern court culture was opposed and criticized from a number of quarters. We have already seen that many nobles were unwilling to accept the decline of chivalry and the accompanying loss of moral autonomy. In addition, a considerable body of literature and theatre had existed for some time poking fun at courtiers and exaggerating their characteristics. They were ridiculed as sycophants and parasites – lascivious, cunning, ambitious, corrupt, effeminate, extravagant, ineffectual, degenerate, and otiose.[153] Diarists have left us some of the flavour of the hostility of the public towards courts. L'Estoile frequently complained about the decadence and extravagance of the court of Henry III and especially about the king's favourites, his *mignons.* "These beautiful *Mignons* wear their hair long, artificially curled and recurled, capped by little velvet bonnets, like those of the prostitutes of the brothels." According to l'Estoile "their activities are to play, blaspheme, jump, dance, swing around, quarrel, and fornicate, and to follow the king everywhere and in all company."[154] It has to be acknowledged that Henry and his *mignons* were unusually degenerate by contemporary standards, but even less outrageous courts, such as that of Charles II, could come under criticism from those of stern morals. Acquaintances of Samuel Pepys referred to the "lewdness and beggary" of Charles's court, its "baseness and looseness," its "mad doings," its "viciousness," its "vices," its "loose amours," and its "gaming, swearing, women, and drinking."[155]

In France, there was a significant social cleavage between the court nobility and the provincial nobility. This cleavage was yet another way in which the old nobility was seriously divided. The nobility of the court looked down on the provincial nobility, while many of the latter repudiated the aristocratic culture of Paris and even ridiculed it.[156] The satires of the courtier were popular among the nobility of the provinces. Their moral codes emphasized religion and patriarchy and despised the pleasure-seeking life of the metropolis.[157]

Yet this criticism did not seriously disable the cultural and ideological power of the court. Ultimately it was the urbanite aristocratic culture that triumphed. The principal reason was the association of the court with the crown. Given the immense prestige and political power of the sovereign, it was difficult to undermine the influence of a culture in which he or she participated. Moreover, many of the so-called effeminate parasites were extremely powerful persons, making it difficult to dismiss the court as nothing more than a degenerate playground. And the criticism of outsiders was often hypocritical. Many aristocrats devoured manuals on court etiquette and tried to live up to the court mode, while at the same time they read satires of courts and attended plays ridiculing them. Sometimes the ridicule was not recognized. One satire, the *Philosopher of the Court* by Philibert de Vienne, appears to have been taken as a serious manual in England, even by its translator George North.[158] The value that courtiers placed on *civilité* was adopted outside the court even by those, like Erasmus, who found much in the court to deplore.[159]

The Bipolarization of Courts

There were no dynamic courts in the peripheries by the eighteenth century. The papal court at Avignon disappeared in 1376.[160] The Medieval ducal court in Brittany had been the equal of many others in Europe for its achievement of the ideals of courtly culture, but the marriage of Anne of Brittany to Charles VIII in 1491 and Louis XII in 1499, and the subsequent union of France and Brittany, put an end to it. Anne's retinue went with her to Paris and there became a distinctive element in the French court, but few great Breton lords came to Paris.[161] In the sixteenth century one does not find many Breton nobles at the French court; the king kept a few there so they could not make trouble in Brittany.[162] During the seventeenth and eighteenth centuries the strategy of the Breton nobility leaned towards withdrawal and avoidance of the intrigues of court by staying away from it.[163] The court of the House of Savoy left Savoy for Turin in the sixteenth century. The dukes rebuilt Turin to make the royal palaces the hub of the city and established an illustrious court, which became a centre for the union of French and Italian culture, renowned especially for its music.[164]

The Burgundian court, once the most illustrious in Lotharingia, disappeared. The court of Charles V was debilitated by his life of war and travelling. His court in Brussels in the 1550s was composed of more than five hundred persons, but its lustre was diminished because Charles was withdrawn. There was an absence of members of the higher nobility at court.[165] Philip II established his court at the Escorial in Spain. During the Dutch Revolt many intellectuals and artists fled the Southern Low Countries.[166] The archdukes revived the court in Brussels and it became once more a leading centre of high culture in Western Europe. The greatest accomplishment of the archdukes was to persuade Rubens (whose father had fled Antwerp before he was born) to join their court, though they agreed to let him live in Antwerp.[167] When direct Spanish rule was resumed, the court in Brussels continued to fluctuate in cultural power, depending on the status of the governor – more powerful if the governor was of a person of royal blood, such as the Archduke Leopold Guillaume (1647–56) and the Elector Maximilian Emanuel (1691–1700), but much less powerful under military governors. During the last half of the eighteenth century the court in Brussels again became magnetic under Charles of Lorraine. It was, however, a second-rate cultural centre when compared with the court of the dukes of Burgundy, at least relative to other courts of their respective periods.

The vigorous and informal court of Scottish monarchs disappeared with the Union of the Crowns in 1603. What happened to the Scottish court was similar to what happened to the Breton court, except that Brittany sent a queen-to-be to the centre, while Scotland sent a king. For this and other reasons Scots played a greater role in the post-union royal court than did Bretons. As noted in the preceding chapter, however, the prominence of Scots in the royal court declined over the course of the seventeenth century.

There had once been a court in Dublin. Henry II made his son John lord of Ireland in 1185, but intended that he should become king of Ireland and, for this purpose, provided him with land, officers, and knights, and the means to establish a royal court in Dublin.[168] This court declined when John departed from Ireland, leaving only the household of the chief governor, who was often an absentee. Small and rustic courts, with scholars and officials, had travelled with the eleventh-century Gaelic lords who were trying to act like kings. Even in the fifteenth and sixteenth centuries Gaelic lords typically maintained intellectual circles of brehon legists, bardic poets, and annalists. English cultural domination had been successfully resisted by these writers. They still thought their culture superior to that of the English and would not have believed that in one or two centuries it would be considered merely a peasant culture. During the seventeenth century, they lost the battle for cultural hegemony primarily for political/military reasons. The Gaelic intellectual circles were broken up and many of their members, including Gaelic scholars, fled to the Continent.[169]

The same forces that brought about the decline of these courts led to an increase in the cultural power of the royal courts located in the two political centres that now dominated Western Europe.

France

The French court went through a period of considerable development in the sixteenth century, much of it under Italian influence. The court of Francis I was unrefined and casual in comparison with the English court. Henry II improved its organization and observed ceremony more regularly, but it was still relatively informal. Henry III, however, was of a different temperament and undertook a major restructuring of the court, significantly increasing the regulations that had to be followed and introducing more ceremony, though we do not know how closely these regulations and ceremony were followed.[170] During the reign of Henry IV, who was born in Pau, the court again became less formal, indeed almost rustic, and as a consequence its prestige declined. Whereas in most periods the culture of the court diffused to the periphery, under Henry IV provincial culture came to court. Unlike virtually all other monarchs in Early Modern Western Europe, Henry IV came from the periphery and never altogether shed his provincial manners.[171] The court of Louis XIII was less rustic and flamboyant than that of his father, but still informal and not particularly ceremonious.

All monarchs tried to use the court as a stage for their own display of grandeur, but Louis XIV carried it to unusual lengths, spending vast sums on the building and decorating of sets for this stage primarily (but not exclusively) at Versailles. This activity provided a considerable stimulus to the art and luxury industries in France.[172] In the early years of his reign the court was most noted for its vivacity and hedonism. In subsequent years it became more staid and ceremonious.

The court went with the crown to Paris after the death of Louis XIV. It returned with the crown seven years later, but Versailles was never again as much the centre as it had been under Louis XIV, mainly as a result of the frequency with which the court moved from one residence to another during the reigns of Louis XV and Louis XVI.[173] Louis XV and Louis XVI were also less flamboyant than Louis XIV and sought to separate their private world from their public, and to avoid great public displays.[174] Be that as it may, Versailles was still the symbolic centre of France. Nothing else could match the king's *grandes fêtes* for grandeur.[175]

The British Isles

Sixteenth-century English courts were more formal than French courts and the monarch less accessible. Henry VIII did not use the court as much as Francis I to create ties between himself and the aristocracy.[176] Elizabeth took greater advantage of her court. That of James I was comparatively informal, but James himself not especially accessible.[177] The court of Charles I, in contrast, was extremely formal, with great emphasis on decorum, ceremony, and ritual.[178]

Under Charles II the pendulum swung back again to a less formal court. His was lavish and stylish, a site of entertainment and gaiety, the social and cultural centre of the British aristocracy. However, from the later years of the reign of Charles II the British court waned as a social and cultural centre. Patronage of the arts shifted to the greater aristocracy.[179] The decline of the court continued until the reign of George II, who restored its attractiveness in some measure, though it was still pale in comparison with the French court. It experienced a further decline after 1788.[180]

We saw in the preceding chapter that one of the major reasons for the decline of the British court was financial. Yet some contingencies and a few peculiarities of the British monarchs were also at least partly responsible. Several revolutions broke up the continuity of the court. James II, William III, and Anne were not by nature inclined toward lavish display or much merriment. Two monarchs, William III and George I, were foreigners, with few social ties among the English aristocracy. Anne suffered from a lack of social skills and poor health.[181] William III and George I were also aloof. George I was particularly inaccessible, except for the years 1717 and 1718 when he opened his doors to compete with the rival court of the Prince and Princess of Wales.[182]

Court and Town

From the time the great palace was built at Versailles it was the centre of French aristocratic society. Even under Louis XV and Louis XVI, Versailles led Paris. Parisians had to adapt if they wanted to enter court society.[183] There was considerable snobbery at Versailles vis-à-vis the Parisian nobility, a snobbery that coincided to some extent with that of old high nobility towards newer nobility and towards the nobility of finance and robe. In order to become acceptable at Versailles, Jeanne Antoinette Poisson (later mistress of Louis XV and marquise of Pompadour), who came from the financial milieu, had to adopt a different manner of speaking and shed her bourgeois airs.[184]

True, Paris was also a great centre of aristocratic culture. More nobles lived in Paris rather than at Versailles. It was in Paris that they had their grand *hôtels*. It was here, in what later came to be called the "salons,"[185] that nobles encountered the Enlightenment. And Paris was a supreme musical centre, particularly of opera. Elias underestimated the cultural power of the city vis-à-vis the court.[186] The town did not by any means always defer to the court. In the 1680s a distinction emerged in women's dresses between the *grand habit* of the royal court and the less conservative, more fashionable *habit de ville* worn in Paris. Men's *steinkerques* (cravats drawn through a hole) became a rage in the 1690s; they were regarded as *habit de ville* and were not worn at court.[187] A portion of the literature that mocked courtiers came from Paris, especially from the *philosophes*. During what was called the "Quarrel of the Bouffons," some of the *philosophes* celebrated Italian opera and criticized French opera in an effort to undermine the court at Versailles.[188] Paris was the centre of aristocratic education. The academies in Paris were in various ways linked with court society and located in the most aristocratic parts of the city, near the Louvre in the early seventeenth century, later around St Germain des Prés.[189]

In the British centre, however, town prevailed over court to an extent unimaginable in Paris. Two powerful alternatives drew people away from the British royal court.

The first was the City. Here were to be found financiers, as one could find them in Paris. Yet there was a difference. London could claim to be a financial centre for commerce as well as for the state, whereas financiers in Paris dealt mostly in state finance. London also had a large and very wealthy merchant population, of which there was no equivalent in Paris. These merchants were able to live in a style comparable to all but the greatest aristocracy. They controlled the City government. "There has formerly been," wrote Daniel Defoe in the 1720s, "a great emulation between the court end of town and the City." Although the court had sought to humble the City, at this time the City "has gained the ascendant, and is now made so necessary to the court (as before it was thought rather a grievance) that now we see the court itself the daily instrument to encourage and increase the opulence of the City."[190] It should be acknowledged that there remained a social gulf between the aristocracy and the business elite, but the English aristocracy was better integrated with the merchant elite than was the case in France. London merchant families intermarried with the landed elite and even participated in the "Season."[191] In varying degrees and forms this integration could be found in other urban centres as well.[192]

The other alternative was Parliament. As we have seen in the preceding chapter, by the eighteenth century the British Parliament was the centre of political power in the British Isles. Much of the social interaction that in France occurred at court, in England occurred in the halls of Parliament. However, the nature of those interactions and the relationship between Parliament and the provinces was altogether different from interaction in the French court, and the relationship between the French court and the provinces. Only a small number of English country gentry could aspire to a parliamentary seat, but most were involved, one way or another, in the electoral process to send a representative. No such central political assembly existed for the French, Savoyard, or South-Netherlandish provincial nobility.

FRENCH CULTURAL IMPERIALISM

The provincial nobility in most parts of France copied the Parisian and court nobility. It should be acknowledged that provincial towns in France – especially those with *parlements*, but others as well, most notably Lyons and Marseilles – provided centres of aristocratic culture to a greater extent than did provincial centres in the British Isles, with the exception of Edinburgh and Dublin. Yet in many respects, the cultures of French provincial towns were imitations of the culture of Paris and Versailles. Provincial academies, for example, had lower status and patterned themselves after the Parisian academies, but were less expensive.[193] Noble families in the provinces, even those living in the countryside, often became urban in their ways and forged links with Paris.[194] Members of the provincial nobility who disliked the Parisian and court nobility could not deny its pre-eminence. The contempt they often expressed for Versailles and Paris did not stop the general movement there of provincial nobility during the Early Modern period. The Parisian and court nobility continued to enjoy higher respect, if not affection, than the lesser nobility that stayed in the countryside. Their cultural power extended to the bourgeoisie as well. As Elias pointed out, the bourgeoisie in France adopted the culture of the royal court to a greater extent than its counterpart in Germany, with the result that French court culture had much greater effect on the evolving French national character.[195] The court and the other institutions that emulated it, most notably the academies, contributed to the nationalization of French culture.[196] English public schools had the same effect, but they did not imitate the culture of a central court in the way that French academies and other educational institutions for the French nobility did.

The pull of the French centre reached beyond French borders. The French court had more impact in Europe than did the English court. Naturally, all the great courts of Europe influenced one another in many ways. Louis XIV imitated a Polish style of wearing a coat and vest. The English long vests spread to other courts in Europe, despite French attempts to impede their diffusion. And the cravat was an English invention that spread to the Continent.[197]

The French court, however, was still the more powerful of the two in shaping the values, manners, dress, and other cultural elements of the European aristocracy. Henry VIII liked to copy the French. Best known is his creation of gentlemen of the Privy Chamber in imitation of the French *gentilshommes de chambre*, though this was done to deal with a problem of precedence during a visit to England of French *gentilshommes de chambre*.[198] The most receptive to French influence was the court of Charles II, partly because Charles had lived in France during the Interregnum. His court was considerably under French influence in furniture, music, dancing, dress, and comportment.[199] Although this court was influenced by Dutch art and architecture, French influence directed the rebuilding of the state apartments by Charles II.[200] Charles had a French tailor. French agents and stores operated in London at this time. English aristocrats going to the Continent would be asked to pick up clothing in Paris.[201]

Of course, there were voices in England that spoke against French cultural influence and in particular against this imitation of French manners and fashions. It is characteristic of the English, however, that this opposition came not from within the aristocracy, but primarily from the business community. Businessmen sought to persuade the crown to ban the import of French fashions and to develop distinctively English modes.[202] There was little they could do, however, to undermine the popularity of French fashions and even less they or anyone else in England could do to interfere with French cultural power elsewhere in Europe.

One place where they succeeded in doing so was in Scotland. Until sometime in the seventeenth century, perhaps the late-seventeenth century, France and the Low Countries constituted a cultural centre for the Scots more than southeastern England. French influence in Scotland may have reached a peak under Mary of Guise, but it definitely did not collapse with the Reformation, though it may have shifted from Paris to other parts of France since French Huguenots played a major role in preserving French cultural influence in Scotland during the late sixteenth and early seventeenth centuries. In any case, by the beginning of the eighteenth century southern England had replaced France as the principal cultural centre of the Scots.

French influence on Scotland never disappeared, however, and in most other parts of Europe French influence was on the increase during the seventeenth and eighteenth centuries. With the decline of Spain, Spanish fashions were giving way to French fashions. A great South-Netherlandish noble could be found wearing French clothes when he represented the King of Spain in London in 1660.[203] During the eighteenth century, especially after 1740, the influence of France on the Southern Low Countries became even greater than in earlier centuries. Three reasons have been suggested: the triumph of French theatre in this period; the toleration of Habsburg officials for the ideas of the Enlightenment; and the example set by the court of Charles of Lorraine in Brussels.[204] Charles's court was an imitation of the court at Versailles; it acted as a radius for the spreading of French court culture in the Southern Low Countries.[205] Yet for the very same reason that Charles's court emulated Versailles most people in the Southern Low Countries were more interested in the court at Versailles than in Charles's court. They read literature on the French court, including clandestine newsletters, known as *nouvelles à la main,* which were written by persons who attended the French court or Parisian salons and disseminated gossip about French high society.[206] French tastes and manners spread to almost all parts of the Low Countries.[207] Nobles from the Southern Low Countries often went to Paris for the social life. Children were routinely sent to French schools. Women, even Flemish women, adopted French manners.[208]

The centre of the Enlightenment was Paris, the capital of the "Republic of Letters."[209] The salons of Paris attracted foreigners from all over Europe, who came to learn and imitate French culture, often remaining in contact with a salon when they returned to their native country.[210] French salons were imitated in many cities, including London.[211] In Vienna, Italian and French drama was more popular among the nobility than German drama.[212] French culture had a considerable influence on Savoy.[213] Savoyard children were sent to colleges in Paris.[214] Many musicians in Savoy were from France, more than from Piedmont. Even Turin was greatly influenced by French culture.[215] Historians have been able to find surviving copies all over Europe of *nouvelles à la main.* There were also official magazines of the French court, such as *Le nouveau mercure galant,* which was nothing less than a propaganda sheet aimed at persuading the European aristocracy of the magnificence of the French court.[216] The *grand habit* became the correct court dress across Europe.[217] Other courts competed to be most like Versailles.[218] After a visit to the West, Peter the Great decreed that his aristocrats must cut off their beards and dress like the French. The British ambassador to Turkey jokingly communicated the impact of the new mode when adopted by the Russian embassy in Turkey. "The Muscovite Ambassador and his retinue have appeared here so different from what they always formerly wore that ye Turks cannot tell what to make of them." He went on to say that "they are all coutred in French habits, with an abundance of gold and silver lace, long perruques, and, which the Turks most wonder at, without beards."[219] Perhaps never before in the history of Europe had power over aristocratic values and norms of style, dress, manners, and comportment been so centralized as they were during the reign of Louis xiv and to a lesser extent his successors.[220]

This process enlarged the social distance between the aristocracy and the general population, increasingly so the farther one travelled from Versailles. In provincial France, in Lotharingia, and in other parts of Europe the highest aristocracy was becoming less and less like the general population because it was adopting an aristocratic culture that was very different from the indigenous culture of the society in which these aristocrats lived. There was now a European aristocratic culture, which distinguished the aristocracy from the general population and shaped its self-image.[221]

Aristocratic cultural power was less centralized in the British Isles. As a consequence of the weakness of the royal court and the lesser urbanization of the aristocracy, aristocratic culture found its centres in the countryside to a greater extent in the British Isles than on the Continent. Many of the great country houses, like Houghton (built by Sir Robert Walpole), Chatsworth (residence of the dukes of Devonshire), and Kedleston (residence of the Curzon family) were leading centres of aristocratic society. It was at the country mansion that the most extravagant spending occurred; it was the country mansion that offered the finest examples of English architecture; it was here that guests were invited to spend a few days, a few weeks, even a few months.[222] Great mansions had to have their great libraries, their music rooms, and their rooms full of collections.[223] Much of this could also be found on the Continent, but not to the same degree.

Moreover, though most provincial urban centres were smaller in the British Isles than they were on the Continent, cultural movements could still emerge in the peripheries. The Enlightenment in France was to be found primarily in Paris, whereas in the British Isles one of the peripheral countries, Scotland, was as much a centre of the Enlightenment as was London. While in some respects Edinburgh declined as a cultural centre after the Union of the Parliaments in 1707, in other respects its cultural power increased.[224] By 1760 Edinburgh was a sizable publishing centre and home for prominent writers in philosophy and history; it had an active theatrical community, a vigorous social life, and an excellent university. Indeed, the University of Edinburgh and the University of Glasgow were at least equal to any other universities in Britain. It is true that English influence, occasional central interference in these universities, and the efforts of Anglified Scots contributed to their development and to the Scottish Enlightenment.[225] The fact remains that Scots living in the periphery had considerable cultural influence, not only on England, but on intellectuals in other parts of Europe as well. Of course, Oxford and Cambridge were located in the southeastern region, but not in London or an adjacent county. Many years ago C.B. Tinker quite rightly stressed that London was regarded as the centre of English literary life in the eighteenth century, but he also suggested that the failure of the English to establish the kind of salons found in France resulted from the decentralization of English literary culture.[226]

A number of factors explain the greater centralization of cultural power in France. I would put the most stress on the ability of the French monarchy to mobilize more resources to impart the culture of the centre. In absolute terms France was a larger and wealthier country. In addition, the capacity of the crown to use the kingdom's wealth to create a glorious centre (especially splendid royal palaces and a magnificent court) was greater in France. French monarchs also spent more money patronizing art and luxury goods. According to Count Kaunitz (Maria Theresa's principal adviser), it was this kind of sponsorship that "put France ahead of all other countries."[227]

THE CULTURAL POWERHOLDERS

Aristocracy and the State

In the eighteenth century the great majority of the French bishops were members of the nobility, mostly nobility of the sword.[228] This was much less the case in the British Isles. From the seventeenth to the nineteenth centuries a significant increase occurred in the proportion of English and Irish bishops from the aristocracy and more precisely from peerage families, but even in the late eighteenth century the British aristocracy did not have the monopoly enjoyed by the French nobility.[229] On the other hand, in the British Isles landowners usually had control over the selection of local clerics, which enabled them to appoint non-inheriting sons from aristocratic families to church livings, though in some places, such as Scotland during the eighteenth century, the falling value of livings led to a decline in the number of men from aristocratic families interested in them.

The aristocracy had always exercised cultural power by patronizing artists and literati. They often held receptions or concerts, collected works of art, subsidized theatres, or employed artists or architects. Even not-so-grand aristocrats might provide maintenance for one or two artists or writers. In sixteenth- and seventeenth-century Ireland, bardic poets were supported by members of the Gaelic aristocracy.[230] Not surprisingly, many of the works of these poets extolled the virtues of the patrons or the society in which they belonged. Aristocratic cultural power is also illustrated by the Parisian salons, which passed judgment on new literature.[231] They could make or break careers of aspiring artists or writers. And they were one of the principal means by which new ideas reached persons in positions of influence. In some countries aristocrats enjoyed the right to make university appointments, usually to chairs they or their ancestors founded. For example, in Scotland the Earl Marischal named five of the seven professors at Marischal College in Aberdeen (until he took part in the Jacobite Rebellion of 1715). In 1732 Ramsay of Balmain founded a chair of Oriental languages, appointments to which were under his control. Local aristocrats often filled chancellorships, rectorships, or other offices in universities.[232]

In addition, the aristocracy had always exercised cultural power by providing models of behaviour for other people in society to follow. The culture of the courtier was shaped by courtiers, particularly the successful ones. This was a very aping culture. Much of what a courtier had to do was to keep track of the latest trends in the culture of the court. Again we must recognize the contradiction that is created by the effort to use cultural power to enhance status power. Aristocrats wanted to maintain a monopoly on aristocratic culture to preserve or enhance their status, while at the same time they wanted other people in the society to revere this culture, which inevitably led them to imitate it. The invention of printing and the increase in public literacy accentuated this contradiction as it became possible to disseminate to a large audience biographies or autobiographies that extolled a particular life style and held it up for imitation. Dewald provides a good analysis of this phenomenon. He examines the growth in the number of nobles in seventeenth-century France who wrote this kind of literature. Dewald is most interested in memoirs, family histories, and letters, in all of which noble authors exposed their private lives to a remarkable extent.[233] Often authors claimed that they had no intention of publishing their memoirs or letters, but they would certainly have been aware that documents of this kind routinely fell into the hands of publishers, who had no hesitation in making them public.[234] We have seen that at the same time there developed a wide variety of journals for the dissemination of court news, which were popular throughout Europe. The printing press and the increase in literacy made the nobility into a cultural commodity, a process that many nobles embraced with considerable enthusiasm.[235]

Aristocratic cultural power was exercised by women as well as men. Women had always been more influential in courts than they were in most other social settings and this influence was often regarded as one of the foundations of proper court behaviour. "Just as no court, however great, can have adornment or splendour or gaiety in it without ladies," declared one of Castiglione's courtiers, "neither can any Courtier be graceful or pleasing or brave, or do any gallant deed of chivalry, unless he is moved by the society and by the love and charm of ladies."[236] In the seventeenth and eighteenth centuries they added to their influence by holding receptions in their salons for famous or up-and-coming artists and literati. While the role of women in salons was in certain respects different from that of men, they exercised real cultural power. Indeed, Parisian hostesses were accused by some men of constraining thought; while this may be unfair, they certainly enforced conversational norms that emerged in the salon culture.[237] It was they who were responsible for the special character of the salon, which was neither an academic colloquium nor a purely social event, but something between the two, with its own unique significance.[238] Women also enjoyed cultural power by writing, particularly private letters that often became public.[239] If a seventeenth-century list of illustrious Parisian women is representative, most were daughters of nobles, both robe and sword.[240]

In the seventeenth century the salons may have been a means of assimilating new nobles and turning them into aristocrats,[241] but in the eighteenth century they played a different role. It is now accepted by most historians that the salons and the aristocracy that frequented them made a major contribution to the French Enlightenment. The salons provided the *philosophes* with an institutional base.[242] The aristocratic character of the hostesses did not make the salons exclusive. On the contrary, in addition to helping nobles to participate in the intellectual changes that were taking place, what these aristocratic women did was to use their own high status and that of their noble guests to raise the status of artists and writers who were from modest backgrounds. The salons brought together persons from different social groups and with different ideas, though it has been argued by Robert Darnton that in the 1770s and 1780s they were less open than they had formerly been.[243]

While the Scottish Enlightenment is generally regarded as less aristocratic than the French, it also benefited from the assistance of the aristocracy. Aristocrats were overrepresented among the members of learned societies, such as the Select Society of Edinburgh.[244] Lords Islay and Bute can be given considerable credit for the advance in learning in Scotland in the last half of the eighteenth century; they were patrons of scientific research and responsible for the appointment of many of the better academics to Scottish universities during the eighteenth century.[245]

Again, however, it is necessary to understand this aristocratic cultural power in the context of an increasing centralization of cultural power. The sovereign had the most cultural power of all. Indeed, the culture of the whole of Europe has been dramatically affected by the fact that, for a period of several centuries, art, literature, and theatre were to an unusual extent under the mercurial influence of particular individuals. In a matter of years an artistic or musical school could be raised to great heights or totally undermined by a royal whim or the accession of a new monarch. Rulers also enjoyed the right to make many "cultural appointments," not only ecclesiastical appointments, but in many cases appointments to educational institutions as well. Such prerogatives could give politicians considerable power to shape an intellectual environment. Islay and Bute were not just aristocrats; they were politicians at the political centre. Decisions on appointments were made in London on the basis of information provided by local contacts and subministers in Edinburgh.[246]

Finally, of course, the state exercised cultural power through censorship. This power was greatest in France. Under Louis XIV the public was subject to severe constraints by the king's inspectors. After he died, control was temporarily reduced, then restored, but during the reigns of Louis XV and Louis XVI the press was not as tightly controlled as it had been under Louis XIV.[247] Yet many of the great works of the Enlightenment (by Voltaire, Diderot, and Rousseau) had to be published clandestinely.

The French state was culturally more powerful than the British – more imitated by other elites in Europe and more influential in the territory ruled from the centre. This may seem to raise questions about the emphasis placed by Philip Corrigan and Derek Sayer on the role of the state in the development of an English national bourgeois culture.[248] Readers here may be more impressed by the comparative weakness of the state cultural revolution in England than by its strength. Yet what we have seen is not inconsistent with Corrigan and Sayer's argument insofar as it assists their effort to explain the development of bourgeois culture in the British Isles, in contrast with the evident triumph of aristocratic culture in France and the role of the French state in that triumph.

We do not want to underrate English cultural power in the Early Modern period. The English did exert considerable cultural influence on the Continent. The origin of the Enlightenment was in seventeenth-century England as much as anywhere else, particularly in the work of John Locke and Sir Isaac Newton. London continued to be a centre of science in the eighteenth century. It was also a centre of music. The best musicians, however, were foreigners (with the exception of Henry Purcell). More significant from our point of view, music was not under the same aristocratic control that it was in other major European centres. London was the place for a musician to go to offer services for public consumption, not aristocratic patronage.[249] From the 1730s, English cultural power in Europe increased. The term "Anglomania" rather overstates it, but there is no doubt that a great variety of "English ways" became fashionable. Yet most popular was what was clearly bourgeois culture in comparison with the dominant culture on the Continent. This included English liberalism and economic principles, and, as we saw in chapter 6, a celebration in some circles of English agricultural practices.

The Vicious Circle of Power

We have seen in previous chapters how economic power and political power reinforced status and how status could be used (though to a much lesser extent) to increase political and economic power. The relationships appear even more recursive when we introduce cultural power.

Economic power was used to increase cultural power. It was primarily their economic resources that enabled rulers and aristocrats to provide illustrious courts, hold tournaments, collect art, and patronize artists and writers. To a lesser extent, status was also used to increase cultural power. This was most visibly the case in the royal court and the salons, whose cultures were respected at least partly because of the status of the persons who maintained or attended them. Similarly, it was more advantageous for an aspiring artist or writer to obtain the patronage of a prestigious aristocrat than of a non-aristocrat with the same wealth. Finally, political power was used to increase cultural power. Most obviously, states and those enjoying state power can use it to impose a certain cultural pattern, especially a religion, on a population. Often those with political power also had the authority to appoint persons to manage cultural institutions. The cultural power of the royal court was a result of the status and political power of the sovereign and the royal court.

Conversely, cultural power can be used to increase the other three types of power, not so much economic power, but certainly political power and status power. As many historians have argued, using cultural power to increase political power was primarily what rulers were doing when they supported spectacular courts, patronized the arts, and put on magnificent ceremonies and pageants. Secular or religious celebrations were routinely held to glorify rulers and their accomplishments. The king often ordered that *Te Deums* be sung to give thanks for recovery from an illness or a royal birth, a military victory, the signing of a treaty, and other events.[250] Handel's *Judas Maccabaeus* was written to celebrate the Duke of Cumberland's victory at Culloden.[251] Charles I believed that harmonious music could be used to overcome civil dis-agreements and that masques could be employed to communicate royal policy.[252] Sovereigns also used chivalric and courtly culture to control the aristocracy. Even etiquette could be used by the sovereign to keep great nobles in their place. Courtly culture called for appro-priate acts of deference from even the highest nobility. It was common for the crown or its agents to accuse their political enemies of failing to observe proper etiquette in order to undermine their political power.[253]

Cultural power can be used to increase or preserve status power. In hundreds of ways, aristocratic culture reinforced the existing status hierarchy. The centralization of cultural power increased its potential to do so. I have already made mention of the processions at the court of Turin with precisely ranked formations. Coronations, including English coronations, could also distinguish aristocratic ranks. In the culture of the French court everyone was carefully ranked.[254] In addi-tion, the very exercise of cultural power could increase or maintain status power. Aristocrats in all countries were anxious to be in tune with the latest cultural developments, out of fear that if they did not they would suffer a loss in status. A particularly good example is provided by a recent study of the successful efforts of the old Viennese aristocracy to preserve its cultural leadership in music under the changing circumstances of the late eighteenth and the early nine-teenth centuries.[255]

The reinforcement of status and political power by cultural power, which was in turn reinforced by the other two, is well illustrated by the court of Burgundy and the Order of the Golden Fleece, with their spectacular tournaments and ceremonies. It is also illustrated by the ceremonies organized by other rulers, such as the dukes of Savoy in Turin. During the seventeenth and eighteenth centuries, however, it was in Paris and Versailles that the vicious circle between cultural power and other types of power was supreme. The salons fused cultural power with status power in a unique way, but the royal court at Versailles fused these with economic and political power as well. Versailles is the quintessential institution of this kind, and Louis XIV the quintessential monarch who achieved this fusion of power. Yet there has been an unfortunate tendency to see Louis XIV as the all-powerful manipulator of people, using courtly etiquette to control the behaviour of his courtiers.[256] The centralization of cultural power does not necessarily mean that even French kings were all-powerful. Louis XIV did not create court etiquette. Nor was he the only one whose conduct shaped it. The culture of the court, demanding as it did exaggerated praise for those of high status, led Louis XIV to believe, or pretend to believe, that he was the greatest man in France and to reward those who declared him to be so. The Duke of Saint-Simon, a courtier in Louis's court, was overstating it when he charged that, as a result, "the coarsest was well received, the vilest even better relished." Nevertheless, Saint-Simon was likely correct in asserting that Louis could be influenced through his "unmeasured and unreasonable love of admiration."[257]

Conclusion

THE DIFFERENTIATION OF
ARISTOCRATIC POWER

Rising monarchies, intentionally and unintentionally, fused status power and political power. The sovereign was elevated to the highest rank in both status and political power. State offices were made ennobling, and letters of nobility were granted to state servants. In varying degrees, status and political power were united in the royal court. Restricting personal access to the royal family to persons of high noble status also served to fuse status and political power. And in varying degrees, aristocrats shared the political power of the emerging monarchies as royal officials.

Yet, in other ways, status and political power were differentiated. The decline of lordship that took place in the British Isles and to a lesser extent in France, Savoy, and the Southern Low Countries increased the differentiation of status and political power. The ennoblement of state servants on the Continent had a side effect that was the opposite of what the crown intended. The aristocracy became differentiated into the nobility of the sword and the nobility of the robe. Speaking very generally, the former had higher status than the latter, but less political power. In addition, the institutionalization of aristocratic status on the Continent meant that high status could be enjoyed by persons without much political power.

Status and political power were less differentiated in the British Isles. Fusion of the two was extreme in the parliaments, the lord lieutenancies, and the commissions of the peace. In addition, most cabinets were composed in the majority by aristocrats, often higher status aristocrats. All in all, there are few societies in world history where status and political power were more fused than in the British Isles during the seventeenth and eighteenth centuries.

Rising monarchies also fuse status power and cultural power. It would also appear that where the monarchy was more powerful, these two types of power were the most fused. It was on the Continent, more precisely in France, that we saw the greatest fusion of status power and cultural power primarily in the royal court, but also in the Parisian salons. Status power and cultural power were also fused in the British Isles, especially in the country seats of the peerage and the wealthier gentry, but on the whole there was more differentiation of status power and cultural power in the British Isles than in France as a result of the lesser centralization of cultural power in the former.

On the other hand, status power and economic power were less differentiated in the British Isles than on the Continent. I am not claiming that there was a perfect correspondence between status power and economic power in the British Isles. Peers and other title-holders enjoyed higher status than untitled members of the gentry with the same wealth. Landowners who were well accepted in county society enjoyed higher status than those who were not, even if they had similar wealth. And non-inheriting younger sons of members of the gentry enjoyed higher status than persons with similar wealth who had no kinship ties with the gentry.

Nevertheless, landed wealth and aristocratic status were closely tied in England by the sixteenth and seventeenth centuries; and this was true almost throughout the British Isles by the late eighteenth century. Without landed wealth it was difficult to sustain aristocratic status in the British Isles. With money and with the land and education it could buy, most wealthy aspirants to aristocratic status were successful, if not for themselves, certainly for their descendants. The fusion of economic and status power also resulted from the role aristocrats played in the English economy, particularly in the reorganization of agriculture and the exploitation of natural resources.

In contrast, status could become separated from wealth and other kinds of economic power more easily in the continental countries. Again I do not want to exaggerate. Status and wealth corresponded to a considerable extent in France, Savoy, and the Southern Low Countries. Seigneurialism continued to fuse status and economic power. More French aristocrats were financiers than British aristocrats. Nobles were on the average much wealthier than non-nobles. Nobles of immense wealth obviously enjoyed higher status than impoverished nobles, if for no other reason because they were better able to pay for the trappings of aristocratic status – a *château*, education at a prestigious academy, a military career, and so on. Just as entrance into the English gentry could be achieved through the purchase of land, admission to the French nobility could be achieved through the purchase of an office. In both cases, obstacles were in the way, but a determined family with money could acquire higher status in this manner in several generations.

All the same, status was more differentiated from economic power in France, Savoy, and the Southern Low Countries than it was in the British Isles. There were many nobles on the Continent who were not wealthy and yet preserved their noble status. While financial weakness might diminish their prestige to a degree, they remained legally members of the nobility, and to this extent status and economic power were differentiated in a way that was less the case in the British Isles. Continental nobles could remain nobles, legally at least, even if they were desperately poor. Wealth varied more in the continental nobility than in the British peerage and gentry.

Differentiation between status and economic power was also promoted by anti-materialist and anti-business aristocratic snobbery. This was true on both sides of the English Channel, but the notion that the aristocracy stood for higher values, and especially their presumption of superiority over those engaged in trade or manufacture, was stronger on the Continent than in the British Isles.[1]

Political and economic power were also more differentiated on the Continent. True, these two types of power were fused among those members of the high French aristocracy who were both wealthy and enjoyed political influence; they were also fused by those were able to exert pressure on politicians; they were fused by those *parliamentaires* who were wealthy; and they were fused by local notables (noble and non-noble) who possessed both political influence and wealth. Political and economic power were more fused in the British Isles, however, where land was the basis of political power far more than on the Continent. Lords and other members of parliament usually fused these two types of power, especially in the eighteenth century when elections had become extremely expensive. The control over local government enjoyed by lords lieutenant, sheriffs, and magistrates also fused political and economic power to a greater extent than was the case of the Continent, though this difference should not be exaggerated; in almost all societies local political power is held disproportionately by the wealthy.

On the whole, aristocratic power was more differentiated from other kinds of power in our continental countries than in the British Isles.

The major exceptions were the greater fusion of status power and cultural power in France and the fusion of status and political power in the French royal court. Leaving these exceptions aside, why was power more differentiated on the Continent?

THE CAUSES OF THE DIFFERENTIATION OF POWER

Spencer held that differentiation came with population growth, but its basic cause was the survival of the fittest: more differentiated societies prevailed over less differentiated ones because differentiation enhanced survival capacity.[2] Durkheim believed that the division of labour resulted from "moral density," the extent to which humans interact with one another, which was in turn related to and could be measured by population or "material density."[3] In Parsons's view, there has been and will continue to be a master trend towards greater differentiation because differentiation is more functionally adaptive. Parsons also stressed conditions for the institutionalization of differentiation, particularly integrative conditions; these conditions may not cause differentiation, but they assist it. This emphasis is also found in the works of Eisenstadt and Habermas.[4] While Habermas gives much attention to the autonomous evolution of normative structures, which depend on communicative and learning processes, the underlying cause of social evolution for Habermas is system adaptation. Drawing on both the Marxian and the Parsonian traditions, he posits that the primary force responsible for social evolution has been the struggle to overcome "system problems" that pose challenges.

These explanations contribute little towards explaining the pattern of aristocratic power differentiation we have found in Early Modern Western Europe. Population was not the decisive variable. True, France was the largest country, and the Southern Low Countries had the highest population density. On the other hand, southern England also had a relatively dense population and aristocratic power was not as differentiated as it was in Savoy, and no more differentiated than it was in Wales, Ireland, and Scotland, where population density was lower. Similarly, adaptive capacity does not explain the differences we have witnessed. It would be difficult to argue that our continental countries were functionally more adaptive than the British Isles.

It is not hard to understand why these historical comparisons do not support the sociological theory. No one can deny that in performing many tasks a division of labour is comparatively efficient and effective. Yet, as Dietrich Rueschemeyer asserts, we cannot assume that historically the division of labour emerged because it is efficient and effective.[5] This is especially the case with respect to the differentiation of power. Powerful interests in society do not give up their power for the sake of societal efficiency and effectiveness. Furthermore, it may not even be true that power differentiation is more efficient and effective. Few historians would agree that commissions of the peace and the British Parliament were inefficient and ineffective because they fused different types of power. Certainly it is difficult to see why the differentiation of status power from other types of power increases efficiency and effectiveness.

Those Marxists who accept that power differentiation has increased assume that this process results from the development of capitalism. Just as capitalism separates workers from the means of production, it separates capitalists from the means of coercion, or at least non-economic coercion. This explanation for power differentiation runs into some serious difficulties, however, particularly of an historical nature. The differentiation of power appeared before capitalism was a major force and advanced furthest on the Continent, where capitalism was weaker – indeed, according to some Marxists, non-existent.

Elias is more helpful. He believed that a close relationship existed between differentiation and the rise of the state. Part of his thesis was functionalist: the concentration of political power provides the coordination that is necessary in a differentiated society.[6] Elias also implied a less functionalist argument. As power monopolizers acquire greater power they depend on the differentiation of power to prevent opposing concentrations of power from developing. The ruler seeks to keep the power of various groups in the society in balance. As an example, he discussed how French monarchs tried to play the nobility and the bourgeoisie off against one another.[7]

This is certainly an oversimplification. Yet the value of Elias's explanation is that it recognizes the critical role of the state and how the state can affect the distribution of power in society.

If there is a general rule about the differentiation of power, I submit it is the following: struggles for power lead to a fusion of power because whoever has one kind of power can use it to obtain others. Yet the consequences of this general tendency were not what we might at first expect. It is true, as just noted, that the rising monarchies fused power by concentrating it in the person of the monarch and the royal court. It is also true that the fusion of status power and cultural power was greater in France than in the British Isles. With respect to political, status, and economic power, however, the fusion of power was greater not in France and Savoy, where the crown fused power the most, but in the British Isles, where power was less concentrated in the crown and the royal court. How is this possible? A number of reasons provide an explanation. These include various factors that made the British aristocracy wealthier (the appropriation of church land, the decline in peasant proprietorship, the rules of inheritance followed by the British), but two general conditions relate to the role of the state.

First, the effect of a rising monarchy varied with the kind of power it confiscated and with what it did with the power that it confiscated. Monarchies that concentrated power in their own hands at the same time disrupted the natural tendency for power to fuse in the larger society. They did this primarily by confiscating more of one kind of power than another. The sovereign confiscated more political (including military) power than other kinds of power. Although the British crown did the same, it confiscated less political power, with the result that political power was free to fuse with status and economic power more than it could on the Continent. Moreover, the way in which power was confiscated made a difference. The vertical absolutism assembled by the French monarchy undercut the political power of the greater nobility, while leaving them as nominal power figures, with their status less diminished than their political power. With some significant differences, the Habsburg and Savoyard states also established vertical absolutism.

Second, again the role played by the monarchy on the Continent in the allocation of status had major repercussions. The institutionalization of aristocratic status differentiated status from political and economic power by preserving and in some cases granting aristocratic status to persons who did not possess comparable political or economic power.

Why then were status power and cultural power more fused on the Continent? Did not the institutionalization of aristocratic status on the Continent preserve the status of nobles who were losing cultural power to the centre? The answer to this question is, partially, yes. Certainly, provincial nobles in France and its peripheries did maintain more status power than cultural power with the development of political centres. Yet what is also important is what happened to the cultural power that became more concentrated in the centre. What made status power and political power more differentiated in the continental centres was that much of the confiscated political power was transferred to non-nobles or to robe nobles. In contrast, most of the cultural power that became concentrated in Paris and its region went to the highest nobility in the royal court and in Paris. Sociologists have always assumed that cultural power and status power were intimately connected, so much so that they typically conflate the two. While this conflation is a mistake, the preceding analysis does support the general assumption that status power and cultural power are closely associated. People tend to be culturally influenced the most by those who enjoy high prestige.

Master Trends

The differences we have found between the British Isles and the Continent do not square easily with conventional views on the development of Western Europe. The great majority of sociologists and historians of Western Europe believe that England modernized more rapidly than continental countries in the sense that it first took on the characteristics that eventually came to be shared by all countries in Western Europe in the nineteenth and twentieth centuries.

Yet we have seen that aristocratic power became more differentiated on the Continent than in the British Isles during the seventeenth and eighteenth centuries. This might lead to some conclusions that I believe do not improve our understanding of the making of Modern Europe. First, one could argue that the above assumptions are all wrong, that the continental countries had in reality advanced further on an evolutionary path. This would be a hard case to make. The conventional wisdom may need revision, but it has not been all wrong. Britain certainly did lead the way in a number of aspects of political and economic development.

Alternatively, one could decide that our findings simply demonstrate that differentiation is not an important phenomenon. Although Marxists implicitly talk about differentiation, explicitly this might be their general reaction: capitalism emerged earlier in England than in France; if differentiation was more advanced in France, this just proves that evolutionary theorists and structural functionalists have been wasting our time with the concept.

The first problem with this reaction is that it throws all evolutionary theory out with the bath water. Even Tilly, who calls Durkheim "useless" and who has pointedly avoided studying differentiation, admits that "many significant processes do involve differentiation." He insists, however, that over the past several hundred years other social processes in Western Europe were more important ("have set the great historical rhythms") and that "many social processes also involve dedifferentiation."[8] Yet surely this dedifferentiation is all the more reason to study differentiation, so long, of course, as one studies dedifferentiation as well. The fact of the matter is that in Western Europe there has been a master trend towards the differentiation of power over the past millennium. I do not think this has been a natural or inevitable process. And I have sought to stress its complexities. All the same, on the whole power has differentiated since the Middle Ages.

Second, it is recognized by some scholars that the British Isles also advanced comparatively slowly with respect to some other measures of modernization. The English oddities that writers have identified include late secularization, the delayed forging of public education, the greater wealth of landowners as compared with industrialists, the later concentration of industrial capital, and the persistence into the twentieth century of an aristocracy, aristocratic values, and a monarchy and all its trappings.[9] I suggested in Part One that the British state in the eighteenth century was not significantly more advanced than the French state whether one measures advancement in terms of infrastructural power or the development of a modern bureaucracy. Even British economic superiority has been exaggerated. These exaggerations have been challenged in some revisionist literature, which insists that the French economy was not so much inferior to the British as simply different.[10] It also needs to be pointed out that most of the comparisons – even by the revisionists – are made between England and France, which conveniently excludes most of the poor regions of the British Isles while including all the poor regions of France and excluding the centre of continental industrialization – the French-speaking part of the Low Countries. Until more comparable geographical regions are examined, we have little idea how superior the British economy was.

British anachronisms have been much debated, especially among Marxists, because they call into question conventional theories of modernization and in particular the classical Marxist theory of the making of capitalism, or what is thought to be the classical Marxist theory – that a bourgeois triumph over the traditional aristocracy coincided with the rise of capitalism. Sayer made a major contribution to the debate by suggesting that it was this very package of peculiarities that led to capitalism in England.[11] In a most engaging *tour de force* Wood has made a similar case, holding that all the so-called archaic features of British state and society were in fact perfectly consistent with the emergence of "pristine" capitalism.[12]

Even though Sayer is highly critical of sociological ideal types, he and Wood have not avoided sociological holism. They are still trying to pull together a variety of characteristics of the English state and society and to use them to explain a number of economic changes that have been collectively referred to as capitalism. I would propose that it is more helpful to distinguish among different kinds of economic change because they may have different causes, patterns, and rates of development. The oddities of the English should not be studied as a package, but rather as a number of different, albeit related, processes. The intellectual problem that Sayer and Wood are trying to solve is of their own making. It is only if one has a holistic conception of social change that the mixture of English economic development with the persistence of monarchy or aristocratic culture becomes a peculiarity that has to be explained.

Similarly, differentiation should not be studied as a single encompassing process, but as a number of processes that may or may not go together. Thus, comparing countries as more or less advanced on the road of differentiation is unwise because differentiation is multi-dimensional. In some ways the French state was more differentiated than the British (a larger state bureaucracy, greater aristocratic power differentiation), while in other respects the British state was more differentiated (differentiated parliaments and greater differentiation between the monarchy and the state). Although the model of a tri-partite agrarian class structure in the British Isles (consisting of land-owners, tenant farmers, and wage labourers in contrast with small peasant proprietorship on the Continent) is an oversimplification, it is no doubt true that the agrarian economy of the British Isles was more differentiated than that of our continental countries. On the other hand, France and Lotharingia were more urbanized in the eighteenth century than was the British Isles.

While there has been a master trend towards power differentiation over the centuries, during the period covered by this book there was no master cause of this trend. Whether or not the reader can accept the proposition that the natural tendency in human society is towards the fusion of power, we can all agree that the differentiation of power we have observed was the result of a number of causal forces, some linked to the rise of the state, but none the inevitable consequence of the rise of the state. The lesson is that if sociologists want to understand the master trend of differentiation they will have to give greater consideration to the particularities of history. As Rueschemeyer maintains, the consequences of struggles for power are highly contingent and render even long-term structural changes extremely unpredictable.[13]

EVOLUTIONARY THEORY AND THE MAKING OF MODERN EUROPE

In doing so, we need to come to better terms with evolutionary theory. Sociologists have something akin to an oedipal complex about it. We are all trained to reject the theory that gave birth to our discipline. Especially in idiographic sociology, evolutionary theory has been repudiated.

Yet one of the purposes of idiographic sociology is to investigate how and why societies differ and change over time – in this case to comprehend how and why Medieval, Early Modern, and Modern Europe have differed. Despite all we might now reject in their work, the evolutionary theorists and those who have followed in their footsteps have contributed to this project. They have done so by constructing concepts and making bold assertions about how Europe changed over the past two to four hundred years.

An unfortunate gulf has emerged between the sociological tradition of Durkheim, Parsons, Smelser, and the neo-functionalists, on the one hand, and the historical sociologists, such as Tilly, Lachmann, Mann, and the Marxists, on the other. If sociologists of the future are going to build on both of these traditions and not just on one of them, the gulf is going to have to be bridged. This will require adaptations to both approaches.

We historical sociologists need to overcome our prejudices against evolutionary and functionalist theory and concepts. If we do not, the study of the various large transformations and processes that went into the making of Modern Europe will forever be partial. We want to reformulate in our own terms the questions they were asking and the answers they suggested. And we need to accept the usefulness of their theorizing, even if we ourselves do not do that kind of thing. Historical sociologists are making a mistake to reject evolutionary theory on the grounds that it precludes the possibility of twists and turns in history. Evolutionary theory can actually aid in detecting these twists and turns.

At the same time, those in the evolutionary and neo-functionalist tradition need to make their models and concepts more adaptable to utilization by those who belong to other schools. Structural functionalists, especially Parsonians, have always made it difficult for others to accept some of their theory without accepting all of it. The first step towards such an *ouverture* is precise conceptualization so that other sociologists are not obliged to assume a large theoretical apparatus in order to employ a particular evolutionary or functionalist concept. In addition, it is necessary to contain, if not eliminate, certain Whiggish ways of thinking – that society progresses, that it goes through stages, that earlier societies are to be understood in terms of how they led to later societies. This still goes on. Neo-functionalists can be found referring to uneven differentiation or a slowdown in differentiation as "reactionary" or as "stagnation."[14]

These Whiggish ways of thinking have not been limited to those in the Durkheimian and Parsonian tradition. Marxism is also, of course, an evolutionary theory; and Marxists have been equally guilty of studying earlier societies in terms of how they led to later ones. Early Modern Europe has been treated as a transitional society between feudalism and capitalism. In true Whig fashion, the focus of attention is on how and why capitalism emerged. This has led to an emphasis on those characteristics of Early Modern Europe that relate to this question. Other questions have been neglected; and periods of history have been evaluated in terms of their contribution to the rise of capitalism.

We witnessed in the 1970s a debate among Marxists over the role of commercialization in the rise of capitalism – one school argued that commercialization caused the decline of feudalism and laid the foundation for the rise of capitalism, while the other side indignantly retorted that commercialism and capitalism are not the same thing and that commercialization has in most places and historical periods emerged without leading to capitalism.[15] The common assumption here is that commercialization is not important unless it led to the rise of capitalism. It is possible to argue, however, that, even if it were not connected to the rise of capitalism (and I doubt that it had no connection), commercialization is still worthy of attention, for two reasons. First, though neither inevitable nor unilinear, there has been a master trend of increased commercialization in Western Europe since the Middle Ages, just as there has been a master trend towards greater differentiation. Second, variations in commercialization, and particularly the commercialization associated with the use of water transport, help to explain differences among Western European societies in the seventeenth and eighteenth centuries. This is less true for the nineteenth and twentieth centuries, when the commercialization of much more of this part of the world and the development of new methods of communication and transportation have reduced the explanatory power of these variables. Yet what accounts for social differences in the nineteenth and twentieth centuries may not account for differences in the seventeenth and eighteenth centuries. I have chosen to build a good part of my analysis on the water-based versus the land-based continuum rather than on a capitalist versus a pre-capitalist dichotomy not only because the concept of capitalism has become overloaded and too systemic, but also because it is less useful for understanding Early Modern society. The Foxian model explains differences in Early Modern society much better than the Marxian. This is all the more true if, as Brenner, Comninel, and Wood want to persuade us, capitalism existed only in English agriculture.[16]

Obviously, all this is not to deny the utility of research on the rise of capitalism or other large processes. Yet the study of large processes has to be combined with an appreciation of the great variety of directions in which different or even the same forces can take societies. Thus the centralization of political power in the Early Modern period made some states small while other states large, and, together with commercialization, took some parts of Europe in very different directions from others. Although I think he has not given sufficient attention to the way in which political centralization created small states, Tilly's version of the Foxian model is a significant advancement. Commercialization caused fundamental differences in European state formation.

The complex interaction of large processes with the twists and turns of history is also evident in the evolution of status. The majority of historical writings on status regard the Early Modern period as a hybrid between the Middle Ages and the Modern period. The seventeenth and eighteenth centuries are thought to be characterized by a mixture of the receding features of the Middle Ages and the emerging characteristics of Modern society. The development of the state in the Early Modern period has been seen as the beginning of a process that ultimately led to a decline in status distinctions and the growth of civil equality. I have tried to demonstrate, however, that Early Modern society was not going in this direction, even though that is where Western Europe has ended up.

Epilogue

In the second volume of this study particular attention will be paid to the institutionalization of status and the development of national status groups. In these closing pages I would like to pull together several conclusions that can been drawn on these two subjects from the first volume.

THE INSTITUTIONALIZATION OF ARISTOCRATIC STATUS AND THE SOCIETY OF ORDERS

I have sought to demonstrate that the role of the state in the institutionalization of aristocratic status increased in the Early Modern period. This process was carried further on the Continent than in the British Isles. This does not mean that the state played no role in the British Isles. Additions to the highest statuses (title-holders) were made by the crown. It was only the lower ranks that were not state appointed. Heraldry, while not regulated very effectively in the British Isles, was regulated more effectively there than it was on the Continent.

Yet it is evident from our inquiry that the state played a still larger role on the Continent. Sovereigns enacted considerable legislation regulating aristocratic status, sometimes denying privilege, often recognizing it and identifying those entitled to it. Much less such legislation was to be found in the British Isles. Moreover, where the crown in the British Isles refused to acknowledge the validity of customs that institutionalized aristocratic status, sovereigns on the Continent accepted many customary laws relating to the nobility, in some cases homologating them. The status of the most numerous segment of the British aristocracy, the gentry, was under very limited state control, through the regulation of heraldry; and even that control deteriorated in the late seventeenth century.

Recognition of the role of the state helps us to understand the sense in which Early Modern continental society was a "society of orders." People living in Medieval and Early Modern Europe were sometimes organized on the basis of three orders and many of those who wrote the records that have survived wanted to think that theirs was a society composed of corporate wholes. As a result, some historians have come to believe that this is the best way to describe the social structure of these societies, which has in turn reinforced, though it did not create, the sociological assumption that status groups are communities. In reality the Early Modern continental nobility was extremely hetero-geneous and disconnected. Nobility was simply a socially attributed characteristic which men and women carried around with them and which entitled them to certain treatment. It did not necessarily elim-inate or even significantly reduce all the other differences that existed among them. No one any longer accepts the absurd notion that the third estate or the peasantry were distinct and homogeneous enough to be considered corporate orders. Indeed, not even Medieval serfs formed a corporate order in this sense. A Medieval specialist, P.R. Hyams, insists that villeinage in twelfth- and thirteenth-century England was simply a "handicap" that put an individual at a disadvan-tage in social competition. Court cases where a lord claimed that a peasant was his villein and the peasant denied it were nothing more or less than contests in which individuals tried to alter the odds in social competition.[1] This way of putting it might underestimate the status power of lordship and certainly ignores the prevailing ideology, but it does identify the most fundamental aspect of Medieval and Early Modern status groups. Corporate holism is not the model that helps us understand the society of orders.

Nor is it clear that the society of orders was one in which greater importance was attached to status than in so-called class societies. Here I cannot present the evidence that it is necessary to challenge this assumption; more will come in the second volume. But let me make a few remarks about the origins of the idea and how it fits Early Modern Europe. It presumably follows from Weber's analysis of status. What Weber actually suggested is that stratification by status predom-inates over stratification by class in times of social stability, while the reverse is true in times of social change. "When the bases of the acquisition and distribution of goods are relatively stable, stratification by status is favoured. Every technological repercussion and economic transformation threatens stratification by status and pushes the class situation into the foreground."[2]

Now, there is little reason to see why people would have less interest in evaluating one another when social change is taking place. What happens during periods of social change is not that status becomes less important; it is rather that social change makes it more difficult to maintain a social consensus on what is better and what values and norms are acceptable for different statuses. Weber was also clearly saying that changes in economic power and the bases of economic power disrupt the existing status structure.

To argue, however, that continental society was a status society in the seventeenth and eighteenth centuries because little social change was occurring would be to underestimate social change in that period. Insofar as Early Modern continental society achieved such a consensus, it was not the absence of social change that was responsible, but the control exercised over status by the state. As we have observed, under state regulation, aristocratic status acquired a firmer basis in law. Although social stability was not responsible for the institutionalization of aristocratic status, the state institutionalization of aristocratic status was the source of greater status stability, at least aristocratic status stability.

If I am correct in this argument, it becomes necessary to reconsider the general perception of the society of orders as traditional. This notion has been stated explicitly by Turner in his *Status*, but he was obviously influenced by Anderson's *Lineages of the Absolutist State*.[3] Anderson would agree with me that Early Modern Western Europe should not be studied for how it prepared the way for Modern Europe, but he would do so on the grounds that Early Modern Europe was still basically "feudal." In his opinion, the absolutist state was not a neutral state, not a product of class equilibrium, but rather a "*redeployed and recharged apparatus of feudal domination.*" It was "never an arbiter between the aristocracy and the bourgeoisie, still less an instrument of the nascent bourgeoisie against the aristocracy." Although many nobles resisted the development of the absolutist state, and it did not always do what they wanted, this state was truly committed to promoting the interests of the nobility. It was an instrument of this feudal class. In a debate with E.P. Thompson, Anderson also claimed that England remained aristocratic in the eighteenth, nineteenth, and even twentieth centuries because it never had a full-scale bourgeois revolution.[4] All this may seem consistent with my argument that aristocratic status was still of concern to the British monarchy as well as its continental counterparts in the Early Modern period.

On closer examination, however, what I have learned differs fundamentally from Anderson's thesis. The eighteenth-century elite was a new development of the late Middle Ages and the Early Modern period. The landed elite had changed dramatically. One could still call it feudal, depending on what definition of feudal one adopts. Yet in doing so one loses sight of a major transformation. The British peerage was a product of the late Middle Ages. The native nobilities were not displaced in some parts of the British Isles until the seventeenth and eighteenth centuries. The French nobility of the Old Regime was in many ways not very old. It changed over the course of the Middle Ages and took on a decidedly different character in the seventeenth and eighteenth centuries, primarily as a result of the increasing regulation of aristocratic status by the state. While Anderson recognized how the landed elite shaped the state, he underestimated how the state shaped the landed elite. He consequently failed to understand the unique character of the Early Modern state and society. States did not simply reproduce Medieval aristocracies. Exaggerating somewhat, we could say that they created the Early Modern aristocracies.

A NATIONAL ARISTOCRACY?

Were these national aristocracies, if by this we mean aristocracies whose contours conformed to those of national states?

Two principal forces operated to nationalize the French nobility. One was the state institutionalization of aristocratic status. Although much noble law varied from one province to another, an increasing body of standardized noble law applied to all the French kingdom. There was also a growing acceptance that the French state had the authority to recognize and regulate aristocratic status for the whole of the kingdom, and a growing expectation that it would do so uniformly, or at least that it would make noble status more uniform than it had been in the past. Foreign nobles were not recognized unless they were accredited by the French government. The aristocrats of territories annexed by France in the Early Modern period became legally part of the French nobility and subject to French state regulation of aristocratic status. And commoners who lived in these annexed territories could aspire to become members of this French nobility, most often by means of an ennobling office.

The nobility was the first national status group in the French population – the first group to hold a status that was institutionalized to an increasing extent according to the same standards throughout the kingdom. Although the state made some attempt to standardize other statuses, such as the "bourgeoisie" of the towns and guild membership, a national status of bourgeois, or a national status of guild master, did not emerge in the way that a national status of noble emerged. The closest thing was the status of "subject," but no body of national legislation regulated this status as it did the status of noble. While the concept of citizen could be used more generally, it also remained linked to the privileged statuses of different towns. Even when used more generally, it was not institutionalized in a corpus of national law. In the seventeenth and eighteenth centuries the foremost emerging national status was that of noble. Although the movement towards increasing state institutionalization of aristocratic status was eventually arrested and there was no direct causal connection between it and the later development of citizenship, the national status of noble was the harbinger of the national status of citizen.

The second force of nationalization in France was cultural assimilation. The most significant of all was religious homogeneity. By the eighteenth century few Protestant nobles remained in France. In a special way even the cultural imperialism of the French centre outside France also helped to nationalize the French nobility. French had become the dominant language in Europe, the language of diplomacy and elites. High French culture was imitated throughout Europe. This meant that in certain respects the European aristocracy was perhaps even more international in the eighteenth century than it had been in the Middle Ages. Yet it was internationalism of a different kind because its centre was tied to a political centre that controlled a limited territory. This internationalism, therefore, promoted the nationalization of the French nobility by elevating the status of French language and culture. For those who lived within the territories controlled by the French political centre, Francization meant nationalization.

The same forces had different consequences in Savoy and the Southern Low Countries. Here as well elites were swept up in the international ascendancy of French language and culture, but this process did not contribute to the development of a national aristocracy in Piedmont-Savoy or in Savoy itself; similarly, French culture in Vienna or the Austrian Low Countries obviously did not contribute to the development of a national aristocracy in the Habsburg dominions or in the Austrian Low Countries. The nobility of Savoy and the South-Netherlandish provinces either remained regionally particularistic or assimilated French international culture.

This left state institutionalization of aristocratic status as the major force nationalizing the South-Netherlandish nobility. The royal legislation of 1595, 1616, and 1754 applied to all the Spanish/Austrian Low Countries. True, as in France, many provincial customary laws still governed aristocratic status, but the legislation of 1595, 1616, and 1754 did more than any other enacted by the Habsburgs to create a national status in the Low Countries. Again it is essential to avoid attributing design to this development. The Habsburgs did not know that the provinces over which they ruled in the Low Countries would become a national state in the nineteenth century. They were standardizing, not nationalizing. Yet in the seventeenth and eighteenth centuries the institutionalization of aristocratic status contributed more than any other force to the evolution of a national aristocracy in what eventually became the Kingdom of Belgium.

Whereas the French aristocracy was nationalized through both the state institutionalization of aristocratic status and cultural assimilation, and the South-Netherlandish nobility was nationalized primarily through the state institutionalization of aristocratic status, the British aristocracy was nationalized primarily through cultural assimilation. This did not occur easily. London was not as powerful a cultural centre as Paris and Versailles. Religious heterogeneity was greater in the British Isles than in France, especially in the period before the destruction of the Catholic aristocracy in Ireland. Yet a united British aristocracy did emerge in the eighteenth century with a common (mostly Anglicized) culture. State institutionalization of aristocratic status contributed little because the state did not regulate membership in the British aristocracy. The exception obviously was the titled aristocracy. And it is notable that the power of the state to set the rules for membership in the peerage eventually assisted Scottish peers in their struggle to be accepted on equal terms with English peers. It was not enough, however, to create a British aristocracy. Whereas in France nobles from a great variety of regions identified with and were accepted as members of the "French nobility," the aristocracy that most aristocrats in the British Isles imitated and tried to join was not the British aristocracy, but the English aristocracy. True, there were some aristocrats in Scotland, Ireland, and even Wales who did not want to join the English aristocracy. Yet most gave in to pressures to imitate English aristocrats in order not to lose status. English aristocrats, for their part, have been equivocal in their acceptance of other aristocrats in the British Isles, setting up some barriers to their assimilation, but not resisting the process altogether. They have, however, never been comfortable with the idea that the English aristocracy should be a subgroup of a larger British aristocracy, just as some English historians are still not comfortable with the idea that English history should be a subtopic within British history.

Terms and Concepts

ABSOLUTISM   As the term is used in this study, a state is absolutist to the extent that political power is concentrated in the head of state and not limited by other civil or state structures.

AIDS (*AIDES*)   Originally referring to any kind of financial assistance provided by a vassal for his lord, and then in the fourteenth century to the taxes collected to ransom King John, in the Early Modern period this term referred usually (though not exclusively) to taxes on consumption, particularly wine.

ALLODIUM (ALLODIAL)   A property held in absolute ownership and not subject to a feudal superior.

ANOBLI   Recently ennobled.

ARISTOCRACY   In classical usage the word "aristocracy" meant the monopolization of political power by a small number of persons regarded as the most fit to rule. Eventually it came to designate those who enjoyed this monopoly, and subsequently those with other advantages besides political power. This is the way European historians employ the concept. Their usage varies, however, in another respect. Some take the term to refer to a small elite, such as French or British peers, while others use it more broadly, in the continental context to cover all nobles, in the British context to cover peers, other title-holders, and members of the landed gentry. In this book it is employed in the broad sense.[1]

ASCRIPTION   For some sociologists this term refers to the treatment of a person according to who he or she is, what position he or she holds, regardless of whether this position was inherited or achieved. When I use the term I am almost always referring to hereditary ascription, i.e., determined by birth.

ATTAINDER   (England) (1) By an act of attainder, Parliament declared that a person was guilty of treason or some other offence against the crown. (2) Abolition of the rights and titles of a person as a result of an act of attainder or conviction for treason. The blood line was attainted and the person's property was confiscated.

BAILLIE   (Scotland) The person in charge of a landed estate.

BAN   (1) The royal power to command. (2) A seigneurial monopoly. (3) Seigneurial jurisdiction. (4) Convocation of vassals.

BANALITÉ, RIGHT OF   The obligatory use of a service provided by a seigneur. Most common was the obligatory use of the seigneur's oven or mill. Payment in lieu of using the service might also be referred to by this word.

CAHIER DE DOLÉANCES   A list of grievances submitted to the crown by each electoral assembly in France in early 1789.

CAPITATION   A head or poll tax based on population.

CASTELLAN   A lord, warden, or governor of a fort or castle.

CASUALTY   (Scotland) A feudal incident of wardholding, such as relief or rights to the land if there was no heir or if the heir was a minor.

CENS   A payment to a lord in lieu of services which acknowledges the lordship.

CESS   (Scotland) Land tax.

CHARGE AULIQUE   Office in a royal court.

CLASS   I adopt a modified Weberian definition of class. A class is composed of people with similar economic resources. This includes control over the means of production, but other economic resources as well. *See also* 18.

COIGN AND LIVERY, RIGHT OF   Food, billeting, and entertainment exacted by Irish chiefs for their soldiers and attendants. People were forced to provide these and other services in return for protection.

COMMISSION OF THE PEACE   (England) The commission of a justice of the peace.

CONTRACTUAL TENANCY   *See* customary tenancy.

COPYHOLD   Customary tenure registered on the manor roll, of which the tenant has a copy.

COURT   (1) The royal court was initially the king's advisory and judicial council, but over time it lost this meaning and, by the Early Modern period, it referred to the monarch's household or to all those who regularly attended entertainments, receptions, and ceremonies held by the crown. (2) In England, a political faction in opposition to the "country." *See also* 282–3.

COURT BARON   (England) A manorial court dealing with manorial administration. It adjudicated local disputes between lords and tenants or among tenants. *See* court leet.

COURT LEET (England) A manorial court of criminal jurisdiction that determined and punished misdemeanours. *See* court baron.

COURT OF BARONY (BARONIAL COURT) (Scotland) Manorial court attached to a barony and overseen by the baron or his baillie. It performed the functions of the English courts baron and courts leet.

CREST A figure or device above the shield of a coat of arms.

CULTURAL CAPITAL This term has been developed primarily by Pierre Bourdieu.[2] It is not cultural power as I use the term, but rather status power, more accurately one kind of status power, that which is based on the possession of esteemed cultural characteristics or cultural objects. Bourdieu is concerned more with status competition (and how culture is used in such competition) than he is with cultural power, though cultural power is what he is talking about in his discussions of cultural production and consumption.[3] *See* cultural power and power.

CULTURAL POWER I use this term to refer to the power to affect the behaviour of others by shaping values, norms, or beliefs. Like most types of power, cultural power and status power are almost always fused to at least some degree. Often they are highly fused, as in the case of pop singers and cult leaders. Yet they need to be conceptually distinguished because a power-holder may have significantly more of one than the other. Newspaper reporters, for example, usually have more cultural power than status power, while professional athletes usually have more status power than cultural power. *See also* power and cultural capital.

CURIA REGIS The early king's court, which advised the king on judicial and political matters.

CUSTOMARY TENANCY This tenancy was based primarily on custom, which might or might not be codified in laws. Contractual tenancy is formed by agreement. The distinction is not dichotomous, but a matter of degree.

DEMESNE Land held directly by the lord and retained for the support of his household.

DÉROGEANCE The loss of noble status and privilege as a result of inappropriate behaviour, such as pursuing a demeaning occupation.

DOMAINE CONGÉABLE A land tenure found in parts of Brittany that required the landlord to reimburse the tenant for his or her buildings in order to remove him or her. If the landlord did not take steps to remove a tenant when his or her lease expired, he or she remained on the land at the existing annual rent.[4]

DON GRATUIT A subsidy granted by the clergy to the king.

ECONOMIC POWER The power to mobilize or distribute natural or material resources. *See also* power.

ÉLECTION (France) (1) A fiscal district. (2) The tribunal that imposed taxes in an *élection*.

ENCLOSURE   Narrowly defined, this term refers to surrounding land with fences. More broadly it means also the consolidation of lands that were formerly divided into open-field segments. More broadly still it includes the extinction of communal rights to land and associated regulations as to its use.[5] And most broadly it includes engrossment.

ENGAGÈRE D'OFFICE   A loan to the state in exchange for an office, to be reimbursed from the revenues of the office. A person obtaining an office was required to pay to his predecessor what was left of the loan.

ENGROSSMENT   A reorganization of property to increase the size of holdings.

ENTAIL   The settlement of an estate on a succession of heirs. The settlement could be broken with the consent of the heir when he came of age.

ESTEEM   In this work, esteem, prestige, and status are synonymous.

EXTENSIVE POWER   See power.

EYRE   Circuit court held by an itinerant justice.

FEU FERME (FEUING)   (Scotland) A tenure by which an owner of land owed monetary payments to the lord enjoying the superiority of his or her land. These payments consisted of a down payment, called a "grassum," and a fixed rent, called a "feu duty."[6] See also 144.

FEUDALISM   This word has numerous usages. Weber employed it to refer to a kind of patrimonial rule in which authority is not concentrated in the household staff of the ruler, but is appropriated by powerful individuals.[7] For Marxists, feudalism is a mode of production in which a surplus is extracted through extra-economic coercion. Most Medieval historians, however, use the word to denote a certain kind of lordship. Feudalism in this sense flourished especially in the eleventh to thirteenth centuries in northwestern Europe. It was based on the granting of a fief, usually but not always land, in return for military service, though other obligations, including advice and monetary payments, could also be owed.

   We should not conclude from the character of early French feudalism that deconcentration is an inherent characteristic of feudalism. Regrettably, this assumption is often made. Weber believed that the appropriation of authority by individuals was the distinguishing feature of feudalism. One is free, of course, to define feudalism any way one likes, but feudalism in the sense that the majority of Medieval historians employ the term did not decentralize authority. Quite the opposite, the feudal bond was a force that held Medieval French society together when most other forces were pulling it apart. One of the few sources of power that the French king had over the duke of Normandy and the count of Flanders was that they were his vassals. Norman England was very much a feudal society; it was also one where the crown was relatively powerful. See also seigneurialism.

FIEF   A feudal term referring to whatever a vassal holds for which he or she owes dues or service to a lord. See feudalism and vassal.

FINE   An initial down payment or sum demanded by the landlord upon entering into or renewing a tenure.

FORMARIAGE, RIGHT OF   Payment that had to be made to the seigneur for permission to marry a person from outside the seigneurie.

GABELLE   (France) A sales tax on salt.

GÉNÉRALITÉ   (France) Administrative and fiscal district that became the district administered by an intendant.

GENTILHOMME   (France) One considered to belong to the noble race. Only those with a long noble ancestry could claim to be *gentilshommes.*

GENTLEMAN   (England) This term usually refers to a member of the British gentry, but some men, professionals for example, might claim to be gentlemen though they would not claim to belong to the gentry. *See also* aristocracy and gentry.

GENTRY   British landowners who do not hold a peerage. The highest ranking are baronets, the lowest ranking, the parish gentry. *See also* aristocracy and peer.

GÎTE, RIGHT OF   The right of a lord or sovereign to lodging and maintenance.

HERIOT   A payment to the lord on the death of a vassal; the usual payment was the vassal's best beast.

HOBEREAU   A country noble of modest means.

HONOUR   I take this word to refer to the deliberate public recognition of status. Thus we honour people by granting them titles or awards or holding banquets or public ceremonies for them. We dishonour people by holding public denigration ceremonies, stripping them of titles, or, at the less institutionalized level, insulting or slandering them.

IDEOLOGICAL POWER   *See* power.

INCIDENT   (1) A due exacted by a lord on certain occasions. (2) A privilege or burden attached to a position.

INTENSIVE POWER   *See* power.

JACOBITE   One who supported the restoration of the Stewart house to the throne in the British Isles.

LORD   (1) The superordinate in a relation of lordship. (2) A British peer.

MAINMORTE (MAINMORTABLES)   (1) The right of a lord to the share of an inheritance. (2) A servile disability that deprived persons of the right to bequeath their property if they had no children. The lord was considered to be their heir.

MAISON DU ROI   (France) The king's household, consisting of the domestic household and the military household.

MANOR   (England) The integral landed holding of a lord.

MANORIAL COURT   For England *see* court baron and court leet. For Scotland *see* court of barony.

MECHANICAL SOLIDARITY   Solidarity in a society resulting from similarity and shared beliefs as opposed to organic solidarity.

MÉDIANATE   A fee paid in the Spanish/Austrian Low Countries to the sovereign on appointment to certain offices.

MEILLEUR CATEL   The French heriot.

MÉTAYAGE   Sharecropping.

MILITARY POWER   The power of physical force. *See also* power.

MUTATION, RIGHT OF   Payment made to the seigneur for permission to sell a non-feudal holding.

NEW ENGLISH   Those who came or whose ancestors came to Ireland from England after approximately the mid-sixteenth century. They were almost all Protestants.

NOBLESSE DORMANTE   The suspension of noble status during a period in which a noble was engaged in a derogatory activity. When the activity was given up, noble status was restored without the necessity of royal dispensation.

OCTROI   A tax on goods.

OLD ENGLISH   Those who came or whose ancestors came to Ireland from England before approximately the mid-sixteenth century. The majority remained Catholic.

ORGANIC SOLIDARITY   Solidarity in a society resulting from interdependence based on the division of labour as opposed to mechanical solidarity.

PARCOURS, RIGHT OF   The right to graze livestock on common land.

PARLEMENTAIRE   Magistrate serving on one of the French *parlements*, the highest courts in France.

PEER   (1) In Medieval France this term was used to refer to one of the great territorial vassals, but in the Early Modern period it was one of the highest ranks of the French nobility. (2) In the British Isles a duke, marquess, earl, viscount, or baron with a right to sit in one of the three parliaments, with the partial except of Scottish peers after 1707.

POLITICAL POWER   I use this term to refer to the power of command over a community. It usually takes the form of issuing orders or decrees, enforcing or interpreting norms, customs, or laws, and in some cases making or changing such norms, customs, or laws. In most of human history, political and military power have been fused, but not always, and so we need to distinguish them conceptually.

   Mann defines political power as state power – that of "centralized, institutionalized, territorial regulation."[8] With this definition it is difficult to talk about differences in the extent to which political power is centralized, and in societies without states or where the arm of the state is weak there is no political power. This kind of conceptualization may be useful to Mann, but it is not to me, since one of the major processes in which I am interested is the transfer of political power from regional lords to centralized states. *See also* power.

POWER As I use the term, power is the ability of *A* to affect the behaviour of *B* in ways intended by or advantageous to *A*.

The classifications examined in this book do not exhaust all types of power, but they have been considered by sociologists to be the most important. Weber distinguished between three types of power: "economic power," the power of rank or "status," and a third category that later writers have conceptualized as political power. Differences in economic power give rise to "classes"; differences in status give rise to "status groups"; and differences in political power give rise to "parties." Mann has made several conceptual contributions, some of which are extremely helpful. He distinguishes between "intensive" and "extensive" power. The former refers to "the ability to organize tightly and command a high level of mobilization or commitment," whereas the latter refers to "the ability to organize large numbers of people over far-flung territories in order to engage in minimally stable cooperation."[9]

To Weber's three sources of power Mann adds "ideological" and "military" power.[10] I prefer the concept "cultural power" to his "ideological power," which I think is simply one kind of cultural power. In any case, a more serious problem is that Mann matches ideological power with status; that is, he believes that ideological power has the same relationship to status as economic power has to classes. It is true that status is often greatly affected by ideological or cultural power, but it is also affected by economic, military, and political power. The primary basis of status groups is, as Weber held, status power. The relationships between power and social groups are shown in table 12. The social groups on the right consist of persons (some organized, some not) who share similar sources of power.

Table 12
Types of Power and Social Groups

Type of Power	*Social Groups*
Political power	Publics, electorates, political elites, parties, political movements
Military power	Military leaders, warlords, warrior chiefs
Economic power	Classes
Status power	Status groups
Cultural power	Cultural elites, intelligentsia, clergy, cultural movements

PRÉCIPUT Right of a person to secure a certain share of an estate before it is divided among the heirs.

PRESTIGE *See* esteem and status.

PROPRIETARY RENT *See* seigneurial rent.

QUARTER OF NOBILITY The largest continuous number of ancestors in the same generation who were noble. If a person has two noble parents, but none of his or her earlier ancestors were noble, he or she possesses two quarters. If his or her four grandparents were noble, but none of his or her earlier ancestors, he or she has four quarters of nobility, and so on.[11]

QUIT-RENT   English *cens.*

RELIEF, RIGHT OF   Payment made to the seigneur for the right to inherit a fief. *See also saisine.*

SAISINE, RIGHT OF   (1) Succession duties paid to the seigneur. (2) Seizure of an inheritance by the seigneur.

SEASON   The periods of time in which the aristocracy went to London when the court was in town, Parliament was in session, and the theatre was active.

SEIGNEURIAL RENT   As I use the term, rent is seigneurial to the extent that it is symbolically reinforced by the status of the seigneur to whom it is owed and legitimated in terms of lordship: dues are owed to a seigneur as a result of the status he holds, not just because he has control over an economic resource. I consider payments to be proprietary (as opposed to seigneurial) to the extent that control over land is what gives the lord power.

There was some tendency for seigneurial rent and customary tenure to go together, and proprietary rent and contractual tenure to go together. Despite the contractual nature of lordship, over time seigneurial rent usually came to be legitimated primarily on the basis of custom. *See also* customary tenancy.

SEIGNEURIALISM   This word may be taken as having the same meaning as lordship. Many historians, however, use it to designate a specific kind of lordship. I sometimes employ it as a synonym for lordship, but I more often employ it to refer to the lordship of lords and peasants. *See* feudalism.

SEIGNEURIE BANALE   Exercise of the *ban* by a lord. *See ban.*

SENESCHAL   An official of a monarch or lord in charge of justice and domestic administration.

STATUS   Status power is the power to elicit respect. It is tempting to say "command respect," but this would be misleading because status power usually does not involve an express command. *See also* power and 15–18.

TAILLE   (1) A seigneurial payment levied on peasants by the king or by their lord. (2) From the late Middle Ages a direct royal tax either on land (*taille réelle*) or on person (*taille personnelle*).

TENANTS-IN-CHIEF   The immediate vassals of the king.

TERRAGE   The right of a lord to a portion of the harvest.

UDAL   *See* allodium.

UNDIFFERENCED ARMS   An inherited coat of arms not altered from that from which it is descended. Usually only the eldest son has the right to inherit undifferenced arms. Daughters and younger sons must alter or "difference" their arms.

VAINE PÂTURE   The obligation to open one's land for common grazing for a limited annual period. Thus also, the right of a member of a community to graze his or her livestock on such land.

VASSAL   A member of a feudal hierarchy owing loyalty or other obligations to a lord.

VILLEIN   (England) An unfree tenant.

VINGTIÈME   (France) A tax levied primarily on landed income.

VOL DU CHAPON   Ditches, barns, stable, etc.

WARDHOLDING   (Scotland) A feudal tenure by which an owner of land owed duties (especially military service) to the lord who enjoyed the superiority of his or her land.

Methodological Problems with the Analysis of Careers of Men Listed in *Dictionary of National Biography*

It is probable that most of the sons of fathers who could not be classified were non-title-holders. Adding the figures in the c columns to those in the a columns alters the percentages, but not enough to lead us to revise our conclusions. To take the most important numbers, the percentage with service in the army whose father did not have a title becomes 4.5 per cent in England (from 4.6), 13.5 per cent in Ireland (from 14.1), and 5.7 per cent in Scotland (from 6.3).

The total percentage of men who entered the military is a function of decisions made by the editors who selected those to be included in the *Dictionary*. This is why we cannot compare these data with those we have for France and Savoy. It is likely that the percentage of men listed in the *Dictionary* who had military experience is higher than in the total population, though those who edited the *Dictionary* do not seem to have been as impressed with military men as with politicians, writers, and religious figures, who could be found in plentiful numbers. Nevertheless, we can legitimately compare the percentages in the a columns with those in the b columns. This gives us the relative participation of the two groups in the military.

Two further methodological problems must, however, be acknowledged. First, the probability that the son of a title-holder would get into the *Dictionary* might have been higher than for a man whose father did not have a title, even if the two men had equally distinguished careers. This assumes that the historians who edited the *Dictionary* were biased in favour of the sons of title-holders. Second, I have included in my sample men born in the British Isles but serving abroad, if, of course, they were in the *Dictionary*; yet the great majority of those who served abroad in the armies of other countries would not have found their way into the *Dictionary*. There is no obvious reason, however, why these two biases in the data should affect the number who served in the military more than the number who did not. Thus they should not alter our conclusions.

Notes

INTRODUCTION

1 For definitions of power and aristocracy see terms and concepts.
2 Tilly, *Big Structures*; and McMichael, "Incorporating comparison."
3 Shils, *Center and Periphery*, 261.
4 Butterflied, *Whig Interpretation*.
5 For a discussion of this debate see Foster-Carter, "Modes of production controversy."
6 Comninel, *Rethinking the French Revolution*, 189.
7 Wood, *Pristine Culture of Capitalism*, 9.
8 Tilly, *As Sociology Meets History*, 195–201; and his "Demographic origins."
9 For discussions of this literature with bibliographies see Tilly, *Big Structures*, and my "Historical anthropology."
10 Wirth, "Urbanism as a way of life"; Redfield, "Folk Society"; Miner, "Folk-urban continuum."
11 Fox, *History in Geographic Perspective*. See also his more recent, "The argument."
12 Fox, *History in Geographic Perspective*, 33–8.
13 Ibid., 60–6.
14 Hochberg, "English Civil War"; Tilly, "Geography of European statemaking and capitalism," and other articles in Genovese and Hochberg, eds., *Geographic Perspectives*; Hochberg and Miller, "Internal colonialism," and other articles in Earle and Hochberg, eds., *Geography of Social Change*.
15 Tilly, *Coercion*, 30, 45–66.

16 Elias, *Civilizing Process*, 2: *State Formation*.

17 Shils, *Center and Periphery*, 3.

18 Rokkan's works on centres and peripheries include "Centre formation" and "Dimensions of state formation"; Rokkan and Urwin, "Introduction: centres and peripheries."

19 Frank, *Capitalism and Underdevelopment*; Frank, "Development of underdevelopment"; Frank, *Latin America Underdevelopment*; Frank, *Sociology of Development*; Frank, *Dependent Accumulation*. Other works in dependency theory that can be mentioned are Emmanuel, *Unequal Exchange*; Wilbur, ed., *Political Economy*; Amin, *Accumulation on a World Scale*; Amin, *Unequal Development*; and Cardosa and Faletio, *Dependency and Development*. Less orthodox are Grieco, *Between Dependency and Autonomy*; Bennett and Sharpe, *Transnational Corporations versus the State*; and Gold, *State and Society in the Taiwan Miracle*.

20 The foremost work on internal colonialism is Hechter, *Internal Colonialism*. The foremost on world-system theory are Wallerstein, *Modern World-System I*; *Modern World-System II*; and *Modern World-System III*. See also Abu-Lughod, *Before European Hegemony*.

21 Rokkan and Urwin, "Introduction: centres and peripheries," 5.

22 Gerald of Wales, *Journey through Wales*, 121.

23 Mann, *Sources of Social Power*, vol. 1, chaps. 13–14, vol. 2, chaps. 1, 3, and 20.

24 Tilly, *Coercion*, 2.

25 Mann, "Autonomous power of the state."

26 Dyson, *State Tradition*.

27 Corrigan and Sayer, *Great Arch*.

28 Spencer, *Principles of Sociology*, 3–6, 437–43, 473–542, 578–85; Durkheim, *Division of Labour*.

29 Hilton, "Feudal society," 166; Hilton, "Feudalism in Europe," 3, 5.

30 Porchnev, *Les soulèvements populaires*, 395–6.

31 One exception is Wood, "Separation of the economic and political." See also my "Landlord domination in nineteenth-century Ireland."

32 Parsons, "Evolutionary universals in society"; Smelser, *Social Change in the Industrial Revolution*, 1–4, 15–17, 29, 50–157, 402–8; Eisenstadt, "Social change, differentiation and evolution"; Eisenstadt, *Modernization: Protest, and Change*, 2–3, 104–5; Eisenstadt, *Political Systems of Empires*.

33 Habermas, *Theory*, 2: *Lifeworld and System*, especially 113–17, 153–79, and 312–13; Habermas, *Communication and the Evolution of Society*, 125, 141–2, 174.

34 Alexander, "Differentiation theory," 12.

35 Ibid., 1; Colomy, "Uneven differentiation," 120.

36 Smelser, "Evaluating the model"; Smelser, "The contest between family and schooling."

37 Alexander, "Differentiation theory," 2.

38 Smelser, "The contest between family and schooling"; see also his *Social Paralysis*, 355–7.

39 Alexander, *Action and Its Environments*, 50; Alexander, "Differentiation theory," 1; Colomy, "Uneven differentiation," 131–2.

40 Keller, *Beyond the Ruling Class.*

41 Works on status crystallization and inconsistency include Lenski, "Status crystallization"; Jackson, "Status consistency"; Geschwender, "Continuities in theories"; Eitzen, "Status inconsistency"; Landecker, *Class Crystallization.*

42 Anderson, *Lineages*, 97; Kimmel, "Ambivalence of absolutism," 63.

43 Marshall, *Class, Citizenship and Social Development*; Bendix, *Nation-building and Citizenship*; Turner, *Status.* Turner's is the best recent work in this school. He argues that until the nineteenth century, Western European society was more a status society than a class society, that during the nineteenth century and the first half of the twentieth it was more a class society than a status society, but that in the late twentieth it has again become more a status society than a class society.

44 Maine, *Ancient Law*, 163–5.

45 References to the status-to-class transition can be found in Mayer, *Class and Society*, 16–21; Bottomore, *Classes in Modern Society*, 15; Krauss, *Stratification, Class and Conflict*, 17–20; Congalton and Daniel, *The Individual in the Making*, 85–6; Kriesberg, *Social Inequality*, 47; Giddens, *Introduction to Sociology*, 258.

46 Mousnier, *Social Hierarchies*; Blum, *End of the Old Order.*

47 Blum, *End of the Old Order*, 8.

48 Weber, *Economy and Society*, 1:305–7.

49 See, for example, Turner, *Status*, especially 5, 11–12.

50 See terms and concepts for a further discussion of the meaning of status and related terms.

51 Spring, "Landed elites compared." For the "embourgeoisement" of the English aristocracy see Thompson, "Peculiarities of the English."

52 Croot and Parker, "Agrarian class structure," 45.

53 Mitford, *Pompadour*, 15–16.

54 Cobban, *History of Modern France*, 1:12, 108, 132–3.

55 Pareto, *Rise and Fall of Elites*, 60–71.

56 Moore, *Social Origins of Dictatorship and Democracy*, 14–15, 37, 42–6, 48, 52–3, 66–7.

57 Bendix, *Kings or People*, 333, 336.

58 Eisenstadt, *Political Systems of Empires*, 86, 181, 183.

59 Wallerstein, *Modern World-System I*, 181–2, 284; Wallerstein, *Modern World-System II*, 121–3.

60 Aulin, *The Cybernetic Laws of Social Progress*, 166–8, 176–8.

61 Chambliss and Ryther, *Sociology*, 190.

62 Forster, *Nobility of Toulouse*; Forster, "Noble wine producers"; Forster, "Provincial noble."

63 Behrens, "Nobles, privileges and taxes"; Behrens, "Revision defended."

64 Zeller, "Une notion: la dérogeance"; Meyer, *La noblesse bretonne*; Taylor, "Non-capitalist wealth"; Richard, *Noblesse d'affaires.*

65 Doyle, "Aristocratic reaction."

66 Chaussinand-Nogaret, *La noblesse au XVIIIème siècle.*

67 Dewald, *Aristocratic Experience*, introduction and chaps. 1, 3, and 5.

68 Bush, *European Nobility*, 1: *Noble Privilege*; Bush, *English Aristocracy*; Bush, *European Nobility*, 2: *Rich Noble, Poor Noble.*

69 Bush, *English Aristocracy*, 1.

70 Cannon, *Aristocratic Century.*

71 Stone and Stone, *Open Elite?*

72 Meyer, *La noblesse bretonne*; Doyle, *Parlement of Bordeaux*; Constant, "Nobles et paysans en Beauce"; Dewald, *Formation: Magistrates of Rouen*; Wood, *Nobility of Bayeux*; Nicolas, *La Savoie au 18e siècle*; Hudemann-Simon, *La noblesse luxembourgeoise*; Dewald, *Pont-St-Pierre*; Janssens, *L'évolution de la noblesse belge.*

73 Books taking a "Britannic" approach include Hechter, *Internal Colonialism*, Davies, ed., *British Isles*; Kearney, *British Isles*; and Frame, *Political Development*. We could also include Colley, *Britons*, though she leaves out Ireland.

CHAPTER ONE

1 Kennedy, *Rise and Fall of the Great Powers*, 21.

2 Périn, *Clovis et la naissance de la France*, 107–10.

3 Bordonove, *Les rois qui ont fait la France*, 155–6.

4 Galliou and Jones, *Bretons*, 149.

5 Einhard, *The Life of Charlemagne*, 51.

6 Werner, "*Hludovicus Augustus*," 7–8.

7 Fox, *History in Geographic Perspective*, 44–5.

8 All of these estimates come from Chandler, *Four Thousand Years of Urban Growth*, 14–17.

9 Clout, "Early urban development," 87.

10 Comninel, "English feudalism," and sources he cites, especially Duby, *Rural Economy*, 186–90, 226–8, 246.

11 For Champagne see Evergates, *Feudal Society*, 146–7, 151–2.

12 Petit-Dutaillis, *Etude sur la vie et règne de Louis VIII*, 329.

13 Labarge, *Saint Louis*, 155.

14 Knecht, *Francis I*, 92.

15 All of the above on Francis 1 comes from ibid., 92–3.

16 Shennan, "Louis xv," 313; Solnon, *La cour de France*, 421–2, 438–9.

17 Cook, "Description of the Courte of Fraunce," 327.

18 This importance has been stressed by Major, *Representative Institutions*. For a critique see Wolfe, *Fiscal System*, 40–52.

19 On French Medieval estates I have learned the most from Strayer, "Consent to taxation," and Lewis, "French Medieval estates."

20 Estoile, *Mémoires-journaux*, 240–1.

21 Richelieu, *Testament politique*, 139.

22 Armstrong, "Old-regime administrative elites," 26, 40.

23 Dawson, "Institutional and sociological study of French intendants," 313; Gruder, *Royal Provincial Intendants*, 98–100.

24 Mousnier, "Le caractère de l'état," 112–15; Mousnier, "Centralisation et décentralisation," 108.

25 Morineau, "Budgets de l'Etat," 291.

26 Armstrong, "Old-regime administrative elites," 35–6.

27 Dawson, "Institutional and sociological study of French intendants," 324.

28 Gail Bossenga has referred to this as the "internal contradiction" of the French state. See her *Politics of Privilege*, 7–8, 12–14.

29 Finer, "State-building," 100.

30 Brewer, *Sinews of Power*, 6.

31 The preceding is based primarily on Galliou and Jones, *Bretons*, 206–7; Touchard, "Le Moyen Age breton," 168; Meyer, "Au rythme du Monde atlantique," 266–7; and Meyer, "Le siècle de l'intendance," 323.

32 Clout, "Industrial development," 451.

33 Asselain, *Histoire économique: De l'acnien régime à la Première Guerre mondiale*, 56; Goldstone, *Revolution and Rebellion*, 190, and sources he cites.

34 Asselain, *Histoire économique: De l'acnien régime à la Première Guerre mondiale*, 56–7; Goldstone, *Revolution and Rebellion*, 203.

35 Morineau, "Budgets de l'Etat," 315.

36 Van Creveld, *Technology and War*, 135.

37 Pritchard, *Louis XV's Navy*, chaps. 11 and 12.

38 The above comes from Finer, "State- and nation-building," 99.

39 Corvisier, *Armies and Societies*, 113; Kennett, *French Armies*, 77; Lynn, "Growth of the French army"; Martin, "Army of Louis xiv"; Ruwet, *Soldats des régiments nationaux*, 22–3, 36; Childs, *British Army of William III*, 103; Barnett, *Britain and Her Army*, 213; Loriga, *Soldats*, 30, 38–9.

40 All of these numbers come from Martin, "Army of Louis xiv," 119–20, 123; Lynn, "Growth of French army," 574–6.

41 Corvisier, *L'armée française*, 430; Corvisier, *Armies and Societies*, 138.

42 Bush, *European Nobility*, 1: *Noble Privilege*, 47–8; Tilly, *Coercion*, 26–7, 29, 53, 63–4, 99–103.

43 Strayer, "Consent to taxation," 91–4.

44 Henneman, *Royal Taxation: Development of War Financing*, 326–8; Henneman, *Royal Taxation: Captivity and Ransom of John II*, 304–5, 310–11; Wolfe, *Fiscal System*, 23–31.

45 Van der Wee, "Monetary, credit and banking systems," 358; Contamine, "Growth of nation state," 23.

46 Collins, *Fiscal Limits*, especially chaps. 1–2.

47 Mathias and O'Brien, "Taxation in Britain and France," 604; Tilly, *Contentious French*, 62; and Goldstone, *Revolution and Rebellion*, 205.

48 French finances have been defended most notably by Morineau, "Budgets de l'Etat." Morineau's position is supported in certain respects by Harris, "French finances"; Dessert, *Argent, pouvoir et société*; Tilly, *Contentious French*; and Goldstone, *Revolution and Rebellion*.

49 Bosher, *French Finances*; Bonney, *King's Debts*; Collins, *Fiscal Limits*.

50 Collins, *Fiscal Limits*, chap. 1.

51 Bosher, *French Finances*, introduction and chaps. 4 and 5.

52 Van der Wee, "Monetary, credit and banking systems," 379–80.

53 Collins, *Fiscal Limits*, 70.

54 Ibid., 48–55.

55 Ibid., 24.

56 Ibid., 38, 42.

57 Bonney, "Failure of French revenue farms," 29.

58 Mathias and O'Brien, "Taxation in Britain and France," 631. They actually conclude that customs made up 7 to 8 per cent of royal indirect tax revenue; I have roughly converted this into a percentage of total royal tax revenue.

59 Ibid., 622–5; Goldstone, *Revolution and Rebellion*, 205.

60 For a discussion of this debate and references see Bossenga, *Politics of Privilege*, 30–1. See also Goldstone, *Revolution and Rebellion*, especially 217, where it is vigorously argued that the urban population was undertaxed.

61 Bonney, "Failure of French revenue farms," 17–18; Bonney, *King's Debts*, 280.

CHAPTER TWO

1 Van der Wee, "Monetary, credit and banking systems," 315.

2 Compare Tilly, *Coercion*, chap. 2.

3 Benecke, *Society and Politics in Germany*, especially ix–xi and 9.

4 De Boom, *Les voyages de Charles Quint*, 6.

5 Dreyfus, *L'Alsace*, 135–6.

6 Parker, *Army of Flanders and the Spanish Road*, 55.

7 Ibid., 60–3.

8 Ibid., 68–70, 72–7.

9 Chevailler, "Emmanuel-Philibert," 57–9.

10 Parker, *Army of Flanders and the Spanish Road*, 60.

11 Symcox, *Victor Amadeus II*, 108–9, 169.

12 G. Stepney to Richard Hill, 8 Sept. 1703, in Hill, *Diplomatic Correspondence of The Right Hon. Richard Hill*, 31.

13 Symcox, "Development of absolutism in the Savoyard state"; Symcox, *Victor Amadeus II*, 56.

14 Nicolas, *La Savoie au 18e siècle*, 2:593–6; Symcox, *Victor Amadeus II*, 32, 59–62, 120; Costamagna, "L'«intendenza»." This paragraph, as well as most of what I say elsewhere about the reign of Victor Amadeus II, is based on Symcox's fine study.

15 Costamagna, "«L'intendenza»," 399–400, 466–7.

16 Devos, "Un siècle en mutation," 239–40.

17 Excerpt from the papers of the Gribaldi family, printed in Guichonnet, *Histoire de la Savoie*, 280–1.

18 Devos, "Un siècle en mutation," 252–3; Nicolas, "Ombres et lumières du xviiie siècle."

19 Bruchet, *Notice sur l'ancien cadastre de Savoie*, 9–10; Devos, "Un siècle en mutation," 235.

20 Devos, "Un siècle en mutation," 254.

21 Chevailler, "Emmanuel-Philibert," 61–2.

22 Barberis, "Continuité aristocratique," 362–3.

23 See 48. Data on Savoyard army come from Loriga, *Soldats*, 30, 38–41.

24 Symcox, *Victor Amadeus II*, 131–3.

25 Hill, *Diplomatic Correspondence of The Right Hon. Richard Hill*, 103, 181, 202–3, 274, 303, 389.

26 Symcox, *Victor Amadeus II*, 118.

27 Daquin, *Topographie medicale de la ville de Chambery*, 77.

28 Lebrun, *L'industrie de la laine à Verviers*, 350 and n. 4, 371–3.

29 Hansotte, *La clouterie liégeoise*, 5–8.

30 A list of the ways in which they did so is provided in a letter written by a chargé d'affaires of the Austrian Low Countries who was stationed in the court of the Prince-Bishop of Liège. See Bastin, Sacré, to the Count of Belgiojoso, 15 Aug. 1786.

31 Bragard, "Liège et la France," 215–16.

32 Genicot, *Histoire de la Wallonie*, 292–3.

33 Gilissen, *Le régime répresentatif avant 1790*, 58.

34 Uyttebrouck, "Une confédération et trois principautés," 233.

35 Harsin, "Histoire des finances publiques," 1:17–18.

36 Van der Wee, "Monetary, credit and banking systems," 322–32, 372; Van der Wee, *Growth of the Antwerp Market*, 2:127–36, 166–207.

37 Mat-Hasquin and Hasquin, "Hainaut," 43.

38 Uyttebrouck, "Une confédération et trois principautés," 222–4.

39 Ibid., 219.

40 Ibid., 219–20.

41 Parker, *Army of Flanders and the Spanish Road*, 57–8.

42 Parker, *Spain and the Netherlands*, 48.

43 Ibid., 48–9, 186–8.

44 Ibid., 45, 81.

45 Ibid., 23–4, 27, 30–2, 67–70.

46 Parker, *Dutch Revolt*, 205–6.

47 Parker, *Spain and the Netherlands*, 35–6.

48 The preceding is based primarily on Schepper and Parker, "Formation of government policy," 247–54.

49 Parker, *Army of Flanders and the Spanish Road*, 70.

50 "L'échec des tentatives de soulèvement aux Pays-Bas sous Philippe IV," 123–9.

51 Gilissen, *Le régime répresentatif avant 1790*, 61–2.

52 See works by Dhondt collected in his *Estates or Powers*.

53 Blockmans, "Typology of representative institutions"; Blockmans, "Introduction" and notes to *Estates or Powers*.

54 This paragraph is based largely on Gilissen, *Le régime répresentatif avant 1790*, 63–4, 71–2, 120; Blockmans in *Estates or Powers*, 259; Van Uytven and Blockmans, "Constitutions and their application," 410, 415, 418–19; Douxchamps-Lefevre, "Les Etats de Namur," 397–403.

55 Poullet, "Constitutions nationales belges," 165.

56 Ibid., 269–70.

57 Polasky, *Revolution in Brussels*, 39–51; Davis, *Joseph II*.

58 What I have said about the Barrier Treaty comes from Hasquin, "Les difficultés financières du gouvernement des Pays-Bas autrichiens," 110–13.

59 Parker, *Army of Flanders and the Spanish Road*, 27, 9, 70, 227, 271–2.

60 Ruwet, *Soldats des régiments nationaux*, 36.

61 Janssens, "De achttiende eeuw," 73–4; Harsin, *Histoire des finances publiques*, 1:10–11.

62 Janssens, "De achttiende eeuw," 104.

63 Harsin, *Histoire des finances publiques*, 1:7; Janssens, "De achttiende eeuw," 68.

64 Janssens, "De achttiende eeuw," 68, and sources he cites.

65 Harsin, *Histoire des finances publiques*, 1:12.

66 Hasquin, "Les difficultés financières du gouvernement des Pays-Bas autrichiens," 113–14, 121.

67 Janssens, "De achttiende eeuw," 62.

68 Hasquin, "Les difficultés financières du gouvernement des Pays-Bas autrichiens," 125.

69 Hasquin, "La vénalité des offices," 244.

70 Ibid.

71 Davis, *Joseph II*, 130–4.

CHAPTER THREE

1 Hechter, *Internal Colonialism*, 49–59; Kearney, *British Isles*, 14.

2 Hill, "Towns as structures and functioning communities," 198.

3 Mack, "Changing thegns," 387.

4 Barrow, *Kingship and Unity*, 25.

5 Simms, *Kings to Warlords*, 11, 21–2, 79–80.

6 Davies, *Domination and Conquest*, 5.

7 Douglas, *William the Conqueror*, chaps. 1–6.

8 Le Patourel, "Norman Conquest of Yorkshire," 7–8; Chibnal, *Anglo-Norman England*, 18, 51.

9 Douglas, *William the Conqueror*, 44.

10 Davies, *Conquest, Coexistence, and Change*, 28.

11 Davies, *Domination and Conquest*, 6–7, 70.

12 This section is based primarily on Byrne, "Trembling sod"; Martin, "Diarmait MacMurchada"; Martin, "Allies and an overlord"; and Martin, "Overlord becomes feudal lord."

13 Martin, "Overlord becomes feudal lord," 122–6.

14 Ibid., 122.

15 Anderson, *Viking Enterprise*, 114–19; Logan, *Vikings in History*, 46, 51.

16 Kirby, *Making of Early England*, 249–53.

17 Ibid., 251–2.

18 Stenton, *Anglo-Saxon England*, 258–9.

19 Kearney, *British Isles*, 42, 60.

20 Chandler, *Four Thousand Years of Urban Growth*, 15.

21 Douglas, *William the Conqueror*, 207.

22 Stenton, *William the Conqueror*, 408–9; Bates, *William the Conqueror*, 112.

23 Chibnall, *Anglo-Norman England*, 122.

24 Kirby, *Making of Early England*, 256.

25 Barrow, *Kingship and Unity*, 87.

26 Dodgshon, "Spatial perspective," 12.

27 See Booton, "Inland trade"; Stevenson, "Trade with the South"; Ditchburn, "Trade with Northern Europe"; and other articles in *The Scottish Medieval Town*.

28 Logan, *Vikings in History*, 46, 51.

29 O'Neill, *Merchants and Mariners* 31, 35, 39, 48–9, 55, 61, 66–7, 71–2, 80, 84–8.

30 For a good discussion of English royal power in relation to the peripheries see Davies, *Domination and Conquest*.

31 Barber, *Henry Plantagenet*, 61.

32 Schlight, *Henry II*, 23, 176.

33 Gillingham, *Richard the Lionheart*, 5, 21–2, 41.

34 Ibid., 57, 66–7, 78, 286.

35 Ibid., 267.

36 Ibid., especially chaps. 12 and 13.

37 Lander, *Limitations*; see also Lander, *English Justices of the Peace*, especially chaps. 1, 5, and 6.

38 Ellis, *Tudor Ireland*, 19.

39 Ibid., 27.

40 Kearney, *British Isles*, 90.

41 Davies, *Conquest, Coexistence, and Change*, 300–7.

42 Elton, *Tudor Revolution*; Elton, *Reform and Reformation*.

43 Coleman and Starkey, *Revolution Reassessed*; Starkey, ed., *English Court*.

44 Ellis, *Tudor Ireland*, 129–30.

45 Jones, *Modern Wales*, 634.

46 On this subject I have made the most use of ibid., chap. 3.

47 Ellis, *Tudor Ireland*, 130.

48 Ibid., especially chaps. 6–8.

49 Canny, *Elizabethan Conquest*, chap. 4.

50 Ellis, *Tudor Ireland*, especially chaps. 8–9.

51 Beckett, *Making of Modern Ireland*, 90–1.

52 MacCurtain, *Tudor and Stuart Ireland*, 180.

53 James, "Active Irish peers," and his more recent *Lords of the Ascendancy*, chaps. 3 and 7. On Catholic landownership and conversion in Tipperary see Power, *Land, Politics, and Society*, 81–3.

54 Simms, "Establishment of Protestant ascendancy," 12–13. See also Simms *Williamite Confiscation*, 160.

55 Young, *Arthur Young's Tour in Ireland*, 2:59.

56 McDowell, *Ireland in the Age of Imperialism and Revolution*, chaps. 10–12; Smith, *Men of No Property*, chaps. 3–7.

57 Smout, *History of the Scottish People*, 99–100.

58 Mitchison, *New History*, 5: *Lordship to Patronage*, 63–5.

59 For the union I have used a number of sources, but especially ibid., chaps. 6–7; Mackie, *History of Scotland*, chap. 14.

60 This paragraph is also based on Mitchison, *New History*, 5: *Lordship to Patronage*, chaps. 7–8; and Mackie, *History of Scotland*, chap. 15.

61 Harriss, "Formation of Parliament," 37.

62 Brown, "Parliament," 111.

63 The literature on the English Civil War is vast. Two major sociological works on the subject are Kimmel, *Absolutism and its Discontents*, and Goldstone, *Revolution and Rebellion*.

64 Kimmel, *Absolutism and Its Discontents*, 223–4.

65 Hochberg, "English Civil War," 742–7.

66 The above is based primarily on Hill, *Century of Revolution*, especially chaps. 1–2.

67 Duncan, "Early parliaments," 51–2.

68 This paragraph is based primarily on Terry, *Scottish Parliament*, 51–3.

69 MacDougall, *James III*, 303.

70 O'Brien, "Scottish parliament."

71 Terry, *Scottish Parliament*, 161–2.

72 See below 112.

73 McCraken, *Irish Parliament*, 5.

74 Beckett, *Making of Modern Ireland*, 51.

75 Ibid., 164.

76 Johnston, *Ireland in the Eighteenth Century*, 55.

77 McGuire, "Irish Parliament," 3–4

78 Beckett, *Making of Modern Ireland*, 225.

79 Wormald [Brown], "Exercise of power," 33–40, 61–3.

80 MacDougall, *James III*, 304.

81 Miller, *Henry VIII and the English Nobility*, 256.

82 Mathew, *James I*, 239.

83 Hatton, *George I*, 134.

84 Trench, *George II*, 140, 151–2, 210, 217, 262.

85 Colley, *Britons*, 235.

86 Plumb, *Walpole*, 1:72.

87 Childs, *Army of Charles II*, 9–11.

88 Barnett, *Britain and Her Army*, 213.

89 See above 48.

90 Van Creveld, *Technology and War*, 135.

91 Brewer, *Sinews of Power*, 257.

92 Childs, *Army of Charles II*, 20.

93 Childs, *British Army of William III*, chap. 8.

94 Hayter, *Army and the Crowd*, 21.

95 Mitchell and Deane, *Abstract of British Historical Statistics*, 389–91.

96 Ibid.; Morineau, "Budgets de l'Etat," 315.

97 Scouller, *Armies of Queen Anne*, 125, 293 and n. 1.

98 Brown, "Scottish lords to British officers," 146.

99 Hayes, "Scottish officers," 30–1.

100 Ibid., 25–6.

101 McDowell, *Ireland in the Age of Imperialism*, 62.

102 Ibid., 59–62.

103 Anderson, *War and Society*, 103.

104 Bruce, *Purchase System*, 17.

105 Ibid., chap. 1.

106 The strengths and weakness of British naval power are examined in articles in Black and Woodfine, eds., *British Navy*.

107 Thompson, "Patrician society, plebeian culture," 403.

108 Hayter, *Army and the Crowd*, 23–4.

109 Simms, "War of the two kings," 485.

110 James, *Ireland in the Empire*, 34, 177–8, 211.

111 Connolly, *Religion, Law, and Power*, 199–203.

112 Rogers, *British Army*, 31.

113 Connolly, *Religion, Law, and Power*, 203–17.

114 Among the works on this subject see Donnelly, "The Whiteboy movement"; and his "The Rightboy movement." See also Clark and Donnelly, eds., *Irish Peasants*, parts I and II; and Smyth, *Men of No Property*.

115 McDowell, *Ireland in the Age of Imperialism*, 255–6.

116 Rogers, *British Army*, 22.

117 The preceding is based on Strayer and Rudisill, "Taxation and community"; Otway-Ruthven, *History of Medieval Ireland*, 166–7.

118 Lander, *Limitations*, 7–14.

119 Alsop, "Theory and practice of Tudor taxation."

120 For tables presenting these data see Mann, *Sources of Social Power*, 1:418–19, 426–7. Mann has taken them from Ramsay, *History of the Revenues of the Kings of England*, 1:195 and 2:86, 287, 426–7. For an analysis of these figures and a discussion of their inaccuracies see Mann, "State and society," 168–73, 177–82.

121 Dietz, "Exchequer in Elizabeth's reign," 80–9.

122 Lander, "Attainder and forfeiture."

123 Beckett, "Land tax or excise," 286–302.

124 Ibid., 299–307.

125 Mitchell and Deane, *Abstract of British Historical Statistics*, 386–8.

126 See above 51, 75–6.

127 Brewer, *Sinews of Power*, 42, 114–26.

128 Ibid., 85, 91–4, 101–14, 127–9.

129 Mathias and O'Brien, "Taxation in Britain and France"; Morineau, "Budgets de l'Etat," 320.

130 Mitchell and Deane, *Abstract of British Historical Statistics*, 389–91.

131 Ibid.; Morineau, "Budgets de l'Etat," 314–15.

132 Hoppit, "Financial crises," 48.

133 Finer, "Princes, parliaments and the public service," 358.

134 Aylmer, "From office-holding to civil service," 96.

135 Ward, "Some eighteenth century civil servants," 27–8, 35.

136 Torrance, "Social class," 65–6.

137 Plumb, *Walpole*, 121–2, 203.

138 Spencer, *Principles of Sociology*, 1:544–75.

139 Parsons, *Evolution of Societies*, chap. 7.

140 Wood, *Pristine Culture of Capitalism*, 24.

141 Hobhouse, *Social Evolution and Political Theory*, 9–10, 18–22, 162, 164.

142 Rueschemeyer, *Power and the Division of Labour*, 177.

143 Kennedy, *Rise and Fall of the Great Powers*, xxv–xxvii.

144 Wallerstein, *Modern World-System II*, 33.

145 Holton, *Transition from Feudalism to Capitalism*, 176–9.

146 Brewer, *Sinews of Power*, xx.

147 Ibid., 55–60, 69–85.

148 Mann, "Autonomous power of the state," 5; Mann, *Sources of Social Power*, 2:59–61; Stanbridge, "European states."

149 Mann, "Autonomous power of the state," 8.

CONCLUSION TO PART ONE

1 Blockmans, "Typology of representative institutions," 202–4.

2 Gilissen, *Le régime réprésentatif avant 1790*, 120; Janssens, "De achttiende eeuw," 52; Douxchamps-Lefèvre, "Les Etats de Namur," 393, 403.

3 Beik, *Absolutism in Languedoc*, 37.

4 Desplat, "Les Etats de Béarn," 89, 92–3, 96, 98–9; Bordes, *L'administration provinciale et municipale*, 91.

CHAPTER FOUR

1 Wormald, *Lords and Men*.

2 See terms and concepts for a discussion of the various meanings of feudalism as well as related concepts – seigneurialism, seigneurial rent, proprietary rent, customary tenancies, and contractual tenancies.

3 The following on *alliances* comes primarily from Lewis, "Decayed and non-feudalism."

4 Duby, *Rural Economy*, 242–3, 248; Fossier, *Peasant Life*, 167; Evergates, *Feudal Society*, 138–43; Verriest, *Le régime seigneurial dans le Comté de Hainaut*, 41, 74–5.

5 Duby, *Rural Economy*, 237–8.

6 Delatte, *Les classes rurales*, 216–23; Devleeshouwer, "Les droits féodaux," 150–7; Hansotte, *Les institutions*, 106.

7 For example, see Dewald, *Pont-St-Pierre*, 222.

8 Van Isterdael, "Belasting en belastingdruk," 346. These and the following data should be treated with caution as a result of the difficulty of distinguishing seigneurial dues from other payments.

9 Nicolas, *La Savoie au 18e siècle*, 1:210–12.

10 Ibid., 1:190; Dewald, *Pont-St-Pierre*, 217–21.

11 Nicolas, *La Savoie au 18e siècle*, 1:220–1.

12 Dewald, *Pont-St-Pierre*, 218.

13 Forster, "Provincial noble," 684–5.

14 Le Goff, *Vannes*, 284–5.

15 Verriest, *Le régime seigneurial dans le Comté de Hainaut*, 264, 332; Yver, "Rédaction officielle."

16 For the Southern Low Countries again see Delatte, *Les classes rurales* 216–23; Devleeshouwer, "Les droits féodaux," 150–7; Hansotte, *Les institutions de Liège*, 106. For Savoy see Nicolas, *La Savoie au 18e siècle*, 1:191–6.

17 Nicolas, *La Savoie au 18e siècle*, 1:194.

18 Bruchet, "Introduction" to Bruchet, ed., *L'abolition des droits seigneuriaux*, xlii–liii; Nicolas, *La Savoie au 18e siècle*, 1:196.

19 Soboul, "La révolution française," 54; Péret, "Bourgeoisie rurale et seigneurs," 358–9 and n. 9; Dewald, *Pont-St-Pierre*, 218.

20 For the Southern Low Countries see Deprez, "Evolution économique et mouvements paysans," 59; Devleeshouwer, "Les droits féodaux"; Perissino-Billen, "Des campagnes"; Van Isterdael, "Belasting en belastingdruk," 201; Hudemann-Simon, *La noblesse luxembourgeoise*, 241. For Savoy see Nicolas, *La Savoie au 18e siècle*, 1:215–16; see also many of the documents printed in Bruchet, ed., *L'abolition des droits seigneuriaux*.

21 Young, *Travels in France*, 296.

22 Root, *Peasants and King in Burgundy*, 164–5.

23 Doyle, "Aristocratic reaction," especially 117.

24 Nicolas, *La Savoie au 18e siècle*, 1:200–1; Hansotte, *Les institutions*, 108.

25 Douglas, *William the Conqueror*, 103.

26 Abels, *Lordship and Military Obligation*, 13–22, 36–7, 42–56, 116–17, 125, 146, 185–6.

27 Douglas, *William the Conqueror*, 273, 281–2.

28 Searle, *Predatory Kinship*, 159–77, 230–49.

29 Comninel, "English feudalism."

30 Chibnall, *Anglo-Norman England*, chap. 6.

31 On these changes I have drawn from Painter, *Studies in English Feudal Barony*, and Waugh, "Tenure to contract."

32 Bennett, *Life on the English Manor*, 291, 294–6.

33 Bean, *From Lord to Patron*, 129, 148.

34 Ibid., chap. 6.

35 Bean, *Decline of English Feudalism*, 21, 38–9, 235, 257–301.

36 Tawney, *Agrarian Problem*, especially 177–80, 183–4, 191, 281, 310, 406–7.

37 Brenner, "Agrarian class structure"; Brenner, "On the origins of capitalist development"; and Brenner, "Agrarian roots of European capitalism."

38 Thirsk, "Enclosing and engrossing"; Kerridge, *Agrarian Problems*; Mingay, *Enclosure*; Thirsk, "Seventeenth-century agriculture"; Croot and Parker, "Agrarian class structure"; Large, "Economic and social change"; Searle, "Custom."

39 Thirsk, "Seventeenth-century agriculture," 99.

40 Ibid., 80; Thirsk, "Enclosing and engrossing."

41 Martin, *Feudalism to Capitalism*, especially 120. The best-known Marxist work on peasant resistance is Hilton, *Bond Men Made Free*. Non-Marxists who emphasize peasant resistance include Hyams, *Kings, Lords, and Peasants*, and Hatcher, "English serfdom."

42 Duby, *Rural Economy*, 196, 554.

43 Comninel, "English feudalism."

44 Clay, "Landlords and estate management."

45 Bettey, "Land tenure and manorial custom in Dorset," 33.

46 Manning, *Village Revolts*, 133, 139–40.

47 Clay, "Landlords and estate management"; Large, "Economic and social change"; Searle, "Custom."

48 Manning, *Village Revolts*, 132, and his "Antiquarianism"; see also Large, "Economic and social change," 53–5.

49 Manning, *Village Revolts*, 37, 137; and his "Antiquarianism."

50 Comninel, "English feudalism."

51 Clay, "Landlords and estate management," 203–14.

52 Manning, *Village Revolts*, 40, 44, 70, 81.

53 Ibid., 94.

54 Skone, "Manorial organization in Medieval Pembrokeshire," 10.

55 Davies, *Lordship and Society*, 66, 130–2; and his *Conquest, Coexistence, and Change*, 69.

56 Davies, *Conquest, Coexistence, and Change*, 417, 451.

57 This paragraph comes mainly from Davies, *Lordship and Society*, 151, 219–20; and his *Conquest, Coexistence, and Change*, 286.

58 Davies, *Lordship and Society*, 152–3.

59 Ibid., 151.

60 Ibid., 149–53.

61 Ibid., 67–8; and his *Conquest, Coexistence, and Change*, 280.

62 Davies, *Conquest, Coexistence, and Change*, 120–1, 160–3, 427; Williams, *Recovery, Reorientation and Reformation*, 40, 104–5.

63 Roberts, "Threshold," 15.

64 Howell, "Landlords," 269.

65 Jenkins, *Foundation of Modern Wales*, 166.

66 Howell, *Patriarchs and Parasites*, 156.

67 Howell, "Landlords," 270; Jenkins, *Making of a Ruling Class*, 53–4.

68 Howell, "Landlords," 271.

69 Ibid., 281 n. 125.

70 Simms, *Kings to Warlords*, 13.

71 Martin, "Overlord becomes feudal lord."

72 Nicholls, "Gaelic society and economy," 421.

73 MacNiocaill, *Ireland before the Vikings*, 60–5; O'Corrain, *Ireland before the Normans*, 42–3.

74 Simms, *Kings to Warlords*, 19–20, 96, 110, 130, 132, 143–4, 149;
   O'Dowd, "Land and lordship," 18.

75 Simms, *Kings to Warlords*, 89–95, 101, 114, 116–18, 143, 149.

76 Ibid., especially 18 and 147.

77 Duffy, "Territorial organization."

78 Nicholls, "Gaelic society and economy," 421–2.

79 Otway-Ruthven, *History of Medieval Ireland*, 115, 125.

80 O'Dowd, "Land and lordship," 17–18.

81 MacCurtain, *Tudor and Stuart Ireland*, 45.

82 O'Dowd, "Gaelic economy and society."

83 Cunningham, "Composition of Connacht."

84 O'Dowd, "Gaelic economy and society"; Duffy, "Territorial organization."

85 O'Dowd, "Land and lordship," 24.

86 Canny, "Flight of the earls," 384.

87 O'Dowd, "Gaelic economy and society," 142–3.

88 Clarke and Edwards, "Pacification," 207.

89 Power, *Land, Politics, and Society*, 4–6, 20, 73, 77.

90 Crawford, "Landlord-tenant relations in Ulster," 7.

91 Ainsworth, "Sidelights on eighteenth-century land tenure," 188.

92 Ainsworth, "Aspects of eighteenth-century Irish land tenure."

93 Smyth, "Estate records ... from County Tipperary," 33, 41.

94 25 Geo. III, c. 44. See Power, *Land, Politics, and Society*, 164.

95 Smout, *History of the Scottish People*, 24.

96 Brown, *Bloodfeud in Scotland*, 18.

97 Wormald, *Lords and Men*.

98 Wormald [Brown], "Exercise of power," 54–6.

99 Grant, *New History*, 3: *Independence and Nationhood*, 200.

100 Wormald, *Lords and Men*, 163.

101 Sanderson, *Scottish Rural Society*, 56–7.

102 Whyte, *Agriculture and Society*, 30.

103 Sanderson, *Scottish Rural Society*, 189.

104 Cregeen, "Tacksmen."

105 Johnson, *Journey to the Western Islands*, 85.

106 Shaw, *Northern and Western Islands*, 31–2.

107 Sanderson, *Scottish Rural Society*; Smout, *History of the Scottish People*,
    127; Shaw, *Northern and Western Islands*, 31–3.

108 Graham, *Social Life of Scotland*, 163–5.

109 Mitchison, *New History*, 5: *Lordship to Patronage*, 79, 147.

110 Whetstone, *Scottish County Government*, 1.

111 Ibid., 2–3.

112 Johnson, *Journey to the Western Islands*, 130.

113 Bush, *European Nobility,* 1: *Noble Privilege,* 170.

114 Bruchet, "Introduction" to Bruchet, ed., *L'abolition des droits seigneur-iaux,* lxii–lxxiii; Symcox, *Victor Amadeus II,* 191–2, 201–2, 204–5, 230; Nicolas, *La Savoie au 18e siècle,* 2:641–2.

115 Fossier, *Peasant Life,* 179; Evergates, *Feudal Society,* 138.

116 Dewald, *Pont-St-Pierre,* 211–12, chap. 6.

117 Root, *Peasants and King in Burgundy,* 45–50, 56–61, 133–40, 193–202, 212–13.

118 Verriest, *Le régime seigneurial dans le Comté de Hainaut,* 168.

119 Ibid., 396.

120 Duby, *Rural Economy,* 245–6.

121 O'Dowd, "Land and lordship," 18, 20.

122 Bean, *Decline of English Feudalism.* especially 301.

123 Ibid., 291–301.

124 Sanderson, *Scottish Rural Society,* 61–2.

125 Smout, *History of the Scottish People,* 137–8; Whyte, *Agriculture and Society,* 31.

126 Smout, *History of the Scottish People,* 137; Whyte, *Agriculture and Society,* 158.

127 For English examples see Clay, "Landlords and estate management," 204–5.

128 On this subject see Martin, *Feudalism to Capitalism,* especially 20, 31, 68–70; Hilton, *Bond Men Made Free,* 75, 85–9, 145–6; Hatcher, "English serfdom"; Bennett, *Life on the English Manor,* chap. 11; Duby, *Rural Economy,* 232–8, 243, 283–4, 312–14, 336–7. See also below 372 for the Marxist debate on commercialization and the decline of feudalism.

129 This correlation is acknowledged in a number of sources, but certain difficulties in its interpretation are also recognized. See Duby, *Rural Economy,* 242–3, 279; 313–14; Hilton, *Bond Men Made Free,* 85–9, 145–6, 156; Evergates, *Feudal Society,* 140–4; Fossier, *Peasant Life,* 182.

130 Delatte, *Les classes rurales,* 217; Devleeshouwer, "Les droits féodaux," 151, 154–6.

131 Bruchet, "Introduction" to Bruchet, ed., *L'abolition des droits seigneu-riaux,* 58; Devos, "Un siècle en mutation, 1536–1684," 236.

132 Bruchet, "Introduction" to Bruchet, ed., *L'abolition des droits seigneu-riaux,* 76–81; Nicolas, "Ombres et lumières du XVIIIe siècle," 319.

133 Confidential memorial from Secchi, the Intendant of Genevois, to the Knight of Mouroux, Secretary of State at the Ministery of the Interior, 20 April 1773, printed in Bruchet, ed., *L'abolition des droits seigneuriaux,* 255.

134 See note 129.

135 Davies, *Conquest, Coexistence, and Change,* 157, 214, 281–2, 400–1.

CHAPTER FIVE

1 Bloch, *La société féodale*, 1–77.

2 Genicot, "La noblesse au Moyen Age"; Bonenfant and Despy, "Noblesse en Brabant"; Warlop, *Flemish Nobility.*

3 Van Winter, "Knighthood and nobility," 91.

4 Evergates, *Feudal Society*; Bouchard, "Origins of the French nobility"; Martindale, "French aristocracy"; Contamine, "Introduction."

5 Duby, *Chivalrous Society*, chap. 3.

6 Martindale, "French aristocracy"; James, *Origins of France*, 125.

7 Evergates, *Feudal Society*, 97, 110; Contamine, "Introduction," 21–2.

8 Fossier, *Terre et hommes en Picardie*, 1:535.

9 Ibid.; Nicholas, "Feudal relationships in the Low Countries," 128.

10 Martindale, "French aristocracy," 12.

11 De Win, "De adel in het hertogdom Brabant"; Mourier, "Nobilitas, quid est?"

12 Perroy, "Social mobility and the French *noblesse.*"

13 De Win, "Lesser nobility," 108–9.

14 Janssens, *L'évolution de la noblesse belge*, chaps. 1, 3, conclusion.

15 Fédou, "La noblesse en France à la fin du Moyen Age"; Fourez, *Le droit héraldique*, 48–9; Constant, "Nobles et paysans en Beauce," 56–61.

16 Strayer, "Consent to taxation," 66–9; Henneman, *Royal Taxation: Development of War Financing*, 40–8; Wolfe, *Fiscal System*, 25–7; Henneman, *Royal Taxation: Captivity and Ransom of John II*, 286–9.

17 Bruchet, *Notice sur l'ancien cadastre de Savoie*, 8; Buttin, "Le Souverain Sénat de Savoie," 2, 6.

18 Major, *Representative Government*, 28.

19 Janssens, *L'évolution de la noblesse belge*, chap. 2.

20 The above is based primarily on Henneman, "Nobility, privilege and fiscal politics," especially 1, 15–17.

21 By now the literature that asserts that the French nobility paid comparatively high taxes is well known. Many English-speaking readers are familiar with Behrens, "Nobles, privileges and taxes," and her *Ancien Régime.* I have already referred to Mathias and O'Brien, "Taxation in Britain and France." This thesis has been challenged by Cavanaugh, "Nobles, privileges, and taxes," defended by Behrens in her "Revision defended," and challenged then again by Cavanaugh in his "Reply to Behrens."

22 Janssens, "Zuidnederlandse adel," 455; and his *L'évolution de la noblesse belge*, chap. 2.

23 Janssens, "De achttiende eeuw," 100.

24 Poullet, "Constitutions nationales belges," 187, 215; Janssens, "Zuidnederlandse adel," 453–4; Godding, *Le droit privé*, 55; Janssens, *L'évolution de la noblesse belge*, chap. 2.

25 Janssens, *L'évolution de la noblesse belge*, chap. 2.

26 Hudemann-Simon, *La noblesse luxembourgeoise*, 245–6.

27 Bruchet, *Notice sur l'ancien cadastre de Savoie*, 10–11; Devos, "Un siècle en mutation," 235.

28 Bruchet, *Notice sur l'ancien cadastre de Savoie*, 11–13.

29 Bruchet, "Introduction" to Bruchet, ed., *Les instructions de Victor Amédée*, 13–14.

30 Nicolas, *La Savoie au 18e siècle*, 2:632–3.

31 See below 169–70.

32 Poullet, "Constitutions nationales belges," 187.

33 Janssens, *L'évolution de la noblesse belge*, chap. 2.

34 Armstrong, "Had the Burgundian government a policy for the nobility?" 17.

35 This discussion of ennoblement by the dukes of Burgundy is based on ibid., 18–19; De Win, "Lesser nobility," 105–7; Janssens, *L'évolution de la noblesse belge*, chap. 1; Fourez, *Le droit héraldique*, 51.

36 Armstrong, "Had the Burgundian government a policy for the nobility?" 18–19.

37 Ibid., 19 and n. 2.

38 Lucas, "Ennoblement in late medieval France," 260.

39 Devos, "Un siècle en mutation," 250–1.

40 Janssens, *L'évolution de la noblesse belge*, chap. 3.

41 Ibid., chap. 4.

42 Duerloo, *Privilegies uitbeelden*, 73.

43 Ibid., 34, 68, 74, 92–6.

44 The data for the fourteenth century through to the mid-seventeenth century were collected by Ellery Schalk. See his "Ennoblement in France." Guy Chaussinand-Nogaret has estimated that, altogether, at least 1000 ennoblements by letter patent were handed out in the eighteenth century; this represents an average of about 11.3 per year. See his *La noblesse au XVIIIème siècle*, 46. The reader should be advised that there was considerable yearly variation and the curve is extremely erratic. This is not surprising. The whims of French kings and the political circumstances in which they found themselves determined the patterns in the short run. It is only in the long run that a more regular pattern emerges.

45 Louis XIV, *Mémoires*, 2:377.

46 Meyer, *La noblesse bretonne*, 1:311–12.

47 Mousnier, *Institutions of France*, 1:127.

48 Cubells, "La politique d'anoblissement," 179–81, 190–3, 195, and n. 50.

49 Chaussinand-Nogaret, *La noblesse au XVIIIème siècle*, 34–42.

50 Bloch, *Anoblissement en France*, 99.

51 This paragraph is based on Bluche and Durye, *L'anoblissement par charges*, 1:23–4; 2:17, 39, 41.

52 Meyer, *La noblesse bretonne*, 1:426–9; Chaussinand-Nogaret, *La noblesse au XVIIIème siècle*, 40–6.

53 Bluche and Duyre, *L'anoblissement par charges*, 2:48.

54 Wood, *Nobility of Bayeux*, 63–4.

55 Fourez, *Le droit héraldique*, 60–1; Janssens, "Les charges anoblissantes."

56 Richard, "Les anoblissements dans les Pays-Bas autrichiens," 144–5.

57 Janssens, "Coûts et profits des structures nobiliaires"; see also his *L'évolution de la noblesse belge*, chap. 6.

58 Richard, "Les anoblissements dans les Pays-Bas autrichiens," 121–4. The author says that exemptions were rare, but her figures do not support this conclusion.

59 Chérin, "Discours préliminaire," in his *Abrégé chronologique d'édits*, cols. 36–7; Mousnier, *Institutions of France*, 1:131–2.

60 Arendt and De Ridder, eds., *Législation héraldique*, 149; or see Janssens, "L'esprit mercantiliste," 245.

61 The above is based on Meyer, *La noblesse bretonne*, 1:318–19; Mousnier, *Institutions of France*, 1:128–9.

62 The above is based mostly on Labatut, *Les ducs et pairs*, 52–3.

63 Puy de Clinchamps, *Chevalerie*, 85.

64 Janssens, "Les charges anoblissantes," 236–7.

65 Arendt and De Ridder, eds., *Législation héraldique*, 210; Fourez, *Le droit héraldique*, 297.

66 Fourez, *Le droit héraldique*, 281.

67 Le Roy Ladurie, "Auprès du roi, la cour," 21–4.

68 Mathieu, *Le système héraldique français*, 60.

69 Billacois, *Duel*, 59, 95.

70 Mousnier, *Institutions of France*, 1:142–5.

71 Billacois, *Duel*, 175–6.

72 Ibid., 183.

73 Keen, *Chivalry*, 128–9.

74 This paragraph is based on Mathieu, *Le système héraldique français*, especially 61–63; Keen, *Chivalry*, especially 136–8.

75 Mathieu, *Le système héraldique français*, 63, 70.

76 Ibid., 206–8.

77 The above comes from ibid., 75–89. For legislation see Chérin, ed. *Abrégé chronologique d'édits*, cols. 220–3, 374–5.

78 Mathieu, *Le système héraldique français*, 183–6.

79 Ibid., 187–95.

80 Arendt and De Ridder, eds., *Législation héraldique*, 151.

81 This paragraph is based on Fourez, *Le droit héraldique*, 81, 111, 119, 149, 174, 204–5; Duerloo, *Privilegies uitbeelden*, 141, 246. For legisla-

tion see Arendt and De Ridder, eds., *Législation héraldique*, 148–9, 151, 211.

82 For these and other examples see Fourez, *Le droit héraldique*, especially 81–3, 111, 121; Duerloo, *Privilegies uitbeelden*, 246.

83 Chérin, ed., *Abrégé chronologique d'édits*, cols. 64–5.

84 Ibid., col. 64.

85 Arendt and De Ridder, eds., *Législation héraldique*, 407; Hansotte, *Les institutions*, 120.

86 Arendt and De Ridder, eds., *Législation héraldique*, 148–9; or see Fourez, *Le droit héraldique*, 81–5.

87 Chérin, ed., *Abrégé chronologique d'édits*, cols. 44–6. See also col. 57.

88 Gérard, *Histoire de la législation nobiliaire*, 225–6; Fourez, *Le droit héraldique*, 190–2.

89 Duerloo, *Privilegies uitbeelden*, 99.

90 This paragraph is based primarily on Duerloo, "Groote ongheregelthe-den," 98–102; Duerloo, *Privilegies uitbeelden*, 68, 108; and Janssens, *L'évolution de la noblesse belge*, chap. 3.

91 Esmonin, *La taille en Normandie*, 210; Sturdy, "Tax evasion, the *faux nobles*, and state fiscalism," 556–7.

92 These data have been put together by Jean-Marie Constant from vari-ous studies. See his "Les structures sociales et mentales de l'anoblisse-ment," 44. The figures he provides represent the number of rejected as a percentage of the number accepted, but I have changed them to indicate the rejected as a percentage of the number adjudicated.

93 Esmonin, *La taille en Normandie*, 202, 216–17, 220.

94 Sturdy, "Tax evasion, the *faux nobles*, and state fiscalism," 552.

95 Fourez, *Le droit héraldique*, 140.

96 Arendt and De Ridder, eds., *Législation héraldique*, 247.

97 Ibid., 248. See also Gérard, *Histoire de la législation nobiliaire*, 224–6.

98 Janssens, *L'évolution de la noblesse belge*, chap. 3.

99 Meyer, *La noblesse bretonne*, 1:141–2.

100 Duerloo, "Groote ongheregeltheden," 98–100, 102–3.

101 Janssens, *L'évolution de la noblesse belge*, 93–5, 98–9.

102 Duerloo, *Privilegies uitbeelden*, 96–7, 111.

103 Bluche and Durye, *L'anoblissement par charges*, 1:25–6.

104 Fourez, *Le droit héraldique*, 52; Godding, *Le droit privé*, 53; Duerloo, *Privilegies uitbeelden*, 76–7.

105 Janssens, *L'évolution de la noblesse belge*, chap. 3.

106 Richard, "Les anoblissements dans les Pays-Bas autrichiens," 19–22; Duerloo, *Privilegies uitbeelden*, 77–8.

107 Richard, "Les anoblissements dans les Pays-Bas autrichiens," 13.

108 Gérard, *Histoire de la législation nobiliaire*, 230–50; Fourez, *Le droit héraldique*, 297–8.

109 Nicolas, *La Savoie au 18e siècle*, 1:18–19.

110 Esmonin, *La taille en Normandie*, 200–1.

111 Bloch, *Anoblissement en France*, 48.

112 Meyer, *La noblesse bretonne*, 1:32–3.

113 Fourez, *Le droit héraldique*, 47.

114 Ibid., 271.

115 Duerloo, *Privilegies uitbeelden*, 36.

116 Fourez, *Le droit héraldique*, 139–40.

117 Duerloo, *Privilegies uitbeelden*, 114.

118 Ibid., 115–16.

119 Ibid., 116.

120 Janssens, *L'évolution de la noblesse belge*, chap. 3.

121 Fourez, *Le droit héraldique*, 307–11; Godding, *Le droit privé*, 52–3.

122 Fourez, *Le droit héraldique*, 311–13.

123 Mathieu, *Le système héraldique français*, 80–5.

124 Bluche and Durye, *L'anoblissement par charges*, 2:18.

125 Cubells, "La politique d'anoblissement," 188.

126 This paragraph is based on Arminjon, *De la noblesse des sénateurs*, 11–12, 20; Bluche and Durye, *L'anoblissement par charges*, 2:51.

127 This paragraph is based on Fourez, *Le droit héraldique*, 60, 67–72; Janssens, "Les charges anoblissantes." For decrees of the Privy Council on the subject see Arendt and De Ridder, eds., *Législation héraldique*, 154–5, 159–60.

128 Esmonin, *La taille en Normandie*, 206–7, 216–17.

129 Ibid., 213–14.

130 Esmonin, *La taille en Normandie*, 220–1.

131 For example see Meyer, *La noblesse bretonne*, 1:53–5.

132 Ibid., 1:65; Sturdy, "Tax evasion, the *faux nobles*, and state fiscalism," 556–7, 568–70.

133 Esmonin, *La taille en Normandie*, 217–18.

134 The best work on this subject is Duerloo, *Privilegies uitbeelden*.

135 Ibid., 86.

136 Chérin, "Discours préliminaire," in his *Abrégé chronologique d'édits*.

137 Meyer, *La noblesse bretonne*, 1:72, 107, 165.

138 Constant, "Nobles et paysans en Beauce," 45–67.

139 Chaussinand-Nogaret, *La noblesse au XVIIIème siècle*, 96–7; Ellis, "Genealogy, history and aristocratic reaction," 430–1 and n. 73; Cubells, "La politique d'anoblissement," 194–6; Schalk, *Valor to Pedigree*, 132–3; see also Motley, *Becoming a French Aristocrat*, for a good analysis of the education of young members of the *noblesse d'épée*.

140 Schalk, *Valor to Pedigree*, especially xiv–xv and chap. 1.

141 Boulle, "François Bernier." See also Jouanna, "L'idée de race."

142 Arendt and De Ridder, eds., *Législation héraldique*, 140; Janssens, *L'évolution de la noblesse belge*, chap. 1.

143 Weber, *Economy and Society*, 2:932.

144 Parkin, *Max Weber*, 97–8.

145 Bush, *European Nobility*, 2: *Rich Noble, Poor Noble*, especially chap. 1.

146 Richard, *Noblesse d'affaires*, 65–6; Meyer, *La noblesse bretonne*, 1:111–12.

147 Janssens, *L'évolution de la noblesse belge*, chap. 2.

148 Ibid., chap. 6; Demoulin, "La réaction de la noblesse," 87; De Win, "Lesser nobility," 107; Hudemann-Simon, *La noblesse luxembourgeoise*, 46, 50; Richard, "Les anoblissements dans les Pays-Bas autrichiens," 124–5, 179.

149 Dewald, *Formation: Magistrates of Rouen*, 119, 130, 160–1, 219–20.

150 Ibid., 15, 102, 109–10; Wood, *Nobility of Bayeux*, 76–7.

151 Lougee, *Paradis de Femmes*, 125.

152 Dewald, *Aristoratic Experience*, 22–3.

153 Mettam, *Power and Faction*, 56–7.

154 Motley, *Becoming a French Aristocrat*, 11.

155 Devos, "Elite et culture."

156 Dewald, *Pont-St-Pierre*, 189–92 and n. 113.

157 Bonenfant and Despy, "Noblesse en Brabant," 42, 58–60; Warlop, *Flemish Nobility*, 1:104, 333; Evergates, *Feudal Society*, 127, 135; Fossier, *Terre et hommes en Picardie*, 2:536–41; Contamine, "Introduction," 20, 25–6; Hunt, "Emergence of the knight"; Van Winter, "Knighthood and nobility," 87–92; Keen, *Chivalry*, 152.

158 Duby, *Chivalrous Society*, 146–7.

159 Arendt and De Ridder, eds., *Législation héraldique*, 139.

160 Louis XIV, *Mémoires*, 2:544.

161 Otway-Ruthven, *History of Medieval Ireland*, 144–5, 168–9; Lydon, *Ireland in the Later Middle Ages*, 28–9.

162 Rosenthal, *Nobles and the Noble Life*, 27–8.

163 Powell and Wallis, *House of Lords*, 470–1.

164 Lydon, *Ireland in the Later Middle Ages*, 32; Richardson and Sayles, *Irish Parliament*, 99.

165 Powell and Wallis, *House of Lords*, 328–9, 448–9, 470–1.

166 Ibid., 527.

167 This is contrary to my usage of the word "aristocracy." See terms and concepts.

168 Powell and Wallis, *House of Lords*, 300, 423–6, 448–9, 527–8.

169 Janssens, "Densité nobiliaire"; Dauvergne, "Problème du nombre"; Meyer, "Noblesse française."

170 Thompson, "Social distribution of landed property," 509.

171 Mayes, "Sale of peerages"; and his "Early Stuarts."

172 James, "Active Irish peers," 55. The "inactive peers" included a small number of Catholic peers.

173 Duncan, "Early parliaments," 42.

174 The above is based on Grant, "Development of Scottish peerage," especially 18–24.

175 Grant, *New History*, 3: *Independence and Nationhood*, 124–5.

176 O'Brien, "Scottish parliament," 70–80.

177 Terry, *Scottish Parliament*, 22–3.

178 Cooper, "Differences," 78.

179 Cannon, *Aristocratic Century*, 54–5.

180 Baldwin, *Sumptuary Legislation*, especially 249; Wormald, *Lords and Men*, 98–9.

181 Pugh and Ross, "English baronage"; Miller, "Subsidy assessments."

182 Whitelock, *Pelican History*, 2: *Beginnings of English Society*, 85–6; Mack, "Changing thegns," 378–9.

183 McFarlane, *Nobility of Later Medieval England*, 142.

184 Smith, *Commonwealth*, 66, cited in Beckett, *Aristocracy in England*, 18; Chamberlayne, *Magna Britannia notitia*, 166–72.

185 Labatut, *Les noblesses européenes*, chap. 3.

186 Beckett, *Aristocracy in England*, 19–20.

187 The literature is too vast to be cited. The critical initial publications were Tawney, "Rise of the gentry, 1558–1640," Stone, "Anatomy of the Elizabethan aristocracy," Trevor-Roper, "Elizabethan aristocracy," Stone, "Elizabethan aristocracy," Trevor-Roper, "Gentry," and Tawney, "Rise of the gentry: a postscript."

188 Davies, *Conquest, Coexistence, and Change*, 68, 115–17; and his *Lordship and Society*, 354–7.

189 Davies, *Conquest, Coexistence, and Change*, 117–18; Williams, *Recovery, Reorientation and Reformation*, 95–7.

190 Davies, *Conquest, Coexistence, and Change*, 121–2.

191 Jones, "Gentry," 10–12; Jones, *Modern Wales*, 7, 66.

192 Howells, "Crosswood estate," 10, 15–21; Howell, "Landlords," 254–7.

193 Pierce, "Landlords in Wales"; Williams, *Recovery, Reorientation and Reformation*, 96–8.

194 In addition to the above sources this and the preceding paragraph are based on Lloyd, *Gentry*, chap. 1; Jones, "Gentry," 10–15.

195 Grant, "Development of Scottish peerage," 1–2.

196 Wormald, "Lords and lairds."

197 Shaw, *Northern and Western Islands*, 43–6.

198 Smout, *History of the Scottish People*, 42–3.

199 The displacement of "udal" landholding by feudal tenure in the Northern Isles is described in Shaw, *Northern and Western Islands*, 34, 37–42.

200 Sanderson, *Scottish Rural Society*, 131–3, 188–9.

201 Wormald, "Lords and lairds," 196.
202 MacNiocaill, *Ireland before the Vikings*, 31–2, 41–3, 60–5; 68–9; O'Corrain, *Ireland before the Normans*, 42–3.
203 McCarthy, "Ulster Office," 5, 177–8, 191–9.
204 James, "Active Irish peers," 60; James, *Lords of the Ascendancy*, chap. 1.
205 Clarke, "The Irish economy," 169–70.
206 Innes of Learney, *Scots Heraldry*, 13–14.
207 Ibid., 11; Adam, *Clans, Septs and Regiments*, 158.
208 This paragraph is based on Wagner, *Heralds of England*, 6, 17, 19–20, 30, 36, 39, 67–8, 186; Squibb, *High Court of Chivalry*, 16–17, 29–33; Wagner *Heralds and Heraldry*, 56–64.
209 Wagner, *Heralds of England*, 274–6, 302–3, 365–6.
210 Innes of Learney, *Scots Heraldry*, 22–4.
211 Wagner, *Heralds and Heraldry*, 11, 78–9; Wagner, *Heralds of England*, 35.
212 Innes of Learney, *Scots Heraldry*, 20–1, 85–8.
213 The following paragraphs are based mostly on McCarthy, "Ulster Office."
214 Ibid., 4, 8–9, 37.
215 Ibid., 208.
216 Ibid., 208–9.
217 For examples of many of these forms of status-seeking in Wales see Howell, *Patriarchs and Parasites*, 171; Jenkins, *Making of a Ruling Class*, 22, 27, 197–9, 201.
218 McCahill, "Peerage creations," 277.
219 Bush, *European Nobility*, 2: *Rich Noble, Poor Noble*, 4.
220 Janssens, *L'évolution de la noblesse belge*, chap. 6 and conclusion.
221 Baldwin, *Sumptuary Legislation*, especially chaps. 5–6.
222 Bruchet, *Notice sur l'ancien cadastre de Savoie*, 58.
223 Victor Amadeus II, *Instructions*, 19.

CHAPTER SIX

1 Asselain, *Histoire économique: De l'ancien régime à la Première Guerre mondiale*, 30.
2 Nicolas, *La Savoie au 18e siècle*, 1:139–40.
3 Delatte, *La vente des biens nationaux*, 21–2; and his *Les classes rurales*, 70; Van Buyten, "Grondbezit en Grondwaarde in Brabant," 103.
4 Again see terms and concepts for definitions of contractual tenure and other terms.
5 For example, see Bettey, "Land tenure and manorial custom in Dorset," 42–3.
6 Dewald, *Pont-St-Pierre*, 57–8; Root, *Peasants and King in Burgundy*, 171–2; De Rammelaere, "Bijdrage tot te landbouwgeschiedenis."

7 Clay, "Landlords and estate management," 199.

8 Watts, "Tenant-right."

9 Crawford, "Landlord-tenant relations in Ulster," 20.

10 Ibid., 7, 10, 20.

11 This paragraph is based largely on Whyte, *Agriculture and Society*, especially chap. 1; Smout, *History of the Scottish People*, chaps. 6 and 12.

12 This paragraph is based on a number of sources, but especially Cregeen, "Tacksmen," and Smout, *History of the Scottish People*, 128–9, 141, 316, 318, 330, 336.

13 Forster, *Nobility of Toulouse*, chaps. 2 and 3; and his "Provincial noble," especially 683–91.

14 Nicolas, *La Savoie au 18e siècle*, 1:311.

15 Ibid., 1:45.

16 Jacquart, "French agriculture," 167–8.

17 Young, *Travels in France*, 296.

18 Mingay, *Gentry*, 107; Richard, *Noblesse d'affaires*, 17.

19 Forster, "Provincial noble," 687.

20 Le Goff, *Vannes*, 67.

21 Smout, "Scottish landowners," 220; Mingay, *Gentry*, 83–4, 95–7.

22 See, for example, the letters of Daniel Eaton, who was an agent of the Third Earl of Cardigan. They reveal the role that the earl played in the management of his estates.

23 Forster, "Provincial noble," 686.

24 Clay, "Landlords and estate management," 206.

25 Ibid., 214–24.

26 Smout, *History of the Scottish People*, especially 271–81.

27 Mokyr, *Why Ireland Starved*, especially 188–91, 210.

28 Maxwell, *Country and Town in Ireland*, 196–7; Beckett, *Anglo-Irish Tradition*, 75–6; Cullen, *Economic History*, 82–3; Cullen, *Emergence of Modern Ireland*, 47–51, 61–2; Power, *Land, Politics, and Society*, 35, 51, 53–4, 60, 169–72, but see also 173.

29 Malcomson, "Absenteeism in eighteenth century Ireland," 22–3.

30 *An Address to the Noblemen and Other Landed Proprietors of Ireland*, 50.

31 Pirotte, *Terre de Durbuy*, 86.

32 Dewald, *Pont-St-Pierre*, 362.

33 Habakkuk, "England," 5; Mingay, *Gentry*, 99–103.

34 The above is from Smout, "Scottish landowners," 220–1.

35 Watelet, *Industrialization sans développement*, 85.

36 The preceding is from Richard, *Noblesse d'affaires*, 185–7.

37 Large, "Wealth of Irish landowners," 2; Cullen, *Emergence of Modern Ireland*, 42; Power, *Land, Politics, and Society*, 51.

38 Taylor, "Non-capitalist wealth," 473.

39 Mingay, *Gentry*, 82.

40 On Lawless see Large, "Wealth of Irish landowners," 29–30.

41 Dewald, *Formation: Magistrates of Rouen*, 167, 208.

42 Mingay, *Gentry*, 90–1.

43 Slicher van Bath, "The rise of intensive husbandry in the Low Countries."

44 Kerridge, *Agricultural Revolution*, 155, 159–60, 208, 212, 330–1; Morineau, *Les faux-semblants*, 73, 76–9, 82, 84; Crouzet, *De la supériorité de l'Angleterre sur la France*, 76 and n.125; Cooper, "In search of agrarian capitalism," 141–2.

45 Morineau, *Les faux-semblants*, 73, 76–9, 82, 84.

46 Large, "Wealth of Irish landowners," 27. This figure does not include commissions that had been bought.

47 Roebuck, "Making of an Ulster great estate."

48 For example, see Howell, *Patriarchs and Parasites*, 34–5.

49 Degryse, "Stadsadel," 471.

50 The income is mentioned in Buttin, "Le Souverain Sénat de Savoie," 6.

51 Nicolas, *La Savoie au 18e siècle*, 1:247.

52 Hudemann-Simon, *La noblesse luxembourgeoise*, 118–19.

53 Ibid., 120–1.

54 Bucholz, *Augustan Court*, 23, 126–33, 137–40, 143–4, 149–51.

55 *Problems of a Growing City*, v; Beckett, *Anglo-Irish Tradition*, 71–2.

56 Dessert, *Argent, pouvoir et société*, chap. 15.

57 Zeller, "Une notion: la dérogeance," 341–2.

58 Cullen, *Emergence of Modern Ireland*, 125–8.

59 Devos, "Un siècle en mutation, 1536–1684," 242.

60 Zeller, "Une notion: la dérogeance," 338–68; Richard, *Noblesse d'affaires*, 62–4; Chaussinand-Nogaret, *La noblesse au XVIIIe siècle*, 128–9.

61 Arendt and De Ridder, eds., *Législation héraldique*, 182–3, 202–5; Janssens, "Zuidnederlandse adel," 460–1; Hudemann-Simon, *La noblesse luxembourgeoise*, 18–19; Richard, "Les anoblissements dans les Pays-Bas autrichiens," 126–7.

62 Richard, "Les anoblissements dans les Pays-Bas autrichiens," 128–30, 144–5; Janssens, *L'évolution de la noblesse belge*, chaps. 6, 8.

63 Richard, *Noblesse d'affaires*, 54–62; Grassby, "Social status," 21–3.

64 Bacon, *Réflexions sur l'état présent du commerce*, 93–4.

65 Zeller, "Une notion: la dérogeance," 337–8.

66 Ibid., 338 n. 1.

67 Chérin, ed., *Abrégé chronologique d'édits*, col. 45; Zeller, "Une notion: la dérogeance," 340.

68 Zeller, "Une notion: la dérogeance," 368.

69 Janssens, "L'esprit mercantiliste," 246.

70 Ibid., 249–50.

71 Ibid., 249; Arendt and De Ridder, eds., *Législation héraldique*, 166–7.

72 Arendt and De Ridder, eds., *Législation héraldique*, 183; Richard, "Les anoblissements dans les Pays-Bas autrichiens," 126; Hudemann-Simon, *La noblesse luxembourgeoise*, 18–19.

73 Janssens, "L'esprit mercantiliste," 254–5.

74 Hudemann-Simon, *La noblesse luxembourgeoise*, 46, 92; Devos, "Un siècle en mutation, 1536–1684," 238; Smout, "Scottish landowners."

75 Richard, *Noblesse d'affaires*, 121, 123–9, 130–6, 148–84, 187, 190–6, 244; Mingay, *Gentry*, 106–7.

76 Richard, *Noblesse d'affaires*, 243.

77 Ibid., 34–6, 238–9.

78 Adams, "Corps of noblesse of Provence," 247–8, 250–2.

79 Nicolas, *La Savoie au 18e siècle*, 1:285, 288–9; Graham, *Social Life of Scotland*, 165.

80 Smout, "Scottish landowners," 228–9.

81 Cullen, "Landlords, bankers and merchants," especially 31–5.

82 Bush, *European Nobility, 2: Rich Noble, Poor Noble*, 149.

83 Beik, *Absolutism in Languedoc*, chap. 11; Hudemann-Simon, *La noblesse luxembourgeoise*, 92.

84 Bonney, *King's Debts*, 18.

85 Durand, *Les fermiers généraux*, 296–301.

86 Richard, *Noblesse d'affaires*, 47–8, 228–9; Chaussinand-Nogaret, *La noblesse au XVIIIe siècle*, 129–30.

87 Mingay, *Gentry*, 105. The estimate was made by T.K. Rabb.

88 Richard, *Noblesse d'affaires*, 197–8, 201–10, 243–4.

89 Smout, "Scottish landowners," 229–30.

90 Ibid., 226–7.

91 Green, *Lagan Valley*, 65–7.

92 Cullen, *Economic History*, 82–3; Mingay, *Gentry*, 99–103; Green, *Lagan Valley*, 35.

93 Goubert, *Beauvais et le Beauvaisis*, 212.

94 Wood, *Nobility of Bayeux*, 122–3.

95 Nicolas, *La Savoie au 18e siècle*, 1:278, 305.

96 Ibid., 1:149.

97 Meyer, *La noblesse bretonne*, 1:21–3.

98 Goubert, *Beauvais et le Beauvaisis*, 213.

99 Nicolas, *La Savoie au 18e siècle*, 1:311.

100 Ibid., 2:787.

101 Beckett, *Aristocracy in England*, 288.

102 Thompson, "Social distribution of landed property," 477.

103 Habakkuk, "English landownership"; Clay, "Marriage, inheritance, and the rise of large estates"; Beckett, "English landownership."

104 Mingay, *Gentry*, 13–14; Chaussinand-Nogaret, *La noblesse au XVIIIème siècle*, 77–8. Mingay estimated income for the seventeenth and nine-

teenth centuries, but I have converted his figures into estimates for the eighteenth century by splitting the differences.

105 Forster, "Survival of the nobility," 71. The estimate was made by C.E. Labrousse.

106 Asselain, *Histoire économique: De l'ancien régime à la Première Guerre mondiale*, 30.

107 Delatte, *La vente des biens nationaux*, 21–2; and his *Les classes rurales*, 70; Van Buyten, "Grondbezit en Grondwaarde in Brabant," 103; Ruwet, *L'agriculture et les classes rurales*, 226; Nicolas, *La Savoie au 18e siècle*, 1:156. The data for Savoy are based on a survey of lands exempted from the taille on account of noble status; the percentage actually refers to the percentage of net revenue from the land.

108 Thompson, "Social distribution of landed property."

109 Spring, "Landed elites compared," 2–3.

110 *Summary of the Returns of Owners of Land in Ireland*, 25.

111 Dessert, *Argent, pouvoir et société*, chap. 14.

112 Bosher, *French Finances*, 73–6.

113 Howell, *Patriarchs and Parasites*, 8–9.

114 Marion, *Dictionnaire des institutions*, 13; Forster, *Nobility of Toulouse*, 121; Meyer, *La noblesse bretonne*, 113; Dewald, *Formation: Magistrates of Rouen*, 249.

115 Beckett, *Aristocracy in England*, 23.

116 Grassby, "Social status."

117 Ibid., 27.

118 This paragraph is based mainly on Asselain, *Histoire économique: De l'ancien régime à la Première Guerre mondiale*, 36; Bourde *Influence on the French Agronomes*, 12–13, 18–21, 99, 200–9; Fox-Genovese, *Origins of Physiocracy*, 50–1.

119 The above is based on Bourde, *Influence on the French Agronomes*, 6–7, 13–24, 42–7, 54–4, 68–9, 102–33, 191–2, 194; Fox-Genovese, *Origins of Physiocracy*, 9, 53–7.

120 Mitchison, "Patriotism and national identity."

121 Fox-Genovese, *Origins of Physiocracy*, 14–16.

122 Ibid., 45–6, 57, 304–5.

123 Briggs, *Early Modern France*, 68–9.

124 Ibid., 70.

125 Woronoff, *L'industrie sidérurgique*, 15–17.

126 Briggs, *Early Modern France*, 72.

127 Barberis, "Continuité aristocratique," 361–2, 380, 383–4.

128 Bruchet, *La cour de Turin*, 19; Barberis, "Continuité aristocratique," 367, 386.

129 Nicolas, *La Savoie au 18e siècle*, 1:46.

130 Dewald, *Formation: Magistrates of Rouen*, 123; Buttin, "Le Souverain Sénat de Savoie," 6.

131 Dessert, *Argent, pouvoir et société*, 343, 355–8.
132 Ibid., conclusion.

CHAPTER SEVEN

1 Perret, *Les institutions dans l'ancienne Savoie*, 26.
2 Finer, "State-building," 87–8.
3 Bordes, *L'administration provinciale et municipale*, 23–5.
4 Kettering, *Patrons, Brokers, and Clients*, 141.
5 Contamine, "De la puissance aux privilèges," 254–5.
6 Bérenger, "Noblesse et absolutisme," 16–17.
7 Labatut, *Les ducs et pairs*, 52–3, 58.
8 Ibid., part 1, book 1. As in chapter 5, what I say about the dukes and peers has come from several sources, but primarily this work.
9 Ranum, "Richelieu and the great nobility," 199–202.
10 Kettering, *Patrons, Brokers, and Clients*, 6, 236.
11 Ibid., 85–97, 142–3, 175–9, 221–2; Dent, "Role of clientèles," 44–9.
12 Lachmann, "Elite conflict," 146.
13 Mettam, *Power and Faction*, 82–4.
14 Solnon, *La cour de France*, 355.
15 Van Kley, *Damiens Affair*, 60.
16 Sieyès, *Qu'est-ce que le tiers état?* 36.
17 Bérenger, "Noblesse et absolutisme," 14–17; Solnon, *La cour de France*, 354.
18 Wolf, *Louis XIV*, 270.
19 Mettam, *Power and Faction*, 93.
20 Solnon, *La cour de France*, 353.
21 Mettam, *Power and Faction*, 94–5.
22 Cobban, *History of Modern France*, 1:21–2.
23 Bluche, "L'origine sociale du personnel ministériel," 10.
24 Kettering, *Patrons, Brokers, and Clients*, 7, 142.
25 For example, see Nicolas, *La Savoie au 18e siècle*, 2:789.
26 Dawson, "Institutional and sociological study of French intendants," 299–300.
27 Gruder, *Royal Provincial Intendants*, 117–18.
28 Bluche, *Les magistrats du Parlement de Paris*, 47.
29 Dewald, *Formation: Magistrates of Rouen*, 78.
30 Doyle, *Parlement of Bordeaux*, 19.
31 Wood, *Nobility of Bayeux*, 74–5.
32 Van Creveld, *Technology and War*, 99–109.
33 Bérenger, "Noblesse et absolutisme," 21.
34 Bien, "La réaction aristocratique," 25.
35 Constant, "Nobles et paysans en Beauce," 158–9.

36 Ibid., 158–61.

37 Wood, *Nobility of Bayeux*, 89–91.

38 Corvisier, *Armies and Societies*, 102.

39 Bien, "La réaction aristocratique," 35–6.

40 Moote, *Revolt of the Judges*, especially 223–7.

41 Bluche, *Les magistrats du Parlement de Paris*, 48.

42 Doyle, *Parlement of Bordeaux*, 19–20.

43 Chérin, ed., *Abrégé chronologique d'édits*, cols. 364–9; Bluche and Duyre, *L'anoblissement par charges*, 2:41.

44 Kettering, *Patrons, Brokers, and Clients*, 142.

45 Dawson, "Institutional and sociological study of French intendants," 299; Gruder, *Royal Provincial Intendants*, 17–18.

46 Ibid., 387. Figures add to more than 100 per cent because many fathers held more than one position.

47 Gruder, *Royal Provincial Intendants*, 120.

48 Mousnier, *Institutions of France*, 2:529, 547.

49 Bluche, "L'origine sociale du personnel ministériel," 10–11.

50 Bordes, *L'administration provinciale et municipale*, 122–5.

51 For a version of the second view see Mettam, *Power and Faction*, especially 211–16.

52 Beik, *Absolutism in Languedoc*, 245–302.

53 Bordes, *L'administration provinciale et municipale*, 149–50.

54 Ibid., 107.

55 Ibid., 155.

56 Beik, *Absolutism in Languedoc*, 78.

57 Ibid., 308–10.

58 Cobban, *History of Modern France*, 1:67.

59 Frotier de la Messelière, *La noblesse en Bretagne*, 44; Bordes, *L'administration provinciale et municipale*, 67–115; Meyer, *La noblesse bretonne*, 76–9, 83–6, Bossenga, *Politics of Privilege*, 18, 24.

60 Meyer, *La noblesse bretonne*, 1:84–6.

61 Bordes, *L'administration provinciale et municipale*, 79–81, 110–11; Beik, *Absolutism in Languedoc*, 46, 121–3.

62 Bordes, *L'administration provinciale et municipale*, 139–40.

63 Wolf, *Louis XIV*, 177.

64 Bordes, *L'administration provinciale et municipale*, 102.

65 Bossenga, *Politics of Privilege*, especially chaps. 1–3, 7.

66 Kettering, *Patrons, Brokers, and Clients*, 5–6, 70–2, 99, 134, 142, 159, 232–7.

67 Hickey, *Coming of French Absolutism*, especially 187–8.

68 Beik, *Absolutism in Languedoc*, 144, 150–4, 177, 245–69, 308–12, 314–16.

69 Bordes, *L'administration provinciale et municipale*, 138. See above 40.

70 Ibid., 80. For Walloon Flanders see Bossenga, *Politics of Privilege*, especially 18, 24, 71–3, 77–85.

71 Beik, *Absolutism in Languedoc*, 122–37.

72 Ibid., 46–7.

73 Frotier de la Messelière, *La noblesse en Bretagne*, 49–50, 56.

74 Frotier de la Messelière, *La noblesse en Bretagne*, 57–9; Meyer, *La noblesse bretonne*, 1:83–7, 98; and Meyer, "Le siècle de l'intendance," 345–52.

75 This paragraph is based primarily on Bordes, *L'administration provinciale et municipale*, 19, 65, 124.

76 Frotier de la Messelière, *La noblesse en Bretagne*, 52–3.

77 Bossenga, *Politics of Privilege*, especially 1–2, 18, 38, 84.

78 Dreyfus, *Histoire de l'Alsace*, 162.

79 The preceding two paragraphs are based largely on ibid., 148–62.

80 Mettam, *Power and Faction*, 11.

81 Ibid., 29–31.

82 Ibid., 38–9.

83 Janssens, "L'échec des tentatives de soulèvement aux Pays-Bas sous Philippe IV," 18; and his "Zuidnederlandse adel," 445–9.

84 Van Uytven, "De Brabantse adel," 87.

85 Janssens, "L'échec des tentatives de soulèvement aux Pays-Bas sous Philippe IV," 8; and his "Zuidnederlandse adel," 462.

86 Born in 1696, he was of Portuguese ancestry. His father had served for the Portuguese government in the Austrian Low Countries and he himself had been working in the Austrian administration in the Low Countries when he was promoted by Maria Theresa.

87 He was born in London when his father was the Austrian ambassador there. After he served as ambassador to France, he was in the Habsburg administration in Vienna until he was sent to the Low Countries.

88 Poullet, "Constitutions nationales belges," 241–3; Janssens, "Zuidnederlandse adel," 462; Janssens, *L'évolution de la noblesse belge*, chap. 2.

89 Mortier and Hasquin, eds., *Etudes sur le XVIIIe siècle*, no. 12: *Une famille noble de hauts fonctionnaires: les Neny*.

90 Janssens, "L'échec des tentatives de soulèvement aux Pays-Bas sous Philippe IV," 19.

91 Janssens, "Zuidnederlandse adel," 462; his *L'évolution de la noblesse belge*, chap. 2, and sources he cites.

92 Lefevre, "La haute magistrature," 944–8; Douxchamps-Lefèvre, *Procureurs généraux*, 211–12; Janssens, "Zuidnederlandse adel," 462, and sources he cites.

93 Lefevre, "La haute magistrature," 950.

94 Poullet, "Constitutions nationales belges," 6; Dhondt and Fredericq-Lilar, "Flandre orientale," 121–2.

95 Gilissen, *Le régime répresentatif avant 1790*, 95–6.

96 For a list of these and other rights see Poullet, "Constitutions natio-nales belges," 160–4.

97 Van Uytven and Blockmans, "Constitutions and their application," 405; Janssens, *L'évolution de la noblesse belge*, chap. 2.

98 Gilissen, *Le régime répresentatif avant 1790*, 92–3.

99 This paragraph is based on Janssens, *L'évolution de la noblesse belge*, chap. 2; Poullet, "Constitutions nationales belges," 142–3.

100 This paragraph is based primarily on Van Geystelen, "Voorouders: adel in het Habsburgse officierencorps," 337, 341–8, 351–2, 387–8, 390, 392–4.

101 The preceding two paragraphs are based on Harsin, *La Révolution lié-geoise*, 18–19; Gilissen, *Le régime répresentatif avant 1790*, 120–1; Demou-lin, "La réaction de la noblesse"; Poullet, "Constitutions nationales belges," 22–5, 77–84, 168–76, 255; Hansotte, *Les institutions*.

102 Genicot, *Histoire de Wallonie*, 296–7.

103 Poullet, "Constitutions nationales belges," 84.

104 Demoulin, "La réaction de la noblesse," 92–3.

105 Poullet, "Constitutions nationales belges," 218–19; Harsin, *La révolution liégeoise*, 18; Demoulin, "La réaction de la noblesse," 90–1, 100–1; Hansotte, *Les institutions*, 120–2.

106 Demoulin, "La réaction de la noblesse," 96 n. 47.

107 Cordey, *Les comtes de Savoie*, 12–13.

108 Symcox, "Development of absolutism in the Savoyard state," 157–9; Chevailler, "Emmanuel-Philibert," 61, 66, 69.

109 Chevailler, "Emmanuel-Philibert," 59.

110 Nicolas, *La Savoie au 18e siècle*, 2:601–2, 607.

111 Ibid., 1:240.

112 Ibid., 2:600–1.

113 Ibid., 2:603.

114 Ibid., 1:44–5, 236–8.

115 See ibid., 45, 226–36, for a good discussion of Savoyard nobles in European armies.

116 Ibid., 1:45, 227.

117 Nicolas, *La Savoie au 18e siècle*, 2:603–5.

118 Ibid., 2:611–12; Symcox, *Victor Amadeus II*, 34, 57–8, 121–2, 192–3; Buttin, "Le Souverain Sénat de Savoie," 26.

119 See letters of state officials printed in Bruchet, ed., *L'abolition des droits seigneuriaux*.

120 Nicolas, *La Savoie au 18e siècle*, 1:30.

121 Symcox, *Victor Amadeus II*, 57, 121, 191–2.

122 Dewald, *Pont-St-Pierre*, 21–12, 282, 284.

123 Rosenberg, *Negotiated World*, 7, 18, 41–2.

124 Nicolas, *La Savoie au 18e siècle*, 1:15–16.

125 Rosenberg, *Negotiated World,* especially 16–17, 40–1.

126 Cameron, *Reformation of the Heretics,* 12–13, 18–22, 37–8, 41, 260–2.

127 Brustein, "Regional social orders," 149–57.

128 Bordes, *L'administration provinciale et municipale,* 176–8.

129 Ibid., 188, 193.

130 Delatte, *Les classes rurales,* 216–23; Vandewalle, "Heerlijkheden," 376–7; Nicolas, *La Savoie au 18e siècle,* 1:190–1, 199–200; Dewald, *Pont-St-Pierre,* 216, 251–63, 267.

131 Goubert, *Ancien Régime,* 84.

132 See, for example, Dewald, *Pont-St-Pierre,* 251–63.

133 See, for example, ibid., 211–12.

134 Symcox, *Victor Amadeus II,* 191–2.

135 Verriest, *Le régime seigneurial dans le Comté de Hainaut,* 91; Deprez, "Evolution économique et mouvements paysans," 59; Verhaegen, *La Belgique sous la domination française,* 2:488.

136 Dawson, "Institutional and sociological study of French intendants," 127–8, 136–8.

137 Bastier, *La féodalité,* 47.

138 Mettam, *Power and Faction,* 216.

139 Dawson, "Institutional and sociological study of French intendants," 132–3, 140–1, 189, 196–9.

140 Ibid., 188–90.

141 Wood, *Nobility of Bayeux,* 118.

142 Bossenga, *Politics of Privilege,* chap. 4; Hickey, *Coming of French Absolutism,* especially 187.

143 Dewald, *Aristocratic Experience,* introduction and chaps. 1, 3, 6, and conclusion.

144 Markoff and Shapiro, "Consensus and conflict," 38–9. See Doyle, *Origins of the French Revolution,* especially chap. 6 for the view that the French nobility struggled with one another during the Revolution of 1789.

145 Hudemann-Simon, *La noblesse luxembourgeoise,* 111–29.

146 Demoulin, "La réaction de la noblesse."

147 Doyle, *Parlement of Bordeaux,* 294–5.

148 I refer here to the Dhondt-Blockmans thesis. See above 71.

149 Ranum, "Courtesy, absolutism, and the rise of the French state."

150 Ibid.; Kettering, *Patrons, Brokers, and Clients,* 57–8.

151 Jackson, "Peers of France."

152 Constant, "Nobles et paysans en Beauce," 169, 176–7; Van Geystelen, "Voorouders: Adel in het Habsburgse officierencorps," 389–90; Dewald, *Aristocratic Experience,* 61.

153 Dawson, "Institutional and sociological study of French intendants," 122–3.

154 Chibnall, *Anglo-Norman England*, 167; Hyams, *Kings, Lords and Peasants*, 137–8.

155 Painter, *Studies in English Feudal Barony*, 135.

156 Hyams, *Kings, Lords and Peasants*, 54–5.

157 Ibid., 151–60.

158 Lander, "Attainder and forfeiture."

159 Powell and Wallis, *House of Lords*, xvi, 162.

160 Ibid., 168, 172–3, 184–200.

161 Lachmann, "Elite conflict."

162 Stone, *Crisis of the Aristocracy*, 124.

163 McCahill, "Tudor peers," 199–204.

164 Miller, *Henry VIII and the English Nobility*, 56–7, 74–5.

165 Bush, *English Aristocracy*, 104.

166 Stone, *Crisis of the Aristocracy*, 123–4.

167 All of the above data come from McCahill, "Tudor peers," 183, 193, 218–19, 230–43.

168 Elton, *Reform and Reformation*, 262–70; Guy, *Tudor England*, 149–53.

169 Guy, *Tudor England*, 273–5.

170 Bush, "Problem of the far North," 60–1.

171 See ibid., and for an alternative argument, James, *Change and Continuity*.

172 Bush, "Problem of the far North," 45.

173 A list of wardens and councillors can be found in Reid, *The King's Council in the North*, 485–98.

174 Grant, *New History, 3: Independence and Nationhood*, 143.

175 Ibid., 171–2, 196–9; Wormald [Brown], "Exercise of power," 39–45, 50–4.

176 Grant, *New History, 3: Independence and Nationhood*, 198–9.

177 These two paragraphs are based mostly on Wormald [Brown], "Exercise of power," and Grant, *New History, 3: Independence and Nationhood*, especially chap. 7.

178 James VI, *The Basilicon Doron*, 85. This is the advice he gave to his son in the second book of *The Basilicon Doron*.

179 Shaw, "Landownership in the Western Isles," 35.

180 Whetstone, *Scottish County Government*, 27.

181 Ibid.

182 Smout, *History of the Scottish People*, 105.

183 Cregeen, "Changing role of the House of Argyll," 5.

184 Wormald, *Lords and Men*, 82–3, 102.

185 Cregeen, "Changing role of the House of Argyll," 5.

186 Mitchison, *New History, 5: Lordship to Patronage*, 15–16.

187 Murdoch, 'People Above,' 7–8, 133–4.

188 Ellis, *Tudor Ireland*, 130.

189 Ibid., 177.

190 This paragraph is based on Davies, *Conquest, Coexistence, and Change*, 355–6, 358–63.
191 Howell, *Patriarchs and Parasites*, 121.
192 Starkey, "Intimacy and innovation"; Cuddy, "Revival of entourage"; Beattie, *English Court*, 217.
193 Starkey, "Introduction," 6–7, 21.
194 Miller, *Henry VIII and the English Nobility*, 83–4, 202–3, 246, 253, 255.
195 Brooke, *King George III*, 466.
196 Plumb, *Sir Robert Walpole*, 76.
197 Beattie, *English Court*, 219–42.
198 Bucholz, *Augustan Court*, 168–9, 179–81.
199 Beattie, *English Court*, 249–55.
200 Starkey, "Introduction," 24.
201 Beattie, *English Court*, 14–15; see also Bucholz, *Augustan Court*, 113–14, 187, 247.
202 Bucholz, *Augustan Court*, 247.
203 Most of what I say about the British royal court from the Restoration until the death of Queen Anne is based on Bucholz, *Augustan Court*.
204 Ibid., 12–22.
205 Ibid., 46–51.
206 Ibid., 52–5, 57–63.
207 Beattie, *English Court*, 18.
208 Ibid., 9.
209 Brooke, *King George III*, 336–49.
210 Bucholz, *Augustan Court*, especially 188–201, and sources he cites.
211 Miller, *Henry VIII and the English Nobility*, 113, 132.
212 Cannon, *Aristocratic Century*, 117.
213 Beckett, *Aristocracy in England*, 407.
214 Kelch, "Dukes," 157.
215 Cannon, *Aristocratic Century*, 116.
216 Ibid., 116–17.
217 Doubts were raised in my own mind by Roger Manning, Louis Cullen, and John Cannon.
218 Razzell, "Social origins of officers," 249.
219 Ibid., 253.
220 Cannon, *Aristocratic Century*, 120.
221 Ibid., 120.
222 Hayes, "Lieutenant-colonel and major-commandants," 12.
223 *Dictionary of National Biography*, vols. 1,3,7, and 10.
224 See above 245 and 262.
225 Roger Manning is currently engaged in a major research project on the role of British gentry in the armed services.

226 On the militarism of the British aristocracy in the late eighteenth and early nineteenth centuries see Colley, *Britons*, chap. 4.

227 Childs, *British Army of William III*, 184–5; Hayter, *Army and the Crowd*, 20.

228 Barnett, *Britain and Her Army*, 167.

229 Bush, *English Aristocracy*, 126.

230 Beckett, *Aristocacy in England*, 413–14.

231 Lowe, "Bishops and Scottish representative peers"; Ditchfield, "Scottish representative peers"; Holmes, *British Politics in the Age of Anne*, chap. 12; McCahill, *Order and Equipoise*, for example 1–11, 213–14; Bucholz, *Augustan Court*, chap. 6. A somewhat different view can be found in Cannon, *Aristocratic Century*, 99–100.

232 Lander, *Government and Community*, 59.

233 Henning, *House of Commons*, 10–11.

234 Howell, *Patriarchs and Parasites*, 122. See 123–8 for other examples.

235 Cannon, *Aristocratic Century*, 112, 114.

236 Bush, *English Aristocracy*, 41.

237 Christianson, "Peers, people and parliamentary management"; and his "Politics and parliaments."

238 Beckett, *Aristocracy in England*, 425–8.

239 McCracken, *Irish Parliament*, 8–10; Howell, *Patriarchs and Parasites*, 131.

240 Namier, *Structure of Politics*, 69–70.

241 Hopkinson, "Electorate of Cumberland and Westmorland," 114–15; O'Gorman, "Electoral deference"; and his *Voters, Patrons and Parties*, 235–44.

242 O'Gorman, "Electoral deference," 403–4, 409; and his *Voters, Patrons and Parties*, 237–8, and n. 40.

243 For an example see Malcomson, "Election politics."

244 Hopkinson, "Electorate of Cumberland and Westmorland," 104.

245 O'Gorman, "Electoral deference," 402, 413–24; and his *Voters, Patrons and Parties*, 237.

246 Howell, "Landlords," 290.

247 O'Gorman, "Electoral deference," 395–6.

248 Malcomson, "Election politics," 51–7.

249 McCracken, *Irish Parliament*, 8–11.

250 Adam, ed., *View of the Political State*, XXXII.

251 Hopkinson, "Electorate of Cumberland and Westmorland," 105–7.

252 Beckett, *Aristocracy in England*, 420–1, 444–5.

253 Cannon, *Aristocratic Century*, 106–7.

254 Smith, *Consitutional and Legal History of England*, 134, 163, 216, 218–19.

255 Eaton, *Letters of Daniel Eaton*, 16–17, 68–71, 70–1, 130–2, 139–40; Wake and Webster, "Introduction," xxv–xxviii. See also Large, "North Worcestershire," 34–5.

256 Large, "Economic and social change," 38.

257 Cannon, *Aristocratic Century,* 121.

258 Lander, *English Justices of the Peace, 1461–1509,* 5.

259 Beckett, *Aristocracy in England,* 122.

260 Teale, "Economy of North Flintshire," 37.

261 Jones, "Caernarvonshire justices of the peace," 40.

262 Lander, *English Justices of the Peace, 1461–1509,* 2–4. I have used this work and Landau, *Justices of the Peace, 1679–1760,* the most on this subject.

263 Lander, *English Justices of the Peace, 1461–1509,* 4.

264 Herbert and Jones, *Tudor Wales,* 23.

265 Lander, *English Justices of the Peace, 1461–1509,* 108–44.

266 Landau, *Justices of the Peace, 1679–1760,* 2, 7–8.

267 Lander, *English Justices of the Peace, 1461–1509,* 8.

268 Ibid., 7–8; Landau, *Justices of the Peace, 1679–1760,* 6.

269 Lander, *English Justices of the Peace, 1461–1509,* 8.

270 Landau, *Justices of the Peace, 1679–1760,* 42.

271 Ibid., 6–7, 44, 213–22.

272 Lander, *English Justices of the Peace, 1461–1509,* 82–3; Landau, *Justices of the Peace, 1679–1760,* 219–20, 228.

273 Jones, "Tudor Glamorgan," 23–4.

274 Lander, *English Justices of the Peace, 1461–1509,* 75–81, 89–90.

275 Landau, *Justices of the Peace, 1679–1760,* 228, 253–62.

276 Lander, *English Justices of the Peace, 1461–1509,* 22.

277 Jones, "Tudor Glamorgan," 23.

278 Landau, *Justices of the Peace, 1679–1760,* 235–9.

279 Ibid., 138.

280 Ibid., 208, 264–5.

281 Lander, *English Justices of the Peace, 1461–1509,* 4.

282 Landau, *Justices of the Peace, 1679–1760,* 36–7.

283 Brown, *Bloodfeud in Scotland,* 271.

284 Ibid., 271.

285 Whetstone, *Scottish County Government,* 4. Most of what I say on Scottish local government comes from this book.

286 For a revised portrait of justices of the peace see Whetstone, *County Government,* and Mitchison, *New History,* 5: *Lordship to Patronage,* 15.

287 Whetstone, *Scottish County Government,* 28.

288 Ibid., 61.

289 Smout, *History of the Scottish People,* 115–18.

290 Terry, *Scottish Parliament,* 16–17, 62.

291 Ibid., 17 n. 1.

292 These figures come from ibid., 2.

293 McDowell, *Ireland in the Age of Imperialism and Revolution,* 120–1.

294 James, "Active Irish peers," 66–8; see also James, *Lords of the Ascendancy,* chap. 4.
295 Cuddy, "Revival of entourage," 175–7, 181–2, 188–9, 203, 220; Cuddy, "Anglo-Scottish Union," 108–10; 112–20; Bucholz, *Augustan Court,* 100.
296 Howell, *Patriarchs and Parasites,* 127.
297 Jones, *Modern Wales,* 86.
298 Dodd, "Landed gentry," 82.
299 Lowe, "Bishops and Scottish representative peers"; McCahill, "Scottish peerage."
300 Shaw, *Management of Scottish Society,* 2.
301 McCahill, "Scottish peerage," 176.
302 Lowe, "Bishops and Scottish representative peers," 103–4.
303 McCahill, "Scottish peerage," 175–7, 178–85, 195–6.
304 Howell, *Patriarchs and Parasites,* 136.
305 Shaw, *Management of Scottish Society,* 125–6.
306 Colley, *Britons,* chap. 3.
307 Shaw, *Management of Scottish Society,* chaps. 1, 3, and 4.
308 Murdoch, *"People Above,"* 133. These paragraphs are based especially on this work and on Shaw, *Management of Scottish Society.*

CHAPTER EIGHT

1 This paragraph is based on Wakelin, *English Dialects,* 15–21.
2 This paragraph is based on Davies, *Conquest, Coexistence, and Change,* chaps. 1, 2, 4, and epilogue.
3 Otway-Ruthven, *History of Medieval Ireland,* 102.
4 Murison, "Historical background," 3.
5 Ibid., 4–5.
6 Smout, *History of the Scottish People,* 22–5.
7 Grant, *New History,* 3: *Independence and Nationhood,* 68, 200–1.
8 Mann, *Sources of Social Power,* 1:377, 379–90.
9 Gazier, ed., *Lettres à Grégoire,* 5.
10 This paragraph is based mainly on Peyre, *La royauté et les langues provinciales,* especially chap. 1.
11 Brun, *Recherches sur l'introduction du français,* especially chaps. 5 and 22.
12 Peyre, *La royauté et les langues provinciales,* 58–90.
13 This paragraph is based on ibid., 140–1, 235–6; Gysseling, "L'origine de la frontière linguistique," 438–40; Brunot, "La langue française en Alsace," especially 602.
14 Brun, *Recherches sur l'introduction du français,* 27.
15 Ibid., 131–3.
16 For Alsace see Brunot and Bruneau, *Histoire de la langue française,* 593–4.

17 The preceding is based largely on reports from different parts of the country in Gazier, ed., *Lettres à Grégoire.*

18 Motley, *Becoming a French Aristocrat,* 70.

19 Solnon, *La cour de France,* 79–81.

20 Kochan and Abraham, *Making of Modern Russia,* 144.

21 Brun, *Recherches sur l'introduction du français,* 423.

22 Devos, "Un siècle en mutation, 1536–1684," 273.

23 Brunot, "La langue française en Alsace," 586–92, but see also 594–5.

24 Armstrong, "Language question," especially 397, 405, 408–9.

25 Defacqz, *Ancien droit belge,* 1:124.

26 Gazier, ed., *Lettres à Grégoire,* 234–5.

27 Deneckere, *Histoire de la langue française,* especially 110–13, 118–23, 127, 337–8; Vanden Berghe et al., "Flandre occidentale," 151; Hasquin, "L'évolution démographique," 140–4.

28 Briggs, *Early Modern France,* 17.

29 Labrousse, *La révocation,* 71–2.

30 My major source for this paragraph is ibid., especially chaps. 5–8.

31 This paragraph is drawn from ibid., especially 14, 193, 199–200; Benedict, "La population réformée."

32 Wood, *Nobility of Bayeux,* 5, 169; Constant, "Nobles et paysans en Beauce," 333–5, 354.

33 Lüthy, *La banque protestante,* 1:19; Constant, "Nobles et paysans en Beauce," 322.

34 Constant, "Nobles et paysans en Beauce," 340.

35 Wood, *Nobility of Bayeux,* 161.

36 Lüthy, *La banque protestante,* 20.

37 Labrousse, *La révocation,* 20.

38 Ibid., 20.

39 Ibid., 143.

40 Hildesheimer, *Le Jansénisme,* 85–9.

41 Ibid., 156.

42 Ibid., 91–5.

43 Wilson, "English and French"; Wakelin, *English Dialects,* 22.

44 Wakelin, *English Dialects,* 27.

45 Stone, *Crisis of the Aristocracy,* 345.

46 Cannon, *Aristocratic Century,* 61.

47 Bossy, *English Catholic Community,* 37.

48 Ibid., 173–81.

49 Cosgrove, "Position of the recusant gentry," 23–29, 77, and 152.

50 1 Eliz., c. 1.

51 1 Eliz., c. 2.

52 4 Eliz., c. 1.

53 13 Eliz., c. 2.

54　27 Eliz., c. 2.

55　3 James I, c. 5.

56　7 James, c. 6.

57　24 Charles II, c. 2.

58　Bossy, *English Catholic Community*, 182–94.

59　Davies, *Conquest, Coexistence, and Change*, 366.

60　Lydon, *Ireland in the Later Middle Ages*, 94–5.

61　Smyth, "Making the documents of conquest speak," 249–52.

62　Murison, "Historical background," 6–8.

63　Davies, *Conquest, Coexistence, and Change*, 459.

64　Jones, *Modern Wales*, 57–61.

65　Williams, "Religion and belief," 113–14.

66　Evans, *History of Wales*, 34.

67　Ford, "Protestant Reformation," 57, 61–3.

68　The preceding three paragraphs are based primarily on ibid., 52–9, 61, 73; Lennon, "Counter-Reformation," 77, 82, 87–9; Bottigheimer, "Why the Reformation failed in Ireland."

69　Cullen, *Emergence of Modern Ireland*, 53–4.

70　Ibid., 37.

71　Burke, "Tracts relative to the laws against popery in Ireland," 33–4.

72　James, "Active Irish peers," 56.

73　Ibid., 56.

74　The major source for this paragraph is Wall, *Penal Laws*, especially 11–16, 21.

75　Ibid., 9–10; Cullen, *Emergence of Modern Ireland*, 195–6.

76　Simms, "Establishment of Protestant ascendancy," 16–21.

77　See above 96 and 200.

78　Cullen, *Emergence of Modern Ireland*, 195–6.

79　Colley, *Britons*, 156–8.

80　Jenkins, *Making of a Ruling Class*, especially xxi–xxii, 40–1; Howell, *Patriarchs and Parasites*, 26–7.

81　Howell, *Patriarchs and Parasites*, 192.

82　Dodd, "Landed gentry," 84–5.

83　Jenkins, *Making of a Ruling Class*, 213–14.

84　Jenkins, *History of Modern Wales*, 3, 105–6, 109–10.

85　Jenkins, *Making of a Ruling Class*, 217–18, 223–4.

86　Jones, "Caernarvonshire justices of the peace," 26–7.

87　Howell, *Patriarchs and Parasites*, 199.

88　For example, see ibid., 175; Humphreys, "Rural society in Montgomeryshire," 44.

89　Jenkins, *Making of a Ruling Class*, 219.

90　Ibid., 11.

91　Whyte, *Agriculture and Society*, 114–16.

92 Graham, *Social Life of Scotland,* 56–60.

93 Aitken, "Scottish speech," 92.

94 Shaw, *Northern and Western Islands,* 185–6.

95 Ibid., 195–6.

96 Smout, *History of the Scottish People,* 322.

97 Aitken, "Scottish speech," 94–6.

98 Ibid., 100.

99 O'Dowd, "Gaelic economy and society," 145–7.

100 Cullen, *Emergence of Modern Ireland,* 26–8, 44.

101 This paragraph is based on Adams, "Dialects of Ulster"; Bliss, "Emergence of modern English dialects in Ireland."

102 For a very different (in my view erroneous) interpretation see Wuthnow, "State structures and ideology," 806–13.

103 Colley, *Britons,* chap. 1.

104 Ibid, 113–17, 120–2.

105 Hechter, *Internal Colonialism,* chaps. 1–2.

106 Ibid., 73–8.

107 Scaglione, *Knights at Court,* 48–9, 63–4.

108 Ibid., 8.

109 See essays collected in Newman, *Meaning of Courtly Love.* A good summary of the academic work concerning idealized love can be found in Boase, *Origin and Meaning of Courtly Love.*

110 Hunt, "Emergence of the knight," 96–7; Keen, *Chivalry,* 23, 42.

111 Scaglione, *Knights at Court,* 80.

112 Ibid., 71.

113 Keen, *Chivalry,* 9.

114 Gillingham, *Richard the Lionheart,* 118–19.

115 Neushel, *Word of Honor,* especially 1–16, 23–5, 196–8, 205–6.

116 Keen, *Chivalry,* 8, 12; Vale, *War and Chivalry,* 15.

117 Keen, *Chivalry,* 21–2; Scaglione, *Knights at Court,* 11, 81, 85–6, 305.

118 Anglo, "The courtier," 38–9.

119 Cox, *Green Count of Savoy,* 348–9.

120 Dickens, "Monarchy and cultural revival," 22–8.

121 Ibid., 21–2; Seward, *Eleanor of Aquitaine,* 110–14.

122 Puy de Clinchamps, *Chevalerie,* 78.

123 Keen, *Chivalry,* 54.

124 Armstrong, "Golden age"; see Vale, *War and Chivalry,* for an appreciative examination of the chivalric culture of the fifteenth century, especially as found in the court of Burgundy.

125 Puy de Clinchamps, *Chevalerie,* 77–88.

126 Ormrod, *Reign of Edward III,* 18–19.

127 Cox, *Green Count of Savoy,* 78–9, 180–1, 343, 346–7.

128 Armstrong, "Golden age," 70; Jones, "Order of the Golden Fleece," 35–8.

129 Jones, "Order of the Golden Fleece," 38, 43.

130 Vale, *War and Chivalry*, 40, 48, 51; Jones, "Order of the Golden Fleece," 33–4, 43.

131 Baelde, "De Orde van het Gulden Vlies"; Vale, *War and Chivalry*, 44.

132 Manning, "Poaching."

133 Colley, *Britons*, 170–3.

134 Chaussinand-Nogaret, *La noblesse au XVIIIème siècle*, 112–17. Chaussinand-Nogaret interprets this criminal activity as a breakdown in aristocratic standards of conduct, and certainly much of it, especially deviant sexual behaviour, offended generally accepted norms. Yet some of this behaviour resulted from a conflict of norms.

135 Janssens, *L'évolution de la noblesse belge*, 36.

136 Billacois, *Duel*, 121–2.

137 Brown, *Bloodfeud in Scotland*, 204–5.

138 Billacois, *Duel*, chaps. 15–16.

139 Trevor-Roper, *Princes and Artists*, 8–9.

140 Castiglione, *Book of the Courtier*, 70.

141 Ibid., 74.

142 Baldwin, *Sumptuary Legislation*, 21–2, 69–70, 78–9, 96–7, 110–11, 131–2, 188–9, 250–1.

143 Le Roy Ladurie, "Auprès du roi, la cour," 28–9.

144 Elias, *Civilizing Process*, 1: *Development of Manners*, 80–2.

145 Elias, *Court Society*, 106–10; Anglo, "The courtier."

146 Castiglione, *Book of the Courtier*, 109.

147 Elias, *Civilizing Process*, 2: *State Formation*, 281; Mettam, *Power and Faction*, 52.

148 Castiglione, *Book of the Courtier*, 43.

149 Dewald, *Aristocratic Experience*, introduction and chaps. 1, 3, 6, and conclusion.

150 Symcox, "City as theatre."

151 Hexter, *Reappraisals in History*, 50, 63–4.

152 This paragraph is based primarily on Motley, *Becoming a French Aristocrat*, chaps. 2, 3, and 4, especially 158, 164–5, 170–2.

153 Anglo, "The courtier," 33–5, 51–3.

154 Estoile, *Mémoires-journaux*, 1:143.

155 Pepys, *Diary*, 96, 329, 356, 378, 429, 430, 531.

156 For example, see Forster, *Nobility of Toulouse*, 156–7.

157 Bluche, *La vie quotidienne de la noblesse*, 223–6.

158 Javitch, "*The Philosopher*," 98, 107–14; Anglo, "The Courtier," 51.

159 Elias, *Civilizing Process*, 1: *Development of Manners*, 53–7.

160 Mollat, *Popes at Avignon*, 62–3.

161 Frotier de la Messelière, *La noblesse en Bretagne*, 34.

162 Ibid., 38.

163 Ibid., 45.

164 Symcox, "City as theatre"; Bouquet-Boyer, "Turin et les musiciens de la cour," 1:44–5, 58–9, 739.

165 Janssens, "Willem van Dranjeaan het Brussels hof," 177–8.

166 Trevor-Roper, *Princes and Artists*, 118–20.

167 Ibid., 131–51.

168 Martin, "Overlord becomes feudal lord," 122.

169 Canny, "Formation of the Irish mind," 54.

170 Solnon, *La cour de France*, 140–4; Potter and Roberts, "Englishman's view."

171 Seward, *First Bourbon: Henri IV*, 162, 177; Solnon, *La cour de France*, 164–5.

172 Solnon, *La cour de France*, 382–4.

173 Ibid., 421–2, 437–42.

174 Shennan, "Louis xv," especially 319.

175 Solnon, *La cour de France*, 452–3.

176 Miller, *Henry VIII and the English Nobility*, 100–1.

177 Cuddy, "Anglo-Scottish Union," 110–11.

178 Sharpe, "Image of virtue."

179 Rykwert, "Seventeenth century," 38.

180 Brooke, *King George III*, 473–4.

181 Bucholz, *Augustan Court*, 23–5, 30, 153–4, 244–6.

182 Hatton, *George I*, 132–4.

183 Solnon, *La cour de France*, 448–9.

184 Ibid., 449.

185 Goodman, "Enlightenment salons," 330 n. 2.

186 Elias, *Court Society*, 36.

187 Marly, *Louis XIV*, 64, 88.

188 Solnon, *La cour de France*, 463–4.

189 Motley, *Becoming a French Aristocrat*, 154.

190 Defoe, *Tour*, 1:340.

191 Rogers, "Money, land and lineage," 445–6.

192 Wilson, *Gentlemen Merchants*, 153–4, 177–9, 212, 213–15, 231–2; Devine, *Tobacco Lords*, 24–7.

193 Motley, *Becoming a French Aristocrat*, 136.

194 For example, see Dewald, *Pont-St-Pierre*, chap. 5.

195 Elias, *Civilizing Process*, 1: *Development of Manners*, 35–6, 100–1.

196 Motley, *Becoming a French Aristocrat*, 13, 140.

197 Marly, *Louis XIV*, 36, 38, 42, 69.

198 Starkey, "Intimacy and innovation," 81–2.

199 Mellers, "Music: paradise and paradox," 211; Bucholz, *Augustan Court*, 16.

200 Beattie, *English Court*, 5.

201 Marly, *Louis XIV*, 39–40.

202 Ibid., 40, 54–6.

203 Ibid., 40.
204 Smeyers et al., "La vie culturelle dans nos provinces."
205 Denekere, *Histoire de la langue française*, 118.
206 Douxchamps-Lefevre, "Un magazine de la cour de France."
207 Deneckere, *Histoire de la langue française*, 118; Van den Berg, "De adel in de 18de eeuw," 148.
208 Deneckere, *Histoire de la langue française*, 119.
209 Goodman, "Governing the republic of letters," 183–4.
210 Glotz and Maire, *Salons du XVIIIe siècle*, 24; Tinker, *Salon*, chap. 4.
211 Tinker, *Salon*, chaps. 1, 8.
212 Wangermann, "Maria Theresa," 294, 297–8.
213 Nicolas, *La Savoie au 18e siècle*, 2:936–40.
214 Devos, "Elite et culture," 217–18.
215 Bouquet-Boyer, "Turin et les musiciens de la cour," 1:14, 30, 32–3, 48, 62–5, 70–1, 738.
216 Marly, *Louis XIV*, 60.
217 Ibid., 68.
218 Ibid., 76.
219 Kochan and Abraham, *Making of Modern Russia*, 124.
220 Elias, *Civilizing Process*, 2: *State Formation*, 4–6.
221 Elias, *Civilizing Process*, 1: *Development of Manners*, 38–9.
222 Stone and Stone, *Open Elite?*, 297, 299, 307–10.
223 Ibid., 318–22.
224 That Edinburgh was still a cultural centre in the eighteenth century is stressed by a number of writers, particularly Roger Emerson and N.T. Phillipson. See Phillipson, "Culture and society," and his "Lawyers, landowners, and the civic leadership."
225 Emerson, *Professors, Patronage and Politics*, 104–5.
226 Tinker, *Salon*, 5, 213.
227 Wangermann, "Maria Theresa," 302–3.
228 Ravitch, *Sword and Mitre*, 71–4.
229 Ibid., 123–4, 144–6.
230 Canny, "Formation of the Irish mind," 52, 74.
231 Glotz and Maire, *Salons du XVIIIe siècle*, 27–8.
232 These Scottish examples come from Emerson, "Lord Bute," 148–9.
233 Dewald, *Aristocratic Experience*, chap. 6.
234 Ibid., 182–7.
235 Ibid., 200–1.
236 Castiglione, *Book of the Courtier*, 204–5.
237 Goodman, "Governing the Republic of Letters," 189–92.
238 Tinker, *Salon*, 16.
239 Goodman, "Enlightenment salons," 342, 345; Dewald, *Aristocratic Experience*, 193.

240 Lougee, *Paradis des Femmes*, 116–27.

241 See above 186.

242 Goodman, "Enlightenment salons," 330; Goodman, "Governing the Republic of Letters," 184.

243 This paragraph is based mainly on Glotz and Maire, *Salons du XVIIIe siècle*, 17–18; Darnton, *Literary Underground*, 23; Gordon, "'Public opinion,'" 304–6; Goodman, "Enlightenment salons," 331–2, 338; Goodman, "Governing the Republic of Letters," 195–6.

244 Emerson, "Select Society of Edinburgh," 301.

245 Emerson, "Lord Bute," 150–1, 162–3, 169–70; his *Professors, Patronage and Politics*, chaps. 4, 5 and the Conclusion; and his "Medical men, politicians, and the medical schools," 195–6, 199, 206.

246 Emerson, *Professors, Patronage and Politics*, 5–6.

247 Doyle, *Origins of the French Revolution*, 80–2.

248 Corrigan and Sayer, *Great Arch*, introduction and chaps. 4 to 7.

249 Anderson, "Music," 275–8.

250 Wolf, *Louis XIV*, 173, 203, 220, 225, 260, 409, 444, 487, 470, 523, 595.

251 Anderson, "Music," 286.

252 Rykwert, "Seventeenth century," 27.

253 See Ranum, "Courtesy, absolutism, and the rise of the French state," for the best discussion of this subject.

254 Le Roy Ladurie, "Auprès du roi, la cour," 23–4.

255 DeNora, "Musical patronage."

256 Elias has contributed much to this misconception. See in particular *Court Society*, 120–1, 126–8.

257 Saint-Simon, *Memoirs*, 2:360.

CONCLUSION TO PART TWO

1 In an earlier paper I overstated the fusion of power in the Southern Low Countries during the eighteenth century, though I correctly identified the subsequent trend. See my "Nobility, bourgeoisie and the Industrial Revolution in Belgium," 145–6.

2 Spencer, *Principles of Sociology*, 1:38–9, 437–8, 451–7, 461.

3 Durkheim, *Division of Labour*, 257.

4 Eisenstadt, "Social change, differentiation and evolution," 377–8; Eisenstadt, *Political Systems of Empires*; Habermas, *Communication and the Evolution of Society*, 97–8, 120–2.

5 Rueschemeyer, *Power and the Division of Labour*, chap. 3.

6 Elias, *Civilizing Process*, 2: *State Formation*, 149–50, 163–5.

7 Ibid., 171–201, 223–4.

8 Tilly, *As Sociology Meets History*, 95; Tilly, *Big Structures*, 48–9.

9 Anderson, "Figures," 35–7, 41–2; Smelser, *Social Paralysis*, 3; Sayer, "Notable administration."

10 Roehl, "French industrialization"; Cameron and Freedeman, "French economic growth."
11 Sayer, "Notable administration," 1382, 1391–1411.
12 Wood, *Pristine Culture of Capitalism*, chaps. 2–6.
13 Rueschemeyer, *Power and the Division of Labour*, 194.
14 Alexander, "Differentiation theory," 1. The best recent work that seeks to make evolutionary theory more palatable to historical sociologists is Sanderson, *Social Evolution*. In my view, his approach is still too holistic, but he does overcome many of the other problems in evolutionary theory.
15 This debate has been published in Hilton et al., *Transition from Feudalism to Capitalism*. Brenner, "On the origins of capitalist development," is also critical of Marxists for confusing commercialism and capitalism.
16 Brenner, "Agrarian class structure and economic development"; and his "Agrarian roots of European capitalism."

EPILOGUE

1 Hyams, *King, Lords, and Peasants*, 268.
2 Weber, *Economy and Society*, 2:938.
3 Turner, *Status*, 37–8; Anderson, *Lineages*, especially 17–20. See also Beik, *Absolutism in Languedoc*, 339. Beik regards the France of Louis XIV as either the "final, highest phase" of feudalism, or as a "society in transition, if you like, from feudalism to capitalism."
4 Anderson, "Origins of present crisis"; Thompson, "Peculiarities of the English"; Anderson, "Socialism."

TERMS AND CONCEPTS

1 Two recent works that also adopt the broad usage of the term aristocracy are Bush, *English Aristocracy*, and Beckett, *Aristocracy in England*. In both cases "aristocracy" refers to the gentry as well as the peerage.
2 He makes use of this concept in a number of works. See, for example, "Forms of capital," *Distinction, Language and Symbolic Power, Reproduction*, and *Homo Academicus*.
3 See, for example, *Distinction*, chaps. 2 and 4.
4 Le Goff, *Vannes*, 160.
5 Comninel, "English feudalism."
6 Smout, *Scottish People*, 127.
7 Weber, *Economy and Society*, 1:235.
8 Mann, *Sources of Social Power*, 1:11.
9 Ibid., vol. 1, chap. 1.
10 Ibid., 1:10–11.
11 Fourez, *Le droit héraldique*, 103–4.

Bibliography

Abels, R.P. *Lordship and Military Obligation in Anglo-Saxon England.* Berkeley: University of California Press 1988

Abu-Lughod, Janet L. *Before European Hegemony: The World System A.D. 1250–1350.* New York: Oxford University Press 1989

Adam, C.E., ed. *View of the Political State of Scotland in the Last Century: A Confidential Report on the Political Opinions, Family Connections, or Personal Circumstances of the 2662 County Voters in 1788.* Edinburgh: Douglas 1887

Adam, Frank. *The Clans, Septs and Regiments of the Scottish Highlands,* edited by Thomas Innes of Learney. Edinburgh: Johnston 1952

Adams, G.B. "The dialects of Ulster." In *The English Language in Ulster,* edited by Diarmaid O Muirithe. Dublin: Mercier 1977

Adams, R.C. "The corps of noblesse of Provence in the eighteenth century: a besieged order defends its privileges," PhD dissertation, University of Minnesota 1973

Ainsworth, John. "Sidelights on eighteenth-century land tenure." *Royal Society of Antiquaries Journal* 79 (1949)

– "Some aspects of eighteenth-century Irish land tenure." *Bulletin of the Irish Committee of Historical Sciences* 87 (1959)

Aitken, A.J. "Scottish speech: a historical view, with special reference to the standard English of Scotland." In *Languages of Scotland,* edited by A.J. Aitken and Tom McArthur. Edinburgh: Chambers 1979

Alexander, J.C. *Action and Its Environments: Toward a New Synthesis.* New York: Columbia University Press 1988

– "Differentiation theory." In *Differentiation Theory and Social Change: Comparative and Historical Perspectives,* edited by J.C. Alexander and Paul Colomy. New York: Columbia University Press 1990

Alsop, J.D. "The theory and practice of Tudor taxation." *English Historical Review* 97 (1982)

Amin, Samir. *Accumulation on a World Scale.* New York: Monthly Review Press 1974

– *Unequal Development: An Essay on the Social Formations of Peripheral Capitalism.* New York: Monthly Review Press 1976

An Address to the Noblemen and Other Landed Proprietors of Ireland by a Gentleman. Dublin: Powell 1769

Anderson, M.S. *War and Society in Europe of the Old Regime.* London: Fontana 1988

Anderson, Nicholas. "Music." In *The Cambridge Cultural History of Britain,* 5: *Eighteenth-Century Britain,* edited by Boris Ford. Cambridge: Cambridge University Press 1991

Anderson, Perry. "Origins of the present crisis." *New Left Review,* no. 23 (1964)

– "Socialism and pseudo-empiricism." *New Left Review,* no. 35 (1966)

– *Lineages of the Absolutist State.* London: Verso 1974

– "The figures of descent." *New Left Review,* no. 161 (1987)

Anderson, Sven Axel. *Viking Enterprise.* New York: AMS 1966

Anglo, Sydney. "The courtier: the Renaissance and changing ideals." In *The Courts of Europe: Politics, Patronage and Royalty, 1400–1800,* edited by A.G. Dickens. London: Thames and Hudson 1977

Arendt, Léon, and Alfred De Ridder, eds. *Législation héraldique de la Belgique, 1595–1895: jurisprudence du Conseil héraldique, 1844–1895.* Brussels: Société belge de librairie 1896

Arminjon, Henri. *De la noblesse des sénateurs au Souverain sénat de Savoie.* Annecy: Gardet 1971

Armstrong, C.A.J. "Had the Burgundian government a policy for the nobility?" In *Britain and the Netherlands,* vol. 2, edited by J.S. Bromley and E.H. Kossmann. London: Chatto and Windus 1964

– "The language question in the Low Countries: the use of French and Dutch by the Dukes of Burgundy and their administration." In *Europe in the Late Middle Ages,* edited by J.R. Hale et al. London: Faber 1965

– "The golden age of Burgundy: dukes that outdid kings." In *The Courts of Europe: Politics, Patronage and Royalty, 1400–1800,* edited by A.G. Dickens. London: Thames and Hudson 1977

Armstrong, J.A. "Old-regime administrative elites: prelude to modernization in France, Prussia, and Russia." *International Review of Administrative Sciences* 38 (1972)

Asselain, J.-C. *Histoire économique de la France du XVIIIe siècle à nos jours,* 1: *De l'ancien régime à la Première Guerre mondiale.* Paris: Seuil 1984

Aulin, Arvid. *The Cybernetic Laws of Social Progress: Towards a Critical Social Philosophy and a Criticism of Marxism.* Oxford: Pergamon 1982

Aylmer, G.E. "From office-holding to civil service: the genesis of modern bureaucracy." *Transactions of the Royal Historical Society* 30 (1980)

Bacon, Nicolas. *Réflexions sur l'état présent du commerce, fabriques et manufactures des Païs-Bas autrichiens,* edited by Hervé Hasquin. 1765. Brussels: Académie royale de Belgique 1978

Baelde, M.E.J. "De Orde van het Gulden Vlies." *Spiegel historiael* 19 (1984)

Baldwin, F.E. *Sumptuary Legislation and Personal Regulation in England.* Baltimore: Johns Hopkins University Press 1926

Barber, Richard. *Henry Plantagenet: A Biography.* London: Barrie and Rockliff 1964

Barberis, Walter. "Continuité aristocratique et tradition militaire du Piémont de la dynastie de Savoie xvie–xixe siècles." *Revue d'histoire moderne et contemporaine* 34 (1987)

Barnett, Correlli. *Britain and Her Army, 1509–1970: A Military, Political and Social Survey.* London: Allen Lane 1970

Barrow, G.W.S. *Kingship and Unity: Scotland 1000–1306.* Toronto: University of Toronto Press 1981

Bastier, Jean. *La féodalité au siècles des lumières dans la région de Toulouse, 1730–1790.* Paris: Bibliothèque nationale 1975

Bastin, Sacré, to the Count of Belgiojoso, 15 Aug. 1786, edited by René Bragard. *La Vie Wallone,* new series, 55 (1981)

Bates, David. *William the Conqueror.* London: Philip 1989

Bean, J.M.W. *The Decline of English Feudalism, 1215–1540.* Manchester: Manchester University Press 1968

– *From Lord to Patron: Lordship in Late Medieval England.* Manchester: Manchester University Press 1989

Beattie, J.M. *The English Court in the Reign of George I.* Cambridge: Cambridge University Press 1967

Beckett, J.C. *The Making of Modern Ireland, 1603–1923.* New York: Knopf 1969

– *The Anglo-Irish Tradition.* Ithaca: Cornell University Press 1976

Beckett, J.V. "English landownership in the later seventeenth and eighteenth centuries: the debate and the problems." *Economic History Review,* 2nd series, 30 (1977)

– "Land tax or excise: the levying of taxation in seventeenth- and eighteenth-century England." *English Historical Review* 100 (1985)

– *The Aristocracy in England, 1660–1914.* Oxford: Basil Blackwell 1986

Behrens, Betty. *The Ancien Régime.* London: Thames and Hudson 1967

– "A revision defended: nobles, privileges, and taxes in France." *French Historical Studies* 9 (1976)

Behrens, C.B.A. "Nobles, privileges and taxes in France at the end of the Ancien Régime." *Economic History Review,* 2nd series, 15 (1963)

Beik, William. *Absolutism and Society in Seventeenth-Century France: State Power and Provincial Aristocracy in Languedoc.* New York: Cambridge University Press 1985

Bendix, Reinhard. *Nation-building and Citizenship: Studies of Our Changing Social Order.* New York: John Wiley 1964

- *Kings or People: Power and the Mandate to Rule*. Berkeley: University of California Press 1978

Benecke, G. *Society and Politics in Germany 1500–1750*. London: Routledge and Kegan Paul 1974

Benedict, Philip. "La population réformée française de 1600 à 1685." *Annales: ESC* 42 (1987)

Bennett, D.C., and K.E. Sharpe. *Transnational Corporations versus the State: The Political Economy of the Mexican Auto Industry*. Princeton: Princeton University Press 1985

Bennett, H.S. *Life on the English Manor: A Study of Peasant Conditions, 1150–1400*. Cambridge: Cambridge University Press 1937

Bérenger, Jean. "Noblesse et absolutisme de François 1er à Louis XIV." In *Noblesse française, noblesse hongroise, XVI–XIXe siècles*, edited by Béla Köpeczi and E.H. Balázs. Paris and Budapest: CNRS and Akadémiai Kiadó 1981

Bettey, J.H. "Land tenure and manorial custom in Dorset, 1570–1670." *Southern History* 4 (1982)

Bien, D.D. "La réaction aristocratique avant 1789: l'exemple de l'armée." *Annales: ESC* 29 (1974)

Billacois, François. *The Duel: Its Rise and Fall in Early Modern France*, edited and translated by Trista Selous. New Haven: Yale University Press 1990

Black, Jeremy, and Philip Woodfine, eds. *The British Navy and the Use of Naval Power in the Eighteenth Century*. Leicester: Leicester University Press 1988

Bliss, A.J. "The emergence of modern English dialects in Ireland." In *The English Language in Ulster*, edited by Diarmaid O Muirithe. Dublin: Mercier 1977

Bloch, Jean-Richard. *L'anoblissement en France au temps de François 1er: essai d'une définition de la condition juridique et sociale de la noblesse au début du XVIe siècle*. 1934. Geneva: Mégariotis Reprints 1977

Bloch, Marc. *La société féodale: les classes et le gouvernement des hommes*. Paris: Michel 1940

Blockmans, Willem. "Introduction" and notes to *Estates or Powers: Essays in the Parliamentary History of the Southern Netherlands from the XIIth to the XVIIIth Century*, by Jan Dhondt. Heule: UGA 1977

- "A typology of representative institutions in late Medieval Europe." *Journal of Medieval History* 4 (1978)

Bluche, François. "L'origine sociale du personnel ministériel français au XVIIIe siècle." *Bulletin de la Société d'histoire moderne* 56 (1957)

- *La vie quotidienne de la noblesse française au XVIIIe siècle*. Paris: Hachette 1973
- *Les magistrats du Parlement de Paris au XVIIIe siècle*. Paris: Economica 1986

Bluche, François, and Pierre Durye. *L'anoblissement par charges avant 1789*, 2 vols. Paris: Cahiers Nobles 1962

Blum, Jerome. *The End of the Old Order in Rural Europe*. Princeton: Princeton University Press 1978

Boase, Roger. *The Origin and Meaning of Courtly Love*. Manchester: Manchester University Press 1977

Bonenfant, P., and G. Despy. "La noblesse en Brabant aux XIIe et XIIIe siècles." *Le Moyen Age* 64 (1958)

Bonney, R.J. "The failure of the French revenue farms, 1600–60." *Economic History Review*, 2nd series, 32 (1979)

– *The King's Debts: Finance and Politics in France, 1589–1661*. Oxford: Clarendon Press 1981

Booton, H.W. "Inland trade: a study of Aberdeen in the Later Middle Ages." *The Scottish Medieval Town*, edited by Michael Lynch, Michael Spearman, and Geoffrey Stell. Edinburgh: Donald 1988

Bordes, Maurice. *L'administration provinciale et municipale en France au XVIIIe siècle*. Paris: Société d'édition d'enseignement supérieur 1972

Bordonove, Georges. *Les rois qui ont fait la France*. Paris: Pygmalion 1988

Bosher, J.F. *French Finances, 1770–1795: From Business to Bureaucracy*. Cambridge: Cambridge University Press 1970

Bossenga, Gail. *The Politics of Privilege: Old Regime and Revolution in Lille*. Cambridge: Cambridge University Press 1991

Bossy, John. *The English Catholic Community, 1570–1850*. London: Darton, Longman and Todd 1975

Bottigheimer, K.S. "Why the Reformation failed in Ireland: a continuing question," unpublished paper

Bottomore, T.B. *Classes in Modern Society*. London: George Allen and Unwin 1965

Boulle, P.H. "Around François Bernier's 'Nouvelle division de la terre' (1684): race and colour in sixteenth- and seventeenth-century France," paper presented at the Annual Meeting of the Canadian Society for Renaissance Studies, Carleton University 1993

Bouchard, Constance. "The origins of the French nobility: a reassessment." *American Historical Review* 86 (1981)

Bouquet-Boyer, Marie Thérèse, "Turin et les musiciens de la cour, 1619–1775: vie quotidienne et production artistique," Thèse de doctorat d'état, Université de Paris-Sorbonne 1987

Bourde, A.J. *The Influence of England on the French Agronomes, 1750–1789*. Cambridge: Cambridge University Press 1953

Bragard, René. "Liège et la France à la fin de l'Ancien Régime." *La Vie Wallone*, new series, 55 (1981)

Brenner, Robert. "Agrarian class structure and economic development in pre-industrial Europe." *Past and Present*, no. 70 (1976)

– "On the origins of capitalist development: a critique of neo-Smithian Marxism." *New Left Review*, no. 104 (1977)

– "The agrarian roots of European capitalism." In *The Brenner Debate: Agrarian Class Structure and Economic Development in Pre-industrial Europe*, edited by

T.H. Aston and C.H.E. Philpin. Cambridge: Cambridge University Press 1985

Brewer, John. *The Sinews of Power: War, Money and the English State, 1688–1783.* Cambridge: Harvard University Press 1990

Briggs, Robin. *Early Modern France: 1560–1715.* Oxford: Oxford University Press 1977

Brooke, John. *King George III.* St Albans: Panther Books 1972

Brown, A.L. "Parliament, *c.* 1377–1422." In *The English Parliament in the Middle Ages,* edited by R.G. Davies and J.H. Denton. Manchester: Manchester University Press 1981

Brown, Jenny. *See* Wormald

Brown, K.M. *Bloodfeud in Scotland, 1573–1625.* Edinburgh: Donald 1986

– "From Scottish lords to British officers: state building, elite integration and the army in the seventeenth century." In *Scotland and War, AD 79–1918,* edited by Norman MacDougall. Edinburgh: Donald 1991

Bruce, Anthony P.C. *The Purchase System in the British Army, 1660–1871.* London: Royal Historical Society 1980

Bruchet, Max. *La cour de Turin au milieu du XVIIIe siècle d'après le journal d'un gentilhomme savoisien.* Chambéry: Ménard 1894

– *Notice sur l'ancien cadastre de Savoie.* Annecy: Archives départementales 1896

– "Introduction." In *Les instructions de Victor Amédée II sur le gouvernement de son duché de Savoie en 1721,* edited by Max Bruchet. Paris: Imprimerie nationale 1901

– "Introduction." In *L'abolition des droits seigneuriaux en Savoie, 1761–1793,* edited by Max Bruchet. Annecy: Hérisson 1908

– ed. *L'abolition des droits seigneuriaux en Savoie, 1761–1793.* Annecy: Hérisson 1908

Brun, Auguste. *Recherches historiques sur l'introduction du français dans les provinces du Midi.* Paris: Champion 1923

Brunot, Ferdinand. "La langue française en Alsace après l'annexion à la France." *Revue de Paris* 23 (1916)

Brunot, Ferdinand, and Charles Bruneau. *Histoire de la langue française des origines à 1900* [later volumes *à nos jours*], 13 vols. Paris: Colin 1905–72

Brustein, William. "Regional social orders in France and the French Revolution." *Comparative Social Research* 9 (1986)

Bucholz, R.O. *The Augustan Court: Queen Anne and the Decline of Court Culture.* Stanford: Stanford University Press 1993

Burke, Edmund. "Tracts relative to the laws against popery in Ireland." In *Irish Affairs,* edited by Matthew Arnold. London: Century Hutchison 1988

Bush, M.L. "The problem of the far North: a study of the crisis of 1537." *Northern History* 6 (1971)

– *The European Nobility,* 1: *Noble Privilege.* Manchester: Manchester University Press 1983

– *The English Aristocracy: A Comparative Synthesis.* Manchester: Manchester University Press 1984
– *The European Nobility,* 2: *Rich Noble, Poor Noble.* Manchester: University of Manchester Press 1988

Butterfield, Herbert. *The Whig Interpretation of History.* London: Bell 1931

Buttin, Anne. "Le Souverain Sénat de Savoie." *L'histoire en Savoie* 17 (1983)

Byrne, F.J. "The trembling sod: Ireland in 1169." In *A New History of Ireland,* 2: *Medieval Ireland, 1169–1534,* edited by Art Cosgrove. Oxford: Clarendon Press 1987

Cameron, Euan. *The Reformation of the Heretics: The Waldenses of the Alps, 1480–1580.* Oxford: Clarendon 1984

Cameron, Rondo, and C.E. Freedeman. "French economic growth: a radical revision." *Social Science History* 7 (1983)

Cannon, John. *Aristocratic Century: The Peerage in Eighteenth-Century England.* Cambridge: Cambridge University Press 1984

Canny, Nicholas P. *The Elizabethan Conquest of Ireland: A Pattern Established, 1565–76.* Hassock: Harvester Press 1976

– "The flight of the earls, 1607." *Irish Historical Studies* 17 (1971)
– "The formation of the Irish mind: religion, politics and Gaelic literature, 1580–1750." In *Nationalism and Popular Protest in Ireland,* edited by C.H.E. Philpin. Cambridge: Cambridge University Press 1987

Cardosa, F.H., and Enzo Faletto, *Dependency and Development in Latin America.* Berkeley: University of California Press 1979

Castiglione, Baldesar. *The Book of the Courtier,* translated by C.S. Singleton. New York: Doubleday 1959

Cavanaugh G.J. "Nobles, privileges, and taxes in France: a revision reviewed." *French Historical Studies* 8 (1974)

– "Reply to Behrens." *French Historical Studies* 9 (1976)

Chamberlayne, Edward. *Magna Britannia Notitia: or, The Present State of Great Britain.* London: Midwinter 1729

Chambliss, W.J., and T.E. Ryther. *Sociology: The Discipline and Its Direction.* New York: McGraw-Hill 1975

Chandler, Tertius. *Four Thousand Years of Urban Growth: A Historical Census.* Lewiston: St David's University Press 1987

Chaussinand-Nogaret, Guy. *La noblesse au XVIIIème siècle: de la féodalité aux lumières.* Paris: Hachette 1976

Chérin, L.N.H., ed. *Abrégé chronologique d'édits, déclarations, réglements, arrêts et lettres patentes des rois de France de la troisième race concernant le fait de la noblesse.* Paris: Royez 1788

Chevailler, Laurent. "Emmanuel-Philibert et la réorganisation de l'Etat savoyard, 1559–1580." *Revue savoisienne* 118 (1978)

Chibnall, Marjorie. *Anglo-Norman England, 1066–1166.* Oxford: Basil Blackwell 1986

Childs, John. *The Army of Charles II.* London: Routledge & Kegan Paul 1976
– *The British Army of William III, 1689–1702.* Manchester: Manchester University Press 1987
Christianson, Paul. "The peers, the people, and parliamentary management in the first six months of the Long Parliament." *Journal of Modern History* 49 (1977)
– "Politics and parliaments in England, 1604–1629." *Canadian Journal of History* 16 (1981)
Clark, Samuel. "Nobility, bourgeoisie and the Industrial Revolution in Belgium." *Past and Present* no. 105 (1984)
– "Landlord domination in nineteenth-century Ireland." In *UNESCO Yearbook on Peace and Conflict Studies, 1986.* New York: Greenwood 1988
– "Historical anthropology, historical sociology, and the making of modern Europe." In *Approaching the Past: Historical Anthropology through Irish Case Studies,* edited by Marilyn Silverman and P.H. Gulliver. New York: Columbia University Press 1992
Clark, Samuel, and James S. Donnelly, Jr, eds. *Irish Peasants: Violence and Political Unrest.* Madison: University of Wisconsin Press 1983
Clarke, Aiden. "The Irish economy." In *A New History of Ireland,* 3: *Early Modern Ireland,* edited by T.W. Moody. Oxford: Clarendon Press 1976
Clarke, Aiden, and R. Dudley Edwards. "Pacification, plantation, and the Catholic question, 1603–23." In *A New History of Ireland,* 3: *Early Modern Ireland,* edited by T.W. Moody, F.X. Martin, and F.J. Byrne. Oxford: Clarendon Press 1976
Clay, Christopher. "Marriage, inheritance, and the rise of large estates in England, 1660–1815." *Economic History Review,* 2nd series, 21 (1968)
– "Landlords and estate management in England." In *The Agrarian History of England and Wales,* 2: *1640–1750: Agrarian Change,* edited by Joan Thirsk. Cambridge: Cambridge University Press 1985
Clout, H.D. "Early urban development." In *Themes in the Historical Geography of France,* edited by H.D. Clout. London: Academic Press 1977
– "Industrial development in the eighteenth and nineteenth centuries." In *Themes in the Historical Geography of France,* edited by H.D. Clout. London: Academic, 1977
Cobban, Alfred. *A History of Modern France,* 1: *Old Régime and Revolution, 1715–1799.* Harmondsworth: Penguin 1957
Coleman, Christopher, and David Starkey, eds. *Revolution Reassessed: Revisions in the History of Tudor Government and Administration.* Oxford: Clarendon Press 1986
Colley, Linda. *Britons: Forging a Nation 1707–1837.* New Haven: Yale University Press 1992
Collins, J.B. *The Fiscal Limits of Absolutism: Direct Taxation in Early Seventeenth-Century France.* Berkeley: University of California Press 1988

Colomy, Paul. "Uneven differentiation and incomplete institutionalization: political change and continuity in the early American nation." In *Differentiation Theory and Social Change: Comparative and Historical Perspectives*, edited by J.C. Alexander and Paul Colomy. New York: Columbia University Press 1990

Comninel, George. *Rethinking the French Revolution: Marxism and the Revisionist Challenge*. London: Verso 1987

- "English feudalism and the origins of capitalism" (forthcoming)

Congalton, A.A., and A.E. Daniel. *The Individual in the Making: An Introduction to Sociology*. Sydney: John Wiley 1976

Connolly, S.J. *Religion, Law, and Power: The Making of Protestant Ireland, 1660–1760*. Oxford: Clarendon Press 1992

Constant, Jean-Marie. "Nobles et paysans en Beauce aux xvième et xviième siècles," Thèse de doctorat d'état, Université de Paris iv, 1978

- "Les structures sociales et mentales de l'anoblissement: analyse comparative d'études récentes xvi-xvii siècles." In *L'anoblissement en France XVème–XVIIIème siècles: théories et réalitiés*, edited by Bernard Guillemain. Bordeaux: Université de Bordeaux iii 1985

Contamine, Philippe. "De la puissance aux privilèges: doléances de la noblesse française envers la monarchie aux xive et xve siècles." In *La noblesse au Moyen Age, XIe–XVe siècles: essais à la mémoire de Robert Boutruche*, edited by Philippe Contamine. Paris: Presses universitaires de France 1976

- "Introduction." In *La noblesse au Moyen Age, XIe-XVe siècles: essais à la mémoire de Robert Boutruche*, edited by Philippe Contamine. Paris: Presses universitaires de France 1976

- "The growth of the nation state." In *Britain and France: Ten Centuries*, edited by Douglas Johnson, François Crouzet, and François Bédarida. Folkestone: Dawson 1980

Cook, Richard. "The description of the Courte of Fraunce," edited by David Potter and P.R. Roberts. *French History* 2 (1988)

Cooper, J.P. "Differences between English and continental governments in the early seventeenth century." In *Britain and the Netherlands*, vol. 1, edited by J.S. Bromley and E.H. Kossmann. London: Chatto and Windus 1960

- "In search of agrarian capitalism." In *The Brenner Debate: Agrarian Class Structure and Economic Development in Pre-Industrial Europe*, edited by T.H. Aston and C.H.E. Philpin. Cambridge: Cambridge University Press 1985

Coornaert, Emile. *Les corporations en France avant 1789*. Paris: Editions ouvrières 1968

Cordey, Jean. *Les comtes de Savoie et les rois de France pendant la Guerre de cents ans, 1329–1391*. Paris: Ecole des hautes études 1911

Corrigan, Philip, and Derek Sayer. *The Great Arch: English State Formation as Cultural Revolution*. Oxford: Basil Blackwell 1985

Corvisier, André. *L'armée française de la fin du XVIIe siècle au ministère de Choiseul: le soldat*, 2 vols. Paris: Presses universitaires de France 1964

– *Armies and Societies in Europe, 1494–1789*, translated by Abigail T. Siddall. Bloomington: Indiana University Press 1979

Cosgrove, John. "The position of the recusant gentry in the social history of Lancashire, 1570–1642," MA thesis, University of Manchester 1964

Costamagna, Henri. "Pour une histoire de l'«intendenza» dans les états de terre-ferme de la Maison de Savoie à l'époque moderne." *Bollettino Storico-Bibliografico Subalpino* 83 (1985)

Cox, E.L. *The Green Count of Savoy: Amadeus VI and Transalpine Savoy in the Fourteenth Century.* Princeton: Princeton University Press 1967

Crawford, W.H. "Landlord-tenant relations in Ulster, 1609–1820." *Irish Economic and Social History* 2 (1975)

Cregeen, E.R. "The tacksmen and their successors: a study of tenurial reorganization in Mull, Morvern and Tiree in the early eighteenth century." *Scottish Studies* 13 (1969)

– "The changing role of the House of Argyll in the Scottish Highlands." In *Scotland in the Age of Improvement: Essays in Scottish History in the Eighteenth Century,* edited by N.T. Philipson and Rosalind Mitchison. Edinburgh: Edinburgh University Press 1970

Croot, Patricia, and David Parker. "Agrarian class structure and the development of capitalism: France and England compared." *Past and Present,* no. 78 (1978)

Crouzet, François. *De la supériorité de l'Angleterre sur la France: l'économique et l'imaginaire XVIIe–XXe siècles.* Paris: Perrin 1985

Cubells, Monique. "La politique d'anoblissement de la monarchie en Provence de 1715 à 1789." *Annales du Midi* 94 (1982)

Cuddy, Neil. "The revival of entourage: the bedchamber of James I, 1603–1625." In *The English Court: From the Wars of the Roses to the Civil War,* edited by David Starkey. London: Longman 1987

– "Anglo-Scottish Union and the Court of James I, 1603–1625." *Transactions of the Royal Historical Society,* 5th series, 39 (1989)

Cullen, L.M. *An Economic History of Ireland since 1660.* London: Batsford 1972

– *The Emergence of Modern Ireland, 1600–1900.* Dublin: Gill and Macmillan 1983

– "Landlords, bankers and merchants: the early Irish banking world, 1700–1820." *Hermathena,* no. 135 (1983)

Cunningham, Bernadette. "The composition of Connacht in the lordships of Clanricard and Thomand, 1577–1641." *Irish Historical Studies* 24 (1984)

Daquin, Joseph. *Topographie medicale de la ville de Chambery et ses environs.* 1787. Chambéry: Société savoisienne d'histoire et d'archéologie 1987

Darnton, Robert. *The Literary Underground of the Old Regime.* Cambridge: Harvard University Press 1982

Dauvergne, Robert. "Le problème du nombre des nobles en France au XVIIIe siècle". In *Hommage à Marcel Reinhard: sur la population française au XVIIIe et au XIXe siècles.* Paris: Société de démographie historique 1973

Davies, R.R. *Lordship and Society in the March of Wales, 1282–1400.* Oxford: Clarendon Press 1978

– *Conquest, Coexistence, and Change: Wales, 1063–1415.* Oxford: Clarendon Press 1987

– ed. *The British Isles, 1100–1500: Comparisons, Contrasts, and Connections.* Edinburgh: Donald 1988

– *Domination and Conquest: The Experience of Ireland, Scotland and Wales, 1100–1300.* Cambridge: Cambridge University Press 1990

Davis, W.W. *Joseph II: An Imperial Reformer for the Austrian Netherlands.* The Hague: Nijhoff 1974

Dawson, J.M.W. "An institutional and sociological study of the French intendants, 1652–1715," PhD dissertation, University of Toronto 1978

De Boom, Ghislaine. *Les voyages de Charles Quint.* Brussels: Office de publicité 1957

Defacqz, Eugène. *Ancien droit belge ou précis analytique des lois et coutumes observées en Belgique avant le Code civil,* 2 vols. Brussels: Méline, Cans 1846 and Bruylant Christophe 1873

Defoe, Daniel. *A Tour thro' the Whole Island of Great Britain,* 2 vols. 1724–6. London: Frank Cass 1968

Degryse, K. "Stadsadel en stadsbestuur te Antwerpen in de 18e eeuw: een sociaal-economische benadering." *Tijdschrift voor geschiedenis* 93 (1980)

Delatte, Ivan. *La vente des biens nationaux dans le département de Jemappes.* Brussels: Académie royale de Belgique 1938

– *Les classes rurales dans la principauté de Liège au XVIIIe siècle.* Liège: Université de Liège 1945

Demoulin, B. "La réaction de la noblesse et la défense de ses privileges dans la Principauté de Liège au début du XVIIIe siècle." In *Etudes sur le XVIIIe siècle,* no. 11: *Idéologies de la noblesse,* edited by Roland Mortier and Hervé Hasquin. Brussels: Editions de l'Université de Bruxelles 1984

Deneckere, Marcel. *Histoire de la langue française dans les Flandres, 1770–1823.* Ghent: Université de Gand 1954

DeNora, Tia. "Musical patronage and social change in Beethoven's Vienna." *American Journal of Sociology* 97 (1991)

Dent, Julian. "The role of clientèles in the financial élite of France under Cardinal Mazarin." In *French Government and Society: Essays in Memory of Alfred Cobban,* edited by J.F. Bosher. London: Athlone 1973

Deprez, Paul. "Evolution économique et mouvements paysans en Belgique à la fin du 18e siècle." *Revue belge d'histoire contemporaine* 4 (1973)

De Rammelaere, C. "Bijdrage tot de landbouwgeschiedenis in Zuid Oost-vlaanderen, 1510–1790." *Handelingen der Maatschappij voor geschiedenis en oudheidkunde te Gent,* new series, 16 (1962)

Desplat, Christian. "Les Etats de Béarn et la définition de la souveraineté béarnaise à l'époque moderne." *Parliaments, Estates and Representation* 3 (1983)

Dessert, Daniel. *Argent, pouvoir et société au Grand Siècle.* Paris: Fayard 1984

Devine, T.M. *The Tobacco Lords: A Study of the Tobacco Merchants of Glasgow and Their Trading Activities, c. 1740–90.* Edinburgh: Donald 1975

Devleeshouwer, Robert. "Les droits féodaux et leur abolition en Belgique." *Annales Historiques de la Révolution Française* 41 (1969)

Devos, Roger. "Un siècle en mutation, 1536–1684." In *Histoire de Savoie,* edited by Paul Guichonnet. Toulouse: Privat 1973

– "Elite et culture: les magistrats savoyards au XVIIe siècle." In *Cahiers de civilisation alpine,* 4: *Culture et pouvoir dans les Etats de Savoie du XVIIe siècle à la Révolution,* edited by G. Mombello, L. Sozzi, and L. Terreaux. Geneva: Slatkine 1985

Dewald, Jonathan. *The Formation of a Provincial Nobility: The Magistrates of the Parlement of Rouen, 1499–1610.* Princeton: Princeton University Press 1980

– *Pont-St-Pierre, 1398–1789: Lordship, Community, and Capitalism in Early Modern France.* Berkeley: University of California Press 1987

– *Aristocratic Experience and the Origins of Modern Culture: France, 1570–1715.* Berkeley: University of California Press 1993

De Win, Paul. "De adel in het hertogdom Brabant van de vijftiende eeuw; een terreinverkenning." *Tijdschrift voor geschiedenis* 93 (1980)

– "The lesser nobility of the Burgundian Netherlands." In *Gentry and Lesser Nobility in Late Medieval Europe,* edited by Michael Jones. Gloucester: Alan Sutton 1986

Dhondt, Jan. *Estates or Powers: Essays in the Parliamentary History of the Southern Netherlands from the XIIth to the XVIIIth Century,* edited by Willem Blockmans. Heule: UGA 1977

Dhondt, Luc, and Marie Fredericq-Lilar. "Flandre orientale." In *La vie culturelle dans nos provinces au XVIIIe siècle,* edited by Hervé Hasquin. Brussels: Crédit communal de Belgique 1983

Dickens, A.G. "Monarchy and cultural revival: courts in the Middle Ages." In *The Courts of Europe: Politics, Patronage and Royalty, 1400–1800,* edited by A.G. Dickens. London: Thames and Hudson 1977

Dictionary of National Biography, edited by Leslie Stephen and Sidney Lee. Oxford: Oxford University Press 1917

Dietz, F.C. "The Exchequer in Elizabeth's reign." *Smith College Studies in History* 8 (1923)

Ditchburn, David. "Trade with Northern Europe, 1297–1540." In *The Scottish Medieval Town,* edited by Michael Lynch, Michael Spearman, and Geoffrey Stell. Edinburgh: Donald, 1988

Ditchfield, G.M. "The Scottish representative peers and parliamentary politics, 1787–1793." *The Scottish Historical Review* 60 (1981)

Dodd, A.H. "The landed gentry after 1660." In *Wales through the Ages,* 2: *From 1485 to the Beginning of the 20th Century,* edited by A.J. Roderick. Aberystwyth: Davies 1960

Dodgshon, R.A. "A spatial perspective." *Peasant Studies* 6 (1977)

Donnelly, James S., Jr. "The Rightboy movement." *Studia Hibernica*, nos. 17 and 18 (1977–8)

– "The Whiteboy movement, 1761–5." *Irish Historical Studies* 21 (1978)

Douglas, D.C. *William the Conqueror: The Norman Impact upon England.* Berkeley: University of California Press 1964

Douxchamps-Lefèvre, Cécile. *Procureurs généraux du Conseil de Namur sous le régime autrichien.* Namur: Société archéologique 1961

– "Le commerce du charbon dans les Pays-Bas autrichiens à la fin du XVIIIe siècle." *Revue belge de philologie et d'histoire* 46 (1968)

– "Les Etats de Namur sous le Régime autrichien." *Anciens pays et assemblées d'états* 70 (1977)

– "Un magazine de la Cour de France au début du règne de Louis XVI." *Revue historique* 271 (1984)

Doyle, William. "Was there an aristocratic reaction in pre-revolutionary France?" *Past and Present*, no. 57 (1972)

– *The Parlement of Bordeaux and the End of the Old Regime, 1771–1790.* New York: St Martin's Press 1974

– *Origins of the French Revolution.* Oxford: Oxford University Press 1980

Dreyfus, F.-G. *Histoire de l'Alsace.* Paris: Hachette 1979

Duby, Georges. *La société aux XIe et XIIIe siècles dans la région mâconnaise.* Paris: Colin 1953

– *Rural Economy and Country Life in the Medieval West*, translated by Cynthia Postan. London: Edward Arnold 1968

– *The Chivalrous Society.* Berkeley: University of California Press 1977

Duerloo, Luc. "'Seer groote ongheregeltheden ... aengaende de titulen': evaluatie van de rol en het belang van het heraldisch proces." In *De Adel in het Hertogdom Brabant.* Brussels: Universitaire Faculteiten Sint-Aloysius 1985

– *Privilegies uitbeelden: de Zuidnederlandse wapenkoningen en wapenkunde in de eeuw der verlichting.* Brussels: AWLSK 1991

Duffy, P.J. "The territorial organization of Gaelic landownership and its transformation in County Monaghan, 1591–1640." *Irish Geography* 14 (1981)

Duncan, A.A.M. "The early parliaments of Scotland." *Scottish Historical Review* 45 (1966)

Durand, Yves. *Les fermiers généraux au XVIIIe siècle.* Paris: Presses universitaires de France 1971

Durkheim, Emile. *The Division of Labour in Society.* New York: Free Press 1984

Dyson, K.H.F. *The State Tradition in Western Europe: A Study of an Idea and Institution.* Oxford: Robertson 1980

Earle, Carville, and L.J. Hochberg, eds. *The Geography of Social Change.* Stanford: Stanford University Press (forthcoming)

Eaton, Daniel. *The Letters of Daniel Eaton to the Third Earl of Cardigan 1725–1732*, edited by Joan Wake and D.C. Webster. Northampton: Northamptonshire Record Society 1971

Einhard. *The Life of Charlemagne,* translated by S.E. Turner. Ann Arbor: University of Michigan Press 1960

Eisenstadt, S.N. *The Political Systems of Empires.* New York: Free Press 1963

– "Social change, differentiation and evolution." *American Sociological Review* 29 (1964)

– *Modernization: Protest and Change.* Englewood Cliffs: Prentice-Hall 1966

Eitzen, D.S. "Status inconsistency and Wallace supporters in a Midwestern city." *Social Forces* 48 (1970)

Elias, Norbert. *The Civilizing Process: Sociogenetic and Psychogenetic Investigations,* 1: *The Development of Manners: Changes in the Code of Conduct and Feeling in Early Modern Times,* translated by Edmund Jephcott. 1939. Oxford: Basil Blackwell 1978

– *The Civilizing Process: Sociogenetic and Psychogenetic Investigations,* 2: *State Formation and Civilization,* translated by Edmund Jephcott. 1939. Oxford: Basil Blackwell 1982

– *The Court Society,* translated by Edmund Jephcott. Oxford: Basil Blackwell 1983

Ellis, H.A. "Genealogy, history and aristocratic reaction in early eighteenth-century France: the case of Henri de Boulainvilliers." *Journal of Modern History* 58 (1986)

Ellis, S.G. *Tudor Ireland: Crown, Community and the Conflict of Cultures, 1470–1603.* London: Longman 1985

Elton, G.R. *The Tudor Revolution in Government: Administrative Changes in the Reign of Henry VIII.* Cambridge: Cambridge University Press 1953

– *Reform and Reformation: England, 1509–1558.* Cambridge: Harvard University Press 1977

Emerson, R.L. "The social composition of enlightened Scotland: the Select Society of Edinburgh, 1754–1764." *Studies on Voltaire and the Eighteenth Century* 114 (1973)

– "Lord Bute and the Scottish universities 1760–1792." In *Lord Bute: Essays in Re-interpretation,* edited by K.W. Schweizer. Leicester: Leicester University Press 1988

– *Professors, Patronage and Politics: The Aberdeen Universities in the Eighteenth Century.* Aberdeen: Aberdeen University Press 1992

– "Medical men, politicians, and the medical schools at Glasgow and Edinburgh, 1685–1803." *William Cullen and the Eighteenth-Century Medical World,* edited by Reginald Passmore et al. Edinburgh: Edinburgh University Press 1993

Emmanuel, Arghiri. *Unequal Exchange: A Study of the Imperialism of Trade.* New York: Monthly Review 1971

Esmonin, Edmond. *La taille en Normandie au temps de Colbert, 1661–1683.* Paris: Hachette 1913

Estoile, Pierre de l'. *Mémoires-journaux de Pierre de l'Estoile,* edited by Paul Lacroix et al. 12 vols. Paris: Lemerre 1888

Evans, E.D. *A History of Wales, 1660–1815.* Cardiff: University of Wales Press 1976

Evergates, Theodore. *Feudal Society in the Bailliage of Troyes under the Counts of Champagne, 1152–1284.* Baltimore: Johns Hopkins University Press 1975

Fédou, René. "La noblesse en France à la fin du Moyen Age (du milieu du XIVe à la fin du XVe siècle)." *Acta Universitatis Lodziensis,* 1st series, 71 (1980)

Finer, S.E. "State-building, state boundaries and border control: an essay on certain aspects of the first phase of state-building in Western Europe considered in the light of the Rokkan-Hirschman model." *Social Science Information* 13 (1974)

– "State- and nation-building in Europe: the role of the military." In *The Formation of National States in Western Europe,* edited by Charles Tilly. Princeton: Princeton University Press 1975

– "Princes, parliaments and the public service." *Parliamentary Affairs* 33 1980

Ford, Alan. "The Protestant Reformation in Ireland." In *Natives and Newcomers: Essays on the Making of Irish Colonial Society 1534–1641,* edited by Ciaran Brady and Raymond Gillespie. Dublin: Irish Academic Press 1986

Forster, Robert. *The Nobility of Toulouse in the Eighteenth Century: A Social and Economic Study.* Baltimore: Johns Hopkins University Press 1960

– "The noble wine producers of the Bordelais in the eighteenth century." *Economic History Review* 14 (1961)

– "The provincial noble: a reappraisal." *American Historical Review* 68 (1963)

– "The survival of the nobility during the French Revolution." *Past and Present,* no. 37 (1967)

Fossier, Robert. *La terre et les hommes en Picardie,* 2 vols. Paris: Faculté des Lettres et Sciences Humaines de Paris-Sorbonne 1968

– *Peasant Life in the Medieval West,* translated by Juliet Vale. Oxford: Basil Blackwell 1988

Foster-Carter, Aiden. "The modes of production controversy." *New Left Review* no. 107 (1978)

Fourez, Lucien. *Le droit héraldique dans les Pays-Bas catholiques.* Louvain: Université de Louvain 1932

Fox, E.W. *History in Geographic Perspective: The Other France.* New York: Norton 1971

– "The argument: some reinforcements and projections." In *Geographic Perspectives in History,* edited by E.D. Genovese and L.J. Hochberg. Oxford: Basil Blackwell 1989

Fox-Genovese, Elizabeth. *The Origins of Physiocracy: Economic Revolution and Social Order in Eighteenth-Century France.* Ithaca: Cornell University Press 1976

Frame, Robin. *The Political Development of the British Isles, 1100–1400.* Oxford: Oxford University Press 1990

Frank, André G. "The development of underdevelopment." *Monthly Review* 18 (1966)

– *Capitalism and Underdevelopment in Latin America* New York: Monthly Review 1967

– *Latin America – Underdevelopment or Revolution.* New York: Monthly Review 1969

– *Sociology of Development and Underdevelopment of Sociology.* London: Pluto 1971

– *Dependent Accumulation and Underdevelopment* London: Macmillan 1978

Frigio, Niccolò, to Francesco II Gonzaga, Brussels, 24 Jan. 1501, edited by W.F. Prizer. *Early Music History* 5 (1985)

Frotier de la Messelière, Henri. *La noblesse en Bretagne avant 1789.* Rennes: Université de Rennes 1902

Galliou, Patrick, and Michael Jones. *The Bretons.* Oxford: Basil Blackwell 1991

Gazier, Augustin, ed. *Lettres à Grégoire sur les patois de France, 1790–1794.* Paris: Durand and Pedone-Lauriel 1880

Genicot, Léopold. "La noblesse au Moyen Age dans l'ancienne 'Francie': continuité, rupture, ou évolution." *Comparative Studies in Society and History* 5 (1962)

– *Histoire de la Wallonie.* Toulouse: Privat 1973

Genovese, E.D., and L.J. Hochberg, eds. *Geographic Perspectives in History.* Oxford: Basil Blackwell 1989

Gerald of Wales, *The Journey through Wales/The Description of Wales,* translated by Lewis Thorpe. Harmondsworth: Penguin 1978

Gérard, P.A.S. *Histoire de la législation nobiliaire de Belgique.* Brussels: Vandale 1846

Geschwender, J.A. "Continuities in theories of status consistency and cognitive dissonance." *Social Forces* 46 (1967)

Giddens, Anthony. *Introduction to Sociology.* New York: W.W. Norton 1991

Gilissen, John. *Le régime répresentatif avant 1790 en Belgique.* Brussels: Renaissance du livre 1952

Gillingham, John. *Richard the Lionheart.* London: Weidenfeld and Nicolson 1978

Glamann, Kristof. "The changing patterns of trade." In *The Cambridge Economic History of Europe,* 5: *The Economic Organization of Early Modern Europe,* edited by E.E. Rich and C.H. Wilson. Cambridge: Cambridge University Press 1977

Glotz, Marguerite, and Madelaine Maire. *Salons du XVIIIe siècle.* Paris: Nouvelles éditions latines 1949

Godding, Philippe. *Le droit privé dans les Pays-Bas méridionaux de 12e au 18e siècle.* Brussels: Académie royale de Belgique 1987

Gold, T.B. *State and Society in the Taiwan Miracle.* Armonk: Sharpe 1986

Goldstone, J.A. *Revolution and Rebellion in the Modern World.* Berkeley: University of California Press 1991

Goodman, Dena. "Enlightenment salons: the convergence of female and philosophic ambitions." *Eighteenth-Century Studies* 22 (1989)

– "Governing the Republic of Letters: the politics of culture in the French Enlightenment." *History of European Ideas* 13 (1991)

Gordon, Daniel, "'Public opinion' and the civilizing process in France: the example of Morellet." *Eighteenth-Century Studies* 22 (1989)

Goubert, Pierre. *Beauvais et le Beauvaisis de 1600 à 1730: contribution à l'histoire sociale de la France du XVIIe*. Paris: SEVPEN 1960

– *The Ancien Régime: French Society, 1600–1750*. New York: Harper and Row 1973

Graham, H.G. *The Social Life of Scotland in the Eighteenth Century*. London: Black 1906

Grant, Alexander. "The development of the Scottish peerage." *Scottish Historical Review* 57 (1978)

– *The New History of Scotland*, 3: *Independence and Nationhood: Scotland 1306–1469*. London: Edward Arnold 1984

Grassby, R.B. "Social status and commercial enterprise under Louis XIV." *Economic History Review* 13 (1960)

Green, E.R.R. *The Lagan Valley, 1800–50: A Local History of the Industrial Revolution*. London: Faber and Faber 1949

Grieco, J.M. *Between Dependency and Autonomy: India's Experience with the International Computer Industry*. Berkeley: University of California Press 1984

Gruder, V.R. *The Royal Provincial Intendants: A Governing Elite in Eighteenth-Century France*. Ithaca: Cornell University Press 1968

Guichonnet, Paul, ed. *Histoire de Savoie*. Toulouse: Privat 1973

Guy, John. *Tudor England*. Oxford: Oxford University Press 1990

Gysseling, Maurits. "L'origine et fluctuations de la frontière linguistique dans le nord de la France." *Bulletin du comité flamand de France* 19 (1974)

Habakkuk, H.J. "English landownership, 1680–1740." *Economic History Review*, 1st series, 10 (1940)

– "England." In *The European Nobility in the Eighteenth Century: Studies of the Nobilities of the Major European States in the Pre-reform Era*, edited by A. Goodwin. London: Black 1953

Habermas, Jürgen. *Communication and the Evolution of Society*, translated by Thomas McCarthy. Boston: Beacon 1979

– *The Theory of Communicative Action*, 2: *Lifeworld and System: A Critique of Functionalist Reason*, translated by Thomas McCarthy. Boston: Beacon 1981

Hansotte, Georges. *La clouterie liégeoise et la question ouvrière au XVIIIe siècle*. Brussels: Librairie encyclopédique 1972

– *Les institutions politiques et judiciaires de la Principauté de Liège aux temps modernes*. Brussels: Crédit communal de Belgique 1987

Harris, R.D. "French finances and the American War, 1777–1783." *Journal of Modern History* 48 (1976)

Harriss, G.L. "The formation of Parliament, 1272–1377." In *The English Parliament in the Middle Ages*, edited by R.G. Davies and J.H. Denton. Manchester: Manchester University Press 1981

Harsin, Paul. *Histoire des finances publiques en Belgique*, 2 vols. Brussels: Institut belge de finances publiques 1950

– *La Révolution liégeoise de 1789*. Brussels: Renaissance du livre 1954

Hasquin, Hervé. "Les difficultés financières du gouvernement des Pays-Bas autrichiens au début du XVIIIe siècle, 1717–1740." *International Review of the History of Banking*, no. 6 (1973)

– "La vénalité des offices dans les Pays-Bas autrichiens." *Annales de la Fédération des cercles d'archéologie et d'histoire de Belgique, XLIVe session congrès de Huy* 44 (1976)

– "L'évolution démographique et sociale: les débuts de la francisation: une ville flamande qui se francise lentement." In *Bruxelles: croissance d'une capitale*, edited by Jean Stengers. Antwerp: Mercator 1979

Hatcher, John. "English serfdom and villeinage: towards a reassessment." *Past and Present*, no. 90 (1981)

Hatton, Ragnhild. *George I: Elector and King*. Cambridge: Harvard University Press 1978

Hayes, James. "Lieutenant-colonel and major-commandants of the Seven Years War." *Journal of the Society for Army Historical Research* 36 (1958)

– "Scottish officers in the British army, 1714–63." *Scottish Historical Review* 37 (1958)

Hayter, Tony. *The Army and the Crowd in Mid-Georgian England*. Towtowa: Rowman and Littlefield 1978

Hechter, Michael. *Internal Colonialism: The Celtic Fringe in British National Development, 1536–1966*. Berkeley: University of California Press 1975

Henneman, J.B. *Royal Taxation in Fourteenth-Century France: The Development of War Financing 1322–1356*. Princeton: Princeton University Press 1971

– *Royal Taxation in Fourteenth-Century France: The Captivity and Ransom of John II, 1356–1370*. Philadelphia: American Philosophical Society 1976

– "Nobility, privilege and fiscal politics in late Medieval France." *French Historical Studies* 13 (1983)

Henning, B.D. *The House of Commons, 1660–1690*, 1: *Introductory Survey, Appendices, Constituencies, Members A–B*. London: Secker and Warburg 1983

Herbert, Trevor, and G.E. Jones. eds. *Tudor Wales*. Cardiff: University of Wales Press 1988

Hexter, J.H. *Reappraisals in History: New Views on History and Society in Early Modern Europe*. Chicago: University of Chicago Press 1979

Hickey, Daniel. *The Coming of French Absolutism: The Struggle for Tax Reform in the Province of Dauphiné, 1540–1640*. Berkeley: University of California Press 1974

Hildesheimer, Françoise. *Le Jansénisme*. Paris: Publisud 1991

Hill, David. "Towns as structures and functioning communities through time: the development of central places from 600 to 1066." In *Anglo-Saxon Settlements*, edited by Della Hooke. Oxford: Basil Blackwell 1988

Hill, John E.C. *The Century of Revolution 1603–1714*. Edinburgh: Nelson 1961

Hill, Richard. *The Diplomatic Correspondence of The Right Hon. Richard Hill, Envoy Extraordinary from the Court of St. James to the Duke of Savoy, in the Reign of Queen Anne from July 1703 to May 1706*, edited by W. Blackey, 2 vols. London: Murray 1845

Hilton, Rodney. *Bond Men Made Free*. New York: Viking 1973

– et al. *The Transition from Feudalism to Capitalism*. London: Verso 1978

– "Feudal society." In *A Dictionary of Marxist Thought*, edited by Tom Bottomore. Cambridge: Harvard University Press 1983

– "Feudalism in Europe: problems for historical materialists." *New Left Review*, no. 147 (1984)

Hobhouse, Leonard T. *Social Evolution and Political Theory*. New York: Columbia University Press 1911

Hochberg, L.J. "The English Civil War in geographical perspective." *Journal of Interdisciplinary History* 14 (1984)

Hochberg, L.J., and D.W. Miller, "Internal colonialism in geographic perspective: the case of pre-famine Ireland." In *The Geography of Social Change*, edited by Carville Earle and L.J. Hochberg. Stanford: Stanford University Press (forthcoming)

Hodges, Richard. "Anglo-Saxon England and the origins of the modern world economy." In *Anglo-Saxon Settlements*, edited by Della Hooke. Oxford: Basil Blackwell 1988

Hollingsworth, H.T. "The demography of the British peerage," supplement to *Population Studies* 18 (1964)

Holmes, Geoffrey S. *British Politics in the Age of Anne*. New York: St Martin's 1967

Holton, R.J. *The Transition from Feudalism to Capitalism*. London: Macmillan 1985

Hopkinson, R. "The electorate of Cumberland and Westmorland in the late seventeenth and early eighteenth centuries." *Northern History* 15 (1979)

Hoppit, Julian. "Financial crises in eighteenth-century England." *Economic History Review*, 2nd series, 39 (1986)

Howell, D.W. "Landlords and estate management in Wales." In *The Agrarian History of England and Wales*, 5: *1640–1750: Agrarian Change*, edited by Joan Thirsk. Cambridge: Cambridge University Press 1985

– *Patriarchs and Parasites: The Gentry of South-West Wales in the Eighteenth Century*. Cardiff: University of Wales Press 1986

Howells, J.N. "The Crosswood estate, 1683–1899," MA thesis, University of Wales 1956

Hudemann-Simon, Calixte. *La noblesse luxembourgeoise au XVIIIe siècle*. Luxembourg and Paris: L'Institut Grand-Ducal and La Sorbonne 1985

Humphreys, T.M. "Rural society in eighteenth-century Montgomeryshire," PhD dissertation, University of Wales 1982

Hunt, Tony. "The emergence of the knight in France and England, 1000–1200." *Forum for Modern Language Studies* 17 (1981)

Hyams, P.R. *Kings, Lords and Peasants in Medieval England: The Common Law of Villeinage in the Twelfth and Thirteenth Centuries.* Oxford: Clarendon Press 1980

Innes of Learney, Thomas. *Scots Heraldry: A Practical Handbook on the Historical Principles and Modern Application of the Art and Science.* Baltimore: Genealogical Publishing 1971

Jackson, E.F. "Status consistency and symptoms of stress." *American Sociological Review* 27 (1962)

Jackson, R.A. "Peers of France and princes of the blood." *French Historical Studies* 7 (1971)

Jacquart, Jean. "French agriculture in the seventeenth century." In *Essays in European Economic History, 1500–1800,* edited by Peter Earle. Oxford: Clarendon Press 1974

James, Edward. *The Origins of France: From Clovis to the Capetians, 500–1000.* London: Macmillan 1982

James, F.G. *Ireland in the Empire, 1688–1770: A History of Ireland from the Williamite Wars to the Eve of the American Revolution.* Cambridge: Harvard University Press 1973

– "The active Irish peers in the early eighteenth century." *Journal of British Studies* 18 (1979)

– *Lords of the Ascendancy: The Irish House of Lords and Its Members, 1634–1800* (forthcoming)

James, M.E. *Change and Continuity in the Tudor North.* York: Borthwick Institute 1965

James VI. *The Basilicon Doron of King James VI,* edited by James Craigie. Edinburgh: Blackwood 1944

Janssens, Paul. "Coûts et profits des structures nobiliaires dans une société de type pré-industriel: les Pays-Bas méridionaux du xème au xviième siècle," unpublished paper 1976

– "L'échec des tentatives de soulèvement aux Pays-Bas sous Philippe IV, 1621–1665." *Revue d'histoire diplomatique* 92 (1978)

– "De Zuidnederlandse adel tijdens het Ancien Régime, 17e–18e eeuw: problemen en stand van het onderzoek." *Tijdschrift voor Geschiedenis* 93 (1980)

– "La densité nobiliaire dans les Pays-Bas autrichiens à la fin de l'ancien régime." *Actes du Congrès de la Fédération des cercles d'archéologie et d'histoire de Belgique* 46 (1982)

– "Willem van Oranje aan het Brussels hof 1549–1559." *Spiegel historiael* 19 (1984)

– "De achttiende eeuw: een lage, maar zware belastingdruk." In *Drie eeuwen belgische belastingen: van contributies, controleurs en belastingconsulenten.* Brussels: Maeckelbergh 1990

– "L'esprit mercantiliste et la notion de dérogeance dans les Pays-Bas espagnols et autrichiens." In *Studia historica œconomica: liber amicorum & liber
alumnorum Herman Van der Wee*, edited by Erik Aerts, Brigitte Henau, Paul
Janssens, and Raymond Van Uytven. Leuven: Universitaire pers Leuven
1993

– "Les charges anoblissantes dans les conseils des Pay-Bas espagnols et autrichiens." In *Beleid en bestuur in de Oude Nederlanden: liber amicorum prof. dr. M.
Baelde*, edited by Hugo Soly and René Vermeir. Ghent: Universiteit Gent
1993

– *L'évolution de la noblesse belge depuis la fin du Moyen Age*. Brussels: Crédit
communal de Belgique (forthcoming)

Javitch, Daniel. "*The Philosopher of the Court*: a French satire misunderstood."
Comparative Literature 23 (1971)

Jenkins, G.H. *The Foundation of Modern Wales, 1642–1780*. Oxford: Clarendon
Press 1987

Jenkins, Philip. *The Making of a Ruling Class: The Glamorgan Gentry, 1640–1790*.
Cambridge: Cambridge University Press 1983

– *A History of Modern Wales, 1536–1990*. London: Longman 1992

Johnson, Samuel. *A Journey to the Western Islands of Scotland*. 1775. Oxford:
Oxford University Press 1924

Johnston, E.M. *Ireland in the Eighteenth Century*. Dublin: Gill and Macmillan 1974

Jones, G.E. "Tudor Glamorgan and the historian." *Morgannwg* 18 (1975)

– *Modern Wales: A Concise History c. 1485–1979*. Cambridge: Cambridge University Press 1984

Jones, G.G. "The Order of the Golden Fleece: form, function, and evolution,
1430–1555," PhD dissertation, Texas Christian University 1988

Jones, Gwynfor. "The gentry." In *Tudor Wales*, edited by Trevor Herbert and
G.E. Jones. Cardiff: University of Wales Press 1988

Jones, J.G. "The Caernarvonshire justices of the peace and their duties during
the seventeenth century," MA thesis, University of Wales 1966

Jouanna, Arlette. "L'idée de race en France au XVIème siècle et au début du
XVIIème siècle, 1498–1614," Thèse de doctorat d'état, 5 vols., Université
de Paris IV 1975

Kearney, Hugh. *The British Isles: A History of Four Nations*. Cambridge: Cambridge University Press 1989

Keen, Maurice. *Chivalry*. London: Yale University Press 1984

Kelch, R.A. "The dukes: a study of the English nobility in the eighteenth
century," PhD dissertation, Ohio State University 1955

Keller, Suzanne. *Beyond the Ruling Class*. New York: Arno 1979

Kennedy, Paul. *Rise and Fall of the Great Powers: Economic Change and Military
Conflict from 1500 to 2000*. London: Fontana 1988

Kennett, Lee. *The French Armies in the Seven Years' War*. Durham: Duke University
Press 1967

Kerridge, Eric. *The Agricultural Revolution.* London: George Allen and Unwin 1967

– *Agrarian Problems in the Sixteenth Century and After.* London: George Allen and Unwin 1969

Kettering, Sharon. *Patrons, Brokers, and Clients in Seventeenth-Century France.* New York: Oxford University Press 1986

Kimmel, M.S. "The ambivalence of absolutism: state and nobility in 17th century France and England." *Journal of Political and Military Sociology* 14 (1986)

– *Absolutism and Its Discontents: State and Society in Seventeenth-Century France and England.* New Brunswick, NJ: Transaction Books 1988

King, Gregory. *Natural and Political Observations and Conclusions upon the State and Condition of England, 1696.* 1696. London: Gregg 1973

Kirby, D.P. *The Making of Early England.* London: Batsford 1967

Kiser, Edgar, and Michael Hechter. "The role of general theory in comparative-historical sociology." *American Journal of Sociology* 97 (1991)

Knecht, R.J. *Francis I.* Cambridge: Cambridge University Press 1982

Kochan, Lionel, and Richard Abraham. *The Making of Modern Russia.* London: Macmillan 1983

Krauss, Irving. *Stratification, Class and Conflict.* London: Collier MacMillan 1976

Kriesberg, Louis. *Social Inequality.* Englewood Cliffs: Prentice-Hall 1979

Labarge, M.W. *Saint Louis: The Life of Louis IX of France.* Toronto: Macmillan 1968

Labatut, Jean-Pierre. *Les ducs et pairs de France au XVIIe siècle.* Paris: Presses universitaires de France 1972

– *Les noblesses européennes de la fin du XVe siècle à la fin du XVIIIe siècle.* Paris: Presses universitaires de France 1978

Labrousse, Elisabeth. *La révocation de l'Edit de Nantes: une foi, une loi, un roi?* 1985. Paris: Payot 1990

Lachmann, Richard. "Elite conflict and state formation in 16th- and 17th-century England and France." *American Sociological Review* 54 (1989)

Landau, Norma. *The Justices of the Peace, 1679–1760.* Berkeley: University of California Press 1984

Landecker, W.S. *Class Crystallization.* New Brunswick, NJ: Rutgers University Press 1981

Lander, J.R. "Attainder and forfeiture, 1453 to 1509." *Historical Journal* 4 (1961)

– *Government and Community: England, 1450–1509.* Cambridge: Harvard University 1980

– *English Justices of the Peace, 1461–1509.* Gloucester: Alan Sutton 1989

– *The Limitations of English Monarchy in the Later Middle Ages.* Toronto: University of Toronto Press 1989

Large, David. "The wealth of the greater Irish landowners, 1750–1815." *Irish Historical Studies* 15 (1966)

Large, P.F.W. "Economic and social change in North Worcestershire during the seventeenth century," PhD dissertation, Oxford University 1980

Laslett, Peter. *The World We Have Lost.* London: Methuen 1971

Lebrun, Pierre. *L'industrie de la laine à Verviers pendant le XVIIIe et le début du XIXe siècle: contribution à l'étude des origines de la Révolution industrielle.* Liège: Université de Liège 1948

Lefevre, Joseph. "La haute magistrature belge du XVIIIe siècle." *Revue générale belge* 87 (1952)

Le Goff, T.J.A. *Vannes and Its Region: A Case Study of Town and Country in Eighteenth-Century France.* Oxford: Clarendon Press 1981

Lemoine, Robert-J. "Classes sociales et attitudes révolutionaires: quelques réflexions sur un chapitre d'histoire belge." *Annales d'histoire économique et sociale* 7 (1935)

Lennon, Colm. "The Counter-Reformation in Ireland." In *Natives and Newcomers: Essays on the Making of Irish Colonial Society 1534–1641,* edited by Ciaran Brady and Raymond Gillespie. Dublin: Irish Academic Press 1986

Lenski, G.E. "Status crystallization: a non-vertical dimension of social status." *American Sociological Review* 19 (1954)

Le Patourel, John "The Norman Conquest of Yorkshire." *Northern History* 6 (1971)

Le Roy Ladurie, Emmanuel. "Auprès du roi, la cour." *Annales: ESC* 38 (1983)

Lewis, P.S. "The failure of the French Medieval estates." *Past and Present,* no. 23 (1962)

– "Decayed and non-feudalism in later medieval France." *Bulletin of the Institute of Historical Research* 37 (1964)

Lloyd, H.A. *The Gentry of South-West Wales, 1540–1640.* Cardiff: University of Wales Press 1968

Logan, F.D. *The Vikings in History.* London: Collins 1991

Loriga, Sabina. *Soldats: un laboratoire disciplinaire: l'armée piémontaise au XVIIIe siècle.* Paris: Mentha 1991

Lougee, Carolyn C. *Le Paradis des Femmes: Women, Salons and Social Stratification in Seventeenth-Century France.* Princeton: Princeton University Press 1976

Louis XIV. *Mémoires de Louis XIV pour l'instruction du dauphin,* edited by Charles Dreyss, 2 vols. Paris: Didier 1860

Lowe, W.C. "Bishops and Scottish representative peers in the House of Lords, 1760–1775." *Journal of British Studies* 18 (1978)

Lucas, R.H. "Ennoblement in late medieval France." *Mediaeval Studies* 39 (1977)

Lüthy, Herbert. *La banque protestante en France de la Révocation de l'Edit de Nantes à la Révolution,* 2 vols. Paris: SEVEN, 1959, 1961

Lydon, James. *Ireland in the Later Middle Ages.* Dublin: Gill and Macmillan 1973

Lynn, J.A. "The growth of the French army during the seventeenth century." *Armed Forces and Society* 6 (1980)

McCahill, B.A.K. "The Tudor peers: their demographic profile and role in government administration," PhD dissertation, Tufts University 1978

McCahill, Michael W. "The Scottish peerage and the House of Lords in the late eighteenth century." *Scottish Historical Review* 51 (1972)

– *Order and Equipoise: The Peerage and the House of Lords, 1783–1806.* London: Royal Historical Society 1978

– "Peerage creations and the changing character of the British nobility, 1750–1850." *English Historical Review* 96 (1981)

McCarthy, S.T. (The MacCarthy Mor), "Ulster Office, 1552–1800," MA thesis, Queen's University of Belfast 1983

McCracken, J.L. *The Irish Parliament in the Eighteenth Century.* Dublin: Dublin Historical Association 1971

MacCurtain, Margaret. *Tudor and Stuart Ireland.* Dublin: Gill and Macmillan 1972

MacDougall, Norman. *James III: A Political Study.* Edinburgh: Donald 1982

McDowell, R.B. *Ireland in the Age of Imperialism, 1760–1801.* Oxford: Clarendon Press 1979

McFarlane, K.B. *The Nobility of Later Medieval England: The Ford Lectures for 1953 and Related Studies.* Oxford: Clarendon Press 1973

McGuire, J.I. "The Irish Parliament of 1692." In *Penal Era and Golden Age,* edited by Thomas Bartlett and D.W. Hayton. Belfast: Ulster Historical Foundation 1979

McMichael, Philip. "Incorporating comparison within a world-historical perspective: an alternative comparative method." *American Sociological Review* 55 (1990)

Mack, Katherin. "Changing thegns: Cnut's conquest and the English aristocracy." *Albion* 16 (1984)

Mackie, J.D. *A History of Scotland,* revised and edited by Bruce Lenman and Geoffrey Parker. 1964. Harmondsworth: Penguin 1978

MacNiocaill, Gearóid. *Ireland before the Vikings.* Dublin: Gill and Macmillan 1972

Maine, H.S. *Ancient Law: Its Connection with the Early History of Society, and Its Relation to Modern Ideas.* 1864. Tucson: University of Arizona Press 1986

Major, J. Russell. *Representative Institutions in Renaissance France, 1421–1559.* Madison: University of Wisconsin Press 1960

– *Representative Government in Early Modern France.* New Haven: Yale University Press 1980

Malcomson, A.P.W. "Election politics in the borough of Antrim, 1750–1800." *Irish Historical Studies* 17 (1970)

– "Absenteeism in eighteenth century Ireland." *Irish Economic and Social History* 1 (1974)

Mann, Michael. "The autonomous power of the state: its origins, mechanisms and results." In his *States, War and Capitalism*. Oxford: Basil Blackwell 1988
– "State and society, 1130–1815: an analysis of English state finances." In *Political Power and Social Theory*, vol. 1, edited by M. Zeitlin. Greenwich: JAI 1980
– *The Sources of Social Power*, 2 vols. Cambridge: Cambridge University Press 1986, 1993
Manning, R.B. *Village Revolts: Social Protest and Popular Disturbances in England, 1509–1640*. Oxford: Clarendon Press 1988
– "Antiquarianism and the seigneurial reaction: Sir Robert and Sir Thomas Cotton and their tenants." *Historical Research* 63 (1990)
– "Poaching as a symbolic substitute for war in Tudor and early Stuart England." *Journal of Medieval and Renaissance Studies* 22 (1992)
Marion, Marcel. *Dictionnaire des institutions de la France aux XVIIe et XVIIIe siècles*. Paris: Picard 1979
Markoff, John, and Gilbert Shapiro. "Consensus and conflict at the onset of revolution: a quantitative study of France in 1789." *American Journal of Sociology* 91 (1985)
Marly, Diana de. *Louis XIV and Versailles*. New York: Holmes and Meier 1987
Marshall, T.H. *Class, Citizenship and Social Development*. New York: Doubleday 1964
Martin, F.X. "Allies and an overlord." In *A New History of Ireland, 2: Medieval Ireland, 1169–1534*, edited by Art Cosgrove. Oxford: Clarendon Press 1987
– "Diarmait MacMurchada and the coming of the Anglo-Normans." In *A New History of Ireland, 2: Medieval Ireland, 1169–1534*, edited by Art Cosgrove. Oxford: Clarendon Press 1987
– "Overlord becomes feudal lord, 1172–85." In *A New History of Ireland, 2: Medieval Ireland, 1169–1534*, edited by Art Cosgrove. Oxford: Clarendon Press 1987
Martin, J.E. *Feudalism to Capitalism: Peasant and Landlord in English Agrarian Development*. London: Humanities 1983
Martin, Ronald. "The army of Louis the XIV." In *The Reign of Louis XIV*, edited by Paul Sonnino. Atlantic Highlands: Humanities Press International 1990
Martindale, Jane. "The French aristocracy in the early Middle Ages: a reappraisal." *Past and Present*, no. 75 (1977)
Mat-Hasquin, Michèle, and Hervé Hasquin. "Le Hainaut." *La vie culturelle dans nos provinces au XVIIIe siècle*, edited by Hervé Hasquin. Brussels: Crédit communal de Belgique 1983
Mathew, David. *James I*. London: Eyre and Spottiswoode 1967
Mathias, Peter, and Patrick O'Brien. "Taxation in Britain and France, 1715–1810: a comparison of the social and economic incidence of taxes collected for the central governments." *Journal of European Economic History* 5 (1976)
Mathieu, Rémi. *Le système héraldique français*. Paris: Janin 1946

Maxwell, Constantia. *Country and Town in Ireland under the Georges*. London: Harrap 1940

Mayer, K.B. *Class and Society*. New York: Random House 1955

Mayes, C.R. "The sale of peerages in early Stuart England." *Journal of Modern History* 29 (1957)

– "The early Stuarts and the Irish peerage." *English Historical Review* 73 (1958)

Mellers, Wilfred. "Music: paradise and paradox in the seventeenth century." In *The Cambridge Cultural History of Britain*, 4: *Seventeenth-Century Britain*, edited by Boris Ford. Cambridge: Cambridge University Press 1989

Mettam, Roger. *Power and Faction in Louis XIV's France*. Oxford: Basil Blackwell 1988

Meyer, Jean. *La noblesse bretonne au XVIIe siècle*, 2 vols. Paris: Ecole pratique des hautes études 1966

– "La noblesse française au XVIIIème siècle: aperçu des problèmes." *Acta polonaie historica* 36 (1977)

– "Au rythme du Monde atlantique." In *Histoire de la Bretagne*, edited by Jean Delumeau. Paris: Privat 1991

– "Le siècle de l'intendance." In *Histoire de Bretagne*, edited by Jean Delumeau. Paris: Privat 1991

Miller, Helen. "Subsidy assessments of the peerage in the sixteenth century." *Historical Research* 28 (1955)

– *Henry VIII and the English Nobility*. Oxford: Basil Blackwell 1986

Miner, Horace. "The folk-urban continuum." *American Sociological Review* 17 (1952)

Mingay, G.E. *Enclosure and the Small Farmer in the Age of the Industrial Revolution*. London: Macmillan 1968

– *The Gentry: The Rise and Fall of a Ruling Class*. London: Longman 1976

Mitchell, B.R., and Phyllis Deane. *Abstract of British Historical Statistics*. Cambridge: Cambridge University Press 1962

Mitchison, Rosalind. "Patriotism and national identity in eighteenth-century Scotland." *Historical Studies* 11 (1978)

– *A New History of Scotland*, 5: *Lordship to Patronage: Scotland, 1603–1745*. London: Edward Arnold 1983

Mitford, Nancy. *Madame de Pompadour*. Harmondsworth: Penguin 1958

Mokyr, Joel. *Why Ireland Starved: A Quantitative and Analytical History of the Irish Economy, 1800–1850*. Winchester: George Allen and Unwin 1983

Mollat, Guillaume. *The Popes at Avignon, 1309–1376*, translated by Janet Love. London: Thomas Nelson 1963

Moore, Barrington, Jr. *Social Origins of Dictatorship and Democracy: Lord and Peasant in the Making of the Modern World*. Boston: Beacon 1966

Moote, A. Lloyd. *The Revolt of the Judges*. Princeton: Princeton University 1971

Morineau, Michel. *Les faux-semblants d'un démarrage économique: agriculture et démographie en France au XVIIIe siècle*. Paris: Colin 1971

– "Budgets de l'Etat et gestion des finances royales en France au dix-huitième siècle." *Revue historique* 264 (1980)

Mortier, Roland, and Hervé Hasquin, eds. *Etudes sur le XVIIIe siècle*, no. 12: *Une famille noble de hauts fonctionnaires: les Neny.* Brussels: Editions de l'Université de Bruxelles 1985

Motley, Mark E. *Becoming a French Aristocrat: The Education of the Nobility, 1580–1715*. Princeton: Princeton University Press 1990

Mourier, Jacques. "Nobilitas, quid est? Un procès à Tain l'Hermitage en 1408." *Bibliothèque de l'Ecole des Chartres* 142 (1984)

Mousnier, Roland. *Social Hierarchies: 1450 to the Present*. New York: Schocken 1973

– *Recherches sur la stratification sociale à Paris aux XVIIe et XVIIIe siècles*. Paris: Pedone 1976

– *The Institutions of France under the Absolute Monarchy, 1598–1789*, 2 vols. Chicago: University of Chicago Press 1979

– "Le caractère de l'état français au moment de la Révolution." In *La Révolution fançaise–produit de la contingence ou la nécessité? Actes du colloque à l'Université de Bamberg du 4 au 7 Juin 1979*. Munich: Oldenbourg 1983

– "Centralisation et décentralisation." *XVIIe siècle*, no. 155 (1987)

Murdoch, Alexander. *'The People Above': Politics and Administration in Mid-Eighteenth-Century Scotland*. Edinburgh: Donald 1980

Murison, David. "The historical background." In *Languages of Scotland*, edited by A.J. Aitken and Tom McArthur. Edinburgh: Chambers 1979

Namier, L.B. *The Structure of Politics at the Accession of George III*. London: Macmillan 1957

Neushel, Kristen B. *Word of Honor: Interpreting Noble Culture in Sixteenth-Century France*. Ithaca: Cornell University Press 1989

Newman, F.X., ed. *The Meaning of Courtly Love*. Albany: State University of New York Press 1968

Nicholas, Karen. "Feudal relationships in the Low Countries: a comparative study of nine principalities," PhD dissertation, Brown University 1972

Nicholls, Kenneth. "Gaelic society and economy in the High Middle Ages." In *A New History of Ireland*, 2: *Medieval Ireland, 1169–1534*, edited by Art Cosgrove. Oxford: Clarendon Press 1987

Nicolas, Jean. "Ombres et lumières du XVIIIe siècle." In *Histoire de Savoie*, edited by Paul Guichonnet. Toulouse: Privat 1973

– *La Savoie au 18e siècle: noblesse et bourgeoisie*, 2 vols. Paris: Maloine 1978

O'Brien, I.E. "The Scottish parliament in the fifteenth and sixteenth centuries," PhD dissertation, University of Glasgow 1980

O'Corrain, Donncha. *Ireland before the Normans*. Dublin: Gill and Macmillan 1972

O'Dowd, Mary. "Gaelic economy and society." In *Natives and Newcomers: Essays on the Making of Irish Colonial Society 1534–1641*, edited by Ciaran Brady and Raymond Gillespie. Dublin: Irish Academic Press 1986

- "Land and lordship in sixteenth- and early seventeenth-century Ireland." In *Economy and Society in Scotland and Ireland, 1500–1939*, edited by Rosalind Mitchison and Peter Roebuck. Edinburgh: Donald 1988
O'Gorman, Frank. "Electoral deference in 'unreformed' England: 1760–1832." *Journal of Modern History* 56 (1984)
- *Voters, Patrons and Parties: The Unreformed Electoral System of Hanovarian England, 1734–1832*. Oxford: Clarendon Press 1989
O'Neill, Timothy. *Merchants and Mariners in Medieval Ireland*. Dublin: Irish Academic Press 1987
Ormrod, W.M. *The Reign of Edward III: Crown and Political Society in England, 1327–1377*. New Haven: Yale University Press 1990
Otway-Ruthven, A.J. *A History of Medieval Ireland*. London: Ernest Benn 1968
Painter, Sidney. *Studies in the History of English Feudal Barony*. Baltimore: Johns Hopkins University Press 1943
Pareto, Vildredo. *The Rise and Fall of the Elites: An Application of Theoretical Sociology*. Totowa: Bedminster 1968
Parker, Geoffrey. *The Army of Flanders and the Spanish Road, 1567–1659: The Logistics of Spanish Victory and Defeat in the Low Countries' Wars*. Cambridge: Cambridge University Press 1972
- *The Dutch Revolt*, revised edition. Harmondsworth: Penguin 1985
- *Spain and the Netherlands, 1559–1659: Ten Studies*. London: Fontana 1990
Parkin, Frank. *Max Weber*. Chichester and London: Ellis Horwood and Tavistock 1982
Parsons, Talcott. "Evolutionary universals in society." *American Sociological Review* 29 (1964)
- *The Evolution of Societies*, edited by Jackson Toby. Englewood Cliffs: Prentice-Hall 1977
Pepys, Samuel. *The Diary of Samuel Pepys*, edited by G.G. Smith. London: Macmillan 1925
Péret, Jacques. "Bourgeoisie rurale et seigneurs au XVIIIe siècle: les fermiers généraux du duché de la Meilleraye." *Bulletin de la Société des antiquaires de l'ouest et des musées de Poitiers*, 4th series, 12 (1974)
Périn, Patrick. *Clovis et la naissance de la France*. Paris: Sogemo/Denoël 1990
Perissino-Billen, Claire. "Des campagnes sous le joug des traditions." *La Wallonie: le pays et les hommes–histoire, économies sociétes*, vol. 1, edited by Hervé Hasquin. Brussels: Renaissance du livre 1975
Perret, André. *Les institutions dans l'ancienne Savoie du onzième au seizième siècle*. Chambéry: Département de la Savoie 1981
Perroy, Eduard. "Social mobility and the French *noblesse* in the later Middle Ages." *Past and Present*, no. 21 (1962)
Petit-Dutaillis, Charles. *Etude sur la vie et règne de Louis VIII, 1187–1226*. Paris: Bouillon 1894
Peyre, Henri. *La royauté et les langues provinciales*. Paris: Presses modernes 1933

Phillipson, N.T. "Culture and society in the eighteenth century province: the case of Edinburgh and the Scottish Enlightenment." In *The University in Society*, vol. 2, edited by Lawrence Stone. Princeton: Princeton University Press 1974

– "Lawyers, landowners, and the civic leadership of post-Union Scotland: an essay on the social role of the Faculty of Advocates 1661–1830 in 18th century Scottish society." *Judicial Review* 21 (1976)

Pierce, T. Jones. "Landlords in Wales: the nobility and gentry." In *The Agrarian History of England and Wales*, 4: *1500–1640*, edited by Joan Thirsk. Cambridge: Cambridge University Press 1967

Pirotte, Fernand. *La Terre de Durbuy aux XVIIe et XVIIIe siècles: les institutions, l'économie et les hommes.* Liège: Centre belge d'histoire rurale 1974

Plumb, J.H. *Sir Robert Walpole: The Making of a Statesman.* Boston: Houghton Mifflin 1956

Polasky, Janet. *Revolution in Brussels, 1787–1793.* Brussels: Académie royale de Belgique 1987

Porchnev, B.F. *Les soulèvements populaires en France de 1623 à 1648.* Paris: SEVPEN 1965

Potter, David, and P.R. Roberts. "An Englishman's view of the court of Henri III, 1548–1585: Richard Cook's 'Description of the court of France.'" *French History* 2 (1988)

Poullet, Edmond. "Les constitutions nationales belges de l'ancien régime à l'époque de l'invasion française de 1794." *Mémoires couronnés et autres mémoires de l'Académie royale des sciences, des lettres et des beaux-arts de Belgique* 26 (1875)

Powell, J.E., and Keith Wallis. *The House of Lords in the Middle Ages: A History of the English House of Lords to 1540.* London: Weidenfeld and Nicolson 1968

Power, Thomas. *Land, Politics, and Society in Eighteenth-Century Tipperary.* Oxford: Clarendon Press 1993

Pritchard, *Louis XV's Navy, 1748–1762: A Study of Organization and Administration.* Montreal: McGill-Queen's University Press 1987

Problems of a Growing City: Belfast, 1780–1870. Belfast: Public Record Office of Northern Ireland 1973

Pugh, T.B., and C.D. Ross. "The English baronage and the income tax of 1436." *Bulletin of the Institute of Historical Research* 26 (1953)

Puy de Clinchamps, Philippe du. *La Chevalerie.* Paris: Presses Universitaires de France 1961

Ramsay, J.H. *A History of the Revenues of the Kings of England, 1066–1399*, 2 vols. Oxford: Clarendon Press 1925

Ranum, Orest. "Richelieu and the great nobility: some aspects of early modern political motives." *French Historical Studies* 3 (1963)

– "Courtesy, absolutism, and the rise of the French state, 1630–1660." *Journal of Modern History* 52 (1980)

Ravitch, Norman. *Sword and Mitre: Government and Episcopate in France and England in the Age of Aristocracy.* The Hague: Mouton 1966

Razzell, P.E. "Social origins of officers in the Indian and British Home Army: 1758–1962." *British Journal of Sociology* 14 (1963)

Redfield, Robert. "The Folk Society." *American Journal of Sociology* 52 (1947)

Reid, R.R. *The King's Council in the North.* London: Longman 1921

Richard, Guy. *Noblesse d'affaires au XVIIIe siècle.* Paris: Colin 1974

– *Les institutions politiques de la France de Louis XV à Giscard d'Estaing.* Paris: Flammarion 1979

Richard, Viviane. "Les anoblissements dans les Pays-Bas autrichiens," Mémoire de licence, Université de Bruxelles 1960

Richardson, H.G., and G.O. Sayles. *The Irish Parliament in the Middle Ages.* Philadelphia: University of Philadelphia Press 1952

Richelieu, duke of. *Testament politique d'Armand du Plessis, cardinal duc de Richelieu.* Amsterdam: Desbordes 1696

Roberts, G. "The threshold of the modern age." In *Wales through the Ages,* 2: *From 1485 to the Beginning of the 20th Century,* edited by A.J. Roderick. Aberystwyth: Davies 1960

Roebuck, Peter. "The making of an Ulster great estate: the Chichesters, barons of Belfast and viscounts of Carrickfergus, 1599–1648." *Proceedings of the Royal Irish Academy* 79 (1979)

Roehl, Richard. "French industrialization: a reconsideration." *Explorations in Economic History* 13 (1976)

Rogers, Hugh C.B. *The British Army of the Eighteenth Century.* London: George Allen and Unwin 1977

Rogers, Nicholas. "Money, land and lineage: the big bourgeoisie of Hanoverian London." *Social History* 4 (1979)

Rokkan, Stein. "Centre formation, nation-building and cultural diversity." In *Building States and Nations,* vol. 1, edited by S.N. Eisenstadt and Rokkan. Beverly Hills: Sage 1973

– "Dimensions of state formation and nation-building: a possible paradigm for research on variations within Europe." In *The Formation of National States in Western Europe,* edited by Charles Tilly. Princeton: Princeton University Press 1975

Rokkan, Stein, and D.W. Urwin. "Introduction: centres and peripheries in Western Europe." In *The Politics of Territorial Identity: Studies in European Regionalism,* edited by Rokkan and Urwin. London: Sage 1982

Root, H.L. *Peasants and King in Burgundy: Agrarian Foundations of French Absolutism.* Berkeley: University of California Press 1987

Rosenberg, Harriet G. *A Negotiated World: Three Centuries of Change in a French Alpine Community.* Toronto: University of Toronto Press 1988

Rosenthal, J.T. *Nobles and the Noble Life, 1295–1500.* London: George Allen and Unwin 1976

Rueschemeyer, Dietrich. *Power and the Division of Labour.* Cambridge: Polity 1986

Ruwet, Joseph. *L'agriculture et les classes rurales au pays de Herve sous l'ancien régime.* Liège: Université de Liège 1943

– *Soldats des régiments nationaux au XVIIIème siècle: notes et documents.* Brussels: Palais des académies 1962

Rykwert, Joseph. "The seventeenth century." In *The Cambridge Cultural History of Britain, 4: Seventeenth-Century Britain,* edited by Boris Ford. Cambridge: Cambridge University Press 1989

Saint-Simon, duke of. *Memoirs of Louis XIV and the Regency,* translated by Bayle St John, 3 vols. London: Dunne 1901

Sanderson, Margaret H.B. *Scottish Rural Society in the Sixteenth Century.* Edinburgh: Donald 1982

Sanderson, S.K. *Social Evolutionism: A Critical History.* Oxford: Basil Blackwell 1990

Sayer, Derek. "A notable administration: English state formation and the rise of capitalism." *American Journal of Sociology* 97 (1992)

Scaglione, Aldo. *Knights at Court: Courtliness, Chivalry, and Courtesy from Ottonian Germany to the Italian Renaissance.* Berkeley: University of California Press 1991

Schalk, Ellery. "Ennoblement in France from 1350 to 1660." *Journal of Social History* 16 (1982)

– *From Valor to Pedigree: Ideas of Nobility in France in the Sixteenth and Seventeenth Centuries.* Princeton: Princeton University Press 1986

Schepper, Hugo de, and Geoffrey Parker. "The formation of government policy in the Catholic Netherlands under the archdukes, 1596–1621." *English Historical Review* 91 (1976)

Schlight, John. *Henry II, Plantagenet.* New York: Twayne 1973

Scouller, R.E. *The Armies of Queen Anne.* Oxford: Clarendon Press 1966

Searle, C.E. "Custom, class conflict and agrarian capitalism: the Cumbrian customary economy in the eighteenth century." *Past and Present,* no. 110 (1986)

Searle, Eleanor. *Predatory Kinship and the Creation of Norman Power, 840–1066.* Berkeley: University of California Press 1988

Seward, Desmond. *The First Bourbon: Henri IV, King of France and Navarre.* London: Constable 1971

– *Eleanor of Aquitaine: The Mother Queen.* New York: Dorset 1978

Sharpe, Kevin. "The image of virtue: the court and household of Charles I, 1625–1642." In *The English Court: From the Wars of the Roses to the Civil War,* edited by David Starkey. London: Longman 1987

Shaw, Frances J. "Landownership in the Western Isles in the seventeenth century." *Scottish Historical Review* 56 (1977)

– *The Northern and Western Islands of Scotland: Their Economy and Society in the Seventeenth Century.* Edinburgh: Donald 1980

Shaw, J.S. *The Management of Scottish Society, 1707–1764: Power, Nobles, Lawyers, Edinburgh Agents and English Influences.* Edinburgh: Donald 1983

Shennan, J.H. "Louis XV: public and private worlds." In *The Courts of Europe: Politics, Patronage and Royalty, 1400–1800,* edited by A.G. Dickens. London: Thames and Hudson 1977

Shils, Edward. *Center and Periphery: Essays in Macrosociology.* Chicago: University of Chicago Press 1975

Sieyès, Emmanuel. *Qu'est-ce que le tiers état?* Paris: Société de l'histoire de la Révolution française 1888

Simms, J.G. *The Williamite Confiscation in Ireland, 1690–1703.* London: Faber and Faber 1956

– "The war of the two kings, 1685–91." In *A New History of Ireland,* 3: *Early Modern Ireland, 1534–1691,* edited by T.W. Moody, F.X. Martin, and F.J. Byrne. Oxford: Clarendon Press 1976

– "The establishment of protestant ascendancy, 1691–1714." In *A New History of Ireland,* 4: *Eighteenth Century Ireland, 1691–1800,* edited by T.W. Moody and W.E. Vaughan. Oxford: Clarendon Press 1986

Simms, Katherine. *From Kings to Warlords: The Changing Political Structure of Gaelic Ireland in the Later Middle Ages.* Woodbridge: Boydell 1987

Skone, G.W. "Manorial organization in Medieval Pembrokeshire," MA thesis, University College of Wales, Aberystwyth 1928

Slicher van Bath, B.H. "The rise of intensive husbandry in the Low Countries." In *Britain and the Netherlands,* vol. 1, edited by J.S. Bromley and E.H. Kossmann. London: Chatto and Windus 1960

Smelser, N.J. *Social Change in the Industrial Revolution: An Application of Theory to the British Cotton Industry.* Chicago: University of Chicago Press 1959

– "Evaluating the model of structural differentiation in relation to educational change." In *Neofunctionalism,* edited by J.C. Alexander. Beverly Hills: Sage 1985

– "The contest between family and schooling in nineteenth-century Britain." In *Differentiation Theory and Social Change: Comparative and Historical Perspectives,* edited by J.C. Alexander and Paul Colomy. New York: Columbia University Press 1990

– *Social Paralysis and Social Change: British Working-Class Education in the Nineteenth Century.* Berkeley: University of California Press 1991

Smeyers, Joseph, et al. "La vie culturelle dans nos provinces au XVIIIe siècle: le Brabant." *Bulletin trimestriel du Crédit communal de Belgique,* no. 141 (1982)

Smith, Goldwin, *A Constitutional and Legal History of England.* New York: Scribner 1955

Smout, T.C. "Scottish landowners and economic growth, 1650–1850." *Scottish Journal of Political Economy* 11 (1964)

– *A History of the Scottish People, 1560–1830.* Glasgow: Collins 1969

Smyth, Jim. *The Men of No Property: Irish Radicals and Popular Politics in the Late Eighteenth Century.* Houndsmills: Macmillan 1992.

Smyth, W.J. "Estate records and the making of the Irish landscape: an example from County Tipperary." *Irish Geography* 9 (1976)

– "Making the documents of conquest speak: the transformation of property, society, and settlement in seventeenth-century Counties Tipperary and Kilkenny." In *Approaching the Past: Historical Anthropology through Irish Case Studies*, edited by Marilyn Silverman and P.H. Gulliver. New York: Columbia University Press 1992

Soboul, Albert. "La Révolution française et la 'féodalité': notes sur le prélèvement féodal." *Revue historique* 240 (1968)

Solnon, Jean-François. *La cour de France.* Paris: Fayard 1987

Spencer, Herbert. *The Principles of Sociology.* 3 vols. London: Williams and Norgate 1897–1906

Spring, David. "Landed elites compared." In *European Landed Elites in the Nineteenth Century*, edited by David Spring. Baltimore: Johns Hopkins University Press 1977

Squibb, G.D. *The High Court of Chivalry.* Oxford: Clarendon Press 1959

Stanbridge, Karen. "European states and their North American colonies" (forthcoming)

Starkey, David. "Intimacy and innovation: the rise of the Privy Chamber, 1485–1547." In *The English Court: From the Wars of the Roses to the Civil War*, edited by David Starkey. London: Longman 1987

– "Introduction: court history in perspective." In *The English Court: From the Wars of the Roses to the Civil War*, edited by David Starkey. London: Longman 1987

– ed. *The English Court: From the Wars of the Roses to the Civil War.* London: Longman 1987

Stenton, F.M. *William the Conqueror and the Rule of the Normans.* New York: Barnes and Noble 1966

– *Anglo-Saxon England*, 3rd edition. Oxford: Clarendon Press 1971

Stevenson, Alexander. "Trade with the South." In *The Scottish Medieval Town*, edited by Michael Lynch, Michael Spearman, and Geoffrey Stell. Edinburgh: Donald 1988

Stone, Lawrence. "The anatomy of the Elizabethan aristocracy." *Economic History Review* 18 (1948)

– "The Elizabethan aristocracy: a restatement." *Economic History Review*, 2nd series, 4 (1952)

– *Crisis of the Aristocracy, 1558–1641*, abridged edition. New York: Oxford University Press 1967

Stone, Lawrence, and Jeanne C. Fawtier Stone. *An Open Elite? England 1540–1880.* Oxford: Clarendon Press 1984

Strayer, J.R. "Consent to taxation under Philip the Fair." In *Studies in Early French Taxation*, edited by J.R. Strayer and C.H. Taylor. Cambridge: Harvard University Press 1939

Strayer, J.R., and George Rudisill. "Taxation and community in Wales and Ireland, 1272–1327." *Speculum* 29 (1954)

Sturdy, D.J. "Tax evasion, the *faux nobles*, and state fiscalism: the example of the *généralité* of Caen, 1634–35." *French Historical Studies* 9 (1976)

Summary of the Returns of Owners of Land in Ireland, Showing, with Respect to Each County, the Number of Owners below an Acre, and in Classes up to 100,000 Acres and Upwards, with the Aggregate Acreage and Valuation of Each Class, United Kingdom, House of Commons, 1876 (422), 80

Symcox, Geoffrey. *Victor Amadeus II: Absolutism in the Savoyard State 1675–1730*. London: Thames and Hudson 1983

– "The development of absolutism in the Savoyard state." *Studies in History and Politics* 4 (1985)

– "The city as theatre: ceremonial use of urban space in Turin, 1650–1750." In *Absolutism and Urban Space in Early Modern Italy*, edited by Geoffrey Symcox and R. Burr Litchfield. Ithaca: Cornell University Press (forthcoming)

Tawney, R.H. *The Agrarian Problem in the Sixteenth Century*. New York: Burt Franklin 1912

– "The rise of the gentry, 1558–1640." *Economic History Review* 11 (1941)

_ "The rise of the gentry: A postscript." *Economic History Review*, 2nd series, 7 (1954)

Taylor, George. "Non-capitalist wealth and the origin of the French Revolution." *American Historical Review* 72 (1967)

Teale, Adrian. "Economy and society of North Flintshire, c.1660–1714," MA thesis, University of Aberytswyth 1979

Terry, C.S. *The Scottish Parliament: Its Constitution and Procedure, 1603–1707*. Glasgow: MacLehose 1905

Thirsk, Joan. "Enclosing and engrossing." In *The Agrarian History of England and Wales*, 4: *1500–1640*, edited by Joan Thirsk. Cambridge: Cambridge University Press 1967

– "Seventeenth-century agriculture and social change." In *Seventeenth-century England: Society in an Age of Revolution*, edited by P.S. Seaver. New York: New Viewpoints 1976

– ed. *The Agrarian History of England and Wales*, 5: *1640–1750: Agrarian Change*. Cambridge: Cambridge University Press 1985

Thomas, David. "The social origins of marriage partners of the British peerage in the eighteenth and nineteenth centuries." *Population Studies* 16 (1972)

Thompson, E.P. "The peculiarities of the English." In *The Socialist Register, 1965*. New York: Monthly Review 1965

– "Patrician society, plebeian culture." *Journal of Social History* 7 (1974)

– *Whigs and Hunters: The Origin of the Black Act*. Harmondsworth: Penguin 1975

Thompson, F.M.L. "The social distribution of landed property in England since the sixteenth century." *Economic History Review*, 2nd series, 19 (1966)

Thomson, J.K.J. "Variations in industrial structure in pre-industrial Languedoc." In *Manufacture in Town and Country before the Factory*. Cambridge: Cambridge University Press 1983

Tilly, Charles. *As Sociology Meets History*. New York: Academic Press 1981

- "Five French regions, four contentious centuries, two fundamental processes." CRSO Working Paper no. 262 (1982)

- *Big Structures, Large Processes, Huge Comparisons*. New York: Russell Sage Foundation 1984

- "Demographic origins of the European proletariat." In *Proletarianization and Family History*, edited by David Levine. New York: Academic Press 1984

- *The Contentious French*. Cambridge: Belknap Press 1986

- "The geography of European statemaking and capitalism since 1500." In *Geographic Perspectives in History*, edited by E.D. Genovese and L.J. Hochberg. Oxford: Basil Blackwell 1989

- *Coercion, Capital, and European States, AD 990–1990*. Cambridge: Basil Blackwell 1990

Tinker, *The Salon and English Letters*. New York: Macmillan 1915

Torrance, John. "Social class and bureaucratic innovation: the commissioners for examining public accounts, 1780–1787." *Past and Present*, no. 78 (1978)

Touchard, Henri. "Le Moyen Age breton." In *Histoire de la Bretagne*, edited by Jean Delumeau. Paris: Privat 1991

Trench, Charles Chenevix. *George II*. London: Allen Lane 1973

Trevor-Roper, Hugh. "The Elizabethan aristocracy: an anatomy anatomized." *Economic History Review*, 2nd series, 3 (1951)

- "The gentry, 1540–1640." *Economic History Review*, supplement 1 (1953)

- *Princes and Artists: Patronage and Ideology at Four Habsburg Courts, 1517–1633*. London: Thames and Hudson 1976

Turner, B.S. *Status*. Minneapolis: University of Minnesota Press 1988

Uyttebrouck, André. "Une confédération et trois principautés." In *La Wallonie: Le Pays et les Hommes–Histoire, Economies, Sociétés*, edited by Hervé Hasquin. Brussels: Rennaissance du Livre 1975

Vale, Malcolm. *War and Chivalry: Warfare and Aristocratic Culture in England, France and Burgundy at the End of the Middle Ages*. Athens: University of Georgia Press 1981

Van Buyten, L. "Grondbezit en grondwaarde in Brabant en Mechelen, volgens de onteigeningen voor de aanleg der verkeerswegen in de achttiende eeuw." *Bijdragen voor de geschiedenis der Nederlanden* 18 (1963)

Van Creveld, Martin. *Technology and War: From 2000 B.C. to the Present*. New York: Free Press 1989

Van den Berg, Magda. "De adel in de 18de eeuw: een 'leisure class'?" In *De adel in het Hertogdom Brabant*. Brussels: Universitaire faculteiten Sint-Aloysius 1985

Vanden Berghe, Yvan, Joseph Smeyers, and Andries Van den Abeele. "Flandre occidentale." In *La vie culturelle dans nos provinces au XVIIIe siècle*, edited by Hervé Hasquin. Brussels: Crédit communal de Belgique 1983

Van der Wee, Herman. *The Growth of the Antwerp Market and the European Economy, Fourteenth to Sixteenth Centuries*, 2 vols. The Hague: Martinus Nijhoff 1963

– "Monetary, credit and banking systems." In *The Cambridge Economic History of Europe, 5: The Economic Organization of Early Modern Europe*, edited by E.E. Rich and C.H. Wilson. Cambridge: Cambridge University Press 1977

Vandewalle, A. "Heerlijkheden op het einde van het ancien regime: het voorbeeld van Gits-Ogierlande, Kringen en Hagebroek in het land van Wijnendale." *Revue belge de philologie et d'histoire* 56 (1978)

Van Geystelen, P. "Voorouders in 't gelid: Zuidnederlandse adel in het Habsburgse officierencorps (1725–1780)." *Belgisch tijdschrift voor militaire geschiedenis* 29 (1992)

Van Isterdael, Herman. "Belasting en belastingdruk: het Land van Aalst, 17de-18de eeuw," Doctoraatsverhandeling Vrije universiteit Brussel 1983

Van Kley, Dale K. *The Damiens Affair and the Unraveling of the Ancien Regime, 1750–1770*. Princeton: Princeton University Press 1984

Van Uytven, R. "De Brabantse adel als politieke en sociale groep tijdens de late Middeleeuwen." In *De adel in het Hertogdom Brabant*. Brussels: Universitaire faculteiten Sint-Aloysius 1985

Van Uytven, R., and Willem Blockmans. "Constitutions and their application in the Netherlands during the Middle Ages." *Revue belge de philologie et d'histoire* 47 (1969)

Van Winter, Johanna Maria. "Knighthood and nobility in the Netherlands." In *Gentry and Lesser Nobility in Late Medieval Europe*, edited by Michael Jones. Gloucester: Alan Sutton 1986

Verhaegen, Paul. *La Belgique sous la domination française, 1792–1814*, 5 vols. Brussels: Goemaere 1922–9

Verriest, Léo. *Le régime seigneurial dans le Comté de Hainaut du XIe siècle à la Révolution*. Brussels: Verriest 1956

Victor Amadeus II. *Les instructions de Victor-Amédée II sur le gouvernement de son duché de Savoie en 1721*, edited by Max Bruchet. Paris: Imprimerie nationale 1901

Wagner, A.R. *Heralds and Heraldry in the Middle Ages: An Inquiry into the Growth of the Armorial Function of Heralds*. Oxford: Oxford University Press 1967

– *Heralds of England: A History of the Office and College of Arms*. London: HMSO 1967

Wake, Joan, and D.C. Webster, "Introduction" to their edited volume *The Letters of Daniel Eaton to the Third Earl of Cardigan 1725–1732*. Northampton: Northamptonshire Record Society 1971

Wakelin, M.F. *English Dialects*. London: Athlone 1972

Wall, Maureen. *The Penal Laws, 1691–1760.* Dundalk: Dundalgan 1967

Wallerstein, Immanuel. *The Modern World-System I: Capitalist Agriculture and the Origins of the European World-Economy in the Sixteenth Century.* New York: Academic Press 1974

– *The Modern World-System II: Mercantilism and the Consolidation of the European World Economy.* New York: Academic Press 1980

– *The Modern World-System III: The Second Era of Great Expansion of the Capitalist World-Economy, 1730–1840.* New York: Academic Press 1988

Wangermann, E. "Maria Theresa: a reforming monarchy." In *The Courts of Europe: Politics, Patronage and Royalty, 1400–1800,* edited by A.G. Dickens. London: Thames and Hudson 1977

Ward, W.R. "Some eighteenth century civil servants: the English revenue commissioners, 1754–98." *English Historical Review* 70 (1955)

Warlop, E. *The Flemish Nobility before 1300,* 2 vols. Kortrijk: Desmet-Huysman 1975

Watelet, Hubert. *Une industrialization sans développement: le Bassin de Mons et le Charbonnage du Grand-Hornu du milieu du XVIIIe siècle au milieu du XIXe siècle.* Ottawa: University of Ottawa Press 1980

Watts, S.J. "Tenant-right in early seventeenth-century Northumberland." *Northern History* 6 (1971)

Waugh, S.L. "Tenure to contract: lordship and clientage in thirteenth-century England." *English Historical Review* 401 (1986)

Weber, Max. *Economy and Society: An Outline of Interpretive Sociology,* 2 vols. Berkeley: University of California Press 1978

Werner, K.F. "*Hludovicus Augustus:* gouverner l'empire chrétien – idées et réalités." In *Charlemagne's Heir: New Perspectives on the Reign of Louis the Pious (814–840),* edited by Peter Godman and Roger Collins. Oxford: Clarendon Press 1990

Whetstone, Anne E. *Scottish County Government in the Eighteenth and Nineteenth Centuries.* Edinburgh: Donald 1981

Whitelock, Dorothy. *The Pelican History of England,* 2: *The Beginnings of English Society.* Harmondsworth: Penguin 1952

Whyte, Ian. *Agriculture and Society in Seventeenth-Century Scotland.* Edinburgh: Donald 1979

Wilbur, C.K., ed. *The Political Economy of Development and Underdevelopment.* New York: Random House 1973

Williams, Glanmor. *Recovery, Reorientation and Reformation: Wales, c. 1415–1642.* Oxford: Clarendon Press 1987

– "Religion and belief." In *Tudor Wales,* edited by Trevor Herbert and G.E. Jones. Cardiff: University of Wales Press 1988

Williams, Penry. "The Tudor gentry." In *Wales through the Ages,* 2: *From 1485 to the Beginning of the 20th Century,* edited by A.J. Roderick. Aberystwyth: Davies 1960

Wilson, R.G. *Gentlemen Merchants: The Merchant Community in Leeds, 1700–1830.* Manchester: Manchester University Press 1971

Wilson, R.M. "English and French in England, 1100–1300." *History* 28 (1943)

Wirth, Louis. "Urbanism as a way of life." *American Journal of Sociology* 44 (1938)

Wolf, J.B. *Louis XIV.* New York: Norton 1968

Wolfe, Martin. *The Fiscal System of Renaissance France.* New Haven: Yale University Press 1972

Wood, Ellen M. "The separation of the economic and the political in capitalism." *New Left Review,* no. 127 (1981)

– *The Pristine Culture of Capitalism: A Historical Essay on Old Regimes and Modern States.* New York: Verso 1991

Wood, J.B. *The Nobility of the Election of Bayeux, 1463–1666: Continuity through Change.* Princeton: Princeton University Press 1980

Wormald [Brown], Jenny. "The exercise of power." In *Scottish Society in the Fifteenth Century,* edited by Jenny Wormald [Brown]. London: Arnold 1977

– *Lords and Men in Scotland: Bonds of Manrent, 1442–1603.* Edinburgh: Donald 1985

– "Lords and lairds in fifteenth-century Scotland: nobles and gentry?" In *Gentry and Lesser Nobility in Late Medieval Europe,* edited by Michael Jones. Gloucester: Alan Sutton 1986

Woronoff, Denis. *L'industrie sidérurgique en France pendant la Révolution et l'Empire.* Paris: L'école des hautes études en sciences sociales 1984

Wuthnow, Robert. "State structures and ideology." *American Sociological Review* 50 (1985)

Young, Arthur. *Travels in France during the Years 1787, 1788 and 1789,* edited by Constantia Maxwell. 1792. Cambridge: Cambridge University 1950

– *Arthur Young's Tour in Ireland (1776–1779),* edited by A.W. Hutton, 2 vols. London: Bell 1892

Yver, Jean. "La rédaction officielle de la Coutume de Normandie (Rouen, 1583): son esprit." *Annales de Normandie* 36 (1986)

Zeller, Gaston. "Une notion de caractère historico-social: la dérogeance." In *Aspects de la politique française sous l'ancien régime.* Paris: Presses universitaires de France 1964

Zumthor, Paul. *Charles le Chauve.* Paris: Jules Tallandier 1981

Index